ROUTLEDGE LIBRARY EDITIONS:
FOLK MUSIC

Volume 2

TRADITIONAL ANGLO-AMERICAN
FOLK MUSIC

TRADITIONAL ANGLO-AMERICAN FOLK MUSIC

An Annotated Discography of Published Sound Recordings

NORM COHEN

Routledge
Taylor & Francis Group

LONDON AND NEW YORK

First published in 1994 by Garland Publishing, Inc.

This edition first published in 2016
by Routledge
2 Park Square, Milton Park, Abingdon, Oxon OX14 4RN

and by Routledge
711 Third Avenue, New York, NY 10017

Routledge is an imprint of the Taylor & Francis Group, an informa business

British Library Cataloguing in Publication Data
A catalogue record for this book is available from the British Library

ISBN: 978-1-138-94398-8 (Set)
ISBN: 978-1-315-66734-8 (Set) (ebk)
ISBN: 978-1-138-96233-0 (Volume 2) (hbk)
ISBN: 978-1-315-65939-8 (Volume 2) (ebk)

Publisher's Note
The publisher has gone to great lengths to ensure the quality of this reprint but points out that
some imperfections in the original copies may be apparent.

Disclaimer
The publisher has made every effort to trace copyright holders and would welcome
correspondence from those they have been unable to trace.

TRADITIONAL ANGLO-AMERICAN FOLK MUSIC

An Annotated Discography
of Published
Sound Recordings

Norm Cohen

GARLAND PUBLISHING, Inc.
New York & London / 1994

Library of Congress Cataloging-in-Publication Data

Cohen, Norm.
  Traditional Anglo-American folk music : an annotated discogra-
phy of published sound recordings / Norm Cohen.
      p.   cm. — (Garland library of music ethnology ; vol. 2)
(Garland reference library of the humanities ; vol. 1469)
  Includes bibliographical references and indexes.
  ISBN 0–8153–0377–7 (alk. paper)
  1. Folk music—United States—Discography. 2. Folk songs,
English—United States—Discography. I. Title. II. Series.
III. Series: Garland library of music ethnology ; 2.
ML156.4.F5C4   1994
016.78162'13'00266—dc20   93–26934
                                                           CIP
                                                           MN

Printed on acid-free, 250-year-life paper
Manufactured in the United States of America

TO
Alexa,
Carson,
Matthew,
and
Verni

CONTENTS

Series Editor's Foreword   ix

Preface   xi

Acknowledgments   xxi

Label Abbreviations   xxiii

Albums Listed   1

I.   Individual artists/groups: primarily noncommercial recordings   15

II.   Anthologies: primarily noncommercial recordings   161

III.   Individual artists/groups: reissues of commercial 78 rpm recordings   275

IV.   Anthologies: reissues of commercial 78 rpm recordings   347

Artist Index   395

Title Index   419

Child Ballad Index   491

Laws Ballad Index   497

Album Label/Number Index   507

SERIES EDITOR'S FOREWORD

The Garland Library of Music Ethnology comprises mainly reference works in ethnomusicology, dance ethnology, music anthropology, and related fields. The series seeks to fill some gaps in reference and research: in specific music areas such as Native American, Arab, Southeast Asian, Latin American, European, and North American, and through works of a more general methodological kind. Further contributions to the series will be in dance ethnology, discography, and filmography. In addition, some important works in translation, as well as the occasional monograph, will form part of the series.

The term "music ethnology" was chosen for a practical reason: to differentiate the series from *The Garland Library of Readings in Ethnomusicology* (7 vols., 1990). There are less obvious reasons for using "music ethnology": "ethnomusicology," though it has flourished in scholarly circles since its invention by Jaap Kunst in 1950, is a cumbersome term for the lay person; a certain ambiguity is built into it through the "ethno" prefix, with its connotations of "other," "different," or "ethnic" (e.g., Western vs. non-Western); and the nominal amalgam appears to emphasize the musicology component over the ethnological (or anthropological) rather than the interaction of musicology and ethnology on equal terms. While no single term is entirely satisfactory, "music ethnology" (like "dance ethnology") at least has the virtue of clarity as well as suggesting a more equable balance between the disciplines.

The second volume in this series represents the filling of a gap of a different sort from the first volume, Ann Briegleb Schuursma's *Ethnomusicology Research: A Select Annotated Bibliography* (1992), which was a more general bibliography of published writings in ethnomusicology since 1960. The gap that the present work aims to fill is of sound recordings of traditional Anglo-American folk music. The author, Norm Cohen, has a distinguished career outside the folk music field (in chemical kinetics), and is currently Senior Scientist at Aerospace Corporation in El Segundo, California. But his association with, and love for American vernacular song and music is reflected in his book *Long Steel Rail: The Railroad in American Folksong* (1981), in his contributions to the John Edwards Memorial Foundation as Executive Secretary (1969–85) and as Editor of its journal, the *John Edwards Memorial Foundation Quarterly* (1966–88), and in his Record Review Editorship for major academic publications such as the *Journal of American Folklore* (1968–69, 1986–90) and *Western Folklore* (1970–75).

Dr. Cohen has also contributed numerous articles on folk music and song to scholarly journals from the mid-1960s to the present, and his other many publications include phonograph album liner and brochure notes e.g., for the Smithsonian Institution Press's recent *Folksong America: The Folk Revival*, a 6-LP/4-CD box set (1991). His discography also covers a somewhat larger time frame than the first volume, namely from the 1920s to the present. The selection of 500 albums includes, moreover, all types of older traditional material, both vocal and instrumental. The listings have also been limited to performers native to the tradition rather than "revival" performers, who probably merit a separate discography. Finally, the album selection is grouped into field recordings and commercial hillbilly (pre-1942) recordings, with subdivisions into individual recordings or anthologies.

The usefulness of this discography will be readily apparent. Within the broad grouping noted above, the main listings are subdivided by label name or number, title, artists, editor (collector, recordist, producer), date and place of recording, date of publication, annotations, selections, and Dr. Cohen's own commentary. A title index grapples with, and largely solves, such practical problems as that of different titles for the same song or the same title for different songs. Particularly useful is the listing of recommended albums for individuals or institutions that want to assemble core collections of significant recordings. The discography reflects not only its author's deep knowledge of Anglo-American folk music's historical development but charts a valuable step forward in the evaluation, as well as the select listing, of available sound recordings.

James Porter, *Editor*
The Garland Library
of Music Ethnology

PREFACE

I. Scope and purpose

In the best of all possible worlds of documentation, the user of folk music material would need only punch a few keys at a computer terminal to gain information on all occurrences of a given ballad or fiddle tune, or by a given performer--whether recorded on commercial 78 or compact disc, in a public or private archive, or simply published in a scholarly popular collection. I believe this world is not only attainable, but will in fact exist within most of our lifetimes. This conviction necessarily undercuts some of the enthusiasm for preparing a reference work such as this. It is much the same as, say, how John Bartlett would have felt if, a few days before completing his 20 years of work on a complete Shakespeare Concordance, IBM had announced the imminence of the first home personal computer and word processing software. I acknowledge, then, that this is not an exhaustive discography of a closed corpus, nor is it a work free of subjective decisions and limitations. In essence, it is a description of 500 recorded "albums" (I use the term as shorthand for phonograph discs, magnetic tape cassettes, and digital compact discs)--or sets of albums--of traditional Anglo-American music that, for the most part, represent the best and most important of the older layers of that continually evolving tradition. Annotations for the albums describe their contents, style, quality, and nature.

Why 500? Simply because space was not unlimited. While all types of older traditional material--vocal and instrumental, secular and religious, commercially and field recorded--are included, some areas are more thoroughly represented than others. For example, I believe that almost every album of traditional vocal music is included; the same cannot be said for recorded stringband dance music, because there is so much of it.

The special genre of commercially recorded "hillbilly" or "country" music, especially that from its earliest years of 1922-24 until World War II, requires some comment. Academic writers first made the point over three decades ago that this material constituted an important corpus of traditional southern American folk and folk-derived music, and what's more, a medium that created many new ballads and songs that subsequently entered oral tradition. Somewhere around 20,000 hillbilly recordings were made prior to WW II, of which perhaps 4000 have been reissued on 400 or so LPs, cassettes, or CDs. Almost 200 of the 500 albums in this listing consist primarily of commercial hillbilly recordings. While I have been most liberally inclusive in field recorded material, the coverage of reissues of commercial 78 rpm records from the 1930s is considerably more selective. I am forced to this position because of (a) the greater quantity of such albums, and (b) the much broader range of material represented in that idiom--from older ballads of British origins to pop songs from Tin Pan Alley (TPA). Among the albums selected from reissues of 78s, then, I have been increasingly selective as the material moves into the later 1930s or into more "pop"- oriented material. For these reasons the reader will find almost no albums of reissues of western swing music, even though its folk roots are as evident as are those of the more familiar southeastern hillbilly string bands. I have included no albums devoted entirely to Jimmie Rodgers (or to his several "imitators"--Gene Autry, Jimmie Davis, Ernest Tubb, and others); in spite of Rodgers' dependence on older tradition, and his later impact on it, by far the bulk of his 113 recordings, and his accompanying styles, owe much more to pop, jazz, and blues music of the 1930s. Even artists as tradition-based as the original Carter Family are extensively but not exhaustively represented. [What is included here is a good, representative sampling of their recorded repertoire, but far from everything that has been reissued.] A useful companion compendium to this discography, though now several years out of date, is Willie Smyth's *Country Music Recorded Prior to 1943: A Discography of LP Reissues*[1]. Smyth's list of approximately 350 reissue albums of hillbilly material fills some of these voids, including all the genres that I have selectively minimized. (However, it contains no comments or evaluations on the albums.)

I have also limited the listings to performers who seemed to me to be native to the traditions that they represented--notwithstanding the frequent fidelity, artistic skill, or knowledgeability of "folk song interpreters" (sometimes called "folk song singers," "folk song interpreters," "city billies," or "revival performers"). The latter artists are not to be ignored or reviled, but they deserve to be the subject of a separate discographic/ bibliographic survey. I have also included very few bluegrass albums, even though the performers meet my other requirements, simply because there are so many qualified examples that they need separate treatment.

I have not been swayed by such mundane factors as availability. Many of the items cited are, and have long been, out of print. Others were published abroad and are obtainable only through specialty shops and mail order outlets. The music business being as capricious as it is, there is no saying what will be available one or ten years from the day this book is published. The approaching world of total informational availability already alluded to will, one hopes, also make available all of the printed and recorded material produced by generations past. The information storage capabilities of new electronic media make it easy to include every folksong collection ever published on a single "CD-ROM"--and not much more will store all the sound recordings as well. Until then, listeners and researchers without private collections at their disposal may obtain assistance in locating and auditioning copies of particular albums by contacting one of the several institutions with substantial collections of folk music and related genres: Library of Congress--both the Recorded Sound Reference Center and the Archive of Folk Culture of the American Folklife Center; the John Edwards Memorial Collection, Wilson Library, University of North Carolina at Chapel Hill; Indiana University Archive of Traditional Music, Bloomington; Center for the Comparative Study of Folklore and Mythology, University of California, Los Angeles; Center for Popular Music, Middle Tennessee State University, Murfreesboro; and Country Music Foundation Archive and Media Center, Nashville. (Practices regarding the making of dubs on tape of out-of-print commercial recordings vary from institution to institution.)

On the 500-plus albums included (careful examination of my counting methods will reveal several more than that rounded number), not every selection is itemized. Non-English language titles are generally excluded on the grounds that they represent other than Anglo-American traditions; the same holds for African-American performers--except in a few cases where the gulf between the two traditions becomes an indistinct blur. These policies will undoubtedly offend or annoy some users. I can only assure readers that there is no implication of superiority or inferiority of material or traditions or artistry; only the recognition that these distinct traditions deserve separate but equal treatment elsewhere. Where my decisions become subjective and questionable is in the few cases of items that straddle traditions: an Anglo-American fiddle tune with a French title; or a Cajun version of a British ballad. I am confident that such instances, though regrettable, are very few. Also omitted are non-musical selections: tales, stories, jokes, sermons, etc. Again, these are important genres and should be treated separately. Although I have not included albums that feature *primarily* non-traditional performers or songs/tunes of fairly recent origins, where such artists or material are to be found on the 500 albums listed they have not been excluded from the listings.

The remainder of the material has all been listed and indexed. This means that one will see titles representing 17th-century British balladry alongside 19th-century TPA tunes and 20th-century hillbilly event ballads. The Anglo-American folk tradition has included all these facets and many others. Attempts to define our folk music on stylistic grounds have all failed badly. This is not to say that the folk music from a narrow chronological period cannot be stylistically characterized, but the broad body of folk music always contains parallel elements originating from different eras, and if these different elements are thrown together willy-nilly, the result is a stylistic hodgepodge. I have found it most useful in my own work to define "folk music" (at least, in 20th-century America) as that music which survives without the need for commercial media. The origin of the song is irrelevant; its content or style secondary at best. The existence of the characteristics once regarded as defining its nature--variation, oral transmission, anonymity, antiquity--are all common consequences of my definition, but are neither necessary nor sufficient criteria. Songs originating in the past decade or two are generally too closely associated with commercial media for us to say whether they will outlive those associations; hence my emphasis on the older layers of the evolving traditions.

II. Organization, guidelines

The 500 or so albums are grouped into four categories:

(I)   Primarily field recordings of individual artists or ensembles

(II)   Primarily anthological field recordings

(III)   Primarily commercial hillbilly (pre-1942) recordings of individual artists or ensembles

(IV)   Primarily anthological commercial hillbilly recordings

"Field recording" and "noncommercial recording" are, for convenience, used interchangeably, though I recognize that, in a sense, any recording, when made available for purchase, becomes a commercial one. Within the first and third sections, albums are arranged alphabetically by principal artist. Within the second and fourth sections, albums are arranged in order of record company name and release number, a reliable procedure in the absence of any method of grouping them consistently on some principle of content. This arrangement is less pedestrian than one might think, since many record companies tended to record particular kinds of music. At the end of this Preface I provide lists of recommended albums in each of several stylistic categories.

A. Main listings

1. Label name/number. This information is generally self-explanatory except for a few comments. Major labels that simultaneously published recordings in different formats--e.g., mono and stereo LP, or stereo LP and cassette, attached different release numbers. I have generally listed the more commonly available format first and affixed other formats where known to me, but these supplemental details are certainly not exhaustive. More troublesome for archivists and discographers is where what appears to be the same release in two different formats actually contains more tracks on one format (e.g., the CD) than the other. I have tried to indicate any such differences in the title listings. A separate problem is the later republication of a record under a very different format--new artwork, different title, new sequencing. Occasionally, a record is reissued by a different company, not always with the original company acknowledged. I believe I have included such happenings in almost all cases.

2. Title. A record title is not always so well defined as a book title. Problems occur when a different title appears on record jacket front cover, back cover, spine, and on the label itself. Also problematic is the common use of subtitles and auxiliary titles, which again may differ in the different positions. Another difficulty is occasioned by the frequently used formula, "John Doe sings Particular Songs," where the verb is in small type and of a different typeface. The "John Doe" may be separated on the cover from the "Particular Songs" by other artwork. Is the entire phrase the title, or only the "Sings Particular Songs" or "Particular Songs"? Because of the inconsistent use of series titles and particular subtitles as product identifiers, users of this discography must be wary in using what I construe the title to be when they are trying to locate the product in a store or library. I have tried to include subtitles and descriptive phrases where they would significantly increase the user's chances of correctly identifying the item sought for but have not been exhaustive in the matter of more subtle subtitles.

3. Artists. These are separately identified only if the title itself is not sufficient for artist identification. Anthology albums generally bear the notation "Artists: Various," with individual performers listed along with the selections listing.

4. Editor, collector, recordist, producer. These terms have different meanings in different circles. "Collector" used to be the designation for the field-worker who recorded traditional material "in the field." With a well-known artist, often with many concerts and albums to his/her credit, and with material recorded in a professional studio, the term seems less appropriate, and "recordist" has become a broad rubric to include both kinds of venues. I have not listed as "recordist" a person identified primarily as a studio engineer. "Editor" generally means the person who selected and programmed the material. "Producer" is the most ambiguous term of all. In different contexts, "producer" may mean simply the person responsible for coordinating the various facets of production, it may mean the person who made all the business arrangements--fees, permissions, etc.; or it may mean what "A&R [Artist and Repertoire] Man" used to mean: the person who supervised the recordings, made decisions regarding accompanists, engineering, studios, selections, etc. Nowadays it generally signifies rather little direct responsibility for any of the artistic or intellectual aspects of the production and packaging. On the many albums of material reissued from commercial 78s of the 1920s and 1930s, the producer and editor, if any, refer to individuals responsible for the LP reissue, not the original recordings. For the most part, I have used the terminology that appears on the album credits. On albums of many independent companies, often none of these roles is identified. I have occasionally identified a name in square brackets when, from other knowledge or information, I was certain it was appropriate--although the product itself contained no clues to identification. A name with a question mark in the brackets indicates "reasonable" certainty. On albums of independent labels, if an individual is named as collector or editor or annotator but the other roles are not identified, it is reasonable to assume that the same individual fulfilled all those functions.

     5. Date and place of recording. Record companies and producers--even individuals who are fully cognizant of the folkloric nature of their material--are often surprisingly lax about giving such fundamental pieces of information. What I give in the listings is what appears in the album credits unless I have given it in square brackets: that indicates I have some other source of information that is reasonably certain. A question mark or "ca." indicates a possible error of 1-2 years.

     6. Date of publication. The date I give is what appears on the album or in the annotations as a copyright date or as the date of signing of the annotations. It can well differ from the actual release date by a year in either direction. A date given in square brackets, again, is inferred from other information and is almost certain to be off by no more than one year. A question mark following the date in brackets indicates somewhat greater uncertainty and may be in error by two or three years. A date in brackets preceded by a "<" sign means publication was no later than the year indicated.

     7. Annotations. Because to the serious user--scholar, student, or other--the annotations can be as important as the material itself, I feel it important to identify the nature of the annotations and the individuals responsible for them. In the Main Listings I have done no more than indicate the physical format: whether printed on the jacket ("liner notes" indicates the back of the album cover), inside a double jacket that opens ("gatefold"), on separate sheets sewn into a double jacket, or as a detachable leaflet, brochure, or booklet. In the prose commentary I always draw attention to important or extensive annotations; the absence of any remarks indicates no annotations at all--or at most a few vague or hyperbolic paragraphs on a jacket cover. If the annotator's name appears in square brackets, it is because I am reasonably certain of his/her undisclosed identity.

     8. Selections. The selections listed are generally complete as appear on the album or label listings but rearranged in alphabetical order. However, I have not striven for obsequious fidelity to grammatical or typographical errors or the whims of the designer or editor. Such errors have been silently corrected. I have been even more liberal in altering titles in the Title Index where I felt that so doing would help the user find a song or tune sought after. (See the comments at the head of the Title Index for more details.) As noted in Section I above, since this is an Anglo-American discography I have generally excluded titles by other types of performers (African-American, Native American, Cajun, Franco-American), or titles in other languages that clearly indicate different traditions, such as French titled fiddle tunes. Selections also exclude titles of tales, anecdotes, and other narratives, though the exclusion of material for any of the above reasons is noted at the end of the title listing by a phrase such as "[also includes five African-American performances and two narratives]."

9. Prose commentary. I have aimed for an objective discussion of the product, with very little aesthetic evaluation. I have found that in many cases my own aesthetic response to a recording is highly dependent on extraneous factors. Consequently, in only those cases where I was really struck by the music have I offered any subjective evaluations. I might forewarn the reader that in the genre of ballad singing, I am somewhat biased in favor of the highly decorated style of some southeastern singers, and less interested in the undecorated midwestern and northern styles. My aesthetic comments should be calibrated accordingly. At the end of the prose discussions is often a reference in brackets to published reviews of the album under consideration. The journals cited are *Journal of American Folklore* [*JAF*], *John Edwards Memorial Foundation Quarterly* [*JEMFQ*], and *Western Folklore* [*WF*]. The journal is identified by an issue number in the cases of *JAF* and *JEMFQ* or a date in the case of *WF*. Unless otherwise noted, the reviews are my own; other reviewers are abbreviated as follows: DD = Diane Dugaw, FF = Frances Farrell, CH = Charles Haywood, AJ = Alan Jabbour, WHJ = William Hughes Jansen, DN = Don Nelson, JJN = John Jacob Niles, WR = Willard Rhodes, CS = Charles Seeger, WS = Willie Smyth, PW = Paul Wells, and DKW = D. K. Wilgus.

B. Title index

The introduction to the Title Index describes the general problems of alphabetization, identification, and what I call "searching problems": what to do about initial "A," "An," and "The;" titles beginning with numerals or non-standard usages (e.g., "bile" or "'round"). Here I simply repeat two important details: (1) While I have tried extensively to group together different titles of the same song--or at least to provide cross-references--I cannot claim 100% success. The user thus cannot take the list of references following "Cripple Creek" as a complete list of all occurrences of that tune among the 500 albums analyzed in this work. Conversely, (2) the reader must be wary of assuming that all citations of a particular *title* indeed refer to the same song or tune. In some cases, one can argue that the boundaries of a lyric song or song cluster are not even that well defined; in others, though, it is a more mundane matter of having failed to compare, for example, different recordings of an instrumental piece of a given title to ascertain musical consanguinity.

C. Child and Laws ballad indexes.

These two separate indexes provide cross references to all the ballads identified either in Francis James Child's monumental work, *The English and Scottish Popular Ballads*[2]--identified by "[C. ###]" where "###" is one of the 305 ballads he discusses; or in one of G. Malcolm Laws' two syllabi, *American Ballads from British Broadsides,*[3] (*ABBB*) and *Native American Balladry*[4] (*NAB*).

Child, an authority on English literature at Harvard University during the latter half of the 19th century, devoted much of his scholarly energies to the compilation of all versions extant of what he called "popular" ballads--what we would call "traditional" or folk balladry--of the British Isles. Because before the turn of the century there was very little fieldwork on folk music either in Britain or North America, Child operated under the premise that the ballads were practically extinct in living memory; "collecting" them, therefore, meant combing the written literature--from old handwritten manuscripts to early published collections of the 18th and 19th centuries. He found 305 ballads that fitted his (unwritten) criteria of popular balladry, most of which could be traced to the 17th and 18th centuries, and many of which had analogs in other European traditions. At the time of his death, he knew of only a handful that were still current in oral tradition, either in the Old World or the New, and regarded most of those as anomalies. Since then, assiduous fieldwork has turned up at least 133 "Child" ballads (and a handful of other dubious survivals) in the New World. This discography includes 62 Child ballads; this is not an indication of the total number of sound recordings because there are many unpublished field recordings that are to be found only in archival collections, such as the Library of Congress' Archive of American Folk Culture (formerly Archive of [American] Folk Song). Child ballads represent the oldest layer of traditional Anglo-American folk song, and most collectors prize them greatly. While frequently voiced fears that American folk music in general is dying out have proven unfounded, there is little doubt that the older strata of folk song do thin out with the passage of time, to be replaced by other songs and ballads more meaningful to singers and audiences. ("Revivalist" singers can reverse this trend in specific instances.)

Laws's two syllabi are devoted to the next layers of traditional balladry; *ABBB* is a catalog of ballads found in North America that derive from cheap print sources, primarily of the 18th and early 19th centuries. The 290 ballads are divided into eight categories:

J	War Ballads
K	Sailors and Sea
L	Crime and Criminals
M	Family Opposition to Lovers
N	Lovers' Disguises and Tricks
O	Faithful Lovers
P	Unfaithful Lovers
Q	Humorous and Miscellaneous

They are organized in a sequential order suggested by the themes or styles of the ballads themselves. *NAB* enumerates 442 ballads divided into nine categories:

A	War Ballads
B	Cowboys and Pioneers
C	Lumberjacks
D	Sailors and the Sea
E	Criminals and Outlaws
F	Murders
G	Tragedies and Disasters
H	Miscellaneous Topics
I	Ballads of the Negro

Most of the ballads seem to have originated in the United States in the late 18th, 19th, or early 20th centuries.

I provide these indexes not out of a sense of reverence for the respective authorities, nor for the special significance of the ballads so identified. I would not be the first to complain about the shortcomings of either classification. Nevertheless, as convenient shorthand identifications of more than 1000 different ballads, they are undeniably useful, and the indexes are provided in that spirit. Scholars will continue to rely on these identifying numbers, at least until a more extensive catalog of American folk song, tunes, and balladry has been compiled and published--and perhaps even after then. Occurrences of a given ballad title are not cited in these two indexes if the recording is an instrumental version only, with no text--as often occurs with several ballads, in particular "Pretty Polly" and "John Henry."

III. Most recorded or most popular pieces

Given the many constraints of my criteria of selection, one can hardly use the song indexes as indicators of America's most popular folksongs and tunes. However, within certain subgenres one can at least identify those titles that have been most frequently recorded. (It takes some leap of faith to move from there to a statement about most "popular" or "well-liked" songs and tunes.) The following are all represented ten or more times.

A. Child Ballads. The ten most frequently recorded, in decreasing order, are: "The House Carpenter" (#243, with 26 recordings), followed closely by "Barbara Allen" (#84, 25) and then "Our Goodman" (#278); then "Blackjack Davy" (#200) tied with "The Unquiet Grave" (#79), "Golden Vanity" (#286), "Two Sisters" (#10), "Lord Thomas and Fair Ellender" (#74) tied with both "Lord Bateman" (#53) and "Edward" (#13). A comparison with other Child ballad compendia,[5,6] of which the most extensive is Bronson's *The Traditional Tunes of the Child Ballads*[7], reveals approximately similar ranking, with the interesting exception that "Our Goodman" seems to have gained in popularity--if not among singers, at least among collectors.

B. Broadside ballads listed in ABBB: "Pretty Polly" (P 36b, with 20 recordings), "Butcher Boy (P 24), and "Knoxville Girl" (P 35).

C. Native ballads listed in NAB: "John Henry" (I 1, with 23 recordings), "John Hardy" (I 2), a four-way tie among "Poor Ellen Smith" (F 11), "Omie Wise" (F 4), "Banks of the Ohio" (F 5), and "Wild Bill Jones" (E 10); "Streets of Laredo" (B 1), and "10,000 Miles from Home" (H 2).

D. Other ballads and songs (in alphabetical order): "Amazing Grace," "Darling Cora," "Don't Let Your Deal Go Down," "Free Little Bird," "Froggie Went a-Courting," "Little Birdie," "Little Maggie," "New River Train," "Nine Pound Hammer," "Old Joe Clark," "Reuben," "Run igger Run," "Short Life of Trouble," and "Wildwood Flower."

E. Instrumentals with few, if any, words (in alphabetical order): "Arkansas Traveler," "Bile Them Cabbage Down," "Billy In the Low Ground," "Black Eyed Susie," "Bonaparte's Retreat," "Cackling Hen," "Cindy," "Cluck Old Hen," "Cotton Eyed Joe," "Cripple Creek," "Cumberland Gap," "Flop Eared Mule," "Fly Around My Pretty Little Miss," "Forked Deer," "Fox Chase," "Hop High Ladies/Miss McLeod's Reel," "Ida Red," "Leather Britches," "Lost John," "Mississippi Sawyer," "Ragtime Annie," "Sally Ann," "Sally Goodin," "Shady Grove," "Shortening Bread," "Soldier's Joy," "Sourwood Mountain," "Sugar Hill," "Turkey in the Straw," and "Whoa Mule."

Without making too much of these listings, it is probably fair to say that they represent the most recorded folk tunes and songs of the second and third quarters of the 20th century--and quite possibly the most widely known and heard during that same period.

IV. Recommended albums

For the benefit of individuals or institutions that wish to assemble core collections of particularly significant recordings, I offer the following lists of albums in each of several categories. I have given particular attention to the quality and utility of the documentation in making these selections but am also conscious of my own (subjective) aesthetic considerations. Unfortunately, not all the albums are still in print.

A. Older ballads and vocal styles.

A list touted as recommending outstanding ballad singers must necessarily provoke the question, what makes a good ballad singer? While the different desiderata pertaining to art song, opera, popular song, and folksong deserve fuller exploration, here I just summarize without elaboration the traits that make a good, or great, traditional ballad singer. Essentially, the singer's role is to present a story in song, without detracting from the listener's understanding. As a corollary, it follows that a good singer is one with a good story--i.e., a good text: complete and sensible. Tempo need not be maintained rigorously but can follow the normal rhythms of ordinary speech (rubato parlando). A great ballad singer is one with a large repertoire of good texts, sung directly and effectively. In the selections for the following list I have also favored singers with older (preferably rare) ballads in their repertoires. "Older style" as defined here means pre-hillbilly singing style--which is to say, before the introduction of characteristics borrowed from Afro-American or pop styles. A certain amount of vocal decoration is acceptable in some regional traditions. In New England, there seems to be almost none. Some of the North Carolina singers mentioned below sing in a very decorated, or melismatic, style: this means with many passing notes (mordents, appoggiatura), turns, slides (portamento), vocal breaks (including "feathering"--a brief, fading, rising slide at the end of a phrase), and rubato. Especially in Kentucky there seems to be a preference for a very intense, high-pitched, declamatory presentation (sometimes called "high lonesome" style). Good singers are generally faithful to consistent pitch, though this does not seem to be important in some communities. Some singers (e.g., bluegrass stars Bill Monroe and Lester Flatt) may regularly sing certain notes of a song sharp or flat. Without some intensive fieldwork on the question, one can only assume, because of its consistency, that this is an intentional device, perhaps meant to heighten tension or effect (which it certainly can do). Devices of popular and art singing, such as change in volume, tempo (particularly decelerando), and vocal quality, or even the slightest histrionics, are not part of the traditional Anglo-American singer's style. Nor is a beautiful voice, or bel canto singing style, requisite for a folksinger. (Cowboy singer Jess Morris recorded "Old Paint" for John Lomax in a gravelly, quavery voice that may repel the uninitiated, but the rendition is one of the finest examples of American folksinging on record.)

In the following list, the first two are general, nationwide surveys; the next two represent northern traditions, and the last six, southern (Appalachian and Ozark) traditions.

1. *Child Ballads Traditional in the United States, Vols. 1 & 2* (Library of Congress AAFS L57 and L58)
2. *Anglo-American Ballads* (Library of Congress AFS L1)
3. *Eight Traditional British-American Ballads from the Helen Harness Flanders Collection of Middlebury College, Middlebury, Vermont* (New England Folksong Series #1)
4. *Sara Cleveland: Ballads and Songs of the Upper Hudson Valley* (Folk Legacy FSA-33)
5. *Traditional Music of Beech Mountain, No. Carolina, Vol. 1* (Folk Legacy FSA-22)
6. *Old Love Songs & Ballads from the Big Laurel, North Carolina* (Folkways FA 2309)
7. Horton Barker: *Traditional Singer* (Folkways FA 2362)
8. Almeda Riddle: *Ballads and Hymns from the Ozarks* (Rounder 0017)
9. Nimrod Workman: *Passing thru the Garden* (June Appal 001)
10. Jean Ritchie: *Child Ballads in America, Vol. 1/2* (Folkways FA 2301/2)

B. Fiddle music

The first album below is the best single anthology available of fiddling in the United States. The five following albums are regional collections from New England, Mississippi, Ohio, Missouri, and Texas, respectively; #s 2-4 are particularly well annotated; #5 is musically outstanding and excellently recorded. The remaining albums focus on individual fiddlers of outstanding ability and repertoire, though some are old recordings and technically inferior.

1. *American Fiddle Tunes* (Library of Congress AFS L62)
2. *New England Traditional Fiddling: An Anthology of Recordings, 1962-1975* (JEMF 105)
3. *Great Big Yam Potatoes* (Miss. Dept. of Archives & History AH-002)
4. *Seems Like Romance To Me: Traditional Fiddle Tunes--Ohio* (Gambier Folklore Soc. GFS 901)
5. *Now That's a Good Tune* (Grey Eagle / University of Missouri 101)
6. Bartow Riley / Vernon Solomon / Benny Thomasson: *Texas Hoedown* (County 703)
7. Tommy Jarrell: *Sail Away Ladies* (County 756)
8. *Emmett Lundy* (String STR 802)
9. Ed Haley: *Parkersburg Landing* (Rounder 1010)
10. *Fiddlin' Arthur Smith, Vol. 1/2* (County 546/547)
11. *Fiddling Doc Roberts: 1927-1933* (Davis Unlimited DU 33015)
12. *Eck Robertson* (Sonyatone STR 201)
13. *The Legend of Clark Kessinger* (County 733 [Folk Promotions FP 828])

C. Other Instrumental music

The first two collections are anthologies of stringband music from commercial 78s. #3 demonstrates the more recent (1950s) bluegrass stringband style. #4 is a collection of several outstanding instrumentalists from North Carolina. #s 5-7 highlight banjo instrumental music. #s 8 and 9 are devoted to two other instruments. The final album features three outstanding Tennessee musicians on banjo, fiddle, and guitar.

1. *Going Down the Valley: Vocal and Instrumental Styles in Folk Music* (New World NW 236)
2. *Early Rural String Bands* (RCA Victor LPV 552)
3. *Mountain Music Bluegrass Style* (Folkways FA 2318)
4. *Instrumental Music of the Southern Appalachians* (Tradition TLP 1007)

5. *The Library of Congress Banjo Collection* (Rounder 0237)
6. *More Clawhammer Banjo Songs & Tunes from the Mountains* (County 717)
7. *American Banjo Tunes & Songs in Scruggs Style* (Folkways FA 2314)
8. *Old-Time Mountain Guitar* (County 523)
9. Kilby Snow: *Country Songs and Tunes with Autoharp* (Asch AH 3902)
10. McGee Brothers and Arthur Smith: *Mountain Songs and Instrumentals* (Folkways FA 2379)

D. Religious music

The first item below is an excellent anthology of religious music from commercial 78s of the '20s and '30s, but, unfortunately, without much annotation. #2 is also from commercial 78s, mostly of the '30s. #s 3-5 are general field collections. #s 6-8 are excellently annotated but of more limited geographic and stylistic content. #s 9 and 10 are two specific styles, both well annotated.

1. *A Joyful Noise, Vol. 1/2* (Marimac [cass] 9100/9101)
2. *Something Got a Hold of Me: A Treasury of Sacred Music* (RCA 2100-2-R [CD])
3. *The Gospel Ship* (New World NW 294)
4. *Southern White Spirituals: Southern Journey 11* (Prestige INT 25011)
5. *White Spirituals* (Atlantic SD-1349)
6. *Primitive Baptist Hymns of the Blue Ridge* (UNC Press 0-8078-4083-1)
7. *Powerhouse of God* (UNC Press 0-8078-4084-X)
8. *Children of the Heavenly King* (Library of Congress AFC L69-L70)
9. *White Spirituals from the Sacred Harp* (New World NW 205)
10. *Early Shaker Spirituals* (Rounder 0078)

E. Individual artists or families

These albums are all excellently annotated collections of particular artists or groups that do not fit well into any of the above categories. The last six are from commercial 78s of the '20s and '30s; the others are field recordings from the '50s and later.

1. Luther Davis, Roscoe Parish, and Leone Parish: *The Old Time Way* (Heritage 070)
2. *The Watson Family* (Smithsonian/Folkways SF 40012 [CD])
3. *Old Time Music at Clarence Ashley's* (Folkways FA 2355)
4. *The Hammons Family* (Library of Congress AFS L65-L66)
5. *Ernest V. Stoneman and the Blue Ridge Corn Shuckers* (Rounder 1008)
6. Gid Tanner and His Skillet Lickers: *The Kickapoo Medicine Show* (Rounder 1023)
7. *Uncle Dave Macon* (Decca DL 4760)
8. *Grayson and Whitter* (County 513)
9. Fiddlin' John Carson: *The Old Hen Cackled and the Rooster's Going To Crow* (Rounder 1003)
10. *The Songs of Dick Burnett and Leonard Rutherford* (Rounder 1004)

F. Regional collections

Except for the first item, each of the following albums is devoted to a single state or a few contiguous counties. Except for #2, which is almost exclusively vocal music, the albums include instrumentals and vocals. The last four entries are from commercial 78s from the '20s and '30s.

1. *Brave Boys: New England Traditions in Folk Music* (New World NW 239)
2. *Wolf River Songs* (Folkways FE 4001)
3. *Mountain Music of Kentucky* (Folkways FA 2317)
4. *Fine Times at Our House: Indiana Ballads, Fiddle Tunes, Songs* (Folkways FS 3809)
5. *Traditional Music from Grayson & Carroll Counties* (Folkways FS 3811)
6. *The New Beehive Songster Volume 1/2* (Okehdokee OK 75003/75004)

7. *Echoes of the Ozarks, Vol. 1/2/3* (County 518/519/520)
8. *Kentucky Fiddle Band Music, Vol. 1/2/3* (Morning Star 45003/4/5)
9. *Nashville, the Early String Bands, Vol. 1/2* (County 541/542)
10. *Round the Heart of Old Galax, Vol. 1/2/3* (County 533/4/5)

G. Occupational and work songs

Unfortunately, there is no single package available that surveys broadly the important occupational musical genres of the United States--namely, cowboy, mining, textile mill, lumbering, maritime/whaling, and railroading. Cowboy songs are best represented in general, and the first five of the following are devoted to this genre.

1. Harry Jackson: *The Cowboy: His Songs, Ballads, & Brag Talk* (Folkways FH 5723)
2. Glen Ohrlin: *The Hell-Bound Train* (Campus Folksong Club University of Illinois CFC 301)
3. *Cowboy Songs*, Vols. I and II (Arizona Friends of Folklore AFF 33-1 and AFF 33-2)
4. *Cowboy Songs, Ballads, and Cattle Calls from Texas* (Library of Congress AAFS L28)
5. *Back in the Saddle Again* (New World NW 314/315)
6. *Songs of the Michigan Lumberjacks* (Library of Congress AAFS L56)
7. *Songs and Ballads of the Bituminous Miners* (Library of Congress AFS L60)
8. *Songs and Ballads of the Anthracite Miners* (Library of Congress AAFS L16)
9. *Railroad Songs and Ballads* (Library of Congress AFS L61)
10. *The Railroad In Folksong* (RCA Victor LPV 532)

REFERENCES

1. Published by the John Edwards Memorial Foundation (1984), now available from the Center for Popular Music at Middle Tennessee State University, Murfreesboro, TN.

2. Originally published in installments between 1882-98, reprinted in 1965 by Cooper Square Press, New York.

3. (Philadelphia: American Folklore Society Bibliography & Special Series, 1957).

4. (Philadelphia: American Folklore Society Bibliography & Special Series, rev. ed., 1964)

5. Branford P. Millar, "The American Ballad List," *Southern Folklore Quarterly* 17, 2 (1953).

6. Reed Smith, "A Glance at the Ballad and Folksong Field," *Southern Folklore Quarterly* 1, 2 (1936).

7. Published in four volumes, Princeton University Press, 1959-72.

ACKNOWLEDGMENTS

I am grateful to Alexa Cohen for undertaking the tedious tasks of assembling and typing much of the discographic data from the album jackets and brochures and proofreading the final copy. My thanks also to Keith Cunningham, David Freeman, Bobby Fulcher, Ken Irwin, Gordon McCann, Bill McNeil, John Morris, Ralph Rinzler, Mike Seeger, Carolyn Sturgill, Richard Weize, Hedy West, and Charles Wolfe for supplying some otherwise unobtainable information.

LABEL ABBREVIATIONS

ACM	Archive of Country Music		Ldr	Leader [England]
AH	Augusta Heritage		Mar	Marimac
AlaTrad	Alabama Traditions		MC	Middlebury College, Vermont
Alp	Alpine		MCA	MCA (formerly Decca)
Arb	Arbor		Mer	Meriweather
Arh	Arhoolie		MFFA	Missouri Friends of Folk Arts
ArkTrad	Arkansas Traditions		MFP	Montana Folklife Project
Atl	Atlantic		Min	Minstrel
AFF	Arizona Friends of Folklore		Miss	Mississippi Dept. of Archives and History
BB	(RCA) Bluebird			
BF	Bear Family [Germany]		Mtn	Mountain
Bio	Biograph		MS	Morning Star
Brch	Birch		N&T	Now and Then
BRI	Blue Ridge Institute		NW	New World
Brun	Brunswick		OFA	Traditional Arts Program /Ohio Foundation on the Arts
Cam	(RCA) Camden			
CFCUI	Campus Folksong Club, University of Illinois		OH	Old Homestead
			OHS	Ohio Historical Society
CMF	Country Music Foundation		Ok	Okedokee
CMH	CMH [Germany]		OT	Old Timey
Col	Columbia		OTC	Old Time Classics
CT	Country Turtle		PB	Pine Breeze
Cty	County		Ph	Philo
De	Decca		Prst	Prestige
DU	Davis Unlimited		Pu	Puritan
Elek	Elektra		RCA	RCA Victor
FC	Flying Cloud		Rim	Rimrock
Fleg	Folk Legacy		Riv	Riverside
Fly	Flyright [England]		Rndr	Rounder
FPrm	Folk Promotions (later Kanawha)		RRT	Rich-R-Tone
FSSM	Folksong Society of Minnesota		SH	Sugar Hill
FV	Folk Variety [Germany]		Shoe	Shoe String
Fwys	Folkways		Sm/Fwys	Smithsonian/Folkways
GFS	Gambier Folklore Society		Str	String [England]
GHP	GHP [Germany]		Sytn	Sonyatone
GnHys	Green Hays		Tak	Takoma
GV	Global Village		TFS	Tennessee Folklore Society
GyEg	Grey Eagle (University of Missouri)		TL	Time-Life
Har	Harmony		Tpc	Topic
Her	Heritage		Trad	Tradition
Hist	Historical		Tst	Testament
HMM	Home Made Music		UIP	University of Illinois Press
Hoop	Hoopsnake		UMP	University of Missouri Press
JEMF	John Edwards Memorial Foundation		UNC	University of North Carolina Press
JnAp	June Appal		UTP	University of Texas Press
Kan	Kanawha		Van	Vanguard
KM	Kicking Mule		Vet	Vetco
LC	Library of Congress Archive of Folk Song/Culture		Wstm	Westminster
			WVUP	West Virginia University Press

ALBUMS LISTED

Section I. Primarily non-commercial, or "field" recordings of individual artists/groups

1	County 777	Virgil Anderson: *...On the Tennessee Line*
2	Philo 1022	Ted Ashlaw: *Adirondack Woods Singer*
3	Folkways FA 2355	*Old Time Music at Clarence Ashley's*
4	Folkways FA 2359	*Old Time Music at Clarence Ashley's, Part 2*
5	Folkways FA 2350	*Clarence Tom Ashley and Tex Isley*
6	Leader LEE 4045	*Lonnie Austin & Norman Woodlieff*
7	Rounder 0026	*E. C. Ball*
8	Rounder 0072	E. C. and Orna Ball: *Fathers Have a Home Sweet Home*
9	Pine Breeze 006	Barbee/Bice Family: *Traditions of a Tennessee Family*
10	Folkways FA 2362	Horton Barker: *Traditional Singer*
11	June Appal JA 025	Andrew F. Boarman: *Mountain State Music*
12	Folkways FA 2392	*Dock Boggs, Vol. 2*
13	Asch AH 3903	*Dock Boggs, Vol. 3*
14	JEMF 104 (< Cap. T 2483)	*Presenting the Blue Sky Boys*
15	Rounder CD 11536	Blue Sky Boys: *In Concert, 1964*
16	County 709	*Camp Creek Boys*
17	Folk Legacy FSA-24	*Carolina Tar Heels*
18	Augusta Heritage AHR 003	Ernie Carpenter: *Elk River Blues*
19	Folkways FA 2418	Dillard Chandler: *The End of an Old Song*
20	Folk Legacy FSA-33	Sara Cleveland: *Ballads and Songs of the Upper Hudson Valley*
21	Philo 1020	*Sara Cleveland*
22	Rounder 0143	*Wilma Lee Cooper*
23	Arkansas Traditions 002	Noble Cowden: *Songs My Family Loves*
24	Kanawha 305	Billy Cox: *The Dixie Song Bird*
25	Mountain 303	Kyle Creed et al.: *Mountain Ballads*
26	Mountain 304	Kyle Creed, Emily P. Spencer and Brian Yerman: *Liberty*
27	Folkways FA 2342	*Rufus Crisp*
28	County 788	Clyde Davenport: *Clydeoscope: Rare & Beautiful Tunes from the Cumberland Plateau*
29	Folkways FTS 31016 (FA 2343)	George Davis: *When Kentucky Had No Union Men*
30	Testament T-3301	Dorsey Dixon: *Babies in the Mill*
31	Rounder 0047	Wilson Douglas: *The Right Hand Fork of Rush's Creek*
32	County 718	Ernest East and the Pine Ridge Boys: *Old-Time Mountain Music*
33	Davis Unlimited DU-33002	Norman Edmonds: *Train on the Island*
34	Flyright LP 546	Eller Brothers & Ross Brown: *Goin' to Georgia*
35	Folk Legacy FSA-13	Hank Ferguson: *Behind These Walls*
36	Rounder 0037	J. P. and Annadeene Fraley: *Wild Rose of the Mountain*
37	Rounder 0133	Art Galbraith: *Dixie Blossoms*
38	Rounder 0157	Art Galbraith: *Simple Pleasures: Old Time Fiddling from the Ozarks*
39	Kanawha 307	Franklin George & John Summers: *Traditional Music for Banjo, Fiddle, and Bagpipes*

40	Rimrock Rlp-495	*Aunt Ollie Gilbert Sings Old Folk Songs to Her Friends*
41	June Appal JA 020	Addie Graham: *Been a Long Time Traveling*
42	Davis Unlimited DU 33014	W. L. Gregory and Clyde Davenport: *Monticello Tough Mountain Music*
43	Folk Legacy FSA-26	Sara Ogan Gunning: *Girl of Constant Sorrow*
44	Rounder 0051	Sara Ogan Gunning: *The Silver Dagger*
45	Rounder 1010	Ed Haley: *Parkersburg Landing*
46	Lib. of Congress AFS L65-L66	*Hammons Family*
47	Rounder 0018	Hammons Family: *Shaking Down the Acorns*
48	W. Va. U. Press Sound Arch. 001	*Edden Hammons Collection*
49	Kanawha 310	Curley Herdman: *Old Time Country Music*
50	County 789	Dee and Delta Hicks: *Ballads and Banjo Music from the Tennessee Cumberland Plateau*
51	Tenn. Folklore Soc. TFS 104	*Hicks Family*
52	Folkways FA 2036	L. M. Hilton: *Mormon Folk Songs*
53	Arhoolie 5001	Hodges Bros: *Watermelon on the Vine*
54	Folkways FA 2368	Roscoe Holcomb: *The High Lonesome Sound*
55	Folkways FA 2374	Roscoe Holcomb: *Close to Home*
56	Birch 1945	*Doc Hopkins*
57	Rounder 0009	Clint Howard, Fred Price, and Sons: *The Ballad of Finley Preston*
58	Folk Legacy FSA-11	Max Hunter: *Ozark Folksongs and Ballads*
59	Rounder 1002	Aunt Molly Jackson: *Library of Congress Recordings*
60	Folkways FH 5723	Harry Jackson: *The Cowboy: His Songs, Ballads, & Brag Talk*
61	County 713	Fred Cockerham, Tommy Jarrell, and Oscar Jenkins: *Down to the Cider Mill*
62	County 723	Fred Cockerham, Tommy Jarrell, and Oscar Jenkins: *Back Home in the Blue Ridge*
63	County 741	Fred Cockerham, Tommy Jarrell, and Oscar Jenkins: *Stay All Night and Don't Go Home*
64	County 748	*Come and Go with Me: Tommy Jarrell's Banjo Album*
65	County 756	Tommy Jarrell: *Sail Away Ladies*
66	County 778	Tommy Jarrell: *Pickin' on Tommy's Porch*
67	County 791	Tommy Jarrell: *Rainbow Sign*
68	Mountain 302	Tommy Jarrell, Kyle Creed, Audine Lineberry, and Bobby Patterson: *June Apple*
69	Arhoolie 5011 [< Folklyric 123]	Jenkins and Sherrill: *Carolina Bluegrass*
70	Rounder 0005	Jenkins and Sherrill: *33 Years of Pickin' and Pluckin'*
71	Augusta Heritage AHR 001	John Johnson: *Fiddlin John*
72	Folkways FS 3810	*Buell Kazee Sings and Plays*
73	June Appal JA 009	*Buell Kazee*
74	County 733 [< Folk Prom. FP 828]	*The Legend of Clark Kessinger*
75	Kanawha 306	Clark Kessinger: *Sweet Bunch of Daisies*
76a	Old Homestead OHCS-314	Bradley Kincaid: *Old-Time Songs and Hymns--Vol. 1*
76b	Old Homestead OHCS-315	Bradley Kincaid: *Old-Time Songs and Hymns--Vol. 2*
76c	Old Homestead OHCS-316	Bradley Kincaid: *Old-Time Songs and Hymns--Vol. 3*
76d	Old Homestead OHCS-317	Bradley Kincaid: *Old-Time Songs and Hymns--Vol. 4*
77	County 712	Lily May Ledford et al.: *Coon Creek Girls*
78	Greenhays GR712	Lily May Ledford: *Banjo Pickin' Girl*
79	Rounder 0008	Steve Ledford: *Ledford String Band*

80	County 729	*Early Recordings of the Lilly Brothers*
81	Folkways FA 2433	Lilly Brothers: *Folk Songs from the Southern Mountains*
82	Prestige Folklore 14010	Lilly Brothers: *Bluegrass Breakdown*
83	Prestige Folklore 14035	*Country Songs of the Lilly Brothers*
84	Arhoolie 5010 [< Folklyric LP 122]	Louisiana Honeydrippers: *Bayou Bluegrass*
85	Prestige INT 13035	*Louisiana Bluegrass with the Louisiana Honeydrippers*
86	String STR 802	*Emmett Lundy*
87	Rounder 0020	Ted Lundy and the Southern Mountain Boys: *The Old Swinging Bridge*
88	Folkways FA 2040	Bascom Lamar Lunsford: *Smoky Mountain Ballads*
89	Riverside RLP 12-645	Bascom Lamar Lunsford: *Minstrel of the Appalachians*
90	Birch 1944	Lester McFarland and Robert Gardner: *Mac and Bob*
91	Bear Family BFX 15214	Uncle Dave Macon ...*At Home*
92	Arhoolie F5002	J. E. Mainer: *The Legendary Family from the Blue Ridge Mountains*
93	Augusta Heritage AHR 008	Phyllis Marks: *Folksongs and Ballads, Vol. 2*
94	Rounder 0034	Asa Martin & Cumberland Rangers: *Dr. Ginger Blue*
95	Folkways FD 5272	Harry McClintock: *Haywire Mac*
96	Arhoolie 5012	Sam McGee: *Grand Dad of the Country Guitar Pickers*
97	Folkways FA 2379	McGee Brothers and Arthur Smith: *Mountain Songs and Instrumentals*
98	Folkways FT 1007	McGee Brothers and Arthur Smith: *Milk 'em in the Evening Blues*
99	Rich-R-Tone LP-8073	Artus Moser: *North Carolina Ballads and Folk Songs*
100	County 720	*Mountain Ramblers, with Joe Drye*
101	Leader LEA 4040	*North Carolina Boys*
102	CFC U. of Ill. CFC 301	Glen Ohrlin: *The Hell-Bound Train*
103	Philo 1017	Glen Ohrlin: *Cowboy Songs*
104	Rounder 0158	Glen Ohrlin: *The Wild Buckaroo*
105	Folkways FA 2356	Old Harp Singers of Eastern Tennessee: *Old Harp Singing*
106	Folk Legacy FSA-15	Lawrence Older: *Adirondack Songs, Ballads, and Fiddle Tunes*
107	June Appal JA 049	Uncle Charlie Osborne: *Relics and Treasure*
108	Heritage 070	Luther Davis, Roscoe Parish, and Leone Parish: *The Old Time Way*
109	Arhoolie 5018	Uncle John Patterson: *Plains, Georgia Rock*
110	Riverside RLP 12-650	Pegram & Parham: *Pickin' and Blowin'*
111	Rounder 0001	*George Pegram*
112	Davis Unlimited DU-33009	Perry County Music Makers: *Sunset Memories*
113	Ariz. Friends of Folklore AFF 33-4	*Bunk and Becky Pettyjohn*
114	Folkways FA 2375	*Phipps Family*
115	Mountain 305	Pine River Boys: *Hoedown Time*
116	Marimac 9200	Everett Pitt: *Up Ag'in' the Mountain*
117	Folkways FA 2306	*Poplin Family of Sumter, South Carolina*
118	Folk Legacy FSA-1	*Frank Proffitt*
119	Folk Legacy FSA-36	*Frank Proffitt Memorial Album*
120	Folkways FA 2360	*Frank Proffitt Sings Folk Songs*
121	Riverside RLP 12-649	Obray Ramsey: *Banjo Songs of the Blue Ridge and Great Smokies*

122	Prestige INT 13020	*Obray Ramsey Sings Folksongs from the Three Laurels*
123	Prestige INT 13030	*Obray Ramsey Sings Folksongs from the Gateways to the Great Smokies*
124	Folkways FA 2493	Ola Belle Reed: *My Epitaph*
125	Rounder 0021	*Ola Belle Reed*
126	Rounder 0077	*Ola Belle Reed and Family*
127	Vanguard VRS-9158	Almeda Riddle: *Songs and Ballads of the Ozarks*
128	Rounder 0017	Almeda Riddle: *Ballads and Hymns from the Ozarks*
129	Minstrel JD-203	*Granny Riddle's Songs and Ballads*
130	Rounder 0083	Almeda Riddle: *More Ballads and Hymns from the Ozarks*
131	Arkansas Traditions 003	Almeda Riddle: *How Firm a Foundation & Other - Traditional Hymns*
132	Elektra EKLP-2	*Jean Ritchie Sings*
133	Riverside RLP 12-620	Jean Ritchie: *Saturday Night and Sunday Too*
134	Westminister SWN 18021	Jean Ritchie: *Songs from Kentucky*
135a	Folkways FA 2301	Jean Ritchie: *Child Ballads in America, Vol. 1*
135b	Folkways FA 2302	Jean Ritchie: *Child Ballads in America, Vol. 2*
136	Folkways FA 2427	Jean Ritchie: *Precious Memories*
137	Folkways FA 2426	*Jean Ritchie and Doc Watson and Folk City*
138	Greenhays GR714	Jean Ritchie: *The Most Dulcimer*
139	June Appal JA 037	Jean Ritchie: *Sweet Rivers*
140	Folk Legacy FSA-3	*Edna Ritchie of Viper, Kentucky*
141	County 202	Eck Robertson: *Famous Cowboy Fiddler*
142	Folk Legacy FSA-27	Grant Rogers: *Songmaker of the Catskills*
143	Kanawha 308	Grant Rogers: *Ballad Singer*
144	Kanawha 313	Grant Rogers: *Ballads and Fiddle Tunes*
145	Marimac 9013	Ross County Farmers: *Farmer's Frolic*
146	Biograph RC 6004	Betsy Rutherford: *Traditional Country Music*
147	Prestige INT 25007	Alabama Sacred Harp Singers: *All Day Singing from "The Sacred Harp": Southern Journey 7*
148	New World NW 205	*White Spirituals from the Sacred Harp*
149	June Appal JA0055	Morgan Sexton: *Rock Dust*
150	Rounder 0078	*Early Shaker Spirituals*
151	June Appal JA 032	Luke Smathers String Band: *In Full Swing*
152	June Appal JA 018	Betty Smith: *For My Friends of Song*
153	Folk Legacy FSA-17	Hobart Smith: *America's Greatest Folk Instrumentalist*
154	Elektra EKL-316	*Oliver Smith*
155	Asch AH 3902	Kilby Snow: *Country Songs and Tunes with Autoharp*
156	County 201	J. W. Spangler: *The Old Virginia Fiddlers*
157	Bear Family BCD 15456	Carl T. Sprague: *Classic Cowboy Songs*
158	June Appal JA 010	I. D. Stamper: *Red Wing*
159	County 739	*Stanley Brothers of Virginia, Vol. 2*
160	Folkways FS 3828	Pete Steele: *Banjo Tunes and Songs*
161	Folk Legacy FSA-18	Arnold Keith Storm: *Take the News to Mother*
162	Rounder 0194	John W. Summers: *Indiana Fiddler*
163	June Appal JA 030	Marion Sumner: *Road to Home*
164	Folkways FES 31089	Gordon Tanner et al.: *Down Yonder Old-Time String Band Music From Georgia*
165	Testament T-3302	Jimmie Tarlton: *Steel Guitar Rag*
166	Rounder 0032	Buddy Thomas: *Kitty Puss: Old Time Fiddle Music from Kentucky*

167	Takoma A 1013	Tony Thomas: *Old Style Texas and Oklahoma Fiddlin'*
168	County 724	Benny Thomasson: *Country Fiddling from the Big State*
169	Folk Legacy FSA-2	*Joseph Able Trivett*
170	Marimac 9025	Troxell Brothers: *Troxsong*
171	Rounder 0064	*George Tucker*
172	Folkways FA 3830	Virginia Mountain Boys: *Country Bluegrass from Southwest Virginia*
173	Folkways FA 3833	*Virginia Mountain Boys, Vol. 2: Blue Grass String Band*
174	Folkways FS 3839	*Virginia Mountain Boys, Vol. 3: Old Time Blue Grass from Grayson & Carroll Counties, Virginia*
175	Folkways FS 3829	*Cullen Galyean, Bobby Harrison and the Virginia Mountain Boys, Vol. 4*
176	Biograph RC-6002	*Fields and Wade Ward*
177	Biograph RC-6003	Wade Ward et al.: *Original Bogtrotters*
178	Folkways FA 2380	Wade Ward: *Uncle Wade*
179	Rounder 0036	Fields Ward: *Bury Me Not on the Prairie*
180	Smithson./Folkways SF CD 40012	*Watson Family*
181	Topic 12TS336	*Watson Family Tradition*
182	Vanguard VRS-9152	*Doc Watson*
183	Vanguard VRS-9170	*Doc Watson & Son*
184	Vanguard VRS-9213	Doc Watson: *Southbound*
185	Vanguard VRS-9239	Doc Watson: *Home Again*
186	Vanguard VSD-9/10	*Doc Watson on Stage*
187	Vanguard VCD-45/46	*Essential Doc Watson*
188	Vanguard VSD-107/108	Doc Watson, Clint Howard, and Fred Price: *Old Timey Concert*
189	Vanguard VSD-6576	Doc Watson: *Ballads from Deep Gap*
190	Sugar Hill SH-CD-3779	Doc Watson: *On Praying Ground*
191	Sugar Hill SH-CD-3786	*Doc Watson Sings Songs for Little Pickers*
192	Sugar Hill SH-CD-3795	Doc Watson: *My Dear Old Southern Home*
193	Vanguard VRS 9124	*Hedy West*
194	Vanguard VRS 9162	*Hedy West, Vol. 2*
195	Folk Legacy FSA-32	Hedy West: *Old Times and Hard Times*
196	Bear Family BF 15003	Hedy West: *Love, Hell, and Biscuits*
197	Topic 12T146	Hedy West: *Pretty Saro and other Appalachian Ballads*
198	Folkways FA 2357	Harry and Jeanie West: *Favorite Gospel Songs*
199	Folkways FA 2352	*Songs of Harry and Jeanie West*
200	Prestige INT 13038	*Roaming the Blue Ridge with Jeanie West*
201	Prestige INT 13049	Harry and Jeanie West: *Country Music in Blue Grass Style*
202	Augusta Heritage AHR 007	Everett White: *Folksongs & Ballads, Vol. 1*
203	Arkansas Traditions 004	Williams Family: *All in the Family*
204	June Appal JA 001	Nimrod Workman: *Passing Thru the Garden*
205	Rounder 0076	Nimrod Workman: *Mother Jones' Will*
206	Rounder 0089	Oscar and Eugene Wright: *Old Time Fiddle and Guitar Music from West Virginia*

Section II. Primarily non-commercial, or "field" recordings: Anthologies

207	Alabama Traditions 103	*Possum up a Gum Stump*
208	Ariz. Friends of Folklore AFF 33-1	*Cowboy Songs*
209	Ariz. Friends of Folklore AFF 33-2	*Cowboy Songs, Vol. II*

210	Ariz. Friends of Folklore AFF 33-3	*In an Arizona Town*
211	Arkansas Traditions [no #]	*Not Far from Here...Traditional Tales and Songs Recorded in the Field*
212	Asch AA 3/4	*Asch Recordings/1939-1945, Vol. 2*
213	Asch AH 3831	*Ballads and Songs of the Blue Ridge Mountains: Persistence and Change*
214	Atlantic SD-1346	*Sounds of the South*
215	Atlantic SD-1347	*Blue Ridge Mountain Music*
216	Atlantic SD-1349	*White Spirituals*
217	Atlantic SD-1350	*American Folk Songs for Children*
218a	Augusta Heritage AHR 009	*Folksongs & Ballads, Vol. 3*
218b	Augusta Heritage AHR 010	*Folksongs & Ballads, Vol. 4*
219	Blue Ridge Inst. BRI 002	*Virginia Traditions: Ballads from British Tradition*
220	Blue Ridge Inst. BRI 004	*Virginia Traditions: Native Virginia Ballads and Songs*
221	Blue Ridge Inst. BRI 005	*Virginia Traditions: Blue Ridge Piano Styles*
222	CFC U. of Ill. CFC 201	*Green Fields of Illinois*
223	County 703	Riley / Solomon / Thomasson: *Texas Hoedown*
224	County 707	Franklin / Franklin / Solomon: *Texas Fiddle Favorites*
225	County 717	*More Clawhammer Banjo Songs & Tunes from the Mountains*
226	County 757	*Clawhammer Banjo, Vol. 3*
227a	County 786	*Traditional Music from the Cumberland Plateau, Vol. 1: Gettin' Up the Stairs*
227b	County 787	*Traditional Music from the Cumberland Plateau, Vol. 2: Five Miles Out of Town*
228a	Folk Legacy FSA-22	*Traditional Music of Beech Mountain, NC, Vol. 1, The Older Ballads*
228b	Folk Legacy FSA-23	*Traditional Music of Beech Mountain, NC, Vol. 2, The Later Ballads*
229	Folk Promotions 41942	*Old-Time Music from Calhoun County, West Virginia*
230	Folk Promotions [no #]	*Old-Time Songs and Tunes from Clay County, West Virginia*
231	Folkways FA 2309	*Old Love Songs and Ballads from the Big Laurel, North Carolina*
232	Sm/Fwys CD SF 40037 (FA 2314)	*American Banjo Tunes & Songs in Scruggs Style*
233	Folkways FA 2315	*Stoneman Family / Old-Time Tunes of the South (Sutphin, Foreacre, and Dickens)*
234	Folkways FA 2317	*Mountain Music of Kentucky*
235	Sm/Fwys CD SF 40038 (FA 2318)	*Mountain Music Bluegrass Style*
236	Folkways FA 2358	*Jean Thomas, the Traipsin' Woman American Folk Song Festival*
237	Folkways FA 2363	*Music of Roscoe Holcomb and Wade Ward*
238	Folkways FA 2365	*Mountain Music*
239	Folkways FA 2390	*Friends of Old Time Music*
240	Folkways FA 2434	*Old Time Fiddlers' Convention at Union Grove, North Carolina*
241	Folkways FA 2435	*Galax Virginia Old Fiddlers' Convention*
242	Folkways FS 3809	*Fine Times at Our House: Indiana Ballads, Fiddle Tunes, Songs*
243	Folkways FS 3811	*Traditional Music from Grayson & Carroll Counties*
244	Folkways FS 3832	*Bluegrass from the Blue Ridge*

245	Folkways FS 3848	*Between the Sound and the Sea: Music of the North Carolina Outer Banks*
246	Folkways FE 4001	*Wolf River Songs*
247	Folkways FES 34151	*Hand Me Down Music 1. Traditional Music of Union County, North Carolina*
248a	Folkways FE 34161	*Folk Visions & Voices, Vol. 1: Traditional Music & Song in North Georgia*
248b	Folkways FE 34162	*Folk Visions & Voices, Vol. 2: Traditional Music & Song in North Georgia*
249	Gambier Folklore Society GFS 901	*Seems Like Romance to Me: Traditional Fiddle Tunes--Ohio*
250	Global Village SC 03	*Georgia Folk: A Sampler of Traditional Sounds*
251	Grey Eagle (U. of Mo.) 101	*Now That's a Good Tune*
252	Heritage 12	*2nd Annual Brandywine Mountain Music Convention, '75: Traditional Music of West Virginia*
253	Heritage XXII	Shelor/ Kimble Family: *Eight Miles Apart: Old Time Music From Patrick & Carroll County, Virginia*
254	Heritage XXXIII	*Visits*
255a	Home-Made Music LP001	*Appalachia - the Old Traditions - Vol. 1*
255b	Home-Made Music LP002	*Appalachia - the Old Traditions - Vol. 2*
256	Hoopsnake 101	*Down By the Rio Grande*
257	JEMF 105	*New England Traditional Fiddling: An Anthology of Recordings, 1962-1975*
	June Appal JAA001 [3 LP box]	*Anthology of Appalachian Music, Vol. 1. The Ballad Tradition*
	June Appal JAA002 [3 LP box]	*Anthology of Appalachian Music, Vol. 2. Mountain Instrumental*
	June Appal JAA003 [3 LP box]	*Anthology of Appalachian Music, Vol. 3. Mountain Swing and Blues*
258	June Appal JA0059C	*Best of Seedtime on the Cumberland Traditional Mountain Arts*
259	Kicking Mule KM 204	*Old-Time Banjo in America*
260	Leader LEA 4012	*Blue Ridge Mountain Field Trip*
261	Lib. of Congress AFS L1	*Anglo-American Ballads*
262	Lib. of Congress AFS L2	*Anglo-American Shanties, Lyric Songs, Dance Tunes and Spirituals*
263	Lib. of Congress AFS L7	*Anglo-American Ballads*
264	Lib. of Congress AAFS L9	*Play and Dance Songs and Tunes*
265	Lib. of Congress AAFS L11	*Sacred Harp Singing*
266	Lib. of Congress AAFS L12	*Anglo-American Songs and Ballads*
267	Lib. of Congress AAFS L14	*Anglo-American Songs and Ballads*
268	Lib. of Congress AAFS L16	*Songs and Ballads of the Anthracite Miners*
269	Lib. of Congress AAFS L20	*Anglo-American Songs and Ballads*
270	Lib. of Congress AAFS L21	*Anglo-American Songs and Ballads*
271	Lib. of Congress AAFC L26/27	*American Sea Songs and Shanties*
272	Lib. of Congress AAFS L28	*Cowboy Songs, Ballads, and Cattle Calls from Texas*
273	Lib. of Congress AFS L29	*Songs & Ballads of American History /Assassination of Presidents*
274	Lib. of Congress AAFS L30	*Songs of the Mormons and Songs of the West*
275	Lib. of Congress AAFS L54	*Versions and Variants of Barbara Allen*
276	Lib. of Congress AAFS L55	*Folk Music from Wisconsin*

277	Lib. of Congress AAFS L56	*Songs of the Michigan Lumberjacks*
278a	Lib. of Congress AAFS L57	*Child Ballads Traditional in the United States (I)*
278b	Lib. of Congress AAFS L58	*Child Ballads Traditional in the United States (II)*
279	Lib. of Congress AFS L60	*Songs and Ballads of the Bituminous Miners*
280	Lib. of Congress AFS L61	*Railroad Songs and Ballads*
281	Lib. of Congress AFS L62	*American Fiddle Tunes*
282	Lib. of Congress AFS L68	*"Folk Songs of America": The Robert Winslow Gordon Collection*
283	Lib. of Congress AFC L69-L70	*Children of the Heavenly King*
284	Meriweather 1001-2	*I Kind of Believe It's a Gift*
285	Middlebury College, #1	*Eight Traditional British-American Ballads*
286	Miss. Dept. Arch. & Hist. AH-002	*Great Big Yam Potatoes*
287	Mo. Friends of Folk Arts 1001	*I'm Old But I'm Awfully Tough*
288	Montana Folklife Project MFP 001	*When the Work's All Done This Fall*
289	Montana Folklife Project MFP 002	*If You Can't Dance to it, It's Not Old Time Fiddle Music*
290	New World NW 223	*I'm on My Journey Home: Vocal Styles and Resources in Folk Music*
291	New World NW 226	*That's My Rabbit, My Dog Caught It: Southern Instrumental Styles*
292	New World NW 239	*Brave Boys: New England Traditions in Folk Music*
293	New World NW 245	*Oh My Little Darling: Folk Song Types*
294	New World NW 291	*Old Mother Hippletoe: Rural and Urban Children's Songs*
295	New World NW 294	*The Gospel Ship*
296	New World NW 314/315	*Back in the Saddle Again*
297	Now and Then 1001	*Down Around Bowmantown*
298	Ohio Trad. Arts TALP-001	*Traditional Music from Central Ohio*
299	Ohio Historical Soc. OF 1001	*Folk Music of Ohio 1938 through 1940*
300	Okehdokee OK 75003	*New Beehive Songster, Vol. 1*
301	Okehdokee OK 76004	*New Beehive Songster, Vol. 2*
302	Pine Breeze 003	*A Bottle of Wine and Gingercake*
303	Pine Breeze 004	*Skip to My Lou*
304	Pine Breeze 005	*In the Field*
305	Prestige Folklore 14030	*Old Time Fiddling at Union Grove*
306	Prestige INT 25003	*Ballads and Breakdowns from the Southern Mountains: Southern Journey 3*
307	Prestige INT 25004	*Banjo Songs, Ballads, & Reels from Southern Mountains: Southern Journey 4*
308	Prestige INT 25006	*Folk Songs from the Ozarks: Southern Journey 6*
309	Prestige INT 25009	*Bad Man Ballads: Southern Journey 9*
310	Prestige INT 25011	*Southern White Spirituals: Southern Journey 11*
311	Riverside RLP 12-610	*Banjo Songs of the Southern Mountains*
312	Riverside RLP 12-617	*Southern Mountain Folksongs and Ballads*
313	Rounder 0028	*High Atmosphere*
314a	Rounder 0057	*Old Originals, Vol. 1: Old Time Instrumental Music*
314b	Rounder 0058	*Old Originals, Vol. 2: Old Time Instrumental Music*
315	Rounder 0065	*Lunsford / Pegram & Parham: Music From South Turkey Creek*
316	Rounder 0237	*Library of Congress Banjo Collection*
317	Rounder SS-0145	*Traditional Music on Rounder: A Sampler*

318	Shoestring Tape SGB 1	*Stone County Singing*
319	Tenn. Folklore Soc. [cass, no #]	*Some Ballad Folks*
320	Tenn. Folklore Soc. TFS-103	*The Mountains*
321	Tenn. Folklore Soc. TFS-105	*Historical Ballads of the Tennessee Valley*
322	Tenn. Folklore Soc. TFS-106	*The Kirkland Recordings*
323	Tenn. Folklore Soc. TFS-108	*It's Just the Same Today*
324	Tradition TLP 1007	*Instrumental Music of the Southern Appalachians*
325	U. of Ill. Press [cass, no #]	*Songs from Joe Scott the Woodsman-Songmaker*
326	U. of Missouri Press	*Old-Time Fiddler's Repertory*
327	U. of No. Car. Press 0-8078-4083-1	*Primitive Baptist Hymns of the Blue Ridge*
328	U. of No. Car. Press 0-8078-4084-X	*Powerhouse of God*
329	U. of Texas Press [cass, no #]	*Sing Me a Song* (to accompany the book, *Tell Me a Story...*)
330	Vanguard VRS-9147	*Old Time Music at Newport*
331a	Vanguard VRS-9182	*Traditional Music at Newport 1964, Part 1*
331b	Vanguard VRS-9183	*Traditional Music at Newport 1964, Part 2*

Section III. Hillbilly Reissues: Individual Artists/Groups

332	Bear Family BF 15501 (FV 12501)	Allen Brothers: *Country Ragtime*
333	Bear Family BF 15502 (FV 12502)	Jules Allen: *The Texas Cowboy*
334	Old Homestead OHCS 190	Emry Arthur: *I Am a Man of Constant Sorrow*
335	County 407	*Blue Ridge Highballers*
336	Folkways RBF 654	*Dock Boggs' Original Records*
337	RCA Bluebird AXM2-5525	*Blue Sky Boys*
338	RCA Camden CAL 797	*Blue Sky Boys*
339	Rounder 1006	Blue Sky Boys: *The Sunny Side of Life*
340	Rounder 1004	*Songs of Dick Burnett and Leonard Rutherford*
341	Old Homestead OHS 90031	*Callahan Brothers*
342	GHP LP 1001	*Carolina Tar Heels*
343	Bear Family BF 15507	*Can't You Remember the Carolina Tar Heels?*
344	Rounder 1003	Fiddlin' John Carson: *The Old Hen Cackled and the Rooster's Going To Crow*
345	U. of Ill. Press [cass, no #]	Fiddlin' John Carson: *Recordings To Accompany the Book, Fiddlin' Georgia Crazy*
346	RCA Camden CAL 586	*Original and Great Carter Family*
347	RCA Camden CAL 2473	Carter Family: *Lonesome Pine Special*
348	RCA Camden CAL 2554(e)	*More Golden Gems from the Original Carter Family*
349	RCA Camden ACLI-0047(e)	Carter Family: *My Old Cottage Home*
350	RCA Camden ACLI-0501	Carter Family: *Happiest Days of All*
351	CMH CMH 107	Carter Family: *Old Family Melodies*
352	CMH CMH 112	Carter Family: *Original and Essential, Vol. 1*
353a	CMH CMH 116	*Carter Family, Vol. 3*
353b	CMH CMH 118	*Carter Family, Vol. 4*
354	Decca DL 4404	Carter Family: *A Collection of Favorites*
355	Decca DL 4557	Carter Family: *More Favorites*
356	Harmony HL 7280/HS 11332	*Famous Carter Family*
357	Harmony HL 7300	*Great Original Recordings by the Carter Family*
358	Harmony HL 7344	Carter Family: *Home Among the Hills*
359	Harmony HL 7396	Carter Family: *Great Sacred Songs*
360	Harmony HL 7422	*Country Sounds of the Original Carter Family*
361	JEMF 101	*Carter Family on Border Radio 1938-1942*

362	MCA VIM-4012	*Carter Family*
363	MCA MCAD-10088 [CD]	Carter Family: *Country Music Hall of Fame Series*
364a	Old Homestead OHCS 111	*Original Carter Family in Texas -- Radio Transcriptions*
364b	Old Homestead OHCS 112	*Original Carter Family in Texas, Vol. 2--Radio Transcriptions*
365	Old Homestead OHCS 116	*Gospel Songs by the Carter Family in Texas, Vol. 3-- Radio Transcriptions*
366	Old Homestead OHCS 117	*Carter Family, Vol. 4--Radio Transcriptions*
367	Old Homestead OHS 90045	*Original Carter Family from 1936--Radio Transcriptions*
368	Old Time Classics OTC 6001	*Carter Family*
369	RCA Victor LPM 2772	Carter Family: *'Mid the Green Fields of Virginia*
370	Time-Life TL CW-06	*Carter Family*
371	County 524	*Da Costa Woltz's Southern Broadcasters 1927--Ben Jarrell and Frank Jenkins*
372	Old Time Classics OTC 6002	*Delmore Brothers*
373	Country Turtle 6000	Dixon Brothers: *Beyond Black Smoke*
374	Country Turtle 6002	Dixon Brothers: *Rambling and Gambling*
375	Old Homestead OHCS 191	Dykes "Magic City" Trio: *String Band Classics, Vol. 1*
376	County 410	*East Texas Serenaders*
377	Rounder 1032	Georgia Yellow Hammers: *The Moonshine Hollow Band*
378	Sonyatone STR 202	*Girls of the Golden West*
379	County 513	*Grayson and Whitter*
380	Davis Unlimited DU 33033	Grayson and Whitter: *Going Down Lee Highway: 1927-1929 Recordings*
381	Old Homestead OHCS 157	Grayson and Whitter: *Early Classics, Vol. 1*
382a	Bear Family BF 15508	*Complete Kelly Harrell, Vol. 1*
382b	Bear Family BF 15509	*Complete Kelly Harrell, Vol. 2*
382c	Bear Family BF 15510	*Complete Kelly Harrell, Vol. 3*
383	County 408	*Kelly Harrell and the Virginia String Band*
384	County 405	*Hillbillies*
385	County 409	*Lake Howard*
386	Rounder 1007	Frank Hutchison: *The Train That Carried My Girl from Town*
387	County 543	Earl Johnson and His Clodhoppers: *Red Hot Breakdown*
388	County 536	*Kessinger Brothers*
389	Kanawha 600	Kessinger Brothers: *Original Fiddle Classics 1928-1930*
390	Old Homestead OHCS 107	Bradley Kincaid: *Mountain Ballads and Old-Time Songs*
391	County 532	*Leake County Revelers*
392	Bear Family BF 15503 (FV 12503)	Uncle Dave Macon: *The Gayest Old Dude in Town*
393	Bear Family BF 15518	Uncle Dave Macon: *First Row, Second Left*
394	Bear Family BF 15519	Uncle Dave Macon: *Fun in Life*
395	County 521	*Recordings of Uncle Dave Macon*
396	County 545	Uncle Dave Macon and the Fruit Jar Drinkers: *Go Mule Go*
397	Decca DL 4760	*Uncle Dave Macon*
398	Folkways RBF 51	*Uncle Dave Macon*
399	Historical HLP 8006	Uncle Dave Macon: *Wait 'til the Clouds Roll By*
400	Rounder 1028	Uncle Dave Macon: *Laugh Your Blues Away*

401	Vetco 101	Uncle Dave Macon: *The Dixie Dewdrop*
402	Vetco 105	*Uncle Dave Macon, Vol. 2*
403a	Alpine ALP 201	*J. E. Mainer's Crazy Mountaineers, Vol. 1*
403b	Alpine ALP 202	J. E. Mainer: *Legendaries from the Blue Ridge Mountains, Vol. 2*
404a	Old Timey 106	*J. E. Mainer's Mountaineers, Vol. 1*
404b	Old Timey 107	*J. E. Mainer's Mountaineers, Vol. 2*
405	County 404	*Wade Mainer and the Sons of the Mountaineers*
406	Old Homestead OHS 90001	Wade Mainer: *Sacred Songs of Mother and Home*
407	Bear Family BF 15505 (FV 12505)	Dave McCarn and Gwen Foster: *Singers of the Piedmont*
408	Rounder 1009	Harry K. McClintock: *Hallelujah! I'm a Bum*
409	Bear Family BF 15517	*Sam and Kirk McGee from Sunny Tennessee*
410	RCA Bluebird AMX2-5510	Monroe Brothers: *Feast Here Tonight*
411	RCA Camden CAL 719	Bill Monroe and His Blue Grass Boys: *The Father of Blue Grass Music*
412	Biograph BLP 6005	*North Carolina Ramblers*
413	County 505	*Charlie Poole and the North Carolina Ramblers*
414	County 509	*Charlie Poole and the North Carolina Ramblers, Vol. 2*
415	County 516	*Legend of Charlie Poole*
416	County 540	*Charlie Poole and the North Carolina Ramblers, Vol. 4*
417	Historical HLP 8005	Charlie Poole & North Carolina Ramblers: *A Young Boy Left His Home One Day*
418	County 411	*Riley Puckett*
419	Old Homestead OHCS 114	Riley Puckett: *Old Time Greats, Vol. 1*
420	County 510	*Red Fox Chasers*
421	Rounder 1001	Blind Alfred Reed: *How Can a Poor Man Stand Such Times and Live?*
422	County 403	*Roane County Ramblers: Original Recordings, 1928-29*
423	Davis Unlimited DU 33015	*Fiddling Doc Roberts, 1927-1933*
424	Sonyatone STR 201	*Eck Robertson*
425	County 506	*Skillet Lickers*
426	County 526	*Skillet Lickers, Vol. 2*
427	Folksong Soc. Minn. LP 15001-D	*Gid Tanner and His Skillet Lickers*
428	Old Homestead OHCS 192	Gid Tanner and His Skillet Lickers: *Early String Band Classics*
429	Old Homestead OHCS 193	Gid Tanner & the Skillet Lickers in Texas: *Early String Band Classics, Vol. 3*
430	Rounder 1005	*Gid Tanner and His Skillet Lickers--With Riley Puckett and Clayton McMichen*
431	Rounder 1023	Gid Tanner and His Skillet Lickers: *Kickapoo Medicine Show*
432	Vetco 107	*Gid Tanner and the Skillet Lickers*
433a	County 546	*Fiddlin' Arthur Smith, Vol. 1*
433b	County 547	*Fiddlin' Arthur Smith, Vol. 2*
434	Bear Family BF 15521	*Carolina Buddies--Walter Kid Smith, Vol. 1*
435	Historical HLP 8004	*Ernest V. Stoneman and His Dixie Mountaineers, 1927-1928*
436a	Old Homestead OHCS 172	E. V. Stoneman: *With Family and Friends, Vol. 1*
436b	Old Homestead OHCS 173	E. V. Stoneman: *With Family and Friends, Vol. 2*
437	Rounder 1008	*Ernest V. Stoneman and the Blue Ridge Corn Shuckers*

438	County 401	Stripling Brothers: *Old Time Fiddle Tunes, 1928-1936*
439	Bear Family BF 15504 (FV 12504)	Darby and Tarlton: *Early Steel Guitar*
440	Old Timey 112	*Tom Darby and Jimmie Tarlton*
441	Puritan PU 3001	Tenneva Ramblers: *Great Original Recordings, 1927-28*
442	Historical HLP 8001 (BC 2433-1)	Fields Ward's Buck Mountain Band: *Early Country Music*

Section IV. Hillbilly Reissues: Anthologies

443	Brunswick 59000	*Mountain Frolic*
444	Brunswick 59001	*Listen to Our Story*
445	CMH CMH 106	*Hoboes and Brakeman*
446	Columbia CS 9660	*Ballads and Breakdowns of the Golden Era*
447	Country Music Foundation CMF 011-L	*Bristol Sessions Historic Recordings from Bristol, Tennessee*
448	Country Turtle 6001	*Gambler's Lament*
449	County 501	*Mountain Fiddle Music*
450	County 502	*Collection of Mountain Ballads*
451	County 503	*Mountain Fiddle Music, Vol. 2*
452	County 504	*Collection of Mountain Songs*
453	County 507	*Old Time Fiddle Classics*
454	County 508	*Mountain Sacred Songs*
455	County 511	*Mountain Blues*
456	County 514	*Hell Broke Loose in Georgia*
457	County 515	*Mountain Banjo Songs and Tunes*
458	County 517	*Texas Farewell*
459a	County 518	*Echoes of the Ozarks, Vol. 1*
459b	County 519	*Echoes of the Ozarks, Vol. 2*
459c	County 520	*Echoes of the Ozarks, Vol. 3*
460	County 522	*Old Time Ballads from the Southern Mountains*
461	County 523	*Old-Time Mountain Guitar*
462	County 525	*A Fiddlers' Convention in Mountain City, Tennessee*
463	County 527	*Old-Time Fiddle Classics, Vol. 2*
464a	County 528	*Traditional Fiddle Music of Mississippi, Vol. 1*
464b	County 529	*Traditional Fiddle Music of Mississippi, Vol. 2*
465	County 531	*Old Time String Band Classics*
466a	County 533	*Round the Heart of Old Galax, Vol. 1*
466b	County 534	*Round the Heart of Old Galax, Vol. 2*
466c	County 535	*Round the Heart of Old Galax, Vol. 3*
467a	County 541	*Nashville, the Early String Bands, Vol. 1*
467b	County 542	*Nashville, the Early String Bands, Vol. 2*
468	County 544	*Georgia Fiddle Bands, Vol. 2*
469	Flyin' Cloud FC-014	*Cotton Mills and Fiddles*
470a	Folkways FA 2951	*[Anthology of] American Folk Music, Vol. 1*
470b	Folkways FA 2952	*[Anthology of] American Folk Music, Vol. 2*
470c	Folkways FA 2953	*[Anthology of] American Folk Music, Vol. 3*
471	Historical HLP 8002 (BC 2433-2)	*Early Country Music, Vol. 2*
472	Historical HLP 8003	*Traditional Country Classics 1927-1929*
473	JEMF 103	*Paramount Old Time Tunes*
474a	Marimac 9100	*A Joyful Noise, Vol. 1*
474b	Marimac 9101	*A Joyful Noise, Vol. 2*
475a	Marimac 9104	*The Cold-Water Pledge, Vol. 1*

475b	Marimac 9105	*The Cold-Water Pledge, Vol. 2*
476	Marimac 9106	*Make Me a Cowboy Again for a Day*
477	Marimac 9109	*Johnny's Gone to War: Old-Time War Songs Recorded in the Golden Age*
478a	Marimac 9110	*It'll Never Happen Again (Old Time String Bands, Vol. 1)*
478b	Marimac 9111	*Goin' Up Town (Old Time String Bands, Vol. 2)*
479a	Morning Star 45003	*Wink the Other Eye: Kentucky Fiddle Band Music, Vol. 1*
479b	Morning Star 45004	*Wish I Had My Time Again: Kentucky Fiddle Band Music, Vol. 2*
479c	Morning Star 45005	*Way Down South in Dixie: Kentucky Fiddle Band Music, Vol. 3*
480	Morning Star 45008	*When I Was a Cowboy: Songs of Cowboy Life*
481	New World NW 236	*Going Down the Valley: Vocal and Instrumental Styles in Folk Music*
482	Old Homestead OHCS 141	*West Virginia Hills--Early Recordings from West Virginia*
483	Old Homestead OHCS 177	*Home in West Virginia: West Virginia Project, Vol. II*
484	Old Timey 100	*The String Bands, Vol. 1*
485	Old Timey 101	*The String Bands, Vol. 2*
486	Old Timey 102	*Ballads and Songs*
487	RCA 2100-2-R [CD]	*Something Got a Hold of Me: A Treasury of Sacred Music*
488	RCA 8416-2-R [CD]	*Ragged but Right: Great Country String Bands of the 1930's*
489	RCA 8417-2-R [CD]	*Are You from Dixie?: Great Country Brother Teams of the 1930's*
490	RCA Victor LPV 507	*Smoky Mountain Ballads*
491	RCA Victor LPV 522	*Authentic Cowboys and Their Western Folksongs*
492	RCA Victor LPV 532	*Railroad in Folksong*
493	RCA Victor LPV 548	*Native American Ballads*
494	RCA Victor LPV 552	*Early Rural String Bands*
495	Rounder 1026	*Rich Man, Poor Man: American Country Songs of Protest*
496	Rounder 1029	*Banjo Pickin' Girl, Vol. 1*
497	Rounder 1033	*Tennessee Strings*
498	Rounder 1035	*Work Don't Bother Me: Old Time Comic Songs from North Georgia*
499	Rounder 1037	*Kentucky Country: Old Time Music from Kentucky, 1927-1937 Recordings*
500	Vetco 103	*Songs of the Railroad Recorded 1924-1934*

SECTION I. Individual Artists/Groups--Primarily Noncommercial Recordings

1   Label Name/Number: County 777
Title: *...On the Tennessee Line*
Artist: Virgil Anderson
Collector/Recordist/Producer: Bobby Fulcher and Barry Poss
Place and Date of Recording: Rockybranch, KY, 1978
Date of Publication: 1981
Annotations: Liner notes by Fulcher
Selections:
   Bed Bug Blues
   Cincinnati Blues
   Green Ford Blues
   I'm Leaving You Woman
   Miner's Dream
   Muskrat
   Rainbow Schottische
   Station House Blues
   Trouble
   Wild Bill Jones [E 10]
   Wild Goose Chase
   You Been Gone So Long

   Cty 777:   Anderson, born in 1902 in the Upper Cumberland Plateau area along the Kentucky-Tennessee border, is a versatile banjo player from a region that has produced many fine banjoists--Dick Burnett, Clyde Davenport and W. L. Gregory among them. Fulcher recorded him at his home and at the local radio station. Anderson's two-finger playing alternates between up-picking and down-picking (frailing). He sings to his own accompaniment. Several of his songs were learned from a local family of black musicians, to whom Anderson attributes a good deal of his style and repertoire.

2   Label Name/Number: Philo 1022
Title: *Adirondack Woods Singer*
Artist: Ted Ashlaw
Collector/Recordist: Robert D. Bethke
Place and Date of Recording: NY, 1975
Date of Publication: 1976
Annotations: Liner notes by Robert D. Bethke
Selections:
   Alan Bain
   Bad Girl's Lament, The [Q 26]
   Barbara Allen [C. 84]
   Driving Saw-Logs on the Plover [dC 29]
   Farmer's Curst Wife, The [C. 278]
   Gentle Boy, The
   Hobo's Life, A
   Joe Bowers [B 14]
   Katie Morey [C. 112 / N 24]
   Mantle So Green [N 38]
   Mickey Brannigan's Pup

Miner Hill
Peggy Gordon
Roving Cunningham, The [H 4]
Two Sons of North Britain [J 12]
When the Work's All Done This Fall [B 3]
Willie Was as Fine a Sailor

Ph 1022: This interesting album offers the first recordings by a 68-year-old northeasterner from a traditional singing family whose material is remarkably free of any contemporary commercial influences. Ashlaw does acknowledge that he learned "Driving Saw-Logs on the Plover" from a 78 rpm disc in the 1920s; this would be the recording (Columbia 15278-D) by Pierre La Dieu (pseudonym for Oscar Grogan--a popular singer whose texts came from Carl Sandburg's anthology, *American Songbag*). Ashlaw's very unornamented singing is characteristic of the Anglo-Canadian style of the northeast; his repertoire, though, shows the pervasive Irish influence of the region. Less characteristic are the two western songs--"Joe Bowers," from the 1850s, and "When the Work's All Done This Fall," from the 1890s--and the relatively unusual "Alan Bain," often thought to be exclusively of Ozark provenance. I was particularly drawn to "Willie Was as Fine a Sailor," a beautiful supernatural tale, set to an Irish tune, that has turned up only rarely. [JEMFQ 53]

3   **Label Name/Number:** Folkways FA 2355
Title: *Old Time Music at Clarence Ashley's*
Artists: Tom Ashley, Doc Watson, Clint Howard, Fred Price, Stella Gilbert, Gaither Carlton, Jack Johnson, Eva Ashley Moore, Tommy Moore
Collector/Recordist: Ralph Rinzler and Eugene Earle
Place and Date of Recording: Shouns, TN, Saltville, VA, and Deep Gap, NC, 1960
Date of Publication: 1961
Annotations: 12 p. booklet by Ralph and Richard Rinzler, discography by Eugene Earle
Selections:
Claude Allen -- Ashley, Watson
East Tennessee Blues -- Price, Howard
Footprints in the Snow -- Howard, Price, Watson, Johnson
God's Gonna Ease My Troublin' Mind -- Ashley, Watson
Handsome Molly -- Watson, Carlton
Haunted Woods, The -- Moore
Honey Babe Blues -- Ashley, Watson, Howard, Price
I'm Going Back to Jericho -- Watson, Carlton, Rinzler
Louisiana Earthquake, The -- Gilbert
Maggie Walker Blues -- Howard, Price, Watson
Old Man at the Mill, The -- Howard, Price
Old Ruben -- Watson, Carlton
Pretty Little Pink -- Howard, Watson, Price, Johnson, Moore
Richmond Blues -- Howard, Price
Sally Ann -- Howard, Watson, Price, Johnson
Skillet Good and Greasy -- Watson, Rinzler
True Lovers [G 21] -- Moore, Watson, Howard, Price

4   **Label Name/Number:** Folkways FA 2359
Title: *Old Time Music at Clarence Ashley's, Part 2*
Artists: Tom Ashley, Doc Watson, Clint Howard, Fred Price, Gaither Carlton, Arnold Watson, the Original Carolina Tar Heels (Ashley, Dock Walsh, Garley Foster), Jack Burchett, Jean Ritchie

Collector/Recordist: Eugene Earle, Mike Seeger, Ed Kahn, and Ralph Rinzler
Place and Date of Recording: Saltville, VA, 1961; Chicago and Los Angeles, 1962
Date of Publication: 1963
Annotations: 16 p. booklet by Ralph Rinzler
Selections:

Amazing Grace -- Watson, Ashley, Howard, Price, Ritchie
Coo-Coo Bird, The -- Ashley, Watson
Corrina, Corrina -- Howard, Watson, Price
Crawdad Song -- Howard, Watson, Price
Daniel Prayed -- Price, Howard, Watson
Free Little Bird -- Ashley, Howard, Watson, Price
Humpbacked Mule -- Price, Watson
Lee Highway Blues -- Price, Howard, Watson
Little Sadie [I 8] -- Ashley, Watson
My Home's Across the Blue Ridge Mts. -- Ashley, Foster, Walsh, Watson
Poor Omie [F 4] -- Ashley, Watson
Rising Sun Blues -- Ashley, Watson
Shady Grove -- Ashley, Burchett
Tough Luck -- Ashley, Watson
Walking Boss -- Ashley
Way Down Town -- Watson, Howard, Price

Folkways FA 2355 / FA 2359: Tom Clarence Ashley (1895?-1967) had enjoyed a successful recording career during the late 1920s and early '30s--as solo artist, in a duo with Gwen Foster, more popularly, as a member of the Carolina Tar Heels, and in other groups as well. When Ralph Rinzler met him at the Union Grove Old Time Fiddlers' Convention in April, 1960, Ashley was 65 years old, hadn't played banjo in years, and would sing only one song. With Rinzler's encouragement, and knowing that there was an emerging interest in old-time music in Northern cities, Ashley decided to brush up his playing and singing and put together a band, which made its first appearance in New York in March 1961. The band was recorded at various locations in the next two years, from which material these two albums were assembled. The release of these albums and the band's many personal appearances from New York to Los Angeles quickly established them as one of the best old timey stringband combinations actively performing--a remarkable evaluation in view of the band's short time together before then. Ashley, during the 20s and 30s, established his reputation as an excellent singer and banjo-player; now, in his sixties, he demonstrated that he had lost none of his musicianship, though his tempos were somewhat slower, and his voice deeper in timbre. He is accompanied by Clint Howard (b. 1930), a first-rate lead singer and back-up guitarist; Fred Price (b. 1915), an outstanding old-time fiddler, and Doc Watson, of whom more is said elsewhere (see notes to his albums later in this Section). In this ensemble, Watson carefully played a supporting role to Ashley's lead; his many talents were not fully revealed until his solo work later. Listening to these albums almost three decades after their first appearance, I still rank them as among the best of old-time stringband music to be recorded since the 1940s. Among the high points of the two albums are Ashley's vocal lead on "Little Sadie," "Coo Coo Bird," and "Walking Boss"--all with his unique clicking sound on the banjo accompaniment; the Ashley/Watson duet on the spiritual, "God's Gonna Ease My Troublin' Mind," the gospel trio on "Daniel Prayed," Price's lead fiddle work on "Lee Highway Blues," and Howard's lead vocal on the ballad, "Maggie Walker Blues." These citations are not meant to imply that the other selections are not noteworthy; these are outstanding albums from beginning to end. [JAF 292--DKW (FA 2355)]

5 Label Name/Number: Folkways FA 2350
Title: *Clarence Tom Ashley and Tex Isley Play and Sing American Folk Music*

Artists: Tom Ashley and Tex Isley
Collector/Recordist: Ralph Rinzler
Place and Date of Recording: Shouns, TN, ca. 1966
Date of Publication: 1966
Annotations: 8 p. booklet by Jon Pankake
Selections:
 Cluck, Old Hen
 Faded Roses
 Frankie Silvers [E 13]
 Hard Luck Blues
 House Carpenter, The [C. 243]
 I'm the Man That Rode the Mule Around the World
 Little Hillside
 Little Log Cabin in the Lane, The
 May I Sleep in Your Barn Mister?
 Prisoner's Song, The
 Rude and Rambling Man [L 12]
 Shout Little Lulu
 Whoa, Mule
 Wild Bill Jones [E 10]

Fwys FA 2350: Ashley's career has been thoroughly documented as a result of Ralph Rinzler's extensive work with him (see above, FA 2355 and FA 2359). Larry "Tex" Isley, from near Spray, North Carolina, was several years younger than Ashley and recorded with Charlie Monroe in 1946 and 1950. He accompanies Ashley on guitar or autoharp. Ashley shows that at age 71 he is still a great singer, wonderfully able to put over a ballad. His "House Carpenter" compares very favorably to his 1928 recording--if anything, it is more listenable because his tempo is slower and his vocal range a little lower and mellower. "Rude and Rambling Man" and "May I Sleep in Your Barn" are also wonderful performances. His "Talking Blues" is a recurrent bit of medicine show humor that he renders with subtle humor and exquisite timing--accompanied by Isley's perfectly-suited finger-picking guitar. [JAF 317--DKW]

6   Label Name/Number: Leader LEE 4045
Title: *Lonnie Austin & Norman Woodlieff*
Artists: Lonnie Austin & Norman Woodlieff (with Janet Kerr and Emery Higginbotham)
Collector/Recordist/Producer: Janet Kerr
Place and Date of Recording: Charleston, WV; Eden, NC; 1971-72
Date of Publication: 1975
Annotations: 7 p. attached booklet by Janet Kerr
Selections: (All by Lonnie Austin except as noted)
 Dan Carter Waltz
 Flop-Eared Mule
 Flying Clouds
 Forked Deer
 Golden Slippers
 He Went in Like a Lion -- Woodlieff
 Heffinger's Fox Chase
 Little Brown Jug
 Mississippi Sawyer
 Pickin' My Way to Georgia -- Woodlieff
 Richmond

  Rickett's Hornpipe
  Rustic Dance
  Sally Gooden
  Silly Bill
  Streets of Glory, The -- Woodlieff
  Under the Double Eagle

  Leader LEE 4045: Lonnie Austin and Norman Woodlieff both grew up in Spray (now Eden), North Carolina; in the late 1920s and early '30s both performed and recorded--Woodlieff as guitarist, Austin as fiddler--with Charlie Poole, one of the most popular musicians of the area. Austin hadn't played fiddle for several years--and Woodlieff hadn't played with him for even longer--when Janet Kerr, with help from Cliff Rorrer, tried to arrange a joint recording session. Unfortunately, circumstances did not permit that, and on this album the two musicians play separately. On most of these selections Austin solos on fiddle; Woodlieff has three quite nice guitar/vocal solos. Sewn-in insert notes give considerable background on the two musicians and their careers.

7 **Label Name/Number:** Rounder 0026
Title: *E. C. Ball*
Artists: Estil C. Ball with Orna Ball and the Friendly Gospel Singers
Collector/Recordist: R. N. Drevo, Bruce Kaplan
Editor: Mark Wilson
Place and Date of Recording: Grassy Creek, NC
Date of Publication: 1973
Annotations: Liner notes by Bruce Kaplan
Selections:
  Ain't No Grave Can Hold My Body Down
  Aunt Dinah's Quilting Party
  Born to Serve the Lord
  Cabin in the Valley, The
  Chow Time
  Do You Call that Religion?
  Early Bird Always Gets the Worm, The
  Give Me Just a Little More Time
  House of Gold
  I See God in Everything
  I'm Glory Bound
  John the Baptist
  Parting Hand, The
  Raggin' the Wires
  Troubles, Trials, Tribulations
  When I Can Read My Titles Clear

8 **Label Name/Number:** Rounder Records 0072
Title: *Fathers Have a Home Sweet Home*
Artists: Estil C. and Orna Ball, with Blair and Elsie Reedy
Collector/Recordist: Mark Wilson
Place and Date of Recording: Rugby, VA, 1976
Date of Publication: 1976
Annotations: Brief liner notes by Rounder Collective
Selections:

Blues in the Morning
Crazy Fingers
Every Time I Kneel and Pray
Fathers Have a Home Sweet Home
Go Down Moses
Here and There
Hold to God's Unchanging Hand
I Want to Know More About My Lord
I've Been a Hard-Working Pilgrim
If You Believe
Jubilee
Old Time Religion
One Day I Will
Plain Old Country Lad
Pretty Polly [P 36b]
Sugarfoot Rag

Rndr 0026 / 0072: Estil C. Ball was first recorded by John A. Lomax for the LC in 1941, and had been playing professionally for over three decades when this album was recorded. In the 1960s and '70s, he and his wife, Orna, performed primarily gospel music in public, several examples of which have been recorded in the '60s and '70s. Rounder 0026 album strives for a broader sampling than the title might suggest, including humorous secular songs and guitar instrumentals as well as gospel music. Both "Chow Time" and "Raggin' the Wires" are unusual guitar instrumentals that illustrate Ball's clean finger picking and rich guitar sound. Orna Ball's harmony singing on this LP is at times weak and uncertain--not representative of her best work.

Rndr 0072 was produced to demonstrate the wide range of material Estil and Orna Ball perform. Although religious material seems to be the backbone of the Balls's performances, Estil's not-flashy-but-rock-solid guitar picking fits equally well on the secular tunes--some of his own composition. The Balls are joined by the Reedys, Orna's brother and sister, on some gospel quartet performances, but Estil's voice is clearly the dominant one. On "Pretty Polly" Ball plays banjo. On instrumentals like "Sugarfoot Rag" and his own "Crazy Fingers," Ball shows his influence from country music of the post-W. W. II decades. [WF 1/75]

9   Label Name/Number: Pine Breeze 006
Title: *Traditions of a Tennessee Family*
Artist(s): The Barbee/Bice Family (Oscar and Eva Barbee, Jimmy Bice, Maudie Ford, Ruth Myers, Eldia Barbee)
Collector/Recordist/Producer: Students of the Traditional Music Project of Pine Breeze Center
Place and Date of Recording: Soddy, TN, and Washington DC, 1976-78
Date of Publication: 1979
Annotations: Liner notes by Ron Williams
Selections:
   Buckin' Mule
   Citico
   Cumberland Gap [3 versions]
   Frank Barbee Hornpipe
   Glory Land Road
   Goin' to Chattanoogie
   He'll Hold to My Hand
   House of Gold

    I'm Living on Higher Ground
    I'm So Glad He Found Me
    Ida Red
    Katy Hill
    Let the Spirit Descend
    March Around the Throne
    Smoke Behind the Clouds

    PB 006: Produced by students of Pine Breeze Center, Chattanooga, this album is divided between recordings of brothers Eldia (fiddle, banjo, vocals) and Oscar Barbee (banjo)--probably both in their late seventies, and of their sister Elzia's children, Maudie Ford, Ruth Myers, and Jimmy Bice. The elder brothers play banjo and fiddle tunes; the younger generation sings religious songs.

10   Label Name/Number: Folkways FA 2362
Title: *Traditional Singer*
Artist: Horton Barker
Collector/Recordist: Sandy Paton
Place and Date of Recording: Beech Creek, NC, ca. 1961
Date of Publication: 1962
Annotations: 7 p. booklet by Sandy Paton
Selections:
    Amazing Grace
    At the Foot of Yonders Mountain
    Blue-Haired Jimmy
    Bow and Balance [C. 10]
    City Four Square
    Dev'lish Mary [Q 4]
    Drunkard's Courtship, The
    Farmer's Curst Wife, The [C. 278]
    Gypsy's Wedding Day, The [O 4]
    Hop, Old Rabbit, Hop
    Lord Thomas and Fair Ellender [C. 73]
    Miller's Will, The [Q 21]
    Paddy Doyle
    Rolly Trudum
    Sweet Mary
    There Was an Old Lady [Q 2]
    Turkish Rebilee, The [C. 286]
    Wayfaring Stranger
    Wondrous Love

    Fwys FA 2362: Horton Barker, sightless from early childhood as the result of an accident, was born in Laurel Bloomery, northeast Tennessee, in 1889 but lived most of his life in Virginia. In the 1930s he came to the attention of folksong collectors and made his first public singing appearance at White Top Mountain Folk Festival in 1933. He made numerous festival appearances in the next three decades and learned many of his songs from other performers at such gatherings. He was recorded in the 1930s by Annabel Buchanan at White Top and by Sarah Gertrude Knott and later Alan Lomax in Washington. Paton's visit with him in ca. 1961 afforded the opportunity to document this wonderful singer with decent recording equipment. Barker has a sweet, gentle tenor voice and sings in rather unornamented style. His "Lord Thomas" and "Bow and Balance" have not changed much in the more than twenty years since he recorded them for the Library of Congress (cf. AFS L7 in Section II), except that his singing seems somewhat mellower and more relaxed. [JAF 299--DKW]

11   Label Name/Number: June Appal JA 025
Title: *Mountain State Music*
Artist: Andrew F. Boarman
Collector/Recordist: Bill Canady
Place and Date of Recording: Berkeley County, WV, 1976-1977
Date of Publication: 1978
Annotations: 4 p. booklet by Jim Steptoe and Dick Kimmel
Selections:
    Buffalo Gals
    Clinch Mountain Backstep
    Dancin' Waves Schottische
    Darktown Dandies
    Darlin' Nellie Gray
    Derby Polka
    Don't Let Your Deal Go Down
    Home Sweet Home
    Medley
    San Antonio Rose
    Smile Awhile
    Soldier's Joy
    Somewhere's in West Virginia
    Turkey in the Straw
    When They Ring Those Golden Bells
    Whoa Mule, Whoa
    Wildflower of the Mountain
    Wreck of the Old 97
    Yes Sir, She's My Baby

JA 025: Boarman, born in 1911 in Berkeley County, West Virginia, plays banjo in both clawhammer and a fairly classical style. He gave up playing professionally during the hard Depression years and didn't start again until the late '50s.

12   Label Name/Number: Folkways FA 2392
Title: *Dock Boggs, Vol. 2*
Artist: Dock Boggs
Collector/Recordist: Mike Seeger
Place and Date of Recording: Wise, VA, 1964
Date of Publication: 1965
Annotations: 8 p. booklet by Jon Pankake & Willard Johnson
Selections:
    Banjo Clog
    Brother Jim Got Shot
    Cole Younger [E 3]
    Danville Girl [H 2]
    Death of Jerry Damron, The
    Glory Land
    John Henry [I 1]

    Little Black Train
    Mixed Blues
    No Disappointment in Heaven
    Old Joe's Barroom [B 1]
    Papa, Papa Build Me a Boat [K 12]
    Poor Boy in Jail [I 4?]
    Railroad Tramp
    Schottische Time
    Sugar Baby
    Wise County Jail

13 Label Name/Number: Asch AH 3903
Title: *Dock Boggs, Vol. 3*
Artists: Dock Boggs
Collector/Recordist/Editor: Mike Seeger
Place and Date of Recording: Roosevelt, NJ; Ann Arbor, MI; Asheville, NC; Norton, VA, 1966?
Date of Publication: 1970
Annotations: 8 p. brochure by Mike Seeger
Selections:
    Calvary
    Careless Love
    Coke Oven March
    Cuba
    Davenport
    Dying Ranger [A 14]
    I Hope I Live a Few More Days
    John Hardy [I 2]
    Leave It There
    Little Ommie Wise [F 4]
    Loving Nancy
    Peggy Walker [P 1b]
    Prayer of a Miner's Child
    Roses While I'm Living
    Sugar Blues
    Turkey In the Straw

     Fwys FA 2392 and Asch AH 3903: Boggs's early life and recording career is synopsized in the comments to Folkways RBF 654 (q. v., in Section III). After his "rediscovery" by Mike Seeger, three albums were issued--the first (Folkways FN 5458) consisting mostly of interviews and these two, of his music. Both albums include mostly traditional ballads, blues, and banjo lyrics together with a few of Boggs's own arrangements of poems written by neighbors or contributors to the *United Mine Workers' Journal.* The brochures include ballet facsimiles introduced by transcriptions of Boggs's comments about the songs taken from interviews. Boggs's style was an almost anomalous combination of black and white influences, unique in the 1920s; in the '60s he sounded much as he had four decades earlier. Several of the same tunes, which he immortalized on 78s, are redone in these LPs. [WF 7/72]

14 Label Name/Number: JEMF 104 (reissued from Capitol T 2483)
Title: *Presenting the Blue Sky Boys*
Artists: Bill and Earl Bolick

Producer: (Paul F. Wells; originally Ken Nelson)
Place and Date of Recording: Los Angeles, CA, May 1965
Date of Publication: 1977 [Capitol issued ca. 1966]
Annotations: Booklet by Paul F. Wells, David Whisnant
Selections:
  Corina, Corina
  Cotton Mill Colic
  I Don't Want Your Greenback Dollar
  Jack O'Diamonds
  Midnight Special
  Oh Marry in Time [C. 2]
  Oh Those Tombs
  Poor Boy [I 4]
  Unquiet Grave, The [C. 79]
  Who's Gonna Shoe Your Pretty Little Feet
  Wild and Reckless Hobo [H 2]
  Will the Circle Be Unbroken

15 Label Name/Number: Rounder CD 11536 (also LP 0236)
Title: *In Concert, 1964*
Artists: Blue Sky Boys [Bill and Earl Bolick]
Producer: Bill Bolick and Ken Irwin
Place and Date of Recording: 1964, U. of Illinois, Champaign IL
Date of Publication: 1989
Annotations: Song notes insert by Charles Wolfe
Selections:
  After the Ball
  Are You from Dixie? (2)
  Beautiful
  Behind These Prison Walls of Love
  Butcher's Boy, The [P 24]
  Don't Trade
  Fox, The
  I'm Just Here To Get My Baby out of Jail
  I'm Saved
  If I Could Hear My Mother Pray Again
  In the Hills of Roane County
  It Was Midnight on the Stormy Deep
  Kentucky
  Last Letter, The
  Only One Step More
  Quit That Ticklin' Me
  Sweetest Gift, The
  Sweetheart Mountain Rose
  Whispering Hope
  Worried Man Blues

JEMF 104 / Rndr CD 11536:   Among the many old time hillbilly artists of the 1930s and '40s who were brought back to the concert stage by the folk revival were North Carolinians Bill and Earl Bolick, the Blue Sky Boys. They had enjoyed great popularity on both radio and records in the 1930s. After the hiatus in their careers caused by the War, they resumed activity until 1951, making records for several labels; then Earl chose to quit the profession for family reasons. In 1963, Archie Green and Ed Kahn located Bill Bolick in Greensboro, North Carolina, and then Earl, in Atlanta; they persuaded the brothers to reunite for a concert at the University of Illinois in October 1964, the first of several campus appearances. The Blue Sky Boys' *In Concert, 1964* (Rounder) recaptures some of the highlights from that memorable concert. Although on their Bluebird recordings of the 1930s, the brothers' repertoire included many older native American and Anglo-American ballads and songs, with the exception of "The Fox" and "The Butcher's Boy" [Laws P 24] (the latter on the CD only) the selections on this album are no older than the late 1800s (e. g., their theme song, "Are You from Dixie?" and "After the Ball"), and several were popular hillbilly songs of the 1930s ("I'm Just Here To Get My Baby out of Jail," "The Last Letter," "Midnight on the Stormy Deep") or inspirational songs of comparable vintage ("Only One Step More," "The Sweetest Gift"). They also recreated one of the comedy routines they used to perform over radio or in live shows, with Earl taking the part of the old hillbilly rube, Uncle Josh. The CD includes 22 of the 26 songs done at the concert; the LP version has 13. There are some flubbed lines, but considering that the brothers hadn't performed together in over a dozen years, they sounded much as they had two decades earlier: smooth, carefully blended duet singing, accompanied by their own guitar and mandolin. The CD brochure and LP jacket notes include song notes by Charles Wolfe that incorporate Bill Bolick's comments on their sources for the material. In addition, the LP jacket has an historical note by Green on finding the brothers and working with them. (This pair of releases foreshadows what has become a nuisance for librarians, archivists, and discographers, if not purchasers as well: the issue of what appears to be the same material in two or more formats--identical title and cover art--but with different contents. The problem may be resolved in a few years as companies phase out entirely the LP format.) While they were in Los Angeles to play at the 1965 UCLA Folk Festival, Ed Kahn arranged a recording session for them with Capitol Records. The album did not stay in print long; and a dozen years later, the JEMF reissued the material with an elaborate booklet, documenting in depth the Bolicks' musical careers and repertoires. Highly sophisticated musicians who perceived clearly the different interests of their Folk Festival audiences from those of their southern rural fans, the Bolicks stressed the older numbers in their repertoires for these recordings. In fact, the Bolicks had not previously recorded any of these songs. [JAF 314--DKW (Capitol)]

16   Label Name/Number: County 709
Title: *The Camp Creek Boys*
Artist: Camp Creek Boys (Fred Cockerham, Kyle Creed, Ernest East, Paul Sutphin, Verlin Clifton, Ronald Collins)
Producer/Recordist: Charlie Faurot
Place and Date of Recording: 1967?
Date of Publication: [1967]
Annotations: Liner notes by Dave Freeman
Selections:
   Cider Mill
   Cotton Eyed Joe
   Fall on My Knees
   Fire in the Mountain
   Fortune
   Honeysuckle
   June Apple
   Let Me Fall
   Lonesome Road Blues
   Old Joe Clark
   Soldier's Joy

Cty 709:   The Camp Creek Boys consists of six musicians from Surry County, North Carolina, and adjacent regions who have been playing music at social functions and fiddlers' conventions since the 1930s. Cockerham and Creed, who play both fiddle and banjo; and East, fiddle and guitar, are also represented on other albums in this discography. Sutphin and Collins play guitars; Clifton, mandolin. All the selections on this album are familiar traditional dance tunes, though some are particularly associated with the Mt. Airy-Galax area ("Fortune," "Cider Mill, "Let Me Fall," "Fall on My Knees"). The album is a fine selection of old-time instrumental stringband music.

17   Label Name/Number: Folk Legacy FSA-24
Title: *The Carolina Tar Heels*
Artists: Dock Walsh, Drake Walsh, Garley Foster
Collector/Recordist: Archie Green, Eugene Earle
Place and Date of Recording: Taylorsville, NC, 1961-62
Date of Publication: 1964/65
Annotations: 33 p. booklet by Archie Green and Eugene Earle
Selections:
  Ain't Gonna Be Treated This-A-Way
  Bull Dog in Sunny Tennessee
  Courtin' in the Rain
  Crescent Limited
  Dango
  Drake's Reel
  Garley's Fox Chase
  Go Wash in That Beautiful Pool
  Goin' to Georgia
  Hide-A-Me
  I Was Born Four Thousand Years Ago
  If I Was A Minin' Man
  Jimmie Settleton
  Knockin' on the Henhouse Door
  Mama Scolds Me For Flirtin'
  My Brushy Mountain Home
  This Morning, This Evening, Right Now

FLeg FSA-24:   Dock Walsh (1901-1967) was born in Wilkes County, North Carolina, into a family of musically talented siblings. He made his first commercial "hillbilly" recordings in 1925, singing and accompanying himself on banjo; in 1927 he and Gwen Foster recorded for Victor as a duo named, by A&R Man Ralph Peer, the Carolina Tar Heels. The following year Garley Foster and Clarence Ashley joined the band and Gwen Foster dropped out. Walsh and Garley Foster continued to play together well after their last recordings in 1932. Both men gave up music except on a very occasional basis as supporting their new families required more reliable occupations. In 1962, Green and Earle visited Walsh and Foster and learned that Dock's son, Drake, also a musician, had learned much of the Tar Heels' repertoire; the three men thus constituted a somewhat rejuvenated Carolina Tar Heels. The recordings are divided between remakes of some of the Tar Heels' old 78s and other tunes, mostly well known; a few are original compositions. The band's full history and detailed notes on the selections and text transcriptions are provided by Green's brochure notes. [JAF 310--DKW]

18   Label Name/Number: Augusta Heritage AHR 003
Title: *Elk River Blues: Traditional Fiddle Tunes from Braxton County, West Virginia*
Artist: Ernie Carpenter
Producers: Gerry Milnes and Michael Kline
Place and Date of Recording: Elkins, WV, 1980s
Date of Publication: 1986
Annotations: 11 p. booklet, reprinted from *Goldenseal Magazine* (Summer 1986) by Gerald
     Milnes and Michael Kline
Selections:
     Betty Baker
     Camp Run
     Cripple Creek
     Elk River Blues
     Flippin' Jenny
     Forked Deer
     Gunboat
     Horney Ewe, The
     Jack of Diamonds
     Jimmy Johnson
     Old Sledge
     Pretty Little Girl I Left Behind Me
     Ryestraw
     Shelvin' Rock
     Twin Sisters
     Wild Horse
     Yew Piney Mountain

     AHR 003: Carpenter, old-time fiddler from West Virginia, learned his music from older
relatives and friends in Braxton and neighboring counties. He is accompanied by Gerry Milnes on
banjo or guitar and Michael Kline on guitar. The long booklet consists mostly of transcripts of Carpenter's stories and reminiscences relating to his music and life. Jacket notes give brief comments
on the tunes and Carpenter's sources.

19   Label Name/Number: Folkways FA 2418
Title: *The End of an Old Song*
Artist: Dillard Chandler
Collector/Recordist: John Cohen
Place and Date of Recording: Marshall, NC, 1968
Date of Publication: 1975
Annotations: 6 p. booklet by Robert Balsam
Selections:
     Black Jack Daisy [C. 200]
     Carolina Lady, The [O 25]
     Drunken Driver
     Gastony Song
     Gathering Flowers
     Going Down the Road
     Hicarmichael
     Jesus Says Go
     Little Farmer Boy [C. 243]
     Meeting Is Over

    Old Shop
    Rain and Snow
    Short Time Here
    Sport in New Orleans
    Young Emily [M 34] -- Doug Wallin

    Fwys FA 2418: This is an outstanding collection by the star performer of Cohen's earlier
album from the Big Laurel, North Carolina (Folkways FA 2309, q.v.)--and the subject of a
documentary film by Cohen, *The End of an Old Song.* Chandler is one of the best traditional
singers on record in terms of highly ornamented, melismatic vocal style. In this style, which, in this
country, seems to be found almost exclusively in the southeast--but is certainly not universal there--
the singer decorates his/her melody line lavishly with grace notes, slides, passing tones, and feathering (ascending vocal breaks at the end of a phrase)--all within the compass of the metrically free
rhythm (rubato). A six-page booklet includes only a brief autobiographical sketch (inasmuch as the
companion film documents Chandler's life), text transcriptions, and brief song notes. Doug Wallin,
another excellent singer, is Chandler's nephew. Chandler's "Rain and Snow" is a fuller text than the
few other recordings of this song--enough of a story line to demonstrate convincingly that there was
a full ballad behind what now survives. "Gastony Song" is a "Midnight Special" variant. Although
Chandler's repertoire and style bespeak the older layers of Appalachian tradition, his "Old Shep,"
Red Foley's popular sentimental ballad of 1940, demonstrates that new compositions can push their
way into the hoariest of repertoires. All in all, a fine sampling of an excellent traditional singer.

20   Label Name/Number: Folk-Legacy FSA-33
Title: *Ballads and Songs of the Upper Hudson Valley*
Artist: Sara Cleveland
Collector/Recordist: Sandy Paton
Place and Date of Recording: Brant Lake, NY, 1966
Date of Publication: 1968
Annotations: 25 p. booklet by Kenneth S. Goldstein
Selections:
    Before the Daylight in the Morning
    Captain Webster
    Come All You Maidens
    Every Rose Grows Merry in Time [C. 2]
    In Bonny Scotland [N 2]
    Maiden's Lament, The
    Molly Bawn [O 36]
    My Bonny Bon Boy [C. 12]
    Queen Jane [C. 52]
    To Wear a Green Willow [P 31]

21   Label Name/Number: Philo 1020
Title: *Sara Cleveland*
Artist: Sara Cleveland
Collector/Recordist: William H. Schubart
Producer: John Diamond
Place and Date of Recording: North Ferrisburg, VT
Date of Publication: 1975
Annotations: Liner notes by Kenneth Goldstein
Selections:
    Boy That Lives Here, The

Georgia Volunteer, A
Great Milwaukee Fire, The [G 15]
James Bird [A 5]
James MacDonald [P 38]
Mines of Irvingdale, The [G 6]
One and a Few
Queenstown Warning, The [H 14]
Utah Carl [B 4]
Woodsman's Alphabet, The

FLeg FSA-33 / Philo 1020: Unaccompanied ballad singer Cleveland (1905-87), born in Hartford, up-state New York, was hailed by Kenneth Goldstein as our "best living traditional female singer in New England." Her singing style, though, is rather undistinguished (at 70 years of age), and she offers her songs in a sweet and gentle voice. The enclosed booklet to FSA-33 includes a list of some 200 songs in her repertoire. She tends to sing at a more stately pace than most singers with much use of head tones. Among her ballads is Child 52, which has not been found outside of Scotland. Other imported items include "The Maiden's Lament," a combination of "Sprig of Thyme" and "Seeds of Love"; "Before the Daylight in the Morning," on the theme of the slovenly wife; and "Captain Webster," about a young man who commits suicide because his mother opposes his marriage to a girl of insufficient means. The brochure notes by Goldstein contain a brief but revealing quotation from Mrs. Cleveland on northern vs. southern styles, although Goldstein has interpreted her characterization of southern singing as referring to popular music.

The Philo album samples further her extensive repertoire (some 200 ballads and songs, all learned from a relatively small circle of relatives and friends), and offers proof of its breadth: unusual ballads of British origins, Amerian ballads from the West as well as from the Northeast, homiletic and sentimental pieces from TPA, religious pieces, and hillbilly songs. (Not all of these categories are represented on this album.) Her distinction lies in the extent of her repertoire and the completeness of her texts (her "Queenstown Warning" runs to more than 10½ minutes), while "Utah Carl" and "James Bird" exceed 7 and 6 minutes, respectively. Goldstein's back jacket notes on the songs are adequate, but some fuller annotations--details concerning the circumstances of the recordings, text transcriptions, and at least minimal biographical background--could have been provided. [JAF 325, WF 10/74 (FLeg); JEMFQ 53 (Philo)]

22 Label Name/Number: Rounder Records 0143
Title: *Wilma Lee Cooper*
Artists: Wilma Lee Cooper with Stoney Cooper, Butch Robins, Bill Carver, Jerry Shook, Jim Brock, Jr., Carol Lee Cooper
Place and Date of Recording: Some at Starday Studios, Nashville, 1976; some at Pete's Place, Nashville, TN
Date of Publication: 1982
Annotations: Liner notes by Robert K. Oermann
Selections:
Bury Me Beneath the Willow
Cowards over Pearl Harbor
Curly Headed Baby
Far Beyond the Starry Sky
Forsaken Love
Nobody's Darling but Mine
Sinful to Flirt [G 19]
Still There's a Spark of Love
What'll I Do with the Baby-O

Who's Gonna Shoe Your Pretty Little Feet
You Tried to Ruin My Name

Rndr 0143:   Wilma Lee Cooper (b. 1921) began her professional musical career with her gospel-singing family, the Learys, but was best known for her musical partnership of nearly forty years with her husband, fiddle-player Stoney Cooper. After Stoney's death in 1977, Wilma Lee continued as a solo act. Her rich, resonant voice made her one of the most distinctive country singers of the 1940s and '50s. Her repertoire ranges from contemporary country gospel back to the mid-19th century, as this album demonstrates. Some of the tracks on this album were recorded shortly before Stoney's death.

23   Label Name/Number: Arkansas Traditions 002
Title: *Songs My Family Loves*
Artist: Noble Cowden accomp. by Lina Lee
Collector/Recordist: Aubrey Richardson
Place and Date of Recording: Cushman and Mountain View, AR; 1979, 1982
Date of Publication: 1984
Annotations: 8 p. booklet by W. K. McNeil; liner notes by George West
Selections:
   Beaver Cap
   Come Take a Trip in My Airship
   Drunkard's Dream
   False Hearted Lover [F 1]
   Horrid Boy, The
   Little Bessie
   Little Oma [F 4]
   May I Sleep in Your Barn Tonight, Mister
   My Mother Was a Lady
   Nobody's Darling on Earth
   Pretty Little Miss
   Prisoner at the Bar
   Put My Little Shoes Away
   They Say It Is Sinful To Flirt [G 19]

Ark Trad 002:   Mrs. Noble Cowden sings fourteen Ozark ballads and songs with guitar accompaniment by her daughter Lina Lee. These songs, selected by the singer or her kin, represent the family favorites. For the most part they are the sentimental--nay, heartrending--"Tin Pan Alley" songs that originated in the last half or third of the 19th century but were rejuvenated via the repertoires of early hillbilly recording artists of the 1920s. Mrs. Cowden is a very listenable singer whose style is unornamented. The guitar backup--and vocal harmony in two selections--are appropriate and unobtrusive. For some of her otherwise familiar songs she has unusual melodies. [JAF 391]

24   Label Name/Number: Kanawha 305
Title: *The Dixie Song Bird*
Artist: Billy Cox
Collector/Recordist/Editor: [Ken Davidson?]
Date of Publication: 1967
Annotations: 2 p. insert sheet
Selections:
   Alimony Woman

Battle Axe and the Devil, The [C. 278]
Blind Baggage Blues
Blue and Low
Brown's Ferry Blues
Dang My Pop-Eyed Soul
Democratic Donkey, The
Fiddling Soldier, The [P 14]
Filipino Baby
Franklin D. Roosevelt's Back Again
Girl in the Hillbilly Band
Jailer's Daughter
Old Pinto and Me
Rolling Pin Woman
Sweet Eloise
They Sent Her Gun to War
Wino's Last Prayer

Kan 305: William Jennings Cox (1897-1968) was born in Charleston, West Virginia. In the late 1920s he built up a local reputation for singing and playing guitar and harmonica, which led to a regular show in the newly opened radio station WOBU. He made numerous 78 rpm recordings between 1929 and 1940 for the Gennett family of labels and for Columbia. From then his musical career remained dormant for over two decades. Over the years, Billy built up the repertoire that began with songs he had learned from his mother with later songs and many of his own compositions. This album consists of fresh recordings of some of his best-known songs. "Battle Axe and the Devil" and "Fiddling Soldier" are the only songs in the set that Cox learned from oral tradition. "F. D. R.'s Back Again" and "Democratic Donkey" were written on Election Day, 1936, and capture the jubilant spirit of young southern democratic supporters looking forward to the repeal of prohibition with Roosevelt's reelection. "Filipino Baby" was Cox's best-known composition after a very successful recording by Cowboy Copas. [JAF 320--DKW]

25 Label Name/Number: Mountain 303
Title: *Mountain Ballads*
Artists: Kyle Creed, Bobby Patterson, Katie Golding, James Lindsey, Bob Flesher, Pete Lissman, and Thomas Norman
Place and Date of Recording: 1974, Galax, VA
Date of Publication: 1974
Annotations: Brief liner notes by Kyle Creed
Selections:
Blackberry Blossom
Cackling Hen
Jimmy Clark
Little Maggie
Love Somebody
Mississippi Sawyer
No One To Love Me [K 12]
Pretty Polly [P 36b]
Raggedy Ann
Sadie Goodwin
South
Sweet Sunny South

26 **Label Name/Number:** Mountain 304
Title: *Liberty*
Artists: Kyle Creed; vocals by Emily P. Spencer or Brian Yerman
Place of Recording: Galax, VA
Date of Publication: 1977
Selections:
    Big Liza
    Cumberland Gap
    Katy Kline
    Let Me Fall
    Liberty
    Little Liza Jane
    Lost Indian
    Nellie Grey
    Roust-a-bout
    Sail Away Ladies
    Shady Grove
    Sinful Flirt [G 19]

Mtn 303 / Mtn 304: Kyle Creed, well-known banjoist/fiddler in the Galax area, started his own record company in the early 1970s and has issued several enjoyable albums--including these--of old-time dance music--mostly pre-bluegrass style. These two albums consist of familiar tunes well rendered by Creed and various friends. Mtn 303 includes mostly dance tunes, with a few vocals by Thomas Norman. Bob Flesher plays lead banjo on the impressive onomotopoetic tune, "Cackling Hen." Emily P. Spencer offers three splendid vocals on Mtn 304.

27 **Label Name/Number:** Folkways FA 2342
Title: *Rufus Crisp*
Artists: Rufus Crisp; also Palmer Crisp, Betty Lafferty, Pharmer Howell
Collector/Recordist: Margot Mayo, Stuart Jamieson
Place and Date of Recording: Allen, KY, 1946
Date of Publication: 1972
Annotations: 8 p. booklet by Margot Mayo
Selections: (all by Rufus Crisp unless noted otherwise)
    Ball and Chain
    Blue Goose
    Blue-Eyed Girl
    Brighter Days
    Cumberland Gap
    Do, Little Bobby
    Fall, Fall, Build Me a Boat [K 12]
    Farewell to Old Beaver -- Mrs. Lafferty
    Old Joe Clark-- w/Howell
    Roll on John -- Palmer Crisp
    Shady Grove
    Shoofly
    Shout Little Lulie
    Sourwood Mountain
    Sourwood Mountain -- w/Howell
    Trouble on My Mind
    Walk Light Ladies
[Also some stories]

recorder and recorded a selection of songs for deposit at the LC AFS. Several of these were issued on LC LPs. Ms. Mayo recorded him again on tape in 1955, but the material on this LP is compiled from the 1946 sessions. Many of the pieces are familiar banjo tunes, including the fine rendition of "Walk Light, Ladies." "Trouble on My Mind" is to the "Molly and Tenbrooks"/"Skipping and Flying" tune; "Ball and Chain" is a melange of lyrics to the "Roving Gambler" tune. "Fall, Fall" is a fragment of K 12 to the tune of "Waterbound." Also included is a discussion of banjo tunings and some anec- dotes by Crisp and an unaccompanied ballad, "Farewell to Sweet Beaver," by neighbor Betty Laf- ferty. Rufus' son, Palmer, sings and plays guitar on the beautiful "Roll On, John," a variant of "Roll on Buddy," and popularized much later by the revival band, The Greenbriar Boys. Brochure notes by Mayo discuss the music, the tunings, Crisp's life, and the history of Floyd County, Kentucky. [WF 1/75]

28 Label Name/Number: County 788
Title: *Clydeoscope: Rare & Beautiful Tunes from the Cumberland Plateau*
Artist(s): Clyde Davenport, with Sharon Poss and Bobby Fulcher
Collector/Recordist: Barry Poss and Bobby Fulcher
Producer: Bobby Fulcher
Place and Date of Recordings: KY, 1977
Date of Publication: 1986
Annotations: Liner notes by Bobby Fulcher
Selections:
> Boatin' Up the Sandy
> Callahan
> Coal Creek March
> Five Miles
> Flatwoods
> Flower from the Fields of Alabama
> Jenny in the Cotton Patch
> Kitty Puss
> Ladies on the Steamboat
> Meriweather
> Old Cow Died in the Forks of the Branch, The
> Old Mister Rabbit
> One Eyed Rosie
> Polecat's Den
> Roses in the Morning
> Rye Straw

Cty 788: Clyde Davenport (b. 1921), of Monticello, Kentucky, plays both banjo and fiddle. With D. L. Gregory (q. v.) he has recorded a series of banjo-fiddle duets highly reminiscent of the style of old-time musicians Dick Burnett and Leonard Rutherford. On this album, we hear mostly his fiddle but some banjo also with guitar and banjo accompaniment. As Fulcher observes in his notes, Davenport has "...a large repertory of 'solo' fiddle tunes, played in an archaic style character- ized by cross tunings, elaborate bowings and eccentric melody lines.... He may well have the largest repertory of solo fiddle tunes among any living southern mountain fiddler." Davenport played with a contemporary country/bluegrass group in the 1940s, but this is not apparent in his breakdown numbers.

29 Label Name/Number: Folkways FTS 31016 (also issued as FA 2343)
Title: *When Kentucky Had No Union Men*
Artist: George Davis, some with accomp. on fiddle or 2nd guitar by Marion Sumner

29 **Label Name/Number:** Folkways FTS 31016 (also issued as FA 2343)
Title: *When Kentucky Had No Union Men*
Artist: George Davis, some with accomp. on fiddle or 2nd guitar by Marion Sumner
Collector/Recordist/Editor: John Cohen
Place and Date of Recording: All but two in Hazard, KY, 1966
Date of Publication: 1968
Annotations: Liner notes by John Cohen (booklet in FA 2343)
Selections:
    Buggerman in the Bushes
    Callahan
    Child of Desertion, A
    Coal Miner's Boogie
    Death of the Blue Eagle
    Glory in the Meeting House
    Harlan County Blues, The
    Jesus Appeared in a Barroom
    Little Lump of Coal, The
    Love of Polly and Jack Monroe [N 7]
    Miner's Dream Come True
    Rocking Chair Money
    Sixteen Tons
    Three-Day Blues, The
    When Kentucky Had No Union Men
    White Shotgun
    Why Are You Leaving?
    Wreck of Main Line Number 4, The

    Fwys FTS 31016: Davis was born in 1906 in Campbell County, east Tennessee; when still in his teens he moved to Kentucky and began 28 years of working in the coal mines. He took up playing guitar and writing songs about mining life in the '30s, several of which are included here; his "Harlan County Blues" was also collected by George Korson (see LC AFS L60). Davis claimed also to have written "Sixteen Tons" in the '30s also, and accused Merle Travis of plagiarizing it. Travis has related the story of his own composition in such convincing detail that it taxes credulity to concede substantial borrowing from someone else's work. Davis's own version--to a somewhat different tune--is also included here. Davis also recorded two songs for the Rich-R-Tone label in 1949 (RRT 435), one side of which ("Coal Miner's Boogie") is reissued here. "Miner's Dream" is an earlier studio recording. "Old Age Pension Check," learned from a Roy Acuff recording, is given a bouncy and bluesy (if somewhat unpolished) treatment.

30 **Label Name/Number:** Testament T-3301
Title: *Babies in the Mill*
Artists: Dorsey Dixon, Nancy Dixon, and Howard Dixon
Collector/Recordist: Gene Earle and Archie Green
Editors: Gene Earle and John Schmidt
Place and Date of Recording: Most in East Rockingham, NC, 1962; 3 (with Howard Dixon)
    from commercial 78s of 1936-37
Date of Publication: 1964
Annotations: 12 p. brochure and liner notes by Archie Green
Selections: (all by Dorsey Dixon except as noted)
    Across the Shining River
    Babies in the Mill

Be at Home Soon Tonight
Burglar Man [H 23]
Christmas Cake
Factory Girl
Factory Girl--Nancy Dixon
Girl I Left in Danville [H 2]--duet with Howard Dixon
Hard Times in Here
Hard Times in Here--Nancy Dixon
I Saw the Wood
Our Johnny
Pin Ball Machine
Somebody Touched Me
Weave Room Blues--duet with Howard Dixon
Weaver's Life--duet with Howard Dixon
Will the Circle Be Unbroken
Wreck of the Old 97 [G 2]
Wreck on the Highway

Testament T-3301: Dorsey Dixon (1897-1967), born in Darlington, South Carolina, worked most of his life in the cotton mills, and many of his songs reflect that association. Dixon was an excellent steel-guitar player (influenced strongly by fellow South Carolinian Jimmie Tarlton) who recorded and played on local radio as a duet with his brother, Howard; he was also a prolific songwriter for whom songwriting was not a commercial venture but an act of personal catharsis. His best-known song, "Wreck of the Highway," popularized by Roy Acuff (unaware at the time of recording it of Dixon's authorship), is an example of just that. His career has been well documented--on this album and elsewhere. The album consists mostly of recordings made in 1962, but includes for comparison three of Dorsey and Howard's RCA Bluebird duets from 1936-37. [JAF 310--DKW]

31 Label Name/Number: Rounder Records 0047
Title: *The Right Hand Fork of Rush's Creek*
Artist: Wilson Douglas, accomp. by Douglas Meade and Roy O. "Speedy" Tolliver
Collector/Recordist/Producer: Guthrie T. Meade & Mark Wilson
Place of Recording: Waldorf, MD
Date of Publication: 1975
Annotations: Gatefold notes by Nancy McClellan
Selections:
Brushy Run
Camp Chase
Chicken Reel
Cotton-Eyed Joe
Elzic's Farewell
Forked Buck
Little Rose
Old Christmas Morning
Old Mother Flanagan
Paddy on the Turnpike
Rocky Road to Dublin
Shelvin' Rock
Walking in the Parlor
West Fork Girls
Yew Piney Mountain

Rndr 0047: Wilson Douglas has lived all his life in Clay County, West Virginia, where he was born in 1922. He learned from several prominent fiddlers in the region, including Ed Haley, French Carpenter--from whom many of the tunes on this album come--and J. P. Fraley. The notes include a long essay by Douglas titled "How I Came To Be a Fiddler" and his own comments on where he learned the tunes. Douglas plays with a short bowstroke, resulting in a rather rough tonal quality. The banjo provides nice accompaniment, often more or less following the melody rather than simply offering rhythmic back-up. The tunes are local ones, some not widely known. [JEMFQ 42-PW]

32   Label Name/Number: County 718
Title: *Old-Time Mountain Music*
Artists: Ernest East and the Pine Ridge Boys (Mac Snow, Gilmer Woodruff, Scotty East)
Collector/Recordist/Producer: Charles Faurot and Richard Nevins
Date of Publication: [1969]
Annotations: Liner notes by Nevins
Selections:
  Fortune
  Greenback Dollar
  Hand Me Down My Walking Cane
  Hell Among the Round Peakers
  June Apple
  Knoxville Girl [P 35]
  Mississippi Sawyer
  Pig in a Pen
  Richmond
  Roll on Buddy
  Sally Ann
  Suzanna Gal

Cty 718: This fine old-time band from the Mt. Airy region of western North Carolina centers on fiddler Ernest East and his son, Scotty, who provides guitar backup and vocals (not, unfortunately, miked very well) on some numbers.   Many of the tunes ("Fortune," "Suzannna Gal," "June Apple") are characteristic of the Mt. Airy/Galax area's rich musical tradition. The tune titled "Richmond" is very close to "Flop Eared Mule," and "Hell among the Round Peakers" is a tongue-in-cheek renaming of "Hell amongst the Yearlings." "Greenback Dollar" and "Pig in a Pen" were learned from Fiddling Arthur Smith's Grand Ole Opry performances.

33   Label Name/Number: Davis Unlimited Records DU-33002
Title: *Train on the Island*
Artist: Norman S. Edmonds
Collector/Recordist: Robert Nobley and Stephen Davis
Place and Date of Recording: VA, 1970
Date of Publication: [1971]
Annotations: 1 page insert
Selections:
  Angeline the Baker
  Black Eyed Susie
  Breaking Up Christmas
  Chinquapin Hunting
  Cricket on the Hearth
  Hawks and Eagles

Lucy Neil
Old Cotton Eyed Joe
Pretty Little Girl
Ship in the Clouds
Train on the Island
Walking in the Parlor

DU 33002:   Virginia fiddler Norman Edmonds (b. 1889) was in his eighties when this album was made and still an active fiddler in the Galax area. The program of relatively uncommon fiddle tunes was recorded at his home with unidentified guitar and banjo accompaniment. Edmonds appeared on one commercial 78 rpm disc in 1927, and, in the 1960s and '70s, on several LPs made at various fiddle conventions. [WF 7/72].

34   Label Name/Number: Flyright LP 546
Title: *Goin' to Georgia*
Artists: Eller Brothers and Ross Brown
Collector/Recordist: Art and Margo Rosenbaum
Place and Date of Recording: Hiawassee, GA, 1977-78
Date of Publication: 1978
Annotations: 18 p. brochure by Art Rosenbaum
Selections:
Barbara Allen [C. 84]
Cindy in the Summertime
Count the Days I'm Gone
Cripple Creek
Dance All Night
Don't Go Riding Down That Old Texas Trail
Ellen Smith [F 11]
Fly Around My Blue-Eyed Girl
John Henry [I 1]
Little Maggie
Little Red Shoes
Lonesome Valley
My Home's in Charlotte, North Carolina
Short Life of Trouble
Shout Lulu
Weepin' Willow
Goin' to Georgia

Flyright LP 546: Brothers Lawrence and Vaughn Eller were born in north Georgia in 1916 and 1918, respectively; by the time they were in their teens they were playing for local dances and in front of the county courthouse on Saturday afternoons when court would recess. In the 1930s, they were often joined by fiddler Ross Brown (b. 1909) at Saturday night dances. After World War II musical activity in the community declined and did not re-emerge for some thirty years, at which time the Eller Brothers and Brown began to play again together after the long hiatus. The trio, playing some combination of guitar, banjo, and fiddle (except for "Cindy" and "Cripple Creek," on which Vaughn plays mouth bow), offer a collection of old-time standards (except for the unusual "Don't Go Riding") in a style that shows no influence of musical developments after about 1940. Most of the lead singing is by Lawrence, who sings in a rather stark, piercing style that at times is quite arresting (e. g., "My Home's in Charlotte"). Rosenbaum's brochure includes photos, biographies, song texts, and notes to the selections.

35 Label Name/Number: Folk-Legacy FSA-13
Title: *Behind These Walls*
Artist: Hank Ferguson
Collectors: Henry Felt, Lee B. Haggerty, Bruce Jackson
Place and Date of Recording: Michigan City, IN, 1962, and Lenoir City, TN, 1963
Date of Publication: 1963
Annotations: 25 p. booklet by Bruce Jackson
Selections:
    Busted
    Get a Little Dirt on Your Hands
    I'm Not Living
    Interstate 40
    Jolly Old-Time Farmer
    Long Black Veil
    Nine Pound Hammer
    One Life's As Long as Any Man Can Live
    Rich Girl, Poor Girl
    Shackles and Chains
    Thunder Road
    Trouble Just Got in My Way
    Wabash Cannonball
    Waiting For a Train [H 2]
    Walls, The
    Wreck of Old #9, The [G 26]
    Wreck of the Old 97, The [G 2]
    You Ain't Heard Nothing Yet

      FLeg FSA-13: Folklorist/sociologist Bruce Jackson was collecting prison folklore at Michigan City, Indiana, prison, when he met and recorded Hank Ferguson. Ferguson's style is clearly contemporary country/western, but most of his songs are his own compositions, dealing primarily with prison life and matters of concern to someone behind bars. Others were learned from commercial recordings by Marvin Rainwater, Hank Snow, and others. [JAF 305--DKW]

36 Label Name/Number: Rounder Records 0037
Title: *Wild Rose of the Mountain*
Artists: J. P. and Annadeene Fraley
Collector/Recordist/Producer: Guthrie T. Meade & Mark Wilson
Place and Date of Recording: Rush, KY, 1973
Date of Publication: 1974
Annotations: Gatefold liner notes by Guthrie T. Meade and Mark Wilson
Selections:
    Birdie
    Cluckin' Hen
    Dusty Miller
    Forked Deer
    Fun's All Over, The
    Going back to Kentucky
    Going down the River
    Granny, Take a Look at Uncle Sam
    Little Liza Jane
    Miller's Reel

    Mud Fence
    Red Headed Irishman, The
    Roosian Rabbit, The
    Run, Johnnie, Run
    Sail Away Ladies
    Swing Nine Yards of Calico
    White Rose Waltz
    Wild Rose of the Mountain

    Rndr 0037: This album was to be the first in a series devoted to the fiddle music of eastern Kentucky by Meade and Wilson. One of the best-known fiddlers in the region is J. P. Fraley, of Rush, Kentucky, who had appeared at many fiddlers' conventions and folk festivals before this album was recorded. Fraley, who plays with a smooth bowing style and strong vibrato, is accompanied by his wife on guitar. Several of Fraley's tunes were learned from an older Kentucky fiddler, Ed Haley (see Rounder 1010). The title tune is fairly rare--except for the Fraleys' own numerous public performances--and is a beautifully haunting piece. Jacket notes include a biographical sketch by Fraley himself and program notes with discographic references. [JAF 395; JEMFQ 42--PW]

37 Label Name/Number: Rounder Records 0133
Title: *Dixie Blossoms*
Artist: Art Galbraith
Producer: Charles Wolfe
Place and Date of Recording: Mountain View, AR, 1979-80
Date of Publication: 1980
Annotations: Liner notes and 4 p. insert by Charles Wolfe and Galbraith
Selections:
    4th of July Waltz
    Arkansas Turnback
    Billy in the Low Ground
    Blue Mule
    Coming up the Pike
    Dixie Blossoms
    Down Home Waltz
    Flowers of Edinburgh
    I Don't Love Nobody
    Ladies' Fancy
    McCraw's Ford
    Peek A Boo Waltz
    Rocky Mountain Hornpipe
    Shamus O'Brien
    Sunday Night Reel
    Waverley

38 Label Name/Number: Rounder Records 0157
Title: *Simple Pleasures: Old-time Fiddling from the Ozarks*
Artist: Art Galbraith, accompanied by Gordon McCann
Producer/Recordist: Mark Wilson
Place and Date of Recording: La Jolla, CA, 1981
Date of Publication: [1982]
Annotations: Liner notes and 4 p. booklet by Art Galbraith

Selections:
Daddy Blues
Doc Jessup's Schottische
Durang's Hornpipe #2
Fat Back Meat and Dumplings
Flock of Birds
Flowers from Heaven
Just from the Fountain
Lay Your Good Money Down
Lost Indian
Old Dubuque
Over the River to Charley's
Piedmont
Possum Trot
Red Hawk Waltz
Seth Thomas Clock
Tennessee Wagoner
Walk Along, John
Want to Go to Memphis So Bad
Whiskers
Wideman's Quickstep
Wild Rose Waltz

Rndr 0133 / Rndr 0157: Born in Greene County, Missouri, Art Galbraith (1909-93) descended from a long line of prominent local fiddlers. He taught English for a while, then took a job with the post office. Before retirement he had played frequently for local dances and social gatherings; afterwards he began appearing at numerous folk festivals and fiddle contests. On 0157 he is accompanied on guitar by Gordon McCann, who only a few years earlier had begun to develop a serious interest in the folk music of the Ozarks and in Vance Randolph, the region's pre-eminent folklore collector. Galbraith plays mostly local tunes that are unfamiliar outside of Missouri; as Wolfe observes in his liner notes, he plays "...in a distinct regional style that can be traced back in southwest Missouri over one hundred years. It is a delicate, stately, lilting style that has seldom been commercially recorded...." Insert notes to 0133 consist mostly of Galbraith's comments on the tunes; he traces his "Flowers of Edinburgh" directly back to his great-great uncle. Rounder 0157 contains more of the same, with Mark Wilson's notes on tune identifications supplementing Galbraith's own comments. Each album contains several of Galbraith's own compositions.

39   Label Name/Number: Kanawha 307 [reiss. in England on Matchbox SDM 229]
Title: *Traditional Music for Banjo, Fiddle, and Bagpipes*
Artists: Franklin George, John W. Summers, Pat Dunford
Collector/Recordist: Pat Dunford
Place and Date of Recording: Indianapolis, IN, 1966
Date of Publication: 1967; [Matchbox ca. 1973]
Annotations: Liner notes by Pat Dunford
Selections:
Franklin George
      Boatsman
      Pipe Medley I: Wearin' of the Green / All the Way to Galway
      Salt River
      Rickett's Hornpipe
      Teetotaler

Pipe Medley II: Minstrel Boy / O'Donnell Abu
Turkey in the Straw
Cumberland Gap
Nancy Ann
Grey Eagle
Franklin George and Pat Dunford
Angeline
Old Molly Hare
John W. Summers and Franklin George
Londonderry Hornpipe
Forked Horn Deer
Fisher's Hornpipe
Round Town Girls
Top of Cork Road
Arkansas Traveler
Summers, George, and Dunford
Medley: Wake Up Susan / Devil's Dream
Mississippi Sawyer

Kan 307: This album features primarily Bluefield, West Virginia, fiddler/banjo player/bagpiper Franklin George, accompanied on four tracks by the older Indiana fiddler John W. "Dick" Summers--with whom he had never played prior to these recordings--and with occasional guitar or banjo by collector Dunford. George learned to play the pipes while in Scotland serving a stint in the army. (Summers can also be heard on Folkways FS 3809, q. v.) The recording quality is not always faultless (the guitar in particular often sounds muddled, and the one track recorded at a coffee house performance has some background clatter), but the performances have an engaging spontaneity about them. [JAF 329--DKW]

40 Label Name/Number: Rimrock Rlp-495
Title: *Aunt Ollie Gilbert Sings Old Folk Songs to Her Friends*
Artist: Aunt Ollie Gilbert
Collector: Jimmy Driftwood
Date of Publication: [1975]
Annotations: Liner notes by Jimmy Driftwood
Selections:
Barbrie Allen [C. 84]
Go Wash in the Beautiful Pool
Green Corn
Home Halley Home
How Came That Blood on Your Shirt Sleeve [C. 13]
If He's Gone Let Him Go God Bless Him
It Rained a Mist [C. 155]
Jimmy Randolph [C. 12]
Lady Beauty Bride [M 3?]
Little Willow Green
Lord Bateman [C. 53]
Sugar Hill
Three Little Babes [C. 79]
Utah Carl [B 4]
White Kitty, The

Rimrock Rlp-495:   "Aunt" Ollie Gilbert was born in 1892 in the Arkansas Ozarks and started amassing her huge repertoire (Driftwood says he has taped over 500 of her songs) from her mother's singing. Apart from this poorly distributed album, little is available of her music, though in the 1960s she did travel about and appear at various folk festivals. At age 83, her voice is somewhat scratchy, and she sings in a plain, almost casual style, as if she were just singing to herself. In view of her huge repertoire, it seems a pity we do not have recordings from her at a younger age. Most of this album consists of unaccompanied singing, but on a few selections she also plays banjo.

41   Label Name/Number: June Appal JA 020
Title: *Been a Long Time Traveling*
Artist: Addie Graham
Collector/Recordist/Producer: Rich Kirby, Barbara Edwards
Date of Publication: 1978
Annotations: 8 p. booklet by Barbara Edwards and Rich Kirby
Selections:
>   Been a Long Time Traveling
>   Darling Don't You Know That's Wrong
>   Dear Friends Farewell
>   Dummy, The
>   Guide Me O Thou Great Jehovah
>   Hungry and Faint and Poor
>   I Am a Little Scholar
>   Ida Red / Went Up on the Old Hillside
>   Indian Tribes of Tennessee, The
>   Jesus Reigns
>   Lonesome Scenes of Winter [H 12]
>   Long and a Country Jake
>   Lord Will Provide, The
>   My Head and Stay Is Called Away
>   O & K Train Song
>   Omie Wise [F 4]
>   Pretty Polly [P 36b]
>   Sisters Thou Art Mild and Lovely
>   Three Little Babes [C. 79]
>   We're Stole and Sold from Africa
>   When Moses and the Israelites
>   Wouldn't Mind Working from Sun to Sun

JA 020: Addie Graham was born in Wolfe County, Ky, and grew up in the eastern part of the state. She learned her songs from her parents and neighbors, including Grant Reed, "...the only colored man there was around there... He'd go along the road pickin' the banjo and I'd stand and listen to him." In the late 1970s, Addie's grandson, Rich Kirby, recognizing the wealth of traditional song lore that his grandmother possessed, conceived this album to share the music he had loved during his childhood with a wider audience. Mrs. Graham sings in a husky voice, in a slightly decorated style that is neither ornate nor monotonous. This evaluation may sound like very faint praise, but in truth I would rate her an outstanding folksinger in the older style. Though well past her singing prime when she was recorded at close to 80 years of age, her rhythm and phrasing are without fault.   Her repertoire, as represented on this disc, holds several surprises in the very rare items such as "The Indian Tribes of Tennessee," "We're Stole and Sold from Africa," "Long and a Country Jake," and "O & K Train Song." Side One consists of secular ballads and songs; Side Two, hymns and religious songs. On one pair of tunes ("Ida Red/Went Up on the Old Hillside") she accompanies herself on piano; the other items are all unaccompanied. On side one are two imported ballads, "The Three Little Babes" and "Pretty Polly," both to somewhat unusual melodies. The former is sung to practically the same tune as that popularized by Buell Kazee (see below), but with one striking difference: she has changed the cadence from A-G-A to A-A-G. Her "Pretty Polly" is also pentatonic, but π^3 rather than the more usual π^4. Also pentatonic are her "The Lonesome Scenes of Winter" [Laws H 12], "Omie Wise" [F 4], and "Ida Red/Went Up on the Old Hillside"; as well as the less common "Indian Tribes of Tennessee" and "Darling Don't You Know That's Wrong." She also recasts "The Dummy Can't Run" in a pentatonic scale, but not one of the usual (i.e., playable on the black keys) ones. Also set to unusual scales are her "When Moses and the Israelites" and "The Lord Will Provide," among her religious pieces. The brochure includes a biography and broad evaluation of her music and its role in her life. Song notes, the brevity of which should not be allowed to impugn their scholarship, sketch--where known--each song's history, and where she learned it, and offer some pertinent published references. The LP was published in 1978 but the recordings themselves are undated. [JEMFQ 65/66]

42 Label Name/Number: Davis Unlimited DU 33014
Title: *Monticello: Tough Mountain Music*
Artist(s): W. L. Gregory and Clyde Davenport, with Gary Gregory
Collector/Recordist: Steve Davis and Charles K. Wolfe
Place and Date of Recording: Monticello, KY, 1974
Date of Publication: [1975]
Annotations: Liner notes by Charles K. Wolfe
Selections:
> Are You Happy or Lonesome?
> Bed Bug Blues
> Billy in the Low Ground
> Cumberland Gap
> Jenny in the Cotton Patch
> Ladies on the Steamboat
> Lime Street Blues
> Lost John
> Monticello
> Over the Waves
> Pig in the Pen
> Rockin' the Boat
> Rocky Road to Dublin
> Rutherford's Waltz
> Sally Johnson
> Sleeping Lulu
> Taylor's Quickstep
> Weeping Willow

DU 33014: 1920s recording artists Dick Burnett and Leonard Rutherford were highly regarded in their native southeastern Kentucky, where they made their living touring and performing. W. L. Gregory (b. 1905) and Clyde Davenport (b. ca. 1921) live in Monticello, Kentucky, where Burnett still lived in the 1980s. Their music is as close to the fiddle-banjo style (no vocals) of Burnett and Rutherford as one could expect without consciously slavish imitation: Gregory plays fiddle or banjo, Davenport plays banjo, and Gary Gregory, W. L.'s son, accompanies on guitar on several tracks. "Lime Street Blues" is an interesting example of the rarely heard knife-blade slide style banjo. Needless to say, the majority of the tunes are associated with Burnett and Rutherford and generally follow closely their style of fiddle and banjo playing melody together rather than the banjo providing rhythmic accompaniment.

43   Label Name/Number: Folk Legacy FSA-26
Title: *Girl of Constant Sorrow*
Artist: Sarah Ogan Gunning
Collector/Recordist: Archie Green, with Ellen Stekert and Oscar Paskal
Place and Date of Recording: Detroit, 1964
Date of Publication: 1965
Annotations: 32 p. booklet by Archie Green
Selections:
   Battle of Mill Spring [A 13]
   Captain Devin [L 13a]
   Christ Was a Wayworn Traveler
   Davy Crockett
   Down on the Picket Line
   Dreadful Memories
   Gee Whiz, What They Done to Me
   I Am a Girl of Constant Sorrow
   I Hate the Company Bosses
   I Have Letters from My Father
   I'm Going to Organize
   Just the Same Today
   Loving Nancy [?K 14/P 5]
   May I Go with You, Johnny [O 33]
   Oh Death
   Old Jack Frost
   Old Southern Town
   Sally [P 9]
   Why Do You Stand There in the Rain

44   Label Name/Number: Rounder Records 0051
Title: *The Silver Dagger*
Artist: Sarah Ogan Gunning
Producer: Mark Wilson
Place and Date of Recording: Medford, MA, 1974
Date of Publication: 1976
Annotations: 16 p. booklet by Jim Garland & Mark Wilson
Selections:
   Davy Crockett
   Down in the Valley to Pray
   Downward Road, The [H 6]
   Drunkard's Dream, The
   God Moves in a Windstorm
   House Carpenter, The [C. 243]
   I Am a Traveling Creature
   I Hate the Capitalist System
   I Hear the Low Winds Sweeping
   I Love Little Willie
   "Indian" Songs
   Lonesome Dove, The
   Miller's Will, The [Q 21]
   Mister Bartender
   Papa's Billy Goat

Ring Dang Rantigan
Silver Dagger, The [G 21]

FLeg FSA 26/ Rndr 0051: Sara Gunning is perhaps best known as the sister of Aunt Molly Jackson and Jim Garland and, like them, for her involvement in the folk song/protest song movement in New York in the late 1930s. She herself composed several bitter pieces reflecting her experiences when she grew up in the coal fields of southeastern Kentucky in the 1920s. Her repertoire, a mixture of older traditional folksongs and protest material, is sampled on these two albums recorded a decade apart. Each album includes primarily traditional songs and a few of her own compositions: "Down on the Picket Line," "I'm Going to Organize," ("covered" by Woody Guthrie in 1941 as "Babe O' Mine"), "Dreadful Memories," "Old Southern Town," "I Have Letters from My Father," and, perhaps her best known composition, "I Hate the Capitalist System." It is all too easy to offer subjective comments on her singing, but her biting voice, sounding as if she sings with considerable tension in her throat muscles, certainly lends itself well to the themes of her own protest song material. The unusual items on the Rounder disc are the rare temperance piece, "Mister Bartender," and the fine example of American frontier humor, "Davy Crockett," a briefer verison of which apeared on her earlier LP. Her version of "The Silver Dagger," a native American ballad of parental opposition to young lovers, is a fine one but certainly not the "first commercial recording by an authentic singer" as the notes suggest. In general, though, the brochure notes to both albums are admirable: the biographical essays warm and personal, the song notes extensive (though more complete bibliographic and discographic references could have been provided on the Rounder disc). [JEMFQ 53; JAF 313--DKW (FLeg)]

45 Label Name/Number: Rounder 1010
Title: *Parkersburg Landing*
Artist: Ed Haley
Collector/Recordist: Home recordings
Producers: Mark Wilson and Guthrie T. Meade
Place and Date of Recording: KY, 1946
Date of Publication: 1976
Annotations: Gatefold and liner notes by Wilson and Meade
Selections:
  Cherokee Polka
  Cherry River Rag
  Cuckoo's Nest
  Done Gone
  Dunbar
  Flower of the Morning
  Forked Deer
  Grey Eagle Jig
  Humphrey's Jig
  Lost Indian
  Man of Constant Sorrow
  Parkersburg Landing
  Stackolee [I 15]
  Wake Susan

Rndr 1010: James Edward Haley was born in 1883 in Logan County, West Virginia, and was blinded at the age of three. He early showed a natural musical ability and before long had developed a local reputation that continued to grow throughout his life. These home recordings-- the only recordings Haley made--were made by his son, Ralph, who also played guitar on some selections, in 1946, in order to preserve for the family their father's music. In spite of the tinny sound, the fact that he was already suffering from heart trouble, and the almost ukulele-like quality of the guitar strumming, Haley's brilliant playing is still apparent in these historically important recordings. "Cherry River Rag" is a virtuoso performance that demonstrates Haley's technical skill; the mournful "Man of Constant Sorrow" shows what he can do with a simple, slow melody. On "Stackolee" he shows himself well able to sing to his own fiddle accompaniment. Notes by Meade and Wilson sketch Haley's life and music, discuss the tunes, and comment on his style and why he is musically so significant. [JEMFQ 42-PW]

46   Label Name/Number: Archive of Folk Song, Library of Congress, AFS L65-L66 [2-LP box set]
Title: *The Hammons Family: A Study of a West Virginia Family's Traditions*
Artists: Burl Hammons, Maggie Hammons Parker, Sherman Hammons
Collector/Recordist: Carl Fleischhauer, Alan Jabbour, and Dwight Diller
Editor: Fleischhauer and Jabbour
Place and Date of Recording: Wash. DC, 1972, 1970, 1971
Date of Publication: 1973
Annotations: 36 p. 12 x 12" booklet by Carl Fleischhauer and Alan Jabbour
Selections:
    Sherman Hammons
        Bringing Back the Sheep
        Muddy Roads
    Burl Hammons
        Camp Chase
        Fine Times at Our House
        Old Sledge
        Route, The
        Sandy Boys, The
        Sugar Babe
        Sugar Grove Blues
        Three Forks of Cheat
        Turkey in the Straw
        Wilson's Clog
    Maggie Hammons Parker
        In Scotland Town [C. 17]
        Jay Legg
        Jimmy Johnson
        Little Omie [F 4]
        Mercian Tittery-Ary-A
        We're Marching Around the Levees
        When This World Comes to an End
        Young Henerly [C. 68]
[Also some narrations]

47   Label Name/Number: Rounder 0018
Title: *Shaking Down the Acorns*
Artists: Maggie Hammons Parker, Burl Hammons, Mose Coffman, Sherman Hammons
Collector/Recordist: Dwight Diller, Carl Fleischhauer, Alan Jabbour
Editors: Carl Fleischhauer & Alan Jabbour
Place and Date of Recording: WV, 1970-72
Date of Publication: 1973

Annotations: 12 p. booklet by Alan Jabbour
Selections:
Big Scioty, The
Cranberry Rock
Greasy Coat
Hard Times in the Charleston Jail
Haunted Wagon, The
Ireland's Green Shore [Q 27]
Johnny Booger
Lonesome Pines, The
Lost Indian
Old Man, Can I Have Your Daughter?
Panther in the Rock, The
Rocky Mountain Goat
Shaking Down the Acorns/ Hink Cogar's Deer Ride
Singing Birds
Sugar Babe
Walking in the Parlor
Who's Been Here Since I've Been Gone?

Rndr 0018 / LC AFS L65-L66: The Hammons family (now) of Pocahantas County, West Virginia, retains in family lore fiddle and banjo tunes, ballads, play party songs, riddles, ghost and witch tales, and family anecdotes. Fleischhauer and Jabbour have assembled a beautiful package (LC 65/66) documenting this rich heritage on this 2-disc set that features three members of the family: Maggie Hammons Parker (b. 1899), Sherman Hammons (1903), and Burl Hammons (1908). The handsome brochure is divided between a history of the family by Fleischhauer and detailed notes on the recordings by Jabbour. Included are 8 fiddle tunes by Burl, 3 banjo tunes by Burl, a banjo tune by Sherman, 7 ballads and songs by Maggie, and narratives by all three. Among the ballads are "In Scotland Town," the first recovery of C. 17 in the U. S. outside of New England; "Little Omie," to an unusual tune; and "Jay Legg," a West Virginia ballad arising from a 1904 Clay County murder. Mrs. Parker is a fine traditional ballad singer, with a rubato parlando style between those of Texas Gladden and Molly Jackson in terms of extent of vocal decorations. When these recordings were made she seemed to have a little difficulty controlling her voice; one longs to have heard her three or four decades earlier, when she might have been genuinely great. The instrumental pieces range from relatively common to extremely rare. The common tunes are often rendered in uncommon variations (e.g., Burl's "Turkey in the Straw"). Jabbour's annotations are exemplary throughout, dwelling in turn on questions of fiddle tune ancestries, fiddle tunings and bowings, origins of banjo picking styles, significations of anecdotal matter, and textual matters. Fleischhauer's notes combine documents with oral history to reconstruct a family history for the past century and relate it to the family folklore and folk music. This album is one of the finest the LC-AFS has produced.

The material on Rndr 0018 comes from the same sessions as that on LC AFS L65/66. The same three artists are represented, joined by William Moses Coffman of Greenbriar County and Lee Hammons of Pocahontas County. The composition of the LP, like the LC package, consists of ballads, fiddle and banjo tunes, and a few tales. Unfortunately, annotation is confined to a biographical sketch of the performers, with no details on who is performing which selections or on the selections themselves. Mrs. Parker sings "The Lonesome Pines," a strange variant with a moral admonishing kindness to tramps because "you may be a tramp some old day"; "Hard Times in the Charleston Jail," a localization of the widely known native American ballad, though set to a tune close to that of "Ground Hog"; and Q 27. The instrumentals are not at all common. "Cranberry Rock" sounds to me like a variant of "Billy in the Lowground"; "Walking in the Parlor" is the

"Johnson Boys" tune, not the minstrel song about the creation of the world; "Singing Birds" is reminiscent of "Little Birdie"; "Lost Indian" is different from a couple of other tunes by that name; "Rocky Mountain Goat" is the same tune recorded commercially in 1927 and 1929 by Doc Roberts of Kentucky; "Sugar Babe" and "Johnny Booger" [Booker] are the usual tunes. Other pieces are less familiar. Obviously the Hammons family repertoire is large enough to justify this supplementary LP (and perhaps more), but better documentation should have been provided. [WF 10/74 (LC); JAF 343--DKW (Rndr)]

48   Label Name/Number: West Virginia University Press Sound Archives 001
Title: *The Edden Hammons Collection*
Artist: Edden Hammons
Collector/Recordist: Louis Watson Chappell
Editor: John A. Cuthbert, Alan Jabbour
Place and Date of Recording: WV, 1947
Date of Publication: 1984
Annotations: 18 p. booklet by John A. Cuthbert and Alan Jabbour
Selections: (All unaccompanied fiddle)
Arkansas Traveller
Big Fancy
Digging Potatoes
Falls of Richmond
Fine Times at Our House
Forked Deer
Love Nancy
Mississippi Sawyer
Old Greasy Coat
On My Way to See Nancy
Queen of the Earth and Child of the Stars
Sandy Boys
Shaking Off the Acorns
Washington's March
Waynesboro

W. Va. Univ. Press Sound Archives 001:   This album consists of 15 field recordings made in 1947 on aluminum discs by folklorist Louis Watson Chappell featuring one of the finest West Virginia fiddlers of his generation (ca. 1874-1955). The booklet includes photos, map, genealogy, biography, program notes, musical transcriptions, and bibliodiscography. Chappell's metallic-sounding recordings of a fiddler somewhat past his prime may not be very listenable, but they are all we have of one of the great fiddlers of the now-well-documented, musically remarkable, Hammons family. Cuthbert's long and leisurely biographic narrative, and Jabbour's impeccable program notes, not only on Hammons and his repertoire but on upper South fiddle music in general, make this an exemplary document. [JAF 391]

49   Label Name/Number: Kanawha 310
Title: *Old Time Country Music*
Artist: Curley Herdman, accomp. by Troy Gerdman, Bob Tanner, Joe Tanner
Place and Date of Recording: Phila., PA, 1967
Annotations: Unsigned brief liner notes
Selections:
Big Tracy
Billy in the Low Ground

Dixie Hoedown
Meigs County Reel
Moonlight Waltz
Old Joe Clark
Rachael
Rocus's Reel
Run Rabbit Run
Running Bear
Turkey in the Straw
Under the Double Eagle

Kan 310: Curley Herdman was born in West Virginia in 1918, scion of a long line of fiddlers, and began playing at local square dances at age nine. In later years he played on various radio stations, notably Renfro Valley Barn Dance in Kentucky. Half of the tunes on this album are of his own composition. He is accompanied by his brother, Troy, on guitar; and Bob Tanner, mandolin and Joe Tanner, banjo. Herdman plays in a smooth style with long, even bowstrokes and alternates melody lead with the banjo, played bluegrass style, and the mandolin.

50   Label Name/Number: County 789
Title: *Ballads and Banjo Music from the Tennessee Cumberland Plateau*
Artists: Dee and Delta Hicks
Collector/Recordist: Barry Poss, Bobby Fulcher
Producer: Bobby Fulcher
Place and Date of Recording: TN, 1980?
Date of Publication: 1985
Annotations: 7 p. booklet by Bobby Fulcher
Selections:
Fox Chase, The
Hairy Buck
He Who Died on Calvary's Mountain
In the Pines
Ketter Gun
Lather and Shave [Q 15]
Lily of the West [P 29]
Lone Cow Trail
Lost Gander, The
Man of Constant Sorrow
Poor Man's Song
Sea Fowl, The
Shout Lulu
Susie Girl
Vulture, The
Young Johnny Sailed from London [K 36]

Cty 789: When one works intensively with a traditional singer having a large repertoire, one often encounters odd and curious pieces that are unique or unidentifiable, along with the familiar standards. Such is the case with Dee and Delta Hicks, members of a family from Fentress County, Tennessee, with a musically rich tradition. Between the two of them they have contributed some 400 songs and tunes to the LC AFC. This album includes recordings made by Fulcher in the late 1970s and features primarily Dee Hicks (1906-83), with two selections by his wife, Delta (b. 1910). Other recordings appeared in 1982 on TFS 104 (see below). Dee died of emphysema, and it is apparent from some of the selections on the 2 LPs that by the 1980s he did not always have the vocal control that he must have had in earlier years. Among the 14 selections performed by Dee are excellent a capella renditions of [K 36] and the humorous Irish ballad [Q 15]. Unusual, but not unknown, are the cante fable "Susie Gal" and the banjo piece, "The Lost Gander." Scarcer yet are "The Sea Fowl," a fragmentary piece that Dee believed was about a shipwreck; the wonderfully sung "The Vulture," according to Fulcher's notes derived from a Hutchison family standard of the 1840s; and Dee's father's satirical composition, "Ketter Gun." Delta's contributions are two strong unaccompanied vocals: "Lily of the West" and "Man of Constant Sorrow." The brochure includes extensive historical/biographical information on the Hickses, their music, and their attitudes, written by collector Fulcher. As he notes, the Hickses set a high premium on the old, established traditions with which they grew up--what they described approvingly as "old-fashioned." Dee's unusual rendition of the widespread "In the Pines" is, according to him, the "old-fashioned" version he learned from his father. Until recently, the Hickses had little public exposure and were not commercially oriented. Dee himself was particularly shy on stage. Song notes are confined to a few brief sentences on the back jacket cover and only hint at the efforts Fulcher had made to identify many of the unusual items in the Hicks repertoire. [JAF 395]

51   Label Name/Number: Tennessee Folklore Society TFS 104
Title: *The Hicks Family*
Artists: Dee, Delta, Lily Mae, Joe, Besford Hicks, Nancy Hicks Winningham
Collector/Recordist: Bobby Fulcher
Editor: Charles Wolfe
Place and Date of Recording: TN, 1978-1982
Date of Publication: 1982
Annotations: 24 p. booklet by Charles Wolfe and Bobby Fulcher
Selections:
    Dee Hicks
        Bill Staples [H 1]
        Crocodile's Mouth
        Froggie Went A-Courting
        Old Brady [I 9]
        Pretty Polly (Six Kings' Daughters) [C. 4]
        There Was an Old Man Lived in the West [C. 277]
    Delta Hicks
        As I Walked Out Into Her Hall
        Once in the Saddle [B 1]
        Willie Moore
    Joe Hicks
        Exile of Arion, The
        Good Old Man, The
        In Came the Owl
        Kate and the Cowhide [N 22]
        Kentucky Boys
        Sow Took the Measles
        True Blue Bill
    Lily Mae Hicks
        Apple Brandy
    Besford Hicks
        Dog and Gun (The Jolly Farmer) [N 20]
    Nancy Hicks Winningham
        Lady Margaret [C. 74]

> To Be A Farmer's Boy [Q 30]
> Besford Hicks Family
>   Nineteen Years Old [cf. H 24]
>   Pizen Sarpent, The (Springfield Mountain) [G 16]

TFS 104: Dee and Delta Hicks are joined by other members of the Hicks Family on this album of songs and ballads, all but one of which are unaccompanied solos. The booklet includes biographical essays by Fulcher and Wolfe, and song annotations by Wolfe, text transcriptions by James Satterwhite, and photos. The family has an outstanding repertoire of very old ballads and songs, but one wishes the older singers (Dee, b. 1906; Joe, b. 1899) could have been recorded when they were younger and must have had more vocal control. All the singing on this album is relatively unornamented, with Delta Hicks having the surest, strongest voice. [JAF 391]

52   Label Name/Number: Folkways FA 2036 (10") [Formerly FP 36]
Title: *Mormon Folk Songs*
Artist: L. M. Hilton
Collector/Recordist: Willard Rhodes
Place and Date of Recording: Ogden, UT, 1946?
Date of Publication: 1952
Annotations: 11 p. booklet by Willard Rhodes
Selections:
> Come, Come Ye Saints
> Echo Canyon Song
> Gather Round the Camp Fire, Brethren
> Hand Cart Song, The
> Hard Times Come Again No More
> Have Courage My Boy To Say No
> Oh Babylon, Oh Babylon!
> Sago Lily
> Sea Gulls and Crickets
> What's the Use of Repining
> Whoa! Ha! Buck & Jerry Boy
> Zack, the Mormon Engineer

Fwys FA 2036: Hilton was Superintendent of the Bureau of Identification and Records after having served as police officer in Ogden City, Utah, when Willard Rhodes recorded the songs his grandmother and parents had taught him. His singing is plain, undecorated, and without accompaniment. Austin Fife had recorded Hilton in 1946, from which session two of the titles issued here were released on AFS L30 (q.v.). The booklet gives text transcriptions and historical background on Mormons themselves and some of the events in Mormon history reflected in the song texts, most of which (with the exception of "Have Courage My Boy To Say No") have direct references to Mormon life.

53   Label Name/Number: Arhoolie 5001
Title: *Watermelon Hangin' on the Vine*
Artists: Hodges Brothers (Felix, Ralph, and James Hodges and John White)
Collector/Editor: Chris Strachwitz
Place and Date of Recording: McComb, MS, 1961-62, 1967
Date of Publication: 1971 (earlier edition, numbered F5001, issued ca. 1961)
Annotations: Liner notes by Strachwitz
Selections:

Bile Dem Cabbage Down
Bogue Chitto Fling Ding
Carrol County Blues
Charmin' Betsy
Fifty Year Waltz
Hooknose in Town [= Big Balls in Town]
Ida Red
It Won't Be Long
Leaves Is Falling on the Ground, The
Little Church House on the Hill
Mississippi Baby
Never Alone Waltz
On the Banks of the Ohio [F]
Six White Horses
Watermelon Hangin' on the Vine

Arh 5001: Chris Strachwitz encountered the Hodges Brothers on his first field trip through the South in 1960 and recorded them in McComb, Mississippi, then and in the following year. From these recordings he issued the first Arhoolie album (F 5001) in ca. 1961. In 1969 he recorded them there again (by now their playing showed considerably more polish), and completely revised the album (now numbered 5001); the titles listed here are from this second, 1971 release, which includes only nine of the 16 original tracks. The three Hodges Brothers, were born and reared in Bogue Chitto, Mississippi, where they still live and farm. Their music is typical of hillbilly music of the late 1930s and early '40s. [JAF 297--DKW]

54   Label Name/Number: Folkways FA 2368
Title: *The High Lonesome Sound*
Artist: Roscoe Holcomb
Collector/Recordist: John Cohen/Peter Bartok
Place and Date of Recording: NYC?, 1964
Date of Publication: 1965
Annotations: 8 p. booklet by John Cohen
Selections:
Baby Let Your Hair Roll Down
Barbara Allen Blues
Boat's Up the River
Charles Guiteau [E 11]
Combs Hotel Burned Down
Coney Isle
Fair Miss in the Gardens [N 42]
Fox Chase
Free Little Bird
Hook and Line
In the Pines
Little Bessie
Married Life Blues
Omie Wise [F 4]
Swanno Mountain
Wandering Boy
Willow Tree

55 Label Name/Number: Folkways FA 2374
Title: *Close to Home*
Artist: Roscoe Holcomb
Collector/Recordist: John Cohen
Place and Date of Recording: Daisy, KY, 1972
Date of Publication: 1975
Annotations: 4 p. booklet by John Cohen
Selections:
    Motherless Children
    Train that Carried My Girl from Town
    Frankie and Johnny [I 3]
    Roll on Buddy
    Darlin' Cory
    Walk Around My Bedside
    Mississippi Heavy Water Blues
    Milk Cow Blues
    In London City [P 24]
    Got No Honey Baby Now
    Village Churchyard, The

Fwys FA 2368 / FA 2374: One of John Cohen's most important finds during his fieldwork in Kentucky was Roscoe Holcomb (1912-1981), a singer of incredible emotional intensity, who not only projected that emotion but so overwhelmed himself while singing that the performance act was often an ordeal for him. FA 2368, the first album devoted entirely to him, demonstrates his intense style, his skills on both banjo and guitar, and his ability to adapt material from old Anglo-American ballads to Afro-American blues to his inimitable style. Some of his songs come (at least, indirectly) from hillbilly 78s--e.g., Frank Hutchison's "Coney Isle" and "Train..." On FA 2374, Holcomb sings one unaccompanied Baptist hymn, "Village Churchyard," and otherwise accompanies himself on either guitar or banjo. His high, shrill, piercing voice is the essence of what is called the Kentucky "high lonesome" style. [JAF 313--DKW (FA 2368)]

56 Label Name/Number: Birch 1945
Title: *Doc Hopkins*
Artist: Doc Hopkins
Collector/Recordist: D. K. Wilgus & Barret E. Hansen
Editor: D. K. Wilgus
Place and Date of Recording: Los Angeles, CA, 1965
Date of Publication: [1971]
Annotations: 14 p. booklet by D. K. Wilgus and others
Selections:
    Fate of the Battleship Maine
    Free Little Bird
    Great Titanic, The
    J. B. Marcum [E 19]
    Jesse James [E 1]
    John Henry [I 1]
    Last Old Dollar
    Pearl Bryant [F 2]
    Poor Ellen Smith [F 11]
    Trouble at the Coal Creek Mines
    Wild Bill Jones [E 10]

Wreck of the Titanic [D 24]
Wreck on the C. & O. [G 3]

Brch 1945: Doc Hopkins (1899-1988), born in Harlan County, Kentucky, enjoyed great popularity on Chicago's WLS and various other radio stations through the 1930s and '40s. His success on radio and in personal appearances was not matched on phonograph record: a handful of scarce recordings on the Broadway label in 1931, another batch in 1936 for the American Record Corp. with the Cumberland Ridge Runners, and a few more in 1941 for Decca constituted the extent of his recordings during the same period. Doc left show business in 1949 and worked as a machinist, in Chicago for many years, and then in Los Angeles. While in L. A., Doc was persuaded to perform at two UCLA Folk Festivals, at which time he also recorded the material for this album. In 1965 he sounded much as he did three decades earlier: competent, intricate banjo and guitar accompaniment, bland but pleasant vocal style. The selections are not representative of Hopkins' repertoire in that they concentrate on the older, traditional pieces. Ballads form the bulk of the material, but of particular interest are a unique cante fable version of "Trouble at the Coal Creek Mines," with instrumental imitations on the banjo, and an unusual "Fate of the Battleship Maine." In editing and preparing the brochure for this LP, Wilgus sought to establish a new model for folk music scholarship, hoping it would eventually become the norm as the field grew to maturity and increased specialization took over. Although himself able to write more than adequate annotations to the songs, he chose to hand over certain items to other scholars who had special knowledge in those areas. Likewise, the meticulous musical transcriptions and the discography were prepared by experts in their fields. Unfortunately, this labor of love was flawed by limitations imposed by a low budget, so the packaging is not nearly so pleasing aesthetically as it might have been. [WF 1/75; JAF 341--WHJ]

57 Label Name/Number: Rounder Records 0009
Title: *The Ballad of Finley Preston*
Artists: Clint Howard, Fred Price, and their sons (Clarence and Kenneth)
Collector/Recordist: Ted Osborn
Place and Date of Recording: Trade, TN, 1971
Date of Publication: 1972
Annotations: 7 p. booklet and liner notes by J. Wilson
Selections:
    Ain't Gonna Rain No More
    Ain't No Sense You High Hattin' Me
    Banks of Old Tennessee
    Beefsteaks
    Cackling Hen
    Carroll County Blues
    East Bound Train
    Finley Preston
    Grey Eagle
    Homesick for Heaven
    I Saw a Man at the Close of Day
    Little Pal
    Mt. Zion
    Peg and Awl
    Pretty Little Widow
    Smoke Among the Clouds
    Streets of Glory
    Sunny Tennessee [= Girl I Loved in...]

Surely I Will
Tough Luck
Whoa Mule

Rndr 0009: The title song is a 1903 local murder ballad (to the tune, approximately, of "I Cannot Call Her Mother") from eastern Tennessee/western North Carolina previously collected in both states (by Mellinger Henry and Frank C. Brown, respectively), though rarely available on commercial disc. Guitar player Howard (b. 1930) and fiddler Price (b. 1915) first achieved renown outside of their native area when they played and recorded with Clarence Ashley and Doc Watson, one of the finest old-time stringbands to be recorded since World War II. On this album, Howard and Price are given freer rein, without being overshadowed by their former associates. Nevertheless, the influence of the late Ashley is evident in their music: three of "his" songs are included here-- "Peg and Awl," an early 19th century song protesting the industrial revolution; "Ain't No Sense You High Hattin' Me," and "Tough Luck [Blues]." Fiddler/singer G. B. Grayson, a neighbor of theirs before his accidental death in the 1930s, is also remembered in the selections on this LP: "I Saw a Man at the Close of Day" and "Banks of Old Tennessee" were both recorded by him. The other 13 pieces include fiddle tunes ("Grey Eagle," "Carroll County Blues," "Pretty Little Widow"), sentimental ballads ("The Girl I Loved in Tennessee," "East Bound Train"), and religious pieces, one of which, "Surely I Will," is remarkable for its sentiments unusual in Christian theology and Southern mountain hymnody. The brochure notes dwell at length on the Finley Preston story and on the performers but say nothing about the other selections. [WF 1/75; JAF 343--DKW]

58   Label Name/Number: Folk Legacy FSA-11
Title: *Ozark Folksongs and Ballads*
Artist: Max Hunter
Collector/Recordist/Editor: Sandy Paton
Place and Date of Recording: Springfield, MO, 1960s?
Date of Publication: 1963
Annotations: 21 p. booklet by Mary Celestia Parler and Vance Randolph
Selections:
Battle of Pea Ridge, The [A 12b]
Blue Ridge Mountains, The
Dewy Dens of Yarrow, The [C. 214]
Down By the Greenwood Side [C. 20]
Down by the Sea Shore [=I Never Will Marry]
Drunkard's Wife, The
How Come That Blood? [C. 13]
John Henry (Hardy) [I 2]
Lady Margaret [C. 74]
Oh Miss, I Have A Very Fine Farm
Open the Door
Pretty Suzie
Sporting Molly
Sweet Lovely Jane

FLeg FSA-11: Max Hunter (b. 1921) grew up in Springfield, Missouri, and early developed an interest in older music. When he acquired a tape recorder, he would record anyone who would sing songs for him, erasing the tape after he learned the songs. In 1957 he learned that there was some more serious interest in the old folksongs, and thereafter he was careful to keep his tapes. He has since deposited his collection at the University of Arkansas. Hunter, the collector, became Hunter, the informant for Vance Randolph and Mary Celestia Parker, and they recorded many of his songs, which he tried to render exactly as he had learned them. Hunter sings in an undecorated, plain style, with simple guitar accompaniment. The brochure includes text transcriptions, backgrounds on the songs, and on Hunter's sources for the songs. Several of the songs are rare: in particular, "Dewy Dens of Yarrow" has been found in the New World only a few times. [JAF 305-- DKW]

59   Label Name/Number: Rounder 1002
Title: *Aunt Molly Jackson*
Artist: Molly Jackson
Collector/Recordist: Alan Lomax
Producers: The Rounder Collective
Place and date of recordings: Kentucky, 1939
Date of Publication: [1972]
Annotations: 8 p. brochure by Rounder Collective (Ken Irwin, Bruce Kaplan, Marian Leighton, Bill Nowlin)
Selections:
    Christmas Eve in the East Side
    Crossbones Skully
    Fare Thee Well Old Ely Branch
    Hard Times in Coleman's Mines
    Hungry Disgusted Blues
    I Love Coal Miners, I Do
    Join the C. I. O.
    Just a Little Talk with Jesus
    Let Me Be Your Teddy
    Lone Pilgrim, The
    Lonesome Jailhouse Blues
    Prisoner's Call
[Also some stories and monologues]

Rndr 1002: Mary Magdalene Garland Jackson (1880-1961) was, as D. K. Wilgus described her, not merely a good singer, but a great one. Not many years after her birth, her father went to work in the mines and soon became involved in union organizing; Aunt Molly followed his footsteps. In 1931 she was essentially run out of Kentucky for her radical unionizing, and she moved to New York to raise money for the struggling miners. She fell in among the local liberal folksong singing crowd, and introduced many urbanites to the harsh, tense "high lonesome" Kentucky singing style. For Alan Lomax and Mary Elizabeth Barnacle she recorded her store of traditional Kentucky ballads and songs, some of which have been issued on Library of Congress albums (q. v.). A highly creative singer and songwriter, she composed numerous songs out of her own experiences, and this is the side of her repertoire mainly featured on the present album. In the 1950s she was interviewed extensively by folklorists, and her life and music have been well documented (see, for example, Archie Green's *Only a Miner*; and the memorial issue of *Kentucky Folklore Record*, Vol. 7, No. 4, 1961). While few of her songs will survive in oral tradition, Aunt Molly's status as a folk composer and singer, one who fashions new material out of traditional elements, is unquestioned. [JAF 343-- DKW]

60   Label Name/Number: Folkways FH 5723 [2 lp set]
Title: *The Cowboy: His Songs, Ballads, & Brag Talk*
Artist: Harry Jackson
Collector/Recordist: [Diane Hamilton]
Editor: Kenneth S. Goldstein

Place and Date of Recording: New York [1957?]
Date of Publication: 1957
Annotations: 12 p. brochure by Kenneth S. Goldstein
Selections:
As I Went Walking One Morning for Pleasure
Blood on the Saddle
Clayton Boone [C. 200]
Cowboy Jack [B 24]
Dally Roper's Song, The
Gal I Left Behind, The [P 1b]
Hangman's Song, The [C. 95]
I Ain't Got No Use for the Women
I Ride an Old Paint
I'm Gonna Leave Old Texas Now
Jack O'Diamonds
Little Joe the Wrangler [B 5]
Little Joe the Wrangler's Sister Nell
Old Blue Was Gray Horse
Old Iron Pants Pete
Pot Wrassler, The
Ridge Running Roan, The
Roll On, Little Dogies
Round-Up Cook, The
Saddle Bum, The
Strawberry Roan [B 18]
Streets of Loredo [B 1]
Tying a Knot in the Devil's Tail [B 17]
Utah Carroll [B 4]
When the Work's All Done This Fall [B 3]
Windy Bill
Zebra Dun [B 16]
[Also some shouts and brags]

Fwys FH 5723: Harry Jackson was born (1924) in Chicago and early developed an interest in horses and riding. He learned his first cowboy songs from a one-time cowpuncher then working in the Chicago Stock Yards. At age 13 he got his first job at a stable near DeKalb, Illinois, and later moved to Wyoming, picking up more songs all along. In 1942 he joined the Marines and after the war went to New York to pursue his other love, painting. In his brochure notes, Goldstein proclaimed Jackson "one of the great American cowboy singers." Jackson sings all his songs (and some "good morning" hollers and brags) in a powerful voice, in rubato rhythm--all without accompaniment. Despite his later reputation as a prominent trained visual artist, Jackson's songs were all learned from traditional sources and he is indeed an excellent repository of cowboy and western songs. Goldstein's lengthy brochure provides general background on cowboy songs in general and Jackson's career in particular; text transcriptions, and notes on all the selections. [JAF 288--DKW]

61 **Label Name/Number:** County 713
Title: *Down to the Cider Mill*
Artists: Fred Cockerham, Tommy Jarrell, and Oscar Jenkins
Collector/Recordist: Charles Faurot and Richard Nevins
Producer: Charles Faurot

Date of Publication: [1968]
Annotations: Liner notes by Richard Nevins
Selections:
    Black Eyed Susie
    Cider Mill
    Ground Hog
    John Brown's Dream
    June Apple
    Little Satchel Suzanna Gal
    Old Bunch of Keys
    Policeman
    Reuben
    Rockingham Cindy
    Too Young to Marry

62   Label Name/Number: County 723
Title: *Back Home in the Blue Ridge*
Artists: Fred Cockerham, Tommy Jarrell, and Oscar Jenkins, with Shag Stanley, Mac Snow
Collector/Recordist: Charles Faurot and Richard Nevins
Producer: Richard Nevins
Date of Publication: [1971?]
Annotations: 4 p. insert brochure by Richard Nevins
Selections:
    Arkansas Traveler
    Bile 'em Cabbage Down
    Breaking Up Christmas
    Cumberland Gap
    Dan Carter Waltz
    Jack of Diamonds
    Let Me Fall
    Old Joe Clark
    Rustic Dance
    Sally Ann
    Sally Ann
    When Sorrows Encompass Me 'Round

63   Label Name/Number: County 741
Title: *Stay All Night and Don't Go Home*
Artists: Fred Cockerham, Tommy Jarrell, and Oscar Jenkins, accomp. by Shag Stanley
Collector/Recordist: Charles Faurot and Rich Nevins
Producer: Rich Nevins
Date of Publication: 1973
Annotations: Liner notes by Ray Alden
Selections:
    Birdie
    Boll Weevil [I 17]
    Bravest Cowboy
    Fall on My Knees
    Frankie Baker [I 3]
    Honeysuckle
    John Hardy [I 2]

Old '97
Polly Put the Kettle On
Stay All Night
Sugar Hill
Texas Gals

Cty 713 / Cty 723 / Cty 741: Fred Cockerham, Tommy Jarrell, and Oscar Jenkins are three outstanding sexagenarian musicians, all of whom excel on both banjo and fiddle. Their repertoires are large, strong in tunes not often found outside the Mount Airy (North Carolina)/Round Peak (Virginia) area, where they live. Jarrell and Jenkins are the sons of Ben Jarrell and Frank Jenkins, respectively fiddler and banjoist in the great 1920s band, Da Costa Woltz's Southern Broadcasters (see County 524). Their albums have fine examples of what can be one of the loveliest instrumental combinations: banjo and fiddle playing melody together. Of particular interest on Cty 713 is Jenkins' unusual fourstring banjo down-picking. "Little Satchel" is a curious mixture of several lyric songs along with a fragment of Laws M 4. "Suzzana Gal," is a local title for "Fly Around My Pretty Little Miss." The liner notes provide helpful information on the instrumental styles, although it would have been more convenient if the contents listing indicated which musician played which instrument on each track. The tunes on Cty 723 are largely familiar stringband numbers, but they are rendered with such marvelously well blended banjo-fiddle inter-play as is seldom heard on disc. Nevins' informative and perceptive brochure notes dwell on the chronological overlays of styles that can be heard in the music of this region, noting the difficulty in reconstructing the musical history when even first-rate practitioners such as these artists have quite different perspectives (as on the question of the origins of double-thumbing banjo style).

Cty 741 features Jarrell's fiddle and vocal on 8 of the 14 tracks, including five ballads. "Old '97" is not the familiar trainwreck ballad (G 2) but rather a version of an older antecedent song, "The Train That Never Returned." Jenkins' fiddling style is somewhat more modern than Jarrell's; on both "Honeysuckle" and "Birdie" he shows signs of the bluesy style associated with Arthur Smith. Cockerham's "Texas Gals" is sometimes called "Texas Gales." Both Jenkins and Cockerham play with guitar accompaniment; Jarrell's older style is more aptly accompanied just by banjo (Cockerham). This album is an outstanding selection of old-time music by some of the finest traditional musicians playing in the 1970s. [JAF 324; WF 7/72; WF 1/75]

64 Label Name/Number: County 748
Title: *Come and Go with Me: Tommy Jarrell's Banjo Album*
Artist: Tommy Jarrell
Collector/Recordist: Charles Faurot & Rich Nevins
Producer: Rich Nevins
Date of Publication: [1974]
Annotations: Liner notes by Faurot
Selections:
    Back Step Cindy
    Ducks in the Millpond
    John Hardy [I 2]
    John Henry
    Little Maggie
    Old Reuben
    Poor Ellen Smith [F 11]
    Rockingham Cindy
    Sally Ann
    Sweet Sunny South
    Tempie Roll Down Your Bangs
    Uncle Ned

65   Label Name/Number: County 756
Title: *Sail Away Ladies*
Artist: Tommy Jarrell
Collector/Recordist: Bobby Patterson
Editor: Barry Poss and Charles Ellertson
Date of Publication: 1976
Annotations: 4 p. brochure insert by Poss
Selections:
    Bonaparte's Retreat
    Cluck Old Hen
    Cotton Eyed Joe
    Devil in the Strawstack
    Drunken Hiccups, The
    Fisher's Hornpipe
    Flatwoods
    Forked Deer
    Greasy String
    Joke on the Puppy, The
    Raleigh and Spencer
    Rochester Schottische/Walking in the Parlor
    Sail Away Ladies
    Soldier's Joy
    Step Back Cindy

66   Label Name/Number: County 778
Title: *Pickin' on Tommy's Porch*
Artists: Tommy Jarrell, with Chester McMillan and Andy Cahan
Collector/Recordist: Bobby Patterson
Editor: [Rich Nevins]
Place of Recording: Galax, VA
Date of Publication: [ca. 1978]
Annotations: Liner notes by Mike Seeger
Selections:
    Chilly Winds
    Dance All Night with a Bottle in Your Hand
    Fortune
    Little Brown Jug
    Lonesome Road Blues
    Merry Girl, The
    New River Train
    Old Buck
    Sourwood Mountain
    Tater Patch
    Train on the Island
    Walking in My Sleep
    What're You Gonna Do with the Baby-O

67   Label Name/Number: County 791
Title: *Rainbow Sign*
Artists: Tommy Jarrell, accompanied by Verlen Clifton, Alice Gerrard, and Andy Cahan
Collector/Recordist: Andy Cahan

Place and Date of Recording: Galax, VA, 1984
Date of Publication: 1986
Annotations: Liner notes by Andy Cahan
Selections:
   Chapel Hill Serenade
   Fire on the Mountain
   God Gave Noah the Rainbow Sign
   Granny Will Your Dog Bite
   Ida Red
   Little Maggie
   Little Sadie [I 8]
   Old Molly Hare
   Old Time Backstep Cindy
   Old Time Sally Ann
   Poor Ellen Smith [F 11]
   Say Darling Say
   Sugar Foot Rag
   Tempie

Cty 748 / 756 / 778 / 791: Thomas Jefferson Jarrell (1901-85), one of the most influential traditional fiddlers of the last decade or two, was frequently recorded. The son of Ben Jarrell, an influential musician of the 1920s (he was fiddler with DaCosta Woltz's Southern Broadcasters), Tommy absorbed a rich musical tradition from turn-of-the-century Mt. Airy. Though he rarely played for some thirty-five years, retirement and the death of his wife provided incentive to return to his music, and he shared it with an eager younger generation for two decades as a steady succession of banjo and fiddle players pilgrimaged to Mt. Airy to learn at the master's knee. The subtitle of Cty 748 refers to the fact that Jarrell is regarded by most as primarily a fiddler, but one would never guess it from these recordings. In his jacket notes, Faurot discusses Jarrell's playing technique--a frailing style that makes heavy use of hammering ons, pulling off, slides, and drop-thumbing. Jarrell has a very consistent sound--notwithstanding that he plays on both fretted and fretless banjos. He sings some of his songs in a rather pinched, nasal voice. Cty 756 offers 16 selections representative of the music of the Mt. Airy area current around the turn of the century. The booklet by Poss includes biographical information and program notes.

Cty 778 focuses on Jarrell's banjo playing. Though he is an excellent singer, the emphasis is on instrumental versions: "John Henry," "Sweet Sunny South" (on fretless banjo), and "Rockingham Cindy" are all without the usual vocals. Though, as Faurot points out in his illuminating liner notes, Jarrell is an exceptional banjo player with a flare for adding characteristic nuances to his renditions, there is, as in the case of many traditional musicians, a sameness to his performances that can be, under different circumstances, both a strength and a weakness.

Jarrell made some of his last recordings shortly before his death early in 1985 for Cty 791--14 tunes with accompaniment by Verlen Clifton, mandolin; Alice Gerrard, guitar; and Andy Cahan, banjo. All selections feature Jarrell's fiddling, with his singing on many as well--from dance tunes ("Old Time Sally Ann,' "Granny Will Your Dog Bite") and gospel songs ("God Gave Noah the Rainbow Sign") to old ballads ("Poor Ellen Smith" [Laws F 11], "Little Sadie" [I 8]) and songs ("Little Maggie," "Tempie"). [JAF 395; WF 1/75]

68   Label Name/Number: Mountain 302
Title: *June Apple*
Artists: Tommy Jarrell, Kyle Creed, Audine Lineberry, and Bobby Patterson
Recordist: Bobby Patterson
Producer: Kyle Creed

Place of Recording: Galax, VA
Date of Publication: 1972
Annotations: Liner notes by Zane Bennett
Selections:
  Breaking up Christmas
  Ducks on the Pond
  John Brown's Dream
  June Apple
  Kittie Clyde
  Policeman
  Reuben
  Rockingham Cindy
  Sally Ann
  Sugar Hill
  Susanna Gal

Mtn 302: Jarrell sings and fiddles through another collection of Galax/Mt. Airy old-time dance tunes, accompanied by Creed on banjo, Lineberry on string bass, and Patterson on guitar. Most of these tunes appear on other Jarrell albums also.

69   Label Name/Number: Arhoolie 5011 [orig. issue: Folklyric LP 123]
Title: *Carolina Bluegrass*
Artists: Snuffy Jenkins with Homer "Pappy" Sherrill, Julian "Greasy" Medlin, Bill Rea, Ira Dimmery
Collector/Recordist/Editor: Harry Oster
Place and Date of Recording: Columbia, SC, 1962
Date of Publication: [1981?] (Orig. issue 1962?)
Annotations: Liner notes by Peter J. Welding
Selections:
  Big-Eared Mule
  Boggy Road to Texas
  Born in Hard Luck
  Charmin' Betsy
  Covered Wagon Rolled Right Along, The
  Dixie, There's No Place Like Home
  Gonna Catch That Train an' Ride
  Long Journey Home
  Long Time Gone
  Miller's Reel [= Carroll County Blues?]
  Possum up a Gum Stump
  Snuffy's Talking Blues
  Spanish Fandango
  Step It Up and Go
  Sweetest Gift, a Mother's Smile, The
  Television
  Twinkle, Twinkle, Little Star
  Watermelon Hangin' on a Vine

70   Label Name/Number: Rounder Records 0005
Title: *33 Years of Pickin' and Pluckin'*
Artists: Snuffy Jenkins and Pappy Sherrill with Dick Harmon, Buddy Harmon, Greasy Medlin

Collector/Recordist: Joel Johnson
Editor: Mark Wilson
Place and Date of Recording: West Columbia, SC, 1971
Date of Publication: [1971]
Annotations: Liner notes by Rounder Collective
Selections:
  Alabama Jubilee
  Aunt Liza's Favorite
  Beaumont Rag
  C & NW Railroad Blues
  Cherry Blossom Waltz
  Coney Island
  Dreamy Georgiana Moon
  Fifty Year Ago Waltz
  I Want My Rib
  Kansas City Kitty
  Lonesome Road Blues
  Milk Cow Blues
  Model T Blues
  Mountain Top/Shout Lula [= Hook and Line]
  Nancy Rowland
  Run, Boy, Run
  Sally Johnson (Katy Hill)
  Shortnin' Bread
  Texas Quickstep
  Wagoner
  When the Bumblebee Backed Up to Me and Pushed

Arh 5011 / Rndr 0005: Dewitt "Snuffy" Jenkins (1908-90) was one of the North Carolina three-finger banjo players whose style was a precursor to Earl Scruggs' bluegrass style. Jenkins, born in Harris, North Carolina, played mandolin, guitar, and banjo in his youth. During the 1920s and early 30s he played frequently at local dances in western North Carolina, settling in Columbia, South Carolina in 1937. There he joined a band on radio station WIS, joined two years later by Homer Sherrill, one of the finest fiddlers of the '30s. Their music is a mixture of '30s sounds with a touch of more modern bluegrass influence. The others on this album joined the band (later called "The Hired Hands") in 1947-55. The Arhoolie album marked Jenkins' first extended recorded appearance since the '30s. Jenkins' playing is admirably presented on three instrumental tracks, "Spanish Fandango," "Dixie/There's No Place Like Home," and "Twinkle, Twinkle, Little Star." "Step It Up and Go" is unabashedly borrowed from Blind Boy Fuller; "Born in Hard Luck" and "Snuffy's Talking Blues" are both talking blues with long pedigrees. "Miller's Reel" sounds more like "Carroll County Blues." Unlike the other quasi-bluegrass albums catalogued here, this one features some lead flat-pick and finger-picking guitar playing--not to mention Jenkins' rhythm backup on washboard. The Rounder LP is a similar mix, with three humorous selections featuring the guitar and singing of Julian "Greasy" Medlin, veteran medicine and tent show performer of many years. [WF 7/72; JAF 343--DKW (Rndr)]

71 Label Name/Number: Augusta Heritage 001
Title: *Fiddlin' John*
Artist(s): John Johnson
Collector/Recordist/Producer: Gerald Milnes, Michael Kline, Paul Reisler
Place and Date of Recording: Elkins, WV, 1981

Date of Publication: 1982
Annotations: Liner notes by Michael Kline and John Johnson
Selections:
    Barnyard Serenade
    Billy in the Lowland
    Bonaparte's Retreat
    Camp Chase
    Dixon County Blues
    Forked Deer
    Golden Bells
    Hassett's Retreat
    Jimmy Johnson
    Jimmy Rogers [sic] Mixture
    Roane County Prisoner
    Roving Piper
    Sally Ann Johnson
    Three Forks of Reedy
    Wild Horse in the Red Brush
    Yew Piney Mountain
    I'll Be There

AH 001: John Johnson was born in Clay County, West Virginia, in about 1916. He learned some of his tunes from older relatives and local residents, and others from popular recording artists such as Fiddlin' John Carson and Arthur Smith; he plays (without accompaniment) with a rather choppy, short bow-stroke style. His "Billy in the Lowland" is lovely.

72   Label Name/Number: Folkways FS 3810
Title: *Buell Kazee Sings and Plays*
Artist: Buell Kazee
Collector/Recordist: Gene Bluestein
Place and Date of Recording: Lexington, KY, ca. 1956
Date of Publication: 1958
Annotations: 6 p. booklet by Gene Bluestein
Selections:
    Amazing Grace
    Bread of Heaven
    Butcher Boy [P 24]
    Cock Robin
    Cumberland Gap
    Dance Around My Pretty Little Miss
    Darling Corey
    East Virginia
    Eternity
    John Hardy [I 2]
    John Henry [I 1]
    Little Mohee [H 8]
    Moonshiner Song
    My Christian Friends
    Old Grey Mare
    On Top of Old Smoky
    Wagoner's Lad

When Moses
Yellow Pups (Fox Chase)

73   Label Name/Number: June Appal JA 009
Title: *Buell Kazee*
Artist: Buell Kazee
Collector/Recordist: Mark Wilson, Buell Kazee
Editor: John McCutcheon
Place and Date of Recording: Seattle, WA, 1969 (some, others not identified)
Date of Publication: 1978
Annotations: 11 p. booklet by Loyal Jones and William H. Tallmadge
Selections:

Amazing Grace
Banjo Medley: Blue-Eyed Gal / Rock Little Julie / What'll I Do With the Baby-O
Black Jack Davy [C. 200]
Blind Man, The
Jay Gould's Daughter
Lady Gay, The [C. 79]
Look up, Look down That Lonesome Road
O, Thou in Whose Presence
Orphan Girl, The
Roll On, John
Roving Cowboy, The [P 1 A]
Sporting Bachelors
Steel A-Going Down

Fwys FS 3810 / JA 009:   Buell Kazee of Magoffin County, Kentucky (1900-1976) is probably better known to most folk music aficionados, having recorded considerably for Brunswick in 1927-29 and then enjoyed a second musical career in the 1960s and 70s for folk revival concert audiences. His 1928 recording of "Lady Gay" was considered by Charles Seeger "about the finest variant" he had heard. Kazee's interest in formal folksinging began in college when he realized that the ballads he was reading in English literature classes were still being sung in his native region. Headed for a career in the ministry, Kazee took voice lessons among his classes and learned to sing in what he called "his good voice." When he made his 78s, the record executives wanted him to sing in his "bad" or "hillbilly" voice, and he tried; but as he later acknowledged, he could not completely erase the effect of years of formal training. His singing on his LPs is thus also affected by voice training--which may disappoint some purists but certainly makes his music more accessible to a broader audience. Folklorist/banjo enthusiast Gene Bluestein visited Buell Kazee at his home and taped their casual conversations in which Kazee talked about his music and career and illustrated his comments with musical examples. He never expected the material to be issued on LP and recalled the fact with some consternation years later. Fortunately, Kazee had nothing to worry about; his earlier musical career during the 1920s was well preserved on 78s, and in the 1960s, when he reactivated his musical career, he was recorded several times. JA 009, put together after Kazee's death, is taken mostly from tapes made by Mark Wilson in ca. 1969. Three selections were taped by Kazee himself. Except for two a capella hymns and one song with guitar back-up by Homer Ledford, all the selections are sung to Kazee's own immaculate frailing banjo accompaniment. Kazee's selections include one of his own compositions--"Steel A'Goin' Down," written in the 1920s.

The material on JA 009 presents a good cross section of Kazee's songs. Oldest are the three British ballads (C. 79, C. 200, and P 1b). From the late 19th century is the sentimental ballad, "Orphan Girl." "Steel A'Goin' Down" is his own composition, written and first recorded in the 1920s. His religious repertoire is represented by two unaccompanied hymns, and his banjo virtuosity by a medley of tunes as well as by his banjo accompaniment to his own singing. Kazee's voice is somewhat huskier than it was when he recorded for Brunswick, and he now takes advantage of the freedom from the time constraints of the 78 rpm disc to sing slower and with more verses to his songs (his "Lady Gay" has three additional stanzas), but some--e.g., "Black Jack Davy" [Child 200], to an unusual pentatonic (pi[1]) tune; and "Look Up, Look Down that Lonesome Road," to a melody (almost tetratonic) similar to the "Reuben" tune--are recorded firsts for him. The June Appal LP includes a 12 x 12" booklet with a long biography by Loyal Jones, program notes by Jones and William H. Tallmadge, and a 78 rpm discography. [JAF 408; JEMFQ 57]

74   Label Name/Number: County 733 (first issued on Folk Promotions FP 828, later relabeled Kanawha 304)
Title: *The Legend of Clark Kessinger*
Artists: Clark Kessinger, accomp. by Gene Meade and Wayne Hauser
Collector/Recordist: Ken Davidson
Place and Date of Recording: WV?, 1971 [FP 828 in 1964]
Date of Publication: 1971
Annotations: Liner notes by Guthrie T. Meade and David Freeman
Selections:
  Billy in the Low Ground
  Chicken in the Barnyard
  Chinky Pin
  Dance All Night
  Flop-Eared Mule
  Hell Among the Yearlings
  Leather Britches
  Over the Waves
  Poca River Blues
  Ragtime Annie
  Red Bird
  Sally Ann Johnson
  Sally Goodwin
  Salt River
  Sandy River
  Turkey Knob
  Wednesday Night Waltz

75   Label Name/Number: Kanawha 306
Title: *Sweet Bunch of Daisies*
Artist: Clark Kessinger with Charlie Bill Lemon
Collector/Recordist: Jerry Galyean and Ken Davidson
Place and Date of Recording: WV?, 1966-67
Date of Publication: [1967?]
Annotations: Liner notes by Jerry Galyean, Guthrie T. Meade Jr and Robert P. Christeson
Selections:
  Black Hawk Waltz
  Devil's Dream
  Done Gone
  Durang Hornpipe
  Kanawha March
  Listen to the Mocking Bird
  Old Jake Gillie

Paddy on the Turnpike
Sweet Bunch of Daisies
Three Forks of Sandy
Under the Double Eagle
West Virginia Hornpipe
Wilson's Hornpipe

Cty 733 (orig. Folk Promotions FP 828) / Kan 306: Clark Kessinger and his nephew, Luches, began playing together in 1919 and by 1926 had their own radio show over WOBU, Charleston, West Virginia. Between 1928 and 1930 they recorded over 70 fiddle/guitar duets for the Brunswick Company. After Luches' death in 1943, Clark retired from commercial music (except for local dances) until 1964, when Ken Davidson found him and recorded him for his Folk Promotions label. Subsequently, Clark won the title of "World Champion Fiddler" at the 1966 Union Grove Fiddlers' Convention and performed at numerous fiddle contests and folk festivals. This County LP is a reissue of that first Folk Promotions (now Kanawha) release. Kessinger, in the 1960s, proved to be a hard-driving skillful fiddler, every bit as good as he had been in the 1920s. The album is one of the most exciting collections of fiddling by one of the most technically proficient old-time fiddlers to be recorded.

The Kanawha album, his second, further demonstrates a masterly approach to old-time fiddling--hard driving, vigorous, and technically precise in every way. [WF 7/72 (Cty 733); JAF 314--DKW (FP 828); JAF 325--AJ (Kan 306)]

76a **Label Name/Number:** Old Homestead OHCS 314 (Originally issued as Bluebonnet BL 107)
Title: *Mountain Ballads and Old Time Songs, Number One*
Artists: Bradley Kincaid
Place and Date of Recording: Ft. Worth, TX, 1963
Date of Publication: 1984 (Bluebonnet LP in 1963)
Annotations: Liner by Charles Wolfe (by D. K. Wilgus on Bluebonnet)
Selections:
Barbara Allen [C. 84]
Billy Boy
Down in the Valley
Fatal Derby Day, The
First Whippoorwill, The
Footprints in the Snow
Four Thousand Years Ago
I Gave My Love a Cherry
I Love My Rooster
I'll Remember You, Love, in My Prayers
Legend of the Robin's Red Breast, The
Little Shirt that Mother Made for Me, The
Liza up in the 'Simmon Tree
Methodist Pie

76b **Label Name/Number:** Old Homestead OHCS 315 (Originally issued as Bluebonnet BL 105)
Title: *Mountain Ballads and Old Time Songs, Number Two*
Artists: Bradley Kincaid
Place and Date of Recording: Ft. Worth, TX, 1963
Date of Publication: [1985] (Bluebonnet LP in 1964)

Annotations: Liner notes by D. K. Wilgus
Selections:
    Don't Make Me Go to Bed and I'll Be Good
    Fingerprints upon the Window Pane
    Gypsy's Warning, The
    High Grass Town
    Hunters of Kentucky, The
    In a Village by the Sea
    Just as the Sun Went Down
    Just Plain Folks
    Letter Edged in Black, The
    Life's Railway to Heaven
    My Grandfather's Clock
    My Sweet Iola
    There's No Place Like Home
    Two Little Orphans

76c   **Label Name/Number:** Old Homestead OHCS 316 (Originally issued as Bluebonnet BL 109 but less two titles)
Title: *Mountain Ballads and Old Time Songs, Number Three*
Artist: Bradley Kincaid
Place and Date of Recording: Ft. Worth, TX, 1963
Date of Publication: 1986
Annotations: Liner notes by Charles Wolfe
Selections:
    Blue Tail Fly, The
    Brush the Dust from that Old Bible
    Bury Me out on the Prairie
    Dog and Gun [N 20]
    Get Away Old Man, Get Away
    House Carpenter [C. 243]
    I Wonder When I Shall Be Married
    I'd Like To Be in Texas
    In the Hills of Old Kentucky
    Legend of the Robin's Red Breast, The
    There's a Red Light Ahead
    Three Wishes, The (or Better Than Gold)

76d   **Label Name/Number:** Old Homestead OHCS 317 (Originally issued as Bluebonnet BL 112)
Title: *Mountain Ballads and Old Time Songs, Number Four*
Artist: Bradley Kincaid
Place and Date of Recording: Ft. Worth, TX, 1963
Date of Publication: [1986] (BL 112 in 1966)
Annotations: Liner notes by D. K. Wilgus
Selections:
    Cindy
    Give My Love to Nell
    Hills of Old New Hampshire, The
    Housekeeper's Tragedy, The
    How Beautiful Heaven Must Be

I Loved You Better Than You Knew
Life of Jimmy [sic] Rodgers, The
Only as Far as the Gate
Pearl Bryan [F 16]
Sweet Kitty Wells
True and Trembling Brakeman, The
Wreck on the C & O Road, The [G 3]

OH OHCS 314 / 315 / 316 / 317: Bradley Kincaid's long career on records and radio has been ably documented in Loyal Jones' *Radio's 'Kentucky Mountain Boy': Bradley Kincaid* (Berea College, 2nd ed, 1988). He made his first recordings in 1928 and his last in the early 1970s. Born in the foothills of the Cumberlands of Kentucky (1895-1989), he learned his first songs from his parents and continued consciously to collect long after his career was well underway, until his repertoire was well over 300 songs. He was very popular over radio especially in the midwest, where his pleasant voice and plain singing style, accompanied by his own guitar, were very appropriate. In 1963 he recorded 162 songs in a Ft. Worth, Texas, studio for the Bluebonnet label, 74 of which were subsequently released on six LPs. OHCS-314 and OHCS-317 are reissues of the first and fourth of those Bluebonnet albums; the latter includes the original liner notes by another one-time Kincaid admirer, the late D. K. Wilgus. OHCS-316, with liner notes by Charles Wolfe, reissues all the material from the second Bluebonnet album with two additional titles of Kincaid's own composition ("The Legend of the Robin Red Breast" and "Brush the Dust from That Old Bible"), probably taken from a 1950 Capitol single. [JAF 317--DKW (BL 112)]

77   Label Name/Number: County 712
Title: *The Coon Creek Girls*
Artists: Lily May, Rosie, and Susie Ledford
Collector/Recordist/Editor: Charles Faurot
Date of Publication: 1968
Annotations: Liner notes by Faurot
Selections:
  Banjo Picking Girl
  Darling, Six Months Ain't Long
  East Virginia Blues
  Going Down the Valley
  Hawk Caught the Chicken and Gone
  How Many Biscuits Can You Eat?
  I Have No Mother Now
  Little Birdie
  Pretty Polly [P 36b]
  Red Rocking Chair
  Take Your Time Miss Lucy
  White Oak Mountain
  Wild Bill Jones [E 10]

78   Label Name/Number: Greenhays GR712
Title: *Banjo Pickin' Girl*
Artist: Lily May Ledford with Mike Seeger, Phil Williams, Vivian Williams
Date of Publication: 1983
Annotations: Liner notes by Ledford
Selections:
  Babes in the Woods

Banjo Pickin' Girl
Blue Eyed Boy
Cacklin' Hen
Callahan
Charmin' Betsy
Christmas Eve
East Virginia
Hiccup Oh Lordy
I Have No Mother Now
Jim Along Josie
John Hardy [I 2]
John Henry [I 1]
Please, Papa, Don't Whip Little Benny
Texas Bound
Wake Up Susan
Wild Bill Jones [E 10]

Cty 712 / Gnhys GR712: These LPs feature the Eastern Kentucky hillbilly group that was prominent on the Renfro Valley Barn Dance from 1937 to 1957. Originally consisting of Lily May Ledford (1917-1985), Violet Koehler, and Daisy Lange, the group made commercial recordings for Vocalion in 1938 and performed publicly before President and Mrs. Roosevelt and the King and Queen of England in 1939. Later, Daisy and Violet left the group and were replaced by Lily May's sisters, Susie and Rosie, this being the group that appears on this disc. Although the ladies no longer play regularly, they have lost little of their professional polish. All selections are traditional pieces primarily suited for the driving, frailing banjo style of Kentucky, here played by Lily May Ledford Pennington. A few ballads are included, but most of the pieces are banjo tunes such as "Red Rocking Chair," "How Many Biscuits Can You Eat?," and "Little Birdie." "Take Your Time Miss Lucy" is also known as "Rock the Cradle, Lucy" and is related to "Soldier's Joy." The liner notes provide biographical background.

Lily May Ledford alone is featured on GR 712, and is as striking a singer and banjo-player today as she was a half-century ago. The album includes 17 selections, some with accompaniment by Mike Seeger on guitar or Phil and Vivian Williams on bass and guitar. Back jacket liner notes contain her own brief comments on where and when she learned the pieces, which include "John Henry"--one of the best recorded renditions of the ballad, in my opinion--"John Hardy," "Wild Bill Jones;" the nineteenth-century sentimental songs, "Babes in the Woods" and "Please, Papa, Don't Whip Little Benny," and long-time banjo-frailing favorites, "Charmin' Betsy" and the title song, "Banjo Pickin' Girl." [JAF 324 (Cty 712)]

79   Label Name/Number: Rounder 0008
Title: *Ledford String Band*
Artist(s): Steve Ledford, Wayne Ledford, James Gardner
Place and Date of Recording: Bakersville, NC, 1971
Date of Publication: [1972]
Annotations: Liner notes by Rounder Collective
Selections:
Big-Eyed Rabbit
Blues Take Off Your Shoes
Brown's Dream
Don't Cause Mother's Hair to Turn Gray
Drunken Driver, The
Faded Picture on the Wall

Georgia Railroad
He's Coming from Vietnam
If There Wasn't Any Women in the World
In a Lonely Graveyard
Little Maggie
Look for Me
Makin' Hay
Mitchell Blues
Roan Mountain Breakdown
Shanghai Rooster
Swap a Little Sugar
Tucker's Old Barn

Rndr 0008: The Ledford stringband, featuring Fiddlin' Steve Ledford accompanied by Wayne Ledford and James Gardner on guitars, continues the North Carolina traditions represented by G. B. Grayson in the 1920s and the bands of J. E. and Wade Mainer in the 1930s. Born in Mitchell County, North Carolina, in 1906 ("Mitchell Blues" is his version of the old Narmour and Smith tune, "Carroll County Blues"), Ledford headed the band, the Carolina Ramblers, that recorded for the American Record Corp. in 1932; later he worked with Wade Mainer and Zeke Morris as The Smiling Rangers. Ledford was an eclectic musician, learning songs from other artists both in person and on record. This LP includes "Little Maggie" and "He's Coming from Vietnam" from the Grayson repertoire--the latter an updated version of "He's Coming to Us Dead;" and "If There Wasn't Any Women in the World" and probably "Georgia Railroad" from Fiddlin' John Carson. "Drunken Driver" was popularized in the 1940s by Molly O'Day. These are fine musicians to draw inspiration from, and Ledford has learned well from his mentors: he combines the rich sound of Grayson's fiddle with the melismatic decorations of Carson's. He is also a fine singer (hear "Little Maggie" and "Don't Cause Mother's Hair To Turn Gray"). [WF 1/75]

80 Label Name/Number: County 729
Title: *The Early Recordings of the Lilly Brothers*
Artists: Everett and Bea Lilly and Don Stover; Dave Miller, unidentified bass player
Collector/Recordist: Allerton Hawkes
Producer: David Freeman
Place and Date of Recording: Westbrook, Maine, 1956-57 for Event Label
Date of Publication: [1974]
Annotations: Liner notes by Bill Vernon
Selections:
    Are You Tired of Me My Darling?
    Bring Back My Blue Eyed Boy
    John Henry [I 1]
    Little Annie
    Long Journey Home
    Riding on My Saviour's Train
    Southern Skies
    Tragic Romance
    Weeping Willow
    Wheel Hoss
    When the Saints Go Marching In

81 Label Name/Number: Folkways FA 2433
Title: *Folk Songs from the Southern Mountains*

Artists: Lilly Brothers (Everett and Bea) and Don Stover
Collector/Recordist: Mike Seeger
Place and Date of Recording: Boston, 1961
Date of Publication: 1962
Annotations: 5 p. brochure by Mike Seeger and Pete Kuykendall
Selections:
   Barbara Allen [C. 84]
   'Neath That Cold Grey Tomb of Stone
   Cornbread and 'Lasses and Sassafras Tea
   Down on the Banks of the Ohio [F 5]
   Forgotten Soldier Boy
   In My Dear Old Southern Home
   John Hardy [I 2]
   Little Annie
   Midnight on the Stormy Sea
   Oh, Hide You in the Blood
   Old Joe Clark
   Saints Go Marching In
   Sinner You Better Get Ready
   Waves on the Sea, The [C. 289]
   What Would You Give in Exchange?
   Where Is My Sailor Boy?

82   Label Name/Number: Prestige/Folklore 14010
Title: *Bluegrass Breakdown*
Artists: Bea and Everett Lilly, Don Stover, Herb Hooven, and Fritz Richmond
Editor: Paul A. Rothchild, supervisor
Date of Publication: [1964]
Annotations: Liner notes by Paul Nelson
Selections:
   Beneath the Old Southern Sky
   Billy in the Low Ground
   Bluegrass Breakdown
   Foggy Mountain Breakdown
   Have a Feast Here Tonight
   I Wonder How the Old Folks Are at Home
   Katy Hill
   Miller's Cave
   Rollin' On
   Storms on the Ocean
   That Star Belongs to Me
   We Shall Meet Some Day
   Why Did You Wander?
   Wildwood Flower

83   Label Name/Number: Prestige/Folklore 14035
Title: *Country Songs of the Lilly Brothers*
Artists: Lilly Brothers (Everett Lilly, Bea Lilly, Everett Allan Lilly)
Producer: Samuel Charters
Place and Date of Recording: Studio, 1964?
Date of Publication: 1964

Annotations: Liner liner notes by Art Weiss
Selections:
Butcher Boy [P 24]
Dig a Hole in the Meadow
Goodbye Maggie
Jack and Mae
Knoxville Girl [P 35]
Long Black Veil
Open up Them Pearly Gates
Roll in My Sweet Baby's Arms
Rosewood Casket
There'll Come a Time
Trouble Trouble
Weeping Willow Tree

Folkways FA 2433 / County 729 / Prest 14035 / Prest 14010. Bea and Everett Lilly were born in Clear Creek, West Virginia, in 1921 and 1923, respectively, into a family of several musicians. They started playing in the mid-'30s, and by 1940 were playing professionally on local radio stations. For many years they were regulars at the Hillbilly Ranch, a club in Cambridge (Massachusetts). They made their first recordings for the Event label in 1956-57, only four of which were issued then. The County LP includes all their Event recordings, seven of which were never previously released. "John Henry," one of those that was issued on the Event label, is one of the most hard driving versions on record. The Lillys, though strongly bluegrass oriented, favor (on these albums, at least), the older repertoire of the 1930s generation of the Monroe Brothers, Carter Family, and Callahan Brothers, and some of their recordings could easily be mistaken for dating to that decade. Prestige 14035, without either banjo or fiddle, would not be classed as bluegrass; the title "Country Songs" should not be taken to imply contemporary country music, since the style is very close to the Monroe Brothers or Blue Sky Boys. [JAF 338--DKW (Cty)]

84 Label Name/Number: Arhoolie 5010 [orig. issue: Folklyric LP 122]
Title: *Bayou Bluegrass*
Artists: Louisiana Honeydrippers (Jim Smoak, Bucky Wood, Dewey Edwards, Lum York, V. J. Myers, J. C. Myers)
Collector/Recordist: Harry Oster
Editor: Harry Oster; reissue produced by Chris Strachwitz
Place and Date of Recording: Baton Rouge, LA, 1961
Date of Publication: [1972]
Annotations: Liner notes by Oster
Selections:
Bill Cheatum
Calinda
Chicken Pie
Fisher's Hornpipe, The
Great Big Billy Goat
Kissin' Cousins
Lakes of Ponchartrain, The [H 9]
Liza Jane
My Last Dollar Is Gone
Old Dan Tucker
Pore Man
Rabbit, Where's Your Mammy?

Raisin' a Rukus
Run, Boy, Run
Underneath the Weeping Willow
Whoah, Mule, Whoah
Woodchuck in the Deadnin'

85   Label Name/Number: Prestige International INT 13035
Title: *Louisiana Bluegrass with the Louisiana Honeydrippers*
Artists: Jim Smoak, J. C. Myers, V. J. Myers, Bucky Wood, Lum York
Collector/Recordist: Harry Oster
Producer: Kenneth S. Goldstein
Annotations: Liner notes by Harry Oster
Selections:
   Beautiful Life
   Bugle Call Rag
   Cora Is Gone
   Cotton-Eyed Joe
   Girl in the Blue Velvet Band, The
   Hoedown
   Johnson's Old Gray Mule
   Keep My Skillet Good and Greasy
   Knoxville Girl [P 35]
   Liberty
   Little Maggie
   Mama Blues
   More Pretty Girls Than One
   Old Blue
   Pretty Polly [P 36b]
   Rabbit in the Log
   Soldier's Joy
   Who's Goin' Down to Wilmingtown

     Arh 5010 / Prest INT 13035.   Despite bandleader/banjo player Jim Smoak's professional experience with Bill Monroe and on Grand Ole Opry, this bluegrass band's sound and repertoire are so heavily biased by earlier hillbilly music that their inclusion does not flagrantly transgress my decision to omit the vast field of bluegrass music.   The band is dominated by Smoak's banjo and vocals, with bass and pre-bluegrass guitar and mandolin back-up.   Except for "Calinda" and "Lakes of Ponchartrain," both native to Louisiana, and "Kissin' Cousins," by Louisiana folk composer Dave Rankin, the repertoire on Arh 5010 is typical 1930s hillbilly.   The Prestige album is undated but probably was recorded about the same time.   The repertoire is similar, except for the New Orleans influence evident in "Bugle Call Rag," and the older tradition evident in "Who's Going Down to Wilmingtown," a song about tobacco inspecting that Smoak learned from his grandfather.   [JAF 297--DKW (LP 122)]

86   Label Name/Number: String STR 802
Title: *Fiddle Tunes from Grayson County, Virginia*
Artist: Emmett W. Lundy
Collector/Recordist: Alan and Elizabeth Lomax
Producers: Tom Carter and Tony Russell
Place and Date of Recording: Galax, VA, 1941
Date of Publication: 1977

Annotations: 12 p. booklet by Tom Carter (?)
Selections:
    Belle of Lexington
    Bonaparte's Retreat
    Chapel Hill March
    Cleveland March
    Deaf Woman's Courtship
    Ducks on the Millpond
    Evening Star Waltz
    Fisher's Hornpipe
    Flatwoods
    Forky Deer
    Highlander's Farewell
    Julie Ann Johnson
    Molly Put the Kettle On
    Piney Woods Gal
    Sheep Shell Corn by the Rattlin' of His Horn
    Sugar Hill
    Susanna Gal
    Lost Girl, The
    Waves on the Ocean
    Wild Goose Chase

Str 802: Emmett Lundy (1864-1953) was born in Grayson County, Virginia, great-grandson of an English emigrant. Apart from two recordings with Ernest V. Stoneman in 1925, these LC discs are Lundy's only recordings. Most of his tunes were learned from a legendary Virginia fiddler, Greenberry Leonard (b. ca. 1810), and Lundy's playing thus represents perhaps our best glimpse into southeastern fiddling early in the 19th century. Lundy was immensely popular in Grayson County, and many local fiddlers learned from him--even though he never tried to make a living with his fiddling and played only for his own amusement. In his insightful brochure notes, which also provide biographical information and comments on Lundy's style and tunes, Carter discusses the problem of why Lundy's repertoire is so unusual, even among other fiddlers born early in the 20th century, and seeks explanation in the influence of the banjo on the fiddle repertoire of the region late in the last century. All in all, this is an excellent and important document of traditional American fiddle music.

87 Label Name/Number: Rounder 0020
Title: *The Old Swinging Bridge*
Artists: Ted Lundy and the Southern Mountain Boys (Bob Paisley, Jerry Lundy, Wes Rineer, John Haftl)
Place and Date of Recording: Bethesda, MD, 1972
Date of Publication: 1973
Annotations: Liner notes by Carl Goldstein
Selections:
    Come Home [= Papa Come Home]
    Darlin' Nellie, Across the Sea
    Fiddler's Dream
    Flat Woods
    Goodbye Liza Jane
    It Rained a Mist [C. 155]
    Jack and Joe

Last Old Shovel, The
Little Bonnie
Margie
Mother Knows Best
Old Homeplace, The
Old Swinging Bridge, The
Weary Angel of Death

Rndr 0020: Although this album presents music thoroughly in the bluegrass style, I have included it because of the heavy representation of older material--in particular, the uncommon rendition of Child 155. Ted Lundy (1927-1980) was born and reared in the Galax, Virginia, region, to two very musical families (his cousin, fiddler Jerry Lundy, is grandson of Emmett Lundy--see notes to String STR 802). Ted's musical career started at age eight, when he took up guitar, and he quit school at age 16 to join Jimmy Williams and the Shady Valley Boys, touring schools, theaters, and music halls. His oldest songs (including "It Rained a Mist") he learned from his mother. Also from her is "Come Home," a version of Henry Clay Work's temperance song, "Papa, Come Home."

88   Label Name/Number: Folkways FA 2040 (10") (formerly FP 40)
Title: *Smoky Mountain Ballads*
Artist: Bascom Lamar Lunsford
Collector/Recordist: Ralph auf der Heide
Place and Date of Recording: New York City, 1951-52
Date of Publication: 1953
Annotations: 7 p. booklet by Pete Seeger, Frances Lynne
Selections:
Death of Queen Jane, The [C. 170]
Jennie Jenkins
Little Margaret [C. 74]
Mole in the Ground
Mr. Garfield
On the Banks of the Ohio [F 5]
Springfield Mountain [G 16]
Swannanoa Tunnel

89   Label Name/Number: Riverside RLP 12-645
Title: *Minstrel of the Appalachians*
Artist: Bascom Lamar Lunsford with Freda English
Collector/Recordist: Paul Clayton
Editor: Kenneth S. Goldstein
Place and Date of Recording: Asheville, NC, 1956
Date of Publication: [ca. 1958]
Annotations: Liner notes by Kenneth S. Goldstein
Selections:
Black Jack Davy [C. 200]
Derby Ram, The
Fly Around, My Blue-Eyed Girl
Go to Italy
I Shall Not Be Moved
John Henry [I 1]
Merry Golden Tree, The [C. 286]
Miller's Will, The [Q 21]

Old Man from the North Country, The [C. 10]
Poor Jesse James [E 1]
Sailor on the Deep Blue Sea, The [K 12]
Sundown
Swing Low, Chariot
Weeping Willow Tree

Fwys FA 2040 / Riv RLP 12-645: Bascom Lamar Lunsford, born (1882-1973) in Madison County, North Carolina, was a legendary figure in the Asheville, North Carolina area; trained as a lawyer, his love for his native music led him to collect and learn hundreds of songs and ballads, and to start the annual Mountain Dance and Folk Festival in 1928. His career has been documented by Loyal Jones in his *Minstrel of the Appalachians: The Story of Bascom Lamar Lunsford* (Boone, NC: Appalachian Consortium Press, 1984). He made his first recordings on cylinders in 1922 for Frank C. Brown of the University of North Carolina and his first commercial recordings in 1924 for the OKeh label; then, in 1935, recorded over 300 numbers at Columbia University in New York (subsequently deposited at the Library of Congress Archive of American Folksong). In the 1930s and '40s he appeared regularly at folk festivals and on college campuses; in 1939 he was invited to sing before King George V and Queen Elizabeth at the White House. Several of the songs on the Folkways LP appear on Library of Congress albums as well. Lunsford has a rather hard, abrasive voice, and generally accompanies himself on banjo. The Folkways brochure includes text transcriptions and Lunsford's own comments on where he learned the songs.

The Riverside album captures Lunsford another five years after the Folkways LP and 15 to 20 after the LC recordings, but still sounding much the same. Lunsford observes in the jacket notes that he recognizes his two mutually inconsistent roles of tradition-bearer, trying faithfully to reproduce the songs and ballads as he learned them, and of entertainer, composing, recomposing, and adapting his material to suit his audiences. Many folk performers straddle this line, which exists more in academic conceptualizations than in the world of living music. Lunsford is accompanied by Freda English on guitar and some vocals; Mrs. English was his accompanist for many years at public performances. [JAF 283--DKW]

90 Label Name/Number: Birch 1944
Title: *Mac and Bob*
Artist(s): Lester McFarland and Robert Gardner
Editor: Dave Wiley
Place and Date of Recording: Some from commercial 78s, 1926-30; others, ca. 1969
Date of Publication: [ca. 1971]
Annotations: Liner notes by Dave Wiley
Selections:

Are You Tired of Me Darling?
Hold Fast to the Right
I'm Tying the Leaves So they Won't Come Down
Molly Darling
No Disappointment in Heaven
Old Fashioned Locket
Old Home Down on the Farm
Old Shep
Seeing Nellie Home
Tis Sweet To Be Remembered
Twenty-One Years
When the Roses Bloom Again

Brch 1944: Lester McFarland (1902-1984) and Robert Gardner (1897-1982) were an immensely popular duo on radio and records during the late 1920s. Both blind from youth, they met at the Kentucky School for the Blind in 1915 and began their professional careers in 1922 in personal appearances and in 1925 on WNOX in Knoxville. Their smooth vocals, with competent mandolin-guitar accompaniment, were very popular on the WLS National Barn Dance for many years. Mac was one of the first hillbilly musicians to feature mandolin and contributed to its rising popularity in the 1930s. Seven of these selections are taken from commercial recordings of 1926-30; the others, from Dave Wylie's interviews with them nearly 40 years later. The selections are typical of hillbilly music of the 1930s. "21 Years" is a re-creation of the Bob Miller composition that they popularized in 1928--so much so that it subsequently entered oral tradition. [JAF 338--DKW]

91   Label Name/Number: Bear Family BFX 15214
Title: *Uncle Dave Macon at Home: His Last Recordings, 1950*
Artist: Uncle Dave Macon
Collector/Recordist: Charles Faulkner Bryan
Producer: Charles Wolfe
Place and Date of Recording: Kittrell, TN, 1950
Date of Publication: 1987
Annotations: Liner notes by Charles Wolfe
Selections:
  All In Down and Out Blues
  Bully of the Town
  Chewing Gum
  Cotton Eyed Joe
  Cumberland Mountain Deer Race
  Death of John Henry [I 1]
  Elephant March
  Hungry Hash House
  Jenny Put the Kettle On
  Keep My Skillet Good and Greasy
  Kissing on the Sly
  Lady in the Car
  Long John Green
  Mountain Dew
  No One to Welcome Me Home
  Old Maid's Love Song
  Rabbit in the Pea Patch
  Rock of Ages [fragment]
  Something's Sure to Tickle Me
  That's Where My Money Goes
  Whoa Mule

BF 15214: David Harrison Macon (1870-1952) was one of the greatest hillbilly stars of radio, stage, and records in the 1920s and '30s (see comments to his LPs in Section III). In 1950, a little over a year before his death, Uncle Dave was visited by folklorist Charles Faulkner Bryan, who taped him at the Macon home in Kittrell, Tennessee. In around 1980, Charles Wolfe, on behalf of the Tennessee Folklore Society and in cooperation with Davis Unlimited Records, produced an album (DU-TFS 101) of 21 selections from Bryan's tapes. In 1987, the contents of the then-out-of-print album were reissued on the West German Bear Family label. Wolfe's original liner notes were modified somewhat, and the information about Bryan himself has been omitted, but the aural contents are the same. Though he was eighty years old at the time of the recordings, Macon was still in good form, both instrumentally and vocally, and he gave Bryan a handful of songs that he had never recorded commercially, including "Bully of the Town" [Laws I 14], "Mountain Dew," "Long John Green," "The Lady in the Car," "Whoa Mule," and "No One to Welcome Me Home." Wolfe's comments draw upon Bryan's field tapes and transcripts. It seems there is more unpublished material from Bryan's interviews with Macon; if so, it would be interesting to see a fuller publication.

92 Label Name/Number: Arhoolie F5002
Title: *The Legendary Family from the Blue Ridge Mountains*
Artists: J. E. Mainer's Mountaineers (J. E. Mainer, J. E., Jr., Glenn Thedford Mainer, Carolyn
    Mainer Wilson, Earl Cheeks, Otis Overcash)
Collector/Recordist/Editor: Chris A. Strachwitz
Place and Date of Recording: Concord, NC, 1963
Date of Publication: [1964?]
Annotations: Liner notes by Strachwitz
Selections:
    Greenback Dollar
    Home in Louisiana
    I'm Just Here To Get My Baby out of Jail
    If I Lose Let Me Lose
    Mama Don't Allow
    Maple on the Hill
    Mississippi Sawyer
    Ramshackle Shack
    Run Moountain
    Sally Goodin
    Seven and a Half
    Shake My Mother's Hand for Me
    Short Life of Trouble
    Wild Bill Jones [E 10]

    Arh F5002: Born near Weaversville, North Carolina, J. E. Mainer (1898-1971) learned to play banjo at age nine but switched to fiddle when he was about 24. In 1923 he and his brother, Wade, began to play for dances and shows, and in 1932 their radio careers began. Their extensive repertoire recorded on the Bluebird label in the 1930s has been featured on several reissue albums (see Section III). J. E.'s recording career slowed down after the end of W. W. II, but he continued to make personal appearances. In 1963, Chris Strachwitz recorded him for his then-new Arhoolie label, and through the '60s Mainer recorded several LPs on the Rural Rhythm label, sang at concerts and festivals, issued his own songbook, and enjoyed an active musical career. All told, Mainer has an enormous repertoire, to which he evidently never stopped adding. Most of the numbers on this LP are re-makes of titles recorded by J. E. in the 1930s. On these recordings J. E.'s unpolished singing and fiddling (and banjo-playing on "Wild Bill Jones") are complemented by the quasi-bluegrass style of the rest of the Mountaineers, updating only slightly what is basically a late 1930s style and repertoire.

93 Label Name/Number: Augusta Heritage AH AHR 008 [cass]
Title: *Folksongs & Ballads, Vol. 2*
Artist: Phyllis Marks
Collector/Recordist/Producer: Gerry Milnes
Place and Date of Recordings: Glenville, WV, 1990-91
Date of Publication: 1991

Annotations: Brief insert notes by Milnes
Selections:
   Bluebell
   Bow and Balance to Me [C. 10]
   Cherry Tree Carol, The [C. 54]
   Dandoo [C. 277]
   Devil and the Old Woman [C. 278]
   Friendly Beasts, The
   Froggie Went A-Courtin'
   Get Up and Bar the Door [C. 275]
   Go Down to Old Ireland
   Lord Lovel [C. 75]
   Mary of the Wild Moor [P 21]
   Molly Bender [O 36]
   Nathan Killed the Bell Cow
   Nobody
   Old King Cole
   One Morning in May [P 14]
   Orphan Girl
   Paper of Pins
   Thompson's Mule
   Three Men Went A-Hunting
   Ven'mous Viper [G 16]
   When the Palefaces Came
   Willie My Son [C. 12]
[Also two recitations]

   AH AHR 009 Blind since the age of 14, Phyllis Marks (b. 1927) of Gilmer County, West Virginia, began to sing at an early age and continues to add to her repertoire. The selections on this cassette are all pre-World War I--some substantially earlier. In other words, there is no apparent influence from hillbilly recordings of the 1920s and later. "Nobody" seems derived from the Bert Williams stage song (early 1900s) of the same name. "Nathan Killed the Bell Cow" and "Bluebell" are lighthearted pieces not often heard. Marks is not a great singer, but she has a fine, wide-ranging repertoire, which she renders in undecorated a capella style.

94   Label Name/Number: Rounder 0034
Title: *Dr. Ginger Blue*
Artists: Asa Martin and the Cumberland Rangers (Buz Brazeale, Jim Gaskin, Earl Barnes); Gilbert Thomas
Producers: Guthrie T. Meade and Mark Wilson
Place and Date of Recording: Irvine, KY, 1972-73
Date of Publication: 1974
Annotations: 20 p. booklet by Guthrie T. Meade and Mark Wilson
Selections:
   Cat's Meow, The
   Death of Edward Hawkins, The
   Dr. Ginger Blue
   Dreamy Georgiana Moon
   Going Back to Alabama
   I Tickled Her Under the Chin
   I'm Leaving You, Sweet Florine

Jim Chapman Schottische
Lay Around the Kitchen 'Til the Cook Comes In
Lost John
Rowan County Crew, The [E 20]
Rutherford's Reel
Sweet Bunch of Daisies
There's More Pretty Girls Than One
There's No Place Like Home for the Married Man
Two Old Freight Trains Side by Side

Rndr 0034: Asa Martin, (1900-1979), born in Clark County, Kentucky, was a very popular singer-guitarist in the 1920s, 30s, and 40s who recorded extensively with several other artists, most notably Fiddlin' Doc Roberts and James Roberts. In 1969, Archie Green and I visited and interviewed him extensively and subsequently he came out of musical retirement. His new band, The Cumberland Rangers, included Jim Gaskins, fiddle; Grady "Buz" Brazeale, guitar, mandolin, autoharp; Gilbert Thomas, mandolin; and Earl Barnes, guitar and vocal. Guitar and fiddle are the principal instruments. This album is an excellent sampling of the variegated fare that Martin had put on records in previous decades or worked into his repertoire more recently. The title song is a fine piece of medicine show monologue; "Rowan County Crew" and "The Death of Edward Hawkins" are local ballads, the latter recorded once in the 1920s but never released. Martin was never a great singer, and his guitar playing has lost some of its edge over the years, but on the whole the music is successful and enjoyable. The well-written brochure, extensively illustrated with vintage advertisements, photos, and reproductions from songbooks, is characteristic of the fine work of producers/annotators Meade and Wilson. [JEMFQ 40]

95   Label Name/Number: Folkways FD 5272
Title: ·*Harry K. McClintock: "Haywire Mac"*
Artist: Harry K. McClintock
Collector/Recordist/Editor: Sam Eskin
Place and Date of Recording: San Pedro, CA, ca. 1955
Date of Publication: 1972
Annotations: 3 p. insert by Eskin, McClintock
Selections:
Big Rock Candy Mountain
Casey Jones (I. W. W. version)
Casey Jones (Saunders' version) [G 1]
Hallelujah, I'm a Bum
Jordan Am a Hard Road To Travel
Long Haired Preachers
Paddy Clancy
Poor Boy [I 4]
Uncle Jim's Rebel Soldier
Utah Carl [B 4]
[Also anecdotes and a tale]

Fwys FD 5272: "Haywire Mac" (1882-1957) led a remarkably colorful life. Born in Knoxville, Tennessee, he left home at the age of fourteen to work with a small circus. In the next few decades he worked as a railroad switchman in Africa during the Boer War, was a muleskinner in the Philippines during the Spanish-American War, went to China as a newspaper aide with the Relief Expedition during the Boxer Rebellion, worked his way to London on a steamer to observe the coronation of Edward VII, railroaded in the Northwest on the Oregon Short Line, was ranch foreman in Nevada and mine owner in New Mexico, played bit parts in Hollywood westerns during the Depression, had a radio program in San Francisco in the 1920s, made records for three companies starting in 1928, wrote fiction and factual stories for *Railroad Magazine* and other magazines for a decade, and painted in his spare time. He died in San Francisco in 1957. McClintock was not the typical hillbilly musician of the 1920s. Scarcely 16 when he first started to play on the streets for pay, his repertoire was soon bulging with songs he learned from his circus days; from the many hoboes, bums, and boomers he knew from his long association with the railroads; and from the cowboys, ranch hands, and farmers he met in his years out West. His recordings reflect these aspects of his varied career: a dozen cowboy and western songs and ballads; a couple about the railroads, a few--including his best-known ones--about hoboes; the rest about circuses, novelty songs, and parodies of sentimental vaudeville pieces. Mac claimed authorship of three of his most popular recordings: "The Big Rock Candy Mountain," "The Bum Song," and "Hallelujah! I'm a Bum." Authorship of all three has been disputed; if he didn't compose them in entirety, he certainly rewrote them, and was largely responsible for their great popularity through his records, radio shows, and sheet music versions. (A 1906 copyrighted sheet music version of "Big Rock Candy Mountain" is quite different from Mac's version.)

In keeping with his repertoire, Mac was, stylistically, quite removed from the Southeastern hillbilly music of the 1920s--somewhere between the western/cowboy style of cowboy singers Carl T. Sprague, Jules Allen, and Edward L. Crain, and the urbane pop-novelty manners of Frank Crumit, Peg Moreland, and Carson Robison. While, as Wilson points out in his song notes, Mac learned many of his songs from printed collections such as John A. Lomax's *Cowboy Songs* and Carl Sandburg's *American Songbag*, he also learned from roustabouts on the New Orleans levees and piano players in San Francisco's Barbary Coast dives.

Eskin's interview tapes with Haywire Mac deserved better documentation than this album provides; fortunately one can turn to Rounder 1009 (see Section III) to learn more of Mac's long life. These recordings include Mac's two most famous songs, "Big Rock Candy Mountain" and "Hallelujah, I'm a Bum." Of particular interest is the version of "Casey Jones" that he claimed he learned from Wallace Saunders, the black engine-wiper often credited with writing (a version of) "Casey Jones." [JEMFQ 64]

96   Label Name/Number: Arhoolie 5012
Title: *Grand Dad of the Country Guitar Pickers*
Artists: Sam McGee, with Clifton McGee & Goldie Stewart
Collector/Recordist/Editor: Mike Seeger
Place and Date of Recording: Franklin, TN, 1969-70
Date of Publication: 1971
Annotations: Liner notes by Seeger
Selections:
   Blackberry Blossom
   Buckdancer's Choice
   Burglar Bold
   Ching Chong
   Dew Drop
   Franklin Blues
   Fuller Blues
   How Great Thou Art
   Jesse James [E 1]
   Penitentiary Blues [I 8]
   Pig Ankle Rag
   Railroad Blues
   Sam McGee Stomp

Wheels
When the Wagon Was New

97   Label Name/Number: Folkways FA 2379
Title: *Mountain Songs and Instrumentals*
Artists: Arthur Smith, Sam & Kirk McGee
Collector/Recordist: Mike Seeger
Place and Date of Recording: Nashville, TN, 1957
Date of Publication: 1964
Annotations: 6 p. booklet by Jon Pankake
Selections:

    Bile 'Em Cabbage Down -- Arthur
    Buck Dancer's Choice -- Sam
    Coming from the Ball -- Sam & Kirk
    Cumberland Gap -- Arthur
    Dusty Miller -- Arthur
    Green Valley Waltz -- Arthur
    Guitar Waltz -- Sam
    Hell Among the Yearlings -- Arthur
    Hollow Poplar -- Arthur
    House of David Blues -- Arthur
    Jim Sapp Rag -- Sam
    Kilby Jail -- Arthur
    Knoxville Blues -- Sam
    Needlecase -- Sam
    Polly Ann -- Arthur
    Railroad Blues -- Sam
    Rock House Joe -- Kirk
    Roll On Buddy -- Sam & Kirk
    Sally Long -- Sam
    Sixteen on Sunday -- Arthur
    Snowdrop -- Kirk
    Whoop 'em Up Cindy -- Sam & Kirk

98   Label Name/Number: Folkways FT 1007 / FTS 31007
Title: *Milk 'em in the Evening Blues*
Artists: McGee Brothers and Arthur Smith
Collector/Recordist/Editor: Mike Seeger
Date of Publication: 1968
Annotations: Liner notes by Jon Pankake
Selections:

    Amos Johnson Rag -- Sam
    Boogie -- Sam & Kirk
    Charming Bill -- Kirk
    Chinese Breakdown -- Sam, Kirk, Arthur
    Dance All Night with a Bottle in Your Hand -- Arthur
    Don't Let Your Deal Go Down -- Sam & Kirk
    Drummer Boy -- Sam
    Easy Rider -- Sam
    Evening Shade -- Arthur
    I've Had a Big Time Tonight --Arthur

Keep a Light in Your Window Tonight -- Sam & Kirk
Lafayette -- Kirk and Arthur
Late Last Night -- Sam & Kirk
Memphis Blues -- Sam & Kirk
Milk 'em in the Evening Blues -- Sam & Kirk
Milk Cow Blues -- Sam & Kirk
Peacock Rag -- Arthur
Pig at Home in the Pen -- Arthur
Redwing -- Sam & Kirk
Sally Johnson -- Arthur
Single-Footing Horse -- Arthur
Uncle Buddy -- Arthur
Under the Double Eagle -- Sam & Kirk
Whistling Rufus -- Arthur
Widow Haley -- Arthur

Arh 5012 / Fwys FA 2379 / Fwys FT 1007. Sam (1894-1975) and Kirk (1899-1963) McGee were born into a musical family in Williamson County, Tennessee. They began playing banjo in their teens; later, Sam took up guitar and Kirk, fiddle. Both began playing professionally in the '20s, and made their first commercial recordings in 1926 with Uncle Dave Macon (see listings in Section III). McGee was one of the first hillbilly guitar pickers (as distinguished from accompanists) to record, and has been very influential since his first recordings in 1926. After World War II they continued professional appearances, gradually becoming "old-timers" on Grand Ole Opry (i. e., performers of generally passé songs and styles in the rapidly cosmopolitanizing Opry). It was through their regular Opry appearances that Seeger became acquainted with them and arranged to record them as one of his first efforts at re-recording old-time musicians. The McGees suggested that Arthur Smith, with whom they worked in the 1930s, join them. Arthur Smith of Humphreys County, Tennessee, performed in public with the McGees frequently in the 1930s and recorded with the Delmore Brothers in the same period. The result was one of the finest albums of old-time music to come out of the 1950s. The McGees, in their sixties, were still brilliant instrumentalists; only someone familiar with Sam's 1920s recordings could suspect that his celebrated finger-picking guitar solos--"Buck Dancer's Choice," "Knoxville Blues" and "Railroad Blues"--could ever have been better. Kirk, who in the '30s was generally overshadowed by Sam, reveals himself on this LP as a virtuoso of comparable skill on banjo. Brochure notes to FA 2379 include biographical background, song texts, and comments on the musicians' sources of their selections.

Although it was Smith's bluesy fiddling that was so influential, on FT 1007 we also hear him play the banjo--on which he was too rusty when Seeger recorded the earlier album (FA 2379). Sam McGee was one of the finest hillbilly guitarists to record commercially in the '20s, and his finger-picking style and repertory show heavy blues, ragtime, and jazz influence. He plays both guitar and banjo-guitar on this LP. Pankake has provided thoughtful liner notes, but the earlier Folkways album (FA 2379) includes more extensive biographical information and furthermore is musically stronger.

Though best known for such tours de force on the guitar as his "Buck Dancer's Choice," "Railroad Blues," and "Franklin Blues," McGee is also an able banjo picker. Both instruments, as well as six-string banjo and vocals, are heard on the Arhoolie album, recorded in 1969-70 when he was over 75 years old. The years had, alas, taken some of the edge off his once unsurpassedly nimble fingers, but he entered his fourth quarter-century with talent to spare, and no one could help but admire his creativity. [WF 7/72 (Arh); JAF 310--DKW (FA 2379); JAF 324 (FT 1007)]

99   Label Name/Number: Rich-R-Tone LP-8073
Title: *North Carolina Ballads and Folk Songs*

Artist: Artus Moser
Collector/Producer: Jim Stanton
Place and Date of Recording: Studio, Johnson City, TN
Date of Publication: [1973?]
Selections:
  Barbara Allen [C. 84]
  Black Jack Davy [C. 200]
  Cambric Shirt, The [C. 2]
  Deer Song, The
  Doggett's Gap
  Get Up and Bar the Door [C. 275]
  Lord Thomas and Fair Ellender [C. 73]
  Merry Golden Tree, The [C. 286]
  Three Little Babes, The [C. 79]
  Wife Wrapped in a Wether's Skin, The [C. 277]
  Wildwood Flower

Rich-R-Tone LP-8073: Singer/collector Artus Moser (1894-1992), born in Catawba City, North Carolina, was exposed to traditional music in his youth and then augmented his knowledge through formal university training. He recorded a long series of pieces for the LC in the 1940s and several numbers for commercial companies in the 1950s. This studio-recorded collection includes mostly imported ballads; "The Deer Song" is a lying song to the tune of "Darby Ram"; "Doggett's Gap" is a variant of "Cumberland Gap." "Wildwood Flower" is unusual for not being derived from the influential Carter Family recordings. Moser accompanies himself on dulcimer, which to my ears is often not noted in a manner consonant with the melody. His singing is reminiscent of his fellow North Carolinian folksong collector/performer, Bascom Lamar Lunsford. [WF 10/74]

100   Label Name/Number: County 720
Title: *The Mountain Ramblers, with Joe Drye*
Artists: Mountain Ramblers (Joe Drye, Carson Cooper, James Lindsey, Jim McKinnon, Thurman Pugh)
Collector/Recordist: Charles Faurot
Producer: David Freeman
Date of Publication: [1969]
Annotations: Liner notes by David Freeman
Selections:
  Behind the Eight Ball
  Carolina Rag
  Cripple Creek
  Dance Around Molly
  Linda Sue
  Polk County Breakdown
  Pretty Little Widow
  Sally Ann
  Sugar in the Gourd
  Tennessee Wagoner
  Tommy's Waltz
  Wake Up Susan

Cty 720: This album auditions the Mountain Ramblers about ten years after Alan Lomax first recorded them (see notes to Atlantic 1346 in Section II)--and about 15 years after they were formed to do a regular radio show over WBOB in Galax. As the subtitle indicates, the repertoire here is dance music--no vocals--with fiddle taking primary lead and generally a break by the banjo. An exception to this line-up is the lovely fiddle-banjo duet (alone) on Polk County Breakdown. With mandolin, guitar, and bass providing just back-up, and no bluesy effects or syncopated rhythms, the sound is as much old-timey as bluegrass. Freeman's notes provide brief biographical background.

101   Label Name/Number: Leader [England] LE 4040
Title: *North Carolina Boys*
Artists: Gray Craig and the New North Carolina Ramblers (Kinney Rorrer, Doug Rorrer); Tex
     Isley with Janet Kerr
Collector/Recordist/Producer: Janet Kerr
Place and Date of Recording: VA, NC, 1971?
Date of Publication: 1972
Annotations: 7 p. insewn booklet by Janet Kerr
Selections:
     Gray Craig and the New North Carolina Ramblers
          Dark Town Strutters' Ball
          Fly Around My Pretty Little Miss
          Letter Edged in Black
          Old Joe Clark
          Polecat Blues
          Redwing
          Run Boy, Run!
          Shanty Town
     Tex Isley
          Flop-Eared Mule
          Fourteen Days in Georgia
          Greenfields
          North Carolina Boys
          Precious Memories
          Silver Bells
          Walking in My Sleep
          Will You Be True?

     Leader LEA 4040:   Like Leader LEA 4012 (see Section II), this album is from field recordings made by Janet Kerr ca. 1971, and features eight tracks by Tex Isley (vocal, guitar, and/or autoharp) and the remainder by Gray Craig and the New North Carolina Ramblers. The latter consists of Kinney and Doug Rorrer, great-nephews of both Charlie Poole, leader of the original North Carolina Ramblers, and his brother-in-law fiddler, Posey Rorer. Craig is an older fiddler who played with the original Ramblers in the 1920s. This is an enjoyable collections of old-time music, including an illustrated brochure that provides biographical backgrounds on the artists. [WF 7/72; JAF 338--DKW]

102   Label Name/Number: Campus Folksong Club Records, University of Illinois, CFC 301
Title: *The Hell-Bound Train*
Artist: Glenn Ohrlin
Editor: Judy McCulloh
Place and Date of Recording: Champaign/Urbana, IL, 1963-64
Date of Publication: 1964
Annotations: 18 p. booklet by Archie Green, Judy McCulloh, Harlan Daniel

Selections:
  Big Combine
  Buffalo Skinners [B 10]
  Bull Riders in the Sky
  Chickens Grow Tall
  Cowboy, The
  Dakota Land
  Days of the Forty-Nine
  Guitar Instrumental
  Hell-Bound Train
  Hog Drivers
  I'm a Swede from North Dakota
  My Home in Montana
  Put Your Little Foot
  Sam's "Waiting for a Train" [H 2]
  Talking Memphis
  Ten Thousand Cattle
  Trail to Mexico [B 13]
  Walking John
  Windy Bill
[Also a story]

103   Label Name/Number: Philo 1017
Title: *Cowboy Songs*
Artist: Glenn Ohrlin with Kay Ohrlin
Collector/Recordist: Bill Schubart
Producers: Glenn Ohrlin & Bill Schubart
Place of Recording: VT
Date of Publication: 1974
Annotations: Liner notes by Glenn Ohrlin
Selections:
  Billy Venero [B 6]
  Burial of Wild Bill, The
  Cole Younger [E 3]
  Cowboy in Church, The
  Cowboy, The
  Cowman's Prayer, The
  Dying Ranger, The [A 14]
  Gol Darn Wheel [dB 38]
  High Chin Bob
  Mexican Tune
  Santa Fe Trail
  Short Creek
  Sporting Cowboy, The [E 17]
  Tender Foot, The
  Top Hand, The
  Varsouviana
  Zebra Dun [B 16]
[Also a recitation]

104   Label Name/Number: Rounder Records 0158
Title: *The Wild Buckaroo*
Artist: Glenn Ohrlin with Art Galbraith and Gordon McCann
Producer/Recordist: Mark Wilson & Lou Curtiss
Place and Date of Recording: La Jolla, CA, 1981
Date of Publication: 1983
Annotations: 11 p. booklet by Glenn Ohrlin
Selections:
    Belle Gunness
    Cowboys' Christmas Ball, The
    Days of '49, The
    Fair at Batesland, The
    Flop House Blues
    Goodbye, Old Paint
    High-toned Dance, The
    La Sanja (The Ditch)
    Lee's Ferry
    Mi Caballo Bayo (My Buckskin Horse)
    My Harding County Home
    My Old Stetson Hat
    Powder River, Let 'er Buck
    Punchin' the Dough
    Tipperary
    Walking John
    Wild Buckaroo, The
    Windy Bill [dB 41]

CFC 301 / Ph 1017 / Rndr 0158:   CFC UI's third album marked the recording debut of working cowboy and traditional musician Glen Ohrlin. Born in Minneapolis in 1926, Ohrlin left home (then California) at the age of sixteen to ride horses in Nevada. In 1943 he started working rodeos as well as cowboying on ranches. He enjoyed singing from childhood and frequently entertained friends in bars, bunkhouses, or rodeo arenas. His gravelly voice, laconic presentation, and wry wit (all true to the idiom), make him the ideal cowboy performer; his interest in songs prompted him to collect from friends and associates whenever he could. Besides several albums to his credit, he has written an engaging book on cowboy and western songs, *Hellbound Train* (University of Illinois Press, 1973). Brochure notes include Ohrlin's extensive comments on his sources for most of the numbers, as well as text and tune transcriptions, biographical background information, and some of Ohrlin's own pen-and-ink sketches.

Rndr 0158 is another collection of 17 songs and one poem, many clearly in oral tradition, others composed by cowboy singers firmly within the tradition, sung by the working cowboy from Arkansas who has performed at numerous folk festivals and college concerts. The jacket notes and booklet, written and illustrated by Ohrlin (and with photos and supplementary references and details by producers Wilson and Curtiss), demonstrate his knowledge and comfortable writing style, but the recordings give only a hint of his ability to captivate an audience. His rough singing is backed up by unobtrusive fiddle and guitar accompaniment.

On Ph 1017 Ohrlin sings another collection of cowboy songs and ballads (with second guitar and harmony vocals by Kay Ohrlin on some selections) and illustrates his considerable knowledge of the music in his liner notes. Several of these songs were learned from commercial 78s. "Short Creek" is Ohrlin's own composition. Ohrlin's "Cole Younger" is the loveliest version of this ballad I've heard. [JAF 391 (Rndr); JAF 307--DKW (CFC)]

105 Label Name/Number: Folkways FA 2356
Title: *Old Harp Singing*
Artists: Old Harp Singers of Eastern Tennessee
Date of Publication: 1951
Selections:
  Amazing Grace
  Greenfields
  Hightower
  Liberty
  Morning Trumpet
  Northfield
  Ocean
  Pleasant Hill
  Western Mount Pleasant
  Wondrous Love

Fwys FA 2356: In the 1770s in America a new institution of singing schools appeared. Singing school teachers traveled from town to town, conducting singing school terms of a few weeks' duration, in which pupils were taught music fundamentals. To facilitate teaching methods, very early in the 1800s the idea of shaped notes was introduced, with four shapes corresponding to the then-popular British solmization of fa-so-la-fa-so-la-me rather than the standard European do-re-mi-fa-sol-la-ti. In 1844 a hymnal, *The Sacred Harp*, was first published (using a slightly modified four-shape notation), and it proved so influential for over a century that it gave its name to a style of hymn singing. Sacred Harp (SH) singing can be quite jarring to those who expect standard European church harmonies. SH music is based on four vocal parts with no part dominant: that is, rather than one obvious melody and three harmonies (or two and a bass line), there are four melody lines of comparable importance. SH singing also discards the customary allocation of soprano and alto parts to female singers and tenor and bass to males and distributes male and female singers among the four parts. Another characteristic is for the singers to sing the fa-so-la syllables the first time through the melody, followed by words. Different members of the chorus take turns selecting tunes for singing and leading the group. This album, recorded at a 1951 singing convention, illustrates these traits. A few of the selections out of the enormous and annually growing shaped note repertoire are particularly enduring: e. g., "Amazing Grace" and "Wondrous Love."

106 Label Name/Number: Folk-Legacy FSA-15
Title: *Adirondack Songs, Ballads, and Fiddle Tunes*
Artist: Lawrence Older
Collector/Recordist: Sandy Paton
Place and Date of Recording: Middle Grove, NY, early 1960s?
Date of Publication: 1963-64
Annotations: 28 p. booklet by Peter E. McElligott
Selections:
  Bonaparte's March
  Bonnet Trimmed in Blue
  Bonnie Black Bess [L 9]
  Derby Ram
  Devil's Dream
  Elder Bordee [C. 167]
  Flim-A-Lim-A-Lee [C. 2]
  Frog in the Spring
  Gypsy Davy [C. 200]

Jed Hobson [= Dick Darby the Cobbler]
Jim Along Josie
Johnny Randall [C. 12]
Johnson's Road
My Old Brown Coat and Me
Not Far from Ballston
Old Shoes and Leggings
Once More A-Lumbering Go
Pat Malone [Q 18]
Peg and Awl
Randy Riley [C. 278]
Woman from Yorkshire [Q 2]
[Also three Franco-American fiddle tunes: Ce Pouflas, En Roulant, La Bastringue]

FLeg FSA-15: Lawrence Older (ca. 1913-82), singer and fiddler from the southern Adirondacks, learned most of his songs and tunes from his family, which traces its emigration to America to British Regular Thomas Older, who arrived in 1749. Like most northeastern singers, Older sings in a very confident but undecorated style, accompanying himself competently on guitar. His repertoire is typical for the region, but a few items are not commonly found--for example, his version of Child 167. His very carefully preserved text to "Bonnie Black Bess" exudes a strong aroma of ink fresh from the broadside presses. The brochure includes family history and notes on the selections and Older's sources.

107   Label Name/Number: June Appal JA 049
Title: *Relics and Treasure*
Artist: Uncle Charlie Osborne with Johnny C. Osborne and Tommy R. Bledsoe
Collector/Recordist: Alan & Charlie Maggard and Doug Dorschug
Editor: Charlie Maggard & Tom Bledsoe
Place of Recording: VA
Date of Publication: 1985
Annotations: Poster/foldout notes by Richard Blaustein with Tom Bledsoe, Charles Wolfe, & Charles Seeman
Selections:
Alice Brown
All at One Shot
Brown's Dream
Dan Tucker
Frolic / Calahan's Reel
Ida Red
Joe Bowers [B 14]
Little Brown Jug
Nancy Ann
Never Miss Your Mother   [= You'll Never...]
Old Aunt Katy
'Omie Wise [F 4]
(Shoot That) Turkey Buzzard
Sugar in the Gourd
Walk up Georgia Row

JA 049: Osborne, born in 1890 in what is now Russell County, Virginia, fiddles and sings typical 19th century tunes and songs. An enclosed illustrated brochure includes program notes by Richard Blaustein and biographical sketches on the artists. [JAF 408]

108 Label Name/Number: Heritage 070
Title: *The Old Time Way*
Artists: Luther Davis, Roscoe Parish, and Leone Parish (with Alice Gerrard and Andy Cahan)
Collector/Recordist: Alice Gerrard and Andy Cahan
Editor: Andy Cahan & Alice Gerrard - project directors
Place and Date of Recording: VA, 1960-84
Date of Publication: 1986
Annotations: 53 p. booklet by Andy Cahan & Alice Gerrard
Selections:
  Luther Davis:
> Flatwoods
> Going to See Friel Lowe
> Grasshopper Sitting on a Sweet Potato Vine
> How Beautiful Heaven Must Be
> Molly Put the Kettle On
> Poor Little Johnny's Gone to the War
> Property Auction
> Rocking in a Weary Land
> Sail Away Ladies
> Shady Grove
> Sheep Shell Corn
> Train on the Island
> Travelling to the Grave
> Walking in the Parlor

  Roscoe Parish and Leone Parish:
> Chapel Hill Serenade
> Cleveland's March
> Cousin Sally Brown
> Dance, Boatman, Dance
> Katy Bar the Door
> Liquor Seller
> Little Things, The
> Old Joe Clark
> Ring the Bells
> Rocky Mountain
> Sheep Shell Corn
> Shoo-Fly
> Sugar in the Gourd
> Unnamed tune (similar to Devil in the Strawstack)
> Unnamed tune (version of Bonaparte Crossing the Rhine)
> Unnamed tune (version of Cuckoo's Nest)

Heritage 070: This LP documents the music and times of three patriarchal figures in the Galax, Virginia, area: Luther Davis (1887-1986), Roscoe Parish (1897-1984), and Leone Parish (b. 1902). Editors Andy Cahan and Alice Gerrard have taken 12 fiddle tunes by Davis, recorded between 1974 and 1984 (together with one auction calling and three narratives), and 16 selections by the Parish siblings recorded between 1969 and 1984 as the basis for a lengthy and fascinating narrative about the life and music of the Grayson/Carroll Counties area in the late 19th and early 20th centuries. Their 54-page booklet includes an overview of the Galax region, discussing the music back as far as the legendary fiddler, Greenberry "Green" Leonard, born ca. 1810. Emmett Lundy (1864-1953), whose music has been preserved, learned much of his music from Leonard, and both Davis and Roscoe Parish learned from Lundy and others of his generation who had learned from Leonard. The overview is followed by long biographical accounts of the three musicians, their families, and social lives, with numerous photos, some dating back to the 1870s and '80s. Especially valuable, and a practice to be encouraged among other collectors, is a list, for both Davis and Roscoe Parish, of all the songs and tunes in their repertoires that the musicians played for the editors over a several-year period. Brief program notes identify the selections, their sources, where known, and list other performances where relevant. Side One of the album focuses on Davis, playing mostly unaccompanied fiddle, but with banjo/guitar or banjo/fiddle back-up by Cahan and Gerrard on two selections. Many of the tunes are rare outside of the Galax area, and some (e. g., "Flatwoods," "Train on the Island," "Sheep Shell Corn," "Rocking in a Weary Land," and "Sail Away Ladies"--not the usual tune) are known only by older fiddlers . "Shady Grove" is now widely known, but Davis's recollection of having learned it in 1895 may be the earliest evidence for the tune's currency and suggests it, too, may be a Galax area tune. (How on earth did the title ever come to refer to a young woman?) Side Two is devoted to the Parishes: Roscoe, on either banjo or fiddle, and/or Leone, accompanying him on guitar or playing pump organ. Familiar titles are performed in unusual renditions by the Parishes, such as "Dance, Boatman, Dance," "Sugar in the Gourd," and "Old Joe Clark." Needless to say, the musicians were past their prime when these recordings were made, but there is dignity and beauty in their performances nonetheless, and their renditions forge an unbreakable link with the musical traditions of a century ago. This album makes a valuable contribution to our understanding of one of Appalachia's most distinctive musical regions.

109   Label Name/Number: Arhoolie 5018
Title: *Plains, Georgia, Rock*
Artist: Uncle John Patterson
Collector/Recordist: George Mitchell/Chet Briggs
Place and Date of Recording: Carrollton, GA, 1976
Date of Publication: 1977
Annotations: Liner notes by Mitchell
Selections:
  Bob Murphy
  Bucking Mule
  Bucking Mule (piano)
  Deep Elm Blues
  Draggin the Bow
  First Lady Waltz
  Flat Footed Charlie
  Hen Cackle
  Milk Cow Blues
  Plains, Georgia Rock
  Snowbird in Ashbank
  Summerland
  Uncle John's Rock
  Uncle John's Waltz

Arh 5018: Georgia banjo player Patterson (ca. 1910-80) won his first banjo championship at age 14. He knew and played with Gid Tanner, and Fiddling John Carson; his claim to have recorded with Clayton McMichen in 1924 is unconfirmed as is his alleged (though more likely) membership in the Carroll County Revelers in 1930. On these recordings he plays banjo or piano, many of the tunes his own compositions, accompanied by his son, James, on guitar. Patterson has a firm hand that has ably compensated for the loss of his picking index finger in an accident 20 years earlier. His rousing piano renditions are a delight, though his left hand is rather repetitious.

110   Label Name/Number: Riverside RLP 12-650
Title: *Pickin' and Blowin'*
Artists: George Pegram and Walter "Red" Parham
Collector/Recordist/Producer: Kenneth S. Goldstein
Place and Date of Recording: NC [1957?]
Date of Publication: [1958?]
Annotations: Liner notes by Robert Black
Selections:
    Cackling Hen
    Chicken Reel
    Down in the Valley
    Downfall of Paris
    Fly Around My Pretty Little Miss
    Foggy Mountain Top
    Georgia Buck
    Johnson's Old Grey Mule
    Listen to the Mockingbird
    Lost John
    Old Joe Clark
    Old Rattler
    Roll On Buddy
    Sourwood Mountain
    Turkey in the Straw
    Wildwood Flower
    Will the Circle Be Unbroken
    Wreck of the Old 97, The [G 2]

111   Label Name/Number: Rounder 0001
Title: *George Pegram*
Artists: George Pegram, with Clyde Isaacs, Fred Cockerham, and Jack Bryant
Producers: Ken Irwin, Bill Nowlin
Place and Date of Recording: NC?, 1967
Date of Publication: 1970
Annotations: Liner notes by Anne Gilbert
Selections:
    Are You Washed in the Blood?
    In the Sweet Bye and Bye
    John Henry [I 1]
    Johnson's Old Grey Mule
    Just Because
    Little Old Log Cabin in the Lane
    Mississippi Sawyer
    Never Grow Old
    Over the Waves Waltz
    Reuben
    What a Friend We Have in Jesus
    Where Could I Go but to the Lord
    Wildwood Flower
    Workin' on a Building

Riv RLP 12-650 / Rndr 0001: George Pegram started to play on a home-made cigar box banjo in 1921. Walter Parham had played harmonica (and also guitar) since early youth. They were brought together in 1949 by Bascom Lamar Lunsford (see notes to Rounder 0065) and played together extensively at festivals and fiddlers' conventions until Pegram's death shortly after the 1974 Asheville Mountain Dance and Folk Festival. Pegram plays a driving, raucus two-finger picking banjo style to which Red Parham manages to adapt his lively harmonica playing quite successfully.

The Rounder LP--inaugurating a new label from a Boston area-based group of anti-establishment entrepreneurs (Ken Irwin, Marion Leighton, Bill Nowlin, and Bruce Kaplan)--shows that the exuberant banjo picking and singing of the 59-year-old North Carolinian hadn't changed much since he was first recorded in about 1957 on the Riverside label. The selections include 19th-century pop tunes, gospel hymns, banjo songs, and other hillbilly standards. On some numbers he is accompanied by guitar, mandolin, and/or fiddle. [WF 7/72; JAF 343--DKW]

112   Label Name/Number: Davis Unlimited Records DU-33009
Title: *Sunset Memories*
Artists: The Perry County Music Makers: Nonnie Presson, Bulow Smith, Virginia Clayborne
Producer: Steve Davis, Charles Wolfe
Place and Date of Recording: Pine View, TN, 1974
Date of Publication: [1975?]
Annotations: Liner notes by Charles Wolfe
Selections:
Black Satin
By the Cottage Door
Downfall of Paris
Evalina Waltz
Gypsy Rag
Hawaiian Nights
I'm Sad and Blue
It Might Have Been Worse
Lexington [= Love Somebody]
Maudaline
On the Beach
Silver Bell
Sunset Memories
Take Me to Lincoln
Trail of the Lonesome Pine
Truckdriver's Song

DU 33009: Nonnie Presson and her brother, Bulow Smith, were a popular local band that made a few recordings in the late 1920s as the Perry County Music Makers--Nonnie on zither, Bulow on guitar. They were "rediscovered" in Pine View, Tennessee, in the early '70s, and though they hadn't played together for years, worked up some of their old numbers for some fresh recordings. They are joined by their niece, Virginia Clayborne, on mandolin. Most of the tunes (including the title song) are Presson's own compositions, some dating back to the '30s.

113   Label Name/Number: Arizona Friends of Folklore AFF 33-4
Title: *Bunk and Becky Pettyjohn*
Artists: Bunk and Becky Pettyjohn, some accomp. by Irene Jones
Editor: Keith Cunningham
Place and Date of Recording: [Flagstaff, AZ, 1974]
Date of Publication: [1976]

Annotations: 24 p. booklet (+ pictures) by Keith Cunningham
Selections: (All by Bunk unless noted otherwise)
    Battle of New Orleans [A 7]
    Blind Girl
    God Be with You till We Meet Again
    Green Corn
    I Went Out a'Hunting
    Lightning Express -- Becky
    Little Joe the Wrangler [B 5]
    Little Sod Shanty
    Little Waltz in A
    My Old Kentucky Home
    Old Joe Clark
    Put My Little Shoes Away
    Put My Little Shoes Away -- Becky
    Rye Whiskey
    Soldier's Joy
    Texas Belle
    Uncloudy Day
    When the Roll's Called up Yonder
    Who's Gonna Shoe Your Pretty Little Foot -- Becky
    Wildwood Flower
    Wreck of the Number 9 [G 26]

    AFF 33-4:   Bunk Pettyjohn (1902-88) lived in Texas and Oklahoma before coming to Arizona. His wife, Becky, died shortly before this album was released. His repertoire is largely borrowed from the early 20th century hillbilly repertoire, but the pieces are played (on banjo, guitar, or mandolin) in such an unpolished and unselfconscious style as to suggest the hearth as a proper setting for the music rather than the public stage. Most of Bunk's selections are instrumentals with only two or three vocals; Becky's are unaccompanied vocals. The brochure tells us little about the performers, and is devoted largely to notes on the songs. These consist of alternating paragraphs by Judith McCulloh and Keith Cunningham, the former offering more scholarly comments on the backgrounds of the pieces; the latter, generally more personal observations of Bunk himself. McCulloh also provides a lengthy biblio-discography for each number. [JEMFQ 65/66]

114   Label Name/Number: Folkways FA 2375
Title: *The Phipps Family: Faith, Love, and Tragedy*
Artists: The Phipps Family (A. L. Kathleen, Helen, and Leemon Phipps)
Collector/Recordist/Editor: Ralph Rinzler
Place and Date of Recording: New York City, 1964
Date of Publication: 1965
Annotations: 4 p. insert
Selections:
    Away Over in the Promised Land
    Charles Guiteau [E 11]
    Forsaken Lover
    Gonna Row My Boat
    Great Titanic, The
    I Never Will Marry [K 17]
    Just Another Broken Heart
    My Home Among the Hills

Old Pine Tree, The
Pearl Bryan [F 2]
Red Jacket Mine Explosion, The
Sinking of the Merry Golden Tree [C. 286]
Unclouded Day, The

Fwys FA 2375: The Phipps Family, of Barbourville, Kentucky, were long-time admirers and friends of the Carter Family (q.v.), and they have cultivated a musical sound that is strikingly similar to the Carters. The performers consist of A. L. (lead guitar, baritone), his wife, Kathleen (autoharp, soprano), their daugher Helen (2nd autoharp, alto), and son Leemon (guitar, bass). A number of the songs on this album were obviously learned from the Carters' versions (compare, for example, "Sinking of the Merry Golden Tree"). The recordings were made shortly after the Phipps' appearance at the 1964 Newport Folk Festival. Two songs are Phipps originals, including "The Red Jacket Mine Explosion," a lament about a mine disaster in Hanger, Virginia, in 1938. The jacket insert includes a 1-page biographical sketch by Bill Vernon and song text transcriptions.

115   Label Name/Number: Mountain 305
Title: *Hoedown Time*
Artists: Pine River Boys (Foy James Lewis, Maybelle Harris, Abe Horton, Walter Morris, Howard Hall)
Recordist: Bobby Patterson
Producer: Pine River Boys
Place and Date of Recording: Galax, VA, 1973
Date of Publication: [ca. 1974]
Annotations: Brief liner notes
Selections:
Arkansas Traveler
Banjo Pickin' Girl
Black Eyed Susie
John Henry
Johnny's Gone to War
Man That Rode the Mule 'Round the World
Mississippi Sawyer
Old Joe Clark
Sally Ann
Shake Hands with Mother
Skip to My Lou
Soldier's Joy

Mtn 305: The Pine River Boys (that one member is a woman does not seem to matter), a band from the Hillsville/Fancy Gap area, has a slightly unusual sound resulting from the use of two frailing banjos, both providing back-up to Walter Morris's lead fiddling. The band, whose members are all in their late 40s or older, have played at many regional fiddlers' conventions and entertained at the Veterans' Hospital. The selections are all dance tunes, performed without vocals; only the one gospel song, "Shake Hands with Mother," is sung in duet. Overall, the style is decidedly old-timey except for the use of some more modern runs on the rhythm guitar.

116   Label Name/Number: Marimac 9200 [cass]
Title: *Up Agin' the Mountain*
Artist: Everitt Pitt
Collector/Recordist: Anne Lutz

Place and Date of Recording: NJ, 1944-49
Date of Publication: 1987
Annotations: Insert notes by Angus K. Gillepsie & Anne Lutz
Selections:
  American Frigate [A 4]
  Backwoodsman [C 19]
  Bold Soldier [M 27]
  Boston Burglar [L 16b]
  Butcher Boy [P 24]
  Cumberland [A 26]
  Day I Fought Dwyer
  Farmer's Curst Wife [C. 278]
  Frog and the Mouse
  Give an Honest Irish Lad a Chance
  Gone to Kansas
  Hushabye
  Jimmy Randal [C. 12]
  Little Iron Monitor
  Lord Beekman [C. 53]
  Lord Lover [C. 75]
  Lovely Jimmy
  Mary of the Wild Moor [P 21]
  Merry Brown Field [C. 43]
  Sheffield Apprentice [O 39]
  Springfield Mountain [G 16]
  Tinker's Story [Q 2]
  Young Edmund

Mar 9200: Field recordings of scantily documented Anglo-American regional tradition are represented by this collection of unaccompanied vocals, made on either wire or disc recorder in New Jersey by an amateur folksong enthusiast. The singer, Everett Pitt (1886-1954), was the descendent, according to family tradition, of a British revolutionary war soldier who escaped to the hills when American troops stormed Stony Point in July 1779. The collector, Anne Lutz, was a schoolteacher, now retired, who was active in the New Jersey Folklore Society in the 1940s and had collected a good deal of material in the Ramapo Mountains. Pitt has a very plain singing style, relaxed, rhythmically very steady, but in such a low range that it is often difficult to ascertain his precise pitch. The 23 items included on this cassette include many antiques of British origin. "Gone to Kansas," "Give an Honest Irish Lad a Chance," and "The Day I Fought Dwyer" are all American stage songs from the mid-19th century. Many of Pitt's tunes are modal or in gapped scales. Although Pitt sang with the words written on paper before him ("because he wanted to be sure he would not spoil a recording by getting mixed up"), one gets the impression that the texts, which he learned from his mother, neighbors, or friends, were firmly in oral tradition. Pitt's text of Child 43, a rare American recovery, is a form of Coffin's story type B--except that the broom is scattered not for magical purposes but so that he would know she had been there; and the bird is a hawk--as in the Scottish texts, rather than a parrot. Though he is not a great singer per se, Pitt's repertoire as represented on this cassette is an amazing sampling of the northeastern Anglo-American tradition, and is a valuable collection. [JAF 408]

117   Label Name/Number: Folkways FA 2306
Title: *The Poplin Family of Sumter, South Carolina*
Artist: China Poplin, Edna Poplin Elmore, Bill Poplin, David Jackson

Collector/Recordist: Jack Tottle
Place and Date of Recording: Ft. Jackson and Sumter, SC, 1962
Date of Publication: 1963
Annotations: 7 p. booklet by Jack Tottle
Selections:
    Blues Don't Mean a Thing, The
    Brown's Ferry Blues
    Catfish [= Banjo Sam]
    Cindy Gal
    Crawdad Hole
    Eyes Like Cherries
    Fingers on Fire
    Goin' back to Sumter
    Hammer Ring
    Hannamariah
    I Don't Drinka Your Whiskey
    I Don't Want To Get Married
    Just Because
    My Home Is Not in South Carolina
    Old Reuben
    Panhandle Rag
    Preacher and the Bear, The
    River of Jordan
    Sit at Home
    Somebody's Been Beating My Time
    Steel Guitar Rag
    Sumter Rag
    Sweet Kiss Waltz
    You Gotta See Your Momma Every Night

Fwys FA 2306:   China Poplin (about 58 years old when these recordings were made) and Edna Poplin Elmore, two of eight musical children, learned much of their music from their parents, supplemented by what they heard on local radio as they were growing up. They performed at local shows and square dances and were first heard by Jack Tottle when they were appearing on a Columbia, South Carolina, television station. They developed a rather unique style, with repertoire a blend of hillbilly songs of the early 20th century and turn-of-the-century pop tunes. Edna, a distinctive lead guitarist, also sings lead. ·Both Edna and China have written some of their pieces-- most noteworthy of which is Edna's beautiful "Sit at Home." [JAF 307--DKW]

118   Label Name/Number: Folk-Legacy FSA-1 (Reissued in England as Topic 12T162)
Title: *Frank Proffitt*
Artist: Frank Proffitt
Collector/Recordist: Sandy Paton
Place and Date of Recording: Reese, NC, 1962
Date of Publication: 1962 (Topic, 1967)
Annotations: 22 p. booklet by Sandy Paton
Selections:
    Bonnie James Campbell [C. 210]
    Cluck Old Hen
    Going Across the Mountain
    Gyps of David [C. 200]

Handsome Molly
I'll Never Get Drunk No More
I'm Going Back to North Carolina
Lord Randall [C. 12]
Moonshine
Morning Fair
Reuben Train
Rye Whiskey
Song of a Lost Hunter [C. 68]
Sourwood Mountain
Tom Dooley [F 36]
Trifling Woman
Wild Bill Jones [E 10]

119   Label Name/Number: Folk-Legacy FSA-36
Title: *Frank Proffitt Memorial Album*
Artist: Frank Proffitt
Collector/Recordist: Sandy Paton
Place and Date of Recording: Huntington, VT, 1963?
Date of Publication: 1968
Annotations: 18 p. booklet by Sandy Paton
Selections:
Blackberry Wine
Everybody's Got To Be Tried
Got No Sugar Baby Now
I'm A Long Time Travelling Here Below
Little Birdie
Little White Robe
Lord Lovel [C. 75]
Man of Constant Sorrow
Oh, Lord, What a Morning
Poor Man
Poor Soldier
Satan, Your Kingdom Must Come Down
Shake Hands with Mother Again
Shull's Mills
Single Girl
Will the Circle Be Unbroken

120   Label Name/Number: Folkways FA 2360
Title: *Frank Proffitt Sings Folk Songs*
Artist: Frank Proffitt
Collector/Recordist: Sandy Paton
Place and Date of Recording: Near Reese, NC, 1961
Date of Publication: 1962
Annotations: 7 p. booklet by Anne and Frank Warner and Sandy Paton
Selections:
Baby-O
Beaver Dam Road
Bo Lamkin [C. 93]
Cindy

Dan Do [C. 277]
Down in the Valley
George Collins [C. 85]
Groundhog
John Hardy [I 2]
Johnson Boys
Julie Jenkins
Ninety and Nine
Old Abe
Poor Ellen Smith [F 11]

Fwys FA 2360 / Fleg FSA-1 / FLeg FSA-36:   In the pages of the history of the folk song revival, Frank Proffitt (1913-1965) will earn a footnote as the ultimate source of the Kingston Trio's highly successful "Tom Dooley." Proffitt loved the old songs and ballads and consciously learned and preserved them.   Born in Laurel Bloomery, North Carolina, Proffitt made his living farming tobacco and carpentering, supplementing his income by making and selling fretless banjos and dulcimers. Though Frank and Ann Warner collected songs from him as early as 1938, the first recordings were made in 1961 by Sandy and Caroline Paton and issued on Folkways FA 2360. Highlights on this album are Proffitt's own composition, "Beaver Dam Road," the satirical Civil War song, "Old Abe," and the fine rendition of "Bo Lamkin." The following year, the Patons recorded him again and featured him on the first album on the Patons' new record label (Folk Legacy FSA-1). High points on the album are Proffitt's renditions of Child ballads 200 and 68--the latter, a particularly unusual text, for which Proffitt provides the tale his Aunt Nancy, his source for the song, used to relate.   Most of Proffitt's songs are sung with banjo accompaniment but the latter is unaccompanied. FSA-36 was recorded by the Patons shortly before Proffitt's death at the age of 52. Either unaccompanied or to his own banjo or dulcimer backup, Proffitt sings mostly his own compositions, gospel songs, a few banjo songs, and one older ballad (C. 75). Brochures to all three albums include some biographical information, text transcriptions and annotations to the songs. [WF 7/72 (FSA-36); JAF 299--DKW (FSA 1, FA 2360)]

121   Label Name/Number: Riverside RLP 12-649
Title: *Banjo Songs of the Blue Ridge and Great Smokies*
Artist: Obray Ramsey
Collector/Recordist/Producer: Kenneth Goldstein
Place and Date of Recording: Western No. Carolina State Hospital, 1957
Date of Publication: [ca. 1958]
Annotations: Liner notes by Kenneth Goldstein
Selections:
Cripple Creek
Down by the Sea Shore [K 17]
God Gave Noah the Rainbow Sign
I Am a Pilgrim
Keep on the Sunny Side
Little Margaret [C. 74]
Lonesome Road Blues
My Lord, What a Morning
Polly Put the Kettle On
Rambling Boy, The [L 12]
Shortenin' Bread
Song of the French Broad River
Weeping Willow
Wildwood Flower

122   Label Name/Number: Prestige International INT 13020
Title: *Obray Ramsey Sings Folksongs from the Three Laurels*
Artists: Obray Ramsey with Tommy Hunter
Collector/Recordist: Rudy Van Gelder
Producer: Kenneth S. Goldstein
Date of Publication: [1961]
Annotations: Liner notes by D. K. Wilgus
Selections:
   Battle of King's Mountain, The [L 4]
   Black Jack Davy [C. 200]
   George Collins [C. 85]
   Green Back Dollar
   I'll Not Marry at All
   I'm Gonna Ride on that Cloud
   Jim Gunther and the Steer
   My Lord What a Morning
   Omie Wise [F 4]
   Rain and Snow
   Rich and Rambling Boy, The [L 12]
   Sailor on the Deep Blue Sea [K 12]
   Shady Grove
   Wagoner's Lad, The
   Wild Bill Jones [E 10]

123   Label Name/Number: Prestige International INT 13030
Title: *Obray Ramsey Sings Folksongs from the Gateways to the Great Smokies*
Artists: Obray Ramsey with Tommy Hunter
Collector/Recordist: Rudy Van Gelder
Producer: Kenneth S. Goldstein
Date of Publication: [1962]
Annotations: Liner notes by D. K. Wilgus
Selections:
   Cripple Creek
   Down Beside the Ohio [F 5]
   Hold Fast to the Right
   I Want to Go Home
   I Wish I Were a Single Girl
   Little Margaret [C. 74]
   Little Sparrow
   Man of Constant Sorrow
   Pearl Bryant [F 1b]
   Pretty Fair Miss [N 42]
   Pretty Saro
   Roaming Boy, The [P 1b]
   Shortening Bread
   War Is a-Raging, The [O 33]
   Worried Man

   Riv RLP 12-649 / Prest INT 13020 / Prest INT 13030:   Banjo player/singer Obray Ramsey was born on the edge of the Great Smokies in Western North Carolina, and learned most of his songs from his mother and grandmother.   In early years Ramsey sang mostly unaccompanied, but in

1953 Bascom Lamar Lunsford induced him to sing at his Asheville Folk Festival, and in return gave him a banjo and urged him to learn to play it. The Riverside album was Ramsey's first, featuring his singing and banjo-playing in a program of mostly well-known traditional songs except for "Song of the French Broad River," Ramsey's own composition--a tribute to a local river and to Ramsey's own Cherokee ancestry. One of Ramsey's gems on Prestige 13020 is the white blues song, "Rain and Snow," which he performs movingly. In his liner notes, Wilgus describes this as a "superlative blend of the imageries of the old ballads and the songs of the lonesome Southern roads." Other, fuller versions of the song make it apparent that there must once have been a complete narrative text to this lyric. "The Battle of Kings Mountain" is one of the few recordings of this 17th century broadside ballad from the New World. Wilgus's notes to both Prestige albums considerably enhance the listener's understanding of the musical milieu of Ramsey's material.

124   Label Name/Number: Folkways FA 2493
Title: *My Epitaph*
Artists: Ola Belle Reed with David Reed & Bud Reed
Collector/Recordist: King Street Recording Company
Place and Date of Recording: 1976
Date of Publication: 1976
Annotations: 7 p. booklet (by Kevin Roth?)
Selections:
   Fortunes
   High on Mountain
   I've Endured
   My Epitaph
   Sing Me a Song
   Springtime of My Life

125   Label Name/Number: Rounder Records 0021
Title: *Ola Belle Reed*
Artists: Ola Belle, with Bud Reed, David Reed, Alan Reed, and John Miller
Collector/Recordist: Gei Zantzinger
Producer: Gei and Ruth Zantzinger
Place and Date of Recording: Devault, PA, 1972
Date of Publication: 1973
Annotations: Unsigned liner notes
Selections:
   Billy in the Lowground
   Blues in My Mind
   Flop Eared Mule
   Fly Around My Pretty Little Miss
   Go Home Little Girl
   God Put a Rainbow in the Clouds
   High on a Mountain
   I Believe
   I've Always Been a Rambler [P 1b]
   John Hardy
   My Epitaph
   Rosewood Casket
   Soldier and the Lady, The [P 14]
   Springtime of Life, The
   Wayfaring Pilgrim
   You Don't Tell Me That You Love Me Anymore

126 Label Name/Number: Rounder Records 0077
Title: *Ola Belle Reed and Family*
Artists: Ola Belle Reed and family (Bud Reed and David Reed)
Date of Publication: 1977
Annotations: Liner notes and 2 p. leaflet by David Whisnant
Selections:
> Boat's up the River
> Butcher's Boy, The [P 24]
> Going to Write Me a Letter
> I've Endured
> Lamplighting Time in the Valley
> My Doney, Where Have You Been So Long
> Ninety and Nine, The
> Only the Leading Role Will Do
> Over Yonder in the Graveyard
> Ranger's Command, The [B 8]
> Sing Me a Song
> When I Can Read My Titles Clear
> Where the Wild, Wild Flowers Grow
> You Led Me to the Wrong

Fwys FA 2493 / Rndr 0021 / Rndr 0077:   Ola Belle Reed (b. 1915), from Ashe County, NC, performed for many years with her brother Alec and the New River Valley Boys and Girls over WWVA, Wheeling, West Virginia. After she married in 1949, she and her husband played professionally together. This album explores the wide range of her repertoire, from old hymns (such as the beautifully rendered "Wayfaring Pilgrim"), imported ballads (P 1b, P 14), and sentimental parlor ballads ("Rosewood Casket") to banjo tunes ("John Hardy," "Flop Eared Mule") and some of her own recent compositions (though the liner notes do not identify which these are). She is a fine singer with a rich voice, given to slowing her tempo at the end of each song. The Folkways album consists of lengthy selections from a 1976 interview, interspersed with songs, all of which are Reed's own compositions. Most of her songs treat familiar gospel song themes; some are based on personal experiences. Half of the songs on Rndr 0077 are her own compositions; others were learned from her father, her uncle, or her husband, Bud. Her distinctive voice is backed up by clawhammer banjo (her own), guitar, and, in some case, slide guitar. David or Bud Reed sing some of the songs. Her plaintive rendition of "My Doney," with just banjo accompaniment, is wonderful. [WF 1/75]

127 Label Name/Number: Vanguard VRS-9158
Title: *Songs and Ballads of the Ozarks*
Artist: Almeda Riddle
Producer: Ralph Rinzler
Date of Publication: 1964
Annotations: Liner notes by John Quincy Wolf
Selections:
> Babes in the Woods
> Black Jack Davey [C. 200]
> Chick-a-la-le-o
> Frog Went A-Courtin'
> House Carpenter, The [C. 243]
> How Firm a Foundation
> Lady Gay [C. 79]
> Locks and Bolts [M 13]

Orphan Girl, The
Soldier of the Legion, A
Two Lovers, The [N 28]
Will the Weaver [Q 9]
Young Carlotta [G 17]

128   Label Name/Number: Rounder 0017
Title: *Ballads and Hymns from the Ozarks*
Artist: Almeda Riddle
Editor: Mark Wilson
Place and Date of Recording: Fayville, MA, 1972
Date of Publication: [1972]
Annotations: 8 p. booklet by Mark Wilson
Selections:
Butcher's Boy, The [P 24]
Four Marys, The [C. 173]
How Tedious and Tasteless the Hours
Lady Margaret [C. 74]
Man of Constant Sorrow, A
Merrimac at Sea, The [C. 289]
My Old Cottage Home
Nightingale Song, The [P 14]
Old Churchyard, The
Peggy of Glasgow [C. 228]
Rare Willie Drowned in Yarrow [C. 215]
Rome County

129   Label Name/Number: Minstrel JD-203
Title: *Granny Riddle's Songs and Ballads*
Artist: Almeda Riddle
Date of Publication: 1977
Annotations: Liner notes by Mark Gilston
Selections:
Barbara Allen [C. 84]
Children of the Heavenly King
Come All Ye Texas Rangers [A 8]
Frog Went A-Courtin'
Orphan Girl, The
Oxford Girl, The [P 35]
Poor Wayfaring Stranger
Soldier of the Legion
Tom Sherman's Barroom [B 1]
Water Is Wide, The

130   Label Name/Number: Rounder Records 0083
Title: *More Ballads and Hymns from the Ozarks*
Artist: Almeda Riddle
Collector/Recordist: Bill Nowlin, Mark Wilson
Producer: Mark Wilson
Place and Date of Recording: Boston, 1972, 1975
Date of Publication: 1978

Annotations: Liner notes
Selections:
Allen Bain
Blood of the Old Red Rooster, The [C. 13]
Brisk Young Farmer, The [N 30]
Brokedown Brakeman, The
Comical Ditty, A
I'm a Long Time Traveling Here Below
Last Fierce Charge, The [A 17]
Locks and Bolts [M 13]
Lonesome Dove, The
Prodigal's Career, The
Seashell Song, The
Ten Thousand Miles Away

131   Label Name/Number: Arkansas Traditions 003
Title: *How Firm a Foundation & Other Traditional Hymns*
Artist: Almeda Riddle
Collector/Recordist: Gene Dunaway, Aubrey Richardson
Place and Date of Recording: Greers Ferry, AR, 1983
Date of Publication: 1985
Annotations: 8 p. booklet by W. K. McNeil; liner notes by George West
Selections:
Amazing Grace
Come, Thou Fount of Every Blessing
How Firm a Foundation
My Old Cottage Home
Sons of Sorrow
Star of Bethlehem
Sweet Rivers
There Is a Happy Land
They Sang That Old Time Religion
Time Has Made a Change in Me
Twilight Is Stealing
Vain World, Adieu
Worldwide Peace

Van VRS-9158 / Rndr 0017 / Min JD-203 / Rndr 0083 / Ark Trad 003:   "Granny" Riddle of Heber Springs, Arkansas, who died in 1986 at age 88, was one of our great ballad singers; her extensive repertoire has been the subject of five full LPs and a book-length autobiography edited by Roger Abrahams (*A Singer and Her Songs*, 1970).   Riddle is an especially active tradition-bearer, always seeking out better versions of songs in her repertoire and reshaping her texts accordingly. She was first recorded in 1959 by Alan Lomax after a tip from John Quincy Wolfe; Wolfe had met her in 1952 in an Ozark mountain cabin where he had come to meet and record another singer. Unlike many of the great Appalachian singers with whom she is often compared, "Granny" Riddle's singing style was marked by a rock-solid meter rather than a rubato parlando.   Her principal decorating technique was portamento, or "feathering"--a very brief rising vocal break that other singers employ at the ends of musical phrases, but which she exhibited more frequently throughout a song.   Almeda Riddle's first album, on Vanguard, is an excellent compilation of songs and ballads, heavily stressing the older elements of her enormous repertoire.   Her long version of "Young Carlotta" is wonderfully spellbinding; perhaps the best recording of what is one of the finest of our more literary native ballads. Riddle has done much to popularize the childrens' song "Chick-a-la-le-o" through her recordings and many public appearances; there do not seem to be any other independent occurrences of it. Her 7-plus minutes "House Carpenter," with its unusual long fourth stanzaic line, is an excellent text. Rndr 0017 includes a brochure with a biographical sketch and (not always accurate) text transcriptions.

Almeda Riddle could invariably be counted upon to have the fullest text ever recorded of any ballad that she sang. In her autobiography, she explained how she often collated songs from various sources when she did not remember all the words that she had known in her youth. Her general but not invariable principle seemed to be to try to recreate the song as she must have learned it first. Since it is hard to believe that the versions she learned in her youth were always of such high quality, one wonders whether the end product of her confabulations wasn't more what she wished she had first sung rather than what she actually sang. Rndr 0017 is further proof that whatever the process, there is no doubt of the aesthetic quality of her end product, at least textually. On this album are five Child ballads (including perhaps the only report of C. 228 in the New World), two other Old World ballads, and five native American pieces. The enclosed brochure includes text transcriptions but no comments on the songs, referring the listener instead to the Riddle/Abrahams book. Her "Man of Constant Sorrow" bears little textual resemblance to other recordings of this song, apart from the opening line; obviously one is a recomposition of the other. Her statement that she learned the song from her grandfather, who learned it in the 1850s from a man who was off to California, surely is the oldest dating for the song that we have. Riddle has been highly acclaimed not only for her remarkable texts but also for her singing, and indeed she does put her songs over lucidly. Yet I must confess that I find her ballad singing more educational than enjoyable. The metronomic nature of her presentation, the nearly predictable placement of her "feathering," and what seems to be a lack of enthusiasm all contribute to this impression. Her hymn singing does not share these characteristics, and I find it more enjoyable. The brochure has been prepared with surprising lack of care: the text transcriptions are generally quite inaccurate; in some cases whole stanzas are missing--or inserted where they shouldn't be.

Minstrel JD-203 is another excellent sampling of "Granny" Riddle's songs and ballads, recorded when she was 79 years old. Gilston's jacket notes report Riddle's comments on the songs' sources and/or associations: for example, her mother allowed her to sing "Tom Sherman's Barrom," but another variant, "Young Trooper Cut Down in His Prime," was not acceptable because of the explicit mention of venereal disease as cause of the young man's death; "The Oxford Girl" she dislikes because "it's too bloody."

By the time the Arkansas Traditions album was recorded, her voice had acquired a quaver not encountered on her earlier albums. This is the first album on which she determined the contents to her own specifications, and the result is a collection of 13 hymns dating from 1759 ("Come, Thou Fount of Every Blessing") to the 1940s ("Time Has Made a Change in Me"). The brochure includes text transcriptions and good headnotes for pieces that have generally not been annotated in field collections. The recordings include several brief remarks by Almeda herself about her sources, treatment, likes and dislikes, etc. She says she modified or expanded some of the song texts to suit her tastes. Several of these sacred tunes were long ago borrowed for secular tunes: "How Firm a Foundation" for the murder ballad, "Poor Ellen Smith"; "Time Has Made a Change in Me" (possibly) for "I Ride an Old Paint;" and "Come, Thou Fount of Every Blessing," according to McNeil, for "Go Tell Aunt Rhody." Frequent appearances at folk festivals since the early 1960s, work with folklorists and collectors, and her own inquiring interest in traditional ballads and songs (and her own active role in the production of this album) made her an unusual informant.

According to the unsigned liner notes on Rndr 0083, this is "a lighter compendium of some of her old-time favorites" tempered slightly by the whims of the producers. Two items--"The Broke-Down Brakeman" and "A Comical Ditty"--have not, to my knowledge, been previously recorded; and "The Seashell Song" [K 17] is one of the few American recordings of an early British broadside ballad that is independent of the verison popularized by the Carter Family (as "I Never Will

Marry"). Annotations on the album are brief, but Riddle's career had been documented extensively on previous LPs and in the book by Abrahams and Riddle. [JEMFQ 53, WF 10/74, JAF 395; JAF 310--DKW (Van); JAF 343--DKW (Rndr 0017)]

132 Label Name/Number: Elektra EKLP-2 (10")
Title: *Jean Ritchie Sings*
Artist: Jean Ritchie
Recordist: Edward Tatnall Canby
Editor: Jac Holzman (production supervisor)
Place and Date of Recording: New York, ca. 1952
Date of Publication: 1952
Annotations: Liner notes by Edward Tatnall Canby; song lyrics enclosed inside
Selections:
  Black Is the Color
  Cuckoo, The (2 versions)
  Gypsum Davy [C. 200]
  Hush Little Baby
  Jubilee
  Keep Your Garden Clean
  Little Cory
  Little Devils, The [C. 278]
  My Boy Willie
  O Love Is Teasin'
  Old Virginny
  One Morning in May (*or* The Nightingale) (2 versions) [P 14]
  Short Life of Trouble, A

133 Label Name/Number: Riverside RLP 12-620
Title: *Saturday Night and Sunday Too*
Artist: Jean Ritchie with Roger Sprung
Collector/Recordist/Editor: Kenneth S. Goldstein
Place and Date of Recording: NY, 1956
Date of Publication: [ca. 1957]
Annotations: Liner notes by Jean Ritchie
Selections:
  Baby-O
  Been a Long Time A-Travelling
  Betty Larkin
  Charlie
  Day Is Past and Gone, The
  Dear Companion
  Father Get Ready
  God Bless Them Moonshiners
  Green Grows the Willow Tree
  Guide Me, O Thou Great Jehovah
  Hiram Hubbard
  Hop Up My Ladies
  Huntin' the Buck
  I've Got a Mother
  Lady Margaret [C. 74]
  Lullaby Medley

Shady Grove
Sing to Me of Heaven
Susan Girl
Two Dukes A-Rovin'

134   Label Name/Number: Westminister SWN 18021
Title: *Songs from Kentucky*
Artist: Jean Ritchie
Date of Publication: [1957?]
Selections:
Bachelor's Hall
Barbry Allen [C. 84]
Christ Was Born in Bethlehem
Froggie Went a'Courting
Gentle Fair Jenny
Hush Little Baby
Jackero [N 7]
Jubilee
Little Devils [C. 278]
Oh, Soldier, Soldier
Old Joe Clark
One Morning in May [P 14]
Pretty Polly [P 36b]
Single Girl
Sourwood Mountain
There Was an Old Woman
Turkish Lady, The [C. 53]

135a   Label Name/Number: Folkways FA 2301
Title: *Child Ballads in America, Vol. 1*
Artist: Jean Ritchie
Place of Recording: NY
Date of Publication: 1961
Annotations: 8 p. brochure by Kenneth S. Goldstein
Selections:
Fair Annie of Lochroyan [C. 76]
False Sir John [C. 4]
Gypsy Laddie [C. 200]
Hangman [C. 95]
House Carpenter, The [C. 243]
Lord Bateman [C. 53]
Lord Lovel [C. 75]
Lord Thomas and Fair Ellender [C. 73]
Merry Golden Tree, The [C. 286]
Old Bangum [C. 18]

135b   Label Name/Number: Folkways FA 2302
Title: *Child Ballads in America, Vol. 2*
Artist: Jean Ritchie
Place of Recording: NY
Date of Publication: 1961

Annotations: 8 p. brochure by Kenneth S. Goldstein
Selections:
  Cherry Tree Carol [C. 54]
  Edward [C. 13]
  Gentle Fair Jenny [C. 277]
  Little Devils [C. 278]
  Little Musgrave [C. 81]
  Lord Randall [C. 12]
  Sweet William and Lady Margaret [C. 74]
  There Lived an Old Lord [C. 10]
  Unquiet Grave, The [C. 78]
  Wife of Usher's Wells, The [C. 79]

136 Label Name/Number: Folkways FA 2427
Title: *Precious Memories*
Artists: Jean Ritchie with Eric Weissberg, Arthur Rosenbaum, Marshall Brickman
Date of Publication: 1962
Annotations: 6 p. brochure by Jean Ritchie
Selections:
  Bury Me Beneath the Willow
  Go Dig My Grave
  Great Speckled Bird, The
  Gypsy's Warning, The
  Jim Blake
  Little Rosebud Casket
  Maple on the Hill
  Most Fair Beauty Bright, The [M 3]
  No, Sir
  Poor and Ramblin' Boy, The [L 12]
  Precious Memories
  Pretty Betty Martin
  Printer's Bride, The [G 21]
  Sweet Willie
  Two Little Children
  Wreck on the Highway, The

137 Label Name/Number: Folkways FA 2426
Title: *Jean Ritchie and Doc Watson at Folk City*
Artists: Jean Ritchie and Doc Watson, with Roger Sprung
Collector/Recordist: George Pickow
Place and Date of Recording: New York City
Date of Publication: 1963
Annotations: 2 p. brochure by Jean Ritchie
Selections:
  Amazing Grace -- All
  Cripple Creek -- Watson, Sprung
  Don't Mind the Weather -- Ritchie
  Hiram Hubbard -- Ritchie, Watson
  House Carpenter, The [C. 243] -- Ritchie, accomp. by Watson
  Soldier's Joy -- Watson
  Spike-Driver Blues -- Watson

Sugar on the Floor -- Ritchie, Watson, Sprung
Wabash Cannonball -- Watson
What'll I Do with the Baby-O? -- Ritchie
Willie Moore -- Watson

138   Label Name/Number: Greenhays Recordings GR714
Title: *The Most Dulcimer*
Artist: Jean Ritchie with John McCutcheon, Mike Seeger, Diane Hamilton, Jon Pickow, Peter
    Pickow
Recordist/Producer: Peter Pickow
Place and Date of Recording: New York City
Date of Publication: 1984
Selections:
    Aunt Rhodie R. I. P.
    Dabbling in the Dew
    Edward [C. 13]
    Four Marys [C. 173]
    Haven of Rest, The
    Jubilee
    Killiekrankie
    Locks and Bolts [M 13]
    Mourning Tears
    Movin' on down the River
    Over the River to Feed My Sheep
    Parson's Farewell, The
    Pretty Saro
    Wintergrace

139   Label Name/Number: June Appal 037
Title: *Sweet Rivers*
Artist: Jean Ritchie with Jim Gage, John McCutcheon, Marion Sumner, Jack Wright, & mem-
    bers of the Ritchie family
Collector/Recordist: Dudley Wilson, Jack Wright
Producer: Jonathan Greene
Date of Publication: 1981
Annotations: Liner notes by Jean Ritchie
Selections:
    Brightest and Best
    Evergreen Shore
    Few More Years Shall Roll, A
    I'm Alone in This World
    Jesus, Grant Us All a Blessing
    Long Lonesome Way, The
    Meeting Is Over, The
    Mother in Bright Glory
    My Head and Stay
    Poor Pilgrim of Sorrow
    Resignation
    She Is Gone
    Stream of Time
    Sweet Rivers of Redeeming Love
    White Pilgrim, The

Elek EKL 10 / Riv RLP 12-620 / Wstm SWN 18021 / Fwys FA 2301/2302 / Fwys FA 2427 / Fwys FA 2426 / GnHys GR 714 / June Appal JA 037: Kentucky-born Jean Ritchie went to New York in 1947, after graduating from the University of Kentucky with a degree in social work, to teach children's songs and dances at the Henry Street Settlement House summer camp. There she found an urban audience for the folk music that had been part of her life, and she began an involvement with the folk revival that has never stopped. In the four decades since, she has made some 40 LP recordings. Initially confining herself to her own store of Kentucky ballads, songs, and dulcimer tunes, she has since developed into a song writer of skill and sensitivity; she is able to fill in the lacunae in her own memory, or even write an entirely new composition, without departing from the traditional style that is part of her cultural heritage. This ability to create fresh material within a traditional framework makes her not less, but more of a traditional artist.

Elektra EKLP-2 was her first commercial recording, made several years after she moved to New York. (Earlier recordings, made for the LC, are on AFS L14, q.v.) Canby's primary interest has always been classical music, and this bias clearly colors his liner notes. Jean Ritchie's ability to make an educational lesson out of her repertoire is evident here, with her offering two comparative versions of two of the selections. She accompanies herself on either guitar or dulcimer.

Ken Goldstein's enthusiasm for Jean Ritchie's significance (and, in fact, the entire Ritchie family's significance) as a great tradition bearer is amply justified by Fwys FA 2301 and Fwys FA 2302--two discs offering 21 Child ballads that Ritchie learned from her father, uncle, or other relatives and friends. Few American folksingers can boast such a repertoire; certainly none has been recorded. Because of Ritchie's active public career since 1946 as performer, lecturer, and writer, and because her repertoire has steadily grown and become modernized--with her own compositions as well as with those of others--it is easy to forget that she is a traditional artist. This tendency is further fueled by her singing style: a beautiful high soprano voice with heavy vibrato is not often associated with the Southern Appalachians. But Ritchie should not be penalized on account of it: her style is traditional--she sings her "big ballads" deliberately, in the non-rhythmic tempo called rubato parlando, with subtle but delightful ornamentation. For an audience not familiar or comfortable with folksier singing styles, Ritchie's recordings are an admirable introduction to the best of older Anglo-American balladry. The range of traditional singers stretches from "passive" tradition bearers, those who pass on songs essentially as they learn them, and generally do not go out of their way to augment their repertoires; to "active" bearers--those, like Ritchie, whose love for songs prompts them to seek them out; to find the best or most complete version, or to put together the best from fragments. When, in addition to doing the latter, they are also intelligent, articulate, and self-aware of their own roles as straddlers of two audiences and two cultures, they seem almost too good to be genuine. Most of Ritchie's text are in very good condition, but a few are particularly remarkable: her "Fair Annie of Lochroyan" (C. 76) is one of the best texts reported ever--certainly the best in the New World. "Little Musgrave" (C. 81) is also an unusually full text. Goldstein's notes synopsize then-current scholarship about the selections as well as reporting where she learned the items. Ritchie accompanies herself on a few of the ballads on the plucked dulcimer.

As indicated in the song credits, FA 2426 is a live concert album divided among performances by Jean and by Doc, with a few by the two of them together, with occasional accompaniment by Roger Sprung on several instruments. Ritchie provides brief notes to the selections, with some quotes from Doc. Most of the tunes appear on other albums by Ritchie and/or Watson. Ritchie observes in her notes to Fwys FA 2427 that though some of these songs are not, strictly, hillbilly, they are "sung in the hillbilly style, and for this reason have usually been avoided by the serious singer of the mountain ballad." Also, her mother "never approved of us girls singing these songs because they were 'banjer-pickin' songs and therefore unladylike and even low-down." Several of the pieces are indeed generally associated with the hillbilly style of the '20s and'30s, but some clearly are not--particularly "Most Fair Beauty Bright" and the unusual broadside ballad, "The Printer's Bride"--a rare and lovely variant of "The Silver Dagger." Also unusual is her "Sweet Willie" (sometimes called "Little Willie")--a short fragmentary ballad that has not, to my knowledge, been recovered in a full text. Weissberg, Rosenbaum, and Brickman provide varied instrumental accompaniment--and join in the singing on some numbers. The unidentified other female voices may be Ritchie's, multiply recorded.

On Riv 12-620 Jean Ritchie creates a typical weekend of music with the Ritchie family of Kentucky; side 1, subtitled "Saturday Night," consists of dance tunes, ballads, and children's songs; side 2, "Sunday," consists of hymns (except for the misplaced "Lullaby Medley" and "Shady Grove") from the Old Regular Baptist Church. She accompanies herself on dulcimer, with occasional violin or banjo by Roger Sprung. Westminister SWN 18021, another early album, is edited from two 10" LPs on the Argo label issued in 1954. Issued without any accompanying information, it features Ritchie accompanying herself on guitar or dulcimer. Most of the songs are also available on her other albums.

GR714 includes 14 selections, on some of which her singing and dulcimer playing are accompanied by mandolin, banjo, recorders, guitar, jews harp, harpsichord, and synthesizer by her sons and friends. Older numbers include "Edward" (Child 13), "Four Maries" (173), "Locks and Bolts" (Laws M 13), "Aunt Rhodie R. I. P.," and "Dabbling in the Dew," a love song primarily of English provenance.

JA 037 consists entirely of religious numbers, several traditional, but others written by Jean Ritchie herself or at least supplemented by her. Performances range from unaccompanied solos to choral renditions by Jean and five of her sisters to others with guitar, dulcimer, and/or autoharp accompaniment. The inner sleeve includes text transcriptions; the back jacket, her own comments on the songs. [JAF 266--CH; JAF 295--DKW (FA 2301/2); JAF 305--DKW (FA 2426)]

140   Label Name/Number: Folk-Legacy FSA-3
Title: *Edna Ritchie of Viper, Kentucky*
Artist: Edna Ritchie
Collector/Recordist: Sandy Paton
Place and Date of Recording: Viper, KY, ca. 1961
Date of Publication: 1962
Annotations: 28 p. booklet by D. K. Wilgus
Selections:
    As Joseph Was A'Walking [C. 54]
    Aunt Sal's Song
    Blackest Crow, The
    Cuckoo, The
    Dear Companion
    Down Came an Angel
    Fair and Tender Ladies
    Foreign Lander
    Gentle Fair Jenny [C. 277]
    I Wonder When I Shall Be Married
    Jackaro [N 7]
    May Day Carol
    Old Chimney Sweeper
    Old Crumley [Q 1]
    Old King Cole
    Old Man Came Courting Me, An
    Old Tyler
    Riddle Song, The
    Somebody's Tall and Handsome

FLeg FSA-3: Not surprisingly, Edna Ritchie's repertoire and style are highly reminiscent of her better-known sister, Jean (see above), but Edna did not start performing publicly until 1960.

I find her voice somewhat mellower and less piercing than Jean's and her singing more pensive and relaxed. Some of her songs are quite beautiful--for example, "Dear Companion." In his excellent notes, the late D. K. Wilgus, one of the outstanding folksong scholars of recent decades, draws attention (without implying criticism) to the contribution to the Ritchie family's enormous repertoire (and to Appalachian folk music in general) of the settlement schools. Those institutions--for example, Hindman Settlement School in Knott County and Pine Mountain Settlement School Settlement School, established, respectively, in 1902 and 1911, fostered a conscious effort to preserve (and revive) the older folk cultural strata of Appalachia, resulting in turning to such sources as Cecil Sharp's fieldwork to reinvigorate waning traditions.

141 Label Name/Number: County 202
Title: *Famous Cowboy Fiddler*
Artist: Eck Robertson
Collector/Recordist: John Cohen, Mike Seeger, and Tracy Schwarz
Place and Date of Recording: Amarillo, TX, 1963
Date of Publication: 1991
Annotations: 17 p. booklet by Blanton Owen and Tom Sauber
Selections:
Beaumont Rag
Billy in the Lowground
Bonaparte's Retreat
Done Gone
Dusty Miller
Forky Deer
Get Up in the Cool
Grey Eagle
Grigsby's Hornpipe
Hawk Got the Chicken
Hell Among the Yearlings
Lost Goose
Lost Indian
Rye Whiskey
Sally Johnson
Say Old Man, Can You Play a Fiddle?
Stumptown Stomp
Texas Wagoner
Unnamed D Tune

Cty 202: Eck Robertson (1887-1975) is remembered as the first traditional southern folk musician to make commercial records. (Some of those 1922 recordings, and later ones, are reissued on Sonyatone STR 201, q. v in Section III.) Robertson was born in Delaney, Arkansas, and was already a fairly well-established "cowboy fiddler" by the time he and his fellow fiddler Henry Gilliland wandered into Victor's New York offices and requested an audition. Not only was he the first, but he was unquestionably one of the best fiddlers to be captured in wax. In 1963 Seeger, Cohen, and Schwarz visited Robertson at his home and found that, at age 76, he was still in great form. Some home recordings were made, and several festival appearances followed in the next few years. Not until 1991 were some of those tapes from 1963 issued. The selections include (not surprisingly) several that Robertson immortalized in the 1920s (but not his magnificent "Sally Goodin") and also several he never waxed earlier. Robertson's wonderful recordings are accompanied by a booklet documenting his life of music. Sauber provides an excellent analysis of his fiddling style, with comments on traditional southern fiddling in general. Notes on the selections and a full Robertson discography, repertoire listing, and bibliography are also included. This is an important production that should not be missed.

142   Label Name/Number: Folk-Legacy FSA-27
Title: *Songmaker of the Catskills*
Artist: Grant Rogers
Collector/Recordist/Editor: Sandy Paton
Place and Date of Recording: Walton, NY, 1965?
Date of Publication: 1965
Annotations: 31 p. booklet by Sandy Paton
Selections:
    At the End of Jimmy's Bar
    Bachelor's Reply, The
    Bessie, the Heifer
    Bold Soldier, The [M 27]
    Bullseye Bill
    Butcher's Boy, The [P 24]
    Canadian Rose, The
    Cannonsville Dam
    Down by the Railroad Track
    Freight #1262
    Gravy and Bread
    It's a Wonder
    Kitty Sharp
    Larry O'Gaff
    Legend of Slide Mountain
    Little Red Barn, The
    Pat McBraid
    Place Called Hell, A
    Rogers' Hornpipe
    Tales of My Grandad
    Three Nights Drunk [C. 274]
    When a Fellow is Out of a Job
    Willie Down by the Pond [G 19]

143   Label Name/Number: Kanawha 308
Title: *Ballad Singer*
Artist: Grant Rogers
Recordist: Grant Rogers
Producer: Ken Davidson
Place of Recording: Walton, NY
Date of Publication: [ca. 1965]
Annotations: Liner notes by Grant Rogers
Selections:
    Charley Brooks
    First Whipper-Will Song, The
    From Texas to Alaska
    Good Old Limburger Cheese
    In the Last Chance Saloon
    Little Box of Pine
    My Little Home in Tennessee

Pat Malone
Paving the Highway with Tears
Take Your Time and Think It Over
Too Young to Understand the Sorrow
Twenty Years Behind Time
Wars by the Numbers
Where the Catskills Reach Their Summits
Willie the Weaver

144 Label Name/Number: Kanawha 313
Title: *Ballads and Fiddle Tunes*
Artist: Grant Rogers
Date of Publication: [ca. 1970]
Annotations: Liner notes by Grant Rogers
Selections:

Aunt Emmy's Tea Party
Black Market Reel
Conservation Hornpipe
Little Red Barn, The
May I Sleep in Your Barn
Mother the Queen of My Heart
My Bearded Lover
Opera Reel
Puttin' on the Style
Two Drummers
Weeping Lady, The
When the Snowflakes Fall Again

FLeg FSA-27 / Kan 308 / Kan 313: Grant Rogers was born in Walton, NY, in around 1907. He learned to play the fiddle when quite young, and was already playing for dances in the Delaware River Valley by age seven. Much later, he began to play guitar and write his own songs. By 1950 he was sufficiently well-known as a local performer that Norman Studer invited him to perform at Camp Woodland, where he came to the attention of other folksong enthusiasts. Rogers is a good example of a contemporary regional folk musician, adding to his repertoire of older material with his own locally-based compositions as the need or mood arises. Paton's booklet to FSA-27 includes a brief biographical sketch, text transcriptions, and notes on the selection. On Kanawha 308 Rogers performs traditional and hillbilly material as well as his own compositions. In his liner notes, Rogers acknowledges his debt to phonograph records for several of his songs (e.g., "Charley Brooks," "Little Box of Pine"). Despite the liner notes, "Willie the Weaver" is not Q 9, but rather the grand-daddy of psychedelic pipe-dreams, "Willie the Weeper." Most of the other selections are his own composition. Kanawha 313 consists mostly of sentimental parlor ballads popularized by Jimmie Rodgers, Vernon Dalhart, and others; and fiddles tunes of uncertain traditional content. [WF 4/68, 7/72; JAF 314--DKW (Kan 308); JAF 320--DKW (FSA 27)]

145 Label Name/Number: Marimac 9013 [cass]
Title: *Farmer's Frolic*
Artists: The Ross County Farmers (Lonnie Seymour, Tony Ellis, Jeff Goehring)
Collector/Recordist: Larry MacBride
Place and Date of Recording: OH, 1986
Date of Publication: 1987
Annotations: Insert notes by Jeff Goehring and Larry MacBride

Selections:
    Beautiful Life
    Casey Jones
    Chillicothe Two-Step
    Chum's Hornpipe
    Come Thy Fount of Every Blessing
    Darling Honey
    Dixie Blues
    Evening Shade
    Feast Here Tonight
    Gonna See My Mama
    Gray Eagle
    Log Chain
    Midnight on the Stormy Deep
    Old Coon Dog, The
    Please Come Back Little Pal
    Sally in the Green Corn
    Shortning Bread
    Stand Boys Stand
    Sugar Barrell
    Tomahawk
    Uncle Joe
    Uncle Mitt
    Webb's Tune

Mar 9013: The Ross County (Ohio) Farmers (Seymour, fiddle; Ellis, banjo/vocal; Goehring, guitar/vocal), render 22 songs and fiddle tunes, some from older Ohio tradition ("The Old Coon Dog," "Gonna See My Mama," "Sugar Barrell," "Chillicothe Two-Step," "Uncle Mitt," "Sally in the Green Corn," "Log Chain"), others from popular hillbilly recording artists of the 1930s, such as Fiddlin' Arthur Smith and the Monroe Brothers. The band's sound is basically pre-bluegrass, but with Scruggs-style banjo-picking. The tunes and sources are identified in the cassette insert.

146   Label Name/Number: Biograph RC 6004
Title: *Traditional Country Music*
Artists: Betsy Rutherford accomp. by Tim Woodbridge, Art Bryan, John Coffey, Pete Colby,
    Neil Rossi, Rusty Strange
Producer: Arnold S. Caplin
Date of Publication: [1972?]
Annotations: Liner notes by John Coffey
Selections:
    Amazing Grace
    Blue
    Boys, Be Good to Dear Old Dad
    Drunkard's Doom
    Faded Coat of Blue
    John Hardy [I 2]
    Rain and Snow
    Tramp on the Street
    West Virginia Mine Disaster, The
    Will the Circle Be Unbroken

Bio RC 6004: This LP features Betsy Rutherford (1944-91), a young singer from Galax and a scion of the musical family that includes the well-known Ward clan. She performs gospel hymns, sentimental songs, ballads, and lyric songs in a clear and strong voice, backed tastefully by a band of northern musicians, including her husband, John Coffey. [WF 7/72; JAF 338--DKW].

147 Label Name/Number: Prestige International INT 25007
Title: *All Day Singing from "The Sacred Harp": Southern Journey 7*
Artists: The Alabama Sacred Harp Singers, led by: Maud Quinn, W. W. Kidd, Mrs. King Roberts, Eugene Dawson, M. O. Slaughter, Velma Johnson, Virginia Dell Shrader, Enis Wall, J. Edge, J. H. Lambert, Uncle Will Laminack, Budford King, Martin Blackman, Reba Dell Lacy, M. O. Kennedy
Collector/Recordist: Alan Lomax with Shirley Collins and Anne Lomax
Producer: Kenneth S. Goldstein
Place and Date of Recording: AL, GA, VA; 1959-60
Date of Publication: [1961]
Annotations: Jacket notes and 7-page booklet by Alan Lomax
Selections:

Amsterdam
Cusseta
David's Lamentation
Greenwich
Last Words of Copernicus
Loving Jesus
Melancholy Day
Milford
Montgomery
Morning Trumpet, The
Mt. Zion
Sherburne
Sinner's Friend
Traveling on
Victoria
We'll All Sing Hallelujah
Windham
Wondrous Love

Prest INT 25007: In 1959, Lomax returned to the South with modern stereo tape recording equipment, intent on recapturing in high fidelity the music that had so entranced him and his father two decades earlier. In Fyffe, northeastern Alabama, he was invited to a weekend singing convention, where the songs on the following album and most of those on this album were recorded. The jacket notes describe the setting at that singing convention. The recordings exemplify the sacred harp style that untutored listeners will find very strange indeed (see also notes to Folkways FA 2356 for a fuller description of the music). Lomax notes that he found the tradition to be every bit as strong, if not stronger, in 1959 than it was in 1942 when he first recorded these songs. "David's Lamentation" is, to my ears, one of the most striking pieces of the Sacred Harp repertoire. [JAF 301--DKW]

148 Label Name/Number: New World NW 205
Title: *White Spirituals from The Sacred Harp*
Artists: Daniel Read, William Billings, H. S. Rees, A. M. Cagle, Joyce Smith, S. M. Denson, J. S. James, M. L. A. Lancaster, William Walker, White and Searcy, John Stephenson, B. F.

White, James Nares, David Morgan, R. Osborne, John Massengale, Sarah Lancaster, Howard Denson, Jeremiah Ingalls

Collector/Recordist/Editor: Alan Lomax
Place and Date of Recording: AL, 1959
Date of Publication: 1977
Annotations: 4 p. insewn notes by Alan Lomax
Selections:
> Amsterdam
> Baptismal Anthem
> Cusseta
> David's Lamentation
> Greenwich
> Hallelujah
> Homeward Bound
> Last Words of Copernicus
> Loving Jesus
> Melancholy Day
> Milford
> Montgomery
> Morning Trumpet
> New Harmony
> North Port
> Northfield
> Sherburne
> Soar Away
> Traveling On
> Wondrous Love

NW 205: New World Records was the label of the Recorded Anthology of American Music, Inc., an enterprise established in the mid-1970s with a $4 million grant from the Rockefeller Foundation. Its express purpose was the production of a set of sound recordings of American music to commemmorate the Bicentennial. Eight thousand sets of 100 albums were distributed free of charge to selected libraries and other educational institutions across the country; additional sets were to be sold for a nominal $195 fee to other educational institutions. Initially, the selections were heavily focused on "high culture" music, with some jazz and pop music playing "second fiddle," but the insistence of a few advisers with a broader perspective won a concession of a handful of albums devoted to folk traditions. Several years after their issue, some of the albums were made available through record stores. Seven more New World albums are listed in Section II; another one is listed in Section IV. New World has continued to issue a handful of recordings (e. g., NW 314/315, Section II) subsequent to the initial 100. All the albums are well edited by experts in their respective fields; all are excellent broad surveys of some aspect of traditional American music.

The songs on this LP, recorded at Fyffe, Alabama in 1959 (see notes to preceding album), are all from the Original Sacred Harp (OSH) hymnal, and were written between the early 1800s and 1935. The notes include facsimile reproductions from OSH of the 20 songs.

149   Label Name/Number: June Appal JA0055
Title: *Rock Dust*
Artist: Morgan Sexton with Lee "Boy" Sexton
Collector/Recordist: Doug Dorschug
Producer: D. Gregory White
Place and Date of Recording: KY, 1988

Date of Publication: 1989
Annotations: 8 p. booklet by D. Gregory White
Selections:

> Froggy Went A-Courtin'
> Goin' Down in Town
> Hook and Line
> It's a Beautiful Doll
> Jenny Get Around
> John Henry
> Last of Callahan, The
> Little Bessie
> Little Birdie
> Little Frankie [I 3]
> Little Sparrow
> London City Where I Did Dwell [P 24]
> Lonesome Scene of Winter
> Mexico
> Old Aunt Jenny
> Old East Virginia
> Old Grey Beard
> Omie Wise [F 4]
> Uncle Ned

JA0055: Another fine traditional Appalachian ballad singer recorded by June Appal is Morgan Sexton (1911-92), born in Linefork, eastern Kentucky. Sexton, a retired coal miner suffering from occupational lung disorders, has been playing the banjo for 70 years. *Rock Dust*--the title alludes to the powdered limestone used to prevent coal dust explosions in the mines--presents 19 selections featuring Sexton's singing and playing (two with fiddle accompaniment by his nephew, Lee Sexton) from recordings made in late 1988. Sexton, who has severe pulmonary problems from his years of mine work, is not an easy singer to understand, and the printed song texts (not always completely accurate) are indispensable in trying to decipher his lyrics. Otherwise, he is an enjoyable singer, gentle and relaxed, with an unusual penchant for slowing down on the last phrase of a song. He accompanies himself with a clean, characteristic two-finger Kentucky banjo frailing style, frequently in non-standard tunings. Ballads include "London City Where I Did Dwell" and the 19th-century sentimental piece, "Little Bessie." Of his "Old Grey Beard," Sexton said "that's a song I mostly made up myself." Though the tune is the usual one, possibly some of the stanzas of this imported humorous courting song are his own. He also contributed his own final stanza to "Froggy Went A-Courtin'." [JAF 397]

150 Label Name/Number: Rounder Records 0078
Title: *Early Shaker Spirituals*
Artists: Sister R. Mildred Barker with Sisters Ethel Peacock, Elsie McCool, Della Haskell, Marie Burgess, Frances Carr, & other members of the United Society of Shakers
Collector/Recordist: Jonathan D. Tankel
Place and Date of Recording: Sabbathday Lake, ME; 1963, 1966, 1970, 1976
Date of Publication: 1976
Annotations: 19 p. booklet by Daniel W. Patterson
Selections:

> Blessed, Thrice Blessed
> Bow Down, O Zion
> Come Life, Shaker Life

Down in the Lowly Vale
Down to the Deep and Rolling River
Farewell, Earthly Joy
Gospel is Advancing, The
Gospel Kindred, How I Love You
How Lovely Are the Faithful Souls
I Bless the Day
I Feel the Need of a Deeper Baptism
I Hunger and Thirst
I Looked and Lo a Lamb
I Love Mother, I Love Her Way
I Never Did Believe
I Will Walk with My Children
I'll Spend and Be Spent
Let Me Have Mother's Gospel
Little Children
Love Is Little
Love, More Love
Low Down in the Valley
Low, Low in This Pretty Path
My Home, My Sweet Home in Zion
O Brighter Than the Morning Star
O Give Me a Little Love
O Holy Father
O the Gospel of Mother
On Sister Paulina Springer
On Zion's Holy Ground
Rolling Deep, The
This Gospel How Precious
'Tis the Gift To Be Simple
We Must Be Meek
We Will All Go Home with You
Where Is the Gem
Who Will Bow and Bend Like the Willow
With a New Tongue
Yielding and Simple

Rndr 0078:   The Shakers, formally called the United Society of Believers in Christ's Second Appearing, formed as a group in New York the 1770s, followers of Ann Lee, an English preacher who had fled to America to escape mob violence and harassment from the law. The Shakers gained strength through the 19th century and established several communities. They had very definite ideas about the role of music in their worship: instruments were forbidden, as was part singing and use of trained choirs and hired professional singers. They were dissatisfied with the customary psalms and hymns of the other denominations, such as Presbyterians, Congregationalists, Baptists, or Methodists and felt a need to compose their own new songs, often using familiar secular tunes. The renditions on this album, all by members of the Shaker community at Sabbathday Lake, Maine, are simple and dignified, sung in undecorated and untrained voices. They are "arranged in groupings that show several aspects of the Shaker repertory," and all date from the 1820s through 1880s. Patterson's excellent brochure provides detailed background on the Shakers, their beliefs and history, and their music.

151   Label Name/Number: June Appal 032
Title: *In Full Swing*
Artists: Luke Smathers String Band: Luke Smathers, Harold Smathers, J.T. Smathers with Charles
      Gidney, Bea Smathers, David Holt
Date of Recording: [ca. 1979]
Date of Publication: 1981
Annotations: Liner notes by Charles Wolfe
Selections:
      Alabama Jubilee
      Bill in the Lowground
      Bully of the Town
      Cimarron
      Dinah
      I'll Keep Loving You
      Indian Love Call
      Meet Me by the Ice House Lizzie
      Memphis Blues
      Mona Lisa
      Sally Ann
      Tiger Rag
      Up the Lazy River
      Walking in My Sleep

   JA 032: Luke Smathers's Asheville, North Carolina, band started as a traditional southeastern-styled stringband in the late 1920s and switched to swing style in the early '30s. It thus represents a musical aggregation at the periphery of the traditional styles included in this discographic survey. The music consists of four older traditional fiddle tunes sandwiched between more recent pop-derived one-time favorites. The band's chosen redirection did not leave a traceless path: there is a curious incongruence between Smathers' own fiddle style and the band's repertoire and other instrumental styles. Smathers' short, choppy bowstrokes are still more characteristic of southeastern bands (especially Georgian) of the 1920s, while the music that the band plays is generally associated with a smooth, jazzy, long bowstroke style. [JAF 408]

152   Label Name/Number: June Appal 018
Title: *For My Friends of Song*
Artist: Betty Smith with John McCutcheon, Jack Wright, Grey Larsen
Recordists: Jack Wright & Jeff Kiser
Editors: Jack Wright, Betty & Bill Smith, Mark Beach, Jeff Kiser
Date of Recording: [ca. 1977]
Date of Publication: 1977
Annotations: 13 p. booklet by Betty Smith
Selections:
      Ballad of Bascom Lunsford, The
      Black Waters
      Bury Me Not on the Lone Prairie [B 2]
      Darby's Ram
      Gentle Maiden
      Knoxville Girl [P 35]
      Lady Isabel and the Elfin Knight [C. 4]
      Little Liza Jane
      Little Margaret [C. 74]

Rolling Hills of the Border, The
Softly Come the Gypsy
Starry Night for Ramble, A
There Once Was an Owl
True Lover's Farewell, The
When They Ring the Golden Bells

JA 018: Betty Smith is a collector of folksongs who, though she grew up in North Carolina and Kentucky and has heard traditional music all her life, continues to add to her repertoire from traditional singers she has met and also from published sources. In addition she sings pieces of recent composition (e. g., Bob Beers' setting of John Ciardi's poem, "There Once Was an Owl" and Jean Ritchie's "Black Waters") and has written some of her own, one of which is her tribute to the great singer/collector of North Carolina, Bascom Lunsford. All pieces are sung in her delicate, pretty voice, with pleasant instrumental accompaniment on psaltery, dulcimer, and/or guitar. The brochure includes notes on the songs and text transcriptions. [JEMFQ 53]

153   Label Name/Number: Folk-Legacy FSA-17
Title: *America's Greatest Folk Instrumentalist*
Artist: Hobart Smith
Collector/Recordist: Norm Pellegrini
Place and Date of Recording: Chicago, IL, 1963
Date of Publication: 1964
Annotations: 21 p. booklet by George Armstrong
Selections:
Black Annie
Bonaparte's Retreat
Chinquapin Pie
Cindy
Columbus Stockade
Cuckoo Bird
Devil and the Farmer's Wife, The [C. 278]
Girl I Left Behind, The
Great Titanic, The
John Greer's Tune
John Hardy
Last Chance
Meet Me in Rose Time, Rosie
Peg and Awl
Sally Ann
Short Life in Trouble
Sitting on Top of the World
Soldier's Joy (2 versions)
Stormy Rose the Ocean
Uncloudy Day

FLeg FSA-17: Hobart Smith was born in Smyth County, Virginia, in 1897--the seventh generation of Smiths in Virginia since his ancestors emigrated from England. He began playing banjo when seven years old, and later, guitar, fiddle, and piano. He was first recorded by Alan Lomax (1942) for the Library of Congress and subsequently on the Disc, Tradition, Atlantic, and Prestige labels, but this set of recordings marks his first solo album and the broadest exposure of his considerable talents. Smith was an excellent and versatile musician, but the album's title must be taken *cum granum salis*. The brochure notes include Smith's own recollections of his musical career; Fleming Brown's comments on Smith's banjo style, headnotes to the selections, text transcriptions, and a discography of other Smith recordings. Smith performed locally considerably during the '30s and '40s, and his repertoire includes country tunes of the day, but Smith recalls that it was Alan Lomax who urged him to "pull back into the old folk music"--which is what is represented on this album. [JAF 313--DKW]

154 Label Name/Number: Elektra EKL-316/EKS-7316
Title: *Oliver Smith*
Artist: Oliver Smith
Collector/Recordist: Peter Siegel
Place of Recording: New York City
Date of Publication: 1966
Annotations: Liner notes by Paul Nelson
Selections:

> Blue Ridge Mountain Blues
> Breeze
> Everybody Works But Father
> Gambling on the Sabbath Day [E 14]
> Guitar Pickin' Sam
> I Only Want a Buddy
> Just A Closer Walk With Thee
> K. C. Blow
> Little Box of Pine on the "729"
> Manhattan Blues
> Pickin' the Guitar
> Satisfied
> Six Feet of Earth
> Twenty-One Years [E 16]

Elektra EKL-316: Smith was a 55-year-old blind itinerant street singer in New York when Peter Siegel "discovered" him some time in the 1960s. He had been reared in Atlanta, Ga., and took to supporting himself and his family as a street singer some 37 years earlier. He claimed to have played with Riley Puckett (the very popular hillbilly musician who recorded extensively with Gid Tanner's Skillet Lickers), and his musical style certainly supports the assertion. Smith plays in vigorous, self-assured manner of a good street musician and sings accordingly. [JAF 317--DKW]

155 Label Name/Number: Asch AH 3902
Title: *Country Songs and Tunes with Autoharp*
Artist(s): Kilby Snow
Collector/Recordist: Mike Seeger
Place and Date of Recording: In auditorium of Unionville-Chaddsford Jr./Sr. High School near Kenneth Square, PA, 1966
Date of Publication: 1969
Annotations: 6 p. booklet by Mike Seeger
Selections:

> 'Round Town Girls
> Autoharp Special
> Budded Roses
> Cannonball, The
> Flop-eared Mule

Greenback Dollar
I Will Arise
Lonely Tombs
Mean Women
Molly Hare
No Tears in Heaven
Old Crossroads, The
Road That's Walked by Fools, The
Shady Grove
Sourwood Mountain
Two-Timing Blues
Wind and Rain [C. 10]
Woodrow for President

Asch AH 3902: Some of the best-known autoharp players have come from Virginia, and John Kilby Snow (1905-1980) of Grayson County was one of the finest traditional instrumentalists I have heard. In addition to instrumental numbers, Snow's repertoire includes some older ballads and contemporary country songs. A broad selection, recorded in 1966 by Seeger, is heard on this LP. Most interesting is his "Rain and Snow" (C. 10), basically the same as #93 in Bronson's collection of versions (*Traditional Tunes of the Child Ballads*) but with significant intrusions of "Knoxville Girl," so that the story presented is one of murder by a rejected lover rather than a jealous sister. It is a natural concatenation, joined at the verse in which the victim is thrown into the river to drown. Snow has written some fine songs himself. [WF 7/72]

156   Label Name/Number: County 201
Title: *The Old Virginia Fiddlers: Old Time Fiddle Music from Patrick County, Virginia*
Artist(s): J. W. "Babe" Spangler, Dudley "Babe" Spangler, Maggie Wood, and Harry Pendleton
Producer: Barry Poss and Tom Carter
Place and Date of Recording: Danville, VA, 1948; Mt. Airy, NC, 1948-49; 2 from 1929 commercial 78 recording
Date of Publication: 1977
Annotations: 4 p. insert brochure by Carter and Poss
Selections:

Coon Dog
Georgia Camp Meeting
Hop Light Ladies
Jenny Lind Polka
Leather Britches
Midnight Serenade
Mississippi Sawyer
Patrick County Blues
Rock the Cradle Joe
Saro
Schottische
Susanna Gal
Tommy Love
Walking in My Sleep

County 201: John Watts "Babe" Spangler (b. 1882), was the son of Wallace Spangler (1851-1926), one of the best old-time fiddlers in Patrick County and an influence on many next-generation musicians. J. W. made two commercial recordings in 1929 ("Midnight Serenade" and "Patrick

County Blues"); at the time he had a regular radio program over WRVA, Richmond, under the pseudonym, "The Old Virginia Fiddler." Dudley Spangler was J. W.'s second cousin and brother-in-law. Maggie Reynolds Wood and Harry Pendleton are friends, also from the Meadows of Dan, Virginia, area. The 1948-49 recordings were made in a furniture store in Danville and at station WPAQ, Mt. Airy, at the artists' instigation simply to preserve their music and never intended for public issue. They are somewhat scratchy but listenable. Carter and Poss provide biographical information and tune identifications.

157 Label Name/Number: Bear Family BCD 15456 [CD]
Title: *Classic Cowboy Songs*
Artist(s): Carl T. Sprague
Producer: Richard Weize
Place and Date of Recording: Bryan, TX; 1972, 1974
Date of Publication: 1988 (Most selections previously issued on Folk Variety FV 12001/Bear
       Family BF 15002 [1974], and Bear Family BF 15006)
Annotations: 24 p. insert brochure by John I. White
Selections:

 Bad Companions [E 15]
 Boston Burglar, The [L 16b]
 Chicken
 Club Meeting, The
 Cowboy's Meditation, The
 Cowman's Prayer
 Following the Cowtrail [B 13]
 Gambler, The [E 14]
 Girl I Loved in Sunny Tennessee, The
 Home on the Range
 It Is No Secret
 Just Break the News to Mother
 Kicking Mule, The
 Kissing
 Last Fierce Charge, The [A 17]
 Last Great Roundup, The
 Mormon Cowboy, The
 My Carrie Lee
 Orphan Girl, The
 Red River Valley
 Roll On Little Dogies
 Rounded up in Glory
 Sarah Jane
 Utah Carol [B 4]
 When the Work's All Done This Fall [B 3]
 Zebra Dun [B 16]

Bear Family BCD 15456: One of the first westerners to record cowboy songs was Carl T. Sprague (1895-1978). During his college years at Texas A & M, Sprague had his own band, and after he joined that faculty's athletic department, he hosted a regular program on the college radio station. Vernon Dalhart's phenomenal success with "The Prisoner's Song" convinced Sprague to contact the Victor Talking Machine Company to see if he could record some of his cowboy songs, which he did in the summer of 1925. Sprague recorded several times for Victor in the next four years and then gave up his musical career--until the folk revival of the 1960s lured him back to college campuses to sing some of his old favorites. In 1972-74 he taped a number of his old songs, which were issued on two LPs by Richard Weize on his Folk Variety and Bear Family labels. Classic Cowboy Songs is a CD reissue of those two LPs, with a 24-page enclosed brochure containing a biographical sketch and song annotations by cowboy song authority (and one-time cowboy singer himself) John I. White and text transcriptions. The 26 selections include some of the best known cowboy ballads and songs from the last part of the 19th century ("When the Work's All Done This Fall," "Utah Carrol," "Zebra Dun," "Red River Valley," "Home on the Range," "Following the Cowtrail"); other traditional ballads of older vintage ("Boston Burglar," "The Gambler," "Bad Companions," "The Last Fierce Charge," "The Orphan Girl"); some Tin Pan Alley-derived pieces ("The Girl I Loved in Sunny Tennessee" [1899], "Just Break the News to Mother" [1897], "The Club Meeting ["Down to the Club," 1876]); and one relatively recent composition, Stuart Hamblen's "It Is No Secret What God Can Do" (1951). Except for a few numbers with second guitar, Sprague sings in a very unornamented style to his own simple guitar accompaniment, sounding much as he had some 50 years earlier. [JAF 409]

158   Label Name/Number: June Appal JA 010
Title: *Red Wing*
Artist: I. D. Stamper with John McCutcheon
Collector/Recordist: John McCutcheon, Jack Wright, John Harrod
Editor: John McCutcheon, Jack Wright
Date of Recording: [ca. 1977]
Date of Publication: 1977
Annotations: Liner notes by McCutcheon
Selections:
>Barbry Allen
>Darlin' Corey
>Down South Blues
>Going Round This World
>Ground Hog
>I Can't Change It
>Jack & Joe
>John Henry
>Lost John
>Marching Thru Georgia
>Married Life Blues
>Meet Me Tonight
>900 Miles
>Pretty Polly [P 36b]
>Rattlesnake Bill
>Red Wing
>Sourwood Mountain

JA 010: Septuagenarian I. D. Stamper of eastern Kentucky plays mostly dulcimer, which he himself builds, but also harmonica and banjo in a program of familiar titles, some with vocals. The Appalachian dulcimer, never a common instrument in the United States, is a type of zither. It has three or more strings, all but one of which are drones; the single melody string is fretted diatonically; the strings are strummed either with the fingers, or with a strummer--a plastic pick now but formerly a turkey or goose quill; and stopped with a wooden noter or the fingers of the other hand.

159   Label Name/Number: County 739 (originally issued on Wango 104)
Title: *The Stanley Brothers of Virginia: Vol. 2 -- Long Journey Home*
Artists: Carter and Ralph Stanley, with George Shuffler
Collector/Recordist: Ray Davis
Date of Recording: Early 1960s
Date of Publication: 1973 (early 1960s on Wango)
Annotations: Back jacket liner notes by Bill Vernon
Selections:

> Cluck Old Hen
> East Virginia Blues
> I'll Be True to the One That I Love
> Long Journey Home
> Mountain Pickin'
> Nine Pound Hammer
> No Letter in the Mail Today
> Pig in a Pen
> Pretty Polly [P 36b]
> Rabbit in a Log
> Ramshackle Shack on the Hill
> Two More Years and I'll Be Free
> Wild and Reckless Hobo [H 2]
> Wildwood Flower
> Will You Miss Me
> Your Saddle Is Empty Old Pal

Cty 739:   Ralph and Carter Stanley were one of the three or four most successful and popular bluegrass bands from the early years of the emergence of the genre (mid-1940s) until Carter's death in 1966, after which Ralph continued with his own band. They were born in McClure, Virginia, Carter in 1925 and Ralph in 1927, and learned to play banjo in their youth from their mother. The Stanleys performed many contemporary bluegrass hits, some of their own composition, but also frequently drew upon their own Virginia roots to tap a much more traditional repertoire--a side of their music that they quickly learned was more popular with their Northern college audiences. This unusual album was one of the first that demonstrated how easily the Stanleys could slip into their older repertoire. With just their own guitar and banjo accompaniment, joined by lead guitarist George Shuffler--no fiddle or mandolin--the style is generally much older than bluegrass. The Stanleys' outstanding vocal work--intense, hard-driving, biting--is one of their hallmarks, and this album is an excellent example. Ralph's piercing lead vocal on "Pretty Polly" makes this one of the best versions of an oft-recorded bluegrass standard; the four-part vocal on "Will You Miss Me" (the trio is joined by Jack Cooke accompanied by Shuffler's McReynolds-patterned guitar flat-picking breaks), is hauntingly beautiful.

160   Label Name/Number: Folkways FS 3828
Title: *Banjo Tunes and Songs*
Artist: Pete Steele
Collector/Recordist: Ed Kahn
Place and Date of Recording: Hamilton, OH, 1957
Date of Publication: 1958
Annotations: 7 p. booklet by Ed Kahn
Selections:

> Coal Creek March
> Cuckoo, The

East Virginia
Ellen Smith [F 11]
Galilee
Goin' Around This World Baby Mine
Hard Times
House Carpenter, The [C. 243]
Ida Red
Last Pay Day at Coal Creek
Little Birdie
Pretty Polly [P 36b]
Scoldin' Wife, The [C. 278]
Shady Grove
Train A-Pullin' the Crooked Hill, The
Unclouded Days, The
War Is A-Ragin' for Johnny, The [O 33]

Fwys FS 3828: Ed Kahn was a student at Oberlin College when, in 1957, he and Art Rosenbaum decided to visit Pete and Lillie Steele in Hamilton, Ohio. Kahn knew of Steele through his LC recordings. Steele (1891-1985) was born in Kentucky, but after several moves he and his wife settled in Hamilton in 1937. Alan Lomax recorded them there in the following year for the LC. Steele was a versatile banjo player, and used several different styles (though always using only two fingers--thumb and forefinger), including frailing, double-thumbing, and up-picking. Kahn's brochure notes include a biographical sketch, headnotes for the selections, and comments on Steele's playing style and banjo-tuning. Most of the selections are familiar renditions of songs and tunes fairly well known in the Kentucky area. Kahn notes the interesting final stanzas of Steele's "House Carpenter," which add uncharacteristic moralization to this old tale of infidelity. Steele's singing is unremarkable, except for the charm of his matter-of-fact approach--in particular in his performance of (and introduction to) "The War Is A-Ragin'." [JAF 285--DKW]

161   Label Name/Number: Folk-Legacy FSA-18
Title: *Take the News to Mother*
Artist: Arnold Keith Storm
Collector/Recordist: Pat Dunford
Place and Date of Recording: Indianapolis, IN, 1963-64
Date of Publication: 1964
Annotations: 25 p. booklet by Pat Dunford and Sandy Paton
Selections:
   Blind Child, The
   Boy Who Could Never Come Home, The
   Dream of the Miner's Child, The
   Great Explosion, The
   Jim Blake, Your Wife Is Dying
   Little Joe, the Wrangler [B 5]
   Little Rosewood Casket
   Ninety and Nine
   Patched Up Old Devil
   Poor Little Joe
   Prison Warden's Secret, The
   Sparrow's Question, The
   Take the News to Mother
   There's A Mother Always Waiting You at Home

Two Drummers
Utah Carl [B 4]

FLeg FSA-18: For several years after its release, this was one of the best collections of the sentimental pop songs current in oral tradition. Storm is a young singer who learned many of these songs during his childhood in rural Illinois from his father, who, in turn, learned them from relatives and neighbors. The notes, by collector Dunford and Folk-Legacy's proprietor, Paton, justly take other collectors and scholars to task for their neglect of similar material. However, by their somewhat cavalier disregard for the commercial phonograph tradition, they omit an important link in the development and mar an otherwise sound treatment of, the material. They fail to note, for example, that Storm's rendition of "Two Drummers" (or "Mother Was a Lady"), the Marks-Stern TPA hit of 1896, obviously owes much to the Jimmie Rodgers recording, although in some textual details it is closer to the original. Likewise, Storm's text to "Take the News to Mother," originally written by the successful TPA composer Charles K. Harris in 1897, can be traced more directly to the version recorded in 1935 by the Callahan Brothers and more recently by other country groups. The album also contains two older traditional ballads (B 4 and B 5) and two of Storm's own compositions. He accompanies himself on guitar and harmonica, singing in a bland and undecorated style. [WF 4/68; JAF 307--DKW]

162   Label Name/Number: Rounder 0194
Title: *Indiana Fiddler*
Artist(s): John W. Summers
Collector/Recordist: Judge Dan White, Art Rosenbaum, and Joel and Kathy Shimberg
Producer: Bob Carlin
Place and Date of Recording: KY, 1962-72
Date of Publication: 1984
Annotations: 8 p. brochure by Joel and Kathy Shimberg, assisted by Bob Carlin and Art Rosenbaum
Selections:

Arthur Berry
Black Eyed Susan
Bunch of Chickens
Chicken Reel
Crazy Jim
Durang's Hornpipe
Five Leaf Clover
Forked Deer
Grand Hornpipe
Grey Eagle
Jig
Old Dan Tucker
Opera Reel
Pretty Little Girl with the Blue Dress On
Two unnamed tunes

Rndr 0194: John Summers, an outstanding fiddler from Indiana who never played professionally, was not recorded until late in life. Some of his recordings have been published previously, but this is the first LP devoted fully to him. Rosenberg's essay is aptly titled "An Appreciation" and portrays a musician whom the reader/listener wishes to have known personally. Most of the selections are fiddle solos; a few from the 1962 session have obtrusive surface noise. [JAF 391]

163   Label Name/Number: June Appal 030
Title: *Road to Home*
Artists: Marion Sumner with Dennis Breeding, Sonny Houston, Alfred "Badeye" Combs, Phyllis
      Moyer, Joe Stuart, Josh Graves, Gordon Reid, George Helton, Clyde & Mary Denny
Collector/Recordists: Dudley Wilson & Jack Wright
Producers: Sonny Houston, Marion Sumner, Jack Wright
Date of Recording: 1979
Date of Publication: [1980]
Annotations: Liner notes by Sharon Hatfield
Selections:
      Beaumont Rag
      Bill Cheatum
      Blackey Rag
      Darling Nellie Gray
      Dragging the Bow
      Dreaming of the Georgiana Moon
      Gold Rush
      Hollow Poplar
      Lady Be Good
      Little Rock Getaway
      Sally Goodin
      Steel Guitar Rag
      Sweet Georgia Brown
      Texahoma Boogie
      There'll Be Some Changes Made
      Up the Lazy River
      Waltz You Saved for Me, The
      Whispering
      Who's Sorry Now

     JA 030: Marion Sumner, born in 1920 and reared in Hazard, Kentucky, played profes-
sionally with many hillbilly-country musicians between 1936 and 1965, including Cousin Emmy, Jim
and Jesse McReynolds, Cowboy Copas, Johnny and Jack, and Don Gibson, and thus had experience
with a wide variety of fiddling styles before retiring. His album includes 19 selections (on three of
which he plays lead guitar), from older tunes such as "Sally Goodin'" and "Bill Cheatum" to western-
swing titles ("Dragging the Bow" and "Beaumont Rag") and pop perennials ("Sweet Georgia
Brown," "Whispering," "Lady be Good"). Sharon Hatfield provides back jacket biographical notes
and Charles Wolfe writes program notes on the inner sleeve.

164   Label Name/Number: Folkways FES 31089
Title: *Down Yonder: Old-Time String Band Music from Georgia*
Artists: Gordon Tanner, Smokey Joe Miller, Uncle John Patterson, and Phil Tanner and the Jr.
      Skillet Lickers
Collector/Recordist/Editor: Art Rosenbaum
Place and Date of Recording: Dacula and Campton, GA, 1977-81
Date of Publication: 1982
Annotations: 6 p. booklet by Art Rosenbaum
Selections:
      Arkansas Traveler
      Billy in the Low Ground
      Bully of the Town

Carrol County Blues
Down Yonder
Four Night's Experience [C. 274]
Goin' Down the Road Feelin' Bad
Goodbye, Little Bonnie Blue Eyes
Hand Me Down My Walking Cane
Hop Light, Ladies
I Wish I'd Bought a Half a Pint and Stayed in the Wagon Yard
Listen to the Mockingbird
Lonesome Hungry Hash House
Medley: Cumberland Gap/Gid Tanner's Buckin' Mule/Hen Cackle
Out of My Bondage

Fwys FES 31089: Born in 1916 in Gwinnett County, son of the legendary north Georgia musician, Gid Tanner, Gordon Tanner ably carries on his famous father's legacy. Gordon was playing with his father's bands when he was scarcely 14 years old, and made his first recordings in 1934, taking the lead fiddle on some of the Skillet Lickers' best-selling titles, one of which, "Down Yonder," is re-recorded on this disc. Tanner is joined by Uncle John Patterson, banjo (heard also on Arhoolie 5018, q. v.), long-time friend Joe Miller on guitar, and his son, Phil on some tracks. Many of the titles were associated with Gid Tanner.

165　Label Name/Number: Testament T-3302
Title: *Steel Guitar Rag*
Artist: Jimmie Tarlton
Collector/Recordist/Editor: Eugene Earle
Place and Date of Recording: Roanoke, AL, 1963; and at the Ash Grove, Hollywood, Calif., 1965
Date of Publication: 1967
Annotations: 23 p. brochure by Norm Cohen; liner notes by Anne Cohen
Selections:

Administration Blues
Ain't It a Shame to Gamble on a Sunday
All Bound Down in Birmingham Jail
Banks of the Ohio [F 5]
Fort Benning Blues
Hawaiian March
Jimmie's Blue Heaven
Joe Bowers [B 14]
John Henry [I 1]
Lowe Bonnie [C. 68]
Pretty Little Girl
Put-Together Blues
Steel Guitar Rag
Uncle Joe and His Hounds

Test T-3302: Jimmie Tarlton, born (1892) in Chesterfield County, So. Carolina, learned to play banjo from his father and ballads from his mother and grandmother. After hearing travelling Hawaiian guitarists he began playing Hawaiian style guitar and, with his musical partner, Tom Darby, recorded over 75 songs between 1927 and 1933. He was "rediscovered" in 1963, and for several years enjoyed a second musical career performing at folk festivals and coffee houses during the halcyon folksong revival years. On this album, he plays mostly steel-guitar style but also a few tunes on banjo, as he had in his youth. His repertoire ranges from old Child ballads to his own compositions ("Administration Blues," about Franklin D. Roosevelt's reelection), and recompositions of Tin Pan Alley songs ("My Blue Heaven"). At age 71, Tarlton was still an excellent singer, with a beautiful, high, clear voice, and amazing guitarist, whose near-blindness did not prevent him from keeping an audience spellbound through his deft performances and stories. The lengthy brochure notes include extensive song annotations and references, text and tune transcriptions, and a full Darby/Tarlton discography.

166   Label Name/Number: Rounder 0032
Title: *Kitty Puss: Old Time Fiddle Music from Kentucky*
Artist: Buddy Thomas, accompanied by Leona Stamm
Collector/Recordist/Producer: Mark Wilson and Guthrie Meade
Place and Date of Recording: KY, MD, 1973-74
Date of Publication: 1976
Annotations: Gatefold notes by Mark Wilson and Guthrie Meade
Selections:
> Big Indian Hornpipe
> Blue Goose, The
> Briarpicker Brown
> Brown Button Shoes
> Frankie
> Georgia Row
> John Rawl Jamieson
> Kitty Puss
> Martha Campbell
> Nine Miles out of Louisville
> 'Possum up a 'Simmon Tree
> Sheeps and Hogs Walking Through the Pasture
> Stillhouse Brown
> Sweet Sunny South, The
> Turkey in a Peapatch
> Yellow Barber

Rndr 0032: The late folk music scholar Gus Meade had a particular fondness for Kentucky fiddle music, and had moved to Kentucky after his retirement from the National Archives in Washington, D.C., to spend more time collecting there. Unfortunately, his dream was unfulfilled because he died in 1990, a year after he moved. In the '70s he and Mark Wilson collaborated on several field projects in Kentucky, among them this album of Buddy Thomas, a young fiddler (he died at age 39, shortly after these recordings) who astonished Meade and Wilson with his store of older and unusual tunes beautifully played: "Buddy seems to have been one of the last representatives of a great and distinctive tradition and his performances provide a glimpse of the complex and melancholy music which once flourished in the area." The title tune is a very unusual piece with a shifting tonal center sure to baffle an unexpecting accompanist. Gatefold jacket notes include a long autobiographical essay by Thomas and tune notes by Meade and Wilson.

167   Label Name/Number: Takoma A 1013
Title: *Old Style Texas and Oklahoma Fiddlin'*
Artist: Tony Thomas, accompanied by Rod Thomas and John Fahey
Collector/Recordist: John Fahey & Barry Hansen (recordists)
Producer: John Fahey & Ed Denson
Place and Date of Recording: Hugo, OK, 1966
Date of Publication: [1967?]

Annotations: 8 p. booklet by John Fahey & Graham Wickham
Selections:

 Arkansas Traveler, The
 Back Up and Push
 Bacon Rind [= Soldier's Joy]
 Barbara Allen
 Belled Buzzard, The
 Bonaparte's Retreat
 Carroll County Blues, The
 Cherry Mountain Hoedown
 Chicken
 Goodnight Waltz, The
 Hoof It
 Jack-O Diamonds
 Liberty Hornpipe
 Little River Stomp, The
 Mexicalli [sic] Rose
 Niger [sic] in the Woodpile [= Wild Horse]
 Old Joe Clark
 Over the Sea Waltz
 Rye Straw
 Rye Whiskey
 Sally Goodwyn
 Shall We Gather at the River?
 Sitting on Top of the World
 Stone Rag
 Walk Along John
 Wednesday Night Waltz, The

  Takoma A 1013: Tony Thomas was born in 1911 in Oklahoma, son of a traditional fiddler of some local renown. Tony learned his tunes and some technique from his father and other southwest fiddlers. The album's editors met him while he was playing with his band over a local radio program in Hugo, southeastern Oklahoma. He plays popular southwestern fiddle tunes, but some of his tunes have no obvious relations: e.g., his "Over the Sea Waltz" (not "Over the Waves"), "Rye Straw" (not the usual tune of that title), "Cherry Mountain Hoedown," and "Hoof It." His "Barbara Allen" and "Shall We Gather at the River?" are both rendered as fiddle tunes, no vocals. He is accompanied by his nephew, Rod, on guitar or Hawaiian guitar, and, on some tracks, by John Fahey on guitar.

168 **Label Name/Number:** County 724
Title: *Country Fiddling from the Big State*
Artist: Benny Thomasson
Collector/Recordist/Producer: Charles Faurot
Date of Publication: [1970]
Annotations: Liner notes by Faurot
Selections:

 Bitter Creek
 Black and White Rag
 Bumblebee in the Gourdvine
 Don't Let the Deal Go Down
 Drunkard's Hiccups

    Dry and Dusty
    Dusty Miller
    Jack of Diamonds
    Lost Indian
    Midnight on the Water
    Nigger in the Woodpile
    Tom and Jerry
    Tug Boat

    Cty 724: Benny Thomasson (1909-1984) perhaps did more than any other fiddler to
establish the style of modern Texas contest fiddling (the terms "Texas fiddling" and "contest fiddling" are often used interchangeably)--smooth, long bowstrokes, highly ornamented and decorated
melodies, played with different variations each time through. This album, the first devoted entirely
to Thomasson, shows his mastery of the instrument. As is commonly the case in Texas-style fiddling, the guitar accompaniment consists of closed chords, rather than single-note runs such as one
hears in the southeast. Thomasson's "Don't Let Your Deal Go Down" is as raggy as the tune gets;
the beautifully haunting "Midnight on the Water," learned from his father and uncle (if they didn't
indeed compose it) is sure to win over anyone indifferent to traditional fiddle music.

169   Label Name/Number: Folk-Legacy FSA-2
Title: *Joseph Able Trivett*
Artist: Joseph Able Trivett
Collector/Recordist: Sandy Paton
Place and Date of Recording: Butler, TN, 1961-62
Date of Publication: 1962
Annotations: 24 p. booklet by Sandy Paton
Selections:
    Black Jack David [C. 200]
    Courting Case, The
    Fair and Tender Ladies
    Frank James [L 16b]
    Go Away From Me, Young Man
    Golden Willow Tree, The [C. 286]
    Joe Bowers [B 14]
    Little Mohee, The [H 8]
    Lord Thomas and Fair Ellender [C. 73]
    Mathy Grove [C. 81]
    Mother-In-Law
    Nowhere Road, The
    Rolling Store, The
    That Bloody War
[Also one anecdote]

    FLeg FSA-2: Eighty years old when these recordings were made, Trivett lived all his life
in the northeastern corner of Tennessee. Paton recorded 37 songs from him in 1961-62, 14 of which
are selected here. Trivett has an interesting repertoire with some good texts (his "Mathy Grove" is
22 stanzas long), but he sings in a rather uninteresting style, tending to compress his melodies'
range and occasionally straying from the tune. Possibly had he been recorded earlier in life he
would not have exhibited these tendencies. Paton's brochure gives notes on the songs and a brief
account of the interview and recording events. Two of the songs ("The Nowhere Road" and "The
Rolling Store") are his own compositions. "Frank James" combines elements of "Boston Burglar"
with other broadside ballads. [JAF 299--DKW]

170   Label Name/Number: Marimac 9025 [cass]
Title: *Troxsong*
Artists: Troxell Brothers (Clyde and Ralph)
Collector/Producer: Bobby Fulcher
Place and Date of Recording: Rockybranch, KY, 1990
Date of Publication: 1990
Annotations: Insert notes by Fulcher
Selections:

     Barlow Knife
     Big Eyed Rabbit
     Boll Weevil
     Cacklin' Hen
     Cora Ellen
     Dandy Jim
     Defellum Blues [= Deep Elem Blues]
     French Waltz
     Girl I Left Behind
     Hell Broke Loose in Georgia
     Knoxville Rag
     Lost John
     Marchin' Through Georgia
     Pretty Pink
     Taylor's Quick Step
     Train 45
     Wild Bill Jones [E 10]

Mar 9025: Clyde and Ralph Troxell were born in 1911 and 1920, respectively, in McCreary County, Kentucky, and were given their first musical instruments (fretless banjo and guitar, respectively) at the ages of 4 and 13. While in his twenties, Clyde toured the coal and sawmill camps with brother-in-law Virgil Anderson (q. v.) playing music. Ralph began playing fiddle professionally with another band in 1975. Most of the selections on this tape feature their banjo and fiddle, with unidentified guitar accompaniment; a few have vocals; some are banjo solos. "Pretty Pink" is not the usual variant of "Fly Around My Pretty Little Miss," but a different banjo tune, melodically reminiscent of the common tune to "House Carpenter." Several of the pieces were learned from the very influential Kentucky musicians of the 20s, Burnett and Rutherford. Fulcher's brief notes sketch biographies and identify the selections. "Troxsong" was originally Fulcher's file title on his computer that inadvertently became the title of the cassette.

171   Label Name/Number: Rounder 0064
Title: *George Tucker*
Artist: George Tucker, accompanied by Guy Carawan, Peter Gott, and Sid Blum
Collector/Recordist: Guy Carawan and Gary Slemp
Date of Recording: 1975?
Date of Publication: 1976
Annotations: Brief song notes by Mark Wilson
Selections:

     Amazing Grace
     Barbara Ellen [C. 84]
     Betsy Brown
     Bright Morning Stars Are Rising

     Cold Penitentiary Blues [I 4]
     Death of Floyd Collins, The [G 22]
     Get Away, Old Man, Get Away
     Jack Monroe [N 7]
     Johnny Wilson
     Just the Same Today
     Kentucky Moonshiner
     Morning Blues, The
     New Talking Blues
     Old Bill Moser's Ford
     Old Dan Tucker
     Old Mother Rhyme, The
     On the Dixie Bee Line
     Poor Little Turtle Dove
     Pretty Green Island
     Scab's Toast, A
     State of Arkansas, The [H 1]
     That Thirty Inch Coal
     Two Old Soldiers
     Uncle Eef's Got the Coon

     Rndr 0064:   George Tucker was born in Letcher County, Kentucky, in 1917. He worked in the coal mines for nearly thirty years and retired a victim of black lung disease. The majority of the songs on this album were learned from commercial 78s; exceptions include the older "Jack Monroe" and "Barbara Ellen" and the more recent composition, "That Thirty Inch Coal."

172   Label Name/Number: Folkways FA 3830
Title: *Country Bluegrass from Southwest Virginia*
Artists: Glen Neaves & the Virginia Mountain Boys (Cullen Galyean, Bobby Harrison, Ivor
        Melton)
Collector/Recordist: Eric H. Davidson; Paul Newman, Lyn Davidson, Jane Rigg, Caleb E. Finch
Place and Date of Recording: VA, 1961-74
Date of Publication: 1974
Annotations: 4 p. booklet by Caleb Finch and Eric Davidson
Selections:
     Barbara Allen [C. 84]
     Careless Love
     Cripple Creek
     Don't Go Out Tonight My Darlin'
     Drinkin' from the Fountain
     Drunkard's Dream
     Fortune
     Hangman (Song) Ballad [C. 95]
     Man of Constant Sorrow
     Nigger Trader
     On the Banks of the Old Tennessee
     Poor Ellen Smith [F 11]
     Someday We'll Meet Again Sweetheart
     Two Dollar Bill
     What a Friend We Have in Mother
     When the Roses Bloom Again

173   Label Name/Number: Folkways FA 3833
Title: *The Virginia Mountain Boys 2: Blue Grass String Band*
Artists: Cullen Galyean, Glen Neaves, Bobby Harrison, Ivor Melton, Herman Dalton, Marvin
        Cockram and others
Collector/Recordist: Eric Davidson with Lyn Davidson, Paul Newman, Caleb Finch, Jane Rigg
Place and Date of Recording: VA, 1961-1974
Date of Publication: 1977
Annotations: 11 p. booklet by Eric Davidson, Jane Rigg, Brooke Moyer
Selections: (all band performances unless single performer noted)
        Clinch Mountain
        I'm Glad My Wife's in Europe -- Neaves
        In the Pines
        John Hardy [I 2]
        Knoxville Girl [P 35]
        Little Birdie
        Little Frankie Baker [I 3] -- Neaves
        Lonesome Road Blues
        Lost Train Blues
        Love Me, Darling
        Nobody's Darling
        Poor Rambler -- Galyean
        Red and Green Signal Lights
        Red Rocking Chair
        Sunny Side of the Mountain -- Neaves
        Train 45
        Whitehouse Blues

174   Label Name/Number: Folkways FS 3839
Title: *Vol. 3: Old Time Bluegrass from Grayson & Carroll Counties, Va.*
Artists: Virginia Mountain Boys (Cullen Galyean, Glen Neaves, Ivor Melton, Bobby Harrison,
        Herman Dalton, Marvin Cockram, and others)
Collector/Recordist: Eric Davidson, Lyn Davidson, and Jane Rigg
Place and date of recordings: Fries and Pipers Gap, VA, 1963-74
Date of Publication: 1980
Annotations: 8 p. brochure by Eric Davidson, Jane Rigg, and Brooke Moyer
Selections:
        Bill Cheatum
        Charming Betsy
        Fire on the Mountain
        I'm Goin' To Walk with My Lord
        John Henry [I 1]
        Let That Circle Be Unbroken [= Will the...]
        Lily Shaw
        Philadelphia Lawyer
        Pig in a Pen
        Prisoner's Song
        Run, Nigger, Run
        Tragic Romance
        Wednesday Night Waltz
        Where Are You Going, Alice? [cf. N 40]

175   Label Name/Number: Folkways FS 3829
Title: *Cullen Galyean, Bobby Harrison and the Virginia Mountain Boys, Vol. 4*
Artists: Cullen Galyean, Bobby Harrison, David Lambeth, John Jackson, Jerry Steinberg
Collector/Recordist: Eric H. Davidson
Place of Recording: Southwestern VA
Date of Publication: 1983
Annotations: 6 p. booklet by Paul Newman and Eric Davidson
Selections:
>   Dream of a Miner's Child
>   East Virginia
>   Fair and Tender Ladies
>   Little Willie
>   Maple on the Hill
>   More Pretty Girls Than One
>   New River Train
>   Sand Mountain Blues
>   Shackles and Chains
>   Wayfaring Stranger
>   What Would You Give
>   Wild Bill Jones [E 10]

Fwys FS 3829 / Fwys FS 3830 / Fwys FS 3833 / Fwys FS 3839. For reasons stated in the Introduction, I have included very few albums of bluegrass music in this Discography. These four albums by the Virginia Mountain Boys are included because this Southwest Virginia bluegrass band is heavily steeped in older traditional stringband musical repertoire. The presence of mandolin, banjo, guitar, fiddle, and bass do not of themselves distinguish a bluegrass band from an older style stringband. The appelation "bluegrass" is generally applied if there are Scruggs-style three-finger banjo picking, lead mandolin, and (sometimes) rotation of instrumental "breaks"--lead with varia- tions on the melody--rather than several instruments playing melody if not in unison at least simultaneously. The Virginia Mountain Boys exhibit these characteristics, but dobro and drums, which became common in bluegrass bands in the 1950s and '60s, are absent. The Virginia Mountain Boys are well known in Southwest Virginia and neighboring North Carolina counties, appearing on radio, at local fiddle conventions, dances, and other social gatherings. All the band members make their livings at other occupations--in factories or mills, doing maintenance work, operating construction machinery. FS 3839 contains two unusual items: a "Where Are You Going, Alice?," probably learned from a Grayson and Whitter 78 rpm recording; and "Lily Shaw," a rare criminal's "last goodnight" lament from a 1903 murder. The albums are all carefully documented, with background information on the musicians, their musical milieux, and on the selections, with text transcriptions as well.

176   Label Name/Number: Biograph RC-6002
Title: *Fields and Wade Ward*
Artists: Fields and Wade Ward with Jimmy Edmonds, John Rector
Producer: Arnold S. Caplin
Collector/Recordist: [Richard Nevins?]
Place and Date of Recording: Galax, VA, 1968
Date of Publication: [1968]
Annotations: Liner notes by Richard Nevins
Selections:
>   Allen Clan, The [E 5]
>   Cold Icy Floor

Cruel Slavery Days
Don't Let Your Deal Go Down
Hobo John
John Hardy
Little Birdie
One Eyed Sam
Riley and Spencer
Round Town Girls
Sweet William [C. 7]
Wade's Fox Chase
Winkin' Eye

177   Label Name/Number: Biograph RC-6003
Title: *The Original Bogtrotters*
Artists: Fields Ward, Crockett Ward, Eck Dunford with Dr. W. P. Davis, Walter Alderman, Marvin Evans, Dr. W. E. Dalton
Collector/Recordist: John Lomax, Alan Lomax and others
Producer: Arnold S. Caplin
Place and Date of Recording: Galax, VA, 1937-1942; two from commercial 78s, 1927
Date of Publication: [1968]
Annotations: Liner notes by Richard Nevins
Selections: [brackets indicate additions to titles on LP credits not from original LC recording data]
    [Ain't That] Trouble in Mind
    Cold Icy Floor
    Deadheads and Suckers
    Fortune
    Hop Up Ladies
    Jess[i]e James [E 1]
    John Henry [I 1]
    Make Me a Pallet on the Floor
    Old Jimmy Sutton
    Piney Woods Girl of North Carolina
    Shoo Fly
    Sugar Hill
    Western Country
    Who Broke the Lock

178   Label Name/Number: Folkways FA 2380
Title: *Uncle Wade: A Memorial to Wade Ward, Old Time Virginia Banjo Picker, 1982-1971*
Artists: Uncle Wade with Glen Smith, Bogtrotters (Wade, Crockett, & Fields Ward)
Collector/Recordist: John A. Lomax; Eric H. Davidson & Jane Rigg
Editor: Davidson & Rigg
Place and Date of Recording: VA, 1937; 1957-1970
Date of Publication: 1973
Annotations: 6 p. booklet by Eric Davidson & Jane Rigg
Selections:
        Arkansas Traveler -- Wade, Glen
        Billy in the Low Ground -- Wade
        Black Mountain Rag -- Wade
        Chicken Reel -- Wade, Glen
        Chilly Winds -- Wade

       Cluck Old Hen -- Bogtrotters
       Foxchase -- Wade
       Half-Shaved -- Wade
       Ida Red -- Wade
       John Lover Is Gone -- Wade, Glen
       June Apple -- Wade
       Mississippi Sawyers -- Wade
       Nancy Blevins -- Wade
       Old Jimmy Sutton -- Wade, Glen
       Old Joe Clark -- Wade, Glen
       Old Reuben -- Wade
       Peach Bottom Creek -- Wade
       Polly Put the Kettle On -- Wade
       Ragtime Annie -- Wade, Glen
       Sally Ann -- Wade, Glen
       Sally Goodin -- Wade, Glen
       Sourwood Mountain -- Wade, Glen
       Western Country -- Wade, Glen, Fields

179   **Label Name/Number:** Rounder Records 0036
Title: *Bury Me Not on the Prairie*
Artists: Fields Ward with Nancy Ward, Jerry Lundy and Burt Russell
Producer: Mark Wilson
Place and Date of Recording: Bel Air, MD, 1973
Date of Publication: 1974
Annotations: Liner notes by Mark Wilson
Selections:
       Bury Me Not on the Lone Prairie [B 2]
       Cotton Blossom
       County Road Gang
       In the Concert Garden
       Leaving Dear Old Ireland
       Little Stream of Whiskey, The [H 3]
       McKinley March
       No Low Down Hanging Around
       Old Zeke Perkin
       Peekaboo Waltz
       Piney Woods Girl
       Rockhouse Gambler
       Sweet Bird
       Train That Carried My Girl from Town, The

     Bio RC-6003 / Bio RC-6002 / Fwys FA 2380 / Rounder 0036: The Bogtrotters' band generally consisted of fiddler Crockett Ward, his son Fields (guitar), and brother Wade (banjo), and neighbors Alec ("Eck") Dunford (fiddle) and Dr. W. P. Davis (autoharp). Most of the recordings on RC-6003 were made by John Lomax for the LC at the Galax Old Time Fiddlers' Convention in October 1937. "Make Me a Pallet" is a much later recording by Fields Ward alone. Although the jacket credits are inconsistent on this point, "Deadheads and Suckers" and "Sugar Hill" are commercial 1927 recordings for the OKeh label by Crockett Ward and his Boys (Fields and Sampson Ward). When it appeared, this was a particularly important reissue from the LC because so much of the Anglo-American material reissued from the Archive of American Folk Song by the LC itself was devoted to the noncommercial, domestic tradition. For it can hardly be denied that this music, although technically "field recorded," is thoroughly hillbilly and part of the commercial tradition--a good example of the difficulties inherent in any attempt to categorize music as either commercial or field recorded. The Bogtrotters played no differently for John Lomax at the 1937 Galax Fiddlers' Convention than they did for OKeh's A&R man in New York in 1927. Fortunately, we do not have to rest our appraisal of the band on their LC material, which was technically very poor. The songs are typical hillbilly numbers: ballads, dance tunes, and lyric songs, with some Afro-American elements ("Make Me A Pallet on the Floor" and "Ain't that Trouble in Mind"). "Cold Icy Floor" has been recorded by other Virginia musicians as "What Will I Do For My Money's All Gone; "Western Country" is better known as "Fly Around My Pretty Little Miss."

In 1968 Fields Ward no longer played regularly with his uncle, Wade, having moved near Forest Hill, MD; Bio RC-6002's recordings were made on one of his visits back to Galax. The music is mostly Ward family standards, with vocal and guitar by Fields, banjo by Wade, and occasional fiddle by John Rector (on "Riley and Spencer") and Jimmy Edmonds (on "John Hardy"), both of Galax. Fields's unaccompanied rendition of "Sweet William" is a lovely, full (14 stanzas) text--very similar to the one he recorded three decades earlier for John A. Lomax (see County 534), but two stanzas longer. It is not transcribed by Bronson, but is similar to his #37 (see Bronson, *Traditional Tunes to the Child Ballads*, Vol. 1).

With one exception, Fwys FA 2380 is compiled from recordings made between 1958 and 1964 by editor Davidson (four of which were previously issued on Fwys FA 2363). One earlier title, "Cluck Old Hen," is reissued from John A. Lomax's 1937 LC field sessions. The selections are banjo and fiddle tunes (Ward played both instruments consummately) that date mostly from the turn of the century or earlier, many found only in the Grayson-Carroll Counties where Ward lived all his life. Ten of the tunes are banjo-fiddle duets by Ward and his frequent musical associate, Glen Smith. Interspersed with the music are reminiscences of Ward's niece, Mrs. Katy Hill, which, together with the fine notes by Davidson and Rigg, offer a well-rounded picture of this beloved old man and his wonderful music.

Rndr 0036 is devoted to the younger Fields Ward, who was only abut 14 years old when he made his first recordings playing guitar with Crockett Ward and his Boys for the OKeh label; then the band was dominated by Fields' father, Crockett, and older brothers. In around 1934, the Wards joined several other musicians (including Fields' uncle, Wade) to form the Bogtrotters, who first recorded as a group for John A. Lomax in 1937 at the Galax Fiddlers' Convention. Several years later, the older Wards gave up playing regularly and the Bogtrotters disbanded. Fields left the Galax area in 1947 and moved to Maryland, where he continues the rich Ward musical tradition as he can. He is joined on fiddle by Jerry Lundy, grandson of well-known Galax fiddler Emmett Lundy. Fields plays both guitar and banjo on this album; some songs (e. g., "Bury Me Not") are sung unaccompanied. Most of the selections are common in the older Ward family repertoire, but pieces like "No Low Down Hanging Around" and "Train that Carried My Girl from Town" were learned from commercial 78s of the '20s. [WF 1/75 (FA 2380)]

180 Label Name/Number: Smithsonian/Folkways SF 40012 [CD/LP/Cass]
Title: *The Watson Family*
Artists: Doc Watson, Rosa Lee Watson, Arnold Watson, Mrs. Annie Watson, Gaither Carlton, Sophronie Miller Greer, Dolly Greer, Merle Watson
Collector/Recordist: Ralph Rinzler, Eugene Earle, Archie Greene, Peter Seigel
Editor: Ralph Rinzler and Jeff Place
Place and Date of Recording: Deep Gap, NC; 1960-65, 1976
Date of Publication: 1990 [15 tracks (not asterisked) previously issued in 1963 as Folkways FA 2366; 3 of the tracks listed below (#) on the CD and cassette formats of this album are omitted from the LP]
Annotations: Descriptive insert notes by Jeff Place

Selections:

    Bonaparte's Retreat
    Cousin Sally Brown *
    Cuckoo Bird, The *#
    Darling Corey
    Doodle Bug *
    Down the Road
    Every Day Dirt [Q 9]
    Frosty Morn *#
    Ground Hog
    House Carpenter, The [C. 243]
    I'm Troubled
    Keep in the Middle of the Road *
    Lone Pilgrim, The
    Look Down That Lonesome Road *#
    Lost Soul, The
    Muddy Roads
    Old Man Below, The *
    Pretty Saro *
    Rambling Hobo *
    Shady Grove *
    Southbound *
    Texas Gales/Blackberry Rag
    That Train That Carried My Girl from Town
    Triplett Tragedy, The
    When I Die
    Your Long Journey

181   Label Name/Number: Topic 12TS336
Title: *The Watson Family Tradition*
Artists: Gaither Carlton, Doc Watson, Dolly Greer, Rosa Lee Watson, Arnold Watson, Merle
      Watson, Tina Greer, Annie Watson
Collector/Recordist: Ralph Rinzler, Daniel Seeger
Editor: Peter Siegel, Ralph Rinzler, A. L. Lloyd
Place and Date of Recording: Deep Gap, NC; 1964-65
Date of Publication: 1977
Annotations: Liner notes by A. L. Lloyd, 2 p. insert by Ralph Rinzler and A. L. Lloyd
Selections:

    And Am I Born to Die?
    Arnold's Tune
    A-Roving on a Winter's Night
    Baa Nanny Black Sheep
    Bill Banks
    Biscuits
    Early, Early in the Spring [M 1]
    Faithful Soldier, The
    Fish in the Mill-pond
    Georgie
    Give the Fiddler a Dram
    Hushabye
    I Heard My Mother Weeping

    Jimmy Sutton
    Julie Jenkins
    Little Maggie
    Marthy, Won't You Have Some Good Old Cider?
    Omie Wise [F 4]
    One Morning in May [P 14]
    Pretty Saro
    Rambling Hobo
    Reuben's Train
    Sheepy and the Goat
    Tucker's Barn

    Smithsonian/Fwys SF 40012 [CD] / Topic 12TS336: Arthel "Doc" Watson was "discovered" as a musical associate of Clarence Ashley's (see notes to Folkways FA 2355 and 2359); at the time he was playing electric guitar in a contemporary local rockabilly band. Through Ralph Rinzler's urging he returned to his older musical roots and created a new (and far more commercially successful) career for himself. Space does not permit inclusion of all his albums in this book, consequently (in consonance with the principles enunciated in my Introduction) I have focused on albums stressing more traditional material; this has resulted in omitting many of his later (and highly enjoyable) albums on the Poppy and Sugar Hill labels.

    When Folkways FA 2366 appeared in 1963, folk music fans who knew Doc Watson only as the blind, flat-picking guitar accompanist to Clarence Ashley's magnificent old-timey stringband were exposed to a rich musical family tradition that boasted several outstanding performers--most notably Doc, his brother, Arnold, his wife, Rosa Lee, and his father-in-law, Gaither Carlton. The album (especially in its present, considerably augmented form) is a broad selection of ballads and songs, hymns and gospel songs, fiddle and banjo tunes, and, of course, some of Doc's now-legendary transpositions of fiddle tunes to flat-picked guitar. The beautiful "Your Long Journey" is Rosa Lee Watson's own composition; the album closes with "Southbound," a composition by Doc's late son, Merle Watson, written while he was in New York for some concerts and longing for home. D. K. Wilgus's excellent and detailed brochure notes to FA 2366 are not included with the newer packages but are available from the Smithsonian Institution.

    Topic 12TS336 includes more of the same type of material, recorded at about the same time. "Georgie" is a brief fiddle tune by Gaither Carlton, all that remains in the family tradition from the old ballad of the same title (Child 209). Together, these two wonderful albums represent the musical heritage of an outstanding musician at the threshold of his successful commercial career.

182   **Label Name/Number:** Vanguard VRS-9152/VSD-79152
Title: *Doc Watson*
Artist: Doc Watson, some accomp. by John Herald
Place and Date of Recording: New York City, 1963?
Date of Publication: 1964
Annotations: Liner notes by Ralph Rinzler
Selections:
    Black Mountain Rag
    Country Blues
    Deep River Blues
    Doc's Guitar
    Georgie Buck
    Intoxicated Rat
    Nashville Blues
    Omie Wise [F 5]

Saint James' Hospital [B 1]
Sitting on Top of the World
Six Thousand Years Ago
Talk About Suffering
Tom Dooley [F 36]

183   Label Name/Number: Vanguard VRS-9170/VSD-79170
Title: *Doc Watson & Son*
Artists: Doc & Merle Watson
Producer: Ralph Rinzler
Date of Publication: 1965
Annotations: Liner notes by Ralph Rinzler
Selections:

Beaumont Rag
Dream of the Miner's Child
Faithful Soldier, The
Gonna Lay Down My Old Guitar
Little Sadie [I 8]
Little Stream of Whiskey [H 3]
Mama Blues
Medley: Fiddler's Dram, Whistling Rufus, Ragtime Annie [= Raggedy Ann]
Memphis Blues
Muskrat
Otto Wood, the Bandit
Rising Sun Blues
We Shall All Be Reunited
Weary Blues

184   Label Name/Number: Vanguard VRS-9213/VSD-79213
Title: *Southbound*
Artist: Doc Watson with Merle Watson, John Pilla, & Russ Savakus
Date of Publication: 1966
Annotations: Liner notes by Doc Watson
Selections:

Alberta
Blue Railroad Train
Call of the Road
Little Darling Pal of Mine
Nashville Pickin'
Never No More Blues
Nothing to It
Riddle Song
Southbound
Sweet Georgia Brown
Tennessee Stud
That Was the Last Thing on My Mind
Walk On Boy
Windy and Warm

185   Label Name/Number: Vanguard VRS-9239/VSD-79239
Title: *Home Again*

Artist: Doc Watson with Merle Watson & Russ Savakus
Producer: Ralph Rinzler
Date of Publication: [1967?]
Annotations: Liner notes by A. L. Lloyd
Selections:
>Childhood Play
>Dill Pickle Rag
>Down in the Valley to Pray
>F. F. V., The [G 3]
>Froggie Went A-Courtin'
>Georgie [C. 209]
>Katie Morey [N 24]
>Matty Groves [C. 81]
>Old Man Below, The
>Pretty Saro
>Rain Crow Bill
>Sing Song Kitty
>Victory Rag
>Winter's Night

186   Label Name/Number: Vanguard VSD-9/10 [2 record set]
Title: *Doc Watson on Stage*
Artist: Doc Watson with Merle Watson
Recordist: Ed Friedner & Claude Karczmer
Place of Recording: Cornell University and Town Hall, NY
Date of Publication: 1970
Annotations: Brief notes by A. L. Lloyd
Selections:
>Banks of the Ohio [F 5]
>Billy in the Low Ground
>Brown's Ferry Blues
>Clouds Are Gwine to Roll Away, The
>Deep River Blues
>Doc's Guitar
>Don't Let Your Deal Go Down
>Hold the Woodpile Down
>I Am a Pilgrim
>Jimmy's Texas Blues
>Life Gits Teejus Don't It
>Little Sadie [I 8]
>Lost John
>Movin' On
>Open Up Them Pearly Gates for Me
>Roll On Buddy
>Salt River/ Bill Cheatham
>Southbound
>Spikedriver Blues
>Wabash Cannon Ball
>When the Work's All Done This Fall
>Windy and Warm
>Wreck of the 1262, The

[Also 2 tales]

187   Label Name/Number: Vanguard VCD-45/46
Title: *The Essential Doc Watson*
Artist: Doc Watson
Place and Date of Recording: Newport, RI, 1963-64; some studio, 1960s
Date of Publication: 1986 (LP format VSD 45/46 issued in 1973)
Annotations: None
Selections:
> Alberta
> Beaumont Rag
> Black Mountain Rag
> Blackberry Blossom
> Blue Railroad Train
> Blue Ridge Mountain Blues
> Country Blues
> Down in the Valley To Pray
> Froggie Went A-Courtin'
> Going Down This Road Feeling Bad
> Groundhog
> Handsome Molly
> I Want To Love Him More
> I Was a Stranger
> Little Omie Wise [F 4]
> Little Orphan Girl
> Muskrat
> My Rough and Rowdy Ways
> Rambling Hobo
> Rising Sun Blues
> Shady Grove
> St. James Hospital [B 1]
> Tom Dooley [F 36]
> Train That Carried My Girl from Town, The
> Way Downtown
> Whitehouse Blues

188   Label Name/Number: Vanguard VSD-107/108 [2 record set]
Title: *Old Timey Concert*
Artists: Doc Watson, Clint Howard, & Fred Price
Collector/Recordist: engineered by Fritz Richmond from tapes made by Phil Williams
Producer: Manny Greenhill
Place and Date of Recording: Seattle, WA, 1967
Date of Publication: 1977
Annotations: None
Selections:
> Cackling Hen
> Corinna Corinna
> Crawdad
> Eastbound Train
> Fire on the Mountain
> Footprints in the Snow

      I Saw a Man at the Close of the Day
      Little Orphan Girl
      Long Journey Home
      Mountain Dew
      My Home's Across the Blue Ridge Mountains
      My Mama's Gone (Gambler's Yodel)
      New River Train
      On the Banks of the Old Tennessee
      Pretty Little Pink
      Rank Stranger
      Reuben's Train
      Sittin' on Top of the World
      Slewfoot
      Sunny Tennessee
      There's More Pretty Girls Than One
      Walkin' in Jerusalem
      Wanted Man
      Way Downtown
      What Does the Deep Sea Say
      Will the Circle Be Unbroken
[Also one anecdote]

189 Label Name/Number: Vanguard VSD-6576
Title: *Ballads from Deep Gap*
Artists: Doc and Merle Watson with Eric Weissberg
Producer: Jack Lothrop
Place and Date of Recording: New York City, 1971
Date of Publication: 1971
Annotations: Liner notes by Bill Vernon
Selections:
      Alabama Bound
      Cuckoo, The
      Gambler's Yodel
      Lawson Family Murder, The [F 35]
      My Rough and Rowdy Ways
      Roll in My Sweet Baby's Arms
      Stack O'Lee [I 15]
      Texas Gales
      Tragic Romance, The
      Travellin' Man
      Willie Moore
      Wreck of Old Number 9, The [G 26]

190 Label Name/Number: Sugar Hill SH-CD-3779
Title: *On Praying Ground*
Artist: Doc Watson, accomp. by Jack Lawrence, Alan O'Bryant, Stuart Duncan, Jerry Douglas,
      Sam Bush, Roy Huskey, Jr., T. Michael Coleman
Producer: T. Michael Coleman
Place of Recording: Studio, Nashville, TN
Date of Publication: 1990

Annotations: None
Selections:

      Beautiful Golden Somewhere
      Christmas Lullaby
      Did Christ o'er Sinners Weep?
      Farther Along
      Gathering Buds
      I'll Live On
      I'm Gonna Lay My Burdens Down
      Ninety and Nine, The
      On Praying Ground
      Precious Lord
      Uncloudy Day
      We'll Work 'Til Jesus Comes
      You Must Come In at the Door

191   Label Name/Number: Sugar Hill SH-CD-3786
Title: *Doc Watson Sings Songs for Little Pickers*
Artist: Doc Watson
Producer: Mark Greenberg and Mitch Greenhill
Place and Date of Recording: Newport, RI, 1988; Atlanta, GA, 1990; others
Date of Publication: 1990
Annotations: 8 p. insert by Watson
Selections:

      Crawdad Song, The
      Froggy Went A-Courtin'
      Green Grass Grew All Around, And the
      John Henry [I 1]
      Liza Jane
      Mama Blues
      Mole in the Ground
      Riddle Song, The
      Sally Goodin
      Shady Grove
      Sing Song Kitty
      Talkin' Guitar
      Tennessee Stud, The

192   Label Name/Number: Sugar Hill SH-CD-3795
Title: *My Dear Old Southern Home*
Artist: Doc Watson, accompanied by Jack Lawrence, Alan O'Bryant, Stuart Duncan, Jerry
      Douglas, Sam Bush, Roy Huskey, Jr., Mark Schatz, T. Michael Coleman
Producer: T. Michael Coleman
Place of Recording: Studio, Nashville, TN
Date of Publication: 1991
Annotations: None
Selections:

      Don't Say Goodbye If You Love Me
      Dream of the Miner's Child
      Grandfather's Clock
      Life Is Like a River

My Dear Old Southern Home
My Friend Jim
No Telephone in Heaven
Ship That Never Returned, The [D 27]
Signal Light
Sleep Baby Sleep
That Silver Haired Daddy of Mine
Wreck of the Number Nine [G 26]
Your Long Journey

SH 3795 / SH 3779 / SH 3786/ Van VRS-9152 / Van VRS-9170 / Van VRS-9213 / Van VRS-9239 / Van VSD-9/10 / Van VSD-107/108 / Van VCD-45/46 / Van VSD 107-108 / Van VSD 6576: The career of Doc Watson is a refreshing reminder that traditional music is not a static entity (if it were, it would still be played on skin drums and wood flutes) but changes in the hands of its more creative bearers. (At the other extreme of a continuum are those passive tradition bearers who faithfully pass on the music as they have learned it, modifying it negligibly in the process.) An engaging, articulate, and entertaining performer, Watson is one of the best traditional artists "discovered" by the folk revival of the 1960s; and certainly the most successful in commercial terms. Yet commerciality, while providing the impetus to innovation and modification, has not enticed Doc too far from his musical roots, as even his most recent albums attest. When Ralph Rinzler and Gene Earle first encountered Doc Watson in the course of locating old-time banjo-player and singer Clarence Ashley, he was recommended to them as a musician of prodigious talents; but at the time, he was playing electric guitar in a rockabilly band in order to supplement his farm income and was not particularly receptive to performing the kind of music Rinzler and Earle were seeking. Today, folk and country music collectors would be eager to record and document a musician playing 1950s rockabilly music. But the folk revival of the 1950s/60s was not interested in rockabilly or contemporary country; young folksong enthusiasts were coming to the southeast with their portable tape recorders, searching out old ballad singers and banjo frailers. Doc's first appearance on LP was as accompanist for Clarence Ashley's band--one of the best modern old-timey bands ever recorded. But it was Ashley's group, and Watson remained politely in the background, providing competent and innovative guitar backup but not much more. On the first Watson Family album (Folkways FA 2366, recorded 1961-62), he was presented as a traditional musician with a store of early hillbilly and pre-hillbilly ballads and tunes (all but three of the selections on the LP were pre-hillbilly), and no hint (except in the brochure notes) of the music with which he had been earning a livelihood. Clearly, Doc perceived what his patrons wanted and fortunately had the background and repertoire to be able to provide it. With his string of Vanguard albums his repertoire moved forward somewhat in time; on the first six (1964-71) about 30 of the 80-odd selections were pre-hillbilly; 30 more came from hillbilly recordings, and the remainder from more recent sources. On his third Vanguard album he performed one Jimmie Rodgers song, and Rodgers material has been included on most albums since. On his two albums on the Poppy label (1972, 1974--not listed here) only about 5 selections (out of 21) were pre-hillbilly. Of the material on his three Flying Fish albums (1981-85--not listed here) a mere five songs (out of 36) came from pre-hillbilly sources. My numbers are only approximate (some songs evade easy categorization), but the trend is clear. Had Watson stopped making albums after the first three Folkways LPs, we would have had quite a different impression of his music and musicianship. There is nothing unusual about this progression; I expect most traditional musicians who turn professional or semi-professional and remain in the business long enough follow a similar path. The lesson, though, is that the trend is clear when the musician is close enough to us that we can discern his sources; it is harder to be so perspicacious with a repertoire from a hundred years or more ago.

It is difficult to assign any ranking of priority, either in terms of aesthetics or "importance" to these Vanguard albums; there is considerable repetition from one album to another. VSD-6576, in spite of its title, contains only six ballads, but is as strong in terms of traditional contents as the others. Van VCD-45/46 is culled partly from live performances at the Newport Folk Festivals of 1963 and 1964, and partly from studio recordings of the 1960s. The material is derived largely from hillbilly music of the 1920s and '30s, with two Jimmie Rodgers pieces, one each from the recordings of Charlie Poole, Dock Boggs, Frank Hutchison, the Delmore Brothers, and Clarence Ashley, and others with more diverse sources. Doc's reputation for transcribing fiddle tunes to flat-pick guitar will not suffer by the renditions of "Beaumont Rag," "Blackberry Blossom," and "Black Mountain Rag" here, but his skills on old-time banjo and finger-picked guitar should not be overlooked either. Doc is an intelligent and perceptive observer as well as performer, with a warm and ingratiating style that cannot but win over his audience, and these recordings show it.   [WF 1/75; JAF 317--DKW (Van 9170, 9213); JAF 320--DKW (Van 9239); JAF 338--DKW (Van 6576)]

193   Label Name/Number: Vanguard VRS 9124
Title: *Hedy West*
Artist(s): Hedy West
Producers: [Maynard Solomon]
Place and date of recordings: New York City, ca. 1962
Date of Publication: [1962]
Annotations: Liner notes by M[aynard] S[olomon]; Hedy West
Selections:

> Brown Girl, The [C. 73]
> Bury Me Not on the Lone Prairie [B 2]
> Cottom Mill Girls
> Drowsy Sleeper [M 4]
> Erin's Green Shore [Q 27]
> Fare Thee Well
> Five Hundred Miles
> Fragments
> Letter from Down the Road
> Little Willie
> Miner's Farewell (Poor Hardworking Miners)
> Shady Grove
> Single Girl
> Sweet Jane

194   Label Name/Number: Vanguard VRS 9162 / VSD 79162
Title: *Hedy West, Vol. 2*
Artist(s): Hedy West
Producers: [Maynard Solomon]
Place of recordings: New York City
Date of Publication: [ca. 1963]
Annotations: Liner notes by Kenneth S. Goldstein, Hedy West
Selections:

> Anger in the Land
> Boston Burglar [L 16b]
> Don't Go Down That Lonesome Road
> Fair and Tender Ladies
> Farther Along
> Hubbard
> Lady Beauty Bright [M 3]
> Lewiston Factory Mill Girls

    Little Carpenter, The
    Little Margaret [C. 74]
    Little Old Man Lived Out West [C. 277]
    Moonshiner's Lament
    Pans of Biscuits
    Poor Little Lost Baby
    Run, Slave, Run
    William Hall [N 30]

195 Label Name/Number: Folk-Legacy FSA-32 (Reissued from Topic 12T117)
Title: *Old Times and Hard Times*
Artist: Hedy West
Place and Date of Recording: London, 1963 (for Topic Records)
Date of Publication: 1968; (Topic 12T117 in 1964)
Annotations: 18 p. booklet by Hedy West and A. L. Lloyd
Selections:
    Barbara Allen [C. 84]
    Brother Ephus
    Coal Miner's Child, The
    Davison-Wilder Blues, The
    Fair Rosamund
    Gambling Man [H 4]
    Lament for Barney Graham
    Old Joe Clark
    Polly [O 14]
    Rich Irish Lady, The [P 9]
    Shut Up in the Mines at Coal Creek
    Wife of Usher's Well, The [C. 79]
    Wife Wrapt in Wether's Skin, The [C. 277]

196 Label Name/Number: Bear Family [West Germany] 15003
Title: *Love, Hell, and Biscuits*
Artist(s): Hedy West, accomp. by Tracy Schwarz
Producer: Richard Weize
Place and date of recordings: USA and West Germany, 1974-76
Date of Publication: 1976
Annotations: 15 p. booklet by Hedy West
Selections:
    Babies in the Mill
    Come All Ye Lewiston Factory Girls
    Devil Perceived
    Erin's Green Shore [Q 27]
    Green Rolling Hills of West Virginia
    How Can a Poor Man Stand Such Times and Live
    Little Lump of Coal
    Molly Bawn [O 36]
    Pans of Biscuits
    Red River Valley/Rio Jarmana
    Roll On Weary River, Roll On
    Shady Grove
    Single Girl

When I Lay My Burdens Down
Whore's Lament [Q 26]

197   Label Name/Number: Topic 12T146
Title: *Pretty Saro and Other Appalachian Ballads*
Artist(s): Hedy West
Recordist: Bill Leader
Place of recordings: London
Date of Publication: 1986
Annotations: Jacket notes by Hedy West
Selections:
    Blow Ye Gentle Winds
    Frankie Silvers [E 13]
    House Carpenter, The [C. 243]
    I'm an Old Bachelor
    Joe Bowers [B 14]
    Johnny Sands [Q 3]
    Lee Tharin's Bar Room [B 1]
    Little Matty Groves [C. 81]
    My Good Old Man
    My Soul's Full of Glory
    Old Smokey
    Over There
    Pretty Saro
    Promised Land
    Rake and Rambling Boy [L 12]
    Whistle, Daughter, Whistle

    Van VRS 9124 / Van VRS 9162 / FLeg FSA-32 / Topic 12T146 / Bear Fam BF 15003: Hedy West (b. 1938) grew up in north Georgia to a poor family of hill farmers, daughter of poet Don West, who taught her many of the coal mining songs he learned while he was a union organizer for the miners in the 1930s. Most of her other songs come from older family tradition. "Lament for Barney Graham," "Davison-Wilder Blues," "Shut Up in the Mines at Coal Creek," and "The Coal Miner's Child" (a recomposition of "The Orphan Girl") are part of that tragedy-filled legacy. West accompanies her lovely singing with her own graceful banjo-playing. One song, the beautiful "Rair Rosamund," comes from a printed source.
    The West German Bear Family release is a collection of songs "from and about farm workers, millhands and miners," for which Hedy West drew (and continues to draw) from her own family tradition, most strongly represented by the repertoire of her grandmother, Lillie Mulkey West. These are supplemented by selections from other sources, printed and recorded--sometimes to find alternative versions to songs and ballads Hedy West learned in her own youth. On her later albums, West has developed a conversational singing style, moving alternately between straight singing and almost talking. Two of her grandmother's songs, "Devil Perceived" and "Roll On Weary River," are quite unusual if not unique in oral tradition. The bilingual brochure includes text transcriptions and West's own excellent annotations, combining personal reminiscence with ballad scholarship and social history. [JAF 337--DKW (FLeg 32)]

198   Label Name/Number: Folkways FA 2357
Title: *Favorite Gospel Songs*
Artists: Harry and Jeanie West
Editor: Kenneth S. Goldstein

Date of Publication: 1957
Annotations: 4 p. brochure by Goldstein
Selections:

> Amazing Grace
> Campin' in Canaan's Land
> He'll Set Your Fields on Fire
> I'm Gonna Let It Shine
> I'm Only on a Journey Here
> Man of Galilee, The
> Matthew Twenty-Four
> Oh, Hide You in the Blood
> Only One Step More
> Preach the Gospel
> Sea of Life, The
> Sweet Bye and Bye
> Thirty Pieces of Silver
> Walking My Lord up Calvary's Hill
> What Are They Doing in Heaven Today?
> When Our Lord Shall Come Again

199 Label Name/Number: Folkways FA 2352
Title: *Songs of Harry and Jeannie* [sic] *West*
Artists: Harry and Jeanie West
Date of Publication: 1963
Annotations: 6 p. brochure by H. and J. West
Selections:

> Building on the Sand
> Coal Miner's Blues
> Curley Headed Baby
> End of My Journey
> Far Beyond the Starry Sky
> Free Little Bird
> Hills of Roane County
> Jenny Jenkins
> Little Joe
> Nine Pound Hammer
> Rosa Lee McFall
> Somewhere Sombody's Waiting
> Sugar Cane Mamma
> Tennessee Gambler
> Will You Always Love Me, Darling?

200 Label Name/Number: Prestige/International 13038
Title: *Roaming the Blue Ridge with Jeanie West*
Artist: Jeanie West, accompanied by Harry West, Bill Emerson, Artie Rose, Tom Morgan
Producer: Kenneth S. Goldstein
Date of Publication: [1962]
Annotations: Liner notes by D. K. Wilgus
Selections:

> Girl I Left in Sunny Tennessee, The
> Girl in the Blue Velvet Band, The

Green Grows the Violets
Greenback Dollar
Gypsy's Warning, The
Have a Feast Here Tonight
Little Margaret [C. 74]
Poor Ellen Smith [F 11]
Single Girl, Married Girl
Six More Miles
Storms Are on the Ocean, The
Those Dark Eyes
Tramp on the Street
You're a Flower Blooming in the Wildwood

201   Label Name/Number: Prestige/International 13049
Title: *Country Music in Blue Grass style*
Artists: Harry and Jeanie West, accompanied by Bill Emerson, Artie Rose, Tom Morgan
Producer: Kenneth S. Goldstein
Date of Publication: [1962]
Annotations: Liner notes by D. K. Wilgus
Selections:

Banks of the Ohio, The [F 5]
Blue Moon of Kentucky
Bury Me Beneath the Willow
Give Me the Roses Now
Homestead on the Farm
I'd Like to Be Your Shadow in the Moonlight
I'm Coming Back, But I Don't Know When
I'm Sitting on Top of the World
In a Little Village Churchyard
Let Us Be Lovers Again
Take This Hammer
They're at Rest Together
Unclouded Day
Where the Old Red River Flows

Fwys FA 2357 / Fwys FA 2352 / Prest INT 13038 / Prest INT 13049:   Harry West (b. 1926), from Lee County, Virginia, and Jeanie West (b. 1933), from Asheville, NC, met at the 1959 Asheville folk festival and were married the following year. Both came from musical families. In the 1950s they moved to New York, where they continue to operate a record and music shop, and were instrumental in introducing traditional Appalachian musical styles to the urban New York folksong revival. In addition to their older family traditions, the Wests learned many of their songs from commercial 78s of the 1920s and '30s. They accompany their own harmony singing--Jeanie, on guitar or banjo; Harry on most stringed instruments--but their vocal work is their distinctive characteristic, with a hard, biting edge well-suited to bluegrass and hillbilly gospel. Except for one song that Harry co-authored, FA 2357 consists of standard gospel tunes popular in the '40s and '50s. Folkways FA 2352 contains a broader range of selections and shows their heavy debt to commercial artists such as Cliff Carlisle, the Carter Family, and the Monroe Brothers. Wilgus's liner notes on the two Prestige albums help to place the Wests' music in the context of the hillbilly tradition of the 1930s and '40s--and to note what other sources may be involved. For example, their "Little Margaret" is probably not from old family tradition but from a recording (or other performance) by Bascom Lamar Lunsford. Prestige 13049 is heavily weighted in favor of late 19th-century sentimental songs and ballads.

202   Label Name/Number: Augusta Heritage AH AHR 007 [cass]
Title: *Folksongs & Ballads, Vol. 1*
Artist(s): Everett White
Collector/Recordist/Producer: Gerry Milnes
Place and date of recordings: Enterprise, WV, 1990
Date of Publication: 1991
Annotations: Brief insert notes by Milnes
Selections:
> Brisk Young Soldier, The [M 27]
> Brown Birl, The [C. 73]
> Camp Chase
> Claudie Banks [N 40]
> Eugene Butcher
> Girl That Wore the Waterfall, The [H 26]
> Haunted Wood, The
> Jam on Gerry's Rock [C 1]
> Little Johnny [K 36]
> Little Shirt My Mother Made For Me, The
> Logan County Jail [E 17]
> Old Arm Chair, The
> Poor Tuckahoe, The
> Pretty Aggie [C. 4]
> Silk Merchant's Daughter [N 10]
> Young Timmy the Miller [P 8]

AH AHR 007. Everett White (b. 1914) worked most of his adult life as a coal miner in Harrison County, West Virginia. He learned most of his songs from his grandfather and mother but continued to add to his repertoire in later life. Milnes' brief notes point out that this selection represents his older repertoire (as learned from oral sources); presumably he sings songs of more recent origin as well, otherwise he would be an unusual singer indeed. Even so, it is not often (especially as recently as the 1980s) that one finds a singer with so many older ballads in his or her repertoire. Among less familiar items are "Haunted Wood," a ballad about vengeful Indians who murdered a young pioneer wife and her two little children; "Eugene Butcher," about a local train-wreck; and "Poor Tuckahoe," a deprecatory song about lowland Virginians. White sings in an unornamented style without accompaniment.

203   Label Name/Number: Arkansas Traditions 004
Title: *All in the Family*
Artists: The Williams Family
Collector/Recordist: Dan Bracken, Aubrey Richardson
Place and Date of Recording: Mountain View, AR, 1986
Date of Publication: 1986
Annotations: 8 p. booklet and liner notes by W. K. McNeil
Selections:
> Cruel Willie
> Darby's Ram
> Dineo
> Down with the Old Canoe
> George Washington

I Will Arise
I'll Be All Smiles Tonight
Katie Dear [M4]
My Ozark Mountain Home
Rattler Treed a Possum
Rattlesnake Bill
Seneca Square Dance
Tillies and Turnies [E 18]
When the Bees are in the Hive
Wind and Rain [C. 10]
Young Man Who Wouldn't Hoe Corn

Ark Trad 004: The Williams family consists of Bob Williams (b. 1943), his wife, Bonnie Mann (b. 1944), and their five children. The songs in their repertoire of approximately 250 numbers come mostly from the Mann family; the instrumentals (Bob plays both guitar and fiddle) are from the Williams side. Accompaniment to the songs consists of combinations of guitar, fiddle, mandolin, dulcimer, washtub bass, and rhythm washboard. Most of the vocals are by two sweet female voices in unison or parallel thirds. Much of the repertoire on the LP reflects the music popular on hillbilly recordings of the 1930s. "Wind and Rain" [C. 10] represents an unusual branch of this venerable ballad. The most unusual piece is "Cruel Willie," more commonly known as a fiddle tune, but here with a ballad texts suggesting considerable antiquity. McNeil, whose brochure includes text transcriptions, biographical background on the singers, and his typically high-quality headnotes, has not been able to find a source or analog for this ballad. [JAF 395]

204   Label Name/Number: June Appal JA 001
Title: *Passing thru the Garden*
Artists: Nimrod Workman and Phyllis Boyens
Collector/Recordist: Gary Slemp and Jack Wright
Producer: Jack Wright
Date of Recording: 1972-73
Date of Publication: 1974
Annotations: 12 p. booklet by Rich Kirby
Selections:
        Bold Sea Captain [O 25]
        Burglar Man [H 23]
        Cabin in Gloryland
        Dixon Said to Jackson [L 4]
        Forty-two Years
        Ginseng
        Good Morning / Old Owl
        I Am a Traveling Creature
        Lady Gay [C. 79]
        Little Scholar
        Lord Daniel [C. 81]
        Oh Death
        Passin' thru the Garden
        Quil O'Quay [C. 18]
        Two Little Angels

205   Label Name/Number: Rounder Records 0076
Title: *Mother Jones' Will*

Artist: Nimrod Workman
Producer: Mark Wilson
Place and Date of Recording: Chattaroy, WV, 1976
Date of Publication: 1978
Annotations: Liner notes by Nimrod Workman
Selections:
>   Biler and the Boar [C. 18]
>   Black Lung Song
>   City Four Square, The
>   Coal Black Mining Blues
>   Darling Cory
>   Devil and the Farmer, The [C. 278]
>   Drunkard's Lone Child, The
>   I Want to Go Where Things Are Beautiful
>   Lord Baseman [C. 54]
>   Lord Daniel [C. 81]
>   Loving Henry [C. 68]
>   Mother Jones' Will
>   My Pretty Little Pink
>   Remember What You Told Me, Love
>   Rock the Cradle and Cry
>   Sweet Rosie
>   What Is That Blood on Your Shirt Sleeve? [C. 13]
>   Working on This Old Railroad

JA 001 / Rndr 0076: Nimrod Workman is a rare find: it's refreshing to know that the nooks and crannies of rural America still have such musical treasures that they are willing, with a little coaxing, to yield up to us. Born in 1895 in Martin County, Kentucky, Workman grew up in a musical environment, heavily influenced by the hardships of work in Kentucky and West Virginia's coal fields. His repertoire holds some scarce old gems as well as more modern compositions of his own making, many dealing with his own life experiences. He sings in a penetrating, stark voice, with the metrical freedom of the best rubato parlando style. He is joined on some tracks by his daughter, Phyllis, whose beautiful but cutting voice is reminiscent of such young singers as Betsy Rutherford and Hazel Dickens. In spite of the very different vocal qualities of these two singers, so sensitive do they seem to be to one another that their duets are magnificent to hear; in particular, the performance of the rare ballad fragment "Quil O'Quay" and Workman's own composition, "Passing thru the Garden" have a haunting and moving quality rarely heard on disc. Among his ballads are some older pieces--"Lord Daniel" [Child 81], "Lady Gay," "Quil O'Quay," "Bold Sea Captain," and "Dixon Said to Jackson" (to the tune of "Buffalo Skinners"), all of which are pentatonic. In characteristic traditional fashion, Workman confidently localizes the events of the latter to family acquaintances. The duet singing in parallel fourths on "Quil O'Quay" (π^4), almost polyphonic rather than harmonic, is quite arresting. Boyens by herself sings in a smoother, more contemporary style with guitar accompaniment (by Jack Wright), though still with abundant use of the old Appalachian characteristic of "feathering" (a rising, fading vocal break at the end of a phrase). Workman is hardly a passive bearer of tradition: his repertoire includes some of his own compositions, several of which treat quite militantly the problems of his fellow coal miners (he retired from 42 years of mining in 1952 with black lung disease). The 12-page insert booklet includes extensive quotes by Workman from taped interviews together with text transcriptions, compiled by Rich Kirby.

Rndr 0076, recorded when Workman was 81, is almost as impressive as his June Appal album, though it does seem as if he loses control of his voice at some points (and is technically flawed on some tracks by print-through). This album includes six old ballads from the Child canon.

His "Lord Baseman" is an unusually long text (over 8 minutes), and his "Loving Henry", set to a tune usually associated with "The House Carpenter," is noteworthy for preserving the encounter with the little bird, rather than ending with the scene between Henry and his sweetheart. "My Pretty Little Pink" is an unusual folk lyric, and "Sweet Rosie" is a murdered girl ballad I have not encountered elsewhere. This is such an unusual album that its producers should have prepared a booklet to accompany it--to give more details on Workman's own compositions and the circumstances that led to them (his "Black Lung Song" does include a long spoken introduction to that effect), and also to offer comments on the unusual older traditional pieces. [JEMFQ 53 (JA 001)]

206   Label Name/Number: Rounder Records 0089
Title: *Old Time Fiddle and Guitar Music from West Virginia*
Artists: Oscar and Eugene Wright
Collector/Recordist/Producer: Joan Fenton
Place and Date of Recording: WV, 1975
Date of Publication: 1978
Annotations: 3 p. booklet by Joan Fenton
Selections:

      Aggravatin' Papa
      Annie Laurie
      Banks of the Wabash
      Chattanooga Blues
      Cumberland Gap
      Danny Boy
      Davy Dugger
      Ducks on the Pond
      Forks of the Sandy
      Gentle Annie
      Hell Up Hickory Holler
      Katy Hill
      Kitchen Girl
      No Home Cried the Little Girl
      Protecting the Innocent
      Shady Grove
      Shelving Rock
      Shortening Bread
      Snowbird of [sic] the Ashbank
      Stoney Point
      Stoney Ridge Stomp
      Suwanee River
      Walking in the Parlor
      Weevily Wheat

Rndr 0089: Oscar Wright (b. 1895?) and his son, Eugene (b. 1926), live in Princeton, West Virginia, not far from where they were born. Oscar started playing fiddle in his teens and played for many years with one of the great West Virginia fiddlers of the early century, Henry Reed, many of whose tunes are included on this album. Father and son take turns backing up the other's fiddle on guitar or playing fiddle-banjo duets. Eugene's guitar back-up is embellished with long flat-picked single note runs. On several songs, including "Suwanee River"--not the Stephen Foster favorite--Oscar provides a somewhat quavery but charming vocal. Their "Danny Boy" (without vocal), not nearly so sentimental as one usually hears, is nicely adapted to the fiddle.

SECTION II: Anthologies: Primarily Noncommercially Recorded

207 Label Name/Number: Alabama Traditions 103
Title: *Possum up a Gum Stump*
Artists: Various
Collector/Recordist: Joyce and Jim Cauthen, Doug Crosswhite (field recordings)
Editor: Joyce Cauthen
Place and Date of Recording: From commercial 78s, home recordings (1940-49), and in the field (1978-87)
Date of Publication: 1988
Annotations: 24 p. booklet by Joyce Cauthen
Selections:

> All Around the World and Back to Citico -- Noah Lacy
> Bile Them Cabbage Down -- Johnson Family
> Chicken in the Barnyard -- Monte Crowder
> Chickens, Don't Roost Too High -- Leonard Keith
> Coon on a Rail -- Howard Hamil
> Dew Drop -- Matt Hill
> Fifty Years Ago -- Y. Z. Hamilton
> Flop-Eared Mule -- "Fiddling" Tom Freeman
> Georgia Wagoner -- Joe Lee
> Get Off Your Money -- Charlie Stripling
> Hamilton's Special Breakdown -- Y. Z. Hamilton
> Home Again Blues -- Howard Colburn
> Katy Hill -- Johnson Family
> Lost John -- Charlie Stripling
> Possum up a Gum Stump -- Ralph Whited
> Smoke Above the Clouds -- Jess Moore
> Turkey Foot -- Ralph Whited
> Walking in the Parlor -- D. Dix Hollis

Ala Trad 103: Album producers that are not constrained by the common dichotomy between "commercial" and "field" recordings are able to assemble broader surveys than they otherwise could. Joyce Cauthen's impressive overview of Alabama fiddling (companion to her book, *With Fiddle and Well-Rosined Bow: Old-Time Fiddling in Alabama*, 1989) is a good case in point. Five recordings (Stripling, Hollis, Hamilton) are taken from commercial 78s of 1924-29; four are from home recordings of 1940-49; and nine are from field recordings of 1978-87. Items of particular interest include the track by D. D. Hollis--one of the earliest traditional fiddlers (born in 1861) to record; and the 1940 example--regrettably, very scratchy, but listenable--of Joe Lee, one of the legendary southeast fiddlers who influenced many others but never made any commercial recordings himself. The recent set of recordings--all carefully recorded and thoroughly enjoyable--illustrate contemporary Alabama fiddling (all with guitar accompaniment--except for added harmonica on the title tune), with emphasis on the less familiar titles. The handsome booklet opens with a long essay on the history of Alabama fiddling, stressing the role of black musicians in the 19th century.

208 Label Name/Number: Arizona Friends of Folklore AFF 33-1
Title: *Cowboy Songs*
Artists: Frances Roberts, Dave Branch, Joe and Bennie Rodriguez, Gail Gardner
Editor: [Keith Cunningham]

Place and Date of Recording: [Flagstaff, AZ, 1971]
Date of Publication: [1971]
Annotations: 15 p. booklet by Keith Cunningham
Selections:
>   Frances Roberts
>>   Bosky Steer
>>   Bury Me Not on the Lone Prairie [B 2]
>>   Zebra Dun [B 16]
>   Dave Branch
>>   Felipe
>>   Flying U Bull
>   Joe and Bennie Rodriguez
>>   Billy Venero [B 6]
>>   Brown Waltz
>>   When the Work's All Done This Fall [B 3]
>   Gail Gardner
>>   Cowman's Troubles
>>   Moonshine Steer
>>   Tying Knots in the Devil's Tail [B 17]

   AFF 33-1:   The Arizona Friends of Folklore made its debut release with this collection of eleven cowboy ballads and instrumentals performed by Roberts, Branch, the Rodriguezes, and Gardner. Gardner, the celebrated Arizona poet in his 70s, sings three of his own compositions, including the now-traditional "Tying a Knot in the Devil's Tail." An illustrated brochure includes text transcriptions and biographical details. [WF 7/72; JAF 338--DKW]

209   Label Name/Number: Arizona Friends of Folklore AFF 33-2
Title: *Cowboy Songs, Vol. II*
Artists: Frances Roberts, Billy Simon, Horace Crandall, Van Holyoak
Editor: [Keith Cunningham]
Place and Date of Recording: [Flagstaff, AZ, 1972]
Date of Publication: [1972]
Annotations: 12 p. "booklet" by Keith Cunningham & James Bartell
Selections:
>   Frances Roberts
>>   Billy the Kid
>>   High Toned Dance, The
>>   Tenderfoot, The
>   Billy Simon
>>   Border Affair
>>   Old Rooney's Calf's A-Bawlin'
>   Horace Crandall
>>   Casey Jones [G 1]
>>   Irish Washer Woman, The
>>   Peek-A-Boo Waltz
>>   Soldier's Joy
>>   Turkey in the Straw
>   Van Holyoak
>>   Gol-Durned Wheel, The [dB 38]
>>   Terry Sloan
>>   Utah Carl [B 4]

AFF 33-2: This features four performers: octogenarian Billy Simon, who years ago set the poems "Border Affair" and "Tying Knots in the Devil's Tail" [B 17] to music and introduced them to the rodeo (and folk) tradition; Uncle Horace Crandall, 78-year-old fiddler from Clay Springs, Arizona; Van Holyoak, ballad singer also from Clay Springs; and Frances Roberts, traditional singer turned college student, also heard on AFF 33-1. Crandall, who has played fiddle for years at local dances, renders several familiar selections in vigorous and lively style. Holyoak sings three ballads in a very plain and unornamented style, one of which, "Terry Sloan," is a humorous anecdote in song that is not at all widely known. The three ballads by Ms. Roberts are common cowboy pieces, sung to her own accompaniment. [WF 1/75; JAF 343--DKW]

210 Label Name/Number: Arizona Friends of Folklore AFF 33-3
Title: *In an Arizona Town*
Artists: Van Holyoak, Bunk Pettyjohn, Lois "Granny" Thomas, Tim Kizzar, Ralph Rogers, Don
  Goodman
Editor: Keith Cunningham
Place and Date of Recording: [Flagstaff, AZ, 1973]
Date of Publication: [1973]
Annotations: 30 p. booklet (+ pictures) by Keith Cunningham
Selections:
  Van Holyoak
    Clay Town Farm
    Tom Plum's Song
  Bunk Pettyjohn
    Little Mohea [H 8]
    Red River Valley
    Strawberry Roan [B 18]
    Sun's a Gonna Shine
    Texas Bells
    Tom Plum's Run
    Way Back in the Hills
  Lois "Granny" Thomas
    Barefoot Boy
    Brown's Ferry Blues
    Changin' Business
    Kickin' Mule
    Mind Your Own Business
  Tim Kizzar
    Boil Them Cabbage Down
    Bonaparte's Retreat
    Rubber Dolly
    Take Me Back to Tulsa
  Ralph Rogers
    Frank Bole
    Freckles
  Don Goodman
    Walkin' John
    Billy Venero [B 6]
    Cowboy's Shirttail
    Turkey in the Straw

AFF 33-3: This album features six performers from Clay Springs, Arizona. The most enjoyable is Lois "Granny" Thomas, whose bluesy vocal style is almost outstanding. Her five contributions to the album (to her own mandolin accompaniment?) are all humorous or light-hearted pieces, such as "Brown's Ferry Blues," textually different from the standard Delmore Brothers' version; "Mind Your Own Business," reminiscent of the hillbilly and blues standard, "Nobody's Business;" and "Barefoot Boy" (the old "It Was Midnight on the Ocean" recitation). Bunk Pettyjohn offers an unusual banjo instrumental version of "Way Back in the Hills" (= "Hills of Roane County"); a banjo tune titled "Texas Bells" that is antecedent to Bob Wills' popular "Faded Love" tune; a nicely sung but textually garbled version of "Little Mohee," and an unusually cast guitar instrumental version of "Strawberry Roan." Don Goodman sings 24 stanzas of the classic E. E. Rexford composition, "Billy Venero" and some lesser known pieces. Ralph Rogers sings two unaccompanied ballads in a plain, rather unmelodious style. Tom Kizzar plays a scratchy but nice fiddle on "Take Me Back to Tulsa," "Bonaparte's Retreat," and "Rubber Dolly," the last one the western descendant of the ragtime song, "Creole Belles." The extensive brochure notes are commendable. [WF 1/75]

211   Label Name/Number: Arkansas Traditions [2 lps, No #]
Title: *Not Far from Here...Traditional Tales and Songs Recorded in the Arkansas Ozarks*
Artists: Various
Collector/Recordist: George West, W. K. McNeil
Place and Date of Recording: Mountain View, AR, 1979-80
Date of Publication: 1981
Annotations: 32 p. 12" x 12" booklet by Francis A. Reynolds, W. K. McNeil, George West
Selections:
> Noble Cowden
>> Bring Back My Blue Eyed Boy
>> Drunkard's Hell
>> Rattlesnake Song, The [G 16]
>> Two Little Lads
>> House Carpenter's Wife, The [C. 243]
> Kenneth Rorie
>> Rich Old Lady [Q 2]
>> Swing and Turn Jubilee
>> Willie Moore
> Rance Blankenship
>> Boston Burglar [L 16 B]
>> Creole Girl, The [H 9]
> Bob Blair
>> Big Crap Game, The
>> Fatal Wedding, The
>> I Can't Stay Here by Myself
>> Nola Shannon

[Also 23 folk narratives]

Ark Trad [No #]: This well-produced double-album set, issued by the Ozark Folk Center with support from various state and federal agencies, is a valuable documentation of the rich folk traditions of the Ozarks. The two discs are divided between narratives (Record #1) and songs. The four singers, all of whom accompany themselves on guitar, have not previously been heard on commercial recordings. Mrs. Noble Cowden (heard also on Ark. Trad. 002, q.v.), was in her 70s when she was recorded--singing and accompanying herself very competently on guitar. Her singing, though rather scratchy and strained on the high notes, is strong and perfectly in tune. Her "House Carpenter" is an unusually bluesy version of this old and widely popular ballad. Most recordings of "Willie Moore" are traceable to the hillbilly recording by Burnett and Rutherford; Kenneth Rorie's recording is from a completely independent oral source--and more evidence that this ballad is (or at least, was) firmly in oral tradition. [JEMFQ 67/68--DD]

212   Label Name/Number: Asch AA 3/4 [2 LP set]
Title: *Asch Recordings/1939-1945, Vol. 2*
Editors: Moses Asch and Charles Edward Smith
Date of Publication: 1967
Annotations: 11 p. brochure by C. E. Smith
Selections: Among 36 selections are:
      Bonny Labouring Boy [M 14] -- George Edwards
      Dark Scenes of Winter -- Mrs. Texas Gladden
      Down in the Willow Garden [F 6] -- Mrs. Texas Gladden
      Railroad Bill [I 13] -- Hobart Smith
      Springfield Mountain [G 16] -- Bascom Lamar Lunsford

      Asch AA 3/4:   In 1967 two boxed sets were issued to demonstrate the broad catalog of Moe Asch's 78 rpm labels that preceded the Folkways label. Even though only five of the 36 selections in this, the second of the two sets, fall clearly within the perimeters of this discography, I list the album because of the choice nature of those five. The two selections by the great ballad singer, Mrs. Texas Gladden, are among her very few non-Library of Congress recordings available on LP. Her brother, Hobart Smith, was an accomplished instrumentalist, and his recording of "Railroad Bill" in an early 78 rpm on the Disc label (Disc 637) influenced many guitar pickers in the folk revival in the 1950s. The Lunsford recording is the same version that appears in Folkways FA 2040 (q. v.). Two ballads by up-state New York singer George Edwards, including "Bonny Laboring Boy," were issued in a 78 rpm album (Asch 560) in the 1940s; this is his only recording issued on LP.

213   Label Name/Number: Asch AH 3831
Title: *Ballads and Songs of the Blue Ridge Mountains: Persistence and Change*
Artists: Hobart Delp, Cliff Evans, Spud Gravely, Sarah Hawkes, Paul and Polly Joines, Ivor Melton, Glen Neaves, Granny Porter, Kilby Reeves, Glen Smith, Ruby Vass, Wade Ward
Collector/Recordists: Eric Davidson, Paul Newman, Caleb Finch
Place and Date of Recording: VA, NC, 1950s and '60s
Date of Publication: 1968
Annotations: 12 p. booklet by Paul Newman and Eric Davidson
Selections:
      Barbry Allen [C. 84] -- Granny Porter, Wade Ward
      Budded Roses   -- Paul Joines, Cliff Evans
      County Jail -- Kilby Reeves
      Death of the Lawson Family [F 35] -- Glen Neaves
      1809 -- Glen Neaves
      George Allen [C. 85] -- Spud Gravely
      Green Willow Tree [C. 286] -- Paul Joines
      Hanging of Georgie [C. 209] -- Paul Joines
      Ho Lilly Ho [N 7] -- Sarah Hawkes
      Little Maggie -- Ivor Melton
      Little Sparrow -- Sarah Hawkes
      Lonesome Day -- Ruby Vass
      Pig in a Pen -- Spud Gravely & Glen Smith
      Pretty Polly [P 36b] -- Ivor Melton & Neaves Band
      Returning Sweetheart [N 42] -- Sarah Hawkes
      Roving Gambler [H 4] -- Hobart Delp

Roving Ranger [A 8] -- Paul Joines
Ten Thousand Miles -- Ruby Vass
The War Is A-Raging [O 33] -- Polly Joines
Walkin' in the Parlor -- Kilby Reeves
Young Men and Maids [G 21] -- Paul Joines

Asch AH 3831: This was the third album of field recordings by Davidson, Newman, and Finch from the Blue Ridge (see Fwys FS 3811 and FS 3832 later in this Section). The previous two were recorded in Grayson and Carroll counties of Virginia; this album extends into the adjacent counties of North Carolina. Styles range from older, unaccompanied ballads to renditions with fiddle, guitar, hillbilly stringband, or bluegrass accompaniment. Overall, it is a good collection presenting a wide range of styles, the only conspicuous absence being that of the sentimental parlor ballads. The notes are detailed and generally commendable, but a few incautious statements have crept in. [JAF 325]

214   Label Name/Number: Atlantic SD-1346
Title: *Sounds of the South*
Artists: Various
Collector/Recordist: Alan Lomax with Shirley Collins
Place and Date of Recording: Various, 1959
Date of Publication: 1960
Annotations: 4 p. brochure by Lomax
Selections:

Banks of the Arkansas -- Neil Morris
Farmer's Curst Wife [C. 278] -- E. C. Ball
Jesse James [E 1] -- Neil Morris
Jesse James -- Mountain Ramblers
Kenny Wagner [E 7] -- Bob Carpenter
Paddy on the Turnpike -- Wade Ward, Charley Higgins, Charley Poe
Wave the Ocean -- Neil Morris and Charley Everidge
Windham -- Alabama Sacred Harp Singers
[Also 9 African-American performances]

215   Label Name/Number: Atlantic SD-1347
Title: *Blue Ridge Mountain Music*
Artists: The Mountain Ramblers (Cullen Galyen, Charles Hawks, James Lindsey, Elridge Montgomery, Thurman Pugh); Estil C. Ball, Orna Ball, Spence Moore, Hobart Smith
Collector/Recordist/Editor: Alan Lomax with Shirley Collins
Place and Date of Recording: Various, 1959
Date of Publication: 1960
Annotations: 4 p. booklet by Alan Lomax
Selections:

Mountain Ramblers
   Big Ball in Boston
   Big Tilda
   Cotton Eyed Joe
   John Henry [I 1]
   Liza Jane
   Old Hickory Cane, The
   Rosewood Casket
   Shady Grove

      Silly Bill
E. C. Ball
      Jennie Jenkins
Spence Moore
      Jimmy Sutton
Wade Ward
      Chilly Winds
Hobart Smith
      Poor Ellen Smith [F 11]
      John Brown

216   Label Name/Number: Atlantic SD-1349
Title: *White Spirituals*
Artists: Various
Collector/Recordist/Editor: Alan Lomax
Place and Date of Recording: Various, 1959
Date of Publication: 1960
Annotations: 4 p. booklet by Alan Lomax
Selections:
      Estil C. Ball
            Father Adieu
            Father, Jesus Loves You
            Please Let Me Stay a Little Longer
            Poor Wayfaring Stranger, The
            Tribulations
      Estil C. Ball and Blair Reedy
            When I Get Home
      Estil and Orna Ball, Lacey Richardson, and Blair Reedy
            Cabin on the Hill, The
            Lonesome Valley
      Rev. I. D. Back
            Sermon and Lining Hymn
            Alabama Sacred Harp Singers
            Antioch
            Calvary
      Mountain Ramblers
            Baptizing Down By the River
            Old Country Church, The
      Neil Morris
            Little Moses

217   Label Name/Number: Atlantic SD-1350
Title: *American Folk Songs for Children*
Artists: Various
Collector/Recordist/Editor: Alan Lomax with Shirley Collins
Place and Date of Recording: Various, 1959
Date of Publication: 1960
Annotations: 4 p. booklet by Alan Lomax
Selections:
      Mountain Ramblers
            Glen's Chimes

        Johnson's Old Gray Mule
        Old Joe Clark
        Train 111
        Whoa Mule
    Almeda Riddle
        Chick-A-Li-Lee-Lo
        Frog Went A-Courtin'
        Go Tell Aunt Nancy
        Mama Buy Me a Chiney Doll
        My Little Rooster
    Hobart Smith
        Arkansas Traveller, The
        Banging Breakdown
        Soldier, Soldier
    E. C. Ball
        Paper of Pins
    Mrs. Texas Gladden
        The Little Dappled Cow
[Also 6 African-American performances]

Atl SD-1346: In the summer of 1959 Alan Lomax returned to the South, for the first time in fifteen years, with modern stereophonic recording equipment in order to revisit some of the great singers he had recorded earlier. Atlantic Records issued a boxed set of seven albums from these field recordings titled *Southern Folk Heritage Series*: this introductory album, divided equally between black and white traditions; three albums featuring only black performers (#s 1348, 1351, 1352); and three more listed here, devoted primarily to white singers. When they were issued (available individually as well as in a boxed set), the albums immediately attracted considerable interest: at a time when the folk music revival was beginning to take wings and fly, featuring primarily urban revival singers, Lomax drew attention to some of the many outstanding traditional artists still capable of offering first-rate performances. This album introduced on LP Lomax's "discovery," the Mountain Ramblers of Galax, Va., a bluegrass-styled band (without mandolin) whose repertoire was strong in older traditional music. The band has since been recorded frequently on other labels (see County 720).

Atl SD-1347 concentrates on the Virginia Blue Ridge Mountains, prominently featuring the Mountain Ramblers. Except for Spence Moore, the other artists--Wade Ward, Estil C. Ball, and Hobart Smith--had all been recorded much earlier by Lomax under LC auspices.

The title of Atl SD-1349 takes "spiritual" in its broader sense of a song with a religious theme. The moods range from Rev. Back's sermon and "lining out" hymn (a style in which the leader sings the words of a song and the ensemble then repeats them), from the Mt. Olivet Regular Baptist Church of Kentucky, to shaped note singing recorded at the annual Alabama Sacred Harp Singing convention, to bluegrass gospel and narrative religious songs.

Atl SD-1350 featured one of the last recordings by Mrs. Texas Gladden and the first commercial release by Mrs. Almeda Riddle, a "discovery" of John Q. Wolf, and whom Lomax considered the finest singer since Gladden. The selections range from nursery songs to lullabies to other light-hearted pieces that, while not originally intended exclusively for children, would not be out of place in a children's concert. [JAF 301--DKW]

218a   Label Name/Number: Augusta Heritage AH AHR 009 [cass]
Title: *Folksongs & Ballads, Vol. 3*
Artists: Holley Hundley, Wavie Chappell, Homer Sampson, Hazel Stover
Collector/Recordist: Michael Kline and Gerry Mills

Producer: Gerry Milnes
Place and date of recordings: WV, 1987-90
Date of Publication: 1991
Annotations: Brief insert notes by Gerry Milnes
Selections:

Holley Hundley
    Billy Richardson's Last Ride
    Brother Green
    FFV, The [G 3]
    Little Lonie [F 4]
    Lord Level [C. 75]
    Love Henry [C. 68]
    Silver Dagger [G 21]
    Willy Brook
Wavie Chappell
    Beautiful Damsel
Homer Sampson
    Battle of Mill Springs
    House Carpenter [C. 243]
    Salem's Bright King
Hazel Stover
    Guide Me Oh Thou Great Jehovah
    Mary Dowell
    Molly Bender [O 36]
    Plains of Waterloo

218b **Label Name/Number:** Augusta Heritage AH AHR 010 [cass]
Title: *Folksongs & Ballads, Vol. 4*
Artists: Clyde Case, Jim Knicely, William May, Bonnie McKinney
Collector/Recordist/Producer: Gerry Milnes
Place and date of recordings: WV, 1990-91
Date of Publication: 1992
Annotations: Brief insert notes by Gerry Milnes
Selections:

Clyde Case
    Nickety, Nackety
    Old Sow
    Davy Crockett
Jim Knicely
    If the Wind Had Only Blown the Other Way
    Jolly Old Dutchman, The
    Welcome
    British American Fight [H 20]
William May
    Rueben's Train
    Little Bessie
    Little Pink
    Darlin' Cory
    Down by the Riverside [P 18]
    Sweet Sadie [I 8]
Bonnie McKinney

Black Eyed Susie
Code of the Mountains

AH AHR 009 / 010. Davis and Elkins College's Augusta Heritage Center is devoted to the preservation and encouragement of local traditions. In recent years Gerry Milnes has produced a number of cassettes of West Virginia traditional folksingers and musicians that attest to the still-flourishing older layers of folk music in that state. Vols. 1 and 2 in the series, *Folksongs and Ballads*, are listed in Section I under the names of the principal performers (Everett White and Phyllis Marks). Vol. 3 is an excellent compendium. Holley Hundley, 84 when recorded, is a good singer whose "Little Lonie" is particularly lovely. Even more impressive is Homer Sampson (b. 1907), whose fine "House Carpenter" is marred only by the ravages of age on the singer's vocal control. Hundley's daughter, Wavie Chappell, sings a beautiful ballad with dulcimer--the only accompanied selection on 009. Stover's mournful ballad about a young soldier who died at Waterloo does not seem to be closely related to other, more common, ballads about the same event (Laws J 1 - J 4). The star of 010 is William May (b. 1911), who, singing to his own fiddle accompaniment, offers a fine rendition of "Reuben's Train," complete with scratchy train imitations. His "Pretty Little Miss" is a short version of a ballad not often recorded.

219   Label Name/Number: Blue Ridge Institute BRI 002
Title: *Virginia Traditions: Ballads from British Tradition*
Artists: Various
Collector/Recordist: Herbert Halpert & Emory L. Hamilton, Sidney Robertson, Kip Lornell,
          George Foss, Alan & Elizabeth Lomax, Joe Wilson, Mike Seeger, Victor Record Co.
Editor/Producers: Blanton Owen, Roddy Moore, and Kip Lornell.
Place and Date of Recording: From commercial 78s and in the field, VA, Atlanta, GA, New York
          City; 1925-77
Date of Publication: 1978
Annotations: 17 p. 12" x 12" booklet by Blanton Owen
Selections:

As I Walked over London's Bridge [C. 209] -- S. F. Russell
Bad Girl, The [Q 26] -- Mrs. Texas Gladden
Barbara Allen [C. 84] -- Dan Tate
Butcher's Boy [P 24], The -- Kelly Harrell
Devil's Nine Questions, The [C. 1] -- Mrs. Texas Gladden
Farmer's Curst Wife, The [C. 278] -- Joe Hubbard
Froggie Went a-Courtin' -- Robert Russell
House Carpenter, The [C. 243] -- Dorothy Rorick
Jealous Lover, The [F 1] -- Stanley Brothers
Little Massie Grove [C. 81] -- Ruby Bowman Plemmons
Oh Death -- Dock Boggs
Old Ireland [N 30] -- Polly Johnson
Queen Sally [C. 295 / P 9] -- Kate Peters Sturgill
Raging Sea, How It Roars, The [C. 289] -- Ernest V. Stoneman
Three Babes, The [C. 79] -- Spence Moore
Three Maids, The [C. 11] -- Polly Johnson
Turkish Rebelee, The [C. 286]-- Horton Barker
Wild Hog in the Woods [C. 18] -- Eunice Yeatts McAlexander
Wind and Rain [C. 10] -- Dan Tate

BRI 002: Virginia's rich Anglo-American folk music tradition has not escaped documentation. Starting with the founding of the Virginia Folklore Society by C. Alphonso Smith in 1913,

Virginia collectors, led by Smith and Arthur K. Davis, sought to capture the believed-to-be-moribund singing tradition that proved that Child's catalog of old British ballads had migrated to the New World. In 1929 Davis published a collection of over 600 texts of Child ballads and followed it in 1960 with another volume of an additional 150 texts. Meanwhile, a 1949 checklist, *Folksongs of Virginia*, listing nearly 1,000 songs and ballads not in the Child corpus, demonstrated a far broader folk music tradition still thriving. This album includes 13 Child ballads and three later broadside ballads, a native American ballad with British antecedents (F 1), and two other non-ballad-like imported pieces. The presentation styles are arranged chronologically from *a capella* vocals to vocal with banjo or guitar, to string band accompaniment. A few performers are familiar: Mrs. Texas Gladden, Horton Barker, Dock Boggs, Ernest Stoneman, Kelly Harrell, and the Stanley Brothers; but the others have been recorded on LP rarely if at all. Like all the releases in BRI's LP series, the brochure is handsomely laid out and well illustrated. [JEMFQ 61]

220   Label Name/Number: Blue Ridge Institute BRI 004
Title: *Virginia Traditions: Native Virginia Ballads and Songs*
Artists: Various
Collector/Recordist: Various
Editor: Doug DeNatale
Place and Date of Recording: From commercial 78s and a 45; in the field, VA, NC, TX, NY, KY,
        1925-80
Date of Publication: 1981
Annotations: 21 p. 12" x 12" booklet by Doug DeNatale
Selections:

> Ballad of Caty Sage, The -- J. C. Pierce
> Ballad of Fancy Gap, The -- Jim and Artie Marshall
> Claude Allen [E 6] -- Hobart Smith
> Cyclone of Rye Cove, The -- Carter Family
> Fate of Dewey Lee, The -- Spence Moore
> Fate of Talmadge Osborne, The -- Ernest V. Stoneman
> Highway 52 -- Little Doc Raymond and Coleman Pardners
> Life and Death of Charlie Poole, The -- Ted Prillaman
> New River Song, The -- Jim and Artie Marshall
> Pinnacle Mountain Silver Mine, The -- Helen Cockran
> Poor Goins -- James Taylor Adams and Finley Adams
> Sidney Allen [E 5] -- Spence Moore
> Story of Freeda Bolt, The -- Floyd County Ramblers
> Story of the Flood, The -- Stanley Brothers
> Vance Song, The [F 17] -- Branch W. Higgins
> Wreck of the 1256, The -- Vernon Dalhart
> Wreck of the Old 97, The [G 2] -- Kelly Harrell and Henry Whitter

BRI 004: This album offers seventeen native Virginian ballads, ranging from the extremely well known to the quite rare. Three ballads deal with railroad-related accidents: "The Fate of Talmadge Osborne," "The Wreck of the 1256" and "The Wreck of the Old 97," all from commercial 78s of the 1920s--the first and third by native Virginian performers. The other two recordings taken from commercial 78s are the Floyd County Ramblers's and the Carter Family's pieces, both dealing with incidents of 1929. Except for "Old 97," all of these songs, despite the popularity of the artists who recorded them, have been recovered extremely infrequently from oral noncommercial tradition. The immensely popular and influential recording artist Vernon Dalhart is one of the few non-Virginian artists featured on this sampling. The others are Uncle Branch W. Higgins of Kentucky, who sings "The Vance Song," and the Adams cousins, also of Kentucky, who sing "Poor Goins."

Evidently there are no known recordings of these ballads by Virginians; however, no apology should be necessary for any of their inclusions. Higgins's performance, originally made for LC in 1937, is one of the best examples of unaccompanied American ballad singing on record. The Adamses' a capella unison duet is also a strong performance. James Taylor Adams, though Kentucky born, was one of the most productive folksong collectors in Southwest Virginia. Of considerably greater popularity are the two ballads about the Hillsville Courthouse shootout of 14 March 1912 involving the Allen Clan. DeNatale's headnotes provide an excellent summary of the historical details of the event, which spawned two very popular ballads sung on this disc by Hobart Smith and Spence Moore. Moore's version of "Sidney Allen" is not sung to the usual "Casey Jones" tune but to a related melody that is eight, rather than four, lines of text long. Of particular interest is "The Ballad of Caty Sage," an account of an event that occurred in Grayson County in 1792 but was not written until 1940. The story of how this song came to be written a century and a half after the episode it documents is a fascinating example of the complicated chain of events that can lead to folk poetry and folk balladry. The last four ballads on the album all either deal with events of the 1950s or later, or else were written then. They are testimony to the continuing strength of the tradition of folk balladry into the last two decades. The album and accompanying booklet are commendable. The selections are musically strong and well recorded, with the exception of two or three that are dubbed from rather scratchy old 78s. The brochure notes are informative and accurate. [JEMFQ 69]

221   Label Name/Number: Blue Ridge Institute BRI 005
Title: *Virginia Traditions: Blue Ridge Piano Styles*
Artists: Various
Collector/Recordist: Various
Editor: Pete Hartman
Place and Date of Recording: Some from commercial 78s (1925-29); others in VA., ca 1959-81
Date of Publication: 1981
Annotations: 12 p. booklet by Pete Hartman
Selections:

> Big Bend Gal -- Shelor Family
> Blue Ridge Rambler's Rag -- H. M. Barnes' Blue Ridge Ramblers
> Caravan -- Janie Carper
> Cumberland Gap -- Gary Patton
> Dill Pickle Rag -- Thelma Thompson
> Double Quick March -- Haywood Blevins
> Fisher's Hornpipe -- Hillbillies
> Fly Around My Blue-Eyed Girl -- Hobart Smith
> General Grant's Grand March -- Haywood Blevins
> Golden Slippers -- Jennifer Crawford
> St. Louis Blues -- Dorothy Zeh
> T's for Texas -- Gary Patton
> Turn Your Radio On -- Jennifer Crawford

BRI 005: The fifth in Blue Ridge Institute's series of albums documenting the musical traditions of Virginia is devoted to a particular instrument, and one that is not often thought of as a vehicle for folk music. Pete Hartman's excellent introductory essay on the history of piano--both in general and in the Blue Ridge Mountains--leaves the listener/reader without any doubts of the importance of the instrument in folk tradition. An interesting question raised is why the piano, common in the area during the early 20th century, is so poorly represented on hillbilly recordings of the 1920s and '30s. A possible explanation, offered by Charles Wolfe, is that "record company executives very early formed a stereotyped notion of what a mountain stringband should sound like, and they exercised more than a little influence to make sure the bands they recorded conformed to this stereotype." I think there is some truth to this idea; but because Al Hopkins's Hill Billies, the earliest large stringband to record, had a piano, one wonders when those stereotypes were formed, and on what they were based. Most other possible explanations--lack of portability, unavailability of pianos on out-of-town recording expeditions, etc., collapse in the face of the great number of blues pianists recorded in the same years. Like its predecessors this volume draws upon early commercial 78 rpm recordings as well as more recent field recordings. Four selections fall into the former category: those by the Hillbillies, the Shelor Family, the Highlanders, and the Blue Ridge Ramblers. The range of roles taken by the piano is great, from simple back-up accompaniment for other instruments to part of ensemble to solo lead on marches, blues, rags, gospel, jazz/pop, and country songs. Little is said in the brochure notes about the style of the playing per se; a knowledgeable listener will probably realize that most if not all of these instrumentalists are playing by ear and not from sheet music. Though differences between these musicians and classically trained pianists are easy to detect, it is harder to articulate them. In the case of those pieces learned from more "sophisticated" pianists, probably over radio or on discs, such as "Caravan" and "Dill Pickle Rag," the difference is partially a matter of simplification--elimination of technically difficult passages, greater repetition, etc., such as one finds when one compares a popular TPA ballad with a rendition by a folksinger. More interesting are the songs that the performer probably never heard on a piano, but transposed from another instrument, such as "T's for Texas" and "Fly Around My Blue-Eyed Girl." Hobart Smith's rendition of the latter sounds very much like he had in mind a banjo (or fiddle) and guitar, and was trying to reconstruct that sound on the piano. This is not unlikely, since Smith played all those instruments with great proficiency. His piano playing is so idiosyncratic it is regrettable there is not more of it preserved on recordings. Hartman's generally very good brochure notes focus on the performers and their milieu, with little if any commentary on the songs/tunes themselves. The problem of selective vs. exhaustive discography/bibliography is solved by not giving any references to other renditions at all. [JEMFQ 69]

222 **Label Name/Number:** Campus Folksong Club Records, University of Illinois, CFC 201
Title: *Green Fields of Illinois*
Artists: Stelle Elam, Cecil Goodwin, Jim Goodwin, Doris and Lyle Mayfield, Cathy and Lloyd
     Reynolds
Editor: Judy McCulloh
Place and Date of Recording: Champaign-Urbana, IL, 1963
Date of Publication: [1963]
Annotations: 39 p. booklet by Archie Green, Fritz K. Plous, Jr., Judy McCulloh, Preston K. Martin,
     Dick Adams, John & Joke Walsh
Selections:
     Stelle Elam
          Billy in the Low Ground
          Buffalo Nickel
          Green Fields of America
          Stoney Point
     Stelle Elam and Lyle Mayfield
          Crow Creek/Jay Bird/Tennessee Wagoner
     Cecil Goodwin
          Billy Richardson's Last Ride
          Fair Fanny Moore
          Mississippi Flood
          My Little Girl
          Old Age Pension
     Lyle Mayfield

        Black Sheep, The
        Drink 'Er Down
Jim Goodwin
        Apples in the Summertime
        Green Corn
Jim Goodwin, Cecil Goodwin
        Haste to the Wedding
        Old Coon Dog/Mississippi Sawyer
Lyle and Doris Mayfield
        Letter Edged in Black, The
        Put My Little Shoes Away
        Sally Goodin
Cathy and Lloyd Reynolds
        Farther Along
        Lord, Build Me a Cabin in Glory Land
        Tramp on the Street
Cathy and Lloyd Reynolds and Lyle Mayfield
        Life's Railway to Heaven

    CFC UI CFC 201: In his introductory essay in the brochure to this undertaking of U of I's folksong club, then-faculty advisor Archie Green traces the events that led to the album's production: an exploration of some of the traditional music that flourished in the Champaign-Urbana region. The album includes four tunes by fiddler Stelle Elam; fiddle, banjo, and guitar instrumentals by Jim Goodwin; ballads and songs by Cecil Goodwin; sentimental ballads by Doris and Lyle Mayfield; and, perhaps the high points of the album, four wonderfully sung gospel songs by Cathy Reynolds. Goodwin's "Fair Fanny Moore" is a full text of this fairly uncommon ballad. The brochure provides careful documentation on singers and references on the selections as well as complete text and partial tune transcriptions.

223   Label Name/Number: County 703
Title: *Texas Hoedown*
Artists: Bartow Riley, Vernon Solomon, Benny Thomasson
Collector/Recordist: Charles Faurot
Producers: Charles Faurot
Editor: Peter Siegel
Place and date of recordings: Texas, 1965?
Date of Publication: [1965]
Annotations: Liner notes by Faurot
Selections:
    Benny Thomasson
        Ace of Spades
        Billy in the Low Ground
        Black Mountain Rag
        Bonaparte's Retreat
        Lady's Fancy
        Laughing Boy
    Vernon Solomon
        Beaumont Rag
        Cripple Creek
        Sally Johnson
        Sopping the Gravy

> Sunnyside
> Bartow Riley
> > Grey Eagle
> > Sally Goodin
> > Waynesboro Reel

County 703. For many folk music aficionados outside of the Texas-Oklahoma region, this wonderful album provided their first taste of the smooth and highly ornamented music called Texas, or contest, fiddling style. The three fiddlers represented all come from long lines of fiddlers, participate in local fiddling contests, and win more than their share of prizes. Thomasson is best known of the three, having performed considerably outside the southwest in the 1970s. Faurot's notes discuss the distinctive features of the Texas style: long, smooth bowstrokes, melodic variation, accompaniment on piano or "closed-chord" guitar (rather than use of single-note runs, as in the southeast).

224 **Label Name/Number:** County 707
Title: *Texas Fiddle Favorites*
Artists: Major Franklin, Lewis Franklin, Norman Solomon
Collector/Recordist/Producer: Charles Faurot
Place and date of recordings: Texas, 1965-66?
Date of Publication: [1966]
Annotations: Liner notes by Faurot
Selections:
> Lewis Franklin
> > Blue Eagle
> > Cotton Patch Rag
> > Dill Pickle Rag
> > Leather Britches
> > Salt River
> Major Franklin
> > Apple Blossom
> > Durang's Hornpipe
> > Fisher's Hornpipe
> > Forked Deer
> > Tom and Jerry
> Norman Solomon
> > Kaw River
> > Miller's Reel
> > Smith's Reel
> > Wagoner

County 707. Charles Faurot presents another trio of outstanding Texas fiddlers in this follow-up to County 703 (see above). Major Franklin is the best known (and oldest) of the three and has had a great influence on Texas contest fiddling over the years. In his notes, Faurot describes contest fiddling and the Gilmer, Texas, contest, in particular. Norman Solomon and his brother, Vernon (see County 703) were recently inducted into the Texas Fiddlers' Hall of Fame. The tunes are all well-known Texas favorites; several of them are not often encountered outside the southwest.

225 **Label Name/Number:** County 717
Title: *More Clawhammer Banjo Songs & Tunes from the Mountains*

Artists: Various
Collector/Recordist: Charles Faurot and Richard Nevins
Producer: Charles Faurot
Place of Recording: VA, NC
Date of Publication: [1969]
Annotations: Liner notes by Faurot
Selections:

> Big Eyed Rabbit -- Matokie Slaughter
> Cousin Sally Brown -- Willard Watson
> Cripple Creek -- Tommy Jarrell
> Elkhorn Ridge -- Oscar Wright
> Jake Gillie -- Oscar Wright
> John Brown's Dream -- Tommy Jarrell
> Johnny's Gone to War -- Matokie Slaughter
> Little Birdie -- Gaither Carlton
> Omie Let Your Bangs Hang Down -- Gaither Carlton
> Roustabout -- Fred Cockerham
> Sally Ann -- Sidna Myers and Fulton Myers
> Sandy River -- Oscar Wright
> Shady Grove -- Sidna Myers and Fulton Myers
> Stillhouse -- Matokie Slaughter
> Twin Sisters -- Sidna Myers

Cty 717:   The musicians are all from the region straddling the Virginia-North Carolina border--where, Faurot, suggests, the clawhammer style originated. Except for Fulton Myers' fiddle accompaniment, all the banjoists play unaccompanied. The notes give biographical background and observations on playing styles and tunings. These are all very good traditional musicians (one woman among them), playing some common and some rarer tunes, all well recorded.

226   Label Name/Number: County 757
Title: *Clawhammer Banjo, Vol. 3*
Artists: Various
Collector/Recordist: Most by Charlie Faurot and Richard Nevins
Editor: Charlie Faurot
Place of Recording: NC, VA, WV
Date of Publication: 1978
Annotations: Liner notes by Blanton Owen
Selections:

> As Time Draws Near -- Tommy Jarrell
> Georgie -- Matokie Slaughter
> Hollyding -- Wade Ward
> Jimmy Sutton -- Glen Smith
> John Hardy -- Esker Hutchins
> John Henry -- Glen Smith
> Johnson Boys -- Wade Ward
> Let Old Drunkards Be -- Oscar Wright
> Little Birdie -- Glen Smith
> Little Brown Jug -- Mildred & Beverly Thompson
> Liza Jane -- Oscar Wright
> Old True Love -- Dan Tate
> Shaving a Dead Man -- Oscar Wright

Sugar Hill -- Esker Hutchins
Tater Patch -- Charlie Lowe

Cty 757: This sampling of clawhammer, or frailing, banjo playing features mostly musicians from North Carolina, Virginia, and West Virginia. Several of the musicians (Ward, Jarrell, Smith, Wright) are well represented on other albums. The Thompsons, a banjo-and-fiddle husband and wife duo, have not been recorded before. The Charlie Lowe cut is taken from a home recording of many years earlier. Most of the selections are unaccompanied banjo; a few have vocals. Owen's jacket notes are very descriptive of the several musical styles represented.

227a Label Name/Number: County 786
Title: *Traditional Music from the Cumberland Plateau, Vol. 1: Gettin' up the Stairs*
Artists: Various
Collector/Recordist: Barry Poss, Bobby Fulcher
Producer: Bobby Fulcher
Place and Date of Recording: Mostly in the field, TN, KY, 1978-82; one home recording, 1973
Date of Publication: [1988]
Annotations: 10 p. booklet by Bobby Fulcher
Selections:
Clyde Troxell
French Waltz, The
Me and My Old Wife Had a Little Falling Out
Skippin' Through the Frost and the Snow
The Rocky Toppers
Sleepin' Lulu
Candy Gal
Bessford Hicks
Cumberlin' Land
Clyde Davenport
Gettin' up the Stairs
Johnny Booger
Rattlin' Down the Acorns
Wild Goose Chase
Zollie's Retreat
Louie Jones
The Corn Song
Retta Spradlin
Man of Constant Sorrow
Pea Fowl, The
Wild Bill Jones [E 10]

227b Label Name/Number: County 787
Title: *Traditional Music from the Cumberland Plateau, Vol. 2: Five Miles out of Town*
Artists: Various
Collector/Recordist: Barry Poss, Bobby Fulcher
Producer: Bobby Fulcher
Place and Date of Recording: Mostly in the field, KY, TN, 1978-1982; 3 home recordings, 1949
Date of Publication: [1988]
Annotations: 10 p. booklet by Bobby Fulcher
Selections:
Clarence Ferrill and Band

City on the Hill
Goin' Across the Sea
New Five Cents
Virgil and Willard Anderson
Ain't It Awful
Virgil Anderson
Bye Bye Blues
Goin' Around the World
John Sharp and Band
Five Miles out of Town
Sharp's Hornpipe
Three Way Hornpipe
Dee Hicks
Lincoln Was a Union Man
Old Bangum [C. 18]
Young Repoleon [J 5]

Cty 786/787: The Cumberland Plateau, occupying three counties that straddle the Kentucky-Tennessee border, was best known, musically, as the home of two celebrated musicians of the 1920s, Richard Burnett and Leonard Rutherford. That there is still a rich survival of older musical traditions is demonstrated by these two albums produced by Bobby Fulcher. Most of the 27 cuts on the two albums were made by Fulcher and Barry Poss--except for three selections by John Sharp and Band, recorded by Sgt. Alvin York in 1949, and one 1973 home cassette recording of Bessford Hicks. Besides Sharp's band, Vol. 2 includes instrumentals by Clarence Ferrill and Band and by Virgil and Willard Anderson; and three unaccompanied vocals by Dee Hicks. Vol. 1 contains a banjo solo and banjo/vocals by Clyde Troxell, two instrumentals by The Rocky Toppers; five fiddle and banjo tunes by Clyde Davenport; three banjo/vocals by Retta Spradlin; and unaccompanied songs, one each by Bessford Hicks and Louie Jones. Many pieces are rare outside the region; exceptions are Hicks' "Old Bangum" and "Young Repoleon," Spradlin's "Wild Bill Jones" (Laws E 10), and Davenport's banjo/vocal "Johnny Booger" [Booker]. Prior to his death in 1983, Dee Hicks ranked as one of our greatest ballad singers, both in terms of his fine singing style and his extensive repertoire (some 400 songs) of well-preserved older texts. His unusually full text of Child 18 is one of the few recovered in this country that includes the denoument of the hero slaying the wild woman; his Napoleon ballad is rare in North America outside of the northeast. Fulcher's extensive historical and biographical notes, in a profusely illustrated 10-page 12" x 12" booklet, are marred only by the difficult-to-read typography and the unusual layout. [JAF 408]

228a   Label Name/Number: Folk-Legacy FSA-22
Title: *The Traditional Music of Beech Mountain, North Carolina, Vol. 1, The Older Ballads and Sacred Songs*
Artists: Various
Collector/Recordist: Sandy Paton
Place and Date of Recording: Beech Mountain, NC, 1961-64?
Date of Publication: 1964
Annotations: 31 p. booklet by Sandy Paton
Selections:
Lee Monroe Presnell
Awake, Awake, My Old True Lover [M 4]
George Collins [C. 85]
Johnny, Oh, Johnny
Sweet Soldier Boy [K 12]

        Two Sisters, The [C. 10]
Buna Hicks
    Day Is Past and Gone, The
    Fathers, Now Our Meeting Is Over
    Johnny Doyle [M 2]
    Sir Lionel [C. 18]
    Young Beham [C. 53]
Buna Hicks and Rosa Presnell
    Where the Sun Will Never Go Down
Hattie Presnell
    Five Nights Drunk [C. 274]
    Jealous Brothers, The [M 32]
    Pretty Crowing Chicken [C. 248]
    William Hall [N 30]
Lena Armstrong
    The House Carpenter [C. 243]
Lena Armstrong and Etta Jones
    The Farmer's Curst Wife [C. 278]

228b   **Label Name/Number:** Folk-Legacy FSA-23
Title: *The Traditional Music of Beech Mountain, North Carolina, Vol. 2, The Later Songs and Hymns*
Artists: Various
Collector/Recordist: Sandy Paton; Diane Hamilton
Producers: Sandy Paton and Lee B. Haggerty
Place and Date of Recording: Beech Mountain, NC, 1961-64?
Date of Publication: 1964/65
Annotations: 29 p. booklet by Sandy Paton
Selections:
Margie Harmon, R. L. Harmon, Ottie "Coot" Greene
    Angel Band
    I'm Going That Way
    Precious Memories
    Where the Soul of Man Never Dies
Margie Harmon, R. L. Harmon
    Soldier and the Lady, The [P 14]
R. L. Harmon
    Soldier John
Lee Monroe Presnell
    Baldheaded End of the Broom
    I Went to See My Suzie
    In Dublin City [L 12]
    Little Maggie
    Look Up, Look Down That Old Railroad
    Old Virginny
Buna Hicks
    Flying Around My Pretty Little Miss
    Going Away Tomorrow [N 8]
    Johnson Boys
Buna Hicks and Viola Hicks
    Cripple Creek

Lena Armstrong and Etta Jones
    Courting Case
    Rogers' Gray Mare [P 8]
Captain Hicks and Viola Hicks
    More Pretty Girls Than One
    Medley: Poor Ellen Smith / Down in the Willow Garden / Maple on the Hill
Lena Armstrong
    Tobacco Union
Tab Ward
    Little Maggie
Group
    Amazing Grace

FLeg FSA-22 / FSA-23:   These two companion albums demonstrate the rich musical tradition that collector Paton found in the Beech Mountain community of Watauga and Avery Counties, in northwestern North Carolina, in 1961 and thereafter. Though the two albums are subtitled to suggest that the older material is on Vol. I, this division is not accurate. One of Paton's best singers, well-represented on these LPs, was Lee Monroe Presnell (*ca.* 1875-1963), whose age and frail health levied a considerable toll on his singing in his last years, though his grand style and substantial repertoire are still apparent. One can well imagine how magnificent he must have sounded when he wasn't plagued by such shortness of breath. One of his loveliest numbers is the very rare lyric (probably once a ballad), "Johnny, Oh, Johnny." Many of the other singers are kin to Presnell: Lena Armstrong and Etta Jones are his daughters; Buna Hicks is his niece; Captain Hicks and Hattie Presnell, her children. Both Buna and Hattie are also excellent singers. Both albums have booklets that share a common introductory sketch on the region and its people and on the performers in the respective albums. Each also contains song headnotes and text transcriptions. All in all, the pair constitute an excellent collection by outstanding singers. [JAF 310--DKW]

229   Label Name/Number: Folk Promotions 41942
Title: *Old-Time Music from Calhoun County, West Virginia*
Artists: Various
Place of Recording: Calhoun County, WV
Date of Publication: [ca. 1965]
Annotations: None
Selections:
Phoeba Parsons
    Cherry River Line
    Curb Stone, The
    John Hardy [I 2]
    Old House, The
    Pretty Polly [P 36b]
    True Born Irishman
    West Fork Girls [= Come All You West Virginia Girls]
Phoeba Parsons and Roscoe Parsons
    Old Jimmy Johnson
    Shortening Bread
Maude Altizer
    Wealthy Squire [N 20]
    One John Riley
Arthur Nicholas
    Wreck of the Shenandoah, The [dG 52]

    Sara Schoolcraft
        Charming Little Girl [M 3]
    General Custer Nicholas
        Ballad of Jay Legg
    Holly Schartiger
        The Blind Child
    Noah Cottrell
        Fox Chase

     Folk Promotions 41942: The debut album of Ken Davidson's new Folk Promotions label (subsequently renamed Kanawha) was a wonderful collection of traditional music from Calhoun County but unfortunately without any documentation whatever. Much of the album is justifiably devoted to Phoeba Parsons, who sings and plays banjo. Her "Curb Stone" is a wonderful story in double talk with a song interpolated. Also excellent performances are the two old ballads by Schoolcraft and Altizer. The only 20th-century songs are "Wreck of the Shenandoah," from 1925, and "Ballad of Jay Legg," about a 1904 murder in Clay County. Phoeba Parson's brother, Noah Cottrell, offers an unusual cante fable version of "Fox Chase." The two Parsons play two fiddle tunes accompanied by the moribund technique of beating straws (or "fiddle sticks") on the fiddle strings. [JAF 313--DKW]

230 Label Name/Number: Folk Promotions [no #]
Title: *Old-Time Songs and Tunes from Clay County, West Virginia*
Artists: Jenes Cottrell, French Carpenter
Place and Date of Recording: Clay and Calhoun Counties, WV, ca. 1963
Date of Publication: [ca. 1964]
Annotations: Liner notes by Ken Davidson
Selections:
    Jenes Cottrell
        Cherry River Line
        Gospel Plow
        Hesitating Blues
        Minnow on the Hook
        New Titanic
        Sail Away Ladies
        Soldier's Joy
    French Carpenter
        Camp Chase
        Elzics Farewell
        Forked Buck
        Old Christmas Morning
        Shelvin' Rock
        Wild Horse
        Yew Piney Mountain

     Folk Promotions [no #]: Though Jenes Cottrell and David Frank ("French") Carpenter lived about seven miles apart and occasionally made music together, this album is divided between solo performances by each of them--Cottrell on banjo (which he also builds and repairs) and Carpenter on fiddle. Cottrell's unusual banjo style is aptly characterized in Davidson's notes as "one of the most primitive styles of banjo playing known," and his repertoire is similarly unusual. His "Cherry River Line" is a loosely connected love lyric with elements from "Little Maggie"/"Darling Cory." "Sail Away Ladies" is not the usual tune/lyric, and "Hesitating Blues" borrows elements from songs like "Train That Carried My Girl from Town." "New Titanic" is Cottrell's own composition to the tune of "John Hardy." Carpenter's fiddling is lovely--especially on "Wild Horse." [JAF 307--DKW]

231   Label Name/Number: Folkways FA 2309
Title: *Old Love Songs and Ballads from the Big Laurel, North Carolina*
Artists: Dillard Chandler, Lee Wallin, Berzilla Wallin, Cas Wallin, Elisha Shelton
Collector/Recordist: Peter Gott, John Cohen
Place and Date of Recording: Big Laurel, NC, 1963
Date of Publication: 1964
Annotations: 8 p. booklet by Peter Gott and John Cohen
Selections:
>   Dillard Chandler
>   Awake, Awake [M 4]
>   Hicks Farewell
>   Mathie Grove [C. 81]
>   Sailor Being Tired, The [K 43]
>   Soldier Travelling from the North [C. 299]
>   Cas Wallin
>   Fine Sally [P 9]
>   Pretty Saro
>   Lee Wallin
>   Juba
>   Neighbor Girl
>   Elisha Shelton
>   Don't You Remember [M 3]
>   In Zepo Town [M 32]
>   Berzilla Wallin
>   Conversation with Death
>   Johnny Doyle [M 2]
>   Love Has Brought Me to Despair [P 25]

Fwys FA 2309:   This collection of songs and ballads must rank as some of the finest traditional American singing on record. Chandler and Cas Wallin sing in highly decorated styles. Not only are these all fine singers, but the selections include full texts of several ballads not easily recovered in such a good state. (For more on Chandler, see comments on Folkways FA 2418, in Section I.) The booklet includes brief biographical sketches, notes on the music of the Laurel River region, and song headnotes and text transcriptions. [JAF 310--DKW]

232   Label Name/Number: Smithsonian/Folkways CD SF 40037 (originally issued in part as Folkways FA 2314)
Title: *American Banjo Tunes & Songs in Scruggs Style*
Artists: Various
Collector/Recordist: Mike Seeger
Place and Date of Recording: Various, 1956
Date of Publication: 1990 (Folkways FA 2314 issued in 1957)
Annotations: 4 p. insert brochure by Ralph Rinzler and Mike Seeger
Selections: (* titles not on FA 2314; # titles only on FA 2314)
>   Smiley Hobbs
>   Cotton Eye Joe
>   Pig in a Pen

Rosewood Casket
Shortening Bread*
Train "45"
J. C. Sutphin
Don't Let Your Deal Go Down
I Don't Love Nobody
Under The Double Eagle*
Junie Scruggs
Cripple Creek*
Sally Goodin/Sally Ann
Snuffy Jenkins
Big Eared Mule*
Careless Love*
Chicken Reel*
Cumberland Gap*
John Henry (2 versions)*
Kansas City Kitty*
Lonesome Road Blues
Sally Ann*
Sally Goodin*
Shortening Bread*
Twinkle, Twinkle Little Star
Oren Jenkins
Bugle Call Rag*
Cripple Creek
Down the Road
Hey, Mr. Banjo*
Home Sweet Home*
Liza Jane*
Spanish Fandango
Joe Stewart
Cackling Hen*
Cumberland Gap*
(John Henry -- #)
Larry Richardson
Bucking Mule*
Dear Old Dixie*
Little Maggie
Lonesome Road Blues*
Take Me Back to the Sunny South
Don Bryant
Jenny Lynn
Turkey in the Straw
Pete Kuykendall (Roberts)
Irish Washerwoman
Eugene Cox
Wildwood Flower
Veronica Stoneman Cox
Lonesome Road Blues
Mike Seeger (Bob Baker, vocal)
Groundhog

(Pretty Polly -- #)
Dick Rittler (Bob Baker & Pike County Ramblers)
    Cindy
Kenny Miller
    Ruben's Train
    (Please Come Back) Little Pal
Eric Weissberg (with Mike Seeger, Ralph Rinzler)
    Jesse James / Hard, Ain't it Hard

     Smithsonian/Fwys SF 40037 (FA 2314):   These recordings by Mike Seeger, when first issued on the Folkways label in 1957 (asterisked titles were not on the original LP), were the first opportunity for most urban listeners to hear Scruggs-style banjo playing in the context of traditional music of the Southeast. In fact, it was the first *album* of bluegrass music (from the mid-40s through the late '50s, all bluegrass recordings were issued on singles). Most of the performers had had some professional experience: Joe Stewart played with Bill Monroe; Snuffy Jenkins recorded on the Bluebird label in the 1930s; Oren Jenkins played with Jim and Jesse McReynolds; Larry Richardson played with Bill Monroe and other bands; Veronica Stoneman Cox is one of the Stoneman family. Some of the musicians (Seeger, Eric Weissberg, Pete Roberts) are of primarily urban backgrounds. Most importantly, the presentation of this album and Seeger's companion survey on Smithsonian/Folkways SF 40038 (Folkways FA 2318) demonstrated the traditional roots of bluegrass music--something not widely appreciated in 1960. The 1991 release includes Seeger's retrospective discussion of bluegrass music in the late 1950s and the circumstances surrounding his recording venture.

233   Label Name/Number: Folkways FA 2315
Title: *The Stoneman Family / Old-Time Tunes of the South (Sutphin, Foreacre, and Dickens)*
Artists: The Stoneman Family; J. C. Sutphin, Louise Foreacre, H. N. Dickens, J. J. Neese, and
        Vernon Sutphin
Collector/Recordist: Michael Seeger
Place and Date of Recording: MD, VA, 1956-57
Date of Publication: 1957
Annotations: 12 p. booklet by Ralph Rinzler
Selections:
    Stoneman Family
        Bile Them Cabbage Down
        Black Dog Blues, The
        Cumberland Gap
        Hallelujah Side
        Hang John Brown
        New River Train
        Say, Darling, Say
        Stoney's Waltz
        When the Springtime Comes
        Wreck of the Old Ninety-Seven, The [G 2]
    J. J. Neese, J. C. Sutphin, V. Sutphin
        Lonesome Road Blues
    Louise Foreacre
        Frankie Was a Good Girl [I 3]
        Late Last Night
        Little Sadie [I 8]
        Rose in Grandma's Garden

War Is A-Raging, The [O 33]
H. N. Dickens
 I Met a Handsome Lady
 Golden Pen
 The Arkansas Traveller
Vernon Sutphin
 John Henry
Vernon Sutphin, J. C. Sutphin
 Lost John

Fwys FA 2315: This album consists of two wholly unrelated groups of musicians (mostly all from Virginia) on the two sides of the disc. One side features the Stoneman family at their home in Carmody, Maryland, at a period betwen Pop Stoneman's long and successful recording career on 78s in the 1920s and early '30s; and the second generation of the Stonemans' modern Nashville-based career of the 1960s and later. Side 2 features H. N. Dickens (b. 1888) of Carroll County, VA; J. C. Sutphin (b. 1885, Patrick County, VA); his son, Vernon; J. J. Neese (b. 1871, Marshall County, TN); Vernon's father-in-law; and Louise Foreacre--not related to the others. J. C. Sutphin played with Charlie Poole and recorded with Henry Whitter in the '20s. He and Dickens had timbered together in southwest Virginia years before; they were recorded in their homes in Maryland. Together, the two sets of recordings constitute an excellent collection of older traditional banjo and fiddle music, ballads, and dance tunes. Rinzler's lengthy notes provide detailed background on the selections. This was one of the best albums of traditional material (in terms of both music and documentation) to appear in the early years of the urban folksong revival.

234 **Label Name/Number:** Folkways FA 2317
Title: *Mountain Music of Kentucky*
Artists: Various
Collector/Recordist: John Cohen
Place and Date of Recording: Eastern KY, 1959
Date of Publication: 1960
Annotations: 32 p. booklet by John Cohen
Selections:
Old Regular Baptist Church Congregation
 Amazing Grace
George Davis
 Death of the Blue Eagle
Mrs. Martha Hall
 Foreign Lander
 Kitty Alone
 Young and Tender Ladies
Willie Chapman
 Jaw Bone
 Little Birdie
Lee Sexton
 Fox Chase
 St. Louis Blues
Roscoe Holcomb
 Across the Rocky Mountain
 Blackeyed Susie
 East Virginia Blues
 I Wish I Were a Single Girl Again

Stingy Woman Blues
Wayfaring Stranger
James B. Cornett
Barbara Allen [C. 84]
Spring of '65, The
Banjo Bill Cornett
Buck Creek Girls
Cluck Old Hen
Old Age Pension Blues
Sweet Willie
Marion Summer, Ina Jones, John Cohen
Lost Indian
Soldiers Joy
Granville Bowlen
Charlie's Neat
Cotton Eyed Joe
Little Sunshine
Corbett Grigsby and Martin Young
John Henry [I 1]
No Letter in the Mail
Rocky Island
James Crase
Give the Fiddler a Dram
Old Joe Clark

Fwys FA 2317: John Cohen, the exuberant banjo-player with the New Lost City Ramblers, was also actively involved in recording, photographing, and filming traditional musicians, both in the United States and abroad in the 1950s and '60s. This was one of his first productions and is an excellent sampling of older traditional styles of Eastern Kentucky. Prominently featured on the album is Roscoe Holcomb, whom Cohen later made the subject of a full album and a half (Folkways FA 2374, 2363). George Davis (FTS 31016), Marion Sumner (JA 030), and Lee Sexton have all been recorded in greater depth more recently. Cohen's brochure notes include a generous selection of his black-and-white photographs taken in the area. [JAF 290--DKW]

235   Label Name/Number: Smithsonian Folkways CD SF 40038 (originally issued in part as Folkways FA 2318)
Title: *Mountain Music Bluegrass Style*
Artists: Various
Collector/Recordist: Mike Seeger
Place and Date of Recording: Mostly Baltimore-Washington area, New York, and Boston; 1958-59
Date of Publication: 1991 (Folkways FA 2318 issued in 1959)
Annotations: 4 p. insert brochure by Mike Seeger
Selections: (* titles not on FA 2318)
Tex Logan
Katy Hill
Natchez Under the Hill
Earl Taylor & the Stoney Mountain Boys
All the Good Times Have Passed and Gone
Foggy Mountain Top *
Fox Chase
Sally Ann *

> Short Life of Trouble
> They're at Rest Together *
> Whitehouse Blues
> Bob Baker & the Pike County Boys
> > Drifting Too Far from the Shore *
> > Feast Here Tonight
> > Little Willie
> > Philadelphia Lawyer, The
> > Snow Dove [P 24]
> Smiley Hobbs
> > Leather Britches
> > Nine Pound Hammer
> Don Stover, Bea Lilly, Chubby Anthony
> > Bile 'em Cabbage Down
> > Cricket on the Hearth
> > Katy Cline
> > There Ain't Nobody Gonna Miss Me
> Jerry Stuart, Smiley Hobbs, Pete Kuykendall, Tom Gray
> > Rocky Run
> Mike Seeger & Bob Yellin
> > Old Joe Clark
> Anthony, Seeger, Yellin
> > New River Train

Smithsonian/Fwys CD SF 40038 (Fwys FA 2318). This album is in many ways a sequel to CD SF 40037; Seeger's "field recordings" feature many of the same musicians, recorded a few years later. Unlike the earlier album, which focused on the banjo *per se* and had minimal vocals or breaks by other instruments, this album presents bluegrass music as it was being played in the late '50s by bands other than the handful who were commercially prominent at the time. Like its predecessor, though, the emphasis is on the older facet of the musicians' repertoires; Seeger observes in his 1990 notes that that was certainly his major interest at the time of the recordings; he also stresses that such a biased selection would not be typical of what one would have heard in a bar or club--even from many of the same bands. Introductory notes by Seeger define bluegrass music broadly and provide biographical sketches of the musicians. Some material included in the 1959 notes (lists of bluegrass bands, radio stations that play bluegrass, etc.) is missing from the 1990 notes because of space limitations, but most of it would be too dated to be useful. Bluegrass music has matured and diversified greatly since these recordings were made; also a great deal has been written about the music from a sophisticated, analytic point of view. None of this should demean these pioneering musicians nor denigrate the significance of the Seeger's efforts to define and explain a new musical phenomenon: the music was (and still sounds) first rate. Of particular interest are Bob Baker's "Little Willie" and "Snow Dove," both learned from his mother, and hauntingly beautiful performances--the latter one of the finest recordings of what is often a dull broadside ballad.

236 Label Name/Number: Folkways FA 2358
Title: *Jean Thomas, The Traipsin' Woman: American Folk Song Festival*
Artists: Various
Place of Recording: KY
Date of Publication: 1960
Annotations: 3 p. booklet
Selections:
> The Children

        Billy Boy -- Donnie Stewart & Terry Perkins
        Bonnie George Campbell [C. 210] -- Margaret Caudil Hurst & daughter
        I Love My Rooster -- Marieda Perkins
        Lord Lovell [C. 75] -- Lucinda Perkins
        Paper of Pins -- Linda Brown & Donnie Stewart
        Paw Paw Patch, The -- Group
    The (Young) People
        Ballad of Peace -- Dave Varney
        Cambric Shirt [C. 2] -- Diane Tincher & Margaret Winters
        Courting Song -- Pleaz Mobley & Olive Mobley
        Give Me One More Chance -- Ruby Dean & Journeymen's Quartet
        Keys of Canterbury -- Ray Napier & Margaret Winters
        Love of Rosanna McCoy -- Dave Varney
        Warning Song -- Rose Day
    The Elders
        Amazing Grace -- Group
        Barbara Ellen [C. 85] -- Rose Day
        Boatin' up Sandy -- George Davidson
        Civil War March -- Aunt Dora Harmon
        Down in the Valley -- Group
        Hi, Said the Blackbird -- Pleaz Mobley
        I'll Never Be Lonesome in Heaven -- Lula M. Curry
        Lord, You've Been So Good to Me -- Aunt Alice Williams
        Pretty Polly [P 36b] -- Pleaz Mobley
        Prodigal Son, The -- Aunt Dora Harmon
        Sally Goodin' -- George Davidson
        Squire's Daughter, The [C. 10] -- Lula M. Curry
        Turkey in the Straw -- Curley Smith & Bob Ramey
[Also Introduction; Cherokee song]

    Fwys FA 2358: Jean Thomas, a native of the Kentucky mountain country with a passionate love for the music and lore of the region, established an annual event in the Cumberlands, "The Singin' Gatherin'," which later became "The American Folksong Festival," and attracted considerable interest during the 1930s when there was little concern with questions of authenticity of performer or presentation. The "festivals" were staged, with performers in costumes playing assigned roles. Thomas's long spoken introduction presents a highly romanticized and sentimentalized framework for her event, and song notes must also be taken with some grains of salt. The distinctions on this album of "Children," "Young People," and "Elders" reflects as much the style of the music as the performers themselves. Nevertheless, there is some good music here (9-year-old Ruby Dean's "Give Me One More Chance" is wonderful, and so is nonagenarian Rose Day's "Barbara Ellen"), but one needs to be aware of the nature of the packaging. [JAF 292--DKW]

237   **Label Name/Number:** Folkways FA 2363
Title: *The Music of Roscoe Holcomb and Wade Ward*
Artists: Roscoe Holcomb and Wade Ward
Collector/Recordist: John Cohen; Eric Davidson, Mike Seeger, or Alan Lomax
Editor(s): John Cohen and Eric Davidson
Place and Date of Recording: (Holcomb) NYC; (Ward) VA, 1937-61
Date of Publication: 1962
Annotations: 8 p. booklet by John Cohen & Eric Davidson
Selections:

Roscoe Holcomb
  Graveyard Blues
  Hills of Mexico
  Little Birdie
  Little Grey Mule
  Man of Constant Sorrow
  Moonshiner
  Old Smokey
  Rising Sun, The
  Trouble in Mind
  True Love
Wade Ward
  Arkansas Traveller
  Cluck Old Hen
  Cumberland Gap
  Half Shaved
  Little Sadie [I 8]
  Lone Prairie [?]
  Mississippi Sawyer (2 renditions)
  New River Train
  Old Jimmy Sutton
  Old Reuben
  Peachbottom Creek
  Sally Ann
  Sourwood Mountain
  Uncle Eef Got a Coon
  Waterbound

Fwys FA 2363: This curious portmanteau album is divided between two excellent musicians who have no connection with each other, and nothing more in common than that both played traditional banjo. John Cohen recorded Holcomb while the latter was in New York City concertizing. The Ward material consists of two 1937 LC field recordings by Alan Lomax ("Cluck Old Hen" and "Waterbound"--with the Bogtrotters band), the balance recorded by Eric Davidson or Mike Seeger between 1956 and 1961. Cohen and Davidson provide biographies of their subjects, notes on the sources of the songs, and text transcriptions where appropriate. Holcomb also accompanies himself on guitar; Ward plays fiddle as well as banjo but does little singing. (For more comments on Holcomb, see notes to Folkways FA 2374; for more on Ward, see Folkways FA 2380, both in Section I.)

238   Label Name/Number: Folkways FA 2365
Title: *Mountain Music Played on the Autoharp*
Artists: Ernest Stoneman, Kilby Snow, Neriah & Kenneth Benfield
Collector/Recordist: Mike Seeger
Place and Date of Recording: VA, 1957, 1961
Date of Publication: 1965
Annotations: 8 p. booklet by Mike Seeger
Selections:
Ernest Stoneman
  All I Got's Gone
  Bile 'Em Cabbage Down
  Flop-eared Mule

Great Reaping Day, The
I'm Alone, All Alone
May I Sleep in Your Barn Tonight, Mister?
She'll Be Coming 'Round the Mountain
Stoney's Wife
Sweet Marie
Wreck of Number Nine [G 26]
Neriah and Kenneth Benfield
'Way Down in the Country
Benfield Hoedown
Ella's Grave
Jacob's Ladder
Old Joe Clark
Shortenin' Bread
Waltz
Kilby Snow
Ain't Goin' to Work Tomorrow
John Henry
Mule Skinner Blues
Precious Jewel
Red River Valley
Tragic Romance
Weeping Willow Tree
Wildwood Flower

Fwys FA 2365: Most city listeners were exposed to the autoharp in elementary grades, where it enabled a teacher with minimal musical experience to accompany singers and choruses. Such a background will not prepare the listener for the innovative and virtuosic displays on autoharp of these musicians, all from Virginia or North Carolina. In his brochure notes, Seeger outlines the history of the autoharp (it was patented in 1881 by Charles F. Zimmerman, who thought it would help him to promote his new system of music notation) and discusses the technical aspects of the musicians' playing that makes their music (especially Kilby Snow's) so unique. Clearly, the autoharp has long outgrown Zimmerman's aims, not to mention your first-grade teacher's efforts.

239   Label Name/Number: Folkways FA 2390
Title: *Friends of Old Time Music*
Artists: Various
Recordist: Peter Siegel, Ralph Rinzler, Michael Seeger, Jerry Goodwin, John Cohen, Ed Kahn
Editor: Peter Siegel and John Cohen
Place and Date of Recording: NYC, 1961-63
Date of Publication: 1964
Annotations: 4 p. brochure by Richard Rinzler
Selections:
Chick-a-la-lee-o -- Almeda Riddle
Claude Allen [E 6] -- Hobart Smith
Come All Ye Tender Hearted -- Carter Stanley
Dark Holler Blues -- Tom Ashley & Doc Watson
Double File -- Doc Watson and Gaither Carlton
He's Coming in Glory Some Day -- Clint Howard, Fred Price, Doc Watson
Hick's Farewell -- Doc Watson and Gaither Carlton

Hook and Line -- Roscoe Holcomb
Little Birdie -- Stanley Brothers
Mistreated Mama Blues -- Dock Boggs
Pretty Fair Miss All in a Garden [N 42] -- Roscoe Holcomb
Rabbit in the Log -- Stanley Brothers
Soldier's Joy -- Hobart Smith
[Also three African-American selections]

Fwys FA 2390: The Friends of Old-Time Music was founded in December 1960 in New
York by Margot Mayo, Jean Ritchie, John Cohen, Ralph Rinzler, and Israel G. Young; its purpose
was to bring traditional music to New York City. FOTM held its first concert in February 1961,
featuring Kentucky folksinger and musician Roscoe Holcomb. Six more concerts were held in the
next two years; this album draws on tape recordings from those concerts, which represent some of
the finest traditional performances in the very early years of the urban folk music revival boom.
Most of these selections by the same artists were recorded on other albums. Of particular interest
are Carter Stanley's unaccompanied hymn, "Come All Ye Tender Hearted" and Ralph Stanley's
frailing banjo playing (rather than his more usual Scruggs-picking style) on "Little Birdie." [JAF
310--DKW]

240   Label Name/Number: Folkways FA 2434
Title: *The 37th Old-Time Fiddlers' Convention at Union Grove, North Carolina*
Artists Various
Collector/Recordist: Mike Seeger and Lisa Chiera
Editor: Mike Seeger and John Cohen
Place and Date of Recording: Union Grove, NC, 1961
Date of Publication: 1962
Annotations: 6 p. brochure by Harper Van Hoy, Mike Seeger, John Cohen
Selections:
        Back Up and Push -- Friendly City Playboys
        Billy in the Lowground -- John Herald and the Lonesome Strangers of New York City
        Blackberry Blossom -- Uncle Charlie Higgins
        Dance All Night -- Kenneth Edwards & the Sunny Mountain Boys
        Fire on the Mountain -- Dixie Ramblers
        Grey Eagle -- Delmer Starling, Esker Hutchins, & Surry County Ramblers
        Hitchhiker's Blues -- Brushy Mountainn Boys
        I Shall Not Be Moved -- Bascom Lamar Lunsford and the Laurel River Band
        Instrumental -- Norman Edmonds and The Old Timers
        Lost John -- Red Parham & the Haywood County Ramblers
        May I Sleep in Your Barn Tonight, Mister? -- Grandma Davis from Roaring River
        Old Richmond -- A. L. Hall Band
        River Stay Away from My Door -- Charlie Knight & His Country Music Boys
        Ruben -- Blue Grass Mountain Boys
        Sally Ann -- Mountain Ramblers
        Sally Ann -- Norman Edmonds and The Old Timers
        Teardrops in My Eyes -- Friendly City Playboys
        Twinkle Little Star -- Mountain Ramblers
        Whiskey Took My Daddy Away -- Louise Edmonds
        Whoa Mule -- Yadkin County Ramblers

241   Label Name/Number: Folkways FA 2435
Title: *Galax Va. Old Fiddlers' Convention*
Artists: Various
Collector/Recordist: Lisa Chiera, Michael Eisenstadt, Alice Schwebke, and Brian Sinclair
Place and Date of Recording: Galax, VA, 1961-63
Date of Publication: 1964
Annotations: 6 p. brochure by Lisa Chiera
Selections:

> Bill Cheatham -- Southern Mountain Boys
> Bill Cheatham -- Stoney Mountain Boys
> Blackberry Blossom -- Buck Mountain Band (Wade Ward, Charlie Higgins, and Dale Poe)
> Cackling Hen -- Uncle Rufus Blackburn
> Columbus Stockade Blues -- Dot Edwards and Katie Golden
> Concord Rag -- J. E. Mainer's Mountaineers
> Cricket on the Hearth -- Sunny Mountain Boys
> Cumberland Gap -- "Lost John" Ray
> Honeysuckle Rag -- Mountain Ramblers
> John Henry [I 1] -- George Pegram
> Kingdom's Come -- Norman Edmonds
> Leather Britches -- Brushy River Boys
> Old Man at the Mill -- Clint Howard
> Paddy on the Turnpike -- unidentified band
> Sally Ann -- George Stoneman
> Seeing Nellie Home -- Billy Edwards
> Stoney Creek -- Sonny Miller
> Sweetest Gift a Mother's Smile, The -- Udel McPeak and Billy Edwards
> Turkey in the Straw -- Larry Richardson, Sonny Miller, & Johnny Jackson
> Walk in the Parlor -- Norman Edmonds and the Old Timers
> Walking in My Sleep -- Virginia Playboys
> Wandering Boy -- Ivor Melton
> Whoa Mule -- Tom Ashley

    Fwys FA 2434 / Fwys FA 2435: These two albums, recorded at two of the best-known old-time fiddlers' conventions in the Southeast, capture the public face of traditional music of (primarily) North Carolina and Virginia in the early 1960s. Fiddlers' conventions such as these were (and are) not confined to fiddling competitions, but (at least, in the case of Galax), offered prizes in guitar, banjo, fiddle, band music, and folksinging. Without full itineraries of all the contestants, it is difficult to ascertain whether the selections are representative of the styles presented, but they probably are. Instrumental music is divided evenly between pre-bluegrass and later styles--at least, as defined by fiddle and banjo techniques, though there is little mandolin, only one guitar solo break on both discs, and no electric instruments. The Union Grove album features three selections with vocals; the Galax album, six. Many of the performers were well known in the region, and some, through recordings, even more widely. One band at Union Grove featured two northern urban musicians--a new introduction in the early 1960s that continued to grow through the decade, until there were many contestants from outside the southeastern states and even some from outside the country. Both album brochures include historical background information on the respective events and on the performers. As Seeger notes in the Union Grove brochure, the two sides of that disc are divided between older and more modern (*i. e.*, bluegrass-influenced) styles. [JAF 299, 310--DKW]

242   Label Name/Number: Folkways FS 3809
Title: *Fine Times at Our House: Indiana Ballads, Fiddle Tunes, Songs*
Artists: John W. Summers, Mrs. Anna Underhill, Louis Henderson, Dan White, Vern Smelser,
        Virgil Sandage, Oscar Parks, Mrs. Ella Parker, Shorty & Juanita Sheehan
Collector/Recordist: Pat Dunford and Art Rosenbaum
Place and Date of Recording: Various, IN, 1962-1964
Date of Publication: 1964
Annotations: 8 p. booket by Arthur Rosenbaum and Pat Dunford
Selections:
    John W. Summers
        Fine Times at Our House
        Rye Straw
        Same Time Today as it Was Yesterday, The
        Sherman's Retreat
        Unnamed Tune
    Dan White and John W. Summers
        Cuckoo's Nest, The
        Waiting for the Lord to Come
    Anna Underhill
        Away out West in Kansas
        Indiana Hero, The [F 16]
        Play Parties
        Elfin Knight, The [C. 2]
    Louis Henderson
        Turkey in the Straw
    Vern Smelser
        Morning of 1845, The [C 19]
        Young Man Who Wouldn't Hoe Corn, The [H 13]
        Young Charlotte [G 17]
    Virgil Sandage
        Birds' Song, The
    Oscar Parks
        The Battle of Stone River
    Mrs. Ella Parker
        Lord Barnett [C. 68]
    Shorty and Juanita Sheehan
        Soldier and the Lady, The [P 14]

FA 3809: In a period of two years, Rosenbaum and Dunford recorded close to 300 items in southern and central Indiana, from which these recordings were selected "to present a varied and interesting picture of the older songs and tunes remembered by Hoosier singers and fiddlers..." Summers' consummate fiddling (for more of which see Rounder 0167, in Part I) makes a nice contrast with the more primitive (but no less skilled) sound of Henderson's home-made cigar-box fiddle. Several excellent ballad performances are included--among them the rarely heard Civil War relic, "The Battle of Stone River." Also represented is the 1820 love-triangle-murder ballad of Fuller and Warren ("The Indiana Hero"), one of Indiana's most celebrated local event ballads. The brochure notes offer some general comments on the traditional music of the state, noting the different styles of the north and the south. Although the southern region is closer in style to Appalachia, the singers on this album all tend to adhere rather closely to a metronomically regular rhythm. The only recent composition is "Way Out West in Kansas," penned in the 1920s by hillbilly singer/songwriter Carson J. Robison. All in all, this is an outstanding regional collection, well-researched and carefully annotated. [JAF 310--DKW]

243   Label Name/Number: Folkways FS 3811
Title: *Traditional Music from Grayson & Carroll Counties*
Artists: Glen Neaves, Vester Jones, Wade Ward, Ed Spencer, Glen Smith
Collector/Recordist: Eric Davidson, Paul Newman
Place and Date of Recording: VA, 1958-61
Date of Publication: 1962
Annotations: 8 p. booklet by Eric Davidson & Paul Newman
Selections:

> Vester Jones
>> Cluck Old Hen
>> Groundhog
>> Katy Cline
>> Old Jimmy Sutton
>> Old Joe Clark
>> Old Ruby (Old Reuben)
>> Poor Ellen Smith [F 11]
>> Sally Goodin
>
> Glen Smith
>> Cindy
>> Fire in the Mountain
>> Fortune
>> Hell Amongst the Yearlings
>> Johnson Boys
>> Little Love
>> Mississippi Sawyers
>> Old Jimmy Sutton
>> Polly Put the Kettle On
>> Pretty Little Willow
>> Soldier's Joy
>
> Wade Ward
>> Ida Red
>> Cripple Creek
>> Sourwood Mountain
>
> Ed Spencer
>> Pretty Polly [P 36b]
>> Sugar Hill
>
> Glen Neaves
>> Handsome Molly
>
> Glen Neaves' Band (Neaves, Roscoe Russell, Ivor Melton, Warren Brown, Ted Lundy)
>> Dev'lish Mary [Q 4]
>> Tom Dooley [F 36]

244   Label Name/Number: Folkways FS 3832
Title: *Bluegrass from the Blue Ridge*
Artists: Various
Collector/Recordist: Eric H. Davidson, Paul Newman, Caleb Finch
Place and Date of Recording: Grayson and Carroll Counties, VA, ca. 1958-67
Date of Publication: 1967
Annotations: 16 p. booklet by Eric Davidson and Paul Newman
Selections:

> Glen Smith and Wade Ward

John Lover Is Gone
Ragtime Annie
Sally Ann
Sally Goodin'
Soldier's Joy
Walkin' in the Parlor
Western Country
William Marshall and Glen Smith
Cindy
Jenny Put the Kettle On
Wade Ward, Glen Smith, Fields Ward
Don't Let Your Deal Go Down
John Hardy [I 2]
Jesse James [E 1]
Train on the Island
Uncle Charlie Higgins, Cliff Caraco, Kelly Lund
Paddy on the Turnpike
Spud Gravely and Glen Smith
Skip to My Lou
Cotton Eye Joe
Bruce Mastin and Band
Eighth Day of January
Bluegrass Buddies and Glen Neaves
Walkin' in My Sleep
Old Joe Clark
Glen and Mrs. Neaves
Banks of the Ohio [F 5]

Fwys FS 3811 / Fwys FS 3832: Although the title of FS 3832 is a misnomer, both of these are outstanding field collections of (primarily) older traditions in instrumental music. On these albums collectors Davidson and Newman present the results of extensive field recordings and interviews made in the musically rich region of Grayson and Carroll Counties, southern Virginia. Among the treasures on FS 3811 is Glen Smith's fine clawhammer style playing on a fretless banjo. The music on FS 3832 is arranged by chronological styles: (1) the oldest, consisting of eight banjo-fiddle duets; (2) music showing the influence of Charlie Poole's band; (3) music showing Irish influence, probably older than this placement suggests; (4) what is termed the Old Galax Band Style (banjo, fiddle, and guitar); and (5) the Late Galax Band Style, showing significant bluegrass influence. Both albums' brochure notes--FS 3832 in particular--include extensive information on the musical styles of the area and the socioeconomic factors that contributed to the rise and decline of the stringbands. Although there are some inaccuracies (the tune titled "Paddy on the Turnpike" is actually "Blackberry Blossom," and Poole did not compose the songs referred to in the notes) by and large the records and accompanying documentation provide an important survey of the area's instrumental music. More recordings from the same collectors' fieldwork can be heard on Asch AH 3831. [JAF 324; JAF 299--DKW]

245 Label Name/Number: Folkways FS 3848
Title: *Between the Sound and the Sea: Music of the North Carolina Outer Banks*
Artists: Various
Collector/Recordist: Karen G. Helms / Otto Henry
Place and Date of Recording: NC, 1973-1976
Date of Publication: 1977

Annotations: 5 p. brochure
Selections:
> Dile Gallop
>> Johnny O'Lou
> Isabel Etheridge
>> Harmonica Medley: Home Sweet Home / Kitty Wells
>> Nellie Cropsey [F 1c]
> Isabel Etheridge and Mary Basnight
>> Amber Tresses
>> Lullaby/Children's Song
>> Ole Tucky Buzzard
>> Oh, Pray Doctor
> Lawton Howard
>> Mandolin Medley: Little Sydney [Cindy] / Round the Mountain
> Edgar Howard
>> Let's Keep the Holler Alive
> Edgar Howard, Garrish, Ballance
>> Tom Dan'ls
>> Paddy's Hollow
>> Matilda Jane Lee
> Dick Tillett
>> The Sailor Boy [K 13]
>> Seventy-Two
> Charles Stowe
>> Charlie Mason Pogie Boat
>> Carolina Cannonball
> Jule Garrish
>> Harmonica medley: Casey Jones / The Old Sow (Jumped over the Fence, the Little
>>> Ones Crawled Under)
>> Booze Yacht

Fwys FS 3848:   This LP, from the eastern extremity of North Carolina, is of particular interest partly because of the several local, fairly recent compositions that demonstrate that the creative folk process is by no means dead in those parts. "Charlie Mason Pogie Boat," to the tune of "The Death of Floyd Collins," concerns an incident of 1948. "Carolina Cannonball" is a localized version of "Wabash Cannonball." "Paddy's Hollow" and "Let's Keep the Holler Alive" are from the 1940s and 1970s, respectively. All four of these are sung by their composers. "Tom Dan'ls" and "Matilda Jane Lee" are both local ballads from the latter part of the 19th century. "Seventy-Two" appeared in print in the early 1890s. "Amber Tresses Tied in Blue" (the original title) was written in 1874. Although most of these are enjoyable performances, the most striking one on the album is Dile Gallop's rendition of "Johnny O'Lou," a local composition of some 50 years ago but probably with Anglo-Irish antecedents. This interesting album could have been much better annotated. [JEMFQ 65/66]

246   Label Name/Number: Folkways FE 4001 (formerly P 1001)
Title: *Wolf River Songs*
Artists: Robert Walker, Warde Ford, Elizabeth Walker Ford, Clara Hawks Tracy, Carlton Hawks
Collector/Recordist: Sidney Robertson Cowell
Place and Date of Recording: WI, CA, WY, Germany; 1952-54
Date of Publication: 1956
Annotations: 11 p. brochure by Cowell

Selections:
>   Robert Walker
>>   Flying Cloud, The [K 28]
>>   Little Brown Bulls, The [C 16]
>>   Lost Jimmie Whalen, The [C 8]
>>   Sinking of the Cumberland, The [A 26]
>>   We Are Anchored By the Roadside, Jim
>>   Wild Colonial Boy, The [L 20]
>>   Wreck of the Lady Sherbrooke, The
>   Warde Ford
>>   Andrew Batan [C. 250]
>>   Foreman Monroe [C 1]
>>   Keith and Hiles Line, The
>>   Lowlands Low, or the Golden Willow Tree, The [C. 286]
>>   Nightingales of Spring, The [N 29]
>>   River Drivers' Song
>>   Young Johnny [K 38]
>   Elizabeth Walker Ford
>>   Land of Pleasure
>   Clara Hawks Tracy
>>   Pretty Polly or The False-Hearted Knight [C. 4]
>   Carlton Hawks
>>   Brennan on the Moore [L 7]

Fwys FE 4001 (formerly P 1001): The musical lore of Wisconsin's lumber camps is wonderfully represented in this collection, which concentrates on Robert Walker (b. 1883), his sister, Elizabeth Walker Ford, and her son, Warde Ford, whom Cowell first met and recorded under LC auspices in 1937. Carlton Hawks and Clara Hawks Tracy are Mrs. Ford's nephew and niece. Some of the best-loved ballads of the lumbering occupation (C 1, C 8, C 16) are heard here in full, leisurely performances, rendered in the flat, unadorned vocal style characteristic of northeastern and midwestern singers. The early 19th-century come-all-ye ballad, "The Flying Cloud," was once very popular but there are very few recordings of it; Cowell was justly proud of preserving Walker's 15-stanza version. The brochure includes text transcriptions of all the songs, but some are to recordings made by the same singers at different times.

247   Label Name/Number: Folkways FES 34151
Title: *Hand Me Down Music: Old Songs, Old Friends: 1. Traditional Music of Union County, North Carolina*
Artists: Roy Pope and the Carolina Homeboys, Otis High, Flarrie Grimm, Bascom Traywick, John A. Bivens, Seena Helms, Horace Helms, Henry Griffin, Karen Helms
Collector/Recordist: Karen G. Helms and Otto Henry
Place and Date of Recording: Union County, NC, 1976-79
Date of Publication: 1979
Annotations: 15 p. booklet by Karen Helms
Selections:
>   Roy Pope and the Carolina Homeboys
>>   Cacklin' Hen
>>   Fire on the Hillside
>>   Leather Britches
>   Otis High
>>   Captain Karo

Young Ladies Take Warning
Otis High and Flarrie Grimm
      Froggie Went A-Courtin'
Bascom Traywick
      Hook and Line
      In the Resurrection Morning
John A. Bivens
      Jack and Joe
      Grandma's Advice
Seena Helms
      Lady Bride and Three Babes [C. 79]
      Christian Pilgrim
      Pioneer Courtship
Horace Helms
      Katy Kline
Henry Griffin
      Holler Jimmy Riley Ho
      Patsy Beasley
Horace Helms and Karen Helms
      Soldier's Joy
[Also 3 African-American selections]

Fwys FES 34151: Few states have been as well canvassed for folksongs as has North Carolina. Four volumes of the *Frank C. Brown Collection of North Carolina Folklore* document the music of the early decades of this century. In the 1920s and '30s the state's musicians made a major contribution to commercially recorded hillbilly music, thereby unwittingly documenting the continuing and evolving folk tradition of the period. In the 1960s, field recordings, given impetus by the thriving folksong revival, demonstrated that great ballad singers such as Dillard Chandler, Lee Monroe Presnell, or Horton Barker, and great instrumental ensembles, such as the Watson Family and friends, could still be recorded. It is easy, then, to lose interest in performers who cannot match the excellence of those now-familiar names. The artists featured on this (and the similar album, Folkways FS 3848) are not great folk musicians; nevertheless both albums have enough interesting or unusual material to deserve notice.

The album was recorded around the Unionville-Fairview and Marshville-Olive Branch areas of Union County in North Carolina's Piedmont, not far from Charlotte, in 1976-79. With one or two exceptions, the performers are all in their sixties and seventies; and with one exception are all white. There is some nice unaccompanied singing by John A. Bivens, Seena Helms, and Otis High; but the most unusual item is a fragment of a rare murder ballad, "Patsy Beasley," purportedly about an episode from the 1840s--a piece that has not, to my knowledge, been recorded from another singer. Almost as rare is "Grandma's Advice," published before 1870. "Captain Karo" is a variant of "Kimo Kimo," the minstrel stage derivative of "Froggie Went a-Courtin.'" The first stanza of the hymn "Christian Pilgrim" is from the *Sacred Harp*, where it is titled "Pilgrim." "Jack and Joe" is a TPA pop song from the early 1900s. [JEMFQ 65/66]

248a   Label Name/Number: Folkways FE 34161
Title: *Folk Visions & Voices, Vol. 1: Traditional Music and Song in Northern Georgia*
Artists: Various
Collector/Recordist/Editor: Art Rosenbaum
Place and Date of Recording: GA, 1977-83
Date of Publication: 1984
Annotations: 6 p. booklet by Art Rosenbaum

Selections:

As I Walked Out One Morning in Spring -- W. Guy Bruce
Cindy in the Summertime -- Lawrence Eller and Vaughn Eller
Don't Go Ridin' Down that Old Texas Trail -- Lawrence Eller, Vaughn Eller, and Ross Brown
Famous Wedding, The -- Maude Thacker
I'm Going to Georgia -- Berthie Rogers, Paralee McCloud, Lawrence Eller, Leatha Eller
Lily of the West, The [P 29] -- W. Guy Bruce
Little Ship, The [C. 286] -- Paralee McCloud
Once I Had an Old Grey Mare -- Maude Thacker
Shout, Lulu -- W. Guy Bruce
Snowbird -- Ross Brown, Howard Cunningham
What You Gonna Name That Pretty Baby? -- Leatha Eller
[Also 8 African-American selections]

248b   Label Name/Number: Folkways FE 34162
Title: *Folk Visions & Voices, Vol. 2: Traditional Music and Song in Northern Georgia*
Artists: Various
Collector/Recordist/Editor: Art Rosenbaum
Place and Date of Recording: GA, 1978-83
Date of Publication: 1984
Annotations: 6 p. booklet by Art Rosenbaum
Selections:

Dawsonville Jail -- Ray Knight, Ed Teague, Art Rosenbaum
Dying Girl, The -- Mabel Cawthorn
Five Hundred Miles -- George and Bobby Childers
Five to My Five -- Rev. Howard Finster
Goin' Down This Road Feelin' Bad -- George Childers
I Wish I Was a Mole in the Ground -- Chesley, Joe, Ralph, and Don Chancey, Gene Wiggins, Art Rosenbaum
Mulberry Gap -- Chesley Chancey
Prettiest Little Girl in the County-O -- Gordon Tanner, Smoky Joe Miller, Uncle John Patterson
Sally Goodin -- Ray Knight, Ed Teague
Shoot that Turkey Buzzard -- Joe, Chesley, and Ralph Chancy
Some Have Fathers over Yonder -- Rev. Howard Finster
Stagolee Was a Bully [I 15] -- Uncle John Patterson
[Also 9 African-American selections]

Fwys FE 34161 / Fwys FE 34162: Through the first half of the century, the state of Georgia escaped the avid attention ballad and folksong collectors lavished on its neighboring states--the Virginias, the Carolinas, the Ozarks, Mississippi and Alabama, in particular. Yet north Georgia was fertile home to a thriving rural musical tradition, as the successes of the annual Atlanta fiddlers' convention in the early 1900s, and of the long string of remarkable hillbilly musicians in the 1920s and '30s convincingly demonstrated. Between 1977 and 1982, Art and Margo Rosenbaum tape recorded some two thousand items in north Georgia--further evidence that the Cracker State still did not deserve such neglect. These two albums are intended as companions to Rosenbaum's book of the same title (*Folk Visions and Voices: Traditional Music and Song in North Georgia*, University of Georgia Press, 1983), containing over 75 items from their field collections.

In most cases, text and tune transcriptions and more information on informants can be found in the book. Nevertheless, the brochures to these LPs contain sufficient information and documentation to stand alone. Vol. I, which focuses on older ballads and hymns, opens with a very unusual almost hymn-like rendition by the Eller Family (with four-part singing and piano accompaniment) of the lyric song, "I'm Going to Georgia." Octogenarian Leatha Eller also plays piano to accompany her own religious composition, "What You Gonna Name That Pretty Baby?" Lawrence Eller sings "Cindy" to the unusual accompaniment of a mouth bow played by his brother; more of their recordings can be heard on Flyright 546 (see Section I). Also unusual is Maude Thacker's fine rendition of a fragment of a rare ballad, "The Famous Wedding." It was also collected in north Georgia in 1909 by Olive Dame Campbell (as "The Awful Wedding"), but seems to be otherwise unknown in this country (though it was collected several times in Britain). Rev. Howard Finster, whose singing and banjo playing is heard on Vol. 2, is more widely known today as a very idiosyncratic visual artist who does paintings, assemblages, and sculptures on religious themes. Other selections in this LP focus on instrumental music and the stringband tradition. Gordon Tanner and his associates, whose music bears more than an echo of his father's famous Skillet Lickers, is also heard on Fwys FES 31089. The second side of the first album is devoted to "black religious singing"; the first side of the second album, to "black frolic songs, work songs, and blues-- including some pieces found also in Anglo-American tradition.

249   Label Name/Number: Gambier Folklore Society GFS 901
Title: *Seems like Romance to Me: Traditional Fiddle Tunes from Ohio*
Artists: Various
Collector/Recordist/Editor: Jeff Goehring and Howard Sacks
Place and Date of Recording: OH, 1983-84
Date of Publication: 1985
Annotations: 15 p. brochure
Selections:
>   Jimmy Wheeler
>>   Pumpkin Vine
>>   Yellow Barber
>   Arnold Sharp
>>   Fine Times at Our House
>>   Hound Chase
>   Cecil Plum
>>   Laurel Mountain Breakdown
>>   Trumpey's Hoedown
>   Lonnie Seymour
>>   Chillicothe Two-Step
>>   Sugar Barrel
>   John Hannah
>>   Coon in a Treetop
>>   Cumberland Blues
>   Cliff and Telford Hardesty
>>   Heel and Toe Polka
>>   Soldier's Joy
>>   Turkey in the Straw
>   Rollie Hommon
>>   Baltzell's Tune
>>   Snowshoes
>   Kenny Sidle

Durang's Hornpipe
Brushy Fork
Cottage Hill

GFS 901: The annotators take pains to avoid any regional generalizations: "Any attempt to make statements of regional style does a disservice to the unique qualities of these fiddlers". Nevertheless, they do on occasion draw attention to a fiddler's playing style as typical of the style of the region. The 18 recordings on this album were made between December 1983 and March 1984 by Howard Sacks and Jeff Goehring and are technically very good. The nine fiddlers, born between 1905 and 1931, represent relatively late music styles--not only in playing (e.g., more blues, rag, swing, and jazz influences; less frequent nonstandard tunings) but also in accompaniment (guitar, with complex chord progressions; and 3 finger banjo). The music itself is lovely; these are excellent fiddlers, all of whom have had extensive local public exposure at dances and other get-togethers, fiddle contests, and, in some cases, even on radio. None, evidently, made any commercial phonograph recordings. Some of the tunes are widely known; some seem to be confined to the Kentucky-Ohio area ("Pumpkin Vine," "Yellow Barber," "Brushy Fork"); some are played only within the family ("Sugar Barrel," "Hound Chase"); others are original compositions by the fiddlers heard playing them. In the latter category are the two fine pieces by Cecil Plum, both aided by good guitar back-up. Scruggs-style 3-finger banjo accompaniment does much to enhance the beauty of Lonnie Seymour's "Sugar Barrel" and "Chillocothe Two-Step." Considerable western swing influence is heard in Rollie Hommon's strong performance of "Snowshoes"; and Kenny Sidle's "Durang's Hornpipe" could pass for a Texas version. The latter two are ably accompanied by deft guitar backup. Hommon's very contemporary performance on "Snowshoes" contrasts with his 19th-century-like rendition of a John Baltzell piece, possibly learned directly from Baltzell himself during the 1920s. Another highlight on the album is Cliff Hardesty's version of "Turkey in the Straw"--a creative approach to what has for decades been one of the most (if not in fact, the most) frequently recorded American traditional fiddle tunes. The brochure includes a long essay, "Traditional Fiddling in Ohio History," with an extended discussion of John Baltzell, the first Ohio fiddler to make commercial recordings; and of Henry Ford's efforts to revive old-time fiddling in the mid-20s through his sponsorship of numerous fiddle contests. The last section of this essay summarizes the relatively recent influence of phonograph and radio on Ohio fiddling. The effect of both of these media in making fiddlers from distant parts of the country available to Ohioans cannot be ignored. Notes on the individual fiddlers and their performances provide ample biographical details, tune identifications, and helpful discussions of playing characteristics. The booklet also includes photos, a few references to other, related recordings, and a short list of other albums including Ohio fiddle music. All in all, this is an excellent survey of Ohio fiddle music today, which evidences strong 19th-century Southeast antecedents as well as more recent, western, jazz, and country borrowings. [JAF 395]

250   Label Name/Number: Global Village SC 03 [cass]
Title: *Georgia Folk: A Sampler of Traditional Sounds*
Artists: Various
Collector/Recordist: Various
Editor: Maggie Holtzberg-Call
Place and Date of Recording: Various
Date of Publication: 1990
Annotations: Insert notes by Maggie Holtzberg-Call
Selections:

Amazing Grace -- Liberty Church Sacred Harp Singing
Cindy in the Summertime -- Vaughan and Lawrence Eller
Columbus Stockade Blues -- Jimmie Tarlton

Gold Watch and Chain -- Gene Jackson, Doug Martin, and Robert George
Griffin's Fiddle Medley -- John R. Griffin and Arthur Griffin
I Saw the Light -- John "Doodle" Thrower and the Golden River Grass (James Watson, Bill Kee, Lyn Elliott)
Kitty and the Baby -- Lowe Stokes & his Potlickers (Bert Layne, Arthur Tanner, Hoke Rice)
Mulberry Gap -- Chesley Chancy
Northfield -- Liberty Church Sacred Harp Singing
Old Susannah -- John "Doodle" Thrower and the Golden River Grass (James Watson, Bill Kee, Lyn Elliott)
Rare Willie Drowned in the Yarrow [C. 215] -- Betty Smith
Soldier's Joy -- John "Doodle" Thrower and the Golden River Grass (James Watson, Bill Kee, Lyn Elliott)
White River Stomp -- Uncle John Patterson, Ben Entrekin, and James Patterson
Yonder He Goes -- Will Montgomery
[Also eight African-American performances]

Global Village [cass] SC 03: This collection, produced with support from the Georgia Folklife Program, is drawn from vintage 78s (Stokes), a home recording (Montgomery, ca. 1955), a studio recording (Tarlton, 1952), and field recordings of 1964-89 made by individual collectors, by folklore societies, and by regional folk festival presenters. Most of the performers are Georgia natives or residents.

251   **Label Name/Number:** Grey Eagle Records, University of Missouri, 101 [2 record set]
Title: *Now That's a Good Tune*
Artists: Various
Collector/Recordists: Amy E. Skillman, Julie Youmans, Howard Wight Marshall, Margot Ford McMillen, Charles Walden, Bill Shull
Editors: Howard Wight Marshall, Amy E. Skillman, Charles Walden, C. Ray Brassieur, Spencer Galloway, Julie Youmans
Place and Date of Recording: MO, 1982-89
Date of Publication: 1989
Annotations: 64 p. booklet by Charles Walden
Selections:
Carol Hascall
Eighth of January
Heel and Toe Polka
Whiskey Before Breakfast
Spotted Pony
Vesta Johnson
Old Man, Old Woman
Orvetta Waltz
Tennessee Wagner
Walking in My Sleep
Gene Goforth
Billy in the Lowground
Dusty Miller
Rocky Road to Denver
Sail Away Ladies
Wooden Shoe Story
Dean Johnston
Hickory Bow Story

Humansville
East Tennessee Blues
Waldo
R. P. Christeson
Bill Driver Tune
Dallas Stamper
Stone's Rag
Whoa Mule
Nile Wilson
Little Whiskey
Tiehacker Rag
Tiehacker's Tune No. 2
Wes Muir's Tune
Cyril Stinnett
Big John McNeil
Jack Danielson's Reel
Johnny Don't Come Home Drunk
Wake Up Susie
Lyman Enloe
Call Your Dogs and Let's Go Hunting
Forgotten Waltz
Hanging Around the Kitchen Til the Cook Comes Home
The Rough Scotsman
Pete McMahan
Ford One Step
Ozark Mountain Waltz
Pretty Polly
Sally Goodin
Bob Walsh
Blackeyed Peas and Cornbread
Carroll County Blues
The Waltz You Saved for Me
White Water
Howe Teague
Forkey Deer
Fourteen Days in Georgia
White River
Bill Eddy
Leather Britches
Phyllis Gayle Breakdown
Twinkle Little Star
Charlie Walden
Bill Katon's Reel
Marmaduke's Hornpipe
Old Rugged Cross
Soldier's Joy

Grey Eagle (University of Missouri) 101: This 2-LP set is one of the most lavish productions of the 1980s. It includes 52 fiddle tunes performed by 13 Missouri fiddlers--most of them born in the first three decades of the century. The recordings were made between in the 1980s under informal circumstances. Most of the fiddlers are accompanied by guitarists; some also have banjo accompaniment; others are backed up by parlor organ or second violin. The accompanying 12" x 12" booklet includes an introductory essay on traditional fiddle playing in Missouri by Marshall; biographies of the musicians; tune transcriptions and annotations; a bibliography and a discography; and several wonderful old photos of musicians and musical settings, including several dating from the 19th century. In his essay, Marshall distinguishes three broad geographic regional fiddling styles: the Ozark style, largely found south of the Missouri river; the North Missouri style; and the Little Dixie style, confined to the region between the other two. The Ozark is a short bow style, with heavy rhythm and double stops; the Little Dixie style tends toward more intricate melodies and short bow strokes interspersed with longer ones; the North Missouri is a long bow style, slower in pace, rich in hornpipe melodies. The spread of mass media in recent decades has tended to blur the older styles, mixing in a good proportion of bluegrass fiddle and Texas-Oklahoma contest style-- not to mention the availability of recordings of other southeastern fiddlers who influenced the fiddlers of this collection. (Bob Walsh's "Carroll County Blues" does not refer to Carroll County, Tennessee or Missouri, as the notes suggest, but Mississippi, and was learned--at least indirectly-- from Mississippi recording artists Narmour and Smith.) Nevertheless, the emphasis in this collection is clearly on the older regional sounds. [JAF #410]

252   Label Name/Number: Heritage 12
Title: *2nd Annual Brandywine Mountain Music Convention: '75 Traditional Music of West Virginia*
Artists: Various
Place and Date of Recording: Concordville, PA, 1975
Date of Publication: 1976
Annotations: 4 p. brochure by Carl Goldstein and Sheldon Sandler
Selections:

>   Morris Brothers
> .   Wake Up Susan
>   Devil in Georgia
>   Dave Morris
>   Battle of Shiloh
>   Wilson Douglas
>   Yew Piney Mountain
>   Rocky Road To Dublin
>   Wilson Douglas and Mike Seeger
>   Boatin' Up Sandy
>   Ola Belle Reed and Family
>   I've Endured
>   Phoebe Parsons
>   Poem and Song
>   John Morris and Phoebe Parsons
>   Arkansas Traveller
>   Ira Mullins and Phoebe Parsons
>   Shortnin'
>   Ira Mullins
>   Cluck Ole Hen
>   Jenes Cottrell
>   Devil and the Farmer's Wife [C. 278]
>   Tracy Schwarz and Mike Seeger
>   Deceiver/Box the Fox
>   Highwoods String Band
>   Dusty Miller
>   Texas Gales
>   George Booker

Heritage 12: This album samples the music heard at the 1975 Annual Brandywine Mountain Music Convention; the recordings were originally made by National Public Radio. Most of the performers are West Virginia natives--except for Ola Belle Reed, Schwarz and Seeger, and the Highwoods Band. This amalgamation of local performers and visitors, probably rare in the pre-LP era, has become increasingly common since the 1960s. Brief brochure notes comment on the event and the performers.

253 Label Name/Number: Heritage XXII
Title: *Eight Miles Apart: Old Time Music from Patrick and Carroll County, Virginia*
Artist: Shelor Family (Clarice, Jesse, Bill, Jimmy, Paul, Joe, and Susan) / Kimble Family (Taylor,
        Stella, Ivery, Doris, and Pearl Wagoner Richardson)
Producers/Recordists: Ray Alden, Dave Spilkia, and Bobby Patterson
Place and Date of Recording: VA, 1973-77
Date of Publication: 1979
Annotations: 4 p. booklet and liner notes by Alden and Spilkia
Selections:
    Shelor Family
            Callahan -- Jesse, Susan, Jimmy
            Evening Star Waltz -- Paul, Susan, Jimmy
            Fire on the Mountain -- Paul, Susan, Jimmy
            Iowna -- Clarice
            Mississippi Sawyer -- Bill, Clarice, Jimmy
            Mountain Clog -- Paul, Susan, Jimmy
            Old Richmond -- Bill, Clarice, Jimmy
            Rich Mountain -- Bill, Clarice, Jimmy
            Sandy River Belle -- Bill, Clarice, Joe
            Susanna Gal -- Bill, Clarice, Joe
            There's a Lock on the Chicken Coop Door -- Clarice
            Yellow Cat -- Bill, Joe
    Kimble Family
            Brady Why Didn't You Run? -- Taylor, Stella
            Don't Let Your Deal Go Down -- Doris, Taylor
            Florida Blues -- Taylor, Pearl
            Georgie Buck -- Taylor, Pearl
            Rachel -- Taylor, Stell, Pearl
            Red Mountain Wine -- Ivery, Taylor, Stella
            Ship in the Clouds -- Taylor, Stella, Ivery
            Shortening Bread -- Taylor, Stella, George, Cap, Ivery
            Tommy Love -- Taylor Stella, George, Cap, Ivery
            Troubles -- Taylor, Stella

Heritage XXII: The title of this album refers to the fact that these two very musical families, the Shelors and the Kimbles, both well known locally, lived eight miles from each other in the Virginia Blue Ridge Mountains yet never met one another. The Kimbles consist of Taylor Kimble (b. 1892) on fiddle; his son, Doris (autoharp, banjo); daughter Ivery (guitar); second wife, Stella Wagoner Kimble (b. 1892, m. 1968; banjo, guitar); her sister, Pearl (banjo); and two friends, George Wood (autoharp) and Cap Ayers (dulcimer). The Shelors consist of fiddler Jesse Shelor (b. 1894), his wife, Clarice Blackard Shelor (b. 1900; piano), their nephew, Bill Shelor (fiddle), sons Jimmy (guitar), Joe (guitar), and Paul (fiddle), and Paul's daughter, Susan (piano). Old-time music on piano, while in general not very common, is found with greater frequency in southwest Virginia. Two of the Shelors' tunes, "Sandy River Belle" and "Susanna Gal," had been recorded by Jesse and

Clarice with Clarice's father, Joe "Dad" Blackard, for Victor in 1927. The brochure includes biographical notes by Alden and tune identifications by Spilkia.

254   Label Name/Number: Heritage XXXIII
Title: *Visits*
Artists: Various
Collector/Recordist/Editor: Ray Alden
Place and Date of Recording: NC, VA, KY, WV, VT, NY, OH, mostly 1972-81
Date of Publication: 1981
Annotations: Gatefold jacket notes by Alden
Selections:

    Banjo Tramp -- Ward Jarvis, Dana Loomis, Grey Larsen
    Blackberry Blossom -- Buddy Thomas
    Bonaparte's Retreat -- Neil Rossi and Jay Ungar
    Crazy Creek -- Backwoods Band
    Denver Belle -- J. P. and Annadeene Fraley
    Fall on My Knees -- Ace Weems and his Fat Meat Boys
    Fox Chase -- Coy Morton and Roy Hall
    Grey Eagle -- Bruce Molsky and Dave Winston
    Holly Ding -- Fred Cockerham and Tommy Jarrell
    Jenny Johnson -- Pete Peterson, Ray Alden, Dave Howard
    Jump Jim Crow -- Melvine Wine
    Katy Hill -- Puryear Brothers Band
    Link of Chain -- Lisa Ornstein and Andy Cahan
    Little Maggie -- Fred Cockerham, Lawrence Lowe, Ernest East, Mac Snow
    Lost Indian -- Ernest East and Pine Ridge Boys
    Martha Campbell / McMichen's Reel -- Fiddling Doc Roberts and James Roberts
    Natural Bridge Blues -- New Rubatonic Entertainers
    Polecat Blues -- Smokey Valley Boys
    Rattle Down the Acorns -- Delbert Hughes
    Roustabout -- Dan Tate
    Saddle Old Paint -- Forest Pick
    Sal, Won't You Marry Me? -- Judy Hyman, Jeff Claus, John Hoffmann
    Singing Birds -- Burl Hammons
    Soapsuds over the Fence -- Mose Coffman and Dave Spilkia
    St. Anne's Reel / Growling Old Man, Growling Old Woman -- Correct Tone String Band
    Stillhouse -- Delmar Pendleton and Calvin Pendleton
    Tall Timber -- Benny Jarrell and Flint Hill Playboys
    Two White Nickels / Three Thin Dimes -- Arm and Hammer String Band
    Visits -- Tommy Jarrell, Mac Snow, Scotty East, Bobby Patterson, Al Tharp, Scott Ainslie,
        Ray Alden, Patsy East
    Warfield -- Aunt Jenny Wilson
    Waynesburgh -- Ben Steel and His Bare Hands
    Wild Hog in the Woods -- Kimble Family
    Wonderful Love -- Shelor Family

    Heritage XXXIII: Alden has selected these examples representing 103 musicians that he had recorded over a ten-year period of field trips throughout the eastern part of the country. All are from his own fieldwork, except for Doc Roberts, whom he visited in 1972 but who is represented in this collection by a ca. 1954 home recording. The two discs are subtitled, respectively, "The Old Timers" and "The Young Musicians," but the dichotomy is not so clear cut; younger musicians appear as accompanists on the first disc and vice versa, which is a good indication of the continuity of the musical traditions represented. Likewise, many of the ensembles mix musicians of rural roots with urban performers who turned to traditional music in their adult years.

255a   Label Name/Number: Home-Made Music LP001
Title: *Appalachia -- The Old Traditions -- Vol. 1*
Artists: Various
Collector/Recordist/Editor: Mike Yates
Place and Date of Recording: VA and NC, 1979-80
Date of Publication: 1982
Annotations: 4 p. booklet by Mike Yates
Selections:

    Banjo Clog -- Walt Davis and Jay C. McCool
    Black Is the Color -- Dellie Norton
    Bugerboo [O 3] -- Dan Tate
    Christmas Holiday -- Pug Allen
    Cindy -- Dan Tate
    Cluck Old Hen -- Ed Weaver and Pug Allen
    Cripple Creek & Shooting Creek -- Charlie Woods
    Derby Ram -- Cas Wallin
    Don't Get Trouble in Mind -- Sam Connor and Dent Wimmer
    Graveyard Blues -- Walt Davis
    Half Shaved Nigger -- Dent Wimmer
    Hounds in the Horn -- Sherman Wimmer
    Jerusalem Mourn -- Cas Wallin
    Lily of the West [P 29] -- Evelyn Ramsey
    Little Fisherman -- Dan Tate
    Little Soldier [M 27] -- Cas Wallin
    Massa Run Away -- Sam Connor
    McKinley -- Pug Allen
    Nigger Trader Boatman -- Pug Allen
    Oh Come See Me When You Can -- Morris Norton
    Oh, Lord, Ellie -- Dellie Norton
    Old Corn Liquor -- Rob Tate
    Once I Lived in Old Virginia -- Dan Tate
    Pretty Little Girl -- William Marshall and Howard Hall
    Russian Roulette -- Walt Davis and Jay C. McCool
    Sally Gooden -- Ted Boyd
    Silk Merchant's Daughter [N 10] -- Dellie Norton
    Three Little Babes [C. 79] -- Eunice Yeatts McAlexander
    White Oak Stomp -- Walt Davis and Jay C. McCool

255b   Label Name/Number: Home-Made Music LP002
Title: *Appalachia -- The Old Traditions -- Vol. 2*
Artists: Various
Collector/Recordist/Editor: Mike Yates
Place and Date of Recording: VA and NC, 1979-80, 1983
Date of Publication: 1983
Annotations: 3 p. booklet by Mike Yates
Selections:

    Baby-O -- Dent Wimmer

Back-Step Cindy -- William Marshall
Black-Eyed Susie -- Robert Sykes and the Surry County Boys
Brown's Dream -- John Hobson and the Glen Ayre Ramblers
Cotton-Eyed Joe -- Benton Flippen and the Smokey Valley Boys
Dance All Night with the Fiddler's Gal -- Sam Connor
Down the Road -- Stanley Hicks
Gary Dawson's Tune -- Benton Flippen
Here Goes a Bluebird -- Stanley Hicks
Little Honey -- Dellie Norton
Little Sparrow -- Dellie Norton
Molly Van [O 36] -- Dan Tate
Muck on My Heel -- Dan Tate
My Man Will Be Home Some Old Day -- Ed Weaver and Pug Allen
Paddy on the Turnpike -- Robert Sykes and the Surry County Boys
Poison in a Glass of Wine [P 30] -- Garret and Norah Arwood
Riddles & Where's the Ox At? -- Stanley Hicks
Roundtown Gals -- Tommy Jarrell
Shady Grove -- Garret and Norah Arwood
Snowbird on the Ashbank -- Mitchel Hopson
Time Draws Near, The -- Doug Wallin
Train on the Island -- Tommy Jarrell
Up Jumped the Devil -- Pug Allen
We'll Camp A Little While in the Wilderness -- Cas Wallin
Worrysome Woman, The [C. 248] -- Virgie Wallin

Home-Made Music LP001 / LP002:   These two albums document three evidently highly successful collecting trips by Yates, who has done much fieldwork in his native England. Yates compares his field trips to those of his predecessor of over 60 years ago; in fact some of his informants are descendants of Americans who sang to Cecil Sharp. Biographical information is sparse, but one gathers that most of the 18 major performers are 60 years or older. Both albums come with brochures that provide brief headnotes and text transcriptions. Yates offers a good collection of songs and tunes (several delightful instrumentals by Walt Davis on both banjo and guitar), mostly pre-bluegrass styles, mostly--but certainly not all--familiar selections. Probably the real strength of the collection is in the ballad singers, some of whom (Dellie Norton and the Wallins among them) are outstanding. There are a few unusual ballads and songs--including one of Yates's "prizes"--a fragment of "The Grey Cock" [C. 248] (on HMM 002). Also of particular interest (on HMM 001) is the rarely recorded "Little Fisherman," better known as "The Sea Crab"--a bawdy song recovered in the 17th century in England and, before that, traced to a Levantine tale of the 15th century. [JAF 391]

256   Label Name/Number: Hoopsnake 101
Title: *Down by the Rio Grande*
Artists: Various
Place and Date of Recording: St. Louis, MO, 1977-79
Date of Publication: 1980
Annotations: Liner and insert notes by Jane and Barry Bergey
Selections:
      Glenn Ohrlin
            High-Toned Dance
            Jake & Roanie
      Troy P. Lee (with Rex & Ray Offutt)

        Gold Rush
    Art Galbraith & Gordon McCann
        Beaumont Rag
    Bill Neely & Larry Kirbo
        Hard Times Blues
        Lovely Mansion
        Won't You Come Over To My House
[Also Hispanic and Native American selections; two stories and one poem]

      Hoopsnake 101: The album is subtitled "Western Music recorded live at the Frontier Folklife Festival (1977-1979)"--an annual event held in front of St. Louis's Gateway Arch, sponsored by the Missouri Friends of the Folk Arts and the National Parks Service. A poster-size insert provides some information on the performers and their traditions, as well as on the event in general. Not listed above is Van Holyoak's recitation of an old western favorite, "Lasca."

257   **Label Name/Number:** John Edwards Memorial Foundation JEMF-105
Title: *New England Traditional Fiddling: An Anthology of Recordings, 1962-1975*
Artists: Various
Collector/Recordists: Various
Producer: Paul Wells
Place and Date of Recording: Various, 1926-75
Date of Publication: 1978
Annotations: 32 p. booklet by Paul Wells
Selections:
    Bonaparte's March -- Elmer Barton
    Daniel O'Connell's Welcome to Parliament/St. Patrick's Day in the Morning -- L. O. Weeks
    Doon Reel/Quinn's Reel -- Paddy Cronin
    Durang's Hornpipe -- Wes Dickinson
    Grandpa's Waltz -- Leon "Fritz" Carl
    Hull's Victory -- Mellie Dunham's Orchestra
    Jigs in E Minor -- Joseph Cormier
    Maple Sugar -- Duane Perry
    Miss McCloud's Reel/Pigtown Fling/Peel Her Jacket -- Uncle Joe Shippee
    Money Musk -- Ron West
    Newlywed Reel -- Louis and Wilfred Beaudoin
    Off She Goes -- Everett Dwyer
    O'Gaff's Jig -- Camile Dubois
    Portland Fancy -- The Plymouth Vermont Old Time Barn Dance Orchestra
    Portsmouth Hornpipe -- Neal Converse
    Shelburne Reel -- Ben Guillemette
    Westphalia Waltz -- Doug Goodwin

      JEMF 105: The aim of this thoroughly researched album is to document in text and with musical examples the history of traditional fiddling in New England. The 17 selections include 3 commercial 1926 recordings (Dunham, Shippee, Plymouth Orchestra) and one from the 50s; two 1939 field recordings from LC and the remainder, 1975 field recordings by Wells. The brochure includes illustrated social history of fiddling in New England, information on each of the performers, and annotations and musical transcriptions for each tune, including extensive bibliodiscographies. [JAF 395]

Label Name/Number: June Appal JAA001 [3 LP Boxed Set]
Title: *Anthology of Appalachian Music, Vol. 1. The Ballad Tradition.* Boxed set consisting of: JA
        001: *Passing Thru the Garden*; JA 009: *Buell Kazee*; and JA 020: *Been A Long Time
        Traveling*; see individual album listings for details.
Editor: Doug Dorschug, producer
Date of Publication: 1987
Annotations: 8 p. brochure by Loyal Jones; additionally, each individual LP includes a brochure

Label Name/Number: June Appal JAA002 [3 LP Boxed Set]
Title: *Anthology of Appalachian Music, Vol. 2. Mountain Instrumental Styles.* Boxed sed consisting
        of: June Appal JA 025: *Mountain State Music*; JA 010: *Red Wing*; JA 049: *Relics and
        Treasure*; see individual album listings for details.
Editor: Doug Dorschug, producer
Date of Publication: 1987
Annotations: 8 p. brochure by Richard Blaustein in addition to individual brochures to each LP

Label Name/Number: June Appal JAA003 [3 LP Boxed Set]
Title: *Anthology of Appalachian Music, III: Mountain Swing and Blues.* Boxed set consisting of: JA
        035: *Look at the People*; JA 032: *In Full Swing*; and JA 030: *Road to Rome*; see
        individual album listings for details.
Editor: Doug Dorschug, producer
Date of Publication: 1987
Annotations: 6 p. brochure by Charles K. Wolfe

        JAA 001/002/003: These three boxed sets of three albums each are repackagings by June
Appal, affiliated with Appalshop of Whitesburg, Kentucky, of nine of its best albums in a commendable and useful collection. Vol. 1 includes an 8-page insert by Loyal Jones with an overview
on Appalachian life and music, a glossary, study questions, bibliography and discography--in addition to the documentation originally accompanying the separate albums. These LPs constituted
some of the best examples of traditional ballad singing issued in the 1970s, and their value is
enhanced by the new packaging. As such, the set can provide libraries with a valuable introduction
to Appalachian folksong and singing. The four singers represent starkly different singing styles,
though all thoroughly traditional. Vol. 3 includes a six-page overview essay by Charles Wolfe
directed specifically toward helping the teacher use the material in an educational context, posing
and answering such discussion questions as: is Appalachian music synonymous with folk music?; to
what extent can commercial songs be considered traditional?; how do the songs in these albums
illustrate the process of folk tradition?; to what extent do the songs reflect specific historical
attitudes or social values?

258   Label Name/Number: June Appal JA0059C [cass]
Title: *The Best of Seedtime on the Cumberland: A Festival of Traditional Mountain Arts*
Artists: Various
Producer: D. Gregory White
Place and Date of Recording: Whitesburg, KY, 1987-90
Date of Publication: [1990]
Annotations: Insert notes
Selections:
        Bangum and the Wild Boar [C. 18] -- Michael Kline
        Blackeyed Susie --Morgan Sexton
        Cacklin' Hen -- Thorton and Emily Spencer
        Courting in the Rain -- Wade and Julia Mainer

Ebenezer -- Whit Sizemore and the Shady Mountain Ramblers
Hogeyed Man, The -- Marion Sumner
Loving Hannah -- Jean Ritchie
Miss McCloud's Reel -- Lee Sexton Band
Powers' Waltz -- Ada Powers
Sailor On the Deep Blue Sea -- Janette and Joe Carter
Set Me Free -- Levi Gross
Shady Grove -- Morgan Sexton
Traveling Creature -- Nimrod and Molly Workman
[Also 3 African-American selections; one narrative; one sound effects]

JA JA0059C: The performances on this cassette are culled from various years of the annual Seedtime on the Cumberland festivals, sponsored by Appalshop (parent organization of June Appal) and held in Whitesburg, Kentucky. Brief insert notes give a paragraph on each performer/performance, all of whom hail from several Appalachian states.

259 Label Name/Number: Kicking Mule KM 204
Title: *The Old-Time Banjo in America*
Artists: Various
Producer: Art Rosenbaum
Place and Date of Recording: Various
Date of Publication: 1978
Annotations: Liner notes by Art Rosenbaum
Selections:

Backwater Blues -- Dan Gellert
Barbara Allen [C. 84] -- Buell Kazee
Boat's up the River -- Ola Belle Reed
Cacklin' Hen -- Reed Martin
Coocoo's Nest -- Pat Dunford
Elzick's Farewell -- Tommy Thompson
Golden Slippers -- John Burke
Grapevine Twist, The -- Bob Winans
Liza Jane --Dan Gellert
Medley: Sally Ann/Half Shaved -- Pat Dunford
My Doney, Where You Been So Long? -- Ola Belle Reed
Policeman -- Reed Martin
Snowdrop -- Reed Martin
Southern Rose Waltz -- Buzz Fountain, Frosty Lamb
Want To Go to Cuba But I Can't Go Now -- Shorty Ralph Reynolds

Kicking Mule KM 204: Rosenbaum presents a variety of old-time banjo styles by an assortment of practitioners that range from thoroughly traditional (Kazee, Reed) to others of city backgrounds who have taken up the instrument in adulthood. He provides brief comments on the performers and the playing styles.

260 Label Name/Number: Leader [U. K.] LEA 4012
Title: *Blue Ridge Mountain Field Trip*
Artists: Various
Collector/Recordist: Janet Kerr
Editor: Seumus Ewens
Place and Date of Recording: VA & NC, 1969

Date of Publication: 1970
Annotations: 8 p. booklet by Janet Kerr
Selections:
>   Hubert Caldwell
>   Constitution Hornpipe
>   Old Virginia Waltz
>   Oxbow Quadrille
>   Staten Island Hornpipe
>   Sue Draheim, Buddy Pendleton, Mac Benford
>   Peeler Creek Waltz, The
>   Carl Leming, Buddy Pendleton
>   Liberty
>   Rutland's Reel
>   Gray Craig & North Carolina Ramblers
>   Richmond
>   Soldier's Joy
>   John Hilt
>   Medley
>   Sweet Sunny South
>   Tex Isley
>   Buck
>   Live and Let Live
>   Nobody's Business
>   Reidsville Blues
>   Silver Threads Among the Gold
>   Sugar in the Gourd
>   John Hilt, Roger Sprung, Joan Sprung
>   Devil's Dream
>   Gray Craig, Doug Rorrer
>   Under the Double Eagle

Leader LEA 4012: This is a collection from a field trip in the Galax, Va., area by Kerr in 1969. Unusual items on the disc are the quadrilles and hornpipes by 75-year-old fiddler Hubert Caldwell, pieces not common in this part of the country. Caldwell has lived as far west as Kansas and Iowa and, furthermore, reads music, so it is difficult to pinpoint the sources of his tunes. Tex Isley, who performed professionally in the 1920s and '30s and in the '60s with Clarence Ashley, is heard on a selection of variegated guitar and autoharp pieces (including a blues on the latter), demonstrating his breadth of styles. A third old-timer, John Hilt of Tannersville, plays several fiddle solos. Other musicians heard are from a younger generation, including native North Carolinians as well as city folk from New York and California, all attending the Galax fiddlers' convention. [WF 7/72]

THE LIBRARY OF CONGRESS'S ARCHIVE OF (AMERICAN) FOLK SONG.
America's preeminent repository of traditional folk music was established in 1928 when its first head and prime mover, Robert Winslow Gordon, was appointed "specialist and consultant in the field of Folk Song and Literature" in the Library of Congress. Though even such an arcane nook in the LC has not been sheltered from the harsh buffets of political winds, the Archive has, over the years, grown steadily, until today it holds some 40,000 hours of unpublished recordings. The AFS (some of its albums bear the designation, "AAFS," reflecting the period prior to 1955, when its title was "Archive of American Folk-Song;" in 1981 it was renamed the Archive of Folk Culture and was made a section of the recently established American Folklife Center) issued its first six albums of

recordings for sale to the public in 1942 as sets of 78 rpm discs--though preceded in 1941 by a trial issue, under the auspices of the Friends of Music in the LC, of two ten-inch discs with four selections (later incorporated into AFS L1). Each album included leaflets with text transcriptions of the songs and brief notes on the music and performers. In the following years a few more albums followed, but wartime rationing of shellac limited production. The first 22 albums were originally issued in 78 rpm format. The 78s were transferred to 33 rpm LPs in 1956. In 1964-66, the LPs were remastered and reissued. In the course of remastering, occasionally alternate takes were used, and sometimes more complete versions than had been used on the earlier releases were given. (Some abrupt transitions suggest that different "takes" may have been spliced together.) In around 1980, the first four albums were reissued with new jackets and new brochures, including a new and very informative introductory essay by Wayne Shirley, Reference Librarian of the LC's Music Division, chronicling the LC's early sound recording ventures, policies, and guiding principles. However, for the most part, the text transcriptions and original headnotes were allowed to stand. Through the 1940s and '50s, the LC's series of albums constituted one of the few sources available to the general public of traditional American folk singers and instrumentalists.

For much of the lay public, the austerely institutional maroon-and-gray covers, the meager mimeographed-and-stapled inserts, the sometimes scratchy, tinny sound of aluminum disc field recordings, and the often shrill, jarring sound of stark, unaccompanied balladists, defined "folk music." Not to say that there weren't some excellent performers and performances, but many recordings lacked easy listenability, and certainly could not compete with commercially issued recordings in terms of technical quality. By the 1980s, when the albums were reissued in new garb, much had changed; hundreds of albums of excellently recorded and annotated folk music of all sorts were available. The LC was no longer the preeminent purveyor of traditional recordings. Nevertheless, the albums are still well worth having. Under the surface noise, the quality of many of these performances is remarkably high. Alan Lomax, who recorded many of the selections in the field and then edited AFS L1 and L2 (as well as some devoted to African-American traditions), had what I consider a flawless knack for selecting beautiful and/or striking performances. [JEMFQ 60]

261 Label Name/Number: Library of Congress AFS L1
Title: *Anglo-American Ballads*
Artists: Various
Collector/Recordist: Alan & Elizabeth Lomax, Herbert Halpert, Charles Seeger, Charles Draves, John A. and Bess Lomax
Editor: Alan Lomax
Place and Date of Recording: VA, DC, WI, TX, KY, OH, AR, 1934-1941
Date of Publication: 1943 (78 rpm), 1956 (LP reissue)
Annotations: 21 p. booklet by Alan Lomax, introduction by Wayne Shirley
Selections:

     Barbara Allen [C. 84] --Rebecca Tarwater
     Devil's Nine Questions, Devil's [C. 1] -- Mrs. Texas Gladden
     Farmer's Curst Wife, The [C. 278] -- Horton Barker
     Gypsy Davy, The [C. 200] -- Woody Guthrie
     House Carpenter, The [C. 243] -- Mrs. Texas Gladden
     Lady of Carlisle, The [O 25] -- Basil May
     Little Brown Bulls, The [C 16] -- Emery DeNoyer
     Old Kimball [Q 22] -- Mrs. Texas Gladden
     One Morning in May [Q 26] -- Mrs. Texas Gladden
     Pretty Polly [P 36b] -- Estil C. Ball
     Pretty Polly [P 36b] -- Pete Steele
     Rich Old Farmer, The [P 1A] -- Pearl Borusky
     Sioux Indians, The [B 11] -- Alex Moore
[Also 2 African-American selections]

LC AFS L1: The LC's first long-playing album is still one of the best single-disc collections of traditional Anglo-American ballad-singing available, informatively annotated by Lomax. The emphasis is clearly on the older layers of American folk ballads: eleven numbers are of British origin and the remaining two from the late 1800s. Mrs. Texas Gladden, who contributes four numbers, is an outstanding singer--a large repertoire of complete texts and a clear, pitch-perfect singing style that does not intrude on the story. Woody Guthrie is heard on one of his first recordings (made in 1940), before he made any commercial discs. He, Estil Ball, and Pete Steele are the only singers who accompany themselves instrumentally. (All three of them and Horton Barker can be heard on other, non-LC albums.) Because the album included the earlier "Friends of Music in the LC" 78s, there are two versions of "Pretty Polly" (with no acknowledgement thereof in the headnotes) and two totally incongruous African-American selections. In his comments on Ball's rendition of "Pretty Polly" Lomax notes that Ball had learned his version from a commercial Victor recording of 1925--an early signal to folklorists (unfortunately ignored for many years afterward) that commercial recordings could not be ignored in understanding the folk tradition. [JAF 276--WR]

262   Label Name/Number: Library of Congress AFS L2
Title: *Anglo-American Shanties, Lyric Songs, Dance Tunes and Spirituals*
Artists: Various
Collector/Recordist: Alan Lomax (some with Elizabeth Lomax or Pete Seeger), Charles Todd and
          Robert Sonkin, Herbert Halpert
Editor: Alan Lomax
Place and Date of Recording: DC, OH, KY, CA, MS, NC, 1937-1941
Date of Publication: 1943 (78 rpm), 1956 (LP reissue)
Annotations: 13 p. booklet by Alan Lomax, introduction by Wayne Shirley
Selections:

> Chilly Winds -- Wade Ward
> Cindy -- W. E. Claunch
> Coal Creek March -- Pete Steele
> Cripple Creek -- Herbert Smoke
> Eighth of January, The -- W. E. Claunch
> Fod -- Henry King and family
> Glory in the Meetinghouse -- Luther Strong
> Grub Springs -- W. E. Claunch
> Haul Away My Rosy --J. M. (Sailor Dad) Hunt
> Jennie Jenkins -- Estil C. Ball
> John Henry --Wallace Swann and his Cherokee String Band
> Last of Callahan, The -- Luther Strong
> Little Dove, The --Molly Jackson
> Old Joe Clark -- Wade Ward
> Pay Day at Coal Creek -- Pete Steele
> Roll on the Ground -- Thaddeus C. Willingham
> Sally Brown -- J. M. (Sailor Dad) Hunt
> Soldier, Won't You Marry Me? -- Russ Pike
> Ten Thousand Miles -- Molly Jackson
> Texas Bell -- W. E. Claunch
> Train, The -- Chub Parham
> Ways of the World, The -- Luther Strong

LC AFS L2: L2 complements L1 by surveying the various Anglo-American folksong traditions other than balladry: two sea shanties, seven fiddle tunes, four banjo songs, a harmonica instrumental, a square dance performance (recorded at the Asheville Folk Festival), an early spiritual, assorted humorous songs, love songs, and other pieces. The disc demonstrates that the crude aluminum disc recording technique was much kinder to vocal and guitar music than to banjo and fiddle, which sound very tinny. Among the musical high points of the album are "Dad" Hunt's two lively shanties (both rendered faster than they would have been on board ship); two examples of Aunt Molly Jackson's wonderful rubato parlando Kentucky style; and the Balls's dialogue song, "Jennie Jenkins," with Estil Ball's solid (and intricate) guitar accompaniment.

263   Label Name/Number: Library of Congress AFS L7
Title: *Anglo-American Ballads*
Artists: Various
Editor: B. A. Botkin
Place and Date of Recording: VA, KY, NC; 1937-1942
Date of Publication: 1943 (78 rpm), [1956?] (LP reissue)
Annotations: 10 p. insert by B. A. Botkin
Selections:

> Bolakins (Lamkin) [C. 93] -- Mrs. Lena Bare Turbyfill
> Claude Allen [E 6] -- Hobart Smith
> Four Marys, The [C. 173] -- Mrs. Texas Gladden
> Golden Willow Tree, The [C. 286] -- Justus Begley
> Lord Thomas and Fair Ellender [C. 73] -- Horton Barker
> Rambling Boy, The [L 12] -- Justus Begley
> Sanford Barney [H 1] -- I. G. Greer
> Three Babes, The [C. 79] -- I. G. Greer
> Two Brothers, The [C. 49] -- Mrs. Texas Gladden
> Two Sisters, The [C. 10] -- Horton Barker

LC AFS L7: The LC's second ballad album features six singers: Mrs. Texas Gladden, her brother, Hobart Smith, and Horton Barker, from Virginia; the Greers and Lena Turbyfill from North Carolina; and Justus Begley from Kentucky. Begley accompanies himself with a vigorous frailing banjo; the versatile Smith, on guitar; the Greers, on plucked dulcimer. As was common (but not invariable) with the insert notes to these early LC albums, we are told nothing about the performers themselves. The backgrounds of at least two of these important artists (Barker-- Folkways FA 2362, and Smith--Folk Legacy FSA-17) have been documented elsewhere on other albums. All are excellent performances.

264   Label Name/Number: Library of Congress AAFS L9
Title: *Play and Dance Songs and Tunes*
Artists: Various
Collector/Recordist: Various
Editor: B. A. Botkin
Place and Date of Recording: IA, MS, KY, VA, NC, TN, TX, 1936-1942
Date of Publication: 1943 (78 rpm), [1959] (LP reissue)
Annotations: 8 p. insert by B. A. Botkin
Selections:

> Bile Dem Cabbage Down --Estil C. Ball, Blair C. Reedy
> Devil's Dream -- J. C. Fowler, Elic Buckner, Alva Ruffner
> Devil's Dream -- Thomas Mann
> Girl I Left Behind Me, The -- Oscar Harper, Harman Clem, Homer Peters, Ray Hanby
> Haste to the Wedding, Off She Goes, Jig: medley -- Thomas Mann
> Irish Washerwoman --Thomas Mann

Mississippi Sawyer -- J. C. Fowler, Elic Buckner, Alva Ruffner
Nancy's Fancy --Thomas Mann
Oh, Fly Around, My Pretty Little Miss --O. L. Coffey
Old Blue Sow --Enos Canoy, Tim Canoy, and Lola Canoy
Old Sally Brown --Calvin Cole, Dan Tate
Pigtown Fling --Thomas Mann
Pore Little Mary Settin' in the Corner -- Enos Canoy, Jim F. Myers
Sally Goodin -- Justus Begley
Sally Goodin -- Oscar Harper, Harman Clem, Homer Peters, Ray Hanby
Soldier's Joy -- Nashville Washboard Band
Where'd You Git Yo' Whisky -- Enos Canoy, Jim F. Myers
[Also 8 African-American selections]

LC AAFS L9: Samplers such as this suggest that while the AFS's albums in the genre of balladry are indispensable to students and educators, when it comes to instrumental party and dance music today's listener can find a much better (and more listenable) selection on LP releases from the 1960s and later by private companies and other institutions. The handful of hammered dulcimer selections by Thomas Mann of Ortonville, Iowa, recorded in 1937, are noteworthy examples of a musical tradition that may never have been moribund in this country, but neither can it be described as flourishing. Mann's "Devil's Dream" interpolates an unacknowledged "Fisher's Hornpipe" as well. Four of the other selections--the pair by Oscar Harper and group, and the two by Fowler and group were all recorded at dances, and prominently feature the caller at the expense of the musicians, who are all but inaudible. "Bile Dem Cabbage Down" has unusual syncopated guitar backup by E. C. Ball, a musician who was more extensively recorded in the 1950s and on. Begley's hard-driving frailing banjo style is exciting but the usual tune of "Sally Goodin" is barely recognizable. Eight African-American performances (originally labeled "Negro Game Songs") are not listed here because they fall outside my circumscribed limits of inclusion, but the lively performance of "Soldier's Joy," by a black string band from Nashville, is a good example of black musicians no further from Anglo-American tradition than Charlie Poole or the Allen Brothers.

265   Label Name/Number: Library of Congress AAFS L11
Title: *Sacred Harp Singing*
Artists: Dock Owen, Paine Denson, Lee Wells, L. P. Odem, Mrs. Delilah Denson Posey, Mrs. Maude Moncrief, Mrs. M. L. Mann, John M. Dye, Euna Vee Denson Nail, Ernestine Tipton, A. Marcus Cagle, R. M. Hornsby
Collector/Recordist: Alan Lomax and George Pullen Jackson
Editor: George Pullen Jackson
Place and Date of Recording: Birmingham, AL, 1942
Date of Publication: 1943 (78 rpm), [1959] (LP reissue)
Annotations: 4 p. booklet by George Pullen Jackson
Selections:
Ballstown
David's Lamentation
Edom
Evening Shade
Fillmore
Heavenly Vision
Lover of the Lord
Mear
Milford
Mission

Montgomery
Mount Zion
Northfield
Sardis
Sherburne
Stratfield
Vain World Adieu
Windham
Wondrous Love

LC AAFS L11: "Sacred harp singing" refers to the rural church practice, dating to the late 18th century but still surviving in the American southeast, of choral four-part singing of religious songs from the Sacred Harp (or similar) hymnals, each rendition beginning with solmization (singing the tune using the names of the notes instead of the regular text)--generally of the older three syllable (fa-sol-la) style. Following the democratic spirit of the camp meeting movement, musical arrangements of all four parts were equally melodic, thus resulting in choral blends that sound rather strange to contemporary urban listeners. These recordings were made at the 37th annual session of the Alabama Sacred Harp Singing Convention by Alan Lomax and George Pullen Jackson, one of America's foremost experts on religious folksong. The brief brochure is confined to text transcriptions and headnotes for each selection; the listener who would like to know something more general about the music and its social setting must turn to one of Jackson's books, in particular *Down-East Spirituals*. The selections are divided into hymns, "fuguing" songs, and anthems, but the listener must look elsewhere to learn what distinguishes these types.

266   Label Name/Number: Library of Congress AAFS L12
Title: *Anglo-American Songs and Ballads*
Artists: Various
Collector/Recordist: Various
Editor: Duncan B. M. Emrich
Place and Date of Recording: TN, AR, MO, KY, NC, CA, 1941-1946
Date of Publication: 1947 (78 rpm), [1959?] (LP reissue)
Annotations: 11 p. insert by Duncan Emrich
Selections:

Derby Ram, The -- Charles Ingenthron
Edward [C. 13] -- Charles Ingenthron
Expert Town (The Oxford Girl) [P 35] --Mildred Tuttle
Froggie Went A-Courting -- Pleaz Mobley
Lord Bateman [C. 53] -- Pleaz Mobley
My Parents Raised Me Tenderly [P 1 A] --Pleaz Mobley
Naomi Wise [F 5] --Lillian Short
Our Goodman [C. 274] -- Orrin Rice
Rolly Trudum -- May Kennedy McCord
Singing Alphabet, The -- May Kennedy McCord
Sourwood Mountain -- I. G. Greer
Sweet William (Earl Brand) [C. 7] -- I. G. Greer
Tree in the Wood, The -- Doney Hammontree
Widow's Old Broom, The -- Charles Ingenthron

LC AAFS L12: LC's third album of ballads and/or songs (following LC 1 and LC 7) redresses the almost complete lack of representation from the Ozarks on the earlier two with eight performances by informants of Vance Randolph (probably not available in the LC when the earlier albums were compiled): Mrs. Tuttle, Short, and McCord, and Mr. Hammontree and Ingenthron. Short and McCord each contributed over 70 items to Randolph's *Ozark Folksongs* (Missouri Historical Society, 1946-50). May Kennedy McCord was something of a song collector herself, and for many years conducted an old-time songs column in a local newspaper. Mrs. Short's "Naomi Wise" is Carson J. Robison's composition, recorded commercially by Vernon Dalhart, and as such is early testimony to the effect of the Robison/Dalhart duo on oral tradition. The album also departs from its predecessors in giving considerable room to humorous or light-hearted pieces, preeminent among which is Hammontree's wonderful performance of "The Tree in the Wood." The retitling of what singer Charles Ingenthron called "The Little White Dog" with its standard title of "Edward" raises the question about editing policy in general; has this practice other examples on these LC discs?

267   Label Name/Number: Library of Congress AAFS L14
Title: *Anglo-American Songs and Ballads*
Artists: Various
Collector/Recordist: Various
Editor: Duncan B. M. Emrich
Place and Date of Recording: IN, NC, CA, DC, KY, 1941, 1945, 1946
Date of Publication: 1947 (78 rpm), [1959?] (LP reissue)
Annotations: 10 p. booklet by Duncan Emrich
Selections:

> Barbara Allen [C. 84] -- Bill Nicholson
> Billy Grimes --I. G. Greer
> Caroline of Edinboro' Town [P 27] -- Charles Ingenthron
> Common Bill -- I. G. Greer
> Darling Cory --Pleaz Mobley
> Devilish Mary [Q 4] --Paul Rogers
> Father Grumble [Q 1]--Jean Ritchie
> Fiddle-I-Fee --Maud Long
> Frank James, The Roving Gambler (The Boston Burglar) [L 16 b] -- L. D. Smith
> Jack of Diamonds -- Bill Nicholson
> Old Smoky -- I. G. Greer
> The Cherry Tree Carol, The [C. 54] -- Maud Long
> Young Charlotte [G 17] -- I. G. Greer

LC AAFS L14: Among the 13 selections, with one exception recorded after the end of the War, are four (by Nicholson, Rogers and Mobley) recorded at Renfro Valley that reflect the great influences of the Renfro Valley Barn Dance, one of the most successful local musical radio programs of the era. The ballads and songs are old, but the guitar and steel guitar accompaniment were then very up to date. Among the other performers are one of Vance Randolph's most important informants, Charles Ingenthron; the first appearance on LP by Jean Ritchie; and four by Prof. I. G. Greer of Thomasville, NC, an early collector/performer who made a few commercial recordings as well (see Country Turtle CT 6001 in Section IV). Greer's solemn baritone renderings are appropriate for the intensely dramatic (and once very popular) "Young Charlotte" but somewhat too ponderous for the light-hearted "Billy Grimes" (believed to be, when the brochure notes were written, a native American song, but since traced to British sheet music of 1850) and "Common Bill."

268 Label Name/Number: Library of Congress AAFS L16
Title: *Songs and Ballads of the Anthracite Miners*
Artists: Various
Collector/Recordist/Editor: George Korson
Place and Date of Recording: PA, 1946
Date of Publication: 1947 (78 rpm), [1959?] (LP reissue)
Annotations: 12 p. booklet by George Korson
Selections:

> Avondale Mine Disaster, The [G 6] -- John L. Quinn
> Boys on the Hill -- James Muldowney
> A Celebrated Workingman -- Daniel Walsh
> Down in a Coal Mine -- M. Jones
> Down, Down, Down -- W. E. Keating
> John J. Curtis [G 29] -- Andrew Rada
> Me Johnny Mitchell Man -- Jerry Byrne
> Miner's Doom, The -- Daniel Walsh
> Old Miner's Refrain, The --Daniel Walsh
> On Johnny Mitchell's Train --Jerry Byrne
> Shoofly, The -- Daniel Walsh
> Union Man -- Albert Morgan
> When the Breaker Starts Up Full Time -- Jerry Byrne
> Rolling on the Rye Grass -- James Muldowney

LC AAFS L16: George Korson's career as a journalist in Pennsylvania's Schuylkill Valley starting in the 1920s brought him into contact with the anthracite mining industry, and he soon developed a resonant empathy for the miners and their difficult conditions. In 1924 he began collecting their songs and ballads, out of which efforts came his book, *Minstrels of the Mine Patch* (1938). In January of 1946, he undertook the first post-war recording expedition under the auspices of the LC and in one week recorded songs and ballads, many from singers whom he had visited or known two decades earlier. This album highlights the fruits of his labors and is best appreciated as a companion to the book, which adds more information on all but one of the songs recorded. The selections are all performed by men who grew up in the mining industry (all but one informant over 60 years old); most are songs and ballads, sung without accompaniment, indigenous to the hard rock "mine patches." While there are a few light-hearted pieces, appropriate to the saloons and cigar shops on Saturday nights, the tone of many is laden with life's tragedy and tedium. The dirge-like pace of many numbers (for example, "The Old Miner's Refrain," to the tune of "Little Old Log Cabin in the Lane") underscores their pathos. Welsh and Irish influences are strong throughout--in the singers and their accents, in the melodies, and in the songs themselves (one is directly of Welsh origin). Two fiddle tunes illustrate the kind of music that entertained the miners in their leisure. Korson's sensitive comments put the material in its proper context: that of a moribund industry that inflicted hardships on the miners and their families both when it thrived and as it faltered.

269 Label Name/Number: Library of Congress AAFS L20
Title: *Anglo-American Songs and Ballads*
Artists: Various
Collector/Recordist: Various
Editor: Duncan B. M. Emrich
Place and Date of Recording: CA, MO, AR, NC, KY, TN, TX, OK, 1941-46
Date of Publication: 1947 (78 rpm), [1959?] (LP reissue)
Annotations: 8 p. insert by Duncan Emrich
Selections:

Baa, Baa, Black Sheep -- Bascom Lamar Lunsford
Black Mountain Blues -- S. Leslie, P. Crisp
Blue-Eyed Girl -- Rufus Crisp
Cripple Creek -- Henry King and family
Cruel War Is Raging, The [O 33] -- Charles Ingenthron
Dying Cowboy, The [B 1] -- Dick Devall
Git Along Down to Town -- Henry King and family
Give the Fiddler a Dram -- McMinnville Garment Factory Workers' Band
Good Old Rebel -- Booth Campbell
Jesse James [E 1] -- Bascom Lamar Lunsford
Kicking Mule -- Henry King and family
Little Dogies -- Dick Devall
Little Old Sod Shanty -- Jimmy Denoon
My Sweetheart's a Cowboy -- Dick Devall
Nottingham Fair -- Charles Ingenthron
Railroader for Me, A -- Russ Pike
Red Whiskey -- Dick Devall
Soldier's Joy -- McMinnville Garment Factory Workers' Band

LC AAFS L20:   Another unfocused assortment from the AAFS archives, this album includes four cowboy ballads by Dick Devall, who also recorded a few numbers commercially for Victor; four more sides from Todd and Sonkin's field recordings of Ozark migrants in California-- the King Family and Russ Pike (heard also on AAFS L2); more examples of some of Vance Randolph's Ozark informants, Charles Ingenthron, Jimmy Denoon, and Booth Campbell; and some uninspiring dances with calls from McMinnville, Tennessee. "Black Mountain Blues" is early evidence that Leslie Keith's "Black Mountain Rag" was well on its way to becoming traditional by 1946. The King Family's three selections are with banjo and guitar accompaniment, not mandolin and guitar, as the notes and credits indicate.

270   Label Name/Number: Library of Congress AAFS L21
Title: *Anglo-American Songs and Ballads*
Artists: Various
Collector/Recordist: Various
Editor: Duncan B. M. Emrich
Place and Date of Recording: Various, 1938 - 47
Date of Publication: 1947 (78 rpm), [1959?] (LP reissue)
Annotations: 10 p. insert by Duncan Emrich
Selections:
Barnyard Song, The -- Sam D. Hinton
Broken Token, The [N 42] -- Maud Long
Buffalo Boy -- Sam D. Hinton
Death of Queen Jane [C. 170] -- Bascom Lamar Lunsford
False Knight Upon the Road, The [C. 1] -- Maud Long
Heavy-Loaded Freight Train -- Pete Steele
I Wish I Was a Mole in the Ground --Bascom Lamar Lunsford
Jackie's Gone A-Sailing [N 7] -- Maud Long
Loss of the "New Columbia," The -- Carrie Grover
Lowlands of Holland, The -- Carrie Grover
My Grandmother Green -- Maud Long
On a Bright and Summer's Morning -- Bascom Lamar Lunsford
Sandy River; Grey Eagle; Bonaparte's Retreat -- Marcus Martin

Shout, Little Lulu --Pete Steele
Sourwood Mountain; Do Little Bobby, Do; Shoo Fly -- Rufus Crisp
Sweet William [N 8] -- Maud Long
There's More Pretty Girls Than One -- Wayne Dinwiddie
Wild Barbaree, The [K 33]-- Carrie Grover

LC AAFS L21:   This mix of ballads and non-narrative songs opens with two tracks of tuning demonstrations: Crisp on banjo and Martin on fiddle. If the album had been edited by an instrumentalist, the headnotes would doubtless have reported the tunings for the listener's benefit. Maine folksinger Carrie Grover makes her LP debut on this album; her extensive repertoire was recorded in Washington, D. C., in 1941 by Alan Lomax. She is (rather, was) an uninteresting singer musically but knew many long and uncommon ballads; her "Loss of the *New Columbia*" is a rare if not indeed unique recovery. Sam Hinton is one of those collector/singers with academic knowledge but traditional background--so intertwined are the two facets that a listener cannot unravel them without Hinton's help. ("Buffalo Boy" he had learned in his youth in Crockett, Texas; "Barnyard Song," in the 1940s from a sailor in California.)   North Carolina ballad singer Maud Long offers an interesting pair of similar broadside ballads on the theme of the young maid who wants to accompany her lover to war; one does not often find such close relatives in the repertoire of the same singer. Lunsford's "Death of Queen Jane" is a fragmentary recovery of a Child ballad but typical of the manner in which several old ballads have been stripped of most of their narrative con-tent and reduced to a lyric lament. [JAF 283--DKW]

271   **Label Name/Number:** Library of Congress AAFC L26/27 [2 LP set, originally issued
            separately]
Title: *American Sea Songs and Shanties*
Artists: Various
Collector/Recordist: Various
Editor: Duncan Emrich
Place and Date of Recording: NY, WI, CA, VA, 1939, 1941, 1946, 1951
Date of Publication: Single LPs issued 1952
Annotations: 17 p. booklet and 5 p. booklet, both by Duncan Emrich
Selections:
Richard Maitland
        A Long Time Ago
        A-Roving, or The Amsterdam Maid
        Blow the Man Down (II)
        Drunken Sailor, The
        Haul the Bowline
        Heave Away
        Paddy Doyle
        Paddy, Get Back
        So Handy, Me Boys, So Handy
Noble B. Brown
        Blow the Man Down (I)
        Blow, Boys, Blow
        Reuben Ranzo
Leighton Robinson
        Dead Horse, or Poor Old Man, The
        Homeward Bound
        Johnny Boker
        Rio Grande

            Roll the Cotton Down
            Rolling Home
            Sailor's Alphabet, The
            Whisky Johnny
        John M. (Sailor Dad) Hunt
            When Jones's Ale Was New

    LC AAFC L26/27:   In the 1980s the LC reissued in a single jacket these two albums of
shanties, originally issued in 1952 and featuring four men who had had actual shipboard singing
experience. Nineteen of the selections are shanties; the others ("When Jones's Ale Was New" and
"The Sailor's Alphabet") are fo'c'sle songs, sung by sailors during leisure time. As Emrich noted in
the brochures, these were probably the first shanties available to the public by genuine shantymen;
he cautioned listeners to be prepared for a much slower tempo than one usually hears in shanty
interpretations--an almost lethargic pace necessitated by the heavy and lengthy labor that the
shanties accompanied. One can assume all four singers were well past their prime when these
recordings were made; nevertheless the single example of "Dad" Hunt's singing (heard also on LC
AAFS L2) shows a vigor and lightness that requires no apologies. Five selections by Capt.
Robinson, made in 1939, are with accompaniment by Alex Barr, Arthur Brodeur, and Leighton
McKenzie, in an attempt to recreate the sound of shanty-singer and chorus that originally characterized these worksongs. However, since Brodeur was a Professor of English at Berkeley one
wonders about the authenticity of the re-creations. (Robinson's other three recordings were made
in 1951--at the age of 83--by Sam Eskin.)

272   Label Name/Number: Library of Congress AAFS L28
Title: *Cowboy Songs, Ballads, and Cattle Calls from Texas*
Artists: Various
Collector/Recordist: John A. Lomax, Duncan Emrich, Rae Korson
Editor: Duncan B. M. Emrich
Place and Date of Recording: Wash. DC (Library of Congress) and TX; 1941, 1942, 1946, 1948
Date of Publication: 1952 (LP)
Annotations: 20 p. insert by Duncan Emrich
Selections:
        Buffalo Skinners, The [B 10] -- John A. Lomax
        Colley's Run-I-O [C 17c] -- L. Parker Temple
        Cowboy's Life Is a Very Dreary Life, The -- Sloan Matthews
        Dreary Black Hills, The -- Harry Stephens
        Dying Cowboy, The [B 2] -- Sloan Matthews
        Dying Ranger, The [A 14-- Johnny Prude
        Goodbye, Old Paint -- Jess Morris
        Goodbye, Old Paint -- Sloan Matthews
        Night-Herding Song, The -- Harry Stephens
        Streets of Laredo, The [B 1] -- Johnny Prude
        Texas Rangers, The [A 8] -- Sloan Matthews
        Zebra Dun, The [B 16] -- J. M. Waddell

    LC AAFS L28:   As Emrich observes in his introductory notes, all the examples on this disc
are Texas songs sung by Texans save one: "Colley's Run-I-O," a Maine lumberjack song included for
comparison with its western descendant, "Buffalo Skinners." The latter is sung by John A. Lomax
himself; it was one of his favorite pieces and one he often included in lecture-demonstrations. A
more interesting peep into Lomax's persona as field collector is afforded in his recorded attempts to
elicit from Sloan Matthews examples of cattle calls; Matthews is clearly ill at ease re-creating artifi-

cially before the microphone the work calls and cries that for him are inextricably bound to life on horseback out on the range, and only through Lomax's dogged persistence are a few half-hearted examples dragged out of him. (The examples interpolated into Harry Jackson's "Night-Herding Song" are more convincing.) For me, the musical highlight of the album is the marvelous recording of "Goodbye, Old Paint" by 64-year old Jess Morris, who had been a prominent dance musician near Amarillo at the turn of the century. Morris's rendition is not for casual background listening: his gravelly voice and squeaky fiddle are at first hearing almost laughably inept. But the control, the artistry, the emotional depth, and the unselfconsciousness of the performance exemplify the distance that can be measured between the aesthetic of traditional singing and that of concert singing. (Morris's performance is all the more remarkable in light of the fact that he had had some training on the violin in his youth in Bartlett, Texas.) I have found it an excellent benchmark performance to play at the beginning and conclusion of a course of Anglo-American folk music. Morris's version is followed by another by Sloan Matthews--a more typical performance yet by no means a prettified one.

273 **Label Name/Number:** Library of Congress AFS L29
Title: *Songs and Ballads of American History and of the Assassination of Presidents*
Artists: Various
Collector/Recordist: Various
Editor: Duncan B. Emrich
Place and Date of Recording: Wash. DC; Akron, OH; Central Valley, CA; Bells, TX, South Turkey Creek, NC; 1937-49
Date of Publication: 1952
Annotations: 18 p. insert by Duncan Emrich
Selections:
Side A
　　Battle of Antietam Creek, The -- Ward H. Forde
　　Cumberland's Crew, The [A 18] -- Capt. Pearl R. Nye
　　Iron Merrimac, The -- Judge Learned W. Hand
　　Phil Sheridan -- Judge Learned W. Hand
　　Southern Soldier, The -- Mrs. Minta Morgan
　　Washington the Great -- Mrs. Minta Morgan
Side B
　　Booth Killed Lincoln (fiddle tune) -- Bascom Lamar Lunsford
　　Booth Killed Lincoln-- Bascom Lamar Lunsford
　　Charles Guiteau [E 11] -- Bascom Lamar Lunsford
　　Mr. Garfield -- Bascom Lamar Lunsford
　　Zolgotz -- Bascom Lamar Lunsford

　　　　LC AFS L29: Side A of this historical collection is, with one exception, devoted to the Civil War; Side B consists of 5 pieces performed by Bascom Lamar Lunsford dealing with the assassinations of McKinley, Garfield, and Lincoln. Of particular interest are the two brief performances by Supreme Court Justice Learned Hand, both learned by him before the turn of the century and recorded in Washington DC in 1942 by Alan Lomax. Editor Emrich does not resist the opportunity to make the point that "traditional songs are transmitted in the folk manner on all levels of our society." Lunsford's "Mr. Garfield" is in the rather rare format of a cante fable--a combined song-and-story. Several of the pieces ("Phil Sheridan," "Washington the Great," "Booth Killed Lincoln") are very rare.

274 **Label Name/Number:** Library of Congress AAFS L30
Title: *Songs of the Mormons and Songs of the West*

Artists: Various
Collector/Recordist: Various
Editor: Duncan B. M. Emrich
Place and Date of Recording: UT, MO, CA, AR, AZ; 1938-1949
Date of Publication: 1952
Annotations: 12 p. insert by Duncan Emrich
Selections:

> Brazos River, The -- Irene Carlisle
> Custer's Last Charge -- Ward H. Forde
> Echo Canyon or Hooray Hoorah the Railroad Is Begun -- L. M. Hilton
> Freighting from Wilcox to Globe -- Abraham John Busby
> Handcart Song, The -- L. M. Hilton
> Joe Bowers [B 14] -- Charles Ingenthron
> On the Road to California or The Buffalo Bull Fight -- W. T. Mann
> Root Hog or Die [B 21] -- Jimmy Denoon
> Sam Bass [E 4] -- Lannis F. Sutton
> St. George -- Rodger McArthur
> Starving to Death on a Government Claim -- Vance Randolph
> Tittery-Irie-Aye -- Joseph H. Watkins
> Utah Iron Horse, The -- Joseph H. Watkins

LC AAFS L30:   Side A consists of six Mormon songs recorded by Austin E. and Alta Fife on extensive field trips in Utah in 1946-47.   These songs all date from 1840-70; one singer, Joseph H. Watkins, was 85 years old when he was recorded singing songs he had learned in the late 1860s. Side B is "songs of the west"--though in this context "west" means Kansas and beyond.   Most of this set is of much wider provenence than Side A--except for Irene Carlisle's unique "The Brazos River," a tribute to the rivers of Texas.   Carlisle is the only woman singing on this LP.   Of special interest is one of the handful of recordings Vance Randolph made of himself.   (Randolph recorded himself singing songs he had collected from informants prior to the availability of a recording machine.) Only two songs on the LP are sung with accompaniment: "On the Road to California," with piano, and "Root Hog or Die," with guitar.

275   Label Name/Number: Library of Congress AAFS L54
Title: *Versions and Variants of Barbara Allen*
Artists: I. N. Marlor, George Vinton Graham, Mrs. T. M. Bryant, Monroe Gevedan, Kitty Ritchie
>   Singleton, May Kennedy McCord, Mrs. Mary Franklin Farmer, Mrs. L. L. McDowell,
>   Mrs. Ollie Wombell, Mrs. Mary Sullivan, Molly Jackson, Mrs. Emma Dusenbury, Dr.
>   C. L. Watkins, Samuel Harmon, Oscar Parks, Ray Hawks, Bascom Lamar Lunsford,
>   Horton Barker, Mrs. W. L. Martin, Mrs. G. A. Griffin, Warde H. Ford, Clyde (Slim)
>   Wilson, Archie Styes, H. J. Beeker, Mary and Cora Davis, the Gant family, Sunshine
>   Robinson, Bill Carr, Rebecca Tarwater, Moses (Clear Rock) Platt
Collector/Recordist: Various
Editor: Charles Seeger
Place and Date of Recording: Various, 1934-1954
Date of Publication: 1966
Annotations: 83 p. insert by Charles Seeger
Selections:
>   30 Versions of Barbara Allen [C. 84]

LC AAFS L54:   Ethnomusicologist Charles Seeger turned to the LC's Archive of Folk Culture for material with which to examine the theoretical problem of "what is a tune?" How much can two singings differ and still be singings of the same tune? Seventy-six recordings of "Barbara Allen" provided his database; he reported his findings in UCLA Institute of Ethnomusicology's *Selected Reports in Ethnomusicology* (1966; pp. 120-167). That paper was reprinted as the notes to L54. Of admittedly limited interest, this specialized album is a good example of a musicological case study of a particular ballad. Thirty variants are presented, nine of which (including one by a black singer) in their entirety. The arrangement is by musical kinship, two broad families being identified. The booklet includes some selected transcriptions of Seeger's melograph analyses of the recordings--oscillographic traces of singers' pitch and volume. All the singers are from the Southeast (as far west as Texas) except for one from Michigan and one from Indiana. Two renditions are with fiddle accompaniment; four, with guitar. Seeger's discourse touches on far more than a question of musicological epistemology: he has much to say about folk and trained singing in western culture in general. His paper is followed by a few pages by Ed Cray discussing the texts of the ballad variants.

276 Label Name/Number: Library of Congress AAFS L55
Title: *Folk Music from Wisconsin*
Artists: Various
Collector/Recordist/Editor: Helene Stratman-Thomas
Place and Date of Recording: WI; 1940-46
Annotations: 35 p. insert by Helene Stratman-Thomas
Selections:

> Awake, Arise You Drowsy Sleeper [M 4] -- Lester A. Coffee
> Billy Vanero [B 6] -- Luther Royce
> Bold McIntyres, The -- Arthur Moseley
> Brennan on the Moor [L 7] -- William J. Morgan
> Couderay Jig, The -- Mr. & Mrs. Otto Rindlisbacher
> Cranberry Song -- Frances Perry
> How Happy is the Sportsman -- J. L. Peters
> I'll Sell My Hat, I'll Sell My Coat -- Pearl J. Borusky
> Little Brown Bulls, The [C 16] -- Charles Bowlen
> Lord Lovel [C. 75] -- Winifred Bundy
> Lumberjack Dance Tune -- Mr. & Mrs. Otto Rindlisbacher
> Milwaukee Fire, The [G 15] -- Robert Walker
> On the Lake of Pontchartrain [H 9] -- Frances Perry
> Once I Courted A Charming Beauty Bright [M 3]-- Pearl J. Borusky
> Pig Schottische -- Mr. & Mrs. Otto Rindlisbacher
> Pinery Boy, The -- Mr. & Mrs. Otto Rindlisbacher
> Pompey is Dead -- Dora Richards
> Reuben Wright and Phoebe Brown -- Hamilton Lobdell
> Shantyman's Life -- Emery De Noyer
> Swamper's Revenge on the Windfall, The -- Mr. & Mrs. Otto Rindlisbacher
> Young Johnny [G 16] -- Winifred Bundy

LC AAFS L55: In 1939, a joint Library of Congress/University of Wisconsin folk music recording project was inaugurated; Helene Stratman-Thomas was faculty advisor. Extensive recording trips across the state were carried out in the summers of 1941 and '42; the project was interrupted by the war and didn't resume until 1946. Over the years, Ms. Stratman-Thomas and her associates recorded an enormous wealth of material from many different ethnic groups in the state. This album, the LC's first devoted to a single state's musical lore, presents only English-language material. The lore of the lumberjacks is well represented with five instrumentals, two songs and a ballad, all with lumbercamp associations. One of the tunes, "The Pinery Boy," is played on a variant of the "lumberjack cello"--a wooden cracker-box fastened to a pitchfork, with one string running over the pitchfork's handle. "Cranberry Song" is a local composition that was still being revised annually when it was collected in 1946; other pieces are much more widely known. "The Milwaukee Fire," about an 1883 disaster that took 71 lives, was a bathetic Victorian ballad that subsequently entered oral tradition. [JAF 291--DKW]

277   Label Name/Number: Library of Congress AAFS L56
Title: *Songs of the Michigan Lumberjacks*
Artists: Various
Collector/Recordist: E. C. Beck or Alan Lomax and Harry B. Williver
Editor: E. C. Beck
Place and Date of Recording: Various, 1938, 1948
Date of Publication: 1960
Annotations: 10 p. booklet by E. C. Beck
Selections:

> Falling of the Pine, The -- Lester Wells
> Jack Haggerty [C 25] -- John Norman
> Jam on Gerry's Rocks, The [C 1] -- Bill McBride
> Jam on Gerry's Rocks, The [C 1] -- Jim Kirkpatrick
> Johnny Carroll's Camp -- Bill McBride
> Little Brown Bulls, The [C 16] -- Carl Lathrop
> Lumberjack's Alphabet -- Gus Schaffer
> Michigan I-O [C 17 b] -- Lester Wells
> Once More A-Lumbering Go -- Carl Lathrop
> Turner's Camp on the Chippewa [C 23] -- Bill McBride
> Wild Mustard River, The [C 5] -- Carl Lathrop

LC AAFS L56: All but one of these recordings were made by Alan Lomax during a ten-week survey of Michigan folksongs in 1938; Kirkpatrick's "Jam on Gerry's Rocks" was recorded by Williver in 1948. The singers were all ex-lumberjacks, most well advanced in years but still able to render a pleasant tune. Dr. E. C. Beck of the University of Michigan and author of *Lore of the Lumber Camps* (1948) edited and annotated the album, which includes some of the best-known songs of the lumberjacks--"Jam on Gerry's Rocks," "Lumberjack's Alphabet," and "Jack Haggerty" (or "The Flat River Girl)." The songs are all sung unaccompanied and most show prominent Irish characteristics. [JAF 291--DKW]

278a   Label Name/Number: Library of Congress AAFS L57
Title: *Child Ballads Traditional in the United States (I)*
Artists: Various
Collector/Recordist: Various
Editor: Bertrand H. Bronson
Place and Date of Recording: KY, VA, TN, CA, NY; 1937-1946
Annotations: 22 p. insert by Bronson
Selections:

> Bangum and the Boar [C. 18] -- G. D. Vowell
> Bishop of Canterbury, The [C. 45] -- Ward H. Forde
> Cherry Tree Carol, The [C. 54] -- Mrs. Lee Skeens
> Edward [C. 13] -- Mrs. Crockett Ward
> Lazarus [C. 56] -- Molly Jackson
> Lloyd Bateman [C. 53] -- Mary Sullivan
> Lord Bateman [C. 53] -- Molly Jackson

Two Sisters, The [C. 10] -- Jean Ritchie
Wild Boar [C. 18] -- Samuel Harmon

278b   Label Name/Number: Library of Congress AAFS L58
Title: *Child Ballads Traditional in the United States (II)*
Artists: Various
Collector/Recordist: Various
Editor: Bertrand H. Bronson
Place and Date of Recording: VA, CA, FL, WI, KY, DC, 1937-1950
Annotations: 24 p. insert by Bertrand Bronson
Selections:

Andrew Batann [C. 167/250] -- Ward H. Forde
Devil and the Farmer's Wife, The [C. 278] -- Carrie Grover
Golden Willow Tree, The [C. 286] -- Jimmy Morris
King's Love-Letter, The [C. 208] -- Mrs. G. A. Griffin
Mermaid, The [C. 289] -- Emma Dusenbury
Oxford Merchant, The [C. 283] -- Ward H. Forde
Ship Carpenter, The [C. 243] -- Clay Walters
Ship Set Sail for North America, A [C. 286] -- Ollie Jacobs
There Was An Old and Wealthy Man [C. 272] -- Dol Small
Three Babes, The [C. 79] -- Mrs. Texas Gladden
Well Met, My Old True Love [C. 243] -- Pearl J. Borusky

LC AAFS L57 and L58.   These two albums, edited by the late, great ballad scholar, Bertrand Bronson of the University of California at Berkeley, sample the strong collection of older Anglo-American ballads in the LC's Archive of Folk Culture.   The recordings were made in the field by several collectors, including John and Alan Lomax, Sidney Robertson Cowell, Helene Stratman-Thomas, Artus Moser, Herbert Halpert, Charles L. Todd and Robert Sonkin, and Mary Elizabeth Barnicle.   Most of the singers are from the South, but a few are from the Midwest or Northeast.   Unfortunately, the technical quality of several of the selections is distractingly poor. Although the singers range from good to excellent, the fact that all sing a capella gives a biased presentation of the Child ballads in 20th-century America, many of which have been admirably adapted to instrumental accompaniment.   For comparative purposes, Bronson includes two versions of four of the ballads.

Harmon's "Sir Lionel" retains traces of the medieval romance story, while Vowell's lighter version, a 17th-century recomposition, enjoyed great vogue in this country on the stage in the 19th century.   "Lord Bateman" is represented by two very full texts (14 and 19 stanzas); the second recording is to a melody that is better known as "Bury Me Not on the Lone Prairie."   "The House Carpenter," one of the most popular Child ballads in America, is also twice presented, including a beautiful melody by Mrs. Borusky from Wisconsin.   Mrs. Skeens' singing of the ballad of Joseph and Mary is punctuated by an interesting catch in her voice at the end of each line.   "Lazarus" is a good example of Aunt Molly Jackson's fine Kentucky singing style.   "The Suffolk Miracle" had, as Child noted, a wide range of analogues in tale and song; in our own time it is echoed in the modern urban tale, "The Vanishing Hitchhiker."   A Florida version of "Lord Derwentwater" is one of the few (if not only) recoveries of this ballad in oral tradition.   "The Mermaid" represents the LP debut of the blind singer from Mena, Arkansas, Mrs. Emma Dusenbury, who contributed 125 songs and ballads to the LC's archive; Vance Randolph regarded her as the best singer he ever met in the Ozarks--by which he meant that she had the finest repertoire.   Bronson's relatively brief but excellent and superbly written notes exemplify how far the LC had come by the early 1960s from the woefully inadequate inserts of the first several albums. [JAF 291--DKW]

279   Label Name/Number: Library of Congress AFS L60
Title: *Songs and Ballads of the Bituminous Miners*
Artists: Various
Collector/Recordist/Editor: George Korson
Place and Date of Recording: WV, PA, OH, KY, VA, AL, 1940
Date of Publication: 1965
Annotations: 13 p. brochure by G. Korson
Selections:

> Blue Monday -- Michael F. Barry
> Coal Diggin' Blues -- Jerrel Stanley
> Coal Loadin' Blues -- Joe Glancy
> Coal Loading Machine, The -- Evening Breezes Sextet
> Coal Miner's Goodbye, A -- Rev. Archer Conway
> Drill Man Blues -- G. Sizemore
> Dying Mine Brakeman, The -- Orville J. Jenks
> Hard Working Miner, The -- G. C. Gartin
> Harlan County Blues -- George Davis
> Hignite [sic] Blues -- Wesley J. Turner
> Mule Skinnin' Blues -- Joe Glancy
> Payday at the Mine -- Charles Underwood
> Sprinkle Coal Dust on My Grave -- Orville J. Jenks
> That Little Lump of Coal -- William March, Richard Lawson
> This What the Union Done -- Uncle George Jones
> Two-Cent Coal -- David Morrison
> We Done Quit -- Sam Johnson
> Young Lady Who Married a Mule Driver, The -- James T. Downer

   LC AFS L60:   This sampling, Korson's companion album to L16 above, reflects the broader musical and geographical limits of bituminous mining lore compared to anthracite. The latter was almost exclusively in Pennsylvania, strongly showing British influences, while the more widespread bituminous industry (Korson collected in ten states, from Pennsylvania south to Alabama and west to Indiana) produced musical lore reflecting the significant presence of black miners. Several of the selections on this album are very bluesy (some sung by white singers); others, many with guitar accompaniment, are reminiscent of hillbilly styles of the 1930s--especially the one fiddle-guitar instrumental, "Payday at the Mine," and the duet, "That Little Lump of Coal." Otherwise, the overall impression of the two albums is similar, exhibiting the various aspects of life in the mining communities--disasters and sickness, unions and strikes, and very occasional lighter moments. [JAF 313--DKW]

280   Label Name/Number: Library of Congress AFS L61
Title: *Railroad Songs and Ballads*
Artists: Various
Collector/Recordist: Various
Editor: Archie Green
Place and Date of Recording: AL, AR, CA, ID, IL, LA, MI, MO, NY, TN, TX, VA, WI; 1936-1959
Date of Publication: 1968
Annotations: 35 p. insert by Archie Green
Selections:

> Big Rock Candy Mountains, The -- Harry McClintock
> Boss of the Section Gang, The -- Mrs. Minta Morgan
> Dying Hobo, The [H 3] -- George Lay
> Engineer, The -- Lester A. Coffee

George Allen [G 3] -- Austin Harmon
I Rode Southern, I Rode L. & N. -- Merle Lovell
Jerry Will You Ile that Car -- Ward H. Forde
Lightning Express, The -- Jim Holbert
New River Train, The -- Ridge Rangers
Oh I'm a Jolly Irishman Winding on the Train -- Noble B. Brown
Railroader, The -- May Kennedy McCord
Roll On Buddy -- Molly Jackson
T. & P. Line, The -- Mary Sullivan
Train Blues -- Russell Wise, Mr. White
Train is off the Track, The -- Mrs. Esco Kilgore
Way Out in Idaho -- Blaine Stubblefield
Wreck of the Royal Palm, The [dG 51] -- Clarence H. Wyatt
[Also 5 African-American performances]

LC AFS L61:   The album contains 22 selections that range widely in content and style.
Side A focuses on ballads, lyric songs, and work songs that deal with railroading and railroad construction as occupations. Several numbers ("Boss of the Section Gang," "Jerry...," "Way Out in
Idaho," "Oh I'm a Jolly Irishman...") attest to the musical impact of the Irish immigrants who
labored to lay tracks from the Mississippi to the Pacific Coast during postbellum decades. G 3 and
dG 51 represent the trainwreck genre--one of the most popular forms of our native American balladry. Side B surveys the variety of instrumentals, blues, parlor ballads, lyric songs and gospel songs
that utilize railroad imagery or railroad settings. Musically, the album includes some admirable
examples, but there are other pieces that could have been improved upon. (Green did have to con-
tend with some parochial administrative contraints; he was barred from using a "Casey Jones" because the song was protected by copyright. So was "Wreck of the Royal Palm," but LC officials
didn't know that!)   Green's capsule annotations, in his inimitably engaging prose, fix the place of
each piece in the spectrum of America's folk and popular music. [WF 1/73; JAF 322--DKW]

281   Label Name/Number: Library of Congress AFS L62
Title: *American Fiddle Tunes*
Artists: Various
Collector/Recordist: Various
Editor: Alan Jabbour
Place and Date of Recording: WI, MI AZ, CA, VT, KY, VA, AR, NC; 1934-46
Date of Publication: 1971
Annotations: 36 p. booklet by Alan Jabbour
Selections:
Patrick Bonner
       Fisher's Hornpipe
       Maid of Kildare, The
       Wind that Shook the Barley, The
Michael Cruise
       Money Musk
Mrs. Ben Scott
       Haste to the Wedding
       Perry's Victory
L. O. Weeks
       Hull's Victory
Elmer Barton
       Bummer's Reel

      Wake Up Susan/Unnamed

W. M. Stepp
      Bonaparte's Retreat
      Drunken Hiccups, The
      Run Nigger Run
      Ways of the World, The

John Rector
      Old Dad

Luther Strong
      Hog-Eyed Man, The
      Rickett's Hornpipe
      Cumberland Gap

Stephen B. Tucker
      Haste to the Wedding

John Hatcher
      Buffalo Girls
      Grub Springs

Lon Jordon
      Natchez Under the Hill

Marcus Martin
      Sugar in the Gourd
      Cotton-Eyed Joe

Wayne Perry
      Old Joe Clark

[Also 4 Franco-American tunes]

LC AFS L62: Jabbour, who was Head of the Archive of Folksong when he edited this album, combines the scholar's discipline with the musician's ear in producing the first in-depth survey of the American fiddle tradition on LP. He provides his reader/listener with exemplary histories of the 28 tunes recorded, as well as extensive references to other printed and recorded versions. His introductory paragraphs on American fiddle music are enlightening. Side A features fiddlers from the North, Midwest, and West; Side B surveys the Southeast. The selections, mostly rather brief by commercial 78 rpm standards, are almost all unaccompanied, and range in artistic quality from fair to outstanding. Jabbour's references to previously published recordings are far from complete, but he does assure us that every item cited has been heard by him--a wise policy in view of the fluidity of fiddle tunes and their titles. [WF 1/73]

282   Label Name/Number: Library of Congress AFS L68
Title: *"Folk Songs of America": The Robert Winslow Gordon Collection, 1922-1932*
Artists: Various
Collector/Recordist: Robert W. Gordon
Editors: Neil V. Rosenberg and Debora G. Kodish
Place and Date of Recording: CA, NC, GA., PA, KY, WV, DC, ca. 1922-32
Date of Publication: 1978?
Annotations: 29 p. 12" x 12" booklet by Debora G. Kodish & Neil V. Rosenberg
Selections:
      All God's Children Got to Humble Down -- Betty Bush Winger
      Blow Boys Blow -- A. Wilkins
      Blow Boys Blow -- J. A. Spencer
      Brother Jonah -- James G. Stikeleather
      Casey Jones [G 1] -- Francis H. Abbot

Deep Down in My Heart -- W. M. Givens
Finger Ring -- Mary C. Mann
Georgie [C. 209] -- Nancy Weaver Stickeleather
Glory to God, My Son's Come Home -- J. D. Purdy
Haul Away -- A. Wilkins
Haul the Wood Pile Down -- unknown
Hesitation Blues -- Bascom Lamar Lunsford
Isaac Medler -- John W. Dillon
Jesus Is My Only Friend -- Bessie Shaw
Let's Go to Bury -- Rev. A. B. Holly
Milk White Steed [C. 75] -- Nellie Galt
Mississippi Sawyer -- John W. Dillon
Mulberry Hill -- Nellie Galt
Not A-Gonna Lay My Religion Down -- Bascom Lamar Lunsford
Ol' Man Satan/Drive Ol' Satan Away -- Mary C. Mann
Old Granny Hare [= Old Molly Hare]-- W. E. Bird
Old Gray Mare, The -- Bascom Lamar Lunsford
Old Ninety Seven [G 2] -- Fred Lewey
Prisoner's Song -- Ernest Helton
Roll the Old Chariot Along -- unknown
Sally Goodin -- John W. Dillon
Single Girl -- Julius Sutton
Yes Ma'am (Bed Time Quiz) -- Betty Bush Winger
[Also one African-American performance]

LC AFS L68: Issued to commemmorate the 50th anniversary of founding of the Archive of Folk Song in the Library of Congress, this album focuses on the Archive's founder and first director, Robert Winslow Gordon, one of America's preeminent folksong collectors until 1933. By that year Gordon had collected nearly ten thousand song texts from correspondents and made nearly a thousand cylinder recordings--twenty-nine of which are made available here. Among the many fascinating items are probably the earliest recordings of shanties by traditional singers: two ("Haul the Wood Pile Down" and "Roll the Old Chariot Along") cylinders from an unidentified Irish-sounding singer made on the San Francisco waterfront in about 1922 and three others from several years later. These selections, made by younger singers than those on AFS 26/27, suggest that the dirge-like tempo of the latter recordings may have been partly due to the singers' age rather than the customary traditional style of rendition. Of special historical importance were the two 1925 recordings of "Old 97" and "The Prisoner's Song"--especially in light of Gordon's active role in the courtroom battle over authorship of "Wreck of the Old 97." Ben Harney, who recorded "The Wagon," was one of the first composers of ragtime music. Excellently annotated, the album is highly recommended--the only drawback being the poor technical condition of the cylinders. [JEMFQ 59--PW]

283   **Label Name/Number:** Library of Congress American Folklife Center AFC L69-L70 [2-LP box set]
Title: *Children of the Heavenly King: Religious Expression in the Central Blue Ridge*
Artists: The congregation of Cross Roads Primitive Baptist Church, Baywood, VA; congregation of Clarks Creek Progressive Primitive Baptist Church, Ararat, VA; congregation at Macedonia Union Baptist Church, Alleghany County, NC; Rev. Robert Akers; congregation at Laurel Glenn Regular Baptist Church, Alleghany County, NC; congregation of Mountain View Baptist Church, Lowgap, NC; congregation of Community Baptist Church, Alleghany County, NC; congregation at Carson Creek, Alleghany

County, NC; Marshall Largen Family with Bill Scott; Calswell Schuyler Family; Peaceful Valley Quartet; Ella Draughn; Elk Horn Four; Jim and Artie Marshall; Elder and Mrs. Jess B. Higgins

Collector/Recordist: Blue Ridge Parkway Folklife Project
Editor: Charles K. Wolfe
Place and Date of Recording: VA, NC; 1978, 1979
Date of Publication: 1980?
Annotations: 48 p. 12" x 12" booklet by Charles K. Wolfe
Selections:

Children of the Heav'nly King
Doxology
Holding to His Hand of Love
Home in Heaven, A
How Happy Are They
I'm Going Down by the River of Jordan
Jesus Is Coming Soon
Keep on the Firing Line
Must Jesus Bear the Cross Alone
On the Other Side of Jordan
Palms of Victory
Satan, Your Kingdom Must Come Down
The Lord Will Make a Way Somehow
Twilight is Falling
What a Time We're Living in
When the Redeemed Are Gathering In

[Also narrations, sermons, baptizing, services]

LC AFC L69-L70: This package includes two discs and an illustrated 48-page booklet in a boxed set. The recordings were made by the Blue Ridge Parkway Folklife Project, a study conducted by the LC-AFC in cooperation with the National Park Service during fieldtrips in 1978-79. The discs offer "a cross-section of the region's religious expression and include hymn singing, prayer, and sermons from church services, performances of gospel music by local trios and quartets, a baptism at a creek, and stories of religious conversion or a call to the ministry." The brochure includes an introductory essay on religious music of the region by editor Wolfe, followed by annotations to the selections. The annotations include data on performer(s), collector, and time and place of recording; text transcription; commentary on the performance and the selection; and bibliography of printed and recorded variants as well as photos of most of the main performers and some of the recording locations. [JEMFQ 70]

284 Label Name/Number: Meriweather 1001-2 [2 record set]
Title: *I Kind of Believe It's a Gift*
Artists: Various
Producers: Burt Feintuch & Bruce Greene
Place and Date of Recording: KY; 1959-1977
Date of Publication: [1979]
Annotations: 10 p. booklet by Burt Feintuch & Bruce Greene
Selections:

Street Butler
Higgins' Farewell
Jenny Jenkins
Young John Riley

Jim Bowles
    Ida Red
    Miss Dare
    Railroad Through the Rocky Mountains
    Shout Old Lulu
    Walk and Talk Together
John Graves
    Darling
    Getting on the Train
    Shucking Up the Corn
Clorine Lawson
    Charles Guiteau
    Courting Song
    Drunkard's Lone Child
    Old Dan Tucker
    Row Us over the Tide
Isham Monday
    Christmas Eve
    Green Mountain
    Rock Creek Girl
    Susan Loller on Judio
Pat Kingery and Troy Basil
    Nancy Dalton
    Rocky Road Through Georgia
    Yellow Rose of Texas
Gladys Pace
    Lass of Mohea
    Pearl Bryan [F 1a]
    Stern Old Bachelor
J. E. Chelf
    Going Across the Sea
    Hot Times
    Sweet Sunny South
Gusty Wallace
    Chicken Reel
    Give the Fiddler a Dram
    Jennie Put the Kettle On
The Walker Family (Sammie, Bernice, Ivan, and Rickie Walker, Neill Walker Fernandez)
    Hangman [C. 95]
    Old Liberty
    Shortning Bread
    Sinful to Flirt [G 19]
    Sundown
[Also 5 African-American performances]

Meriweather 1001-2: Kentucky has proved fertile ground for folksong collecting for some 60 years--Wyman, McGill, Sharp, Perrow, and Combs in the 1910s and '20s; Lomax, Thomas, and Halpert in the 1930s and '40s,; Wilgus, Montell, and Jones in the '50s, '60s, and '70s. The Western Kentucky Folklore Archive, whence all the recordings on this double album were drawn, had over 5,500 items when I looked through it some 20 years ago. The recordings were made in 1959-77 by Wilgus and Montell, Greene, and Feintuch, featuring 12 different artists or groups; the albums were produced by young folklorists and their students. Not listed here are two selections by Afro-American performer Bud Garrett. The set comes in a double jacket that opens up to display photos of most of the performers. The brochure includes notes on the songs and tunes and performers, as well as song text transcriptions. The performances include unaccompanied ballad singing (by Butler, Lawson, Pace), banjo and fiddle instrumentals and some hillbilly influences. The latter is represented by the Walker Family--a band with two very good vocalists (the old-time ballad singing of "Hangman," set to hillbilly instrumentation, provides an unusual performance indeed). [JEMFQ 65/66]

285 Label Name/Number: Middlebury College, New England Folksong Series No. 1
Title: *Eight Traditional British-American Ballads*
Artists: Various
Collector/Recordist: Helen Hartness Flanders, Marguerite Olney
Place and Date of Recording: RI, VT, ME; 1930s--1953
Date of Publication: 1953
Annotations: 4 p. booklet by Marguerite Olney
Selections:

      Bailiff's Daughter of Islington, The [C. 105]- Phyllis Burditt
      Burly Banks of Barbry-O, The [C. 14] -- Elmer Barton
      Edward [C.13] -- Edith B. Price
      Farmer's Curst Wife, The [C. 278] -- Elmer Barton
      King John and the Bishop [C. 45] -- Elmer George
      Lord Bateman [C. 53] -- Asa Davis
      Robin Hood Rescuing the Three Squires [C. 140] -- Charles Finnemore
      Wife of Usher's Well [C. 79] -- Phyllis Burditt

     Middlebury College, New England Folksong Series No. 1: Along with the Southern Mountains (Appalachians and Ozarks), New England has proven a fertile ground for gathering ballads of British origins. One of the most indefatigable New England ballad collectors was Helen Hartness Flanders, who, with her colleagues, filled an archive with some 9,000 items collected in the 1930s, '40s, and '50s. This LP (now out of print) can give listeners an excellent sampling of New England ballad singing at its starkest. The singers are all model examples of the quintessential traditional ballad singer, whose role is to present a story in song with the least intrusion of vocal artifice or style. Some of the singers had been visited by Flanders and Olney in the 1930s and were rerecorded in 1953 for this LP. More information on the singers and text transcriptions can be found in Flanders' *Ancient Ballads Traditionally Sung in New England*, 4 vols. (Univ. of Pennsylvania Press, 1960-65). A brief 4-page insert gives educators some key ideas to develop in using these recordings as teaching aides (the stated principal purpose of the album). Several of the ballads (all presented in full texts) are extremely rare on LP.

286 Label Name/Number: Mississippi Dept of Archives & History AH-002
Title: *Great Big Yam Potatoes*
Artists: Various
Collector/Recordist: Herbert Halpert and Abbott Ferriss
Editor: Tom Rankin and Gary Stanton
Place and Date of Recording: MS, 1939
Date of Publication: 1985
Annotations: 16 p. booklet by Rankin, Sauber, Ferriss, and Stanton
Selections:
      W. E. Claunch:
          Bear Creek's Up

Great Big Taters
Grub Springs
Miss Sally at the Party
Wolves a-Howling
John Hatcher
Farewell Whiskey
Going up to Hamburg
Leather Britches
Old Miss Sally
Tishomingo County Blues
John Brown
Dusty Miller
Rats in the Meal Barrel
Wolves a-Howling
Frank Kittrell (with Mollie Kittrell)
Indian War Whoop
Ryestraw
Went To Go to Meeting
W. A. Bledsoe (with Horace Kinard or Douglas Williams)
Big Footed Nigger in a Sandy Lot
Farewell Mary Ann
Hardy Sharp (with Horace Kinard or Douglas Williams)
Eighth of January
Great Big Yam Potatoes
Mississippi Sawyer
Puncheon Floor
Enos Canoy (with Tim Canoy and Lola Canoy)
Old Blue Sow
Buck Dancing Charlie
Lost John
Jim Myers
Old Field Rabbit
Stephen B. Tucker
Bragg's Retreat
Christmas Time in the Morning
Circus Piece
Cold Frosty Morning
Indian Eat the Woodpecker
Joke on the Puppy
Raker's Hornpipe
Soldier's Joy
Throw the Soapsuds in the Corner of the Fence
Charles Long (and Sam Neal)
Alabama Waltz
Hard Road to Texas
Jones County
My Little Dony
My Old Dog's Trailing Up a Squirrel

Miss. Dept. of Archives & History AH-002: In 1939, under the auspices of the WPA Federal Writers' and Music Projects and the LC, NY folksong collector Herbert Halpert and Mississippian sociologist Abbott Ferriss spent five weeks driving through Mississippi in an army ambulance converted into a recording truck, garnering over 300 ballads, worksongs, hollers, play party songs, and fiddle tunes from performers who had been lined up in advance by fieldworkers in the Federal Projects. Of the 115 fiddle tunes they collected, only 10 have been issued previously on LC LPs. This album redresses the hitherto regrettable unavailability of this material by publishing a representative 42 selections. Readers may wonder what was edited out in order to permit so many selections on one disc, but these are the complete pieces as Halpert recorded them. Severely limited in the number of acetate blanks at his disposal, Halpert requested his informants to play all parts of each tune once only and then stop. As a result, the selections range from only 33 seconds to slightly over 2 minutes each.

Mississippi state folklorist Tom Rankin edited the material for this album from the recordings on deposit in the LC's AFC and the biographical information in the Mississippi Dept. of Archives and History. The accompanying 12" x 12" booklet includes a background essay by Rankin on the WPA project itself and the results it produced; Ferriss's own recollections of the trip; reproductions of several of Ferriss's photographs; a brief essay, "Fiddling Style in Mississippi" by fiddler/ethnomusicologist Tom Sauber; notes on each of the 10 fiddlers and the selections (some with tune transcriptions) by Rankin and Gary Stanton; a complete list of all the fiddle tunes (save one) recorded by Halpert and Ferriss; a brief bibliography; and a discography of other Mississippi fiddle music albums. Intelligent headnotes to the selections analyze the tune structures and the subtleties of each performance, thereby helping both novice and experienced listener alike to appreciate what is unique, unusual, or typical in each instance. The condition of the recordings is good, considering the technical limitations imposed by the circumstances of the field trip.

The music itself represents almost 3 generations of fiddlers. The oldest fiddler recorded on the trip was Stephen B. Tucker, born in 1859 and 80 years old at the time he was recorded. Nine of the 24 tunes he recorded are included here; in spite of his age and the fact that he hadn't fiddled for many years, the recordings show him to have been an excellent fiddler, with a repertory including both common and very unusual tunes (according to the notes, his "Cold Frosty Morning," "Indian Eat the Woodpecker," and "Throw the Soapsuds in the Corner of the Fence" have not been reported elsewhere). Possibly the most impressive fiddler that Halpert and Ferriss encountered was Jim Hatcher (b. 1886), five of whose tunes are reissued. These include excellent renditions of some standard tunes ("Leather Britches"--all 3 parts), trick fiddling ("Farewell Whiskey"), a local northern Mississippi tune ("Going up to Hamburg"), and one of Hatcher's own compositions ("Tishomingo County Blues"). Evidently the youngest fiddler recorded on the trip was Enos Canoy, whose recordings, with his guitar and mandolin stringband, include "Old Blue Sow," demonstrating that even a 30-year-old could show the WPA folks some marvelous fiddling techniques. Sauber, Rankin and Stanton take pains to identify what is characteristic of the Mississippi regional fiddling style. [JAF 395]

287   Label Name/Number: Missouri Friends of the Folk Arts 1001 [2 record set]
Title: *I'm Old but I'm Awfully Tough*
Artists: Various
Collector/Recordist: Julia Olin, Jim Olin, Barry Bergey
Place and Date of Recording: Southern MO and northern AR, 1975-76
Date of Publication: [1977?]
Annotations: 24 p. booklet by Jim and Julia Olin, Jane and Barry Bergey, Emily Goodson
Selections:

> Lee Finis Cameron "Tip" McKinney
>> Gipson Davy [C. 200]
>> Gone to View That Land
>> Heaven Bells Are Ringing
>> I'm Old But I'm Awfully Tough

Wandering Boy
Emmanuel Wood and Family
    Bear Creek Sally Goodin
    Dixie Blossom
    Lighthouse
    Spokane Waltz
    Walk Along John
Green Berry Horton
    Bunker Hill
    Midnight Shuffle
    Over the Woods and Through the Snow
    Rattlesnake and the Texas Pony
Troy Lee, Rex and Ray Offutt
    Durang's Hornpipe
    Fort Smith
    Kentucky Waltz
    Twinkle Twinkle Little Star
    Unnamed Schottische
    Whiskey Before Breakfast
Jake Hockmeyer and Russ Orchard
    Coming Down from Denver
    Dance Around Molly
    Marmaduke's Hornpipe
Lawrence Baker
    Death of the Old Sow
    Old Man Who Lived in the West, The [C. 277]
Vesta Johnson and Don Womack
    Fat Meat and Dumplings
    She Ought to Been a Lady
Frank Reed and Alva Lee Hendren
    Fox Chase
    Massa Bill
    Middlegrove
    Stoney Point
Joe Politte
    Grand Picnic
    Jenny Put the Kettle On
    Molly Musk
    Old Man Portell's Tune
    Old Rock Road, The
[Also several stories; Missiouri-French fiddle tunes and songs]

Missouri Friends of the Folk Arts 1001 [2 LP set]: Ozark traditional music has, strangely, never received the limelight that Appalachian music has enjoyed. These field recordings provide evidence of still-thriving traditions in the 1970s, featuring performers mostly unknown on commercial recordings. One exception is "Tip" McKinney, vocalist with Pope's Arkansas Mountaineers in the late 1920s. Missouri's Franco-American community is also represented though not itemized here. [JEMFQ 50-FF]

288 Label Name/Number: Montana Folklife Project 001
Title: *When the Work's All Done This Fall*

Artists: Various
Producers: Michael Korn, Jo Rainbolt
Place and Date of Recording: various, MT
Annotations: 12 p. booklet by Michael Korn & Jo Rainbolt
Selections:

> Cowboy's Dream, The -- Ray Grenfell
> Git Along Little Dogies -- Lou Schlautman
> Home on the Range -- Ray Grenfell
> Little Joe, the Wrangler [B 5] -- Lou Schlautman
> Old Chisholm Trail, The -- Lew Ohl
> Strawberry Roan, The [B 18] -- Val Giessler
> Tying a Knot in the Devil's Tail [B 17] -- Earsel Bloxham
> When the Work's All Done This Fall [B 3] -- Earsel Bloxham
> Zebra Dunn, The [B 16] -- Ken Trowbridge

Montana Folklife Project MFP 001:   With the majority of attention given to recordings from the American Southeast, followed by the Northeast, deep South, and Ozarks, collections from states like Montana are a welcome addition to a national library of demonstration folksong and folkloric materials from the entire country. The album includes nine songs and six recitations by nine Montana men. The musical selections are all old western favorites--ballads and songs, listed above; not listed are recitations, including the Robert Service standard, "The Shooting of Dan McGrew," poems written by the tellers, and anecdotes. The singing style is mostly unornamented as is characteristic of traditional western singers, though the rendition of "The Cowboy's Dream" does have some unusual vocal catches and breaks. Recitations have always played an important part in the lore of the Southwest; "When the Work's All Done This Fall" and "Tying a Knot in the Devil's Tail" both began as poems, and there are still cowboy poetry reading gatherings held annually. The brochure includes text transcriptions, notes on the selections, photos, and a list for further reading.

289   Label Name/Number: Montana Folklife Project MFP 002
Title: *If You Can't Dance to It, It's Not Old Time Fiddle Music*
Artists: Various
Producer: Michael Korn
Place and Date of Recording: MT
Date of Publication: 1986
Annotations: 20 p. booklet by Michael Korn, Glenda Bradshaw, & Jo Rainbolt
Selections:

> Alex and Maureen -- Ben Setran
> Buffalo Gals -- Jim Bebee
> Charmaine -- Bernie Rasmusson
> Dixie Hoedown -- Mike Conroy
> Dying Cowboy, The -- Alec Allery
> Foggy Valley -- Mary Trotchie
> Grandma's Chickens -- Tari Conroy
> Kansas City Kitty -- Andy Tesinsky
> Lonesome Moonlight Waltz -- Alice Allen
> Moonlight on the River Colorado -- Ralph Farnes
> N-Bar-N, The -- Muriel Gabisch
> Old Oly Mathieus -- Ernest Christianson
> Old One-Step, The -- Delbert Hanson
> Ragtime Annie -- Jimmy Widner
> Summer Evening in Aalhus, A -- Anund Roheim

> That French-Canadian Tune -- Tom Harwood
> Waltz of the Wildflowers -- Pickles Lehman
> When You and I Were Young, Maggie -- Harold Sprague

Montana Folklife Project MFP 002: The album's title, taken from a quote from one rhythm guitarist, is used to emphasize that Montana's musical tradition is based on dancing. The fiddlers on this album are well known in Montana and were chosen as representative of the range of fiddle styles found in the state. These include Norwegian hardanger fiddle (Christianson, Roheim), Metis (or Mitchif) fiddling--a mixture of French/Canadian/Indian elements (Allery), western swing (Tesinsky), and borrowing from southeast and southwest. The illustrated brochure includes biographical information on all the performers.

290 Label Name/Number: New World NW 223
Title: *I'm on My Journey Home: Vocal Styles and Resources in Folk Music*
Artists: Various
Collector/Recordist: Various
Editor: Charles Wolfe
Place and Date of Recording: From commercial 78s and field recordings, 1928-75
Date of Publication: 1978
Annotations: 6 p. insewn notes by Charles Wolfe
Selections:

> Barbara Allen [C. 84] -- I. N. (Nick) Marlor
> Been a Long Time Traveling Here Below -- Grandpa Isom Ritchie's church congregation
> Black Sheep, The -- Tom Darby and Jimmie Tarlton
> Bold McCarthy, or the City of Baltimore [K 26] -- Bill Cramp
> Bright and Morning Star -- Walter and Lola Caldwell
> Don't Put Off Salvation Too Long -- Southland Ladies Quartette
> Hanging Johnny -- Captain Leighton Robinson and group (Alex Barr, Arthur Brodeur, Leighton McKenzie)
> Hey, Hey, I'm Memphis Bound -- Delmore Brothers (Alton and Rabon)
> I Am O'ershadowed by Love -- Members of the Stamps-Baxter School of Music
> I'm on My Journey Home -- Denson Quartet
> Late One Evening [M 32] -- Barry Sutterfield
> Risselty Rosselty -- Ray R. Denoon
> Sweet Wine -- Mrs. Goldie Hamilton
> Turkey in the Straw -- Neil Morris

[Also hollerin', whooping, eephing, ringing the pig, spelling, tobacco auctioneering]

NW 223: "This album is a loosely structured survey of different types of vocal styles and resources found in rural Anglo-American lower- and middle-class communities....The album is divided into...(1) nonstandard vocal effects that show how much music infuses the everyday communication, instruction, and recreation of the folk community; (2) solo singing; and (3) ensemble singing, from duets to quartets to larger groups" [from Wolfe's introductory notes]. Wolfe's headnotes to the selections, while also providing background information on the singers and the songs themselves, dwell on the singing style per se--ornamentation, tempo, vibrato, coordination among several singers, etc. Five of the recordings (Darby & Tarlton, Delmores, Denson, Stamps-Baxter, Southland Ladies) are from commercial 78s of 1928-35; five others (Denoon, Hamilton, Marlor, Robinson, Caldwells) are from Library of Congress field recordings of 1936-39; the remainder are more recent field recordings. Most of the selections are without instrumental accompaniment to minimize distraction from the singing--an editorial choice that results in most of the non-solo selections being religious pieces. This well-annotated study should be an excellent tool for classroom demonstration purposes.

291   **Label Name/Number:** New World NW 226
Title: *That's My Rabbit, My Dog Caught It: Traditional Southern Instrumental Styles*
Artists: Various
Collector/Recordist: Various
Editor: Mark Wilson
Place and Date of Recording: Commercial 78s and field recordings, 1927-77
Date of Publication: 1978
Annotations: 4 p. gatefold notes by Mark Wilson
Selections:

Bibb County Hoedown -- Seven Foot Dilly and His Dill Pickles
Bigfooted Nigger -- Helton Brothers
Blues -- Hobart Smith
Granny Went to Meeting with Her Old Shoes On -- Mrs. and Mrs. Vernon Judd
Groundhog -- Marion Reese
Hunky Dory -- Alva Greene and Francis Gillum
Jig -- Bill Boyd and his Cowboy Ramblers
Kimball House -- Ezra "Ted" Hawkins and Riley Puckett
Last of Sizemore, The -- Luther Strong
Lights in the Valley -- Neriah and Kenneth Benfield
Lost Boy Blues -- Palmer McAbee
Lost Indian -- Louis H. Propps
My Pretty Little Pink -- I. D. Stamper
Old Gray Horse, The -- Obed Pickard
Peacock Rag --Arthur Smith and his Dixieliners (Alton and Rabon Delmore)
Pearly Dew -- Lena Hughes
Run, Banjo -- Justis Begley
Rymer's Favorite -- Allen Sisson
Spanish Fandango -- Pete Steele
That's My Rabbit, My Dog Caught It -- Walter Family
[Also 2 Cajun selections]

NW 226: Wilson's admirable demonstration selection includes examples of most instruments found in Southern Anglo-American traditional music: fife, jews-harp, dulcimer, banjo, guitar, autoharp, harmonica, accordion, mandolin, and fiddle as lead, with several other supporting instruments. Apart from two Cajun selections (not listed) and Bill Boyd's band, serving up one of the most breathtaking instrumentals in the western swing idiom on record, the musicians are all from the southeast.

292   **Label Name/Number:** New World NW 239
Title: *Brave Boys: New England Traditions in Folk Music*
Artists: Various
Collector/Recordists: Sandy Paton, Edward D. Ives, Jay Iselin, William Gulvin, Wendy Newton
Editor: Sandy Paton
Place and Date of Recording: ME, MA, NY, NH, CT, New Brunswick, 1959-77
Date of Publication: 1977
Annotations: 6 p. insewn notes by Sandy Paton
Selections:

And Now, Old Serpent, How Do You Feel? -- Mrs. Morris Austin
Brave Boys [K 21] -- Gale Huntington
Cherish the Ladies -- Brendan Mulvihill, Kevin Taylor, Seamus Logue
Dreadnaught, The [D 13] -- Gale Huntington

Erin-Go-Bragh [Q 20] -- Edward Kirby
Fair Fannie Moore [O 38] -- Sara Cleveland
Farmer's Curst Wife, The [C. 278] -- Lewis Lund
Flowers of Edinburgh, The -- Phil, Paul, and Sterl Van Arsdale
Frog He Would A-Wooing Go, A -- Gail Stoddard Storm
Give an Honest Irish Lad a Chance -- Sara Cleveland
Good Old Days of Adam and Eve, The -- Rosalie Shaw
Good Old State of Maine, The -- James Brown
I'll Hit the Road Again, Boys -- Grant Rogers
Jam on Gerry's Rock, The [C 1] --Lawrence Older
Johnstown Flood, The [G 14] -- Mack Moody
Knit Stockings -- Wilfred Guillette and Maurice Campbell
Ladies' Walpole Reel -- Newton F. Tolman, Kay Gilbert
Medley of Scottish fiddle tunes -- Harvey Tolman and Rose Tolman
My Man John -- Gail Stoddard Storm
Three Men They Went A-Hunting -- Sara Cleveland
Two Brothers, The [C. 49] -- Ben Mandel
Who Will Bow and Bend like a Willow? -- Mrs. Morris Austin

NW 239: Albums such as this are particularly welcome in view of the general paucity of good surveys of northeastern musical traditions (in contrast to the well-canvassed Southeast). The material ranges from older ballads and stern Shaker spirituals to vigorous maritime songs, lively instrumental music and lighter pieces. Some of the singers are familiar from other albums: Cleveland, Older, and Rogers all have one or more LPs devoted to them (see Section I). Cleveland's "Fair Fannie Moore" must be one of the loveliest tunes in her repertoire--certainly on this album. The instrumental selections include flute/piano, fiddle/piano, hammered dulcimers, and fiddle/accordion/guitar. The ballad about the 1889 flood in Johnstown, Pensylvania, is rarely recorded.

293 Label Name/Number: New World NW 245
Title: *Oh My Little Darling: Folk Song Types*
Artists: Various
Editor: Jon Pankake
Place and Date of Recording: Commercial 78s and field recordings, 1923-39
Date of Publication: 1977
Annotations: 6 p. insewn brochure by Jon Pankake
Selections:

Been on the Job Too Long [I 9] -- Wilmer Watts and the Lonely Eagles
Chick-A-Li-Lee-Lo -- Almeda Riddle
Come All You Coal Miners -- Sarah Ogan (Gunning)
Cotton Mill Blues -- Daddy John Love
Crawling and Creeping -- Asa Martin and James Roberts
Dr. Ginger Blue -- Arthur Tanner and his Blue Ridge Cornshuckers
Farmer is the Man that Feeds them All, The -- Fiddlin' John Carson
Haunted Road Blues -- Tom Clarence Ashley and Gwenn Foster
I'm a Long Time Traveling Away from Home -- J.T. Allison's Sacred Harp Singers
If the Light Has Gone Out in Your Soul -- Ernest Phipps and His Holiness Singers
King William Was King George's Son -- Mr. and Mrs. Crockett Ward
Lexington Murder, The [P 35] -- Wesley Hargis
Lily Schull -- Mrs. Lena Bare Turbyfill and Mrs. Lloyd Bare Hagie
Oh My Little Darling -- Thaddeus C. Willingham

Poor Drunkard's Dream, The -- Wade Mainer and Songs of the Mountaineers
Sweet William [C. 7] -- Fields Ward
Village School, The -- Nelstone's Hawaiians
Whoopee-Ti-Yi-Yo -- John White and Roy Smeck
[Also one Cajun song]

NW 245: Editor Jon Pankake's goal in this collection was to present a sampling of the diverse kinds of folk songs encountered in America; more specifically, his material is drawn from the Southeast and, with one exception, from the Anglo-American tradition. The song types demonstrated are: children's and play-party songs; Child, broadside, and native ballads; agrarian, labor, and cowboy songs; lyric, banjo, and minstrel songs; outlaw song (blues ballad); bawdy song; blues song; sentimental and homiletic songs; evangelical hymn and Sacred Harp hymn. The bawdy example is a commercial 78 rpm recording that is only slightly suggestive--a problem with the honest presentation of bawdy material that has still not completely been overcome. The local ballad, "Lily Schull," has also been recorded as "The Ballad of Finley Preston" and concerns a 1903 Tennessee murder.

294   Label Name/Number: New World NW 291
Title: *Old Mother Hippletoe: Rural and Urban Children's Songs*
Artists: Various
Collector/Recordist: Various
Editors: Kate Rinzler and Bess Lomax Hawes
Place and Date of Recording: Various, 1937-76
Date of Publication: 1978
Annotations: 8 p. sewn-in notes by Kate Rinzler
Selections:

B-A-Bay -- Mrs. A. P. Wilson
Bobby Halsey -- Estil C. Ball
Frog Went A-Courtin' -- Almeda Riddle
Go to Sleep, Little Baby -- Lester Powell
Jim Crack Corn -- Uncle Alec (Eck) Dunford
Little Rooster -- Almeda Riddle
Little Sally Water-- Captain Pearl R. Nye
Mister Rabbit -- Susie Miller and two boys
Oh, Blue -- Thelma, Beatrice, and Irene Scruggs
Old Grandpaw Yet -- Mrs. Nell Hampton
Old John the Rabbit -- Four girls
Old Mother Hippletoe -- J. D. Dillingham
Rabbit -- Four girls
Rabbit in the Pea Patch -- Angie Clark
Robin Hood and the Peddler [C. 132] -- Carrie Grover
Round to Maryanne's -- Kenneth Atwood
Roxie Anne -- Samuel Clay Dixon
Today is Monday -- Mississippi schoolchildren
[Also ring games, fife tune, jump rope rhymes, other African-American, Cajun, Native American, and Hispanic-American selections]

NW 291: Kate Rinzler opens her notes with the observation that "The concept of childhood as a period requiring special institutions, such as schools, is fairly recent....When children's life and labor were integrated with those of their elders, they mimicked them in their play, enacting scenes of child rearing, seasonal work, recreation, religious events, ill health and healing, aging, death, and burial." This conceptual framework helps to understand the presence of many of the selections included here, but some (e.g., the Robin Hood ballad) still seem out of place. The title song is better known by its opening line, "The fox went out one moonlit night."

295 Label Name/Number: New World NW 294
Title: *The Gospel Ship*
Artists: Various
Collector/Recordist/Editor: Alan Lomax
Place and Date of Recording: KY, VA, AR
Date of Publication: 1977
Annotations: 4 p. gatefold notes by Alan Lomax
Selections:

> Airplane Ride, The -- Nell Hampton
> Amazing Grace -- Howard Adams & congregation of Thornton Regular Baptist Church
> Guide Me, O Thou Great Jehovah -- Ike Caudell & congregation of Mount Olivet Regular Baptist Church
> Hicks' Farewell -- Texas Gladden
> I Am a Poor Wayfaring Stranger -- Almeda Riddle
> Jim and Me -- Hobart Smith, Preston Smith, Texas Gladden
> My Lord Keeps a Record -- Mountain Ramblers
> Old Gospel Ship, The -- Ruby Vass
> See That My Grave Is Kept Clean -- Hobart Smith
> The Little Family -- Ollie Gilbert
> When Jesus Christ Was Here on Earth -- Rev. I. D. Beck
> When the Stars Begin to Fall -- Hobart Smith, Preston Smith, Texas Gladden
> Why Must I Wear This Shroud? -- Thornton Regular Baptist Church

[Also testimonies]

NW 294: Lomax's survey opens with several examples, all recorded in church services in Kentucky (undated, but probably in the 1960s and '70s), of "lining-out" hymns--in which the leader intones quickly a line of text to be followed by the congregation singing it at a more leisurely pace. This is one of the earliest Protestant singing styles, probably surviving from England. The second side of the album focuses on later religious ballads, spirituals, and gospel songs--the types of material one is more likely to encounter outside the formal church setting. Lomax is identified in the album credits as co-founder of the (Library of Congress') "Archives of American Folksongs"--an attribution that distorts history by denying the role of Robert W. Gordon (see notes to LC albums above).

296 Label Name/Number: New World NW 314/315 [2 LP set]
Title: *Back in the Saddle Again*
Artists: Various
Collector/Recordist: Various
Editor: Charlie Seemann
Place and Date of Recording: Various, 1925--ca. 1980
Date of Publication: 1983
Annotations: 4 p. insewn notes by Charlie Seemann
Selections:

> Back in the Saddle Again -- Gene Autry
> Cattle Call -- Tex Owens
> City Boarders -- Sam Agins
> Cowboy Song -- Riders in the Sky

Cowboy Stomp -- Bob Wills and the Texas Playboys
Cowboy, The -- Glenn Ohrlin
Cowhand's Last Ride -- Jimmie Rodgers
D-Bar-2 Horse Wrangler -- Slim Critchlow
Dim Narrow Trail -- Texas Ruby
Dying Cowboy, The [B 2] -- Jules Verne Allen
Gol-Durned Wheel, The -- Van Holyoke
I Want to Be a Cowboy's Sweetheart -- Patsy Montana
I Want to Be a Real Cowboy Girl -- Girls of the Golden West
Little Old Log Shack I Always Call My Home -- Wilf Carter
Lone Star Trail, The -- Ken Maynard
My Dear Old Arizona Home -- Rex Allen
Old Chisholm Trail, The -- Harry McClintock
One More Ride -- Sons of the Pioneers
Pot Wrassler, The -- Harry Jackson
Ridge Runnin' Roan -- Glen Rice and his Beverly Hill Billies
A-Ridin' Old Paint -- Tex Ritter
Rusty Spurs -- Chris Le Doux
Sioux Indians [B 11] -- Marc Williams
Strawberry Roan [B 18] -- Arizona Wranglers
Streets of Laredo [B 1] -- John G. Prude
Tying a Knot in the Devil's Tail [B 17] -- Powder River Jack and Litty Lee
When the Work's All Done This Fall [B 3] -- Carl T. Sprague
Whoopee-Ti-Yi-Yo -- John White

NW 314/315 [2 LP set]: This excellent anthology includes 17 selections from 78s, 3 from electrical transcriptions for radio station use, 1 LC field recording, and 6 from commercial LPS. The material is arranged chronologically by style rather than original recording date, starting with older traditional cowboy and western songs and ballads, moving into the era of the silver screen cowboy, and concluding with some fairly recent compositions. Only a few of the singers (Critchlow, Agins, Ohrlin, Le Doux) have had experience as authentic cowboys or rodeo performers. [JAF 391]

297 **Label Name/Number:** Now and Then Records 1001
Title: *Down Around Bowmantown*
Artists: Clyde Dykes, Gilbert (Gib) Broyles, Tom Slagle, Jerome Broyles, Orland Whitaker, Bob
       Crawford, B. G. Williams, Will Keys, Vestal Jackson, Walter Harmon, Kenneth "Bill"
       Adams
Collector/Recordist: Raymond Blanche; Doug Dorschug, Richard Blaustein
Place and Date of Recording: Limestone, TN; 1940-1951, 1987
Date of Publication: 1989
Annotations: 20 p. booklet by Tim Stafford and Richard Blaustein
Selections:
Side 1: ca. 1940-51
    Coal Creek March
    I'll Be Glad When You're Dead You Rascal You
    I'm as Free a Little Bird as I Can Be
    Plant Some Flowers By My Graveside
    Please Mama Please
    Train 45
    Whiskey Joe

Side 2: 1987

> Bury Me Beneath the Willow
> Chicken Reel
> Dead March
> Hold Fast to the Right
> I Wish I Was Single Again
> More Pretty Girls Than One
> Sycamore Shoals
> Whiskey Joe
> Whistlin' Rufus
> Will There Be Any Stars?

Now and Then 1001: From the late 1930s to 1966, Raymond Blanche, a radio repairman in Washington County, eastern Tennessee, used to record on his home disc machine the weekly community jam sessions held every Saturday night. Several years ago, the existence of these acetates came to the attention of Richard Blaustein and others at East Tennessee State University (Johnson City), who researched their history. From these "instantaneous" recordings, the first side of this album was compiled. Then, in 1987, Blaustein and Doug Dorschug gathered together several survivors of that era and some newer musicians to record some contemporary examples of eastern Tennessee dance music. Home recordings predating World War II are quite rare, so that these materials are an important documentary find. Furthermore, Stafford and Blaustein have compiled an excellent brochure to accompany the music, including a general introduction to the region and its music, to the musicians and the man who recorded them, and to the musical examples. Additionally, a two-page "Short History of Home Disc Recordings" discusses the technology, its provenance, and significance.

298   Label Name/Number: Traditional Arts Program/Ohio Foundation on the Arts TALP-001
Title: *Traditional Music from Central Ohio*
Artists: Various
Editor/Producers: Timothy Lloyd & David Brose
Place and Date of Recording: Various in OH; 1978-79
Date of Publication: 1979
Annotations: 16 p. booklet by David Brose
Selections:

> After My Laughter Came Tears -- F. LeRoy Hawkins
> Arkansas Traveler, The -- Clyde C. Riggs
> Cherokee -- Rollie Hammon and Harold Henthorne
> Grey Eagle -- Woody Inboden
> I'm Standing on the Solid Rock -- the Ambassadors
> Icy Mountain -- Ward Jarvis
> Jesus is Real -- the Ebenezer Baptist Church Mass Choir
> Little Bessie -- Ruth Hiles
> News Boy, The -- Rollie Hommon & Harold Henthorne
> Panhandle Country -- Shorty Ratliff and the Bluegrass Mountain Boys
> Pretty Little Indian -- Ward Jarvis
> Schottische -- Harvey Phelps
> Where No One Stands Alone -- Woody Inboden
> Will You Miss Me When I'm Gone? -- Shorty Ratliff & the Bluegrass Mountain Boys

Ohio Foundation on the Arts TALP-001: The differences between this album and the one following (Ohio Folklife OF 1001)--another Ohio field collection--are considerable. Collected some 40 years later (by Brose and Lloyd, 1978-79) it is not surprising that there are stylistic differences. The chronological gap is augmented somewhat by different goals of the respective collectors. Whereas the Lomaxes were consciously seeking out older material, Brose and Lloyd made an effort to document the music that is still vital in today's folk music in Central and Southern Ohio. Side One of this album is devoted to older traditions--banjo and fiddle music, sentimental ballads, and the ubiquitous "Arkansas Traveler" skit--this one done with jews harp accompaniment. Side Two features a popular local professional bluegrass band, a Baptist quartet, a Baptist church choir, and a retired professional pianist/singer, among others. The back jacket contains data on where and when the performances were collected and on the background of the song itself, including in some cases bibliographies and discographies of other versions. The booklet includes photos and biographies of the performers and text transcriptions. [JEMFQ 65/66]

299   Label Name/Number: Ohio Historical Society OF 1001
Title: *Folk Music of Ohio: 1938 through 1940*
Artists: Various
Collector/Recordist: John, Alan & Elizabeth Lomax
Place and Date of Recording: OH, 1938
Date of Publication: 1978
Annotations: 13 p. booklet by David Brose
Selections:
>   Coal Creek March -- Pete Steele
>   Galilee -- Mrs. Pete Steele
>   Hoe Down -- Pete Steele
>   Hogs in a Corn Field -- Henry Davis
>   Hot Corn, Cold Corn -- Edgar S. Smith
>   House Carpenter, The [C. 243] -- Mrs. Pete Steele
>   I'm Just Here to Get My Baby out of Jail -- Vergil and Geneva Bowman
>   John Henry -- Pete Steele
>   Little Birdie -- Pete Steele
>   Liza Jane -- Turner Powers
>   Lynchburg Town -- Edgar S. Smith
>   New River Train -- Ridge Rangers
>   No Work for a Tramp -- Henry Davis
>   One Night in Cleveland -- Pearl R. Nye
>   Red Hill Special -- String Band from Fort Thomas, Kentucky
>   Shortenin' Bread -- Bellbrook String Band
>   Snappin' Bug -- Henry Davis
>   Spanish Fandango -- Pete Steele
>   We're Going to Pump Out Lake Erie -- Capt. Pearl R. Nye

OHS OF 1001: Ohio has not been so well canvassed by folksong collectors as has its neighboring state to the south, Kentucky. The only sizeable printed collection that is accessible is represented by Mary O. Eddy's *Ballads and Songs from Ohio*. The relative extent of collecting activity in the two states is indicated by the Library of Congress Archive of American Folk Song checklist of songs recorded up to July 1940: it lists approximately 150 items from Ohio and more than seven times as many from Kentucky. Although this (and the preceding) album would appear to help redress the comparative neglect given the region north of the Ohio River, the boundary between Ohio and Kentucky, closer inspection proves this collection to be as much a Kentucky as an Ohio collection: Pete Steele and his wife were originally from Kentucky; Edgar Smith was banjoist for the Ft. Thomas, Ky, String Band; and the Bowman sisters were granddaughters of the brother of the famous Kentucky balladeer and fiddler, Blind Jim Day (Jilson Setters). Their appearance on this album is a result of the fact that the Lomaxes did much of their Ohio fieldwork at the Ohio Valley Folk Festivals, which attracted performers from both sides of the Ohio River. And, in truth, the music of Southern Ohio is closer to that of Kentucky than it is to that of the northern part of the state. The only representative of Northern Ohio traditions on this album is Capt. Pearl Nye, who sings two songs associated with the life along the Erie Canal. [JEMFQ 65/66]

300 Label Name/Number: Okehdokee Records OK 75003
Title: *The New Beehive Songster, Volume 1*
Artists: Various
Collector/Recordist: Austin & Alta Fife, Lester Hubbard, others
Editor: Tom Carter, Jan Harold Brunvand, H. Reynolds Cannon
Place and Date of Recording: Various (UT), 1943-1951
Date of Publication: 1975; revised edition, 1979
Annotations: 36 p. booklet by Tom Carter (1975); 18 p. sewn-in booklet (1979)
Selections:

      All Are Talking of Utah -- Ella J. Seegmiller
      Black Hills Waltz, The -- K. C. Kartchner
      Brigham, Brigham Young -- Lewis W. Jones
      Bull Whackers, The -- James Jepson
      Days of '49, The -- George S. Taggart
      Double Tragedy, The -- Otho Murphy
      Gay Paree -- Effie M. Carmack
      Gol Darn Wheel, The [dB 38] -- Buck Lee
      Handcart Song, The -- Margaret Y. Boyle
      None Can Preach the Gospel like the Mormons Do! -- Abraham J.Busby
      Once I Lived in Cottonwood -- George T. Thompson
      Rattlesnake -- K.C. Kartchner
      Strawberry Roan, The [B 18] -- Andrew Somerville
      This Is the Place -- Myron Crandall
      Tittery-Irie-Aye -- Joseph H. Watkins
      Watermelon Smilin' on the Vine -- Long Pete Anderson

301 Label Name/Number: Okehdokee Records OK76004
Title: *The New Beehive Songster, Volume 2*
Artists: Various
Collector/Recordist: Hal Cannon and others
Editor: Hal Cannon, Jan Harold Brunvand, Tom Carter
Place and Date of Recording: Various (UT), 1946-1976
Date of Publication: 1976
Annotations: 12 p. gatefold notes by Hal Cannon & Jan Harold Brunvand
Selections:

      Alexandria -- Kartchner Sisters
      Beautiful Utah -- Myron Crandall
      Clayhole Waltz -- Larkin Gifford
      Contented Bachelor -- Rhythm Wranglers
      Coyote, The -- Vernon Condie
      Dear Heart -- Kartchner Sisters
      Dryland Farmers -- Kenneth Ward Atwood
      Farmer's Curst Wife, The [C. 278] -- Kenneth Ward Atwood
      Grandpa's Quadrille -- James Shupe Family
      Hearing Aid, The -- Stella Day

Hen and the Rooster -- Newell Day
Herding Sheep for Granville Pace -- Della Turner
I Am an Old Time Trapper -- Kenneth Ward Atwood
Mandola Polka -- Rhythm Wranglers
New Spanish Twostep -- Lea Aitken
Paul Bachor's Serenade -- Paul Bachor
Riding on a Humpback Mule -- Emery Peterson
Rockville Waltz -- Larkin Gifford
Shirley's Tune -- Clark Family Orchestra
Teasdale Quadrille -- Peterson Brothers Stringband
Virgin Ditch -- A. Karl Larson
Waltz of Shannon -- James Shupe Family
We Left Our Homes in Utah -- Della Turner

Okehdokee OK 75003/ Okehdokee OK 76004: Vol. 1 is a handsomely packaged collection of 16 selections recorded between 1943 and 1951 from non-professional singers and musicians in the Mormon culture region. The booklet includes brief notes on the Mormons and annotations and text transcriptions to the songs. Eight of the selections are local ballads and songs dealing with the Mormons or events in Mormon history. All but one of these are sung unaccompanied, with pronounced Anglo-Irish elements in text and tune styles. Vol. 2 is a sequel to Vol. 1 in a logical, as well as chronological, sense. The singers of this volume, recorded in 1975-76, are one generation further removed from Utah's pioneer settlers than were the artists of the first volume. In both cases, most of the performers are well past middle age (on Vol. 2 the average age is aproximately 75), which raises the inevitable question about the state of folk music in Utah among the younger generation--if not about the selectivity of the collectors. The 23 pieces offered are divided between songs and ballads (13) and instrumentals (10); in both cases, pieces of strictly local provenance predominate. This lends stature to the collection as a sampling of music truly native to Utah rather than the music that, predictably, drifted into the region with the pioneers themselves. Not unexpectedly, the preponderant evidence for Irish influences in tunes and singing styles observed in the first volume has dwindled considerably in the second. Now the tunes are borrowed from popular, western, or hillbilly melodies. Apart from the Rhythm Wranglers, whose two recordings are evidently taken either from electrical transcriptions or air checks, the performers are all non-professional and of varying degrees of skill. [JAF 357]

302   Label Name/Number: Pine Breeze 003
Title: *A Bottle of Wine and Gingercake: Traditional Music from Southeast Tennessee*
Artists: Various
Collector/Recordist: Traditional Music Class, Pine Breeze Center
Place and Date of Recording: Southeast TN, 1977
Date of Publication: [1977]
Annotations: 6 p. booklet by Charles Wolfe, Ron Williams
Selections:
  Smith, Stewart, and Brandon
      Bottle of Wine and Gingercake, A
      Chattanooga
      Choctaw Bill
      Cincinnati
      Cotton in the Crib
      Jeff Davis
      Run Boy Run
  Eldia Barbee & Stringband

Black Oak Ridge
    Devil Chased Me Around the Stump
    Ike Ward
    Rubber-Tired Buggy
Clay Turner
    Old Account Was Settled, The
    Pick and a Shovel Down in the Mines
    Will the Circle Be Unbroken
Peanut Cantrell
    Sugar Gal
    Sail Away Ladies

303 Label Name/Number: Pine Breeze 004
Title: *Skip to My Lou: Traditional Children's Songs & Dances from Southeast Tennessee*
Artists: Various
Collector/Recordist: Students of the Traditional Music Project
Place and Date of Recording: Southeast TN
Annotations: 1 p. insert
Selections:
All Around the Cedar -- Ella Hughes
Chase the Squirrel -- Ella Hughes
Fox, The -- Ramona Millsaps, "Doc" Cullis, Ron Williams, Eldia Barbee
Girl I Left Behind Me, The -- Eldia Barbee, "Doc" Cullis, Ron Williams
Go in and out the Window -- Ramona Millsaps and group
Green Coffee -- Ella Hughes
Green Gravel -- Ramona Millsaps and group
Johnny Was a Miller Boy -- Ella Hughes
Lazy Mary -- Ramona Millsaps and group
Let's Go Hunting -- Ramona Millsaps, "Doc" Cullis
Poor Scotchee, The [C. 68] -- Ella Hughes
Pop Goes the Weasel -- Eldia Barbee
Shoot the Buffalo -- Ella Hughes
Skip to My Lou -- Blaine Smith, Florrie Stewart, Willie Brandon
Two Little Boys -- Tom, Mary, and Scott Morgan
Unruly Wife, The -- Johnson Swafford, Tom Morgan, Ron Williams, Scott Morgan
Weevily Wheat -- Ella Hughes

304 Label Name/Number: Pine Breeze 005
Title: *In the Field: Traditional Fiddle Music from Southeast Tennessee*
Artists: Eldia & Oscar Barbee; Homer & Calvin Chastain and band; Blaine Smith and band; Lee Trentham and band
Collector/Recordist: Students of the Traditional Music Project at Pine Breeze Center
Place and Date of Recording: Southeast TN
Date of Publication: [1979]
Annotations: Liner notes
Selections:
Barbee and Band
    Cumberland Gap
    Flatwoods
    George Gann
    Liza Jane

Trentham and Band
>   Boneparte's Retreat
>   Mississippi Sawyer
>   Pine Ridge Breakdown
>   Sockeye

Chastain and Band
>   Cindy
>   Cotton-Eyed Joe
>   Greenback Dollar
>   Old Joe Clark

Smith and Band
>   Big Ball's Uptown
>   Buckin' Mule
>   Girl I Left Behind
>   Irish Washerwoman

PB 003/ PB 004 / PB 005: These three albums were recorded, edited, and produced by students of Ron Williams' Traditional Music Project at Pine Breeze Center, Chattanooga, Tennessee. The principal musicians on PB 003 are fiddlers Blaine Smith (b. ca. 1914), Eldia Barbee (ca. 1910), banjoist Clay Turner (ca. 1889), and hammered dulcimer player J. R. Cantrell (1900s). PB 005 is divided among four banjo/fiddle/guitar ensembles. The Barbees, heard on this album as well, are more prominently featured on PB 006 (see Section I). PB 004 includes five ballads and songs, nine play party games (with instructions in the insert) and three dances.

305   Label Name/Number: Prestige Folklore 14030
Title: *Old Time Fiddling at Union Grove*
Artists: Various
Collector/Recordist/Editor: Michael Eisenstadt and Brian Sinclair
Producer: Samuel Charters
Place and Date of Recording: Union Grove, NC, 1961?
Date of Publication: 1964
Annotations: Liner notes by Geoff Gregory
Selections:
>   'Round Town Gals -- Bert Edwards & Randolph Music Club Band
>   Breakdown -- James Lindsay & Mountain Ramblers
>   Cindy -- Thomas Holland & The Crossroad Boys
>   Cotton-Eyed Joe -- Esker Hutchins & Surrey County Ramblers
>   Fire on the Mountain -- Esker Hutchins & Surrey County Ramblers
>   Fortune -- Kenneth Edwards & Sunny Mountain Boys
>   Johnson's Old Grey Mule -- J. E. Mainer & His Mountaineers
>   Old Time Reel -- Grandma Pearlie Davis
>   Orange Blossom Special -- Larry Campbell & Country Playboys
>   Rawhide -- L. W. J. Lambert & Bluegrass Partners
>   Sally Ann -- Ray Childress & Carolina Foothill Ramblers
>   Sally Goodin' -- Charles Hawks & Brushy River Boys
>   Scotland -- Franklin Bailey & Tennessee Pals
>   Train 45 -- Thomas Holland & The Crossroad Boys
>   Walk in the Park, A -- Norman Edmonds & The Old Timers
>   Watermelon on the Vine -- Morris Herbert & the Twin County Boys

Prest Folklore 14030: Recorded at the 38th annual Old Time Fiddler's Convention at Union Grove, No. Carolina, this album offers another cross section of these highly popular southeastern gatherings (see also Fwys FA 2434 and 2435 above). This sampler shows a mixture of older and bluegrass-influenced styles accepted side by side, though the contestants were still all local residents, rather than, as occurred in later years, visitors from outside the rural Southeast. Jacket notes discuss the history of the convention and its social significance. [JAF 310--DKW]

306 Label Name/Number: Prestige International INT 25003
Title: *Ballads and Breakdowns from the Southern Mountains: Southern Journey 3*
Artists: Various
Collector/Recordist: Alan Lomax with Shirley Collins and Anne Lomax
Producer: Kenneth S. Goldstein
Place and Date of Recording: Various, 1959, 1960
Date of Publication: [1961]
Annotations: Booklet by Alan Lomax
Selections:

> Banks of the Ohio, The [F 5] -- Ruby Vass
> Breaking Up Christmas -- Norman Edmonds, Paul Edmonds, and Rufus Quesinbery
> House Carpenter, The [C. 243] -- Almeda Riddle
> It Rained a Mist [C. 155] -- Ollie Gilbert
> Lass of Loch Royale, The [C. 76] -- Neil Morris
> Little Schoolboy, The [C. 49] -- Hobart Smith
> Poor Ellen Smith [F 11] -- E. C. Ball
> Rainbow 'mid the Willows, The [M 13] -- Almeda Riddle
> Sally Anne -- George Stoneman
> Sally Goodin -- Neil Morris and Charlie Everidge
> Scotch Musick, The -- Absy Morrison
> Three Nights Drunk [C. 274] -- J. E. Mainer's Mountaineers (Carolyn Mainer Helmes, J. E.
>   Mainer, Glen Mainer, & Mary Mainer)
> Uncle Charlie's Breakdown -- Wade Ward, Charlie Higgins, and Dale Poe
> Willow Garden -- Wade Ward, Charlie Higgins, and Dale Poe

307 Label Name/Number: Prestige International INT 25004
Title: *Banjo Songs, Ballads, and Reels from the Southern Mountains: Southern Journey 4*
Artists: Various
Collector/Recordist: Alan Lomax with Shirley Collins and Anne Lomax
Producer: Kenneth S. Goldstein
Place and Date of Recording: Various, 1959, 1960
Date of Publication: 1961
Annotations: 8-page booklet by Alan Lomax
Selections:

> Hobart Smith
>> Drunken Hiccups
>> Fly Around My Blue-Eyed Girl
>> Graveyard Blues
>> Parson Burrs
>> Peg an' Awl
> Wade Ward
>> Cluck Old Hen
>> Fox Chase, The
>> June Apple
>> Old Joe Clark
>> Piney Woods Gal

Bob Carpenter
Burglar Man, The [H 23]
Almeda Riddle
Down in Arkansas
Ollie Gilbert
Pretty Polly [N 14]
Spence Moore and Roy E. Birns
Girl I Left Behind, The [P 1b]
Mrs. Texas Gladden
Three Little Babes [C. 79]

308   Label Name/Number: Prestige International INT 25006
Title: *Folk Songs from the Ozarks: Southern Journey 6*
Artists: Various
Collector/Recordist: Alan Lomax with Shirley Collins and Anne Lomax
Producer: Kenneth S. Goldstein
Place and Date of Recording: Various, 1959, 1960
Date of Publication: [1961]
Annotations: 11-page booklet by Alan Lomax
Selections:
Almeda Riddle
Alan Bain
Lonesome Dove
Merry Golden Tree [C. 286]
Neil Morris
Juice of the Forbidden Fruit
Rock All the Babies to Sleep
Soldier and the Lady, The [P 14]
Turnip Greens
Carlos Shannon
Buffalo Gals
Cotton Eye Joe
Eighth of January
Ollie Gilbert
Willow Green
Absy Morrison
My Pretty Little Gal is Gone
Nancy's Got A Party Dress On
Charlie Eldridge
Turkey in the Straw

309   Label Name/Number: Prestige International INT 25009
Title: *Bad Man Ballads: Southern Journey 9*
Artists: Various
Collector/Recordist: Alam Lomax, with Shirley Collins and Anne Lomax
Producer: Kenneth S. Goldstein
Place and Date of Recording: Various, 1959, 1960
Date of Publication: [1961]
Annotations: 11-page booklet by Alan Lomax
Selections:
Claude Allen [E 6] -- Hobart Smith

    Columbus Stockade -- Mainers Mountaineers (J. E. Mainer, Carolyn Mainer Helmes, Mary
        Mainer, Glen Mainer, Floyd Overcash)
    Hangman Tree [C. 95] -- Almeda Riddle
    Hawkins County Jail -- Hobart Smith
    Lawson Murder, The [F 35] -- Spence Moore & Roy Everett Birns
    Pretty Polly [P 36b] -- Estil C. Ball
    Railroad Bill [I 13] -- Hobart Smith
    Willie Brennan [L 7] -- Neil Morris
[Also 4 African-American recordings: Po' Laz'rus (2 versions), Early in the Mornin', Dangerous
    Blues]

310 **Label Name/Number:** Prestige International INT 25011
Title: *Southern White Spirituals: Southern Journey 11*
Artists: Various
Collector/Recordist: Alan Lomax with Shirley Collins, Anne Lomax
Producer: Kenneth S. Goldstein
Place and Date of Recording: Various, 1959, 1960
Date of Publication: [1961]
Annotations: 8-page booklet by Alan Lomax
Selections:
    Bretheren, We Meet Again -- George Spangler & the Thornton Regular Baptist Church
        Congregation
    Guide Me, O Thou Great Jehovah -- George Spangler & the Thornton Regular Baptist
        Church Congregation
    Hick's Farewell -- Texas Gladden
    I Am a Poor Wayfaring Stranger -- Almeda Riddle
    I'm on My Journey Home -- Jesse Drysen leading the Alabama Sacred Harp Singers
    Jim and Me -- Hobart Smith, Texas Gladden, Preston Smith
    Little Family, The -- Ollie Gilbert
    Lonely Tombs -- Hobart Smith, Texas Gladden, Preston Smith
    My Lord Keeps a Record -- Mountain Ramblers
    Old Gospel Ship, The -- Ruby Vass
    Sardinia -- Jesse Drysen leading the Alabama Sacred Harp Singers
    See That My Grave Is Kept Clean -- Hobart Smith
    When Jesus Christ Was Here on Earth -- Rev. I. D. Back & the Mount Olive Regular
        Baptist Church Congregation
    When the Stars Begin To Fall -- Hobart Smith

    Prest INT 25003 / 25004 / 25006 / 25009/ 25011: Following up on the success of his
seven-LP set on the Atlantic label (see Atl SD 1347, 1349, 1350 above), Alan Lomax edited a 12-
volume set on the Prestige label titled *Southern Journey: A Collection of Field Recordings from the
South.* Many of the recordings came from the same field trips as the Atlantic set, and feature many
of the same performers. Half of the albums focused on African-American traditions and are not
discussed here; one album was devoted entirely to the Alabama Sacred Harp Singers and is discussed in Part I. 25009, the set from the Ozarks, includes some less common items in the local "last
goodnight" (i.e., the supposed last words of a criminal about to be hanged) ballad, "Alan Bain;" and
the drinking song,"Juice of the Forbidden Fruit." The mouthbow, played by Charlie Everidge on
"Turkey in the Straw" (25009) and "Sally Goodin" (25003) is a very old instrument now rarely
encountered.

311   Label Name/Number: Riverside RLP 12-610
Title: *Banjo Songs of the Southern Mountains*
Artists: Various
Collector/Recordist: Kenneth S. Goldstein and William A. Grant
Editor: Kenneth S. Goldstein
Place and Date of Recording: Asheville, NC, and New York City (H. & J. West), 1955?
Date of Publication: [ca. 1956]
Annotations: Liner notes by K. S. Goldstein
Selections:
> Obray Ramsey
>> Little Maggie
>> Poor Little Ellen [F 11]
>> Pretty Polly [P 36b]
> George Pegram and Walter Parham
>> Arkansas Traveller
>> Cripple Creek
>> Cumberland Gap
>> Good Old Mountain Dew
>> John Henry [I 1]
>> Old Reuben
> Harry and Jeanie West
>> Awake, Awake, Ye Drowsy Sleepers
>> Boston Burglar, The [L 16b]
>> Careless Love
>> Finger Ring
>> Keep My Skillet Good and Greasy
>> Lost John
> Aunt Samantha Bumgarner
>> Way Down on the Island
>> Fly Around, My Pretty Little Miss

312   Label Name/Number: Riverside RLP 12-617 [reiss. on Washington WLP 734]
Title: *Southern Mountain Folksongs and Ballads* [on Washington: *Bury Me Beneath the Willow: A Treasury of Southern Mountain Folksongs and Ballads*]
Artists: Various
Collector/Recordist: Kenneth S. Goldstein and William A. Grant
Editor: Kenneth S. Goldstein
Place and Date of Recording: Asheville and Swannanoa, NC, and New York City, 1955
Date of Publication: [ca. 1956]
Annotations: Liner notes by Goldstein
Selections:
> Artus Moser
>> Bonny Blue Eyes
>> Cherry Tree Carol, The [C. 54]
>> I Went up on the Mountain
>> Mole in the Ground
>> Sailor on the Deep Blue Sea, The [K 12]
> Harry and Jeanie West
>> Banks of the Ohio [F 5]
>> Bury Me Beneath the Willow
>> Knoxville Girl [P 35]

> Nine Pound Hammer
> Wild Bill Jones [E 10]
> George Pegram
>> Boston Burglar, The [L 16b]
>> Mountain Fox Chase
> Virgil Sturgill
>> Charles Guiteau [E 11]
>> Devilish Mary [Q 4]
> Obray Ramsey
>> Jim Gunter and the Steer
>> On Top of Old Smoky
> George Pegram and Walter Parham
>> I Am a Pilgrim
>> Pickin' and Blowin'

Riv RLP 12-610 and 12-617: These recordings, some of the first made "in the field" apart from LC-sponsored ventures, were the result of a 1955 field trip to Asheville, N. C., to attend Bascom Lamar Lunsford's annual mountain folk dance and music festival. Most of the performers were recorded there; Harry and Jeanie West, North Carolinians then living in New York City but regular performers at the Asheville events, were recorded in New York. Most of the performers have been frequently recorded elsewhere, and appear elsewhere in this discography. Virgil Sturgill, though Kentucky-born, has a more studied presentation manner, probably the result of acquiring much of his material later in life from secondary sources. Samantha Bumgarner, in her eighties in 1955, was one of the first musicians to record commercial hillbilly 78s back in 1924. At the time of their publication, these albums were immensely important as early commercial field recordings, showing city enthusiasts of the then-blossoming folk revival what traditional music could still be heard in the Southeastern states. [JAF 280--DKW (12-610); JAF 280--JJN (12-617)]

313 Label Name/Number: Rounder 0028
Title: *High Atmosphere*
Artists: Various
Collector/Recordist: John Cohen
Producers: Mark Wilson and John Cohen
Place and Date of Recording: VA, NC, 1965
Date of Publication: 1974
Annotations: 9 p. booklet by Cohen and Wilson
Selections:

> Alabama Gals -- Sidna Myers
> Apple Blossom -- Gaither Carlton
> Barker's Creek [B 10] -- George Landers
> Conversation with Death, A -- Lloyd Chandler
> Cumberland Gap -- Frank Proffitt
> Cumberland Gap -- George Landers
> Early, Early in the Spring [M 1] -- Dellie Norton
> Forkey Deer -- Sidna Myers
> Fortune -- Fred Cockerham
> Half Shaved -- Wade Ward
> High Atmosphere -- Wade Ward
> Home Sweet Home -- George Landers
> I Wish My Baby Was Born -- Dillard Chandler
> Old Jimmy Sutton -- Wade Reedy and Estil C. Ball

Pretty Crowing Chicken [C. 248] -- Frank Proffitt
Rambling Hobo -- Gaither Carlton
Remember and Do Pray for Me -- Lloyd Chandler
Rolling Mills are Burning Down -- George Landers
Satan, Your Kingdom Must Come Down -- Frank Proffitt
Shady Grove -- Wade Ward
Twin Sisters -- Sidna Myers
Warfare -- Estil C. Ball
Young Emily [M 34] -- Dellie Norton

Rndr 0028: As John Cohen explains it, the material on this album was originally gathered during a collecting project intended to document different traditional banjo tunings. The result, though, is an outstanding mixture of banjo tunes and old ballads, sung by some of Appalachia's best: Dellie Norton, her brother, Lloyd Chandler, and their cousin, Dillard Chandler. (Another sibling of Dellie and Lloyd's is Berzil Wallin, another excellent singer heard on other albums.) The brochure includes several wonderful black and white photos by Cohen, text transcriptions, and brief notes to the selections--in particular in regard to banjo playing styles.

314a **Label Name/Number:** Rounder Records 0057
Title: *Old Originals, Volume 1: Old Time Instrumental Music*
Artists: Various
Collector/Recordist: Tom Carter and/or Blanton Owen
Producer: Tom Carter & Blanton Owen
Place and Date of Recording: VA and NC, 1973-74
Date of Publication: 1976
Annotations: 7 p. booklet by Tom Carter
Selections:

Bonaparte's March Into Russia -- Sherman Wimmer
Breakin' Up Christmas -- Kimble Family
Dineo -- Ted Boyd and Charlie Woods
Flying Indian -- Clarice and Joe Shelor
Hop Light Ladies -- Frank Dalton & George Wood
Jake Gilly -- Sam McNeil
Old Time Fire on the Mountain -- Sam Connor & Dent Wimmer
Old Virginia March -- New Ballard Fife and Drum Band
Possum Trot -- Bill Shelor
Rich Mountain -- Frank Dalton & George Wood
Roustabout -- Dent Wimmer
Salt River -- Sam Connor
Sandy River Belles -- Doc Williams
Saro -- Calvin Pendleton
Shootin' Creek -- Sam Connor & Dent Wimmer
Shortenin' Bread -- Fred Clifton
Stillhouse -- Grover and Marvin Cockram
Tommy Love -- Calvin Pendleton, Delmar Pendleton, & family
Train on the Island -- Kimble Family
Turkey in the Straw -- Cap Ayers & Darrell Cockram
Twin Sisters -- Sherman Wimmer
Walls of Jericho -- Sam McNeil
You Never Miss Your Mamma 'Till She's Gone -- Dent Wimmer

314b **Label Name/Number:** Rounder Records 0058
Title: *Old Originals, Volume 2: Old-Time Instrumental Music*
Artists: Various
Collector/Recordist: Tom Carter and/or Blanton Owen
Producer: Tom Carter & Blanton Owen
Place and Date of Recording: NC and VA, 1964-74
Date of Publication: 1976
Annotations: 11 p. booklet by Blanton Owen
Selections:

    Ain't Going to Work Tomorrow -- William Marshall, Calvin Cole, & Howard Hall
    Belle Election -- John Patterson
    Chicken in the Bread Tray -- Munsey Gaultney
    Cripple Creek -- Albert Hash, Paul Spencer, & Jones Baldwin
    Cumberland Gap -- Corbit Stamper & Thornton Spencer
    Did You Ever See the Devil, Uncle Joe? -- John Patterson
    Evening Rainbow Waltz -- Luther Davis
    Fanny Hill -- John Rector
    Forked Deer -- John Rector
    Going Home -- Fulton Myers
    Holliding Cindy -- Stuart Carrico
    House Carpenter [C. 243] -- Dorothy Rorick
    Molly Put the Kettle On -- Haywood Blevins
    Nancy Blevins -- Albert Hash & Thornton Spencer
    Old Molly Hair -- Haywood Blevins
    Pearly Blue -- Worley Hash
    Piney Woods Gal -- Luther Davis
    Quit That Ticklin' Me -- Calvin Cole
    Rambling Hobo -- Jont Blevins
    Sally Ann -- Clell Caudill
    Saro -- William Marshall, Calvin Cole, & Howard Hall
    Trap Hill Tune -- Hus Caudill
    Twin Sisters -- William Marshall
    Walls of Jericho, The -- Munsey Gaultney
    Waves on the Ocean -- Hus Caudill

    Rndr 0057 / Rndr 0058: These two albums are drawn from extensive field recordings made with support from the NEH. Vol. 1 is devoted principally to music from Franklin, Floyd, Montgomery, Patrick, Carroll, and Henry Counties. Vol. 2 concentrates on areas further west, centering around Hillsville (Carroll County), Galax and White Top (both Grayson County). In their excellent brochure notes, Carter and Owen delineate the different musical styles found in the five regions into which the area surveyed is divided. In the eastern-most area of FLoyd and Franklin Counties is found a blending of the southern West Virginia and the Virginia Blue Ridge fiddle traditions. There is less ensemble playing than in neighboring Patrick County to the south-west, and separate banjo and fiddle repertoires appear more frequently. The fiddle style is melodically complex, often in the keys of G, C, and A, which are not well-suited to clawhammer banjo playing. The strong banjo-fiddle ensemble tradition in Patrick County links it to the adjacent Grayson/Carroll Counties further to the west. In these regions, fiddlers use gapped scales much more than in Patrick. Fiddle tunes in the key of G are still played by older musicians, but these tunes tend to fall out of use with the introduction of the banjo and the development of the banjo/fiddle ensemble. In the Hillsville area, between Grayson and Patrick Counties, elements of both the bordering regions can be found. However, it has developed stylistic features of its own: a rhythmically straight and hard-driving fiddle style. In the White Top area, in the western tip of Virginia, the fiddling tends to be more chordal than in the Galax area, with longer bowing motions and consequently smoother sounds. These generalizations are by no means iron clad (as some of the selections offered demonstrate), but they are useful.

In addition to their regional characterizations, the editors discuss the changes that have taken place with time, noting that the musicians that are represented on these two discs are all 60 to 90 years old, often no longer recognized as musicians in their own communities.

The music is mostly fiddle and banjo, with guitar accompaniment on a few tracks. There are also three selections featuring piano, and one each of fife, fife and drum band, jew's harp duet, harmonica, and a couple with autoharp. The tune notes include information on performers, date and place of recording, instrument tuning, source and geographic distribution of the tune, and related recordings. The editors have assembled a fine selection of traditional music of the region and presented it in an instructive and insightful manner. [JEMFQ 56]

315   Label Name/Number: Rounder Records 0065
Title: *Music from South Turkey Creek*
Artists: Bascom Lamar Lunsford, George Pegram, and Red Parham
Collector/Recordist: Kenneth Goldstein
Place and Date of Recording: Asheville, NC; 1956
Date of Publication: 1976
Annotations: Liner notes by Loyal Jones
Selections:
       Bascom Lamar Lunsford:
             Drinking of the Wine
             Essie Dear
             Free a Little Bird
             Georgia Buck
             Goodbye Dear Old Stepstone
             Lily of the West [P 29]
             Lord Joshuay [C. 95]
             Old Mountain Dew
             On a Bright and Summer's Morning
             Poor Ellen Smith [F 11]
       George Pegram and Red Parham
             Charlie Lawson [F 35]
             Cindy
             Keep My Skillet Good and Greasy
             Leaf from the Sea, A
             Lost John
             Mama Blues
             Old Joe Clark
             Old Rattler
             Pig in a Pen
             Poor Ellen Smith [F 11]
             Red and George Breakdown
             Roll On, Buddy
             T Model Ford and Train

     Rndr 0065: Though Lunsford, Pegram, and Parham never recorded together, their juxtaposition on this album is natural since Lunsford was responsible for Pegram and Parham's long musical association. Parham lived on the Lunsford farm for many years, running it under Mrs.

Lunsford's direction. When he wasn't farming, he was performing under Lunsford's supervision at one of Lunsford's festivals. Lunsford ran into Pegram in 1949 when his car broke down near Pegram's house. He asked if he could stay the night; when he learned that Pegram played banjo, he invited him to his Asheville festival and introduced him to Parham. These 1956 recordings were not released until 1976, after Lunsford and Pegram had died. This album is typical of all three performers' earlier recordings (see Folkways FA 2040 and Riverside 12-645; Riverside 12-650 and Rounder 0001); of interest is Lunsford's "Lord Joshuay," possibly mistitled on the LP since in earlier recordings of this ballad he used the more standard title of "The Hangman's Tree."

316 Label Name/Number: Rounder Records 0237
Title: *The Library of Congress Banjo Collection*
Artists: Various
Collector/Recordist: John Lomax, Alan Lomax and others, Herbert Halpert, Margot Mayo and others, Charles Seeger, Vance Randolph
Producer: Bob Carlin
Place and Date of Recording: 1937-46
Date of Publication: 1988
Annotations: 7 p. booklet by Bob Carlin
Selections:

> Banjo Solo -- Lifus Gibson
> Bile Dem Cabbages Down -- Belton Reese, Thaddeus Goodson, Israel Alston
> Bonnie Blue Eyes -- Austin Harmon
> Callahan -- McKinley Asher
> Cluck Old Hen -- Bob Bossie
> Durang's Hornpipe -- Bob Bossie
> East Virginia -- Walter Williams
> Hand Me Down My Old White Hat -- McKinley Asher
> It's Nobody's Business -- Theophilus G. Hoskins
> Italian Mulazicci -- Bob Bossie
> John Hardy -- Austin Harmon
> John Henry -- Albert Josey
> John Henry -- Raymond Swinney McKenzie Case -- Belton Reese
> Mississippi Valley Waltz -- Thaddeus Willingham
> Old Dan Tucker -- Austin Harmon
> Reuban -- Ernest and Osey Helton
> Rove Riley Rove -- Thaddeus Willingham
> Shortnin' Bread -- McKinley Asher
> Tune -- Lifus Gibson
> Wild Horse -- Walter Williams & W. M. Stepp

Rndr 0237: The enormous musical repository of the LC's Archive of Folk Culture (previously the Archive of American Folksong, then the Archive of Folk Song) is still not adequately represented on commercially available discs. In recent years, many commercial companies have leased material from the LC, thereby augmenting considerably the archival material available to the public. Afro-American blues and gospel music have been tapped most extensively through this venue by overseas as well as domestic labels. This is the first instrumental survey to follow Jabbour's fiddle LP, and necessarily begs comparison with its predecessor. In two respects, the banjo album surpasses the fiddle album. Carlin has taken great pains to locate the dozen-plus performers--Walter Williams, W. M. Stepp, McKinley Asher, Theophilus G. Hoskins, Austin Harmon, Thaddeus Willingham, Bob Bossie, Lifus Gibson, Belton Reese, Thaddeus Goodson, Israel Alston, Ernest and Osey Helton, Albert Josey, Raymond Swinney (or their heirs)--

represented by 21 tunes, in order to provide his audience with a good sense of these men (no women), their backgrounds, and their relationship to their music. Additionally, his eight-page brochure includes photographs of four of the banjos or their bands. The fiddle LP had no photos and little biographical information. Beyond that, however, the banjo album is weaker both as a collection and as a scholarly document. The technical limitations of some of the recordings are excusable; all recorded between 1937 and 1946 by John and Alan Lomax, Herbert Halpert, Charles Seeger, Vance Randolph, and Margot Mayo et al., they were subject to the severe limitations of early field equipment. (Carlin chose to exclude magnetic tape recordings of ca. 1950 and later, and also performers--such as Bascom Lamar Lunsford, Wade Ward, and Pete Steele, already available on LP--a decision that necessarily precluded use of some of the best musical material. The fact that fiddler W. M. Stepp and Ernest Helton, banjo/vocal, have appeared on LP does not really violate his principle, which can be taken to refer to banjo music per se.) Carlin explains his organization as proceeding from frailing, or clawhammer, style to two-finger and then three-finger picking styles, but there is no detailed information on any of the styles represented. The final cut, Swinney's "John Henry," recorded at the Galax Fiddler's Convention of 1941, shows how far three-finger picking before Earl Scruggs had progressed toward bluegrass banjo, but the opportunity to present any stylistic evolution was not seized. Nor does the album explore Afro-American banjo playing--certainly an important component in the development of Appalachian banjo. Only one of the banjo players on the album (Reese) is black, and though his music clearly signals his identity, the program notes disclose that fact only obliquely. Most of the selections are well-known banjo tunes or songs with vocals: "Wild Horse," "East Virginia," "Callahan," "Shortnin' Bread," "Cluck Old Hen," "Bile Dem Cabbages Down," "Reuban." Reese's "McKenzie Case" is a rare blues ballad to the tune of "Railroad Bill," about a 1910 murder. Neither of the renditions of "John Henry" has any vocal. "Italian Mulazicci" is a mazurka that fiddler Bob Bossie learned from his Italian-born father. Some of the omissions in the descriptive treatment of banjo music could have been excused by reference to the many good articles and instructional manuals on the instrument and its playing styles that have been published in recent years. There is still room, then, for a definitive album/history of American banjo music.

317   Label Name/Number: Rounder Records SS-0145
Title: *Traditional Music on Rounder: A Sampler*
Artists: Various
Collector/Recordist: Jim Carr & Mark Wilson with others
Producer: Mark Wilson
Date of Publication: 1981
Annotations: Liner notes by Mark Wilson
Selections:
> 'Way Down on the Mango Farm -- Bessie Jones, the Georgia Sea Island Singers with children from Roxbury, Mass.
> Al Bowen -- Almeda Riddle
> Captain Devin [L 13A] -- Sarah Gunning
> Cruel Willie -- John Patterson and Annadeene Fraley
> Frankie -- Buddy Thomas
> Granny Went to Meeting with Her Old Shoes On -- Mr. and Mrs. Vernon Judd
> Hunky Dory -- Alva Greene and Francis Gillum
> I Don't Love Nobody -- Snuffy Jenkins, Pappy Sherrill, and the Hired Hands
> Mother's Grave -- Asa Martin and the Cumberland Rangers
> My Buddy -- Van Holyoak
> New Market Reel -- Jerry Holland
> No Tears in Heaven -- E.C. and Orna Ball
> One More River to Cross -- Wilson Douglas

Riley and Spencer -- Fields Ward
Train that Carried My Girl from Town, The -- Ola Belle Reed
Watergate Boogie, The -- Nimrod Workman
[Also one African-American, one French-Canadian, and one Cajun selection]

Rndr SS-0145: Some of the best albums produced in Rounder's 17 years of existence were by Mark Wilson. This album, produced and annotated by him, samples 20 traditional artists, all but one of whom were recorded by Wilson and most of whom have had full Rounder albums devoted to them. Unlike many other samplers, however, this one does not include selections already issued on other albums. [JAF 395]

318   Label Name/Number: Shoestring Tape SGB 1 [LP]
Title: *Stone County Singing*
Artists: Estella Palmer, Floyd Holland, Glenn Ohrlin
Producer: Keith Cunningham
Place and Date of Recording: AR
Annotations: Unsigned jacket notes
Selections:
> Estella Palmer
>> Amazing Grace
>> Please Meet Me Tonight
>> Willow Garden [F 6]
> Glen Ohrlin
>> Billie Venero [B 6]
>> Jake and Rooney and the Bald-Faced Steer
>> Sporting Cowboy, The
>> Trail to Mexico [B 13]
> Floyd Holland
>> City of Sighs and Tears
>> Old Elm Tree, The
>> Susie Licked the Ladle Clean

Shoestring Tape SGB 1:   This features ten selections by three Ozark traditional singers. Ohrlin is the only one who had been recorded previously; on this disc he sings four cowboy ballads, on two of which he accompanies himself on fiddle. Estella Palmer of Mountain View, Arkansas, sings in a flat, unadorned voice that is rather difficult to listen to. Floyd Holland, aged 77, of Stone County, offers a comic monologue with sung chorus ("Suzie Licked the Ladle Clean") and two 19th-century sentimental songs. [JAF 325]

319   Label Name/Number: Tennessee Folklore Society cassette [no #]
Title: *Some Ballad Folks*
Artists: Hattie Presnell, Buna Hicks, Lena Harmon, Bertha Baird
Collector/Recordist: Thomas Burton and Ambrose Manning
Date of Publication: [1978?]
Annotations: Accompanies book of same title
Selections:
> Hattie Presnell
>> George Collins [C. 85]
>> Golden Willow Tree [C. 286]
>> House Carpenter, The [C. 243]
>> Old Devil, The [C. 278]

        Pretty Crowin' Chicken [C. 248]
        Six Nights Drunk [C. 274]
        Two Sisters [C. 10]
Buna Hicks
        Barbry Ellen [C. 84]
        Jobal Hunter [C. 18]
        Lord Thomas [C. 73]
        Young Beham [C. 53]
Lena Harmon and Hattie Presnell
        Massey Grove [C. 81]
Lena Harmon
        Barbry Ellen [C. 84]
        Blackjack Daisey [C. 200]
        George Collins [C. 85]
        Little Guinea Gay Haw [C. 13]
        Mermaid, The [C. 289]
        Wild Boar's Den [C. 18]
Bertha Baird
        Barbry Allen [C. 84]
        Bolamkin [C. 93]
        Brown Girl, The [C. 73]
        House Carpenter, The [C. 243]
        How Came That Blood on Your Shirt Sleeve? [C. 13]

    TFS cassette: Thomas G. Burton's book, *Some Ballad Folks* (East Tennessee State
University, 1978), documents the lives and music of five ballad-singing women from Beech
Mountain, North Carolina; this cassette, to accompany the book, includes selected examples from
recordings Burton and Ambrose Manning made of four of those singers: Buna Hicks (1888-); her
daughter, Hattie Presnell (1907-); Lena Harmon (1911-), Hattie's sister-in-law; and Bertha Baird
(1880-). Full documentation is given in the book.

320   Label Name/Number: Tennessee Folklore Society TFS-103
Title: *Tennessee: The Folk Heritage, Vol. 2--The Mountains*
Artists: Various
Collector/Recordist: Thomas Burton, Ambrose Manning et al.
Producer: Charles Wolfe
Place and Date of Recording: TN, 1966-1978
Date of Publication: 1982
Annotations: 4 p. insert by Charles Wolfe
Selections:
        Ballad of the Braswell Boys, The -- Jesse Hudelston
        Citaco -- Barbee Brothers
        Davy Crockett -- Dee Hicks
        Dog and Cat Rag -- Uncle Jimmy McCarroll
        Fiddler A Dram -- Uncle Jimmy McCarroll
        Grey Eagle -- Clarence Farrill and String Band
        Hills of Roane County, The -- Delsie Hicks
        House Carpenter, The [C. 243] -- Audrey McGuire
        Knoxville Girl, The [P 35] -- Hamper McBee
        Lucky Tiger Ointment -- T. J. "Uncle Jake" Box
        Lunatic Asylum, The -- "Mrs. B. D."

My Parents Raised Me Tenderly [P 1A] -- Delsie Hicks
Nashville Blues -- Lewis Brothers
Polecat Blues -- Nonnie Presson and Bulow Smith
Schoolhouse Song -- Cordell Kemp
Shortenin' Bread -- Payne Brothers and Blaustein
Stone's Rag -- Omer Forster
Train 111 -- Uncle Jimmy McCarroll

TFS-103: The first side of the album is devoted to songs and ballads and includes some outstanding singers, including both Delta and Dee Hicks of Fentress County, Hamper McBee of Grundy County, and others with a nice selection of British ballads and rare native American pieces. Side B, subtitled "instrumentals and songs," includes a couple of performances by one-time commercial artists (Presson & Smith--the Perry County Music Makers; and McCarroll--fiddler for the Roane County Ramblers), and ends with a lovely "cover" of the Delmore Brothers' smooth harmonies on their composition, "Nashville Blues." A small brochure gives essential recording data and brief notes on the performers' backgrounds and the songs themselves. [JEMFQ 72]

321   Label Name/Number: Tennessee Folklore Society TFS-105
Title: *Historical Ballads of the Tennessee Valley*
Artists: Various
Collector/Recordist: Various
Editor: Charles Wolfe
Place and Date of Recording: Various in TN, KY, VA; 1926-1982
Date of Publication: 1982
Annotations: 24 p. booklet by Charles Wolfe
Selections:

Arcade Building Moan -- Leola Manning
Bible's True, The -- Uncle Dave Macon
Big Bend Tragedy, The -- Fred Ford
Death of Floyd Collins [G 22] -- Tom Spencer
Hickman's Boys -- Russ Vandergriff
Hunters of Kentucky, The [A 25] -- Bob Atcher
Kirby Cole -- Aaron Sims
Newmarket Wreck, The -- Mr. and Mrs. J. W. Baker
Old Cumberland Land -- Dee Hicks
Raftman's Song -- Linnie Johnson
She Sleeps Beneath the Norris Dam -- Cope Brothers
Shut Up in the Mines of Coal Creek -- Roy Harper
Steam Arm, The -- Jerry Henderson
Tragedy of Spring City -- Ollan Smith & Dennis Brewer
TVA Song -- Roy Harper

[Also some by African-American artists]

TFS-105: This anthology consists of 10 previously unpublished field recordings, one ca. 1950 aircheck, and 5 reissues from commercial records originally issued in 1926-76. The brochure by Wolfe includes historical background on the subject of the songs, biographies of the performers, and text transcriptions. This album, designed as an education package through MTSU's Environmental Education Program, is an excellent example of what can be done with traditional and commercial-folk-derived music in the context of local social history. Dozens of local historical or folklore societies could do the same for their own regions. Subject matter includes the Scopes Trial, Floyd Collins, local train wrecks, mine disasters, and fires, and the TVA. The selections are arranged chronologically, from "Old Cumberland Land," a fragmentary (in this recording) ballad dealing with the settlement of the upper Cumberland in the early 19th century, to "Tragedy of Spring City," about a 1955 collision between a school bus and a train that resulted in 11 deaths. Five of the songs were previously unrecorded in any form. Altogether the album strikes a good balance between the familiar and the unusual. [JAF 391; JEMFQ 72]

322 Label Name/Number: Tennessee Folklore Society TFS-106
Title: *The Kirkland Recordings: Newly Discovered Field Recordings from Tennessee and North Carolina 1937-39*
Artists: Various
Collector/Recordist: Original recordings by Edwin C. & Mary Kirkland
Editor: Charles Wolfe
Place and Date of Recording: TN, NC, 1937-1939
Date of Publication: 1984
Annotations: 20 p. booklet by Kip Lornell, Willie Smyth, & Charles Wolfe
Selections:

      Crawdad -- W. H. Thomas and group
      Cross Mountain Mines Explosion [G 9] -- Lola Long
      Florella [F 1] -- Buck Fulton
      Green Bed, The [K 36] -- J. B. Cantrell
      Hicks Carmichael -- Sam Hatcher
      I Married Me a Wife -- Marie Walker
      If You Want to Make a Preacher Cuss -- Arthur Anderson
      Johnny Troy [L 21] -- Jack Moore
      Mangrum and Mynatt [E 17] -- Columbus Popejoy
      Never Let the Deal Go Down -- Wheeler Bailey, Preston Fulp
      Old Grumble [Q 1] -- Bob House
      Pretty Polly [P 36b] -- Raymond Stanley
      Roving Boy [P 1b] -- Ashley Moore
      Roving Gambler [H 4] -- J.B. Easter
      Run, Sinner, and Hide Your Face -- tobacco workers
      Sir Patrick Spens [C. 58] -- Clara J. McCauley
      Soldier's Sweetheart, The [N 42] -- Lola Long
      Song of the Cove Creek Dam -- Eugene Wallace
      Wild Bill Jones [E 10] -- Matt Simmons, John Lewis

    TFS-106: One of the best releases of the 1980s from an archival collection was published in connection with the 50th anniversary of the Tennessee Folklore Society. The recordings are taken from over 400 made in 1937-39 by Edwin C. and Mary Kirkland while Edwin was on the faculty of the University of Tennessee, Knoxville. The Kirklands' collecting was facilitated by the loan of a bulky but portable disc recorder from the University's Speech Department. Interestingly, however, much of their collecting was done among students, faculty, and staff at the University. As Kip Lornell notes in his lengthy (but poorly edited) introductory essay, the Kirklands were eager to collect from the well-educated and professionally experienced singers as well as from the more usual objects of the ballad collectors' attentions. For several reasons, the Kirklands' recording activity practically ceased during the WW II years. They moved to Florida in 1946 and remained there until Edwin's death in 1972. The discs remained in Mary's possession until 1984, virtually unheard by anyone alse, when Charles Wolfe and Kip Lornell contacted her to learn more about the Kirklands' recording activity. Given access to the still-playable recordings, Wolfe edited the present collection of 19 selections. The booklet includes the essay by Lornell, who initially helped Mrs. Kirkland sort through the recordings and related materials; a brief essay by Willie Smyth on early Knoxville radio, stressing the Kirklands' utilization of this medium to aid in their collecting activity; song texts; and notes on the songs (perhaps more accurately described as notes on the performers) by Wolfe. For field-recorded aluminum and acetate discs, the recordings are in very good technical condition; they certainly compare favorably with LC field recordings of the same era.

The album includes seven ballads of identifiable Old World origins. The rendition of "Sir Patrick Spens" is evidently the first recording made of this venerable ballad in the U.S. It was performed in 1937 by Clara McCauley, supervisor of Public School Music in Knoxville; she had learned it 40 years earlier from her father. Her tune is very similar to one used for "The House Carpenter" (C. 243); her text is an abbreviated nine stanzas that lacks much of the drama of older texts of the ballad (much of which was still preserved in a text collected in Virginia in the previous year). Of McCauley's text, Bronson noted in *The Traditional Tunes of the Child Ballads* (II, p. 29), that it was so close to one published by Child that "suspicions of direct influence are aroused." But I fail to see the similarity. The other six ballads identified by alphanumerics above are all good but not unusual versions of familiar ballads--well recorded, good texts, and nicely sung (Ashley Moore's unaccompanied "Roving Boy" [P 1b] with old fashioned "feathering" particularly so). Kirkland was unable to find any analogs of "I Married Me a Wife," but it clearly is a longer version of the ballad recorded commercially a decade earlier by G. B. Grayson (of Laurel Bloomery, Tenn.) and Henry Whitter, titled by them "Never Be as Fast As I Have Been," and has speculation-provoking similarities to the piece recovered several times in America--first by Cecil Sharp--titled "Rain and Snow," and also to a song commercially recorded by Buell Kazee as "Sporting Bachelors." In a version of "Rain and Snow" sung by Dillard Chandler of N. C. (FA 2418; 1975) the story ends with the man murdering his nagging wife, suggesting a much fuller original if not simply a later accretion.

New World ballads include the ubiquitous "Florella," "Roving Gambler," and "Wild Bill Jones." Unbeknownst to the Kirklands, Simmons had recorded commercially for the OKeh label ten years earlier. Two other selections are local Tennessee ballads: "Song of the Cove Creek Dam," a topical song concerning events of 1934-35 involving the Norris Dam; and "Hicks Carmichael," about an 1888 murder, sung by professional performer Sam "Dynamite" Hatcher (who had already worked with Acuff by the time the Kirklands recorded him). Both ballads are apparently unrecorded apart from the Kirklands' work. The curiously titled "Mangrum and Mynatt" is not identified in the headnotes but is clearly a variant of "Logan County Jail." [JAF 395]

323 Label Name/Number: Tennessee Folklore Society TFS-108
Title: *It's Just the Same Today: The Barnicle-Cadle Field Recordings from Eastern Tennessee and Kentucky, 1938-1949*
Artists: Various
Collector/Recordist: Mary Elizabeth Barnicle and Tillman Cadle
Editor: Willie Smyth
Place and Date of Recording: TN, 1938-49
Date of Publication: [ca. 1987]
Annotations: 12 p. booklet by Smyth
Selections:
>   Dan Doo [C. 277] -- Jack Johnson
>   God Moves on a Windstorm -- Tillman Cadle
>   Hard Times -- Findlay Donaldson
>   Hold My Dying Head -- Tillman Cadle
>   It's Just the Same Today -- Tillman Cadle
>   Leather Breeches -- Wash, Lawrence, & James Redman
>   Long, Long Ago -- Adams Family Quartet
>   Mother's Love -- Ed Hunter, James E. & Lonzo Honeycutt
>   Mulberry Gap -- Sam & Charley Green
>   Nigger in the Woodpile -- Sam Avery, Bud Green

Oh John the Spirit of the Lord -- Findlay Donaldson
Old Eve She Did the Apple Pull -- Jack Johnson
Ploughboy Down at the Farm -- Adele Luebke
She's Mean I Mean -- Sara Ogan Gunning
Silk and Satin -- Sam Avery, Bud Green
Soldier and the Lady [P 14]- Ed Hunter, James E. Honeycutt
Whoa Larry Whoa -- Jack Johnson

TFS-108: Mary Elizabeth Barnicle was an energetic and enthusiastic collector/educator whose work in the area of Appalachian folklife has not been fully appreciated. While teaching folklore at New York University in the 1930s, she fell under the influence of John Lomax's work, and organized a field trip to Georgia, Florida, and the Bahamas to collect folklore in 1935. In the following years, Barnicle met, and either worked with or influenced, Alan Lomax, Leadbelly, Jim Garland, Sara Ogan Gunning, Aunt Molly Jackson, and Pete Seeger. In 1935 she met her husband-to-be, Tillman Cadle, a Kentucky miner and union activist, who had come to New York to visit his friend Jim Garland after a serious mining injury. In 1938 and thereafter, Cadle accompanied Barnicle on a series of recording trips in Kentucky. Her last teaching position was at the University of Tennessee in 1949-50, but she left there under a cloud, beset by political problems with a very conservative English Department. Just as she was leaving the University, Barnicle was informed that some 200 of her cherished field recordings, which had been on deposit in a campus office, had been misplaced. Deeply hurt by what she and Cadle regarded as the suspicious circumstances of the recordings' disappearance, she lost interest in any further field work until her death in 1979. In 1983, while engaged in a search for various archival field recordings made by collectors Edwin and Mary Kirkland, folklorist Willie Smyth stumbled upon a cache of 150 recordings made by Barnicle, squirreled away on the shelves of the University of Tennessee at Knoxville's radio station. In searching for more recordings and more information about them, Smyth met, interviewed, and worked with the reclusive Tillman Cadle, who had participated in most of his wife's fieldwork and also still possessed over 450 more field-recorded discs.

This album is the result of Smyth's efforts: a carefully researched tribute to the work of Mary Barnicle and Tillman Cadle, including 16 of their field recordings, together with one recent (1986) rerecording by two of Barnicle's performers whose original recording (of "The Soldier and The Lady") was damaged by a bolt of lightning in the middle of the 1949 recording session. The selections include instrumental music ("Nigger in the Woodpile" is not the usual tune associated with this title); Old- and New-World ballads and songs (including an Irish-American "Whoa Larry Whoa," "Dan Doo," and a quaint minstrel-derived "Old Eve She Did the Apple Pull"); and religious or homiletic songs by Cadle himself ("God Moves On a Windstorm," "Hold My Dying Head," "It's Just the Same Today"). Sara Ogan Gunning, well represented on other LPs and a long-time close friend of Barnicle and Cadle, contributes her own composition of complaint about her better-known sister, Aunt Molly Jackson, "She's Mean I Mean," to a tune very close to the Carter Family's "Jealous Hearted Me." Ed Hunter (Cadle's nephew), Lonzo Honeycutt, and James Espent Honeycutt perform "Mother's Love," a composition of Espent Honeycutt's that shows how familiar those men were with hillbilly styles of the 1930s and '40s. Rather unusual is the Adams Family's shape-note-styled performance of Thomas Haynes Bayly's 1843 hit, "Long Long Ago," one of the few antebellum pop songs to turn up with much frequency after a full century. Rare (if not otherwise unknown in oral tradition) is the "Ploughboy Down at the Farm," sung a capella by Adele Luebke in 1949 when she was a student of Barnicle's at the University of Tennessee. The 78-rpm aluminum and acetate discs are not all in good condition; the selections for this LP were made with attention paid to both musical and technical listenability. Smyth's booklet includes a lengthy appreciation of Barnicle's career, importance, and mistreatment; the circumstances of the recordings and the suspicious fate that befell them; and program notes (with text transcriptions) to the selections themselves; all in all, a commendable package. An inventory of all the Barnicle-Cadle recordings, originally intended for inclusion in the booklet, was published separately in the *Tennessee Folklore Society Bulletin.* [JAF 408]

324 Label Name/Number: Tradition Records TLP 1007
Title: *Instrumental Music of the Southern Appalachians*
Artists: Various
Collector/Recordist: Diane Hamilton, Liam Clancy, Paul Clayton
Place and Date of Recording: 1956
Date of Publication: [1956?]
Annotations: Liner notes by Paul Clayton
Selections:

    Hobart Smith
        Cripple Creek
        Drunken Hiccups
        John Brown's Dream
        Pateroller Song
        Pretty Polly
    Edd Presnell
        Amazing Grace
        Sally Goodin
        Shady Grove
    Richard Chase
        Girl I Left Behind Me, The
        Molly Brooks
        Skip to My Lou
    Etta Baker
        Bully of the Town
        Goin' Down the Road Feeling Bad
        John Henry
        One Dime Blues
        Railroad Bill
    Boone Reid
        Johnson Boys
        Sourwood Mountain
    Lacey Phillips
        Marching Jaybird
        Soldier's Joy

      Tradition TLP 1007: Tradition Records was co-founded by American folksong enthusiast Diane Hamilton and the Irish Clancy Brothers, who had recently moved to New York intent on establishing their careers in the theater. Paul Clayton [Worthington] was a trained folklorist who also enjoyed a thriving second career on stage and records as folksong performer. This album made an immense impression on young city folk music enthusiasts, presenting as it did an astonishing array of wonderfully recorded traditional instrumentalists. Etta Baker's finger-picking guitar style in particular was meticulously copied note for note by struggling imitators. Although Baker, her father, Boone Reid, and Reid's son-in-law Lacey Phillips are African-Americans from North Carolina, and I have defined the perimeters of this study to encompass Anglo-American musicians only, I include their performances here because they occupy that slender junction between the Anglo-American and African-American musical traditions: all their songs could be heard from white performers of their native locale. (The album annotations give no clues to the ethnicity of any of the performers.)

325   Label Name/Number: University of Illinois Press cassette [no #]
Title: *Songs from Joe Scott, the Woodsman-Songmaker*
Artists: Various
Collector/Recordist: Edward D. Ives
Place and Date of Recording: Northeast, 1950s-'60s
Date of Publication: 1979
Selections:
>   Benjamin Deane [F 32] -- Chester Price
>   Benjamin Deane [F 32] -- William Bell
>   Benjamin Deane [F 32] -- Wilmot MacDonald
>   Guy Reed [C 9] -- Philip Walsh
>   Howard Carey [E 23] -- John O'Connor
>   Howard Carey [E 23] -- Wesley Smith
>   Norway Bum, The -- James Brown
>   Plain Golden Band, The [H 17] -- Sam Jagoe
>   White Cafe, The -- Fred A. Campbell

U Illinois Press cassette: Joe Scott (1867-1918) was a Maine lumberman and balladmaker who composed several songs that entered northeast oral tradition.   His career and music, in the context of the lumbercamp society, are carefully documented in Edward D. Ives' *Joe Scott, the Woodsman-Songmaker* (U. of Ill. Press, 1979), which this cassette is meant to accompany. All the songs are Scott's compositions, collected by Ives from singers in the northeast and maritimes in the 1950s and '60s. The cassette contains no documentation, which is amply provided in the book.

326   Label Name/Number: University of Missouri Press [2 record set]
Title: *Old-Time Fiddler's Repertory: Historic Field Recordings of Forty-One Traditional Tunes*
Artists: Various
Collector/Recordist: Various
Editor: R. P. Christeson
Place and Date of Recording: 1948-1961
Date of Publication: 1976
Annotations: Liner notes (companion album to book, *Then Old-Time Fiddler's Repertory: 245 Traditional Tunes*, compiled and edited by R. P. Christeson [1973])
Selections:
>   Bob Walters
>>   Adrain's Hornpipe
>>   Art Wooten's Quadrille
>>   Casey's Hornpipe
>>   Done Gone
>>   Frisky Jim
>>   Granny, Will Your Dog Bite?
>>   Hell in Texas
>>   Hooker's Hornpipe
>>   Iberia Breakdown
>>   Jack Danielson's Reel
>>   Jimmy in the Swamp
>>   Jump Fingers
>>   Kelly Schottische
>>   Lantern in the Ditch
>>   Lazy Kate
>>   Old Joe

       Old Melinda
       Old Time Schottische
       Oxford Minuet
       Oyster River Quadrille
       Quadrille in C & F
       Quadrille Melody
       Rose Waltz
       Sleepy Joe
       St. Joe Hornpipe
       Steven's Waltz Number Two
       Stoney Point
       The Missouri Mud
       Thunderbolt Hornpipe
       Tunes from Home Schottische
       Unnamed Tune in D, A, & G
Bill Driver
       Marmaduke's Hornpipe
       Scott Number One
       Scott Number Two
       Unnamed Breakdowns (2)
George Helton
       Jinny Nettles
Tony Gilmore
       Brickyard Joe
       Rustic Dance
       Wait Till You Hear This One, Boy
Cyril Stinnett
       Pacific Slope

     U. of Missouri Press: These two discs of five fiddlers from Missouri and Nebraska, recorded 1948-61 have minimal documentation, but the set is meant to accompany Christeson's comprehensive book, *The Old-Time Fiddler's Repertory: 245 Traditional Tunes* (1973). Most of the recordings are by Bob Walters of Nebraska, who used to perform on local radio for many years. Driver is African-American but his repertoire and style--at least on these recordings--are solidly Anglo-American. Some listeners may find Christeson's spoken commentary on the recordings distracting. [JAF 395, JEMFQ 42--PW]

327 **Label Name/Number:** Univ. of North Carolina Press 0-8078-4083-1 [2 LP set]
Title: *Primitive Baptist Hymns of the Blue Ridge*
Artists: Various
Collector/Recordist: Brett Sutton, Pete Hartman
Place and Date of Recording: Various (VA), 1976
Date of Publication: 1982
Annotations: 27 p. booklet by Brett Sutton
Selections: (first title is tune; second is first line of text)
       Dunlap: My God the Spring of All My Joys -- Danville Primitive Baptist Church
       Devotion: Poor and Afflicted, Lord Are Thine -- Union Primitive Baptist Church
       Pilgrim: On Jordan's Stormy Banks I Stand -- Elder Bennie and Edrie Clifton
       Pisgah: I'm Not Ashamed To Own My Lord -- Old Republican Primitive Baptist Church
       Wayfaring Stranger: Come Thou Long-Expected Jesus -- Old Republican Primitive Baptist
          Church

U. of North Carolina Press 0-8078-4083-1: Doctoral candidate (at the University of North Carolina) Sutton spent nine months in Primitive Baptist churches of Virginia and North Carolina collecting hymns and studying their cultural environment. Of the dozen selections on this LP, seven are from black church groups (and are not listed). For three of the hymn tunes, Sutton pairs black and white church groups singing their respective versions. The illustrated brochure includes a history of "Church, community, and the singing tradition;" discussions of the hymns, the tunes, and the practice of lining out; a musical analysis, and a discussion of the performances per se. The selections were recorded either by congregations or smaller groups of different churches of Patrick, Floyd, Franklin, Henry, and Pittsylvania Counties in Southwestern Virginia. [JEMFQ 70]

328   Label Name/Number: Univ of North Carolina Press 0-8078-4084-X [2 LP set]
Title: *Powerhouse of God: Sacred Speech, Chant, and Song in an Appalachian Baptist Church*
Artists: Various
Collector/Recordist: Jeff Todd Titon, Kenneth M. George
Place and Date of Recording: Stanley, VA, 1977, 1978
Date of Publication: 1982
Annotations: 24 p. booklet by Jeff Todd Titon
Selections:

> I Saw the Face of Jesus -- Betty Cave, Arthur Cave, Welford Cave, Rosalee Cave
> I Shall Not Be Moved and This Little Light of Mine (medley) -- Denise Sherfey, Tammy Sherfey, Missy Owens
> I'm So Glad He Found Me -- Betty Cave, Arthur Cave, Welford Cave, Rosalee Cave
> Little Church Aisle, The -- Belvin Hurt, Delores Hurt Fincham
> Meet Me There -- led by John Sherfey
> Nothing but the Blood -- led by John Sherfey
> Preaching by the Roadside -- John Sherfey, Pauline Sherfey
> Precious Memories -- John Sherfey, Elsie Sherfey McNally, Don Sherfey

[Also prayers, sermons, life story]

U. of North Carolina Press 0-8078-4084-X: This handsomely produced package was edited by Titon and based on five years of his own field research with the Fellowship Independent Baptist Church of Stanley, Virginia. The selections include nine hymns. One entire side of a disc is a sermon, invitation, and prayer by Brother John Sherfey, and another is Sherfey's spoken life story. The brochure includes an introductory essay and annotations for each of the selections that give text transcriptions and comments on performer, performance, and/or selection. [JEMFQ 70]

329   Label Name/Number: University of Texas Press [cass, no #]
Title: *Sing Me a Song*
Artists: Various
Collector/Recordist/Editor: William A. Owens
Place and Date of Recording: Various, 1937-41
Date of Publication: 1983
Annotations: None
Selections:

> Ballad of Jesse James, The [E 1] -- May Kennedy McCord
> Boston Burglar, The [L 16b] -- Mr S. C. H. Burke
> Cowboy Jack [B 24] -- Daniel Jeffus
> Fair Ellender [C. 73] -- May Kennedy McCord
> I Wisht I Was a Single Girl Again -- Maidy Kelly Hendricks
> Keep Your Garden Clean -- May Kennedy McCord

[Also 23 African-American, Hispanic, Cajun, and Czech-American selections]

U. of Texas Press [cass, no #]: This cassette is a companion to William A. Owens' book, *Tell Me a Story, Sing Me a Song* (1983), a collection of songs Owens collected, mostly in his native Texas--though at least one singer on this tape, May K. McCord, is not from Texas but Missouri. Nevertheless, the cassette does much to bring to life the texts and tunes that Owens has gathered over a period of four years just before World War II.

330 Label Name/Number: Vanguard VRS-9147/VSD-79147
Title: *Old Time Music at Newport*
Artists: Various
Place and Date of Recording: Newport, RI, 1963
Date of Publication: 1964
Annotations: Liner notes by Stacey Williams
Selections:
    Doc Watson
        Groundhog
        Little Orphan Girl
        Rambling Hobo
        Train That Carried My Girl from Town
    Clarence (Tom) Ashley
        Coocoo Bird
        House Carpenter [C. 243]
        Little Sadie [I 8]
    Jenes Cottrell
        Devil and the Farmer's Wife, The [C. 278]
    Maybelle Carter
        Storms Are on the Ocean, The
    Dorsey Dixon
        Intoxicated Rat
        Weaveroom Blues
        Wreck on the Highway
    Dock Boggs
        Oh, Death
        Drunkard's Lone Child
        Sugar Baby
    Clarence Ashley, Clint Howard, Fred Price, and Doc Watson
        Amazing Grace (with Jean Ritchie)
        Old Account Was Settled Long Ago, The

331a Label Name/Number: Vanguard VRS-9182/VSD-79182
Title: *Traditional Music at Newport 1964, Part 1*
Artists: Various
Collector/Recordist/Editor: Ralph Rinzler with Jack Lothrop
Place and Date of Recording: Newport, RI, 1964
Date of Publication: 1965
Annotations: Liner notes and 4 p. brochure by Ralph Rinzler
Selections:
    Hobart Smith
        Coo-Coo Bird
        Jack of Diamonds
        Railroad Bill [I 13]
    Sarah Gunning

        Girl of Constant Sorrow
  Ken and Neriah Benfield
        Ella's Grave
        Katy Cline
  Sacred Harp Singers
        Calvary
        Rocky Road
  Chet Parker and Elgia Hickok
        Golden Slippers
        Temperence Reel
  Bill Thatcher
        Job I Left Behind, The
  Doc Watson, Gaither Carlton, and Arnold Watson
        Cripple Creek
        Muskrat
[Also 8 African-American and 2 Cajun selections]

331b   Label Name/Number: Vanguard VRS-9183/VSD-79183
Title: *Traditional Music at Newport: 1964, Part 2*
Artists: Various
Collector/Recordist/Editor: Ralph Rinzler with Jack Lothrop
Place and Date of Recording: Newport, RI, 1964
Date of Publication: 1965
Annotations: Liner notes and 4 p. brochure by Ralph Rinzler
Selections:
  Clayton McMichen
        Bile Them Cabbage Down
        Old Joe Clark
  Phipps Family
        Anchored His Love
        God Gave Noah the Rainbow Sign
  Frank Proffitt
        My Home's Across the Blue Ridge Mountains
        Poor Man
  Glenn Ohrlin
        Chickens They Grow Tall, The
        Montana Is My Home
  Jean Ritchie
        'Tis the Gift to be Simple
        Goin' to Boston
  Almeda Riddle
        Hangman, The [C. 95]
  Phoeba and Roscoe Parsons
        Sourwood Mountain
        Shortening Bread
[Also 4 Irish and 4 African-American selections]

    Van VRS-9147 / Van VRS-9182/ Van VRS-9183: Newport, Rhode Island, already famous as the site of an annual jazz festival, hosted the first Newport Folk Festival in the summer of 1959. In the first two festivals, the performers were mostly city musicians or at least musicians who had become well accepted by the urban connoisseurs. Financially disappointing, the event would have been discontinued but for the determination of Pete and Toshi Seeger, Ewan MacColl and Peggy Seeger, and others to revamp the event, seeking to present traditional artists rather than big-name performers. Seven festivals were held between 1963 and 1969, with that of 1965 being the most successful. From the dozens of hours of tapes made at the 1963 and 1964 events, Vanguard issued several albums that demonstrated the range of traditional performances heard. (Earlier festivals were also immortalized in wax, but the performers were mostly interpreters rather than traditional artists.) Almost all the artists heard on these albums are more fully represented on other LPs.

SECTION III: Individual Artists/Groups--Primarily Reissues of Commercial 78 rpm Recordings

332 Label Name/Number: Bear Family [West Germany] BF 15501 (= Folk Variety 12501)
Title: *Country Ragtime*
Artists: The Allen Brothers
Editor: Richard Weize
Source and Date of Recording: From commercial 78s, 1928-31
Date of Publication: [1974?]
Annotations: Liner notes by Mike Paris
Selections:
    Cheat 'em
    Free Little Bird
    Frisco Blues
    I'll Be All Smiles Tonight
    I'm Always Whistling the Blues
    Jake Walk Blues
    No Low Down Hanging Around
    Old Black Crow in the Hickory Nut Tree
    Preacher Blues
    Price of Cotton Blues
    Prisoner's Dream, The
    Reckless Night Blues
    Roll Down the Line
    Skipping & Flying
    Tiple [sic] Blues
    When You Leave, You'll Leave Me Sad

BF 15501: Austin (1901-59) and Lee Allen (1906-81) were born in Franklin County, Tennessee, and early turned to music as their profession. In around 1923 they settled in Chattanooga and began a long career of radio broadcasts and personal appearances at local theaters. They made their first records in 1927 for Columbia, one of their early numbers being "Salty Dog." Columbia executives thought the recording could "pass" for African-American and issued it in the "race" rather than "hillbilly" series, a gesture some would take as a compliment but one that failed to please the Allens. After an unsuccessful lawsuit, the Allens recorded successively for Victor and American Record Corporation until 1934. Generally, Austin played tenor banjo and harmonica while Lee played guitar and kazoo. Their repertoire included some sentimental and topical songs, but they were best-known for their racy, exuberant, light-hearted blues and raggy pieces. "Jake Walk Blues" is one of a number of topical hillbilly recordings of the Prohibition era dealing with the adverse medical effects (including inability to walk properly) of illicit Jamaica gin, or "jake." "Tiple Blues" (so misspelt by RCA Victor) is a disjointed lyric (to the popular tune of "Deep Elem Blues") with coal mining, not boozing, references.

333 Label Name/Number: Bear Family [West Germany] BF 15502 (= Folk Variety 12502)
Title: *The Texas Cowboy*
Artist: Jules Allen
Editor: Richard Weize
Source and Date of Recording: From commercial 78s, 1928-29
Date of Publication: [1974?]
Annotations: 8 p. brochure by John I. White

Selections:
 Chisholm Trail
 Cow Trail to Mexico [B 13]
 Cowboy's Lament
 Days of 49, The
 Dying Cowboy [B 2], The
 Gal I Left Behind, The
 Home on the Range
 Jack O'Diamonds
 Little Joe, the Wrangler [B 5]
 Little Old Sod Shanty, The
 'Long Side the Santa Fe Trail
 Po' Mourner
 Prisoner for Life, A
 Punching the Dough
 Somebody, but You Don't Mean Me
 Texas Cowboy, The

  BF 15502: This LP includes 16 of the 22 songs recorded between 1928 and 1929 by Jules Verne Allen (1883-1945), one of the most popular singing cowboys of the era. The brochure includes extensive notes on the songs by one-time cowboy singer John I. White, text transcriptions, a brief biography, and a complete Jules Allen discography. Most of the pieces are familiar cowboy ballads and songs (including the first recording of "Home on the Range"), but Allen's repertoire included several non-western pieces, such as "Po' Mourner" and "Somebody, but You Don't Mean Me." The album's sole flaw is that some of the tracks were poorly transferred from the originals, resulting in noticeable speed fluctuations. [WF 7/75]

 334 **Label Name/Number:** Homestead OHCS 190
Title: *I Am a Man of Constant Sorrow*
Artist: Emry Arthur
Source and Date of Recording: From commercial 78s, 1928-29
Date of Publication: 1987
Annotations: Liner notes by Charles Wolfe
Selections:
 Down in the Tennessee Valley
 Going Around This World
 Goodbye, My Lover, Goodbye
 Heart of the City That Has No Heart, The
 Heave-Ho the Anchor
 I Am a Man of Constant Sorrow
 I Shall Know by the Prints of the Nails in His Hand
 Love Lifted Me
 Mother's Going To Leave You Bye and Bye
 Nobody's Business
 Shining for the Master
 Wanderer, The
 Wandering Boy
 Wandering Gypsy Girl [O 4]
 Where the Gates Swing Outward Never
 Where the Silvery Colorado Winds Its Way

OHCS 190: Emry Arthur was born around the turn of the century in Wayne County, Kentucky. His family was noted throughout the area for their singing, and his father was a collector of old songs. In around 1925 Arthur moved north to Indianapolis to find work in the factories; there in 1927 he auditioned successfully for Brunswick, for whom he, with his brothers, recorded for the next years. Arthur's plaintive singing, accompanied by a simple guitar backup (he was handicapped by the loss of a finger on his right hand), is at its best on the title song, which he was first to record (though it had been written by a neighbor of his, Dick Burnett). His repertoire was heavily weighted with sentimental and religious ballads and songs of the post-1870 decades. The oldest of the 17 on this LP is "Wandering Gypsy Girl." Wolfe's liner notes provide much hitherto-unknown biographical information, drawn from extensive correspondence of Arthur to one of his record companies. [JAF 406]

335   **Label Name/Number:** County 407
Title: *The Blue Ridge Highballers*
Editor: [David Freeman]
Source and Date of Recording: From commercial 78s, 1926-27
Date of Publication: 1974
Annotations: Liner notes by C. Kinney Rorrer
Selections:
   Darling Child
   Darneo
   Flop Eared Mule
   Fourteen Days in Georgia
   Going Down to Lynchburg Town
   Green Mountain Polka
   Round Town Girls
   Sandy River Belle
   Skidd More
   Soldier's Joy
   Under the Double Eagle
   Wish to the Lord I Had Never Been Born

Cty 407:   The Blue Ridge Highballers were a popular dance band organized in the mid 1920s by Franklin County, Virginia, fiddler, Charley W. La Prade (1888-1958), who appeared at square dances, fiddlers' conventions, and local theaters. La Prade recorded twice: one session in 1926 for Columbia and a second in 1927 for Paramount. On the 1926 session he was accompanied by guitarist Lonnie Griffith and banjoist Arthur Wells. Luther B. Clarke, a music store proprietor in Danville who helped arrange the recording session, sang three vocals; the other selections are all instrumentals. La Prade was a skilled fiddler (with some formal violin training) who led his band at a sprightly clip; the other instruments provide only rhythmic back-up. Most of the tunes are familiar numbers: "Darneo" is basically "Sail Away Ladies"; "Green Mountain Polka" is better known as "Richmond Cotillion"; "Lynchburg" seems to be a medley of several familiar strains. Clarke's vocal ("Wish to the Lord...") is a local song referring to tobacco farm co-op difficulties of the period. C. Kinney Rorrer provides good biographical liner notes based, apparently, on his own researches. [JEMFQ 40]

336   **Label Name/Number:** Folkways RBF 654
Title: *Dock Boggs' Original Records*
Artist: Dock Boggs
Editor: Mike Seeger and Barry O'Connell
Source and Date of Recording: From commercial 78s, 1927-29

Date of Publication: 1983
Annotations: 18 p. brochure by Barry O'Connell
Selections:
   Country Blues
   Danville Girl [H 2]
   Down South Blues
   False Hearted Lover's Blues
   Hard Luck Blues
   Lost Love Blues
   New Prisoner's Song
   Old Rub Alcohol Blues
   Pretty Polly [P 36b]
   Sammie, Where Have You Been So Long?
   Sugar Baby
   Will Sweethearts Know Each Other There

Fwys RBF 654:   This is the definitive Boggs reissue. Moran Lee "Dock" Boggs (1897-1971), a Virginia-born collier, was a minor hillbilly artists who made a dozen recordings in 1927 and 1929, all of which are reissued here. Relatively unimportant in terms of the history of commercially-recorded hillbilly music, Boggs disappeared from public view with the coming of the Depression (except, of course, locally). Highly idiosyncratic in style, Boggs's dozen recordings are instantly recognizable; yet there is no evidence that any other country artists learned from his recordings or were influenced by them until, over three decades later, Doc Watson began his own recording career. Nevertheless, this is an important, welcome reissue. Why? In the first place, there are aesthetic reasons. Boggs created a unique musical combination of vocal and banjo styles that produced an intense musical experience that no listener can ever forget. Though he learned to play banjo in a frailing style, as his father and other relatives played while he was young, he chose to develop a picking style based on the playing of a black banjoist whom he heard once in his youth and was deeply impressed by. He went on to develop the sounds that he had heard into a style of accompaniment that could provide several different kinds of sounds--an alternate melody line, a bass line, or a rhythmic accompaniment at different times--but basically left the airwaves sufficiently uncluttered to allow maximum vocal embellishments. And it is his singing that is most memorable: a rather gravelly voice, slightly nasal tones, with elaborate slides, scoops, vocal breaks, passing tones, anticipations, and hesitations. Though he sings many old Anglo-American ballads, and with a strong predilection for pentatonic tunes, there is more behind his singing than the style of the unaccompanied ballad singer. Boggs has also incorporated the vocal decorations of black singers into his kit of vocal ornamentations. For example, while white singers tend to use ascending vocal decorations, blacks tend more to use descending ornamentations. Boggs does both. There is also, thanks largely to Mike Seeger, extensive documentation of Boggs's life and music. Subsequent to his "rediscovery" by Seeger in 1963, Boggs was recorded on several occasions, the results being three full song LPs (FA 2351, FA 2392, and Asch AH 3903) and one interview album (FH 5458). Boggs's music, whatever its effect on his contemporaries, made a mark on later urban folk music aficionados. "Pretty Polly" was chosen by Alan Lomax for reissue on one of the two albums he edited for Brunswick/Decca in 1947. Harry Smith reissued "Country Blues" and "Sugar Baby" on his influential set, *Anthology of American Folk Music* (Folkways FA 2951-53) in 1952. In the 1960s, the New Lost City Ramblers offered their own re-creations of some of Boggs's songs for folksong revival audiences, and Doc Watson, in the 1960s, added "Country Blues" to his repertoire and performed it in concerts and on LP. O'Connell's lengthy, thought-provoking, biographical essay dwells not only on the facts of Boggs's life and career but also probes the inner tensions in his psyche: on the conflict between musical career and coal-miner; between being a musician and being a good, dependable husband and provider; between the rural audience of the 1920s and the urban audience of the 1960s; between professional commitment to a musical career and a casual predilection. His notes on the songs give brief comments on Boggs's sources and on other traditional versions. The textual transcriptions are useful but could have been done with greater accuracy. [JEMFQ 70, JAF 391]

337   **Label Name/Number:** Bluebird AXM2-5525
Title: *Blue Sky Boys*
Source and Date of Recording: From studio recordings, 1936-50
Date of Publication: [1976]
Annotations: Liner notes by Douglas B. Green
Selections:
    Beautiful, Beautiful Brown Eyes
    Butcher's Boy, The [P 24]
    Have No Desire To Roam
    Hymns My Mother Sang
    I Need the Prayers
    I'm Just Here To Get My Baby out of Jail
    Kneel At the Cross
    Little Bessie
    Midnight on the Stormy Sea [M 1]
    My Last Letter
    Only One Step More
    Prisoner's Dream, The
    Since the Angels Took My Mother Far Away
    Take Up Thy Cross
    When the Roses Bloom in Dixieland
    Whispering Hope
    Why Not Confess
    You Give Me Your Love

338   **Label Name/Number:** Camden CAL 797
Title: *Blue Sky Boys*
Source and Date of Recording: From studio recordings, 1930s
Date of Publication: 1964
Annotations: Liner notes by Archie Green
Selections:
    Are You from Dixie?
    Asleep in the Briny Deep
    Butcher's Boy, The [P 24]
    Down on the Banks of the Ohio [F 5]
    Fair Eyed Ellen [F 1a]
    In the Hills of Roane County
    Katie Dear [M 4]
    Lightning Express, The
    Mary of the Wild Moor [P 21]
    Short Life of Trouble
    Story of the Knoxville Girl [P 35]
    Sunny Side of Life

339   **Label Name/Number:** Rounder 1006
Title: *The Sunny Side of Life*

Artists: The Blue Sky Boys
Editors: The Rounder Collective
Source and Date of Recording: From commercial 78s, 1936-49
Date of Publication: 1974
Annotations: Liner notes by Rounder Collective
Selections:
    Are You from Dixie?
    Asleep in the Briny Deep
    Don't Say Goodbye If You Love Me
    Down on the Banks of the Ohio [F 5]
    Fair-Eyed Ellen [F 1a]
    In the Hills of Roane County
    Katie Dear [P 35]
    Lightning Express
    Pictures from Life's Other Side
    Sunny Side of Life
    Sweet Allalee
    Turn Your Radio On

Bluebird AXM2-5525: One of the most influential hillbilly duets of the '30s, in terms of both repertoire and style, was the Blue Sky Boys, Bill and Earl Bolick. The brothers were born near Hickory, No. Carolina, in 1917 and 1919, respectively. They learned many songs and ballads from their maternal grandmother, and early decided on music as a career. They recorded 124 selections for RCA Victor/Bluebird between 1936 and 1950, at which time they broke up their musical partnership because Earl wanted to have more time with his new family. They developed a very mellow, smooth singing style, with near-perfectly coordinated timing. Their mandolin and guitar backup were not flashy but proficient and carefully integrated with their singing. Their earlier selections are steeped in older traditional material, with the proportion of more recent hymns and gospel songs growing on their post-war recordings. There is some duplication among the three reissues listed here, with the Camden release, their first reissue LP, concentrating the most on their older repertoire. For post-1960 recordings, and more biographical notes, see comments on Rounder CD 11536 and JEMF 104 in Section I. The very brief liner notes to Rounder 1006 include a statement by the Bolicks--an interesting comment on folk and hillbilly music by a thoughtful team that, nearly four decades ago, was one of the most popular hillbilly acts on radio. [WF 7/75]

340   **Label Name/Number:** Rounder 1004
Title: *The Songs of Dick Burnett and Leonard Rutherford*
Source and Date of Recording: From commercial 78s, 1926-30
Date of Publication: 1975
Annotations: 12 p. brochure by Charles Wolfe
Selections:
    Billy in the Lowground
    Blackberry Blossom
    Cabin with the Roses at the Door
    Going across the Sea
    Going around the World
    Knoxville Rag
    Ladies on the Steamboat
    Little Stream of Whiskey [H 3]
    Lost John
    My Sweetheart in Tennessee

Ramblin' Reckless Hobo [H 2]
Sarah Jane
Short Life of Trouble, A
Taylor's Quickstep
There's No One Like the Old Folks
Two Faithful Lovers

Rndr 1004:   Richard Burnett (1883-1976) and Leonard Rutherford (ca. 1900-54) were one of the best known and most influential musical duos of the '20s and '30s in south central Kentucky. Burnett's impact was not only through his recordings but also via his songbook, which he had printed up in ca. 1913 and sold on his travels.   Their repertoire was largely made up of native folk ballads and pop songs from the latter decades of the 19th century and older fiddle tunes.   Both men played fiddle, but Rutherford was the smoother fiddler and Burnett was willing to accompany him on banjo, producing some of the finest banjo-fiddle duets on record.   The handsomely produced brochure includes biographic information, notes on the songs, illustrations and reproductions from Burnett's songbook, and discography.   [JEMFQ 42]

341   Label Name/Number: Old Homestead OHS 90031
Title: *The Callahan Brothers*
Editor: [John Morris]
Source and Date of Recording: From commercial 78s, 1934-41
Date of Publication: 1975
Annotations: Unsigned liner notes [by John Morris]
Selections:
Corn Licker Rag
Dying Girl's Farewell, The
Gonna Quit My Rowdy Ways
I Got Her Boozy
I Want To Be Where You Are
John Henry [I 1]
Little Poplar Log House on the Hill
Maple on the Hill
On the Banks of the Ohio
Rounders Luck (Rising Sun Blues)
She Came Rollin' down the Mountain
She's Killing Me
She's My Curly Headed Baby, No. 3
St. Louis Blues
Take the News to Mother
Way Out There

OHS 90031:   Walter Callahan (1910-71) and his brother Homer (b. 1912) were born in Madison County, North Carolina, and began learning songs in their youth from their parents.   By the mid '20s they were performing together at schoolhouses and private gatherings.   They began making records in 1933 for the American Record Corp., recording over 90 sides between 1934 and 1941.   They accompanied their own close duet singing with their own guitar playing.   More pungent sounding than such contemporaries as the Blue Sky Boys or the Delmore Brothers, the Callahans still achieved a carefully blended sound with perfectly synchronized singing, even on their yodeling. Most of the selections on this LP are characteristic of the repertoires of the several brother duets that were so popular during the '30s, but a few older songs and ballads can also be found.

342   **Label Name/Number:** GHP [West Germany] LP 1001 [reissued as Old Homestead OH 113]
Title: *The Carolina Tar Heels*
Editor: Gerd Hadeler
Source and Date of Recording: From commercial 78s, 1927-31
Date of Publication: [1969]
Annotations: Unsigned liner notes [by Norm Cohen]
Selections:
   Bulldog Down in Sunny Tennessee, The
   Farm Girl Blues
   Hand in Hand We Have Walked Along Together
   I Don't Like the Blues No How
   I Love My Mountain Home
   My Home's Across the Blue Ridge Mountains
   Oh, How I Hate It
   Old Grey Goose, The
   Roll On Boys
   Rude and Rambling Man [L 12]
   Somebody's Tall and Handsome
   There's a Man Going Round Taking Names
   Washing Mama's Dishes
   Who's Gonna Kiss Your Lips Dear Darling

343   **Label Name/Number:** Bear Family [West Germany] BF 15507
Title: *Can't You Remember the Carolina Tar Heels?*
Editor: Richard Weize
Source and Date of Recording: From commercial 78s, 1927-31
Date of Publication: [1975]
Annotations: Brochure by Richard Weize
Selections:
   Apron String Blues, The
   Bring Me a Leaf from the Sea
   Can't You Remember When Your Heart Was Mine? [C. 243]
   Goodbye, My Bonnie, Goodbye
   Got the Farmland Blues
   Her Name Was Hula Lou
   I'll Be Washed
   I'm Going to Georgia
   My Mama Scolds Me for Flirting
   Peg and Awl
   Roll On Daddy, Roll On
   Shanghai in China
   She Wouldn't Be Still
   There Ain't No Use Working So Hard
   When the Good Lord Sets Me Free
   You're a Little Too Small

     BF 15507 / GHP 1001:   The Tar Heels were one of the finest stringbands from the Carolinas to record in the 1920s--which is noteworthy, since they never recorded with a fiddle, relying instead on strong harmonica (played by either Gwen Foster or Garley Foster) and banjo (by Walsh) leads. Their repertoire ranged from old traditional ballads to white blues to religious numbers to occasional renditions of 1920s pop songs ("Her Name Was Hula Lou"). The Tar Heels' career has been well documented, thanks to their "rediscovery" in the early 1960s by Gene Earle, Ralph Rinzler, and Archie Green, with a full newly recorded album (Folk Legacy FSA 24; see Section I) resulting. The first Tar Heels reissue appeared on the now long-defunct German label, GHP; the Bear Family album was the second reissue LP devoted to the group. On the latter, in general, the technical quality of the tracks is good, though a few are rather scratchy, and one song ("Apron String Blues") slows down markedly toward the end. [JEMFQ 54; JAF 334--DKW (GHP)]

344   Label Name/Number: Rounder 1003
Title: *The Old Hen Cackled and the Rooster's Going To Crow*
Artist: Fiddlin' John Carson
Source and Date of Recording: From commercial 78s, 1923-34
Date of Publication: 1973
Annotations: Brochure by Mark Wilson
Selections:
   Bachelor's Hall, The
   Corn Licker and Barbecue, Part 2
   Do Round My Lindy
   Engineer on the Mogull
   Georgia's Three-Dollar Tag
   Gonna Swing on the Golden Gate
   Honest Farmer, The
   I'm Glad My Wife's in Europe
   I'm Nine Hundred Miles from Home
   It's a Shame To Whip Your Wife on Sunday
   Little Old Log Cabin in the Lane, The
   Old Hen Cackled and the Rooster's Going To Crow, The
   Smoke Goes out the Chimney Just the Same, The
   Sugar in the Gourd
   There's a Hard Time Coming
   Watcha Gonna Do When Your Licker Gives Out?

345   Label Name/Number: University of Illinois Press [no #] [cass]
Title: *Recordings to accompany the book,* Fiddlin' Georgia Crazy, *by Gene Wiggins*
Artist: Fiddlin' John Carson
Editor: Norm Cohen
Source and Date of Recording: From commercial 78s, 1923-34
Date of Publication: 1986
Annotations: None
Selections:
   Alabama Gal (Won't You Come Out Tonight?)
   Boston Burglar, The [L 16b]
   Did He Ever Return?
   Death of Floyd Collins, The [G 22]
   Dixie Boll Weevil [I 17]
   Hop Light, Lady
   I'm Going To Take the Train to Charlotte
   In My Old Cabin Home
   John's Trip to Boston
   Lightning Express, The
   Little More Sugar in the Coffee

Meet Her When the Sun Goes Down
My Ford Sedan
On the Banks of the Old Tennessee
Papa's Billy Goat
Taxes on the Farmer Feeds Them All
Tom Watson Special
When You and I Were Young, Maggie

Rndr 1003: The first LP reissue of Fiddlin' John Carson (ca. 1873-1949) was long overdue; on the other hand, perhaps it should have been expected that the producers of hillbilly reissues would have to cultivate their audience gradually, before turning to such hard-to-take (at least, for most modern listeners) artists as Carson. Carson's importance in the history of early hillbilly music has been well documented (see Gene Wiggins' biography, *Fiddlin' Georgia Crazy: Fiddlin' John Carson, His Real World and the World of His Songs*, University of Illinois Press, 1987, for the most extensive account). Briefly, he was, if not quite the first traditional rural musician to be commercially recorded, surely the one whose first recordings, made in the summer of 1923, awakened the phonograph industry to the vast potential market for this kind of music. A mainstay of the North Georgia rural music scene for decades, Carson was a consistent winner at the famous Atlanta Fiddle Conventions, was one of the first old-time fiddlers to perform over radio (Atlanta's WSB in September 1922), hobnobbed with or campaigned for several populist politicians (the Talmadges, Tom Watson) and recorded nearly a gross of ballads, songs, and fiddle tunes between 1923 and 1934. This LP includes a representative sampling, from the celebrated first 1923 coupling, "The Little Old Log Cabin in the Lane"/"The Old Hen Cackled and the Rooster's Going to Crow" to one of Carson's last recordings, about Eugene Talmadge. Carson's music is often dismissed on aesthetic grounds--the fiddling seems rough and scratchy, the singing arhythmic and droll. In truth, Carson's was not first-rate hoedown fiddling, but it was perfectly suited for accompanying his own singing, which was characterized by a beautifully ornate, melismatic style rarely if ever equalled by an American folksinger, let alone by commercially recorded hillbilly singers. Two excellent examples on this disc are "The Bachelor's Hall," a British composition of the late 18th century, and "The Honest Farmer," one of several songs he recorded cataloguing the hardships of the rural farmer in the 1920s. Carson's career has been admirably documented by Gene Wiggins in his biography, which the cassette cited above was intended to accompany. [WF 7/75 (Rndr)]

346 Label Name/Number: Camden [RCA] CAL 586
Title: *The Original and Great Carter Family*
Source and Date of Recording: From studio recordings, 1928-30
Date of Publication: 1962
Annotations: None
Selections:
    Diamonds in the Rough
    Forsaken Love
    God Gave Noah the Rainbow Sign
    Grave on the Green Hillside, The
    I'm Thinking Tonight of My Blue Eyes
    Kitty Waltz
    Little Moses
    Lula Walls
    On the Rock Where Moses Stood
    Sweet Fern
    Wabash Cannon Ball
    Wildwood Flower

347   Label Name/Number: Camden CAL 2473
Title: *Lonesome Pine Special*
Artists: The Carter Family
Source and Date of Recording: From studio recordings, 1929-41
Date of Publication: 1971
Annotations: Liner notes by Neil Hickey
Selections:
  Darling Little Joe
  Distant Land To Roam, A
  Engine One Forty-Three [G 3]
  Home by the Sea
  Home in Tennessee
  I Cannot Be Your Sweetheart
  Lonesome Pine Special
  My Little Home in Tennessee
  School House on the Hill, The
  When the Roses Come Again
  You Tied a Love Knot in My Heart
  You're Gonna Be Sorry You Let Me Down

348   Label Name/Number: Camden CAL 2554(e)
Title: *More Golden Gems From the Original Carter Family*
Source and Date of Recording: From studio recordings, 1927-33
Date of Publication: 1972
Annotations: Liner notes by Gary Giddins
Selections:
  Anchored in Love
  Hello, Central! Give Me Heaven
  I Have No One To Love Me (But the Sailor on the Deep Blue Sea) [K 12]
  I Never Will Marry
  I'll Be Home Some Day
  Little Darling, Pal of Mine
  Little Log Cabin by the Sea
  Sunshine in the Shadows
  There's No Hiding Place Down Here
  Will the Roses Bloom in Heaven

349   Label Name/Number: Camden ACL1-0047(e)
Title: *My Old Cottage Home*
Artists: The Carter Family
Source and Date of Recording: From studio recordings, 1927-41
Date of Publication: 1973
Annotations: Liner notes by Johnny Cash
Selections:
  Hill Lone and Gray, A
  Keep on the Firing Line
  My Old Cottage Home
  On the Sea of Galilee
  Poor Little Orphaned Boy
  Sweet As the Flowers in May Time

There'll Be Joy, Joy, Joy
Wondering Boy, The
Worried Man Blues

350   Label Name/Number: Camden ACL1-0501
Title: *The Happiest Days of All*
Artists: The Original Carter Family (Featuring A. P. Carter)
Source and Date of Recording: From studio recordings, 1929-41
Date of Publication: 1974
Selections:
Away out on the Old Saint Sabbath
Cowboy's Wild Song to His Herd
Faded Flowers
Fifty Miles of Elbow Room
Happiest Days of All, The
Mountains of Tennessee, The
No More the Moon Shines on Lorena
Spirit of Love Watches Over Me, The
When the Roses Bloom in Dixieland

351   Label Name/Number: CMH (West Germany) CMH 107
Title: *Old Family Melodies*
Artists: Carter Family
Source and Date of Recording: From commercial 78s, 1928-34
Date of Publication: [1972]
Selections:
Anchored in Love
Bring Back My Blue Eyed Boy to Me
Cyclone of Ryecove
Don't Forget This Song
Faded Coat of Blue
Happiest Days of All
I Have An Aged Mother
I Have No One To Love Me
I'll Be All Smiles Tonight
It'll Aggravate Your Soul
Little Log Hut in the Lane
River of Jordan
Room in Heaven for Me
Sunshine in the Shadows
Sweet As the Flowers in Maytime
We Will March Through the Streets of the City

352   Label Name/Number: CMH CMH 112
Title: *Original and Essential, Vol. 2*
Artists: Carter Family
Source and Date of Recording: From commercial 78s, 1936-38
Date of Publication: [1972]
Selections:
Are You Lonesome Tonight
Bonnie Blue Eyes

Broken Down Tramp
Give Me Your Love and I'll Give You Mine
Goodbye to the Plains
Happy in Prison
Honey in the Rock
In a Little Village Church Yard
In the Shadow of the Pines
Lay My Head Beneath the Rose
Lord, I'm in Your Care
My Honey Lou
Only Girl I Ever Cared About, The
That Last Move for Me
When Silver Threads Are Gold Again
Where the Silvery Colorado Winds Its Way

353a   **Label Name/Number:** CMH CMH 116
Title: *The Carter Family, Vol. 3*
Source and Date of Recording: From commercial 78s, 1935-40
Date of Publication: [1972]
Selections:
Answer to Weeping Willow
Charlie and Nellie
Fate of Dewey Lee, The
Heart That Was Broken
Hold Fast to the Right
Homestead on the Farm
It Is Better Farther On
Meet Me by the Moonlight Alone
My Virginia Rose Is Blooming
You Denied Your Love
You're Nothing More to Me
You've Got To Righten That Wrong
Young Freda Bolt
Your Mother Still Prays for You, Jack

353b   **Label Name/Number:** CMH CMH 118
Title: *The Carter Family, Vol. 4*
Source and Date of Recording: From commercial 78s, 1928-41
Date of Publication: [1972]
Selections:
Are You Tired of Me My Darling
Carter's Blues
Church in the Wildwood
Cowboy's Wild Song to His Herd
Dark and Stormy Weather
Fifty Miles of Elbow Room
Girl on the Greenbriar Shore
Happy Or Lonesome
I Ain't Gonna Work Tomorrow
Lonesome Homesick Blues
Mountains of Tennessee, The

My Heart's Tonight in Texas
Sailor Boy [K 13]
Sow 'em on the Mountain
When the World's on Fire
Why Do You Cry Little Darling?

354   Label Name/Number: Decca DE DL 4404
Title: *A Collection of Favorites By the Carter Family*
Source and Date of Recording: From studio recordings, 1936-38
Date of Publication: [< 1969]
Annotations: Unsigned liner notes
Selections:
   Coal Miner's Blues
   Funny When You Feel That Way
   Hello Stranger
   Jealous Hearted Me
   Little Joe
   My Dixie Darling
   Oh Take Me Back
   Stern Old Bachelor
   Sweet Heaven in My View
   Wayworn Traveler, The
   You Are My Flower
   You've Been a Friend to Me

355   Label Name/Number: Decca DL 4557
Title: *More Favorites By the Carter Family*
Source and Date of Recording: From studio recordings, 1936-38
Date of Publication: [< 1969]
Annotations: Liner notes by Ralph Rinzler
Selections:
   Bring Back My Boy
   Cuban Soldier
   Jim Blake's Message
   Just Another Broken Heart
   My Home's across the Blue Ridge Mountains
   My Native Home
   Never Let the Devil Get the Upper Hand of You [P 35]
   No Depression
   Reckless Motorman
   St. Regious Girl
   Walking in the King's Highway
   You Better Let That Liar Alone

356   Label Name/Number: Harmony HL 7280/HS 11332
Title: *The Famous Carter Family*
Source and Date of Recording: From studio recordings, 1935
Date of Publication: [ca. 1962]
Selections:
   Can the Circle Be Unbroken
   Gathering Flowers

Gospel Ship
Keep on the Sunny Side
Little Darling Pal of Mine
Lonesome Valley
Lulu Walls
My Clinch Mountain Home
Wildwood Flower
Worried Man Blues

357 Label Name/Number: Harmony HL 7300
Title: *Great Original Recordings By the Carter Family*
Source and Date of Recording: From studio recordings, 1940
Date of Publication: [1963]
Selections:
Bear Creek Blues
Buddies in the Saddle
Dying Mother, The
Give Him One More As He Goes
Heaven's Radio
I Found You Among the Roses
It's a Long, Long Road To Travel Alone
Kissing Is a Crime
Meeting in the Air
Sea of Galilee

358 Label Name/Number: Harmony HL 7344
Title: *Home Among the Hills*
Artists: The Carter Family
Source and Date of Recording: From studio recordings, 1935-40
Date of Publication: [ca. 1964]
Selections:
Broken Hearted Lover
He Took a White Rose from Her Hair [G 19]
I'll Never Forsake You
Little Poplar Log House on the Hill
My Home Among the Hills
My Old Virginia Home
My Texas Girl
No Other's Bride I'll Be
Sad and Lonesome Day
We Shall Rise

359 Label Name/Number: Harmony HL 7396
Title: *Great Sacred Songs*
Artists: The Original Carter Family
Source and Date of Recording: From studio recordings, 1935-40
Date of Publication: [ca. 1966]
Selections:
Beautiful Home
Beautiful Isle o'er the Sea
Glory to the Lamb

God Gave Noah the Rainbow Sign
Little Black Train, The
Look Away from the Ocean
On the Rock Where Moses Stood
River of Jordan
Storms Are on the Ocean, The
There'll Be No Distinction There

360   Label Name/Number: Harmony HL 7422
Title: *Country Sounds of the Original Carter Family*
Source and Date of Recording: From studio recordings, 1935-40
Date of Publication: [ca. 1967]
Selections:
   Behind Those Stone Walls
   Black Jack David [C. 200]
   By the Touch of Her Hand
   Cannon Ball Blues
   Don't Forget Me Little Darling
   East Virginia Blues No. 2
   I'm Thinking Tonight of My Blue Eyes
   Lonesome for You Darling
   Sinking in the Lonesome Sea [C. 286]
   Will You Miss Me When I'm Gone

361   Label Name/Number: John Edwards Memorial Foundation JEMF 101
Title: *The Carter Family on Border Radio 1938-1942*
Editor: William Koon
Source and Date of Recording: Electrical transcriptions, Del Rio, TX
Date of Publication: 1973
Annotations: Brochure by Archie Green, William Koon, and Norm Cohen
Selections:
   Alabama Gals
   Bonnie Blue Eyes
   Broken Down Tramp
   Broken Engagement
   Chinese Breakdown
   Cyclone of Rye Cove
   Del Rio
   Diamonds in the Rough
   Goin' Back to Texas
   Honey Babe
   I Cannot Be Your Sweetheart
   I Wouldn't Mind Dying
   I'm Sitting on Top of the World
   Just a Few More Days
   Keep on the Sunnyside
   Last Letter, The
   Old Ladies Home
   One Little Word
   Soldier's Sweetheart
   There'll Be Joy, Joy, Joy

What Would You Give in Exchange for Your Soul?
When Our Lord Shall Come Again
Who's That Knocking [M 4]
Why There's a Tear in My Eye

362   Label Name/Number: MCA [Japan] VIM-4012
Title: *The Carter Family*
Producer: Toru Mitsui
Source and Date of Recording: From studio recordings, 1936-38
Date of Publication: 1976
Annotations: Jacket notes by Toru Mitsui
Selections:
Answer to Weeping Willow
Dark Haired True Lover
Farewell Nellie
He Never Came Back
In the Shadow of Clinch Mountain
In the Shadow of the Pines
Just a Few More Days
Little Girl That Played on My Knee
Look How This World Made a Change
Lover's Lane
There's No One Like Mother to Me
They Call Her Mother
When This Evening Sun Goes Down
Who's That Knocking on My Window? [M 4]

363   Label Name/Number: MCA MCAD-10088 [CD]
Title: *The Carter Family: Country Music Hall of Fame Series*
Editor: Bob Pinson
Source and Date of Recording: From studio recordings, 1936-38
Date of Publication: 1991
Annotations: 6 p. enclosed booklet (by Pinson?)
Selections:
Answer to Weeping Willow
Bonnie Blue Eyes
Charlie and Nellie
Coal Miner's Blues
Dark Haired True Lover
Hello Stranger
Hold Fast to the Right
In the Shadow of Clinch Mountain
Just a Few More Days
Lover's Lane
My Dixie Darling
Oh Take Me Back
You Are My Flower
You Denied Your Love
Young Freda Bolt
You're Nothing More to Me

364a   Label Name/Number: Old Homestead OHCS 111
Title: *The Original Carter Family in Texas -- Radio Transcriptions*
Source and Date of Recording: Electrical transcriptions, Del Rio, TX, 1930s-40s
Date of Publication: [1978]
Annotations: Liner notes by Freeman Kitchens
Selections:
  Broken Engagement
  Bury Me Beneath the Willow
  Charlie Brooks
  Cowboy Jack [B 24]
  Cumberland Gap
  Cyclone of Rycove
  Dark Haired True Lover
  God's Gonna Trouble the Waters
  Going back to My Texas Home
  I'm Thinking Tonight of My Blue Eyes
  Keep on the Sunnyside
  Kissing Is a Crime
  Let the Church Roll On
  Maple on the Hill, The
  My Virginia Rose Is Blooming
  Old Lady's Home
  Ole Faithful
  Out on Old Saint Sabbath
  Prisoners Dream, The
  Shortening Bread
  Will the Circle Be Unbroken?
  Will You Miss Me?
  Worried Man Blues

364b   Label Name/Number: Old Homestead OHCS 112
Title: *The Original Carter Family in Texas, Vol. 2--Radio Transcriptions*
Source and Date of Recording: Electrical transcriptions, Del Rio, TX, 1930s-40s
Date of Publication: 1978
Annotations: Liner notes by Ivan M. Tribe
Selections:
  Beautiful Brown Eyes
  Frankie and Johnnie [I 3]
  Give Me Your Love and I'll Give You Mine
  Happiest Days of All
  Hello Stranger
  Homestead on the Farm
  I Cannot Be Your Sweetheart
  I Only Want a Buddy
  I Want To Be Loved
  Just Another Broken Heart
  Keep on the Sunnyside
  No Telephone in Heaven
  Nobody's Darling
  Sinking in the Lonesome Sea [C. 286]
  Something Got Ahold of Me

When the Roses Are Blooming
Winding Stream, The
You Are My Flower
You Denied Your Love

365 Label Name/Number: Old Homestead OHCS 116
Title: *Gospel Songs By the Carter Family in Texas, Vol. 3--Radio Transcriptions*
Source and Date of Recording: Electrical transcriptions, Del Rio, TX, 1930s-40s
Date of Publication: 1978
Annotations: Liner notes by John Morris
Selections:
Anchored in Love
Better Farther On
Death Is Only a Dream
Happy in the Prison
I Have No Loving Mother Now
Just a Few More Days
Keep on the Sunny Side
Kings Highway, The
Lord I'm in Your Care
No One To Welcome Me Home
On a Hill Lone and Gray
On the Sea of Galilee
River of Jordan
Spirit of Love
There's More in Heaven for Me
This Is Like Heaven to Me
Weary Prodigal, The
When the Roll Is Called up Yonder
Will My Mother Know Me There?

366 Label Name/Number: Old Homestead OHCS 117
Title: *The Carter Family, Vol. 4-- Radio Transcriptions*
Source and Date of Recording: Some commercial 78s; mostly electrical transcriptions from Del
   Rio, TX, 1930s
Date of Publication: [1980]
Selections:
Charlie and Nellie
Chinese Breakdown
Coal Miners Blues
Dark and Stormy Weather
Dixie Darling
Don't Forget This Song
Funny When You Feel That Way
God Gave Noah the Rainbow Sign
Gold Watch and Chain
I Have An Aged Mother
I Never Will Marry [K 17]
Oh Death
One Little Word
Orphan Child, The

River of Jordan
Sitting on Top of the World
Soldier's Sweetheart
Sparkling Blue Eyes
Two Sweethearts
Wandering Boy, The

367   Label Name/Number: Old Homestead OHS 90045
Title: *The Original Carter Family from 1936--Radio Transcriptions*
Source and Date of Recording: Electrical transcriptions from New York, 1936
Date of Publication: [1975]
Annotations: Liner notes by Ed Romaniuk
Selections:
Are You Lonesome Tonight?
Cannonball Blues
Distant Land to Roam, A
East Virginia Blues
Happy or Lonesome
I'm Working on a Building
Jealous Hearted Me
Just Another Broken Heart
Keep on the Sunnyside
Kissing Is a Crime
Little Darling Pal of Mine
Lonesome Valley
My Dixie Darling
My Native Home
No Depression in Heaven
Single Girl, Married Girl

368   Label Name/Number: Old Time Classics OTC 6001
Title: *The Carter Family*
Source and Date of Recording: From commercial 78s, 1927-34
Date of Publication: [1979]
Selections:
Amber Tresses
Broken Hearted Lover
Cannonball, The
Chewing Gum
Fond Affection
I'm Working on the Building
Jimmy Brown the News Boy
Lover's Return
On a Hill Lone and Grey
Single Girl, Married Girl
Sun of the Soul
There's Someone A-waitin'
Two Sweethearts
Where Shall I Be?

369   **Label Name/Number:** RCA Victor LPM 2772
Title: *Mid' the Green Fields of Virginia*
Artists: The Carter Family
Producer: Brad McCuen
Source and Date of Recording: From studio recordings, 1927-34
Date of Publication: 1963
Annotations: Liner notes by Archie Green
Selections:
    Bury Me Under the Weeping Willow
    Cowboy Jack [B 24]
    Evening Bells Are Ringing, The
    Foggy Mountain Top
    Homestead on the Farm
    Keep on the Sunny Side
    Longing for Old Virginia
    'Mid the Green Fields of Virginia
    Motherless Children
    My Clinch Mountain Home
    Over the Garden Wall
    Picture on the Wall
    Poor Orphan Child, The
    This Is Like Heaven to Me
    Will You Miss Me When I'm Gone?
    Winding Stream, The

370   **Label Name/Number:** Time Life TLCW-06 [3 LP box set]
Title: *The Carter Family*
Artists: The Original Carter Family (A. P., Sara, and Maybelle Carter); A. P. Sara, Joe, and
    Janette Carter (#); Carter Sisters and Mother Maybelle (*); Sara and Maybelle Carter
    (**); Carlene Carter (***)
Producer: Michael Brooks
Source and Date of recordings: Studio recordings, 1927-1979
Date of Publication: 1982
Annotations: 24 p. booklet by Tony Russell
Selections:
    Bear Creek Blues
    Beautiful Isle o'er the Sea
    Black Jack David
    Blackie's Gunman
    Can the Circle Be Unbroken
    Cannon Ball Blues
    Coal Miner's Blues
    Don't Forget This Song
    East Virginia Blues No. 2
    Fair and Tender Ladies *
    Foggy Mountain Top ***
    God Gave Noah the Rainbow Sign
    Gospel Ship
    Happiest Days of All **
    He Never Came Back
    Hello Stranger

It'll Aggravate Your Soul
Jealous Hearted Me
Keep on the Sunny Side
Kissing Is a Crime
Little Joe
Lonesome Valley
My Dixie Darling
My Home Among the Hills
My Texas Girl
No More Goodbyes **
On the Rock Where Moses Stood
Railroading on the Great Divide #
Sinking in the Lonesome Sea [C. 286]
Storms Are on the Ocean, The
Sun's Gonna Shine in My Back Door *
That's What It's Like To Be Lonesome *
There's a Big Wheel *
Titanic, The #
Wildwood Flower
Will You Miss Me When I'm Gone
Worried Man Blues
You've Been a Friend to Me
You've Got To Righten That Wrong

Cam CAL 586 / Cam CAL 2473 / Cam CAL 2554 / Cam ACL1-0047 / Cam ACL1-501 / CMH 107 / CMH 112 / CMH 116 / CMH 118 / De DL 4404 / De DL 4557 / Har HL 7280 / Har HL 7300 / Har HL 7344 / Har HL 7396 / Har HL 7422 / JEMF 101 / MCA VIM 4012 / MCAD 10088 / OH 111 / OH 112 / OH 116 / OH 117 / OH 90045 / OTC 6001 / RCA LPM 2772 / TW-06: Few hillbilly acts had a greater impact on American country music--or a larger recorded repertoire--than the Carter Family, which originally consisted of A. P. (Alvin Pleasant) Carter (1891-1960), his wife, Sara (neé Dougherty, 1898-1979), and Maybelle (neé Addington, 1909-1978), Sara's cousin and wife of A. P.'s brother Ezra. An exceptional instrumentalist, Maybelle originated the guitar style named after her ("Carter lick"), in which the melody is plucked on the bass strings with the thumb while the other fingers brush rhythmically on the treble strings. Woody Guthrie was one of the many guitarists who used the Carter lick extensively, and through him, Maybelle's style became standard fare among folk revival guitar players in the 1950s and '60s.

The Carters' recording career began in 1927 in Bristol, Tennessee, for the Victor Talking Machine Co.--coincidentally at the same recording session that Jimmie Rodgers waxed his first songs. Their professional career seems to have been the result of A. P.'s determined promotional efforts. Ironically, A. P.'s contribution to the Carters' recordings is rarely audible; Sara and Maybelle did almost all the instrumental accompaniment and lead singing, with A. P. contributing at most choral support. His real role was in repertoire and promotion. He loved the old songs and was always interested in collecting them from friends and visitors as he traveled through the mountains (for many years he made his living as a traveling fruit tree salesman). The Carters recorded together from 1927 to 1941, alternately for Victor, Columbia, and Decca--the major companies of the period. In that interval, they recorded close to three hundred songs--a wide range of religious hymns and gospel pieces, older traditional ballads, one-time Tin Pan Alley sentimental songs, and a few contemporary topical pieces. Several dozen LPs have been reissued from that immense corpus, of which 27 are listed here. Their repertoire is not uniformly strong, but all the albums listed have some items of interest, and none should be dismissed.

Five of the albums listed (OH 111, 112, 116, 117; JEMF 101) are taken not from commercial 78s but from electrical transcriptions--recordings made for use over the radio. These recordings, featuring A. P., Sara, Maybelle, and several of their young children, were made in 1938-41 at Del Rio, Texas, during one of the Carters' many stints at border radio stations XERA, XEG, and XENT. These stations, operating just on the Mexican side of the border, broadcasted 50,000 watt signals that could be heard over a wide area of the U. S. (The stations' high wattage was in deliberate violation of international agreement; it resulted from the Mexican government's perception that the U. S. had pushed through broadcast frequency allocations with contemptuous disregard for the needs of some countries.) A number of country musicians engaged in similar activities. The JEMF album originally was issued with an extensive booklet documenting the Carters' career in Texas and providing extensive song notes and text/tune transcriptions. Also taken from electrical transcriptions is OH 90045 but from ETs made in New York for Associated Program Services.

The Japanese album, VIM-4012, was part of an 11-LP set with the series title, *From the Southeast to the Southwest: 1930's Decca Hillbilly Records*, compiled and annotated by Japanese music critic and Professor of English, Toru Mitsui.

The Time-Life boxed set is the most expansive of those listed above, including three discs and a carefully researched booklet. The selection is a cross section of the Carters' recorded material--primarily from the "original" Carter Family of the 1927-41 period. Four selections are by Maybelle and her daughters, Helen, June, and Anita, who recorded as Carter Sisters and Mother Maybelle; two are by Maybelle and Sara, from 1966; and one is by June's daughter, Carlene Carter, recorded in 1979.   [WF 4/73; 7/75; JAF 296--DKW (CAL 586); JAF 317--DKW (Ha 7396); JAF 338--DKW (CAL 2473); JAF 341--WHJ (JEMF)]

371   **Label Name/Number:** County 524
Title: *Da Costa Woltz's Southern Broadcasters 1927--Ben Jarrell and Frank Jenkins*
Editor: [David Freeman]
Source and Date of Recording: From commercial 78s, 1920s-'30s
Date of Publication: 1972
Annotations: Liner notes by Richard Nevins
Selections:
> Evening Star Waltz
> Home Sweet Home
> John Brown's Dream
> Lonesome Road Blues
> Lost Train Blues
> Merry Girl
> Old Joe Clark
> Richmond Cotillion
> Sweet Sunny South
> Wandering Boy
> When You Ask a Girl To Leave Her Happy Home
> Yellow Rose of Texas

Cty 524:   Features one of the finest stringbands to record during the 1920s. The band's four members were all born in or near Surry County in northwestern North Carolina. The group had one recording session for the Starr Piano Company in 1927 but, evidently for want of any significant response, never recorded again. What was recorded at that one session was a marvelous assortment of fiddle and banjo solos, stringband dance tunes, remnants of the minstrel stage, and late 19th-century sentimental ballads, a dozen of which are included here. All 12 are musically outstanding, but I am particularly drawn to Frank Jenkins' three-finger picking banjo solo, "Home Sweet Home" and Ben Jarrell's vocals on "The Sweet Sunny South" and "Yellow Rose of Texas." Their "Old Joe Clark" may be the best version on record. Nevins' liner notes help to make this an outstanding album in every respect. All that is lacking are details on who plays what on which selections (both Jenkins and Jarrell played both fiddle and banjo). [WF 4/73]

372   Label Name/Number: Old Time Classics OTC 6002
Title: *The Delmore Brothers*
Source and Date of Recording: From commercial 78s, 1940-41
Selections:
> Baby Girl
> Gathering Flowers from the Hillside
> Gospel Cannonball
> I Wonder Where My Darling Is Tonight
> In the Blue Hills of Virginia
> Last Night I Was Your Only Darling
> Make Room in the Lifeboat for Me
> Old Mountain Dew
> Precious Jewel
> Silver Dollar
> There's Trouble on My Mind Today
> Will You Be Lonesome Too?

OTC 6002:   Alton (1908-1964) and Rabon (1916-1952) Delmore were born in north Alabama, Alton in 1908, Rabon in 1916, children of struggling tenant farmers. Their mother sang gospel songs, and her brother not only was an able singer but also taught gospel music. By the time Rabon was scarcely ten years old, the brothers were singing and playing together and made their first recordings in 1931. Between 1933 and 1940, amid their regular radio and live appearances, they recorded extensively for the RCA Bluebird label, often with Arthur Smith adding his fiddle to their smooth harmonies and their own guitar and tenor guitar accompaniment. Between 1945 and 1952 they recorded for the Cincinnati-based King label; secular numbers, often with harmonica and/or electric guitar accompaniment, reflected considerable rockabilly influence, but their gospel numbers, recorded pseudonymously as by the Brown's Ferry Four, were in the older, acoustic style, and are still considered by many some of the finest recordings in the genre. Between the Bluebird and King stints were two sessions for the Decca label, from which the recordings on the OTC album are taken. The Delmores' life has been documented in Alton Delmore's autobiography, edited and supplemented by Charles K. Wolfe, *Truth Is Stranger Than Publicity* (Nashville: Country Music Foundation Press, 1977).

373   Label Name/Number: Country Turtle 6000
Title: *Beyond Black Smoke*
Artists: The Dixon Brothers
Source and Date of Recording: From commercial 78s, 1930s
Date of Publication: [1978]
Annotations: Liner notes by Pat Conte
Selections:
> Always Be Waiting for You
> Beautiful Stars
> Beyond Black Smoke
> Bootlegger's Story, The
> Dark Eyes
> Easter Day
> Girl I Left in Danville [H 2]
> How Can a Broke Man Be Happy?

I Can't Tell Why I Love You
I Didn't Hear Anybody Pray
Jimmie and Sallie
More Pretty Girls Than One, Part 3
Weave Room Blues
Wonderful Day, A

374   Label Name/Number: Country Turtle 6002
Title: *Rambling and Gambling*
Artists: Dorsey Dixon, Howard Dixon, Beatrice Dixon, Mutt Evans
Source and Date of Recording: From commercial 78s, 1936-38
Date of Publication: [1987]
Annotations: Liner notes by Pat Conte
Selections: [All by Dorsey and Howard Dixon except as noted]
Fisherman's Luck
Have Courage To Only Say No
Hobo Jack the Rambler
Old Home Brew, The
Prisoner's Plea -- Rambling Duet (Howard Dixon and Mutt Evans)
Rambling Gambler
Satisfied at Last -- Dorsey & Beatrice Dixon
She Tickled Me
Shining City Over the River -- Dorsey & Beatrice Dixon
There's a Place in My Home for Mother -- Rambling Duet
Two Little Boys
Two Little Rosebuds
Where I Shall Be -- Dorsey & Beatrice Dixon
Wonder Who's Kissing Her Now, Pt. 2 -- Rambling Duet

CT 6000 / 6002: The Dixon Brothers, Dorsey and Howard, from South Carolina, were "rediscovered" in the 1960s and re-recorded, so that their careers have been well documented. The key figure in this group was Dorsey Dixon, born in 1897 in the mill town of Darlington. Throughout their career on records they both played guitar--Dorsey, Spanish style, and Howard, slide style. Their repertoire, though including a large store of older traditional material, was distinguished by Dorsey's own compositions, the most famous of which was "I Didn't Hear Anybody Pray," later recorded by Roy Acuff under the title, "Wreck on the Highway." Other important pieces of theirs were the several textile mill songs (in particular, "Weave Room Blues," "Spinning Room Blues," and "Weaver's Life") that Dorsey wrote or recomposed out of older traditional material. More extensive biographical information was provided in the liner notes to Testament T-3301, discussed in Part I. "Bootlegger's Story" is based directly on "Meet Me By Moonlight Alone," and not, as stated in the liner notes, on the Darby & Tarlton song, "Roy Dixon," which itself uses the tune of the latter piece also. "Beyond Black Smoke," a fine composition that uses railroad imagery in a religious context, is to the tune of "Girl I Left in Danville." "I Can't Tell Why I Love You" was a 1900 pop song written by Gus Edwards and Will D. Cobb. I would question the speculation that "Jimmie and Sallie" is based on "Poor Ellen Smith." Its plot certainly is elusive, as is its relation to any other texts, but it does not seem to be a murder ballad. CT 6002, with very good liner notes by Pat Conte, includes three duets by Dorsey and his wife, Beatrice, who recorded a few religious numbers together; and four numbers by the Rambling Duet. [JEMFQ 54]

375   Label Name/Number: Old Homestead OHCS 191
Title: *Dykes "Magic City" Trio: String Band Classics, Vol. 1*

Source and Date of Recording: From commercial 78s, 1927
Date of Publication: [1987]
Annotations: Liner notes by Charles Wolfe
Selections:
  Callahan's Reel
  Cotton Eyed Joe
  Far Beyond the Blue Skies
  Frankie [I 3]
  Free a Little Bird
  Golden Slippers
  Hook and Line
  Huckleberry Blues
  Ida Red
  Poor Ellen Smith [F 11]
  Red Steer
  Shortening Bread
  Tennessee Girl
  Twilight Is Stealing

   OHCS 191: It is surprising that fiddler John Dykes and his "Magic City" trio had been bypassed in the hillbilly reissue programs for so long; only one of the band's 14 recordings ("Free a Little Bird") had appeared on LP prior to this 1987 release, which includes their complete recorded output. Born in upper east Tennessee in about 1882 (according to Charles Wolfe's liner notes), Dykes was well respected as a square dance fiddler in the mining communities of Wise County, Virginia, by the 1920s. Unable to get work in the mines, he moved to Kingsport, Tennessee, then called "Magic City" by one promotor. He formed the trio with two younger musicians, G. H. "Hub" Mahaffey, guitar/vocals, and Myrtle Vermillion, autoharp, in 1925, and the group recorded for the Brunswick Company in March, 1927. The selections included two traditional ballads, "Frankie" [Laws I 3] (though Brunswick executives identified the song as the Leighton Brothers' vaudeville hit of 1912, it clearly is an older version) and "Poor Ellen Smith" [F 11]; two gospel songs (I don't count "Golden Slippers," which has been rendered almost secular in lyrics); and a handful of fiddle tunes, many with dance calls. Wolfe's liner notes identify the selections, give biographical background (based on interviews with relatives), and comment on musical styles. These are strong selections and a worthwhile reissue all in all. [JAF 406]

   376   Label Name/Number: County 410
   Title: *The East Texas Serenaders*
   Editor: [David Freeman]
   Source and Date of Recording: From commercial 78s, 1927-37
   Date of Publication: [1978]
   Annotations: Liner notes by Nancy Bredenberg
   Selections:
     Acorn Stomp
     Adeline Waltz
     Arizona Stomp
     Babe
     Beaumont Rag
     Combination Rag
     Deacon Jones
     East Texas Drag
     Mineola Rag

    Ozark Rag
    Serenaders Waltz
    Shannon Waltz
    Sweetest Flower Waltz
    Three-in-One Two-Step

      Cty 410:   The East Texas Serenaders were a stringband that straddled the two separate stylistic worlds of the southeast and the southwest, and borrowed heavily from ragtime and Tin Pan Alley for their tune repertoire. The band regularly consisted of Cloet Hamman (guitar) and D. H. Williams (fiddle), both from near Lindale, Texas; and Henry Bogan (cello). John Munnerlyn played tenor banjo on the 1927-30 sessions, and for the 1936-37 recordings, Henry Lester played second fiddle and Shorty Lester, banjo. Their unusual instrumental line-up clearly set them apart from southeastern bands and pretty much put them in a class by themselves. Their deft handling of lively raggy tunes, several of which they composed themselves, helped to launch a new musical style that contributed to the early beginnings of western swing music.

377   **Label Name/Number:** Rounder 1032
Title: *The Moonshine Hollow Band*
Artists: The Georgia Yellow Hammers
Source and Date of Recording: From commercial 78s, 1924-29
Date of Publication: 1979
Annotations: Notes by Charles Wolfe
Selections:
    Black Annie
    Fourth of July at a Country Fair
    G Rag
    I'm S-A-V-E-D
    Johnson's Old Grey Mule
    Moonshine Hollow Band, The
    Old Rock Jail Behind the Old Iron Gate, The
    Pa, Ma, and Me
    Peaches Down in Georgia
    Picture on the Wall
    Raise Rough House Tonight
    Song of the Doodle Bug
    Tennessee Coon
    Warhorse Game
    When the Birds Begin Their Singing in the Trees
    Whoa, Mule

      Rndr 1032:   Prior to this LP, little had been reissued from this very successful group of musicians from Calhoun and Gordon Counties in North Georgia--Bill Chitwood, Bud Landress, Phil Reeve, and Charles E. Moody. In some respects it was an unlikely foursome: Chitwood and Landress were firmly footed in the old-time stringband tradition, while Moody and Reeve also recorded extensively in a sacred music genre--under their own names or in the Calhoun Sacred Quartet, the Gordon County Quartet, the Moody Bible Sacred Singers, or as the Charles Brothers. This LP stays clear of such pieces, but stylistically the sentimental pop songs, or the parody "I'm S-A-V-E-D" are similar. The Yellowhammers did many of the same songs that other coeval North Georgia bands, such as the Skillet Lickers, or Earl Johnson's groups, recorded; yet occasionally, when they indulged in four-part harmony vocals, their sound was practically unique. Their repertoire ranged from old fiddle/banjo tunes, such as the 1924 duet, "Whoa, Mule," to original compositions (Landress's "The Old Rock Jail...," Moody's "Song of the Doodle Bug" and the title song) to reworked pop songs (Kerry Mills's "At a Georgia Camp Meeting" becomes "Peaches Down in Georgia," and Shepard Edmonds's "I'm Goin' to Live Anyhow 'Till I Die" becomes "Tennessee Coon"). Of the Yellowhammers's most successful hit, "Picture on the Wall," it should be noted that evidence is now pretty convincing that Landress wrote it. The issue has been clouded by two 19th-century songs of the same title by Henry C. Work and J. P. Skelley and by a later copyright credit (on record labels) to Carson Robison and Frank Luther. Other nonce titles disguise familiar pieces: "Raise Rough House Tonight" is "Raise a Ruckus Tonight," and "Warhorse Game" is "Old Hen Cackled." "G Rag" is interesting for the inclusion of black fiddler Andrew Baxter on the lead-- one of the very few examples of an integrated old-time stringband on records. [JEMFQ 62]

378 Label Name/Number: Sonyatone STR 202
Title: *The Girls of the Golden West*
Editor: Peter Feldmann
Source and Date of Recording: From commercial 78s, 1933-38
Date of Publication: 1978
Annotations: Notes by Peter Feldmann
Selections:
    Buckin' Broncho
    Cowboy Jack [B 24]
    Cowgirl's Dream, The
    Empty Cot in the Bunkhouse
    Going back to Mississippi
    Hi Yo, Hi Yo
    I Want To Be a Real Cowboy Girl
    Little Old Log Cabin in the Lane
    My Cross-Eyed Beau
    My Dear Old Arizona Home
    Old Chisholm Trail
    Roll Along Prairie Moon
    That Silver-Haired Daddy of Mine
    We'll Meet at the End of the Trail
    Whoopie Ti Yi Yo
    Will There Be Any Yodelers in Heaven?

      Sonyatone STR 202: One of the sweetest-sounding teams of the 1930s was the Girls of the Golden West; I think of them almost as female counterparts of the Delmore Brothers in their soft, smooth harmonies; though without the bluesy sound and hard drive that the Delmores still managed to incorporate into their style. The sisters, Millie (b. 1913) and Dolly (1913-1967) Good, recorded over five dozen selections betwen 1933 and 1938, the majority of which dealt with western themes. This important portion of their repertoire is well represented on this reissue LP. The Goods came by their songs honestly: born in Muleshoe, Texas, they grew up listening to south-western cowboy songs. Their professional career began on radio station WIL in St. Louis, when Dolly was only 14 years old. More radio work followed, until 1933, when they became regulars on WLS Chicago's National Barn Dance. Although they stopped making 78s in 1938, in the 1960s they were recording again. Their songs were divided between older traditional cowboy and western numbers and contemporary songs composed in the 1930s, many for the cowboy movies. [JEMFQ 55]

379 Label Name/Number: County 513
Title: *Grayson and Whitter*

Artists: G. B. Grayson and Henry Whitter
Editor: [David Freeman]
Source and Date of Recording: From commercial 78s, 1927-30
Date of Publication: [1968]
Annotations: Liner notes by Joe Wilson [on 2nd printing]
Selections:
    Dark Road Is a Hard Road to Travel
    Don't Go Out Tonight My Darling
    Handsome Molly
    He Is Coming to Us Dead
    I Saw a Man at the Close of the Day
    I've Always Been a Rambler [P 1b]
    Joking Henry
    Nine Pound Hammer
    Ommie Wise [F 4]
    Short Life of Trouble
    What You Gonna Do with the Baby?
    Where Are You Going Alice? [cf. N 40]

380 Label Name/Number: Davis Unlimited DU 33033
Title: *Going Down Lee Highway*
Artists: Grayson and Whitter
Source and Date of Recording: From commercial 78s, 1927-29
Date of Publication: 1977
Annotations: Liner notes by Frank Mare and Joe Wilson
Selections:
    Cluck Old Hen
    Going down the Lee Highway
    Handsome Molly
    I Have Lost You Darling, True Love
    My Mind Is To Marry
    Nobody's Darling
    Old Jimmy Sutton
    On the Banks of Old Tennessee
    Red and Green Signal Lights
    Sally Gooden
    Shout Lula
    Sweet Rosie O'Grady
    Tom Dooley [F 36]
    Train No. 45

381 Label Name/Number: Old Homestead OHCS-157
Title: *Early Classics, Vol. 1*
Artists: G. B. Grayson & Henry Whitter
Source and Date of Recording: From commercial 78s, 1927-29
Date of Publication: 1984
Annotations: Liner notes by Charles Wolfe
Selections:
    Barnyard Serenade
    I Have Lost You Darling True Love
    Lee Highway Blues

Little Maggie
My Mind Is To Marry
Never Be As Fast [As I Have Been]
On the Banks of the Old Tennessee
Red and Green Signal Lights
Rose Conley [F 6]
Tom Dooley [F 36]
Train 45
You'll Never Miss Your Mother

Cty 513 / DU 33033 / OH 157: Henry Whitter (1892-1941), singer, guitarist, harmonica player from the Fries, Virginia, area, was in 1923 one of the first rural musicians to make phono records. Whitter's influence in the very early years of hillbilly recordings was, strangely enough, due to his mediocrity: many musicians who heard his first few discs made in 1923 felt that they could do better and determined to make recordings themselves. Whitter's career took a distinct turn for the better when he met G. B. Grayson, a blind fiddler-singer from Laurel Bloomery, Tenn, at a 1927 fiddler's convention in Mountain City, Tennessee. Grayson (1887?-1930) was only five years Whitter's senior, but musically he represented an earlier generation--not only in repertoire, but also in singing style and instrumentation. Whitter, who had already recorded several times for OKeh, arranged recording sessions for himself and Grayson first for the Starr Piano Co. of Richmond, Indiana, owners of the Gennett and subsidiary labels; and then for the Victor Talking Machine Company. In the next two years the team recorded some 40 selections--not a huge number, but an important repertoire nonetheless, and one that influenced not only other southeastern musicians during the 1930s but also early bluegrass musicians in the 1950s and then urban folk song revival singers in the 1960s and '70s. When Whitter's early solo discs, on which he accompanied his own singing with guitar and harmonica, are compared with the recordings he made with blind fiddler Grayson, one can only conclude that the high musical quality of the duets was entirely due to the remarkable musicianship of Grayson himself. His beautiful, archaic fiddling and singing exemplify what is perhaps the earliest native American technique of adding instrumental accompaniment to ballad singing. However, his importance in the larger view of the commercial hillbilly tradition lies in the number of songs he himself contributed to tradition. The songs thus represent Grayson's own repertoire. Both as a singer and as a fiddler he was a great performer.

The duo's presentations were uniformly characterized by Grayson's haunting fiddling and penetrating vocals accompanied competently by Whitter's guitar work--with occasional folksy spoken interjections. Whitter, as guitar accompanist, ranged from adequate to very good, being weakest on some of the modal tunes that he was unable to chord appropriately. Understandably, these recordings found their way into the repertoires of many folk revival artists in the 1960s and later; but it should not be forgotten that even while they were still fresh, G&W discs were being bought and used as source material by the Mainer Brothers of North Carolina, the Monroe Brothers of Kentucky, and other hillbilly artists. It is sobering to recall this fact when contemplating arguments that recordings tamper with, or distort, folk tradition. Grayson--at least, on record--was not a "fiddler's fiddler;" compare his "Sally Gooden" with the classic recording by Eck Robertson. But as an accompaniment to his singing, his fiddling was without peer.

Cty 513 contains such standards as "Handsome Molly" (most American recordings of which are traceable to this source), "Short Life of Trouble," "Nine Pound Hammer," and "Ommie Wise." "Where Are You Going, Alice?" is a fragmentary ballad on the returned lover disguised theme, although too little of the narrative remains to permit ready identification. "I Saw a Man..." is a typical turn-of-the-century temperance song. "He Is Coming to Us Dead" is an anti-war song (or so it seems today) from the [Civil?] War that has entered tradition. The first edition of this LP contained no liner notes; it was subsequently reissued with notes by Joe Wilson.

OH 157 includes 12 selections, 3 from Gennett and the others from Victor. "My Mind is to Marry" was never issued on 78s but survived in the Whitter family as a test pressing. Wolfe's jacket liner notes stress the importance of these musicians and summarize biographical details, which in the case of Grayson were, until very recently, woefully sparse. [JAF 323, 394; JEMFQ 55]

382a   Label Name/Number: Bear Family [West Germany] BF 15508
Title: *The Complete Kelly Harrell, Vol. 1*
Editor: Richard Weize
Source and Date of Recording: From commercial 78s, 1925-29
Date of Publication: [1975]
Annotations: Brochure by Richard Weize
Selections:
>Be at Home Soon Tonight
>Blue Eyed Ella [F 1a]
>Butcher's Boy [P 24] (2)
>I Was Born About 10,000 Years Ago
>I Was Born in Pennsylvania [E 15]
>I Wish I Was a Single Girl Again (2)
>I'm Going Back to North Carolina
>New River Train (2)
>Peg and Awl
>Rovin' Gambler [H 4] (2)
>Wild Bill Jones [E 10]
>Wreck on the Southern Old 97 [G 2]

382b   Label Name/Number: Bear Family [West Germany] BF 15509
Title: *The Complete Kelly Harrell, Vol. 2*
Editor: Richard Weize
Source and Date of Recording: From commercial 78s, 1925-29
Date of Publication: [1975]
Annotations: Brochure by Richard Weize
Selections:
>Beneath the Weeping Willow Tree
>Bright Sherman Valley
>Broken Engagement
>Bye and Bye You Will Soon Forget Me
>Cuckoo She's a Fine Bird, The
>Dying Hobo, The [H 3]
>Hand Me Down My Walking Cane
>Henry Clay Beattie
>I Love My Sweetheart the Best
>I Want a Nice Little Fellow
>My Horses Ain't Hungry
>O! Molly Dear Go Ask Your Mother [M 4]
>Oh My Pretty Monkey

382c   Label Name/Number: Bear Family [West Germany] BF 15510
Title: *The Complete Kelly Harrell, Vol. 3*
Editor: Richard Weize
Source and Date of Recording: From commercial 78s, 1925-29
Date of Publication: [1975]
Annotations: Brochure by Richard Weize
Selections:

All My Sins Are Taken Away
Cave Love Has Gained the Day
Charles Guiteau [E 11]
Charley, He's a Good Old Man
For Seven Long Years I've Been Married
Henpecked Man, The
I Have No Loving Mother Now
I Heard Somebody Call My Name
In the Shadow of the Pine
My Name Is John Johanna [H 1]
My Wife Has Gone and Left Me
Nobody's Darling on Earth
Row Us over the Tide
She Just Kept Kissing On

383   Label Name/Number: County 408
Title: *Kelly Harrell and the Virginia String Band*
Editor: [David Freeman]
Source and Date of Recording: From commercial 78s, 1925-29
Date of Publication: 1975
Annotations: Liner notes by C. Kinney Rorrer
Selections:
Cave Love Has Gained the Day
Charles Giteau
Charley He's a Good Old Man
For Seven Long Years I've Been Married
Henpecked Man, The
Henry Clay Beattie
I Have No Loving Mother Now
I'm Nobody's Darling on Earth
In the Shadow of the Pine
My Name Is John Johanna [H 1]
My Wife, She Has Gone and Left Me
Row Us over the Tide

BF 15508/ BF 15509/ BF 15510 / Cty 408: The Bear Family set includes all 43 recordings made by Crockett Kelly Harrell (1889-1942) of Wythe County, Virginia--a textile mill worker for most of his life who was also interested in traditional and then-contemporary country music. He played no instruments but was a good singer and had a good repertoire; he also wrote a few pieces, including "Away out on the Mountain," recorded by Jimmie Rodgers. His earliest recordings for Victor in 1925-26 were with accompaniment by unknown studio guitar and violin--possibly Carson Robison and Murray Kellner. In 1925 for OKeh records he was accompanied by long-time friend Henry Whitter. In 1927 he was accompanied by Alfred Steagal on guitar, Posey Rorer (or Lonnie Austin) on fiddle, and Raymond Hundley, banjo. On the last session, Roy Smeck, harmonica and jews harp, and Sam Freed, fiddle, joined Harrell and Steagal. As C. Kinney Rorrer observes in his liner notes to the County album, Steagal's fine guitar picking, Hundley's 3-finger banjo picking, and Rorer's fiddling created a sound reminiscent of Charlie Poole's No. Carolina Ramblers, though Harrell eschewed the bluesy and raggy tunes that Poole favored, and his singing was somewhat more distinct. Harrell's recorded repertoire was not unusual for early hillbilly recording artists, though the proportion of traditional native and imported folk ballads was quite large. "Henry Clay Beattie" is a relatively rare local ballad about a Virginia murder of 1911 that was at one time dubbed "the crime of the century." Harrell's version of "Old 97" is a fine, long text, and a rare recording, being issued on one of the few 12" hillbilly records of the 1920s. Steagal's guitar accompaniment on "Henpecked Man," an uncommon song on an over-worked topic, is particularly fine. "Wild Bill Jones" is musically unusual because (1) Harrell sings it entirely in the major scale and (2) Whitter accompanies it in the fifth of the scale (doubtless thrown off by Harrell's uncommon choice of mode). Harrell's "Dying Hobo" is only partly the hobo song and principally stanzas from "George Collins" (C. 85). "My Horses Ain't Hungry" is better known as "The Wagoner's Lad," and "Bye and Bye You Will Soon Forget Me" is a variant of "Fond Affection" ("Dear Companion"). Other titles provide no surprises--except for "Cave Love," which seems to have been a scribal error on the original issue for "[Be]ca'se Love Has Gained the Day." The County LP is a good sampler. [JEMFQ 42]

384   Label Name/Number: County 405
Title: *The Hillbillies*
Editor: [David Freeman]
Source and Date of Recording: From commercial 78s, 1925-32
Date of Publication: 1974
Annotations: Liner notes and 4 p. brochure by Joe Wilson
Selections:
    Black Eyed Susie
    Bristol Tennessee Blues
    C. C. and O Number 558
    Cindy
    Cluck Old Hen
    Fisher's Hornpipe
    Johnson Boys
    Round Town Gals
    Sally Ann
    Silly Bill
    Soldier's Joy Medley   [Soldier's Joy, If You Want To Go Courtin', Shoot That Turkey
      Buzzard]
    Texas Gals

Cty 405: Al Hopkins' Galax-based band of the 1920s, the Hill Billies, gave their name to the new genre of music (new, at least, on phonograph records), yet none of their music had been reissued prior to this LP. A dozen selections from their OKeh and Brunswick/Vocalion recordings are reissued, with a brochure by Wilson that sketches in some biographical details. As Wilson notes, the band's personnel varied. Most of their recordings featured Hopkins' vocal; Charlie Bowman and Tony Alderman, fiddles; and, initially, John Rector on banjo. (This Rector is not the same John Rector of Galax who recorded on fiddle for Library of Congress field sessions in the 1930s; see, for example, AFS L62). Rector had recorded in 1924 with Henry Whitter's Virginia Breakdowners but was dissatisfied with the results and wanted to put together another band. He took Hopkins and Alderman to New York in the summer of 1924 for the first recordings of what was to become "The Hill Billies." (The band had been christened by A&R man Ralph Peer when they responded to his query of the group's name with, "we're nothing but a bunch of hillbillies.") A promising career was cut short when Hopkins, the band's able promoter, was killed in an automobile accident in 1932. The selections on this LP are mostly familiar fiddle tunes; like other Galax musicians, the Hill Billies were less influenced by blues and jazz music than artists from other areas. "Bristol Tennessee Blues," a fiddle/flat-pick guitar duet, is the outstanding exception on the LP to this generalization. [WF 7/75]

385   Label Name/Number: County 409
Title: *Lake Howard*
Editor: [David Freeman]
Source and Date of Recording: From commercial 78s, 1934-35
Date of Publication: 1977
Annotations: Liner notes by Ruth Howard Hughes
Selections:
  Chewing Gum
  Duplin County Blues
  Forsaken Love
  Grey Eagle
  I've Lost My Love
  It's None of Your Business
  Little Annie
  Love Me Darling, Love Me
  Lover's Farewell
  New Chattanooga Mama
  Streamline Mama
  Walking in the Light
  Within My Father's House

Cty 409:   Lake Howard (1913-54) of Greensboro, North Carolina, was one of many country music performers of the 1930s who was heavily influenced by the Carter Family, both in repertoire and in instrumental style. What is interesting about his guitar style, however, is that it is every bit as driving, if not more so, than Maybelle Carter's. This album, the first reissue of Howard's music, includes 13 of the 20 sides of his that were issued in the mid-'30s. While the Carter influence is evident in "Lover's Farewell," "Forsaken Love," and "Within My Father's House" ["There'll Be Joy, Joy, Joy"], Howard was adept at other styles as well: "New Chattanooga Mama," a reworking of the Allen Brothers' number, "Streamlined Mama," is a white blues in the style of Jimmie Rodgers or Cliff Carlisle. Other titles are perhaps deceiving: "I've Lost My Love" is a variant of "Careless Love," and "Duplin County Blues" is an instrumental version of "I Don't Love Nobody," with lead fiddle by Roland Cauley. "Chewing Gum" is neither the Carter Family nor Macon song on the same subject; possibly it is Howard's own composition. [JEMFQ 50]

386   Label Name/Number: Rounder 1007
Title: *The Train That Carried My Girl from Town*
Artist: Frank Hutchison
Source and Date of Recording: From commercial 78s, 1927-29
Date of Publication: [1974]
Annotations: Jacket notes by Mark Wilson
Selections:
  All Night Long
  C. and O. Excursion Train
  Chevrolet Six, The
  Coney Isle
  Hell Bound Train
  Hutchison's Rag
  Johnny and Jane, Parts 1 and 2
  K. C. Blues
  Last Scene of the Titanic, The [D 24?]
  Miner's Blues, The

Old Rachel
Railroad Bill [I 13]
Train That Carried the Girl from Town, The
Wild Hogs in the Red Brush
Worried Blues

Rndr 1007: Frank Hutchison's 78s have long been highly prized among collectors; musically he was one of the most interesting of early hillbilly guitarists to record, of whom little was known for some time. This LP is an admirable package of 16 selections recorded between 1927 and 1929, together with informative notes by Wilson that give some biographic data to relate to the music. Born in Logan County, West Virginia, Hutchison (1897-1945) was apparently heavily influenced by a black guitarist in his youth, both in style and repertoire. Many of the selections of this LP seem to come from black tradition: the familiar "Railroad Bill" and the less familiar blues ballads, "Old Rachel" and "Johnny and Jane"; the blues-structured "The Miner's Blues" and "Worried Blues"; and the celebrated "Train That Carried the Girl from Town," a non-blues relative of the blues piece, "I Wish the Train Would Wreck," recorded by Maynard Britton in 1931. "The Last Scene of the Titanic" is an unusual prose narrative about the maritime disaster unlike other Titanic songs (dozens were written). Hutchison accompanied his singing in a variety of guitar styles, sometimes with striking elegance (e.g., the title song, "Worried Blues," and "Miner's Blues") but at other times with astonishing disregard for rhythmic conventions (e.g., "Railroad Bill"). The notes include transcriptions of the texts (unfortunately, with many errors). [WF 7/75]

387 Label Name/Number: County 543
Title: *Red Hot Breakdown*
Artists: Earl Johnson and His Clodhoppers
Editor: [David Freeman]
Source and Date of Recording: From commercial 78s, 1927
Date of Publication: 1976
Annotations: Liner notes by Donald Lee Nelson
Selections:
Ain't Nobody's Business
Bully of the Town [I 14]
Earl Johnson's Arkansaw Traveller
Hen Cackle
I Get My Whiskey from Rockingham
John Henry Blues [I 1]
Johnson's Old Grey Mule
Leather Breeches
Little Grave in Georgia
Old Grey Mare Kicking out of the Wilderness
Red Hot Breakdown
Shortning Bread

Cty 543: Earl Johnson and His Clodhoppers: Robert Earl Johnson (1886-1965) was born in Gwinnett County, Georgia, son of a renowned old-time fiddler. He formed a band with his brothers that enjoyed some success until both brothers died in 1923. He first recorded with Fiddling John Carson's Virginia Reelers (actually a North Georgia band) but was anxious to form his own group, which he soon did. Known variously as the Clodhoppers or the Dixie Entertainers, the band recorded between 1927 and 1931, probably consisting of Johnson on fiddle/vocals, Emmett Bankston, banjo/vocals, and Byrd Moore and Lee Henderson, guitars. Johnson was an exuberant fiddler and singer, who brought an infectious enthusiasm to his recorded performances. This album samples the band's first year's recordings, which some consider its best. Most of the pieces are dance tunes; "Little Grave in Georgia" is a topical ballad about the Mary Phagan murder of 1915.

388   Label Name/Number: County 536
Title: *The Kessinger Brothers*
Editor: [David Freeman]
Source and Date of Recording: From commercial 78s, 1928-30
Date of Publication: 1975
Annotations: Liner notes by Nancy Dols
Selections:
>   Everybody to the Puncheon
>   Garfield March
>   Gippy Get Your Hair Cut
>   Going up Brushy Fork
>   Josh and I
>   Kanawha County Rag
>   Little Betty Brown
>   Old Jake Gillie
>   Rat Cheese Under the Hill
>   Shoo Fly
>   Sixteen Days in Georgia
>   West Virginia Special

389   Label Name/Number: Kanawha 600
Title: *Original Fiddle Classics 1928-1930*
Artists: The Kessinger Brothers
Source and Date of Recording: From commercial 78s, 1928-30
Date of Publication: 1969
Annotations: Liner notes by Bob Kessinger
Selections:
>   Boarding House Bells Are Ringing Waltz
>   Don't Let Your Deal Go Down
>   Forked Deer
>   Garfield March
>   Going up Brushy Fork
>   Goodnight Waltz
>   Mexican Waltz
>   Midnight Waltz
>   Mississippi Sawyer
>   Sixteen Days in Georgia
>   Sopping the Gravy
>   Turkey in the Straw

Cty 536 / Kan 600: As Dols points out in her liner notes to the County LP, West Virginian Clark Kessinger (1896-1975) was a relatively modern old-time fiddler in the 1920s, with considerably more flashy technique and polish than many of his contemporaries. When he was "rediscovered" in 1964, it was found that, at the age of 68, his playing was more brilliant than it had been in the '20s, and he enjoyed another seven years of popularity and acclaim before a serious stroke put an end to his playing. The liner notes give biographical information as well as tune annotations and comment on Kessinger's technique. [WF 7/75]

390   Label Name/Number: Old Homestead OHCS 107
Title: *Mountain Ballads and Old-Time Songs*
Artist: Bradley Kincaid
Source and Date of Recording: From commercial 78s, 1927-34
Date of Publication: 1976
Annotations: Liner notes by Jay Taylor
Selections:
> After the Ball
> Ain't We Crazy
> Barbara Allen [C. 84]
> Blind Child, The
> Down by the Railroad Track
> Fatal Wedding, The
> Four Thousand Years Ago
> Give My Love to Nell
> Gooseberry Pie
> Little Shirt My Mother Made for Me, The
> Liza up a Simmon Tree
> My Mother's Beautiful Hands
> Picture from Life's Other Side
> Some Little Bug Is Goin' To Get You Some Day
> Somebody's Waiting for You
> Two Little Girls in Blue, The

OHCS 107: For biographical notes on Bradley Kincaid, see comments on his four releases (OHCS-314/15/16/17) in Section I. This album is a good sampling from Kincaid's extensive recording career on commercial 78s from 1927 to 1934. Kincaid actively added to the songs he had learned from his family with compositions radio listeners sent him or that he found in published collections. Kincaid sang in a sweet tenor voice that was easy to understand because of his lack of any regional speech characteristics. He always accompanied himself on guitar. The large number of his recordings, made for several different companies (often with considerable duplication of titles) attests to his popularity at that time.

391   Label Name/Number: County 532
Title: *The Leake County Revelers*
Editor: [David Freeman]
Source and Date of Recording: From commercial 78s, 1927-30
Date of Publication: 1975
Selections:
> Dry Town Blues
> Georgia Camp Meeting
> Good Fellow
> I'm Gwine Back to Dixie
> Leather Breeches
> Lonesome Blues
> Mississippi Breakdown
> Monkey in the Dog Cart
> Old Hat, The
> Saturday Night Breakdown
> Sweet Rose of Heaven
> Wednesday Night Waltz

Cty 532: This popular Mississippi stringband consisted of Will Gilmer, fiddle; R. O. Mosley, mandolin; Dallas Jones, guitar; and Jim Wolverton, banjo. Lead was taken by either the fiddle or mandolin, with the other instruments providing rhythm back-up. The few numbers with vocals were not musically enhanced by the singing. [WF 7/75]

392   Label Name/Number: Bear Family [West Germany] BF 15503 (Same as Folk Variety 12503)
Title: *The Gayest Old Dude in Town*
Artist: Uncle Dave Macon
Editor: Richard Weize
Source and Date of Recording: From commercial 78s, 1920s-'30s
Date of Publication: [1974?]
Annotations: Liner notes by Mike Paris
Selections:
    Bake That Chicken Pie
    Gayest Old Dude in Town, The
    He's up with the Angels Now
    Hop High Ladies, the Cake's All Dough
    Keep My Skillet Good and Greasy
    Life and Death of Jesse James [E 1]
    Man Who Rode the Mule Around the World, The
    Molly Married a Travelin' Man
    Peek a Boo
    Poor Old Dad
    Since Baby's Learned To Talk
    Summertime on the Beeno Line
    Travelin' Down the Road
    Uncle Dave's Travels, Parts 1-4

393   Label Name/Number: Bear Family [West Germany] BF 15518
Title: *First Row, Second Left*
Artist: Uncle Dave Macon
Source and Date of Recording: From commercial 78s, 1920s-'30s
Date of Publication: [1975?]
Annotations: Insert with text transcriptions by Willard Johnson and Robert Nobley
Selections:
    Ain't It a Shame To Keep Your Honey out in the Rain
    Are You Washed in the Blood of the Lamb
    Bear Me Away on Your Snowy Wings
    Deliverance Will Come
    Diamond in the Rough
    For Goodness Sakes Don't Say I Told You
    Hush Little Baby Don't You Cry
    I Ain't Got Long To Stay
    Maple on the Hill
    Over the Mountain
    Put Me in My Little Bed
    Sassy Sam
    Stop That Knocking At My Door
    Them Two Gals of Mine

    Uncle Dave's Beloved Banjo
    We Are up against It Now

394 Label Name/Number: Bear Family [West Germany] BF 15519
Title: *Fun in Life*
Artist: Uncle Dave Macon
Source and Date of Recording: From commercial 78s, 1920s-'30s
Date of Publication: [1975?]
Annotations: Insert with text transcriptions by Willard Johnson and Robert Nobley
Selections:
    All Go Hungry Hash House
    Give Me Back My Five Dollars
    He Won the Heart of My Sarah Jane
    I'll Tickle Nancy
    Keeping My Skillet Good and Greasy
    Old Dan Tucker
    Only As Far As the Gate Dear Ma
    Railroading and Gamblin'
    Save My Mother's Picture from the Sale
    Sho' Fly Don't (You) Bother Me
    They're After Me
    Things I Don't Like To See
    Walk, Tom Wilson, Walk
    Watermelon Hanging on the Vine
    When the Harvest Days Are Over (with the Delmore Brothers)
    Working for My Lord

395 Label Name/Number: County 521
Title: *The Recordings of Uncle Dave Macon*
Editor: [David Freeman]
Source and Date of Recording: From commercial 78s, 1925-35
Date of Publication: [1971]
Annotations: Brief unsigned liner notes
Selections:
    Going across the Sea
    Governor Al Smith
    Grey Cat on the Tennessee Farm
    Gwine Back to Dixie
    Just One Way to the Pearly Gates
    Rabbit in the Pea Patch
    Rock About My Sarah Jane
    Sail Away Ladies
    Take Me Home Poor Julia
    Walking in Sunlight
    Way down the Old Plank Road
    Worthy of Estimation

396 Label Name/Number: County 545
Title: *Go Mule Go*
Artists: Uncle Dave Macon and the Fruit Jar Drinkers
Editor: [David Freeman]

Source and Date of Recording: From commercial 78s, 1926-38
Date of Publication: [1981]
Annotations: Liner notes by Bill Knowlton
Selections:
    Buddy Won't You Roll Down the Line
    Carve That Possum
    Death of John Henry [I 1]
    Go Long Mule
    Got the Money, Too
    Hold the Woodpile Down
    I Never Go There Anymore
    Johnny Grey
    Late Last Night When Willie Come Home
    Oh Baby, You Done Me Wrong
    Susie Lee
    Tom and Jerry
    When Reubin Come to Town
    When the Train Comes Alone

397   Label Name/Number: Decca DL 4760
Title: *Uncle Dave Macon*
Editor: Ralph Rinzler
Source and Date of Recording: From studio recordings, 1926-29
Date of Publication: [1966]
Annotations: Liner notes by Ralph Rinzler
Selections:
    Carve That Possum
    Cross-Eyed Butcher and the Cackling Hen, The
    Farm Relief
    I'm A-Goin' Away in the Morn
    I'm the Child To Fight
    Kissing on the Sly
    Late Last Night When My Willie Came Home
    Shall We Gather At the River?
    Sleepy Lou
    Sourwood Mountain Medley
    Tell Her To Come Back Home
    Tennessee Jubilee
    Tom and Jerry
    Uncle Dave's Travels--Part 1 [H 1]

398   Label Name/Number: Folkways RBF 51
Title: *Uncle Dave Macon*
Editor: Norman Tinsley, Bob Hyland, and Joe Hickerson
Source and Date of Recording: From commercial 78s, 1920s-'30s
Date of Publication: 1963
Annotations: 6 p. brochure notes by Pete Seeger and others
Selections:
    All In Down and Out Blues
    Cumberland Mountain Deer Race
    From Earth to Heaven

  Gal That Got Stuck on Everything She Said, The
  Hold That Wood-Pile Down
  I've Got the Mourning Blues
  Johnny Gray
  Jordan Is a Hard Road To Travel
  My Daughter Wished To Marry
  Old Man's Drunk Again, The
  Over the Road I'm Bound To Go
  Rise When the Rooster Crows
  Tom and Jerry
  Two-In-One Chewing Gum
  When the Train Comes Along
  Wreck of the Tennessee Gravy Train

399   Label Name/Number: Historical HLP 8006
Title: *Wait 'til the Clouds Roll By*
Artists: Uncle Dave Macon
Source and Date of Recording: From commercial 78s, 1920s-'30s
Date of Publication: 1975
Annotations: Liner notes by Frank Mare
Selections:
  Arcade Blues
  Buddy Won't You Roll down the Line
  Death of John Henry, The [I 1]
  Fame Apart from God's Approval
  Hop High Ladies, the Cake's All Dough
  I'm the Child To Fight
  Never Make Love No More
  Old Ties
  One More River To Cross
  She Wouldn't Give Me Sugar in My Coffee
  Sleepy Lou
  Wait 'Till the Clouds Roll By

400   Label Name/Number: Rounder 1028
Title: *Laugh Your Blues Away*
Artist: Uncle Dave Macon
Editor: Charles Wolfe
Source and Date of Recording: In the studio, air checks, home recordings, 1930-50
Date of Publication: 1979
Annotations: Liner and 1 p. insert notes by Charles Wolfe
Selections:
  Chewing Gum
  Come Dearest the Daylight Is Dawning/Nobody's Darling
  Come on Buddie, Don't You Want To Go
  Death of John Henry [I 1]
  Don't You Look for Trouble
  Eleven Cent Cotton
  From Jerusalem To Jericho
  Go On, Nora Lee
  How Beautiful Heaven Must Be

I'm Drifting Farther from You
I'm Free, I've Broken the Chains
Laugh Your Blues Away
Mysteries of the World
Oh Lovin' Babe
Over the Mountain
Take Me back to My Old Carolina Home
Travellin' on My Mind

401   Label Name/Number: Vetco 101
Title: *The Dixie Dewdrop*
Artist: Uncle Dave Macon
Source and Date of Recording: From commercial 78s, 1920s-'30s
Date of Publication: [< 1973]
Annotations: Notes by Bob Hyland
Selections:
Bible's True, The
Country Ham and Red Gravy
From Jerusalem to Jericho
Hold On to the Sleigh
Hold That Wood Pile Down
On the Dixie Bee Line
Over the Mountain
Poor Sinners, Fare You Well
Rise When the Rooster Crows
She's Got the Money Too
Shout Monah, You Shall Be Free
Tennessee Red Fox Chase

402   Label Name/Number: Vetco 105
Title: *Uncle Dave Macon, Vol. 2*
Source and Date of Recording: From commercial 78s, 1920s-'30s
Date of Publication: 1974
Annotations: Notes by Bob Hyland
Selections:
Bum Hotel, The
Comin' Round the Mountain
He Won the Heart of Sarah Jane
Honest Confession Is Good for the Soul
Jordan Is a Hard Road To Travel
New Ford Car
Peekaboo
Run, Nigger, Run
Station Will Be Changed After a While
Tossing the Baby So High
Travelin' Down the Road
Whoop 'em Up Cindy

David Harrison Macon (1870-1942) is one of the few artists of the 1920s whose total recorded repertoire (approx. 200 sides) should be available on LP. Born in Warren County, Tennessee, Macon was nearly 50 years old before his first sought payment for his musical ministrations--and then only to rid himself of a pesky farmer who kept importuning him to play at a forthcoming party. Rather than being put off, the farmer agreed to the requested payment and thus began a professional musical career that lasted almost until Uncle Dave's death in 1952 at age 82. By the time he made his first recordings in 1924, he was well known as a local entertainer, banjoist, and raconteur. Records were a secondary career; like most artists in his field, Macon was better known through his personal appearances and radio shows--in particular, Grand Old Opry, on which he was a featured star for many years. His repertoire was immense--in addition to the recorded selections there were another 200 that he performed on radio. Though there were some older Anglo-American traditional ballads and songs, and also a selection of religious songs, the bulk of Macon's recorded material came from the minstrel stage of the 3rd quarter of the 19th century and the TPA era that followed, not to mention many contemporary topical songs and pieces of his own creation. And when he did not compose songs outright, he often created his own capsule vaudeville performances by combining dedication, anecdote, homily, instrumental, and song in one three-minute tour-de-force. In most of Macon's recordings, the inadequacies of 78 rpm disc cannot hide his exuberant personality, his rich catalog of banjo styles, and his effective singing techniques. The eleven Macon albums listed above are not all that have been issued (nor are all currently available), but they give a representative cross section of his work. Macon seldom repeated himself, nor did he produce any uninteresting or inferior products; consequently, all his recordings are of interest and ultimately all should be reissued in a single self-contained set.

Fwys RBF 51 is of particular historical interest as the first LP Macon reissue--and one of the first unauthorized reissues devoted to any single hillbilly artist. Little biographical or discographical information was available at the time, so documentation was sparse; nevertheless, the compilers included several characteristically exuberant performances: the topical satire, "Wreck of the Tennessee Gravy Train," the religious "When the Train Comes Along," and the cante fable, "Cumberland Mountain Deer Chase." The publication, three years later, of Decca DL 4760, carefully annotated by Rinzler, provided more solid information and another outstanding selection of examples.

BF 15503 demonstrates that Macon's immense repertoire was filled with songs that are rare (if not otherwise unknown) in folk tradition. Many must have come from his early association with the vaudeville stage; some may well have been his own creation. Among the selections are Macon's first recording, "I'll Keep My Skillet Good and Greasy"; the narratives, "Uncle Dave's Travels, Parts 2 and 4"; the ballad, "Life and Death of Jesse James"; and 11 others. The brochure includes text transcriptions for all the pieces.

Cty 521/545: Macon's versatility was astonishing: though he often recorded alone, accompanying his singing with his own banjo playing, he also performed and recorded with Fiddling Sid Harkreader, and with some combination of Sam and Kirk McGee and Maize Todd. With the latter three he frequently recorded as Uncle Dave and his Fruit Jar Drinkers, in whose company Macon sang his way through some of the finest stringband numbers on early discs. "Sail Away Ladies" and "Rock About My Saro (Sarah) Jane" were two of his best recordings, and deserve their place among any collection of stringband classics. More of their stringband numbers can be heard on Cty 545.

Most of the selections on Rndr 1028, the eleventh LP fully devoted to Macon, had never been issued commercially in any form. The first four cuts were made in 1930 for OKeh and three were never released but are available thanks to test pressings in the possession of the Macon family. The next seven (omitting "Take Me Back") were recorded privately by Macon in 1945. "Take Me Back" is from the sound track to the 1939 movie, *Grand Ole Opry*. "Chewing Gum" is one of several recordings made in 1950 by Charles F. Bryant when he was interviewing Macon extensively. The remaining titles are from airchecks from *Grand Ole Opry* radio programs of ca. 1946. Considering these diverse sources, the sound quality of the recordings is not bad. Wolfe's notes comment on the various sources or the recordings, the side musicians, and the songs themselves. The records from the 1940s, by which time Macon had become something of an institution, show that, though then in his 70s, Macon's failure to make any more commercial recordings was due more to changing musical styles than to his declining abilities.

Of topical interest on Vetco 101 are "On the Dixie Bee Line," with references to Henry Ford; and "The Bible's True," about the Scopes Trial of 1925. [WF 4/73, 7/75; JEMFQ 41, 44, 62; JAF 409]

403a   Label Name/Number: Alpine ALP 201
Title: *J. E. Mainer's Crazy Mountaineers, Vol. 1*
Artists: J. E. Mainer's Mountaineers
Source and Date of Recording: From commercial 78s, 1935-40
Date of Publication: [ca. 1970]
Selections:
   All Aboard
   City on the Hill
   Don't Leave Me This Way
   Free Again
   Kiss Me Goodbye If You Love Me
   Lights in the Valley
   Longest Train, The
   Lord Promised Me a Place in the Sky, The
   Maple on the Hill
   Old Number 9
   Railroad Blues
   Shang High Rooster [sic]
   Take Me in the Life Boat
   Train 45

403b   Label Name/Number: Alpine ALP 202
Title: *Legendaries From the Blue Ridge Mountains, Vol. 2*
Artists: J. E. Mainer's Mountaineers
Source and Date of Recording: From commercial 78s, 1930s-40s
Date of Publication: [ca. 1970]
Annotations: Liner notes by J. E. Mainer
Selections:
   Crying Holy
   Drunkards Hecups [sic]
   Floating down the Streams of Time
   Had the Key to the Kingdom
   John Henry Was a Little Boy [I 1]
   Little Book
   Preaching by the Road Side
   Ram Shackle Shack on the Hill
   She's My Curley Headed Baby
   Those Blue Eyes I Love So Well
   Train One Hundred and Eleven
   Water Melon on the Vine
   We Can't Be Darlings Anymore
   Working on a Building

404a   Label Name/Number: Old Timey 106
Title: *J. E. Mainer's Mountaineers, Vol. 1*

Source and Date of Recording: From commercial 78s, 1935-40
Date of Publication: [ca. 1968]
Annotations: Liner notes by J. E. Mainer
Selections:
  Answer to Greenback Dollar
  Change All Around, A
  Don't Get Trouble in Your Mind
  Just Over in the Gloryland
  Kiss Me Cindy
  Let Her Go, God Bless Her
  Maple on the Hill, No. 2
  Searching for a Pair of Blue Eyes
  Seven and a Half
  Sparkling Blue Eyes
  Sparkling Blue Eyes, No. 2
  We Will Miss Him
  Why Do You Bob Your Hair, Girls
  Write a Letter to Mother

404b   Label Name/Number: Old Timey 107
Title: *J. E. Mainer's Mountaineers, Vol. 2*
Source and Date of Recording: From commercial 78s, 1935-40
Date of Publication: [ca. 1968]
Annotations: Liner notes by J. E. Mainer
Selections:
  Back to Johnson City
  Blue Ridge Mountain Blues
  Broken Hearted Blues
  Concord Rag
  Country Blues
  Don't Go Out
  Drunkard's Hiccoughs
  Fatal Wreck of the Bus
  Going Back West in the Fall
  I Once Loved a Young Man
  In a Little Village Churchyard
  New Lost Train Blues
  Train No. 111
  When I Reach My Home Eternal

Alp ALP 201 / Alp ALP 202 / OT 106 / OT 107: Joseph E. Mainer was born in Buncombe County, North Carolina, in 1898. From the age of about 10 he worked alternately in the cotton mills or on the farm. He took up the banjo in his teens and before long was playing at local square dances. Subsequently he took up fiddle, which he played on most of his recordings. By 1932 he was popular enough for the Crazy Water Crystals Company to entreat him to appear on their new radio show over WBT, Charlotte, North Carolina. There followed a long and successful career of radio station shows and numerous personal appearances. Between 1935 and 1940 he recorded regularly for RCA Victor; after the War he recorded for King, Rural Rhythm, and other labels. All four albums listed, drawn from RCA Bluebird recordings of the 1930s (except for three later recordings on Alp 202), feature Mainer and the artists he associated with--including Wade Mainer, Zeke Morris, Daddy John Love, Leonard Stokes, George Morris, Snuffy Jenkins, and Homer Sherrill. J. E. and his companions were among the first to assimilate into their repertoires songs learned from commercial recordings of other hillbilly artists. The two Alpine albums are unusual reissues in that they are produced by the artist himself. Many of the titles have been changed from the original 78s. Vol. 1 includes two of Mainer's most popular recordings, "Maple on the Hill" and "Lights in the Valley." [WF 7/71 (Alp)]

405   Label Name/Number: County 404
Title: *Wade Mainer and the Sons of the Mountaineers*
Editor: [David Freeman]
Source and Date of Recording: From commercial 78s, 1937-41
Date of Publication: 1973
Annotations: Unsigned liner notes
Selections:
    Don't Leave Me Alone
    I Won't Be Worried
    Lonely Tombs
    Look On and Cry
    Mansions in the Sky
    Memory Lane
    Old Ruben
    Pale Moonlight
    Poor Drunkard's Dream
    Precious Jewel, The
    Rambling Boy
    Ramshackle Shack
    Wild Bill Jones [E 10]
    You May Forsake Me

406   Label Name/Number: Old Homestead OHS 90001 [renumbered OHCS 135]
Title: *Sacred Songs of Mother and Home*
Artists: Wade Mainer
Source and Date of Recording: From commercial 78s, 1935-41
Date of Publication: 1971
Annotations: Liner notes by John W. Morris
Selections:
    Dear Daddy You're Gone
    Dying Boy's Prayer
    Heaven Bells Are Ringing
    I'm Not Turning Backward
    If I Could Hear My Mother Pray Again
    Little Rosebuds
    Mother Came To Get Her Boy from Jail
    My Mother Is Waiting
    Old and Faded Picture, The
    Precious Memories
    Shake Hands with Mother Again
    Ship Sailing Now
    Take Me Home to the Sweet Sunny South
    What Would You Give in Exchange?

     Cty 404 / OH 90001: Wade Mainer, J. E.'s younger brother, was born in western North Carolina in 1907, and worked during his early years on the farm, in the cotton mill, and in logging camps. During the 1930s he moved to Concord, North Carolina, to work in the mills, and there he and J. E. began to develop their musical style. In 1932 they were hired to play on the Crazy Water Crystal Barn Dance in Charlotte. The brothers split up in 1935, and Wade performed and recorded with various other musicians. The County album includes 14 selections by different ensembles, including his nephews, known as the Little Smiling Rangers, and the Sons of the Mountaineers, including Leonard Stokes, George Morris, and Steve Ledford. OHS 90001 includes 14 selections recorded between 1936 and 1941. Most of the selections are hillbilly gospel standards of the 1930s; a few are sentimental songs from the late 19th century. Mainer came out of retirement in the early 1970s to resume musical activity, and, as of 1993, is still going strong. [WF 4/73; WF 7/75]

407   Label Name/Number: Bear Family [West Germany] BF 15505 (Same as Folk Variety 12505)
Title: *Singers of the Piedmont*
Artists: Dave McCarn, Howard Long, Dave Fletcher, and Gwen Foster
Editor: Richard Weize
Source and Date of Recording: From commercial 78s, 1927-31
Date of Publication: [1974?]
Annotations: 4 p. insert by Mike Paris
Selections:
    Dave McCarn
        Bashful Bachelor, The
        Cotton Mill Colic
        Everyday Dirt [Q 9]
        Gastonia Gallop
        Hobo Life
        Poor Man, Rich Man (Cotton Mill Colic No. 2)
        Serves 'Em Fine (Cotton Mill Colic No. 3)
        Take Them for a Ride
    Dave [McCarn] and Howard [Long]
        Bay Rum Blues
        Fancy Nancy (Every Day Dirt No. 2)
        My Bones Gonna Rise Again
    Gwen Foster
        Black Pine Waltz
        Wilkes County Blues
    Carolina Twins (Fletcher and Foster)
        Off to War I'm Going
        One Dark Stormy Night
        Red Rose Rag

BF 15505: This welcome reissue makes available on LP the complete extant recordings (11) of South Carolina mill-hand, guitarist, poet, and singer, Dave McCarn (1905-64). The remaining selections are divided between harmonica player Gwen Foster and the Carolina Twins (Foster and Dave Fletcher). With the exception of "Everyday Dirt" (McCarn's version of the imported ballad, "Will the Weaver") and the raggy instrumentals, McCarn's recordings were largely his own compositions or re-compositions based on traditional elements. Best known, of course, is his three-part protest song, "Cotton Mill Colic," a cynical though amusing indictment of not only the mill owners but also of the mountain folk who expected the mills to make them rich. "My Bone's Gonna Rise Again" is a recomposition of the spiritual, "These Bones Gonna Rise Again," with any hint of religious elements thoroughly expunged and replaced with surprisingly suggestive erotica. McCarn was an excellent versifier, a very good guitarist, and a pleasing singer who deserves more recognition than he has received. The guitar duet instrumental, "Red Rose Rag" is a delightful bonus. [WF 7/75]

408   Label Name/Number: Rounder 1009
Title: *Hallelujah! I'm a Bum*
Artist: Harry K. McClintock
Editor: Mark Wilson
Source and Date of Recording: From commercial 78s, 1928-29
Date of Publication: [1981]
Annotations: 16 p. booklet by Lou Curtiss
Selections:
> Ain't We Crazy?
> Big Rock Candy Mountain, The
> Billy Venero [B 6]
> Bum Song, The
> Bum Song #2, The
> Circus Days
> Fireman, Save My Child
> Git Along, Little Dogies
> Goodbye, Old Paint
> Hallelujah I'm a Bum
> Jerry, Go Ile That Car
> My Last Dollar
> Old Chisholm Trail, The
> Texas Ranger, The [A 8]
> Trail to Mexico, The [B 13]
> Trusty Lariat, The

Rou 1009:   Harry McClintock's (1882-1957) life and career has already been discussed in the notes to Folkways FD 5272 (q. v.), drawn from recordings "in the field" made in the 1950s. To date, this Rounder LP is the only full album from Mac's commercial 78s and offers a good documentation of his musical career.

409   Label Name/Number: Bear Family [West Germany] BF 15517
Title: *Sam and Kirk McGee From Sunny Tennessee*
Source and Date of Recording: From commercial 78s, 1926-28
Date of Publication: 1975
Annotations: Brochure by Charles Wolfe
Selections:
> As Willie and Mary Strolled By the Seashore [N 28]
> C-H-I-C-K-E-N Spells Chicken
> Charming Bill
> Chevrolet Car
> Easy Rider
> Flower from My Angel Mother's Grave, A
> If I Could Only Blot Out the Past
> Kicking Mule, The
> My Family Has Been a Crooked Set
> Old Master's Runaway
> Only a Step to the Grave
> Rufus Blossom

Salty Dog Blues
Ship Without a Sail, The
Someone Else May Be There While I'm Gone
Tramp, The

BF 15517:   This album offers a delightful excursion into the musical talents of long-time Opry regulars Sam and Kirk McGee. Though their later recordings for Folkways (FA 2379 and FTS 31007) show them to be remarkably adept at Anglo-American fiddle and banjo tunes, their 1920s recordings stressed their borrowings from late 19th-century minstrelsy, blues, TPA balladry. Only two numbers on this LP fall outside these domains: the British broadside balllad, "As Willie and Mary Strolled by the Seashore" [N 28] and the Vaughan gospel song, "Only a Step to the Grave." Sam's excellent finger-picking banjo-guitar work, familiar to reissue collectors through such titles as "Knoxville Blues," "Railroad Blues," "Buck Dancer's Choice," and "Franklin Blues," is heard again on "Easy Rider," actually more closely related to "Salty Dog Blues" than the usual "Easy Rider"; and "Amos Johnson Rag," interpolated at the end of his "The Ship Without a Sail." Kirk's excellent blues-influenced fiddle is heard to distinction on "Salty Dog Blues," more closely related to bluesman Papa Charlie Jackson's versions than the one popularized by hillbilly musicians the Allen Brothers and others after them. Wolfe's notes are up to his usual high standards; fortunately, Wolfe had the opportunity to interview the McGees with a tape of these selections in hand and thereby elicit their comments on the songs and their sources. [JEMFQ 49]

410   Label Name/Number: Bluebird AMX2-5510
Title: *Feast Here Tonight*
Artists: Monroe Brothers
Source and Date of Recording: From studio recordings, 1936-38
Date of Publication: [1975]
Annotations: Liner notes by Douglas B. Green
Selections:
All the Good Times Are Passed and Gone
Beautiful Life, A
Darling Corey
Drifting Too Far from the Shore
God Holds the Future in His Hands
Goodbye Maggie
Have a Feast Here Tonight
He Will Set Your Fields on Fire
In My Dear Old Southern Home
Katy Cline
Little Joe
Little Red Shoes
My Long Journey Home
New River Train
Nine-Pound Hammer Is Too Heavy
On Some Foggy Mountain Top
On That Old Gospel Ship
On the Banks of the Ohio [F 5]
Pearly Gates
Roll in My Sweet Baby's Arms
Roll On Buddy
Rollin' On
Saints Go Marching In, The

Sinner You Better Get Ready
Some Glad Day
Watermelon Hanging on the Vine
Weeping Willow Tree
What Is a Home Without Love?
What Would You Give in Exchange?
When Our Lord Shall Come Again
Where Is My Sailor Boy?
Will the Circle Be Unbroken?

Bluebird AMX2-5510: While Bill Monroe will always be best remembered as progenitor of the music called "bluegrass," his earlier musical activities should not be forgotten: in particular, he and his older brother Charlie created a fiery, virtuosic duet style of intense, fast-paced singing accompanied by driving and intricate mandolin playing and guitar back-up. Their influence on other hillbilly musicians of the '30s was great. The brothers were born in Rosine, Kentucky, in 1903 and 1911, absorbing much music from their mother and her brother. (Bill was also heavily influenced by a local black fiddler/guitarist, Arnold Shultz.)   Between 1936 and 1938 they recorded 60 selections for RCA's Bluebird label--many older, traditional dance tunes and songs, ballads, and gospel pieces but also a goodly proportion of then-current hillbilly numbers. This double album is an excellent sampling of 32 of those recordings, arranged chronologically. Green's gatefold liner notes concentrate on biographical details and comment only briefly on the selections. A five-LP boxed set of all their RCA recordings was issued in Japan.

411   Label Name/Number: Camden CAL 719
Title: *The Father of Blue Grass Music*
Artists: Bill Monroe and His Blue Grass Boys
Source and Date of Recording: From studio recordings, 1940-41
Date of Publication: 1962
Annotations: Liner notes by Frank Sheffield
Selections:
Back Up and Push
Blue Yodel No. 7
Dog House Blues
Honky Tonk Swing
I Wonder If You Feel the Way I Do
In the Pines
Katy Hill
Mule Skinner Blues
No Letter in the Mail
Orange Blossom Special
Six White Horses
Tennessee Blues

Cam CAL 719: After Bill Monroe and his brother split up, Bill formed his own band, the Blue Grass Boys--named for Kentucky, the bluegrass state. The band made its first recordings in 1940-41 for the Bluebird label. This long-out-of-print Camden album, one of the first LP reissues of pre-World War II material, shows Monroe's new band still strongly tradition oriented, with many of their numbers older fiddle tunes ("Katy Hill") and songs ("In the Pines"); but also borrowing from Jimmie Rodgers ("Mule Skinner Blues" and "Blue Yodel") and other hillbilly artists of the '30s (*e. g.*, the Rouse Brothers' "Orange Blossom Special") and also beginning to write their own material. In the 1940s and '50s, Monroe's own compositions became increasingly important in the band's repertoire, but in the 1960s, partly under the influence of the folksong revival and urban interest in bluegrass, Monroe returned somewhat to older traditional material.

412 Label Name/Number: Biograph BLP 6005
Title: *The North Carolina Ramblers*
Source and Date of Recording: From commercial 78s, 1920s-'30s
Date of Publication: 1972
Annotations: Liner notes by Richard Nevins
Selections:
    Bluefield Murder, The
    Flop Eared Mule
    George Collins [C. 85]
    I'll Meet My Mother After All
    Kitty Blye
    Lynchberg Town
    May I Sleep in Your Barn Tonight, Mister?
    My Mother and My Sweetheart
    Old Clay Pipe
    Please Papa Come Home
    Richmond Square
    Tennessee Blues
    Under the Double Eagle
    When the Bees Are in the Hive
    When the Whipperwill Was Whispering Good Night

413 Label Name/Number: County 505
Title: *Charlie Poole and the North Carolina Ramblers*
Editor: [David Freeman]
Source and Date of Recording: From commercial 78s, 1927-31
Date of Publication: [1964]
Selections:
    Don't Let Your Deal Go Down
    He Rambled
    Leaving Home [I 3]
    Letter That Never Came, The
    Mountain Reel
    Ramblin' Blues
    Shootin' Creek
    Sweet Sixteen
    Sweet Sunny South
    Take a Drink on Me
    Took My Gal A-Walkin'
    White House Blues

414 Label Name/Number: County 509
Title: *Charlie Poole and the North Carolina Ramblers, Vol. 2*
Editor: [David Freeman]
Source and Date of Recording: From commercial 78s, 1925-30
Date of Publication: [1967?]
Selections:
    Bill Mason

Can I Sleep in Your Barn?
If I Lose Let Me Lose
If the River Was Whiskey
It's Movin' Day
Monkey on a String
My Gypsy Girl [O 4]
One Moonlight Night
Ragtime Annie
The Baltimore Fire
There'll Come a Time
Wild Horse

415   Label Name/Number: County 516
Title: *The Legend of Charlie Poole*
Source and Date of Recording: From commercial 78s, 1926-30
Date of Publication: [> 1968]
Selections:
Budded Roses
Goodbye Booze
Goodbye Liza Jane
Goodbye Mary Dear
Highwayman, The [I 4]
Hungry Hash House
Leaving Dear Old Ireland
Look Before You Leap
Milwaukee Blues
My Wife Went Away and Left Me
Old and Only in the Way
Write a Letter to My Mother

416   Label Name/Number: County 540
Title: *Charlie Poole and the North Carolina Ramblers, Vol. 4*
Editor: [David Freeman]
Source and Date of Recording: From commercial 78s, 1925-30
Annotations: Unsigned liner notes
Selections:
Baby Rose (Just Keep Waiting till the Good Time Comes)
Coon From Tennessee
Falling by the Wayside
Flying Clouds
Girl I Left in Sunny Tennessee, The
Honeysuckle
I'm the Man That Rode the Mule 'round the World
Jealous Mary
Kiss Waltz
Mother's Last Farewell Kiss
Southern Medley
You Ain't Talking to Me

417   Label Name/Number: Historical HLP 8005
Title: *A Young Boy Left His Home One Day*

Artists: Charlie Poole and the North Carolina Ramblers
Source and Date of Recording: From commercial 78s, 1926-30
Date of Publication: 1975
Annotations: Liner notes by Frank Mare
Selections:
> Forks of Sandy
> Husband and Wife Were Angry One Night
> I Once Loved a Sailor
> Kiss Waltz, A
> Mother's Farewell Kiss
> Only Girl I Ever Loved, The
> Southern Medley
> What Is Home Without Babies
> Where the Whip-poor-will Is Whispering Goodnight
> Wreck of Virginian No. 3, The
> You Ain't Talkin' to Me
> Young Boy Left His Home One Day, A

Bio BLP 6005 / Cty 505 / Cty 509 / Cty 516 / Cty 540 / Hist 8005: The North Carolina Ramblers were one of the most popular of the hillbilly stringbands of the 1920s--and are well represented on LP reissues. The leader of the band was Charlie Poole, born in Randolph County in 1892 the son of a cotton mill worker. He was already playing banjo by the age of eight or nine. Charlie worked in the mills also, but a strong urge to wander took him away from home (and wife) for weeks at a time. In around 1918 he moved to Spray, NC, where he found a thriving stringband tradition. He met fiddler Posey Rorer about that time, and the two of them hung around together for the next decade, joined by various other musicians at different times. They made their first recordings in 1925 for Columbia with Norman Woodlieff on guitar and recorded extensively for the next five years--for Columbia, Gennett, Paramount, Edison, and Brunswick. Poole's was a fast and whiskey-filled life, which brought about his premature death in 1931.

Poole's band (perhaps one should say bands, since the personnel varied from time to time) was justly one of the most popular stringbands of the 1920s in the Southeast and has also been one of the most admired and emulated among latter day folksong revivalists. As was often the case in North Carolina, Poole finger picked rather than frailed the banjo. He and his guitarist, Roy Harvey, provided their fiddlers with a remarkable well-blended and uncluttered accompaniment that gave the impression that every note had been carefully planned in advance. Few bands managed to produce such an integrated euphony as the North Carolina Ramblers. Poole's repertoire was typical early hillbilly, in that it drew upon the older Anglo-American ballad and fiddle tradition as well as the later minstrel stage, the TPA songbag of mostly Victorian sentimentalia, and finally then-contemporary pop song. Notably absent from his recorded work was any trace of religious material. What Poole didn't have in his blood from birth he learned from his sister, his fellow musicians, and from newspaper and magazine song columns and other printed sources. His career has been admirably documented in Kinney Rorrer's *Rambling Blues: The Life and Songs of Charlie Poole* (London: Old Time Music, 1982).

Cty 505, 509, and 516 contain most of the best of the NCR Columbia material, including their influential "White House Blues," "If the River Was Whiskey" (W. C. Handy's "Hesitatin' Blues"), and "Goodbye Booze." Cty 516 includes typical Poole fare, which is mostly late 19th- and early 20th-century pop songs "(Goodbye Booze," "Budded Roses," "Old and Only in the Way") and a few older ballads, such as "The Highwayman." "Milwaukee Blues" is one of the blues ballad ancestors of "Casey Jones." Cty 540 includes "Southern Medley," a banjo/guitar duet in which Poole demonstrates how much he learned from Vess Ossman, Fred Van Eps, and other classical banjoists of the day.

Six of the selections on the Biograph LP are by the NCR: Charlie Poole, Roy Harvey, and Posey Rorer; the other selections are by various other groups of which Harvey was a member. [JEMFQ 43; WF 7/73, 7/75; JAF 314--DKW (505); JAF 320--DKW (509); JAF 327]

418   Label Name/Number: County 411
Title: *Riley Puckett*
Editor: [David Freeman]
Source and Date of Recording: From commercial 78s, 1928-39
Date of Publication: [1979]
Annotations: Liner notes by Joe Wilson
Selections:
    Boots and Saddle
    Curly Headed Baby
    How Come You Do Me Like You Do
    I Wish I Was Single Again
    I'm Getting Ready To Go
    I'm Ragged but I'm Right
    K. C. Railroad
    Old Spinning Wheel
    Other Side of Jordan, The
    Poor Boy [I 4]
    Rambling' Boy
    Riley's Hen House Door
    Waitin' for the Evening Mail
    When I'm Gone You'll Soon Forget Me

419   Label Name/Number: Old Homestead OHCS 114 [Reissue of GHP 902 [West Germany], with 2 added titles marked by *]
Title: *Old Time Greats, Vol. 1*
Artist: Riley Puckett
Source and Date of Recording: From commercial 78s, 1927-39
Date of Publication: [1978]
Annotations: Liner notes [by Norm Cohen]
Selections:
    Away out on the Mountain
    Call Me Back Pal o' Mine
    Clover Blossoms
    Curley Headed Baby
    Darkie's Wail *
    Dissatisfied
    Don't Try It for It Can't Be Done
    Frankie and Johnny [I 3]
    Fuzzy Rag *
    I'm Getting Ready To Go
    I'm Going to Georgia
    Moonshiner's Dream, The
    On the Other Side of Jordan
    Ragged but Right
    Send Back My Wedding Ring
    Wait til the Sun Shines Nellie

Cty 411 / OHCS 114: Although to modern listeners, Riley Puckett is best remembered as the back-up guitarist for the celebrated Atlanta stringband, Gid Tanner's Skillet Lickers, to country audiences of the 1920s and '30s it was as a singer that he was better known. The purpose of the County LP was to sample his talents as a singer on a variety of songs from the traditional Anglo-American folksongs ("I Wish I Was Single Again") to blackface minstrelsy ("The Other Side of Jordan") to TPA sentimentalia ("When I'm Gone You'll Soon Forget Me") to swinging 1930s country novelties ("I'm Ragged but Right"). Puckett's popularity is easy to understand after listening to a collection such as this: he sang in a mellow, rich baritone with careful enunciation and little accent. He could have crossed over to pop music had he come along a decade later. His style was relatively unornamented--frequent vibrato and occasional falsettos but few decorative grace notes, slides, scoops, or other devices. My personal preference is for "How Come You Do Me" and "Ragged but Right," both with mandolin accompaniment by Ted Hawkins; and "I'm Getting Ready To Go," with the touch of yodeling in the chorus, demonstrating his singing at its best. No flashy guitar here, just good vocals. Annotations and documentation are almost nonexistent.

The Old Homestead release was a reissue from the German GHP label, but with two additional titles--both guitar instrumentals. "Darkie's Wail" is a steel guitar version of the "John Henry" melody; "Fuzzy Rag" is a basic circle-of-fifths tune recorded by others under different titles (closest is Frank Hutchison's "Hutchison's Rag"). Apart from these and one or two others, most of this album consists of pop material from the 1920s and '30s--not Puckett's most interesting (or exciting) material. [JEMFQ 55]

420   Label Name/Number: County 510
Title: *The Red Fox Chasers*
Editor: [David Freeman]
Source and Date of Recording: From commercial 78s, 1928-30
Date of Publication: 1967
Annotations: Liner notes by Richard Nevins
Selections:
  Blind Man and His Child, The
  Devilish Mary [Q 4]
  Did You Ever See the Devil, Uncle Joe
  Goodbye Little Bonnie
  Honeysuckle Time
  Katy Cline
  Little Darling Pal of Mine
  Mississippi Sawyer
  Naomi Wise [F 4]
  Pretty Polly
  Stolen Love
  Sweet Fern

Cty 510: This LP highlights a generally neglected North Carolina string band that recorded for the Gennett label in 1928-31. Their repertory was strong in traditional numbers, but their vocal styles and harmonies reflected urban gospel influence. This may be because two vocalists of the group, A. P. Thompson and Bob Cranford of Surry County, took singing school lessons when young. Selections are a representative cross section of this band's recorded output. Most of the pieces are standard hillbilly numbers; two exceptions are compositions by the band's fiddler, Guy Brooks, and guitarist/vocalist Thompson. Liner notes provide helpful if effusive background information on the members of the band and their styles. [JAF 323]

421   Label Name/Number: Rounder 1001
Title: *How Can a Poor Man Stand Such Times and Live?*
Artist: Blind Alfred Reed
Editor: The Rounder Collective
Source and Date of Recording: From commercial 78s, 1927-29
Date of Publication: [1972?]
Annotations: Brochure by the Rounder Collective (Marion Leighton, Ken Irwin, Bill Nowlin,
    Bruce Kaplan)
Selections:
    Always Lift Him Up and Never Knock Him Down
    Beware
    Black and Blue Blues
    Explosion in the Fairmount Mines
    How Can a Poor Man Stand Such Times and Live?
    I Mean To Live for Jesus
    Prayer of the Drunkard's Little Girl, The
    There'll Be No Distinction There
    Walking in the Way with Jesus
    We've Just Got To Have 'em, That's All
    Why Do You Bob Your Hair, Girls?
    Why Don't You Bob Your Hair, Girls, No. 2
    Woman's Been After Man Ever Since
    You Must Unload

Rndr 1001:   Blind Alfred Reed (1880-1956), an outstanding singer, fiddler, and songwriter, was well known and highly admired in Mercer County, West Virginia, where he spent most of his life. Between 1927 and 1929 he recorded two dozen selections for the Victor Talking Machine Company (or its successor as of early 1929, RCA Victor), 14 of which are reissued here. Reed's songbag comprised a catalog of rural fundamentalist attitudes toward the concerns of the world of the 1920s. The title song voiced dissatisfaction of the rural folk, beset by hard times while the rest of the country rode on the crest of prosperity. "There'll Be No Distinction There" is one of the few hillbilly songs on the subject of discrimination. Whether Reed actually was a misogynist or composed such songs as "Why Do You Bob Your Hair, Girls" with tongue in cheek is not known, but he recorded several pieces of similar persuasion: "Black and Blue Blues," and "Woman's Been After Man Ever Since" among them. "Explosion in the Fairmount Mines" is "Don't Go Down in the Mines, Dear Dad," localized to the 1907 Fairmount disasters. "The Prayer of the Drunkard's Little Girl" is Reed's contribution to the temperance motif. Reed's strong, clear vocals and haunting, archaic fiddling make an historically important collection musically exciting as well. Reed was also a highly respected hoedown fiddler; unfortunately, he never saw fit to record any purely instumental selections. The brochure gives song texts, biographical and discographic data.   [WF 4/73; JAF 343--DKW]

422   Label Name/Number: County 403
Title: *The Roane County Ramblers Original Recordings, 1928-29*
Artists: Roane County Ramblers (James McCarroll, John Kelley, Luke Brandon, and Howard
    Wyatt)
Editor: [David Freeman]
Source and Date of Recording: From commercial 78s
Date of Publication: 1971
Annotations: Liner notes by David Freeman
Selections:

Alabama Trot
Callahan Rag
Everybody Two-Step
Free a Little Bird--1930 Model
Green River March
Hometown Blues
Johnson City Rag
McCarroll's Breakdown
Roane County Rag
Southern No. 111
Step High Waltz
Tennessee Waltz

Cty 403: Dance music, primarily instrumental, was one of the mainstays of the hillbilly catalogs of the 1920s. A popular Tennessee stringband was James McCarroll's Roane County Ramblers, whose music seems more closely related to the North Georgia style than to that of other Tennessee groups. Their complete issued recorded output is reissued on this LP. Jacket notes are based on Freeman's interview with McCarroll, who recalled details about the band and their recordings. [WF 4/73]

423 Label Name/Number: Davis Unlimited DU 33015
Title: *Fiddling Doc Roberts: 1927-1933*
Source and Date of Recording: From commercial 78s, 1927-33
Date of Publication: [1974]
Annotations: Liner notes by Ivan Tribe
Selections:
Billy in the Lowground
Black Eyed Susie
Brickyard Joe
Cripple Creek
Cumberland Blues
Did You Ever See the Devil, Uncle Joe?
Farewell Waltz
I Don't Love Nobody
New Money
Old Buzzard
Run Smoke Run
Sally Ann
Waynesboro
Wednesday Night Waltz

DU 33015: Phil (Doc) Roberts (1897-1978), born in Madison County, Kentucky, was an outstanding old-time fiddler of the 1920s whose bluesy technique was almost unique among recording artists of the period ("Cumberland Blues" is an outstanding example, not only of his fiddling but also of his partners' back-up artistry). Roberts was, fortunately, one of the most recorded old-time fiddlers of the 20s and 30s. An excellent fiddler with a wide-ranging repertory, Roberts' smooth long-boy style was remarkably bluesy for its time (there were in fact several black fiddlers in that region of Kentucky from whom Roberts learned some of his tunes, but they do not seem to account for his graceful, fluid bowing style). Though Roberts also fiddled back-up behind several vocalists, this LP samples only his fiddle instrumentals. Some of the tunes are quite rare (e.g., "New Money" and "Farewell Waltz"); in some instances (e.g. "Cripple Creek"), Roberts turns out delightful and unusual variations of well-known standards. Unfortunately, Roberts' fine musicianship is not heard to best advantage because of the poor technical quality of the original 78s and/or the remastering job. Nevertheless, this is a useful LP if for no other reason than that--surprisingly--so little of Martin and Roberts' work has been reissued. This album offers a few of the more unusual tunes in Roberts' repertory, such as "Brickyard Joe," "New Money," and the swinging "Cumberland Blues" but also shows that even on familiar titles, such as "Billy in the Lowground," Roberts' arrangements were often unusual. The two-guitar backup of James Roberts and Asa Martin, with their fancy chords and flat-pick runs, combined with Roberts' smooth style to make a highly distinctive string-band sound that must have seemed "far out" to listeners in the Depression years; even today it has not lost its charm. Liner notes by Tribe provide a biographical skech and tune identifications. [JEMFQ 40, 52]

424   Label Name/Number: Sonyatone STR 201
Title: *Eck Robertson*
Editor: Peter Feldmann
Source and Date of Recording: From commercial 78s, 1922-29
Date of Publication: 1976
Annotations: Brochure notes by Peter Feldmann
Selections:
    Amarillo Waltz
    Arkansas Traveller
    Brilliancy Medley
    Brown Kelley Waltz, Parts 1 and 2
    Done Gone
    Great Big 'Taters in Sandyland
    Island Unknown, The, Parts 1 and 2
    Radio Theme Song
    Ragtime Annie
    Run Boy Run
    Sallie Gooden
    Sallie Johnson/Billy in the Low Ground
    Texas Wagoner
    There's a Brown Skin Girl down the Road Somewhere
    Turkey in the Straw

Sonyatone STR 201: Arkansas-born, Texas-reared Alexander Campbell Robertson was the fiddler who started it all. His brilliant solos and duets (with Henry Gilliland) made in the summer of 1922 before a baffled crew at Victor Talking Machine Company's Camden NJ offices were, to our knowledge, the first commercial recordings by a traditional old-time fiddler, and they still rank as some of the finest ever recorded by anyone at any time. This album reissues, in chronological order, all of his issued commercial recordings and, for extra measure, a 1965 recording of a song that Eck composed and used on his radio programs to solicit mail from listeners. Feldmann's brochure includes a 4-page biography, notes on the songs and tunes, a text transcription of the three selections with words, a complete Robertson discography, and a bibliography listing interviews, articles, and books that refer to Robertson. (See also notes to County 202 in Section I.) [JAF 395; JEMFQ 52]

425   Label Name/Number: County 506
Title: *The Skillet Lickers*
Editor: [David Freeman]
Source and Date of Recording: From commercial 78s, 1926-31

Date of Publication: [1965]
Annotations: Liner notes by Norm Cohen
Selections:
>   Big Ball in Town
>   Cacklin' Hen and Rooster Too
>   Corn Licker Still in Georgia, A
>   Cotton Eyed Joe
>   Devilish Mary [Q 4]
>   Four Cent Cotton
>   In the Woodpile
>   Leather Breeches
>   Molly Put the Kettle On
>   Rock That Cradle Lucy
>   Sal's Gone to the Cider Mill
>   Soldier's Joy

426 Label Name/Number: County 526
Title: *The Skillet Lickers, Vol. 2*
Editor: [David Freeman]
Source and Date of Recording: From commercial 78s, 1920s-'30s
Date of Publication: 1973
Annotations: Liner notes by Richard Nevins
Selections:
>   Broken Down Gambler
>   Bully of the Town [I 14]
>   Dixie
>   Hell Broke Loose in Georgia
>   Liberty
>   Night in a Blind Tiger
>   Pretty Little Widow
>   Ride Old Buck to Water
>   Rocky Pallet
>   Run Nigger Run
>   Shortenin' Bread
>   Watermelon on the Vine

427 Label Name/Number: Folksong Society of Minnesota FSSMLP 15001-D
Title: *Gid Tanner and His Skillet Lickers*
Editors: Lyle Lofgren, Liz Williams, and Louis Claeson
Source and Date of Recording: From commercial 78s, 1920s-'30s
Date of Publication: [1962]
Annotations: 8 p. insert by Lofgren, Williams, and Claeson
Selections:
>   Bee Hunt on Hell-for-Sartin Creek, A
>   Don't You Hear Jerusalem Moan?
>   Georgia Railroad
>   Goodbye Booze
>   Hand Me Down My Walking Cane
>   If You Want To Go A-Courting
>   Liberty
>   Miss McLeod's Reel

Molly Put the Kettle On
Nancy Rollin
S-A-V-E-D
Sal Let Me Chaw Your Rosin Some
You Got To Stop Drinking Shine

428   Label Name/Number: Old Homestead OHCS 192
Title: *Early String Band Classics*
Artists: Gid Tanner and his Skillet Lickers
Source and Date of Recording: From commercial 78s, 1934
Date of Publication: 1988
Annotations: Liner notes by Charles Wolfe
Selections:
Back Up and Push
Cotton Patch
Cumberland Gap
Down in the Valley
Down Yonder
Georgia Waggoner
Git Along
I'm Satisfied
Ida Red
Mississippi Sawyer
Rainbow Waltz
Rufus
Skillet Licker Breakdown
Texas Hop
Three Nights Drunk [C. 274]
Zelma Waltz

429   Label Name/Number: Old Homestead OHCS 193
Title: *Gid Tanner and the Skillet Lickers in Texas: Early String Band Classics, Vol. 3*
Artists: Gid Tanner and the Skillet Lickers
Source and Date of Recording: From commercial 78s, 1934
Date of Publication: 1990
Annotations: Liner notes by Charles Wolfe
Selections:
Flop-Eared Mule
Hawkins Rag
Hinkey Dinkee Dee
Hop High Ladies
I Ain't No Better Now
Keep Your Gal at Home
Kimball House
Raindrop Waltz
Tanner's Boarding House
Tanner's Rag
Tokio Rag
Tra-La-La-La
Whoa, Mule, Whoa

430 Label Name/Number: Rounder 1005
Title: *Gid Tanner and His Skillet Lickers--with Riley Puckett and Clayton McMichen*
Source and Date of Recording: From commercial 78s, 1924-34
Date of Publication: 1973
Annotations: Notes by Mark Wilson
Selections:
  Cumberland Gap
  Flatwoods
  I'm Satisfied
  John Henry [I 1]
  Keep Your Gal At Home
  Pass Around the Bottle and We'll All Take a Drink
  Roll 'em on the Ground
  Run Nigger Run
  Ryestraw
  Settin' in the Chimney Jamb
  Sleeping Lulu
  Slow Buck
  Sugar in the Gourd
  Tanner's Boarding House
  Uncle Bud
  Watermelon on the Vine

431 Label Name/Number: Rounder 1023
Title: *The Kickapoo Medicine Show*
Artists: Gid Tanner and His Skillet Lickers
Editor: Mark Wilson and Charles Wolfe
Source and Date of Recording: From commercial 78s and test pressings, 1924-34
Date of Publication: [1977]
Annotations: 12 p. booklet by Mark Wilson and Charles Wolfe
Selections:
  Arkansas Sheik, The
  Cumberland Gap on a Buckin' Mule
  Don't You Hear Jerusalem Moan?
  Farmer's Daughter, The
  I Ain't No Better Now
  Kickapoo Medicine Show, Pts. 1/2
  Mississippi Sawyer
  Nancy Rollin
  Never Seen the Like Since Gettin' Upstairs
  New Dixie
  Paddy Won't You Drink Some Cider
  Prettiest Little Girl in the County
  Rake and Rambling Boy [L 12]
  You Got To Stop Drinking Shine
  You Gotta Quit Kicking My Dawg Around

432 Label Name/Number: Vetco 107
Title: *Gid Tanner and the Skillet Lickers*
Source and Date of Recording: From commercial 78s, 1920s-'30s
Date of Publication: 1975

Annotations: Liner notes by Bob Hyland
Selections:
    Bile Them Cabbage Down
    Black Eyed Susie
    Buckin' Mule
    Cripple Creek
    Dance All Night with a Bottle in Your Hand
    Fiddler's Convention in Georgia, A
    Fly Around My Pretty Little Miss
    Georgia Waggoner
    Going on Down Town
    It Ain't Gonna Rain No Mo'
    It's a Long Way to Tipperary
    Sal Let Me Chaw Your Rosin

Cty 506 / Cty 526/ / FSSMLP 15001-D / OH 192 / OH 193 / Rndr 1005 / Rndr 1023 / Vetco 107: In his jacket liner notes to Old Homestead OHCS-192, Charles Wolfe refers to the north Georgia aggregation as "[In] 1934, America's most famous string band." It is probably an apt description; from 1924 until the Depression, Tanner, Riley Puckett, and their associates recorded some 300 sides--an amazing catalog of dance tunes, traditional ballads and songs, 19th-century sentimental ballads, and then-current pop tunes--all for the Columbia label. (Additionally, Lowe Stokes, Clayton McMichen and other members of the Skillet Lickers recorded on their own under different band names for different labels.) Adding negligibly to the Skillet Lickers' reputation was their distinction of being the first hillbilly stringband to be documented in the pages of an academic journal (*Journal of American Folklore* 78 [1965], pp. 229-44). The band's central patriarchal figure was fiddler/chicken farmer James Gideon Tanner (ca. 1885-1960), a regular at the area's annual fiddlers' conventions since early in the century. His recording career began in 1924 when he was asked by Columbia's Frank Walker to come to New York to make recordings. He brought with him George Riley Puckett (ca. 1894-1946), blind singer-guitarist whose smooth, listenable singing was largely responsible for the Skillet Lickers' success. The third major figure in the band was Clayton McMichen (1900-1970), a younger fiddler of considerable virtuosity, whose drive for professional success and popularity pushed the band(s) toward more modern styles and selections.

FSSMLP 15001-D is of historical importance as the first hillbilly reissue album devoted to a single artist or group. It, and the two County albums, are drawn entirely from the extensive Columbia repertoire of the Skillet Lickers. In 1966, when County issued 504, the editor dropped the first word from the title of the minstrel song, "Nigger in the Woodpile" for fear of causing offense; by 1973, when 526 was issued, it must have been assumed such locutions would be taken in stride.

County 526 concentrates on their fiddle tunes, though one piece generally labeled a ballad ("Bully of the Town") and one musical skit ("Night in a Blind Tiger") are included. The liner notes by Nevins offer interesting and informative commentary of the group and their music. A reading of all that had been written in recent years about these musicians, however, will reveal some strongly discordant evaluations of the relative merits of the various musicians' contributions. In part, this is a reflection of the in-group rivalries among the various bandmembers themselves. Stokes and McMichen felt a considerable gap between themselves and their older colleagues, Tanner and Puckett, and their criticisms extended well beyond the realm of purely musical matters. Nevins' notes draw heavily on his own interviews with Stokes, and are colored by Stokes' own recollections and feelings. In particular, there is a tendency to embellish Stokes' role in the music-making to the detraction of others. The presence of three fiddle parts, with Stokes in lead, is frequently asserted; this is more on a basis of Stokes' own recollections (which I found often to be at variance with those of other members of the band) than on aural evidence, as it is hard enough sometimes to distinguish two fiddles playing in double stops, let alone three. Nevertheless, I am sympathetic to

Nevins' argument because he is justified in trying to restore to Stokes some of the credit he has long been denied.

In March 1934, RCA Victor, trying to battle the Depression with a new budget-priced Bluebird label, paid the celebrated Gid Tanner to bring his band to San Antonio, Texas, for a recording session. Out of the 48 sides recorded in two frantic days' work, 29 are reissued on OH 192 and 193. The Bluebird sound differed in several ways from the earlier Columbia material. Most noticeable was the prominent mandolin by Ted Hawkins. In place of the stellar fiddling by McMichen and Stokes, lead fiddle was the job of 17-year-old Gordon Tanner. (Gid Tanner, never a first-class fiddler, often left the lead to his companions, excelling at his old-timey singing and raucous humor). The material consisted of the same kind of mix as their Columbia work, as these albums demonstrate: the wildly exuberant traditional fiddle and dance tunes, ("Georgia Waggoner," "Mississippi Sawyer," "Cumberland Gap," "Ida Red," "Git Along [Cindy]," and "Cotton Patch"); one older ballad (a rather dragging version of "Three Nights Drunk" [Child 274]); and versions of pop hits, such as "Down Yonder" (1921) and "[Whistling] Rufus" (1899). "Down Yonder" and "Back Up and Push" were so popular (the first reportedly selling a million copies) they were kept in RCA's catalog for two decades, first on 78s, then on 45s and on early LP reissues.

Rndr 1023 is one of the best single-album cross sections of their work available, exhibiting the full Skillet Lickers' stringband sound, fiddle-guitar duets by McMichen and Puckett, solos by Gid Tanner, a traditional ballad by Puckett (accompanied by the McMichen-Layne String Orchestra), and one of the best two-part skits that the group recorded and was renowned for, "The Kickapoo Medicine Show" (incidentally, an interesting and candid document of a fascinating bit of now-nearly-forgotten Americana). Two selections--"Prettiest Little Girl" and "Rake and Rambling Boy"--were never issued commercially in any form. The brochure includes a 3-p. biographical sketch by Wolfe that offers valuable information on the various musicians and their musical milieu; the song notes include complete recording data, text transcriptions, and headnotes. [JEMFQ 52, JAF 409, WF 7/75; JAF 297--DKW (FSSMLP); JAF 317--DKW (Cty 506)]

433a   Label Name/Number: County 546
Title: *Fiddlin' Arthur Smith, Vol. 1*
Editor: [David Freeman]
Source and Date of Recording: From commercial 78s, 1935-40
Date of Publication: 1978
Annotations: Brochure by Charles Wolfe and Barry Poss
Selections:
  Adieu False Heart
  Bonaparte's Retreat
  Cheatham County Breakdown
  Dickson County Blues
  Fiddler's Blues
  Florida Blues
  Goin' to Town
  I'm Bound To Ride
  I've Had a Big Time Today
  K. C. Stomp
  Lonesome Day Today, A
  Lost Train Blues
  Straw Breakdown
  Take Me Back to Tennessee

433b   Label Name/Number: County 547
Title: *Fiddlin' Arthur Smith, Vol. 2*

Editor: [David Freeman]
Source and Date of Recording: From commercial 78s, 1936-40
Date of Publication: 1978
Annotations: Brochure by Charles Wolfe and Barry Poss
Selections:
Blackberry Blossom
Chittlin Cooking Time
Fiddler's Dream
Freight Train Moan
Girl I Love Don't Pay Me No Mind, The
House of David Blues
In the Pines
Indian Creek
Peacock Rag
Pig at Home in the Pen
Red Apple Rag
Smith's Rag
Sugar Tree Stomp
There's More Pretty Girls Than One

Cty 546 / Cty 547: These two albums comprise an excellent tribute to one of the greatest and most influential country fiddlers of the pre-W. II era. Born in Humphreys County, Tennessee, in 1898, Smith had by 1920 developed a local reputation as a fiddler of note and in 1927 made his first of many appearances on the fledgling Grand Ole Opry out of Nashville, In the next half dozen years Smith was one of the most popular fiddlers in Tennessee, touring first with his cousin, Homer Smith, then with the McGee Brothers, and still later, in 1934, with the Delmore Brothers. It was with the latter duo that Smith made his first recordings in 1935, and he continued to record for RCA Bluebird until 1940. Through the 1940s, though he made no records, he continued to travel and perform with various groups. In the 1960s he enjoyed a second burst of popularity in the folk revival, and three LP albums of his were issued, two of them, with the McGee Brothers, outstanding collections of old-time instrumental music by three of the genre's giants [see Section II above]. Smith died in 1971 from cancer. Throughout his career Smith was an influential fiddler; many of the tunes he popularized or composed have continued to be favorites with other fiddlers--in particular, bluegrass-oriented ones. Smith's tunes are well-suited to bluegrass adaptation, since his own style was so full of fire and dexterity. In these characteristics, he is closest to Clark Kessinger or Clayton McMichen, but there's no confusing his recordings with theirs or anyone else's. Smith also had a penchant for slow, bluesy tunes that became another hallmark of his. These albums are in every way an excellent collection; the selections offer a cross-section of Smith's finest recorded work; the technical quality is faultless, and the brochure notes are informative, readable, and sensitive. Apart from additional information on the backgrounds of some of the tunes one could not ask for more. [JEMFQ 55, JAF 395]

434 Label Name/Number: Bear Family [West Germany] BF 15521
Title: *Carolina Buddies--Walter Kid Smith, Vol. 1*
Source and Date of Recording: From commercial 78s, 1929-36
Date of Publication: [1976?]
Annotations: 4-p. brochure by Willard Johnson, Robert Nobley, Norm Cohen
Selections:
Broken Hearted Lover
He Went in Like a Lion
I Loved You So True

I Went To See My Sweetheart
In a Cottage by the Sea
It's Hard To Leave You Sweet Love
Mistreated Blues
Murder of the Lawson Family, The [F 35]
My Evolution Girl
My Father Doesn't Love Me Anymore
My Sweetheart Is a Shy Little Miss
One More Kiss Before You Go
Otto Wood, the Bandit
Story the Crow Told Me, The
We'll Talk About One Another
Work Don't Bother Me

BF 15521: The musical career of Walter "Kid" (or "Gid") Smith has been documented in *JEMFQ* #31 (Autumn 1973) and *Old Time Music* #17 (Summer 1975). Born in Carroll Cty, Virginia, in 1895, Smith surrounded himself with excellent musicians (he did not play himself) in order to make, between 1929 and 1936, some outstanding recordings of old ballads and songs. With a few scattered exceptions, this is the first offering of his music on LP. Though a few older pieces are included ("I Went To See My Sweetheart," recorded as "If One Won't Another One Will" by the Carter Family, is a descendent of Laws P 10), the majority are from pop music of the latter decades of the 19th century. Probably the oldest of these, "I Loved You So True," is Will S. Hays' "I'll Remember You Love in My Prayers" (1869). A few are Smith's own compositions: "My Evolution Girl," "Otto Wood, the Bandit," and "The Murder of the Lawson Family." The latter two seem to have become traditional in the Virginia/Carolina area. The brochure includes song lyrics and a biography. [JEMFQ 41]

435 Label Name/Number: Historical HLP 8004
Title: *Ernest V. Stoneman and His Dixie Mountaineers, 1927-1928*
Source and Date of Recording: From commercial 78s, 1927-28
Date of Publication: [< 1974]
Annotations: Liner notes by Richard Nevins
Selections:
Careless Love
East Bound Train
Hop Light Ladies
It's Sinful To Flirt
Kitty Wells
Old Maid and the Burglar
Once I Had a Fortune
Sally Goodin
There'll Come a Time
Unlucky Road to Washington

436a Label Name/Number: Old Homestead OHCS-172
Title: *Vol. I: With Family and Friends*
Artists: Ernest V. Stoneman and others
Editor: [John Morris]
Source and Date of Recording: From commercial 78s, 1927-34
Date of Publication: 1986
Annotations: Liner notes by Ivan M. Tribe

Selections:
All I've Got's Gone
Banks of the Ohio [F 5]
Broken Hearted Lover
Fallen by the Wayside
Goodbye Old Stepstone
Hand Me Down My Walking Cane
He's Coming After Me
I Remember Calvary
My First Bicycle Ride -- Uncle Eck Dunford
My Only Sweetheart
Peek-a-Boo Waltz
Resurrection, The
Skip to My Lou
Till the Snowflakes Fall
We Parted by the Riverside
When the Redeemed Are Gathered In

436b   Label Name/Number: Old Homestead OHCS-173
Title: *Vol. II: With Family and Friends*
Artist: Ernest V. Stoneman
Editor: [John Morris]
Source and Date of Recording: From commercial 78s, 1926-28
Date of Publication: 1986
Annotations: Liner notes by Ivan M. Tribe
Selections:
Fate of Talmadge Osborne, The
Girl I Left in Sunny Tennessee, The
I Love To Talk to Jesus
I Will Meet You in the Morning
I'll Be Satisfied
In the Golden Bye and Bye
Kenny Wagner's Surrender [E 8]
Little Old Log Cabin in the Lane
May I Sleep in Your Barn Tonight Mister?
Mountaineer's Courtship, The
Road to Washington
Story of the Mississippi, The
Sweet Summer's Gone Away
Two Little Children
When the Roses Bloom Again
Whip-Poor-Will Song, The

437   Label Name/Number: Rounder 1008
Title: *Ernest V. Stoneman and the Blue Ridge Corn Shuckers*
Source and Date of Recording: From commercial 78s, 1926-28
Date of Publication: 1975/76
Annotations: 12 p. brochure by Tony Russell
Selections:
All Go Hungry Hash House
Are You Washed in the Blood

Dying Girl's Farewell, The
Going up Cripple Creek
Hallelujah Side
I Know My Name Is There
Ida Red
Little Old Log Cabin in the Lane
Old Joe Clark
Poor Tramp, The
Raging Sea, How It Roars, The [C. 289]
Savingest Man on Earth, The
Sinless Summerland, The
Sourwood Mountain
Sweeping Through the Gates
West Virginia Highway

Hist HLP 8004 / OHCS 172 / OH 173 / Rndr 1008: Ernest V. "Pop" Stoneman (1893-1968) was born in the Blue Ridge Mountains of Virginia into a family of musicians and singers. In 1924, while working as a carpenter, he heard the first recordings of his friend, Henry Whitter, and felt he himself could do better, so he wrote to Columbia and OKeh to arrange recording auditions in New York. Thus began, in 1925, a career that spanned cylinder, 78 rpm recordings, LPs, radio, and television. He recorded over 200 selections between 1925 and 1929, and a handful more in 1934. "Pop" was a remarkable preserver of tradition rather than an innovator. He was not an exciting singer or musician but a competent one and felt his first duty as entertainer was to perform a song his audience could understand. He was an intelligent and perceptive musician who appreciated the commercial industry and learned how to work well within it. However, he was also aware of the academic aspects of folk music and was not shy about lifting some of his texts from books such as John H. Cox's *Folk-Songs of the South* (Harvard University Press, 1925). Stoneman's importance includes his training a generation of younger Stonemans, who went on to enjoy a successful career of their own after his death and into the 1980s. The history of the entire family has been meticulously documented by Ivan Tribe in his *The Stonemans* (University of Illinois Press, 1993).

Cty 533, one of three volumes issued by County Records featuring the exciting music of Carroll County, Virginia, centered around the town of Galax, is listed in Section IV. All the selections are by Stoneman and one or more of his musical colleagues or relatives. OH 172 represents an effort to strike a balance between stringband numbers and those that feature Stoneman as a solo artist, according to Ivan M. Tribe's liner notes. The selections range from the traditional ballad, "Banks of the Ohio" (Laws F 5), to 19th-century popular ballads and sacred songs. "My First Bicycle Ride" is a humorous monolog by Stoneman's long-time associate, Alex "Uncle Eck" Dunford.

Rndr 1008 is an excellent all-round survey, with an extensive biographical essay and complete discography. Hist HLP 8004 includes 10 selections all recorded for the Edison company in 1927-28. The disc consists largely of native American pieces from the last half of the 19th century--as did the bulk of Stoneman's repertory. Black influence in Stoneman's work was very slight; even "Careless Love" has elements of older British songs. [JAF 323, 409]

438 Label Name/Number: County 401
Title: *Old Time Fiddle Tunes 1928-1936*
Artists: The Stripling Brothers
Editor: [David Freeman]
Source and Date of Recording: From commercial 78s, 1920s-'30s
Date of Publication: 1971

Annotations: Liner notes by Robert C. Fleder
Selections:
    Big Eyed Rabbit
    Big Footed Man in the Sandy Lot
    Coal Mine Blues
    Dance All Night
    Horse Shoe Bend
    June Rose Waltz
    Kennedy Rag
    Lost Child, The
    Pallet on the Floor
    Ranger's Hornpipe
    Red River Waltz
    Wolves Howling

Cty 401: The Stripling Brothers, fiddler Charles Nevins (b. 1896) and guitarist Ira Lee (b. 1898), were a popular guitar/fiddle duo from Pickens County, Alabama, who began their musical development in their teens and were soon regulars at local fiddle contests. They recorded several times between 1928 and 1936; this album includes a sampling of their 42 issued duets. Charles's "The Lost Child," one of his regular contest pieces, is clearly an antecedent of Leslie Kieth's very popular "Black Mountain Rag." "Big Eyed Rabbit" is not the tune usually associated with that title, and "Ranger's Hornpipe" bears some resemblance to "Flop Eared Mule." The archaic-sounding "Wolves Howling" is a haunting piece that has turned up in tradition but may possibly owe its origin to this, its first recording. [WF 4/73]

439   **Label Name/Number:** Bear Family [West Germany] BF 15504 (Same as Folk Variety 12504):
Title: *Early Steel Guitar*
Artists: Tom Darby and Jimmie Tarlton
Editor: Richard Weize
Source and Date of Recording: From commercial 78s and test pressings, 1928-33
Date of Publication: [1974?]
Annotations: 4 p. brochure by Mike Paris
Selections:
    After the Ball
    After the Sinking of the Titanic [cf. D 24]
    Black Sheep
    By the Old Oaken Bucket, Louise
    Country Girl Valley
    Going Down That Lonesome Frisco Line
    Hobo Tramp
    I Can't Tell Why I Love Her
    I Left Her at the River
    Irish Police, The
    Let's Be Friends Again
    Little Bessie
    New Birmingham Jail
    New York Hobo [H 2]
    Pork Chops
    Whistling Songbird

440   Label Name/Number: Old Timey 112
Title: *Steel Guitar Blues*
Artists: Tom Darby and Jimmie Tarlton
Source and Date of Recording: From commercial 78s, 1927-32
Date of Publication: 1971
Annotations: Liner notes by Graham Wickham
Selections:
> Birmingham Jail, No. 2
> Birmingham Rag
> Birmingham Town
> Dixie Mail
> Down in Florida on a Hog
> Gamblin' Jim [I 4]
> Heavy Hearted Blues
> Lonesome in the Pines
> Lonesome Railroad
> Lowe Bonnie [C. 68]
> Mexican Rag
> Ooze up to Me
> Rainbow Division, The
> Weaver's Blues, The

BF 15504 / OT 112:   An important early team in leading country music from the string-band idiom of the 1920s to the guitar/steel guitar-based style that predominated in the 1930s was Tom Darby and Jimmie Tarlton. It was curious that Jimmie Tarlton, one of the best white blues performers of the 1920s (and still, into the 1960s, after his "rediscovery") insisted to me that he never learned songs from any black guitarists. His music makes this assertion difficult to accept, though he and his partner Tom Darby did record a good deal of non-blues material as well. The Bear Family album seems to stress this latter aspect of their music, including such turn-of-the-century pop songs as "Hobo Tramp," a variant of "Little Red Caboose Behind the Train" that was in print in the 1890s; "After the Ball" (1892), "The Black Sheep" (1897), "By the Old Oaken Bucket, Louise" (tune from the 1870s), and "Let's Be Friends Again" (probably 1890s). More likely of folk origin are "Pork Chops" and "Lonesome 'Frisco Line," respectively variants of "Sweet Thing" and "Going Down the Road Feeling Bad." The latter pieces, as well as "After the Sinking of the Titanic," are dubbed from previously unissued test pressings. The only item on OT 112 predating the late 19th century is Tarlton's "Lowe Bonnie," sung to the tune he claimed to have composed in order that his partner/rival Darby would not learn the original melody. However, the tune was used for "The Drunkard's Dream" well before his borrowing of it. Many of their songs derive from the minstrel and vaudeville stage of the late 1800s, and black influences are apparent throughout. For more on Tarlton's career, see the comments on Testament T-3302 in Section I. [WF 4/73, 7/75]

441   Label Name/Number: Puritan PU 3001
Title: *Great Original Recordings 1927-28*
Artists: The Tenneva Ramblers
Editor: Dave Samuelson
Source and Date of Recording: From commercial 78s, 1927-28
Date of Publication: 1972
Annotations: Liner notes by Dave Samuelson
Selections:
> Curtains of Night, The

Darling Where You Been So Long?
Goodbye My Honey I'm Gone
I'm Goin' to Georgia
If I Die a Railroad Man
Johnson Boys, The
Lonely Grave, The
Longest Train I Ever Saw, The
Miss Lisa, Poor Gal
Seven Long Years in Prison
Sweet Heaven When I Die
Tell It to Me
When a Man Is Married

Puritan PU 3001: The Tenneva Ramblers have long been remembered unfairly only as the band that Jimmie Rodgers took to Bristol, Tennessee, to make their first recordings in 1927. The musicians fell to quarrelling among themselves on the eve of their audition, and Rodgers never recorded with them. The recordings, then, are by Claude Grant, Jack Grant, Jack Pierce and Claude Slagle, and are the typical 1920s stringband melange of traditional ballads, contemporary pop tunes, and their own compositions or recompositions. The overall sound, though, is somewhat modern for the period, with vocals predominant and instruments (guitar, banjo, fiddle, mandolin) taking primarily an accompanying role. The band continued to play together after their last recordings in 1928, well into the '40s, but found it difficult to find jobs during the Depression. Samuelson's informative jacket notes benefited from his interviews with Claude Grant, the last surviving member of the foursome.

442   Label Name/Number: Historical 8001 (originally issued as Historical BC 2433-1)
Title: *Early Country Music*
Artists: Fields Ward's Buck Mountain Band (Fields Ward, Ernest Stoneman, Eck Dunford, Sampson Ward; Sweet Brothers)
Producer: Arnold S. Caplin
Source and Date of Recording: From commercial test pressings, 1928-29
Date of Publication: [ca. 1968]
Annotations: Liner notes by Fields Ward and Arnold S. Caplin
Selections: (Sides marked EVS are by Ernest Stoneman and the Sweet Brothers)
    Ain't That Trouble in Mind
    Birds Are Returning, The
    Goodbye Little Bonnie
    I Am Gonna Marry That Pretty Little Girl -- EVS
    I Got a Bulldog -- EVS
    John Hardy [I 2] -- EVS
    My Only Sweetheart
    New River Train, The -- EVS
    No One Loves You As I Do
    Say Darling Say -- EVS
    Sweetest Way Home, The
    Those Cruel Slavery Days
    Tie Up Those Broken Chords
    Watch and Pray
    Way Down in North Carolina
    You Must Be a Lover of the Lord

Hist BC 2433-1: The Ward Family of Galax has been one of the mainstays of the region's musical tradition--perhaps even more so than the Stonemans. The group's career on commercial 78s, though was not nearly so felicitous. Besides the albums listed here, they are also represented on County 534, listed in Section IV. The Wards also recorded for the LC several times between 1937 and 1941. In fact, the Ballard Branch Bogtrotters, with Crockett, Wade, and Fields Ward, Eck Dunford and Doc Davis, was one of the very few stringbands to be recorded by the Archive of Folk Music. "Jimmy Sutton" is from a 1937 recording supervised by John A. Lomax at the Galax Fiddlers' Convention. "Sweet William," a solo by Fields, "The Raging Sea," and "Jackie Munroe," duets by Crockett and Perline Ward, are from the 1937 and 1940 LC field recordings. Wade has been more extensively recorded than the other Wards; in addition to his participation in the Bogtrotters' recordings he was recorded several times for the LC between 1937 and 1970, has been featured prominently on three LPs (Biograph RC-6002A and Folkways FA 2380--discussed in Section I, and Folkways 2363--in Section II), and given lesser billing on several other discs. He justly deserved his reputation as one of the great clawhammer banjo pickers captured on disc. His solo banjo pieces, "Lost Indian" and "Die in the Field of Battle," from undated LC recordings, exemplify his skills. Among the most unusual and striking pieces on this Ward Family sampler are the two unaccompanied ballads, "Jackie Munroe" and "Sweet William."

The recordings credited to Fields Ward's Buck Mountain Band on the Historical LP were taken from test pressings in Ward's possession; they were cut at sessions in Richmond, Indiana, in 1929 intended for the Gennett label, but, because of contractual disagreements, were never issued in any form prior to this album. The sides marked "EVS" were from a different session, without Ward, in 1928. All these sides are technically and musically adequate, and illustrate that decisions to issue or not issue often have nothing to do with aesthetics. The titles in general are characteristic of the music of the area and appear on other labels also. Most are traditional, even though Fields Ward claimed composition of several pieces. [JAF 320--DKW]

SECTION IV: Anthologies--Reissues of Commercial 78 rpm Recordings

443   Label Name/Number: Brunswick 59000
Title: *Mountain Frolic*
Editor: Alan Lomax
Source and Date of Recordings: Studio recordings, 1927-31
Date of Publication: 1947 (78 rpm format)
Annotations: 18-p. booklet by Alan Lomax
Selections: [all reissued in Japan on Coral MH 174 except *]
   Arkansas Traveler -- Tennessee Ramblers
   Black Eyed Susie -- Al Hopkins and His Buckle Busters
   Cindy -- Bradley Kincaid
   Cluck, Old Hen -- Al Hopkins and His Buckle Busters
   Old Joe Clark -- Bradley Kincaid
   Sail Away, Ladies -- Uncle Dave Macon and His Fruit Jar Drinkers
   Sally Goodin / Sally In the Garden / Sourwood Mountain -- Crockett Family *
   Sugar Hill -- Dad Crockett

444   Label Name/Number: Brunswick 59001
Title: *Listen to Our Story*
Editor: Alan Lomax
Source and Date of Recordings: Studio recordings, 1927-31
Date of Publication: 1947 (78 rpm format)
Annotations: 20-p. booklet by Alan Lomax
Selections: [all reissued in Japan on Coral MH 174 except *]
   Death of John Henry, The [I 1] -- Uncle Dave Macon
   Derby Ram, The -- Bascom Lamar Lunsford
   Girl I Left Behind Me, The [Original 78 rpm title: Always Marry Your Lover] [P 1b] -- Dick
      Reinhart *
   Lady Gay [C. 79] -- Buell Kazee
   Pretty Polly [P 36b] -- Dock Boggs
   Rock About, My Saro Jane -- Uncle Dave Macon and His Fruit Jar Drinkers
[Also two African-American performances]

   Brunswick 59000 and Brunswick 59001: These two albums, first issued as 78 rpm sets (B-1024 and B-1025, respectively), then as 10" LPs, are of particular historic interest as being among the first hillbilly reissues aimed at a general urban audience. (See also comments on RCA LPV 507.) For 59000, Lomax selected eight items that demonstrated the closeness between commercial hillbilly recordings of the 1920s and '30s and the kind of music he and his father had been recording under the auspices of the Library of Congress. The result was an excellent collection of dance songs and tunes featuring some of the best commercially recorded stringbands of the period. Lomax's brochure interweaved his descriptions of the songs with "The Knob Dance, A Tennessee Frolic"--a short story from 1845 written by George W. Harris: "...Having somewhat rearranged Mr. Harris's tale and amplified it for dramatic purposes, I have woven into it the best recordings of Southern mountain frolic tunes that Brunswick has in its files." 59001 is, as its title suggested, devoted to ballads and songs (including two performances by black musicians as well). Kazee's "Lady Gay" won the praise of ethnomusicologist Charles Seeger as possibly the best recording of Child 79 available; it is a stunning performance. Macon's version of "John Henry" and Boggs's "Pretty Polly" are also outstanding examples of ballad singing with instrumental accompaniment. Both album brochures included text and tune transcriptions. [JAF 240--CS]

445   Label Name/Number: CMH (West Germany) CMH 106
Title: *Hoboes and Brakeman*
Source and Date of Recordings: From commercial 78s, 1926 - 1930s (except *)
Date of Publication:
Selections:
> At the End of the Hobo's Trail -- Goebel Reeves
> Barber's Blues -- Frankie Marvin
> Big Rock Candy Mountains, The -- Harry McClintock
> Billy Venero [B 6] -- Harry McClintock
> Bum Song, No. 2, The -- Harry McClintock
> Bum Song, The -- Harry McClintock
> Hallelujah, I'm a Bum -- Harry McClintock
> Hand Me Down My Walking Cane -- Kelly Harrell
> Jailhouse Blues -- Gene Autry
> New River Train -- Kelly Harrell
> Oh, For the Wild and Woolly West -- Frankie Marvin
> Oklahoma Kid, The -- Goebel Reeves
> Texas Rangers, The [A 8] -- Harry McClintock
> When the Old Age Pension Check Comes to Our Door -- Chris Comber *
> Who Said I Was a Bum -- Wendell Hall
> Wild Cat Mama -- Gene Autry
> Yodeling Ranger -- Jimmie Rodgers

CMH 106: This strange assortment is not always true to its title. Except for two 1926 selections by Harrell with studio musician accompaniment, all the tracks are vocal solos with guitar backup. Hobo/bum songs are performed by McClintock, Hall, and Reeves. McClintock also offers two traditional western ballads (A 8 and B 6). Among the other artists is contemporary Englishman, Chris Comber, who offers a remarkable performance of "The Old Age Pension Check" in 1930s hillbilly style. [WF 4/73]

446   Label Name/Number: Columbia CS 9660
Title: *Ballads and Breakdowns of the Golden Era*
Source and Date of Recordings: Studio recordings, 1926-31
Date of Publication: 1968
Annotations: Liner notes by Richard Nevins
Selections:
> Bill Mason -- Charlie Poole and the North Carolina Ramblers
> Darling Child -- Blue Ridge Highballers
> Fly Around My Pretty Little Miss -- Frank Blevins and His Tar Heel Rattlers
> Frankie Dean -- Tom Darby and Jimmie Tarlton
> Free a Little Bird -- Roane County Ramblers
> In the Pines -- Dock Walsh
> Johnson Gal -- Leake County Revelers
> Ladies on the Steamboat -- Burnett and Rutherford
> Moonshiner and His Money -- Charlie Bowman and His Brothers
> Murder of the Lawson Family [F 35] -- Carolina Buddies
> Paddy Won't You Drink Some Cider -- Clayton McMichen and Riley Puckett
> Sally Johnson -- Lowe Stokes and Riley Puckett
> Soldier's Joy -- Gid Tanner and His Skillet Lickers
> Standing by a Window -- Clay Everhart and the North Carolina Cooper Boys

Whitehouse Blues -- Charlie Poole and the North Carolina Ramblers
Willie Moore -- Burnett and Rutherford

Columbia CS 9660:   Although Columbia Records had in its vaults an enormous collection of wonderful hillbilly music from the mid 1920s on, the company was very slow to reissue any of it in LP format. In the mid-60s, producer John Hammond conceived and initiated a fine three-disc set that would have sampled some of the best of Columbia's artists of the 1020s and early '30s. Unfortunately, illness forced Hammond to hand the project over to others, and the decision to consummate production was repeatedly delayed. What finally did appear was a single, rather poorly mastered disc, by the time of publication of which most of the selected material--and much more-- had already been reissued elsewhere on bootleg LPs, and the disc's impact was considerably blunted. All the items on this LP are traditional, including "Frankie Dean" (I 3) and "Murder of the Lawson Family" (F 35). "Willie Moore" is a beautiful ballad, surely of British origin, that has been recovered only a handful of times; this 1927 recording is the source of most other recoveries. Several outstanding instrumental numbers are included, representing a variety of styles from Mississippi, Tennessee, Georgia, Kentucky, and North Carolina. The notes give complete recording data. [JAF 323]

447   Label Name/Number: Country Music Foundation CMF 011-L [2-LP set]
Title: *The Bristol Sessions: Historic Recordings from Bristol, Tennessee*
Editor: Bob Pinson
Source and Date of Recordings: Studio recordings, Bristol, TN, 1927
Date of Publication: 1987
Annotations: Gatefold jacket notes by Charles K. Wolfe
Selections:

Are You Washed in the Blood? -- Ernest V. Stoneman and his Dixie Mountaineers
Billy Grimes, the Rover -- Shelor Family
Black-Eyed Susie -- J. P. Nestor
Bury Me Under the Weeping Willow -- Carter Family
Greasy String -- West Virginia Coon Hunters
Henry Whitter's Fox Chase -- Henry Whitter
I Am Bound for the Promised Land -- Alfred G. Karnes
I Want To Go Where Jesus Is -- Ernest Phipps and his Holiness Quartet
I'm Redeemed -- Alcoa Quartet
Jealous Sweetheart, The -- Johnson Brothers
Johnny Goodwin -- Bull Mountain Moonshiners
Little Log Cabin by the Sea -- Carter Family
Longest Train I Ever Saw, The -- Tenneva Ramblers
Midnight on the Stormy Deep -- E. Stoneman, Miss I. Frost, E. Dunford
Mountaineer's Courtship, The -- E. Stoneman, Miss I. Frost, E. Dunford
Newmarket Wreck, The -- Mr. & Mrs. J. W. Baker
O Molly Dear [M 4] -- B. F. Shelton
Old Time Corn Shuckin', Pts. 1 & 2 -- Blue Ridge Corn Shuckers [sketch w/songs]
Passing Policeman, A -- Johnson Brothers
Poor Orphan Child, The -- Carter Family
Pot Licker Blues -- El Watson
Resurrection, The -- Ernest V. Stoneman and his Dixie Mountaineers
Sandy River Belle -- Dad Blackard's Moonshiners
Single Girl, Married Girl -- Carter Family
Skip to Ma Lou, My Darling -- Uncle Eck Dunford
Sleep, Baby, Sleep -- Jimmie Rodgers

Soldier's Sweetheart, The -- Jimmie Rodgers
Standing on the Promises -- Tennessee Mountaineers
Storms Are on the Ocean, The -- Carter Family
Tell Mother I Will Meet Her -- E. Stoneman, K. Brewer, M. Mooney
To the Work -- Alfred G. Karnes
Walking in the Way with Jesus -- Blind Alfred Reed
Wandering Boy, The -- Carter Family
When They Ring the Golden Bells -- Alfred G. Karnes
Wreck of the Virginian, The -- Blind Alfred Reed

CMF 011-L: As I recall, it must have been 25 years ago when Ed Kahn first suggested reissuing in chronological sequence the complete recordings from Victor Talking Machine Company's historic 1927 field sessions made in Bristol, Tennessee. Collectors and historians have always viewed those two weeks as a watershed in the history of hillbilly/country music, including, as they did, the first recordings of both Jimmie Rodgers and the Carter Family. This set didn't quite fulfill Kahn's aims, but it did include, in one two-disc set, 36 of the 76 recordings that the remarkable A&R man, Ralph S. Peer, made in Bristol between 25 July and 5 August, offering at least one example by every hillbilly artist that Peer recorded (only one item of the 76 was by a jazz band; the rest were all--so far as we know--hillbilly musicians.) Collectors welcomed the six previously unissued takes and the two previously unissued songs--"Midnight on the Stormy Deep" by Ernest V. Stoneman and company, and the Johnson Brothers' "A Passing Policeman." Charles Wolfe's informative (as usual) liner notes, filling the insides of the gatefold jacket, provide information not only on the various performers, but on the circumstances of the sessions, why Peer chose Bristol, and how he drew prospective talent. The inner sleeves include complete discographic data and photographs, many never previously published. Interestingly, in Peer's view, what really attracted would-be talent was a newspaper article about the first week's recordings that mentioned how much money some of the musicians were receiving for making records. Clearly, Peer was not going to attract the same kind of singers who had performed a decade earlier for Cecil Sharp, and vice versa. What we *don't* know about Peer's operation is how many performers auditioned for him but failed to pass his criteria for recording. What he did select for recording varied between good and outstanding. Though Rodgers and the Carters proved the most valuable to Victor (and the most important to country music history), there were outstanding traditional folksingers (Alfred G. Karnes is, in my opinion, one of the best ever recorded commercially) and instrumentalists in older styles: fiddler/singer Alfred Reed, banjoist/singers B.F. Shelton and J. P. Nestor, the Blackard/Shelor stringband, and others. [JAF 406]

448   Label Name/Number: Country Turtle 6001
Title: *Gambler's Lament*
Source and Date of Recordings: From commercial 78s, 1920s-'30s
Date of Publication: [1980]
Annotations: Brochure notes by Pat Conte and Frank Mare
Selections:
As We Sat Beneath the Maple on the Hill -- Posey Rorer
Cabin with the Roses, The -- Virginia Dandies
Frank DuPree -- Blind Andy
Gambler's Lament -- Zack Hurt
I Truly Understand You Love Another Man -- Shortbuckle Roark and His Family
Italy -- Bascom Lamar Lunsford
Jim Blake the Engineer -- Frank Wheeler and Monroe Lamb
On the Banks of the Old Tennessee -- Mr. and Mrs. J. W. Baker
Shut Up in Coal Creek Mine -- Green Bailey

Sweet William and Fair Ellen, Parts 1 and 2 [C. 7] -- Professor and Mrs. I. G. Greer
Tim Brooks [H 27] -- Carver Boys
Wreck of the Number Four, The -- Green Bailey
[Also one African-American ballad]

CT 6001: This excellent reissue features many performers not heard on LP previously. Among the best performances (in my opinion) are Green Bailey's powerfully moving "Shut Up in Coal Creek Mine," a song based on communications written by trapped miners who died in a horrible mine explosion (see notes to Rounder 1026, below); and George "Shortbuckle" Roark's wistful "I Truly Understand." The curiously titled "Italy" is a lyric song named, according to Lunsford, for a small mountain community. [JEMFQ 61]

449   Label Name/Number: County 501
Title: *A Collection of Mountain Fiddle Music*
Editor: [David Freeman]
Source and Date of Recordings: From commercial 78s, 1927-30
Date of Publication: [1963]
Selections:
Billy in the Low Ground -- Burnett and Rutherford
Cluck Old Hen -- Hill Billies
Darneo -- Blue Ridge Highballers
Forked Deer -- Taylor's Kentucky Boys
Greenback Dollar -- Weems String Band
Johnson City Rag -- Roane County Ramblers
Little Rabbit -- Crockett Mountaineers
Old Molly Hare -- McMichen and Puckett
Ragtime Annie -- Solomon and Hughes
Sally Johnson -- Lowe Stokes
Shootin' Creek -- North Carolina Ramblers
Wednesday Night Waltz -- Leake County Revelers

Cty 501: David Freeman of New York City debuted his new label in late 1963 with this sampler album of choice material from the late 1920s. Like Cty 502/3/4 (see below), it had no annotations, other than lists of titles and performers, but by listing individual artists, some of whom were not named on the original 78 rpm labels, the compiler revealed his considerable knowledge of early hillbilly recordings. The source of early County LPs was a well-kept secret (the first three listed no company address) partly for legal reasons, but in subsequent years County Records/County Sales has grown to be a major force in the preservation and production of traditional southeastern folk-derived music--both old-time hillbilly and bluegrass.

450   Label Name/Number: County 502
Title: *A Collection of Mountain Ballads*
Editor: [David Freeman]
Source and Date of Recordings: From commercial 78s, 1926-30
Date of Publication: [1964]
Selections:
Dark Holler Blues -- Clarence Ashley
Darling Cora -- B. F. Shelton
Fate of Ellen Smith, The [F 11] -- Green Bailey
George Collins [C. 85] -- North Carolina Ramblers
Henry Clay Beattie -- Kelly Harrell

I've Always Been a Rambler [P 1b] -- Grayson and Whitter
Six Months Ain't Long -- John Foster
Sunny Tennessee -- Floyd County Ramblers
Sweet Sunny South -- Piedmont Log Rollers
Wreck of the Virginian -- Blind Alfred Reed
Wreck on the Mountain Road -- Red Fox Chasers
[Death of] John Henry [, The] [I 1] -- Uncle Dave Macon and Sam McGee

Cty 502: When collector/proprietor David Freeman compiled County's second anthology of old-time hillbilly recordings, he didn't have a folklorist's rigorous definition of "ballad" in mind; consequently, the narrative strengths of the selections on this delightful compendium are not all as coherent as the title might suggest. With the exception of "George Collins" and "Always Been a Rambler," all the songs and ballads seem to be of New World origin. High points of the collection include the two banjo-accompanied vocals by Ashley and Shelton; Macon's oft-reissued "John Henry," one of the best versions on 78s; G. B. Grayson's masterful rendition of an old British ballad, to his own fiddle and Henry Whitter's guitar accompaniment; and the sentimental "Sweet Sunny South" by Red Patterson's band--one of the few popular 19th-century compositions to enter oral tradition that has resisted source identification.

451   Label Name/Number: County 503
Title: *A Collection of Mountain Fiddle Music, Vol. 2*
Editor: [David Freeman]
Source and Date of Recordings: From commercial 78s, 1927-30
Date of Publication: [1965]
Selections:
   Bull at the Wagon -- Dempson and Dennison Lewis
   C. and N. W. Railroad Blues -- Byron Parker's Mountaineers
   Charleston -- Narmour and Smith
   Free Little Bird -- Dykes Magic City Trio
   Going Down the Lee Highway -- Grayson and Whitter
   Green Valley Waltz -- McCartt Brothers and Patterson
   Hen Cackle -- Earl Johnson and Byrd Moore
   Old-Time Medley -- Crockett Mountaineers
   Rabbit up the Gum Stump -- Hiter Colvin
   Rat Cheese Under the Hill -- Clark and Luches Kessinger
   Searcy County Rag -- Ashley's Melody Men
   Wolves Howling -- Charles and Ira Stripling

Cty 503: This collection follows Cty 501 as an anthology of early fiddle music, mostly with stringband accompaniment and some with vocals. An excellent collection musically, this album and its other early companions on County have, to a considerable extent, been superseded by more recent collections that cover the same stylistic material and provide the listener some background information as well. [JAF 314--DKW]

452   Label Name/Number: County 504
Title: *A Collection of Mountain Songs*
Editor: [David Freeman]
Source and Date of Recordings: From commercial 78s, 1927-30
Date of Publication: [1965]
Selections:
   All Night Long Blues -- Burnett and Rutherford

Big Ball in Memphis -- Georgia Yellow Hammers
Careless Love -- Byrd Moore and His Hot Shots
George Washington -- Pope's Arkansas Mountaineers
Groundhog -- Jack Reedy and His Walker Mountain String Band
I'll Rise When the Rooster Crows -- Binkley Bros. Dixie Clodhoppers
In the Shadow of the Pine -- Kelly Harrell
Milwaukee Blues -- North Carolina Ramblers
Preacher Got Drunk and Laid His Bible Down, The -- Tennessee Ramblers
Sandy River Belle -- Dad Blackard's Moonshiners
Wish I Had Stayed in the Wagon Yard -- Lowe Stokes and His North Georgians
Your Low Down Dirty Ways -- Carolina Tar Heels

Cty 504: This lively collection of stringband-accompanied vocals offers performers from Kentucky, Georgia, North Carolina, Arkansas, and Tennessee. African-American influences are more evident than in the companion album, Cty 502 (see above)--especially in the very liquid, bluesy fiddling of Leonard Rutherford and Posey Rorer (in the North Carolina Ramblers) and "Careless Love" and "Wish I Had Stayed...," probably both more common in African-American than Anglo-American tradition. [JAF 314--DKW]

453 Label Name/Number: County 507
Title: *Old Time Fiddle Classics*
Editor: [David Freeman]
Source and Date of Recordings: From commercial 78s, 1920s-'30s
Date of Publication: [1965]
Selections:

Bill Cheathem -- Arthur Smith with the Delmore Brothers
Billy in the Low Ground -- Lowe Stokes and Riley Puckett
Brilliancy Medley -- Eck Robertson
Done Gone -- Clayton McMichen and Riley Puckett
I Get My Whiskey from Rockingham -- Earl Johnson
Johnson City Rag -- Roane County Ramblers
Lost Child -- Stripling Brothers
Moonshiner and His Money -- Charlie Bowman
New Lost Train Blues -- Clarence Todd and Ollie Bunn
Ragtime Annie -- Kessinger Brothers
Sugar in the Gourd -- Kahle Brewer with Stoneman's Dixie Mountaineers
Sunny Home in Dixie -- Frank and Oscar Jenkins, Ernest Stoneman

Cty 507: Subtitled "...played by champion fiddlers," this collection presents some of the best from the late 1920s and '30s, including Clayton McMichen, Lowe Stokes, James McCarroll of the Roane County Ramblers, Frank Jenkins, Eck Robertson, Clark Kessinger, Arthur Smith and Kahle Brewer-- representing Georgia, North Carolina, Alabama, Tennessee, Virginia, and Texas. [JAF 325--AJ]

454 Label Name/Number: County 508
Title: *Mountain Sacred Songs*
Editor: [David Freeman]
Source and Date of Recordings: From commercial 78s, 1920s-'30s
Date of Publication: [1965]
Annotations: Unsigned liner notes [by Archie Green]
Selections:

Ain't Going To Lay My Armor Down -- McVay and Johnson
Are You Sure -- Dixon Brothers and Mutt Evans
Are You Washed in the Blood of the Lamb -- Da Costa Woltz's Southern Broadcasters
Bathe in That Beautiful Pool -- Dock Walsh
Called to the Foreign Field -- Alfred G. Karnes
Don't Grieve After Me -- Ernest Phipps Holiness Quartet
Going Down the Valley -- Ernest Stoneman's Dixie Mountaineers
Great Reaping Day -- Roy Harvey and Jess Johnson
I Am on My Way to Heaven -- Hill Brothers and Willie Simmons
It Won't Be Long till My Grave Is Made -- Walter Smith, Norman Woodlieff and Posey Rorer
No Drunkard Can Enter There -- Delmore Brothers
Row Us over the Tide -- Kelly Harrell and Henry Norton

Cty 508: One of the few anthologies to explore the treatment of religous themes by old-time stringbands, this album filled a major gap in hillbilly music scholarship; unaccountably, the album was soon allowed to go out of print, and no similar collection has been assembled. However, two anthologies on the Marimac label [see below] offer a broader collection of religious music.

455   Label Name/Number: County 511
Title: *Mountain Blues*
Editor: [David Freeman]
Source and Date of Recordings: From commercial 78s, 1920s-'30s
Date of Publication: [1966?]
Selections:
Brown Skin Blues -- Dick Justice
Cannon Ball Blues -- Frank Hutchison
Careless Love -- Jimmie Tarlton
Carroll County Blues -- Narmour and Smith
Cumberland Blues -- Doc Roberts
Curley Headed Woman -- Burnett and Rutherford
Down South Blues -- Dock Boggs
Farm Girl Blues -- Carolina Tar Heels
Johnson City Blues -- Clarence Greene
Leake County Blues -- Leake County Revelers
Left All Alone Again Blues -- Lowe Stokes and his North Georgians
Railroad Blues -- Sam McGee

Cty 511: Presents a dozen different artists who demonstrate the heavy black influence in some styles of hillbilly music. This is perhaps most evident in the five vocal/guitar selections by McGee of Tennessee, Tarlton of South Carolina (steel guitar), Justice and Hutchison of West Virginia, and Green of North Carolina. Stokes' band shows heavy urban influence -- as often was the case with the music of these musicians from the Atlanta area. Many of the artists represented (McGee, Tarlton, Green, Boggs, Walsh, Burnett) were interviewed and recorded in the late '50s or '60s. Though most openly acknowledged their indebtedness to black musicians, others were adamant in denying any such influence. [JAF 323]

456   Label Name/Number: County 514
Title: *Hell Broke Loose in Georgia*
Source and Date of Recordings: From commercial 78s, 1927-34
Date of Publication: [1967?]

Selections:

Arkansas Traveler -- Earl Johnson and His Dixie Entertainers
Christmas Time Will Soon Be Over -- Fiddlin' John Carson's Virginia Reelers
Diamond Joe -- Georgia Crackers
Don't You Cry My Honey -- Gid Tanner's Skillet Lickers
Four Cent Cotton -- Lowe Stokes' Georgia Potlickers
Georgia Blues -- Bill Helms Upson County Band
Goin' Crazy -- Shores Southern Trio
Katy Did -- Lowe Stokes and Mike Whitten
Kiss Me Quick -- Georgia Yellow Hammers
Soldier's Joy -- Gid Tanner's Skillet Lickers
Swamp Cat Rag -- Swamp Rooters
12th Street Blues -- Dupree's Rome Boys

Cty 514: North Georgia was an active center of rural music in the early decades of this century, and that activity manifested itself in a highly popular annual fiddlers' convention, early appearances on WSB, one of the first radio stations in the country, and numerous recordings by local musicians starting in 1924. The Georgia stringband style was generally a wildly exuberant one, prominently featuring one or often more lead fiddles, strong rhythmic backup on guitar, and banjo generally playing rhythm backup rather than melody line. At least, this characterized the bands of John Carson, Earl Johnson, Bill Helms, Gid Tanner, and Lowe Stokes, all of whom can be heard on this lively collection.

457 Label Name/Number: County 515
Title: *Mountain Banjo Songs and Tunes*
Source and Date of Recordings: From commercial 78s, 1925-33
Date of Publication: 1968
Annotations: Liner notes by John Burke
Selections:

American and Spanish Fandango -- R. B. Smith and S. J. Allgood
Charming Betsy -- Land Norris
Cheat 'Em -- Red Headed Fiddlers
Coal Creek March -- Marion Underwood
Don't Get Weary Children -- Uncle Dave Macon
Going Back to Jericho -- Dock Walsh
Home Sweet Home -- Frank Jenkins
Leather Breeches -- W. A. Hinton
Little Turtle Dove -- Bascom Lamar Lunsford
Orphan Girl, The -- Buell Kazee
Railroad Bill -- Riley Puckett and Gid Tanner
Shuffle Feet Shuffle -- Fisher Hendley and J. Small

Cty 515: This is an enjoyable and informative collection of a dozen pieces originally recorded in 1925-33. Liner notes call attention to the various regional styles represented, including two-finger picking from Kentucky (Underwood), three-finger picking from North Carolina (Jenkins), and a variety of frailing techniques (Macon, Puckett, Hinton). [JAF 327]

458 Label Name/Number: County 517
Title: *Texas Farewell*
Source and Date of Recordings: From commercial 78s, 1922-30
Date of Publication: 1969

Annotations: Liner notes by Charles Faurot
Selections:
Arkansas Traveler -- Eck Robertson and Henry Gilliland
Babe -- East Texas Serenaders
Beaumont Rag -- Smith's Garage Fiddle Band
Bull at the Wagon -- Dempson Lewis and Denmon Lewis
Dallas Bound -- Oscar Harper and Doc Harper
Fatal Wedding, The -- Red Headed Fiddlers
Great Big Taters -- Eck Robertson and J. B. Cranfill
Sally Johnson -- Ervin Solomon, Joe Hughes and Jim Solomon
Sally Johnson -- Lewis Brothers
Texas Farewell -- Fiddlin' Jim Pate
Texas Quick-Step -- Red Headed Fiddlers
Three-in-One Two-Step -- East Texas Serenaders

Cty 517:   The Lone Star State, with its curious blend of folklore imported by settlers of Irish, German, and Mexican ancestry, has given birth to one of the most melodic, ornamental, and fluid styles of American folk fiddling. This album surveys some popular fiddlers when the tradition was in a somewhat different stylistic period. Faurot's liner notes point out that Texas fiddling is heavily ornamented because bands in this area played strictly instrumental numbers rather than providing accompaniment for vocalists; and in fact all 12 of the selections on this album are instrumentals. Biographical data are provided where known. [WF 7/71]

459a   Label Name/Number: County 518
Title: *Echoes of the Ozarks, Vol. 1*
Editor: [David Freeman]
Source and Date of Recordings: From commercial 78s, 1928-32
Date of Publication: 1970
Annotations: Liner notes by David Freeman
Selections:
Bath House Blues -- Ashley's Melody Men
Birmingham -- Pope's Arkansas Mountaineers
Booneville Stomp -- Dutch Cole and Red Whitehead
Cotton Eyed Joe -- Pope's Arkansas Mountaineers
Dry and Dusty -- Morrison Twin Brothers String Band
Eighth of January -- Arkansas Barefoot Boys
Get Along Home Miss Cindy -- Pope's Arkansas Mountaineers
Give the Fiddler a Dram -- Carter Brothers and Son
Hog Eye -- Pope's Arkansas Mountaineers
Jaw Bone -- Pope's Arkansas Mountaineers
Ozark Waltz -- Morrison Twin Brothers String Band
Searcy County Rag -- Ashley's Melody Men

459b   Label Name/Number: County 519
Title: *Echoes of the Ozarks, Vol. 2*
Editor: [David Freeman]
Source and Date of Recordings: From commercial 78s, 1928-32
Date of Publication: 1970
Annotations: Liner notes by David Freeman
Selections:
Drunkard's Hiccoughs -- Reaves White County Ramblers

Flying Engine -- Reaves White County Ramblers
Ft. Smith Breakdown -- Luke Highnight's Ozark Strutters
Going Down the River -- Dr. Smith's Hoss Hair Pullers
I'm Going To Leave Old Arkansas -- A. E. Ward and His Plowboys
Kansas City Reel -- Fiddlin' Bob Larkan and Family
Rattler Treed a Possum -- Reaves White County Ramblers
Saturday Night Waltz -- Fiddlin' Bob Larkan and Family
Shortenin' Bread -- Reaves White County Ramblers
Ten Cent Piece -- Reaves White County Ramblers
There's No Hell in Georgia -- Luke Highnight's Ozark Strutters
Where the Irish Potatoes Grow -- Dr. Smith's Hoss Hair Pullers

459c   Label Name/Number: County 520
Title: *Echoes of the Ozarks, Vol. 3*
Editor: [David Freeman]
Source and Date of Recordings: From commercial 78s, 1928-32
Date of Publication: 1970
Annotations: Liner notes by David Freeman
Selections:

Corn Dodger Special No. 1 -- George Edgin's Corn Dodgers
Cotton Eyed Joe -- Carter Brothers and Son
Davy, Davy -- Weems String Band
Echoes of the Ozarks -- Fiddlin' Sam Long
Greenback Dollar -- Weems String Band
I'm Sad and Blue -- Perry County Music Makers
Indian War Whoop -- Hiter Colvin
Liza Jane -- Carter Brothers and Son
My Ozark Mountain Home -- George Edgin's Corn Dodgers
Nancy Rowland -- Carter Brothers and Son
Old Jaw Bone -- Carter Brothers and Son
Rabbit up a Gum Stump -- Hiter Colvin
Robinson County -- Birkhead and Lane
Seneca Square Dance -- Fiddlin' Sam Long

Cty 518 / 519 / 520: Of all the regional styles to be presented on hillbilly records, that of the Ozarks seems to have been the freest of pop, jazz, and blues influences, and therefore possibly the oldest. Neither the recordings nor the performers seem to have found their way out of the Ozarks very much, and producer/annotator Freeman had to do considerable field work to find the biographical information he provides in his liner notes. Based on the 17 groups represented on the three discs, typical instrumentation in this region was fiddle(s) and guitar(s); only four groups used banjo. There is an apparent contradiction here between the assertion that the Ozark music is archaic and the frequent appearance of the guitar, considered a late comer into the mountains -- at least in the Appalachians. Perhaps in the Ozarks the guitar gained a foothold earlier than did the banjo. Other instruments represented are harmonica and piano, with occasional appearance of a string bass and a unique recording of a zither. [WF 7/71]

460   Label Name/Number: County 522
Title: *Old Time Ballads from the Southern Mountains*
Source and Date of Recordings: From commercial 78s, 1927-31
Date of Publication: [1972]
Selections:

Banks of the Ohio, The [F 5] -- Grayson and Whitter
Broken Wedding -- Emry Arthur
Burial of Wild Bill -- Frank Jenkins' Pilot Mountaineers
Charles Guiteau [E 11] -- Kelly Harrell and the Virginia String Band
Fate of Chris Lively and Wife -- Blind A. Reed with Orville Reed
Louisville Burglar [L 16b] -- Hickory Nuts
My Mama Always Talked to Me -- John Hammond
Newmarket Wreck, The -- Mr. and Mrs. J. W. Baker
Otto Wood the Bandit -- Carolina Buddies and Walter Smith
Pearl Bryan [F 2] -- R. D. Burnett and L. Rutherford
Pretty Polly [P 36b] -- B. F. Shelton
Sporting Cowboy, The [E 17] -- Watts and Wilson

Cty 522: This includes a dozen commercially recorded items from the late 1920s -- some well-known ballads (E 11, E 17, F 1b, F 5, L 16b, P 36b), others quite rare. "Burial of Wild Bill" by Jenkins' Pilot Mountaineers is based on a poem by Capt. Jack Crawford published in 1879. The Baker duo's "Newmarket Wreck" reports a train collision in Tennessee in 1904. Alfred Reed's "Fate of Chris Lively and Wife" describes the death of a couple when their car was struck by a train. "Otto Wood the Bandit," performed by the Carolina Buddies, sympathizes with a young man who shot a Jewish pawnbroker for failing to keep a watch that was in hock. The song was written by the group's singer, Walter Smith, who also composed "The Lawson Family Murder." The excellent fiddle and guitar accompaniment to "Otto Wood" make it one of the highlights of the album. Also musically outstanding are John Hammond's blues ballad, "My Mama Always Talked to Me," and Emry Arthur's "The Broken Wedding," sung to the same beautiful one-line mixolydian melody as his "I Am a Man of Constant Sorrow." The album's only flaw is lack of any annotation. [WF 4/73; JAF 338--DKW]

461   **Label Name/Number:** County 523
Title: *Old-Time Mountain Guitar*
Source and Date of Recordings: From commercial 78s, 1926-30
Date of Publication: 1972
Annotations: Liner notes by Robert Fleder
Selections:

Back to the Blue Ridge -- Roy Harvey and Leonard Copeland
Charlotte Hot-Step -- David Fletcher and Gwen Foster
Fresno Blues -- Johnny and Albert Crockett
Greasy Wagon -- Roy Harvey and Leonard Copeland
Guitar Rag -- Roy Harvey and Jess Johnson
Jailhouse Rag -- David Miller
Jefferson St. Rag -- Roy Harvey and Jess Johnson
Knoxville Blues -- Sam McGee
Logan County Blues -- Frank Hutchison
Lonesome Weary Blues -- Roy Harvey and Leonard Copeland
Red Rose Rag -- David Fletcher and Gwen Foster
Spanish Fandango -- John Dilleshaw and the String Marvel
Take Me to the Land of Jazz -- Lowe Stokes' North Georgians

Cty 523: Over half of the pieces on this interesting sampling are guitar duets. Fleder's fine notes help to place folk guitar in proper perspective against the broader backdrop of American popular music, but they also indicate that very little was known about most of the artists represented on this disc at the time of its publication: only Harvey, the Crockett Family, and Sam

McGee had received any detailed biographical treatment. Since then, more has been written about Dilleshaw, Miller, Johnson, and Hutchison as well. The guitar has been such a strong backbone to much of American country, blues, and folk music, and pop music since the 1950s that it may surprise some listeners to learn that its role as a solo or lead instrument during the 1920s was very uncommon. This album, then, hardly presents the typical but rather the unusual; and while lead guitar was rare, those few practitioners who pioneered the art were very successful artistically, if not always commercially. [WF 4/73; JAF 341--DKW]

462 **Label Name/Number:** County 525
Title: *A Fiddlers' Convention in Mountain City, Tennessee*
Source and Date of Recordings: From commercial 78s, 1925-30
Date of Publication: 1972
Annotations: 3 p. insert booklet by Joe Wilson
Selections:
>   Blue-Eyed Girl -- Hill Billies
>   Boatin' up Sandy -- Hill Billies
>   Buck Eyed Rabbits -- Hill Billies
>   Dark Holler Blues -- Clarence 'Tom' Ashley
>   Don't Let Your Deal Go Down -- Fiddlin' John Carson
>   Hell Bound for Alabama -- Fiddlin' John Carson and His Virginia Reelers
>   Never Be As Fast As I Have Been -- G. B. Grayson and Henry Whitter
>   Old John Hardy [I 2] -- Clarence 'Tom' Ashley
>   Patty on the Turnpike -- Fiddlin' Powers Family
>   Roll on Buddy -- Charlie Bowman and His Brothers
>   Tennessee Breakdown -- Vance's Tennessee Break-downers
>   Tennessee Mountain Fox Chase -- Vance's Tennessee Breakdowners

Cty 525: This album is organized around a novel theme: the artists were all present at the important May 1925 Mountain City fiddlers' convention -- although the recordings themselves were taken from various different sessions between 1925 and 1930. Wilson sees this event as "a watershed in the development of professional country music: it brought together four of the earliest groups [Carson, Hill Billies, Powers, Stuart] to pioneer in radio and recording in a 'package' show. More important, it demonstrated the power of these new media." Among the best performances are Carson's outstanding "Don't Let Your Deal Go Down" (not the usual melody, nor tempo) and Ashley's two banjo songs. "Dark Holler Blues" is his variant of "East Virginia Blues." Particularly interesting is Grayson's variant of what is usually titled "Rain and Snow." [WF 7/75]

463 **Label Name/Number:** County 527
Title: *Old-Time Fiddle Classics, Vol. 2*
Source and Date of Recordings: From commercial 78s, 1927-34
Date of Publication: 1973
Annotations: Liner notes by Richard Nevins
Selections:
>   8th of January -- Ted Gossett's Band
>   Citaco -- Swamp Rooters
>   Cumberland Gap -- Leonard Rutherford, Byrd Moore, and R. D. Burnett
>   Forky Deer -- Charlie Bowman and His Brothers
>   Last Days in Georgia -- Melvin Robinette and Byrd Moore
>   Mineola Rag -- East Texas Serenaders
>   Old Molly Hare -- Clayton McMichen and Riley Puckett
>   Paddy on the Handcar -- Red Headed Fiddlers

Pike's Peak -- Sharp, Hinman, and Sharp
Rye Straw -- Fiddlin' Doc Roberts
Salt River -- Clark Kessinger and Luches Kessinger
Texas Wagoner -- Eck Robertson

Cty 527: This is an eclectic sampling of fiddle music from 1927-34; some of the fiddlers are familiar enough (Kessinger, McMichen, Robertson, Stokes), but others had not been previously heard on LP (Robinette, Gossett, Sharp). Some, like Roberts and Rutherford, were very popular in their day and recorded extensively, yet little of their work had been reissued. [WF 7/75]

464a   Label Name/Number: County 528
Title: *Traditional Fiddle Music of Mississippi, Vol. 1*
Source and Date of Recordings: From commercial 78s, 1925-30
Date of Publication: 1975
Annotations: Liner notes by David Freeman
Selections:
    Avalon Quick Step -- Narmour and Smith
    Carroll County Blues -- Narmour and Smith
    Cotton Eyed Joe -- Carter Bros. and Son
    Indian War Whoop -- Floyd Ming and His Pep-Steppers
    Jake Leg Wobble -- Ray Brothers
    Jenny on the Railroad -- Carter Brothers and Son
    Last Shot Got Him, The -- Mississippi Possum Hunters
    Miss Brown -- Carter Brothers and Son
    Mississippi Breakdown -- Narmour and Smith
    Mississippi Echoes -- Ray Brothers
    Nancy Rowland -- Carter Brothers and Son
    Possum on a Rail -- Mississippi Possum Hunters
    Rufus Rastus -- Mississippi Possum Hunters
    Tupelo Blues -- Floyd Ming and His Pep-Steppers

464b   Label Name/Number: County 529
Title: *Traditional Fiddle Music of Mississippi, Vol. 2,*
Source and Date of Recordings: From commercial 78s, 1925-30
Date of Publication: 1975
Annotations: Liner notes by David Freeman
Selections:
    Bankhead Blues -- Nations Brothers
    Been to the East, Been to the West -- Leake County Revelers
    Captain George Has Your Money Come? -- Narmour and Smith
    Charleston No. 1 -- Narmour and Smith
    Croquet Habit -- Freeny's Barn Dance Band
    Don't You Remember the Time? -- Freeny's Barn Dance Band
    Johnson Gal -- Leake County Revelers
    Magnolia One-Step -- Nations Brothers
    Mississippi Square Dance (Sally Ann) -- Freeny's Barn Dance Band
    Molly Put the Kettle On -- Leake County Revelers
    Sales Tax Toddle -- Nations Brothers
    Sullivan's Hollow -- Freeny's Barn Dance Band
    Sweet Milk and Peaches -- Narmour and Smith

Cty 528 / Cty 529:   Together these albums, by some of the best Mississippi stringbands to make commercial recordings, go a long way toward correcting the great lack of Mississippi string-band music available on LP.   The 28 selections feature mostly fiddle(s), played with short bow strokes, accompanied by guitar, with occasional banjo or vocal.   However, Freeman in his liner notes warns against drawing generalizations to Mississippi stringband styles in general on the basis of these examples.   The bands range from the widely known and successful Leake County Revelers and Narmour & Smith to the obscure Freeny's Barn Dance Band; from the fairly typical styles (for the '20s) of the Leake County Band to the much older sound of the Carters, whose tunes are often mixolydian (or nearly so), with frequent mouth music vocalizations.   (The fiddling Carter Brothers were both born in the 1870s).   Freeman's liner notes include biographical information gathered during a field trip in 1973 that sheds light on several of the musicians who hitherto were completely unknown entities to collectors and scholars.   Although some commentary on the more obscure fiddle tunes would have been useful, these are outstanding reissues. [JEMFQ 41, JAF 395]

465   Label Name/Number: County 531
Title: *Old Time String Band Classics*
Source and Date of Recordings: From commercial 78s, 1927-33
Date of Publication: 1975
Annotations: Liner notes by Tom Carter
Selections:
>Camp Nelson Blues -- Booker Orchestra
>Carolina Stompdown -- Aiken County String Band
>Eighth of January -- Fox Chasers
>Going to Jail -- Ted Gossett's Band
>Granny Will Your Dog Bite -- Floyd County Ramblers
>Ham Beats All Meat -- Dr. Humphrey Bate and His Possum Hunters
>Johnny Lover -- Roanoke Jug Band
>L and N Rag -- Alex Hood and His Railroad Boys
>Mississippi Jubilee -- Earl Johnson and His Clodhoppers
>Robinson County -- Sharp, Hinman and Sharp
>Sailing on the Ocean -- Luke Highnight and His Ozark Strutters
>Saro -- Caplinger's Cumberland Mountain Entertainers

Cty 531:   The recordings are all delightful.   I find particularly enjoyable Ted Sharp's fiddle-led "Robinson County" (with piano accompaniment), the raggy "Going to Jail" by the Gossett Band, and the musical miscegenation represented by the Booker Orchestra -- one of the few black aggregations to be recorded playing in the white (well, nearly white) stringband style.   Carter's notes stress the changes that took place in the music when new styles, such as blues, ragtime, and swing permeated the South.   Most of the selections on this LP are products of the influences of such 20th-century genres on the older survivals of Anglo-American instrumental music.   In this sense, then, the appellation "old-time," which was used as a frequent descriptive even in the 1920s, was a misnomer: this music was quite modern in the sense that it would never have been heard 2 or 3 decades earlier.   Yet to contemporary listeners--in particular the city-bred record company executives who created the advertising terminology to describe their product--the difference between what they heard here and what they knew as up-to-date styles (e.g., blues, jazz, etc.) was more apparent than the difference between these stringbands and the much older styles of, say, an Emmett Lundy or an Ed Haley. [JEMFQ 49]

466a   Label Name/Number: County 533
Title: *Round the Heart of Old Galax, Vol. 1*

Artists: Ernest V. Stoneman, Eck Dunford, George Stoneman, Kahle Brewer, Irma Frost, Tom Leonard, W. Mooney, Herbert Sweet, Earl Sweet, Hattie Stoneman, I. Edwards, Bolen Frost, Edna Brewer

Editor: [David Freeman]

Place and Date of Recording: From commercial 78s, 1920s-'30s

Date of Publication: 1980

Annotations: Liner notes by Wayne Martin

Selections:

    Barney McCoy -- Eck Dunford and band

    Buffalo Gals -- Kahle Brewer, Bolen Frost and E. V. Stoneman

    Flop Eared Mule -- Kahle Brewer, Bolen Frost and E. V. Stoneman

    I Am Resolved -- E. V. Stoneman, Kahle Brewer and Irma Frost

    John Hardy -- Sweet Brothers and E. V. Stoneman

    Lonesome Road Blues -- E. V. Stoneman, Kahle Brewer, and Bolen Frost

    New River Train -- Herbert Sweet, Earl Sweet and E. V. Stoneman

    No More Goodbyes -- E. V. Stoneman and band

    Sweet Bunch of Violets -- E. V. Stoneman and Kahle Brewer

    Tell Mother I Will Meet Her -- E. V. Stoneman, Kahle Brewer and W. Mooney

    There's a Light Lit Up in Galilee -- E. V. Stoneman, Hattie Stoneman, Eck Dunford

    Too Late -- E. V. Stoneman, Hattie Stoneman and Eck Dunford

    Two Little Orphans -- E. V. Stoneman, Eck Dunford, George Stoneman

    Old Hickory Cane, The -- E. V. Stoneman

466b   Label Name/Number: County 534

Title: *Round the Heart of Old Galax, Vol. 2*

Artists: The Ward Family and others

Collector/Recordist: Some from commercial 78s, 1920s-'30s; others from Library of Congress field recordings by John Lomax

Editor: Wayne Martin

Place and Date of Recording: Mostly in Galax, VA: 1923-1941

Date of Publication: 1980

Annotations: Liner notes by Martin

Selections:

    Crockett Ward & his Boys

        Ain't That Trouble in Mind

        Sugar Hill

    Wade Ward

        Die in the Field of Battle

        Lost Indian

        Married Man's Blues, A

    Fields Ward & Grayson County Railsplitters

        My Only Sweetheart

        Watch and Pray

        Way Down in North Carolina

    Crockett and Perline Ward

        Jackie Munroe [N 7]

        Raging Sea, The [C. 289]

    Ballard Branch Bogtrotters

        Jimmy Sutton

    Fields Ward

        Sweet William [C. 7]

Dunford, Stoneman, Edwards
    Ain't That Trouble in Mind
    Skip to My Lou

466c   **Label Name/Number:** County 535
Title: *Round the Heart of Old Galax, Vol. 3*
Place and Date of Recording: Some from commercial 78s, 1920s-'30s; others from Library of Congress field recordings of 1941
Date of Publication: 1980
Annotations: Liner notes by Wayne Martin
Selections:
    Black Eyed Susie -- J. P. Nestor and Norman Edmonds
    Chilly Winds -- Wade Ward
    Ducks on the Millpond -- Emmett Lundy, Kelly Lundy, and Geedy Lundy
    Fox Chase -- Wade Ward
    I Ain't Nobody's Darling -- Piper Gap Ramblers
    I'm Going To Marry That Pretty Little Girl -- Sweet Brothers
    I've Got a Bulldog -- Sweet Brothers and E. V. Stoneman
    Mississippi Sawyer -- Emmett Lundy, Kelly Lundy, and Geedy Lundy
    Old Dad -- John Rector
    Piney Woods Girl -- Emmett Lundy and E. V. Stoneman
    Say Darling Say -- Sweet Brothers and E. V. Stoneman
    Train on the Island -- J. P. Nestor and Norman Edmonds
    Waves on the Ocean -- Emmett Lundy and Kelly Lundy
    Yankee Doodle -- Pipers Gap Ramblers

Cty 533 /534 /535: The Galax area has fascinated collectors of old-timey and folk music for many years. Rural until the turn of the century, Fries and Galax were established in the very early 1900s, both based on the just-starting lumber milling and wood products industries. Railroads had come into the area in the preceding decade, probably exposing for the first time the residents to the music of the Afro-Americans and to their instruments. Nevertheless, much of what is preserved on these three discs and on other recordings by these artists and others who recorded commercially in the 1920s from Grayson/Carroll Counties, shows very little minstrel, blues, jazz, or ragtime influence. Although Martin, in his brief general notes repeated on the jackets of all three albums, wisely cautions against generalizing about a "Galax sound," it does seem generally true that the lead fiddling (double fiddle does not seem to be common) is, as Martin notes, "characterized by intricate bowing and complex melody lines," using "double stops as points of emphasis rather than as continuous drones." The banjo playing is usually but not invariably in the clawhammer, rather than finger-picking style; guitar is used as a rhythmic backup with simple chordal strumming and short bass runs. Everything from old British ballads to turn-of-the-century TPA sentimental ballads survived on records. The recorded evidence also suggests that many dance tunes which subsequently became widespread may have originated in this area of Southern Virginia -- including "Old Joe Clark," "Cripple Creek," and "New River Train." Of course, we must be wary of treating the small sampling of music that has survived on 78s as representative: how much, for example, is our image of Galax music shaped by the extensive and influential recordings of the likes of Ernest Stoneman?

Wade Ward recorded a pair of banjo pieces in 1926 for OKeh, one of which, "Married Man's Blues," is issued on Cty 534 for the first time. Crockett, Fields, and Sampson Ward recorded a half-dozen stringband tunes the following year as Crockett Ward and His Boys, two cuts of which, "Sugar Hill" and "Ain't That Trouble in Mind," are included here. In 1929 Fields and Sampson joined Stoneman and Eck Dunford as Fields Ward and the Grayson County Railsplitters, in a recording session for the Gennett label, but none of the recordings was issued on 78s. "My Only Sweetheart," "Way Down in North Carolina," and "Watch and Pray" are from that session.

County 535 is divided among several performers. Three more cuts from the 1928 Gennett sessions of Ernest Stoneman and the Sweet Brothers are heard. The only two issued banjo-fiddle duets by Hillsville musicians J. P. Nestor and Norman Edmonds, made in 1927 for Victor, are reissued here. Similarly, the two selections by the Pipers Gap Ramblers, a Coal Creek band featuring Ike and Haston Lowe and Josh and Walter Hanks, are the only issued recordings from their sole recording session in 1927 for OKeh. Emmett Lundy from Delhart was reputed to be one of the finest fiddlers of the Galax area. He made only two commercial recordings -- both in 1925 for OKeh when he accompanied Ernest Stoneman to New York for a recording session. One of these, "Piney Woods Girl," is reissued here for the first time. Lundy was recorded again in 1941 for the LC; from that session are the three other pieces by him on this LP. (For a more extensive sampling of his 1941 recordings see String STR 802.) The remaining numbers on this album are also LC recordings. Perhaps the most exciting piece is the fiddle solo, "Old Dad" (a version of "Stoney Point") by Galax musician John Rector. The final two selections are both banjo solos by Wade Ward from undated LC sessions. Both of them were pieces that he played frequently and are more fine examples of his skills. These albums comprise an excellent set, and Martin, a young student of old-time music who has had his own band in the Chapel Hill, NC, area, put a great deal of effort into their production. They are highly recommended on both historical and aesthetic grounds. [JEMFQ 63]

467a   Label Name/Number: County 541
Title: *Nashville, the Early String Bands, Vol. 1*
Source and Date of Recordings: From commercial 78s, 1925-34
Date of Publication: 1976
Annotations: Same 14 p. brochure and liner notes by Charles Wolfe and Barry Poss for both
      Vols. 1 and 2
Selections:
    Candy Girl -- Uncle Bunt Stephens
    Chevrolet Car -- Sam McGee
    Eighth of January -- Dr. Humphrey Bate and His Possum Hunters
    Give Me Back My Fifteen Cents -- Binkley Brothers
    Green Backed Dollar Bill -- Dr. Humphrey Bate and His Possum Hunters
    I'm Going Away in the Morn -- Uncle Dave Macon and His Fruit Jar Drinkers
    My Wife Died Saturday Night -- Dr. Humphrey Bate and His Possum Hunters
    Old Joe -- Sid Harkreader and Grady Moore
    Railroadin' and Gamblin' -- Uncle Dave Macon
    Robertson County -- Paul Warmack and His Gully Jumpers
    Salt Lake City Blues -- Sam and Kirk McGee
    Stone Rag -- Paul Warmack and His Gully Jumpers
    Throw the Old Cow Over the Fence -- Dr. Humphrey Bate and His Possum Hunters

467b   Label Name/Number: County 542
Title: *Nashville, the Early String Bands, Vol. 2*
Source and Date of Recordings: From commercial 78s, 1925-34
Date of Publication: 1976
Annotations: Same 14 p. brochure and liner notes by Charles Wolfe and Barry Poss for both
      Vols. 1 and 2
Selections:
    Bake That Chicken Pie -- Uncle Dave Macon and His Fruit Jar Drinkers
    Bill Cheatam -- Blind Joe Mangrum and Fred Schreiber
    Billy Wilson -- Uncle Jimmy Thompson
    Brown's Ferry Blues -- Sam McGee

Going Across the Sea -- Crook Brothers String Band
Hale's Rag -- Theron Hale and Daughters
Jobbin Gettin' There -- Crook Brothers String Band
Jolly Blacksmith -- Theron Hale and Daughters
Karo -- Uncle Jimmy Thompson
Old Master's Runaway -- Sam and Kirk McGee
Over the Road I'm Bound To Go -- Uncle Dave Macon
[Also two by African-American DeFord Bailey]

Cty 541 / Cty 542: Wolfe has already written an excellent account of the formative years of the Grand Ole Opry [*Grand Ole Opry: The Early Years, 1925-1935*]; these two albums provide aural documentation to many of the musical figures that are discussed in his book. All of the musicians heard on these companion albums were featured on the Opry in those early years; some (Bate, Macon, Thompson) were major mainstays for varying lengths of time. We have, then, a fairly good representation of what the early Opry sound must have been like, and the overriding impression is one of rather raucus and highly spirited stringbands. There are, of course, exceptions, such as the relatively archaic fiddling of Stephens and Thompson, the trace of the parlor room sound in Theron Hale's band, and the harmonica blues of the Opry "mascot," DeFord Bailey. Apart from Macon, not much singing; mostly good fiddle, banjo, and harmonica. There are some fine examples here: of course, Macon and the McGee Brothers can be counted on to provide outstanding performances, and it's good to have the McGees' "Salt Lake City Blues" reissued at last. Harkreader & Moore's fiddle-guitar work makes the listener wonder why more of this duo hasn't been reissued. The same can be said for the Mangrum-Schreiber duets, although unfortunately only two sides by these men (of the five recorded) were ever issued. Warmack's band offers a lively version of "Stone Rag," a piece generally attributed to Oscar Stone, fiddler for Dr. Bate's band; yet I wonder if the piece could be older, as elsewhere it is known as "Lone Star Rag," or "48 Dogs in the Meathouse." Stone's fine fiddling can be heard on "Green Backed Dollar Bill." [JEMFQ 49]

468   Label Name/Number: County 544
Title: *Georgia Fiddle Bands, Vol. 2*
Source and Date of Recordings: From commercial 78s and test pressings, 1924-34
Date of Publication: [1977?]
Annotations: Liner notes by Gene Wiggins
Selections:

Cindy -- Clayton McMichen and Riley Puckett
Cotton Eyed Joe -- Fiddlin' John Carson
Cotton Patch -- Skillet Lickers
Georgia Man -- Georgia Organ Grinders
Hometown Rag -- Hometown Boys
I've Got a Gal on Sourwood Mountain -- Earl Johnson's Clodhoppers
Johnnie Get Your Gun -- Earl Johnson's Clod-hoppers
Liberty -- Hershal Brown's Washboard Band
Raccoon on a Rail -- Hometown Boys
Rock That Cradle Lucy -- Cofer Brothers
Sally Johnson -- Lowe Stokes and Riley Puckett
Slim Gal -- Clayton McMichen and Riley Puckett
Walburn Stomp -- Walburn and Hethcox
White Lightning -- Georgia Yellow Hammers

Cty 544: Whether North Georgia actually had an unusually rich musical folk tradition or whether it was just particularly well represented on commercial recordings of the 1920s is hard to say. Unfortunately, we have no great collection of field recordings to parallel the surveys of Frank C. Brown in North Carolina or Arthur K. Davis in Virginia, for comparison. This collection includes some of the most popular and influential North Georgia musicians, such as McMichen, Tanner, Stokes, Carson, Johnson, and Puckett but also some outstanding lesser-known performers. Georgia bands almost always featured lead on one or more fiddles and subordinate role of clawhammer style banjo. Guitar backup was influenced by the very idiosyncratic style of Riley Puckett; compare the backup on the Cofer Brothers' selection for evidence of Puckett's stylistic influence. There are some fine moments on this collection: the Stokes-Puckett duet on "Sally Johnson" is one of the great pieces from the period and thoroughly deserves to be readily available. Less common but also delightful are the old-timey "White Lightning," the bluesy "Georgia Man," and the previously unissued "Walburn Stomp." The fine liner notes by Wiggins bespeak a good deal more research into Georgia stringband music than has hitherto been published. [JEMFQ 52; JAF 327]

469   Label Name/Number: Flyin' Cloud FC-014
Title: *Cotton Mills and Fiddles*
Editor: Doug Rorrer
Source and Date of Recordings: From commercial 78s, 1926-1931
Date of Publication: 1990
Annotations: Liner notes by Kinney Rorrer
Selections:

   As We Sat Beneath the Maple on the Hill -- Posey Rorer with the North Carolina Ramblers
   Battleship of Maine, The -- Red Patterson's Piedmont Log Rollers
   Bill Morgan and His Girl -- Buster Carter and Preston Young
   I Want a Nice Little Fellow -- Kelly Harrell with the Virginia String Band
   Jule Girl -- Blue Ridge Highballers
   Little Bessie -- Kid Smith and Family
   Long Eared Mule -- Dixie Ramblers
   Mother's Plea for Her Son, The -- Charlie Poole with the North Carolina Ramblers
   Murder of the Lawson Family, The [F 35] -- Carolina Buddies
   New Coon in Town -- Four Virginians
   Too Young to Marry -- Charlie Poole with the North Carolina Ramblers
   Wayward Boy, The -- Charlie Poole with the North Carolina Ramblers
   When I Was a Baby -- Four Pickled Peppers

       Flyin' Cloud FC-014: Rorrer's album title suggests rather more direct relationship to the cotton mill industry of North Carolina than is justified; these songs are simply a collection, without specific theme, by some of the many outstanding "tarheel" bands to record in the late '20s and '30s-- the occurrence of "Virginia" in two bands' names notwithstanding. Rorrer himself is related to Posey Rorer, the celebrated fiddler of the North Carolina Ramblers.

470a   Label Name/Number: Folkways FA 2951 [2-lp box set, formerly numbered FP 251]
Title: *[Anthology of] American Folk Music, Vol. 1*
Editor: Harry Smith
Source and Date of Recordings: From commercial 78s, 1926-32
Date of Publication: 1952
Annotations: Same brochure in all three boxes by Harry Smith
Selections:

   Butcher's Boy, The [P 24] -- Buell Kazee
   Charles Giteau [E 11] -- Kelly Harrell
   Cole Younger [E 3] -- Edward L. Crain

Engine 143 [G 3] -- Carter Family
Farm Land Blues -- Carolina Tar Heels
Fatal Flower Garden [C. 155] -- Nelstone's Hawaiians
Gonna Die with My Hammer in My Hand [I 1] -- Williamson and Curry
Henry Lee [C. 68] -- Dick Justice
House Carpenter [C. 243] -- Clarence Ashley
John Hardy [I 2] -- Carter Family
King Kong Kitchie -- "Chubby" Parker
Lazy Farmer Boy -- Carter and Young
Old Lady And Devil [C. 278] -- Bill and Belle Reed
Ommie Wise [F 4] -- G. B. Grayson
Peg And Awl -- Carolina Tar Heels
Pennys Farm -- Bentley Boys
Shoes And Leggins -- Uncle Eck Dunford
Stackalee [I 15] -- Frank Hutchison
Wagoners Lad, The -- Buell Kazee
White House Blues -- Charlie Poole and North Carolina Ramblers
Willie Moore -- Burnett and Rutherford
[My Name Is] John Johanna [H 1] -- Kelly Harrell
[Also other titles]

470b   Label Name/Number: Folkways FA 2952 [2-lp box set, formerly numbered FP 252]
Title: *[Anthology of] American Folk Music, Vol. 2*
Editor: Harry Smith
Source and Date of Recordings: From commercial 78s, 1926-32
Date of Publication: 1952
Annotations: Same brochure in all three boxes by Harry Smith
Selections:
Brilliancy Medley -- Eck Robertson Family
Dry Bones -- Bascom Lamar Lunsford
Indian War Whoop -- Floyd Ming Pep-Steppers
Little Moses -- Carter Family
Present Joys -- Sacred Harp Singers
Rocky Road -- Sacred Harp Singers
Sail Away Lady -- Uncle Bunt Stephens
Shine on Me -- Phipps Singers
Wake Up Jacob -- Prince Albert Hunt's Ramblers
Wild Wagoner, The -- J. W. Day
[Also other titles]

470c   Label Name/Number: Folkways FA 2953 [2-lp box set; formerly numbered FP 253]
Title: *[Anthology of] American Folk Music, Vol. 3*
Editor: Harry Smith
Source and Date of Recordings: From commercial 78s, 1926-30
Date of Publication: 1952
Annotations: Same brochure in all three boxes by Harry Smith
Selections:
Coo Coo Bird, The -- Clarence Ashley
Country Blues -- Dock Boggs
Down Plank Road -- Uncle Dave Macon
East Virginia -- Buell Kazee

I Wish I Was a Mole -- Bascom Lamar Lunsford
Lone Star Trail -- Ken Maynard
Mountaineer's Courtship -- Mr. and Mrs. Ernest Stoneman
One Morning in May -- Didier Herbert
Roll Down the Line -- Uncle Dave Macon
Single Girl -- Carter Family
Spanish Merchant's Daughter -- Stoneman Family
Sugar Baby -- Dock Boggs
Train on the Island -- J. P. Nestor
  [Also other titles]

Fwys FA 2951/2/3 [3 2-lp boxes]: When Folkways' proprietor Moe Asch issued this 6-disc set drawn from commercial 78s in the collection of an eccentric New York some-time anthropologist and folklorist, he produced the first significant "bootleg" album, and created a resource that influenced the repertoire and style of the urban folksong revival for two decades. Harry Smith had accumulated thousands of hillbilly and race 78s from the "golden" period of 1924-41 and offered to sell the collection to Asch. Asch counterproposed that Smith edit an anthology to parallel a jazz compendium that he had recently published. Smith agreed, and from his collection selected 84 sides for this anthology, divided almost equally between white (hillbilly) and black (race, or blues & gospel) artists with a few Cajun as well; the idiosyncratic annotations gave no clue to the artists' ethnicity--one likes to think that this was Smith's deliberate way of focusing on the unity rather than the separateness of America's folk music. Of course, at the time next to nothing was known about most of the commercial artists of the 20's and '30s, but more importantly, the focus was on the music and not the performers; virtually every title was well-known from other, non-commercial sources. (The organization, from "Child Ballads" to other ballads to songs to religious material, echoed the common arrangement of early scholarly folksong collections.) The range of material was panoramic insofar as pre-Depression styles were concerned: ballads, occupational songs, stringbands, religious songs, Sacred Harp singers, fiddle tunes, white blues. Musically, the material has held up remarkably well and still provides an excellent anthology of commercially recorded traditional ballads, songs, and tunes. But for the fact that so much more has been reissued in the intervening four decades--and with much better annotation--the set could be recommended as highly today as when it first appeared. Aesthetically, though, it is still an outstanding collection, many selections of which justly deserve the overworked label of "classics." Smith eventually sold his collection to Moe Asch, whose archives were all sold to the Smithsonian Institution after has death. Needless to say, there was much more outstanding music whence these 84 selections came. (For more on Smith, see John Cohen's "A Rare Interview with Harry Smith," *Sing Out!* 9 [April-May 1969], pp. 2-11, 41; and Robert Cantwell's "Smith's Memory Theater: The Folkways Anthology of American Folk Music," *New England Review* 13, pp. 364-97.)

471   Label Name/Number: Historical HLP 8002 (formerly BC 2433-2)
Title: *Early Country Music, Vol. 2*
Editor: [Arnold S. Caplin]
Source and Date of Recordings: From commercial 78s, 1928-31
Date of Publication: [ca. 1968]
Annotations: Liner notes by Arnold S. Caplin
Selections:
  Break Melody -- Golden Melody Boys (Demps and Phil)
  Cotton Patch Rag -- John Dilleshaw
  Cross-Eyed Butcher -- Golden Melody Boys (Demps and Phil)
  Guitar Rag -- Golden Melody Boys
  New Huntsville Jail -- Joe Evans

    Nothin' Doin' -- Nap Hayes and Matthew Prater
    Old Hen Cackle -- Joe Evans and Arthur McClain (Coleman and Harper)
    Sabula Blues -- Golden Melody Boys (Demps and Phil)
    Sittin' on Top of the World -- Joe Evans
    Somethin' Doin' -- Nap Hayes and Matthew Prater
    Sourwood Mountain -- Joe Evans and Arthur McClain (Coleman and Harper)
    Spanish Fandango -- John Dilleshaw
    Take a Look at That Baby -- Joe Evans
    Way Down in Arkansas -- Golden Melody Boys (Demps and Phil)

    Hist BC 2433-2: Caplin's sampling of early hillbilly recordings demonstrates a distinctly different aesthetic from those of similar anthologies on other labels, such as County, Old Timey, or Old Homestead, each of which attests to its compiler's personal taste. Here, jazz and blues influences are strong; most of the selections are primarily (if not entirely) instrumental with lead mandolin and guitar prominent. Although Evans and McClain were almost certain African-Americans, some of their recordings were so hillbilly-sounding (e. g., "Sourwood Mountain" and "Old Hen Cackle") that they were originally released in record series devoted entirely to hillbilly music. I have included all their titles in the above listing inasmuch as there is no neat way to include some and exclude others. [JAF 320--DKW]

472   Label Name/Number: Historical HLP 8003
Title: *Traditional Country Classics, 1927-1929*
Source and Date of Recordings: From commercial 78s, 1927-29
Date of Publication: [ca. 1968]
Annotations: Liner notes by Richard Nevins
Selections:
    Georgia Wobble Blues -- Carroll County Ramblers
    Gray Eagle -- Taylor's Kentucky Boys
    Honeysuckle Time -- Cranford, Miles and Thompson
    Just Keep Waiting till the Good Time Comes -- Charlie Poole's North Carolina Ramblers
    Kenny Wagner Surrender -- Ernest Stoneman
    Leather Breeches -- Earl Johnson and His Clodhoppers
    Lye Soap Breakdown -- Seven Foot Dilly and His Dill Pickles
    Oh Molly Dear [M 4] -- B. F. Shelton
    Red Hot Breakdown -- Earl Johnson and His Clodhoppers
    She's a Flower from the Fields of Alabama -- Burnett and Rutherford
    Sugar Hill -- George and Dad Crockett
    Take Me Back to the Sweet Sunny South -- DaCosta Woltz's Southern Broadcasters
    What You Gonna Do with the Baby -- Grayson and Whitter
    Yellow Rose of Texas -- DaCosta Woltz's Southern Broadcasters

    Hist HLP 8003: The selections, compiled by Joe Bussard, Jr., represent all the major recording companies and provide an excellent sampling of a variety of styles from 1927 to 1929. Dilly's band, from the Atlanta region, was among the first to add a string bass to its instrumentation. The Southern Broadcasters were one of the outstanding bands from northern North Carolina. "Gray Eagle," a widely known fiddle tune, is an outstanding example of banjo and fiddle (by a black musician) both playing as melody instruments. [JAF 323]

473   Label Name/Number: John Edwards Memorial Foundation JEMF 103
Title: *Paramount Old Time Tunes*
Editor: Norm Cohen

Source and Date of Recordings: From commercial 78s, 1927-32
Date of Publication: [1974]
Annotations: Brochure by Norm Cohen
Selections:

    Alabama Square Dance, Pt. 1 -- Chumber, Coker, and Rice
    Blue Eyes -- Carolina Ramblers and Roy Harvey
    Brave Engineer, The [G 3] -- Carver Boys
    Bully of the Town [I 14] -- Sid Harkreader and Grady Moore
    Cabin Home -- Golden Melody Boys
    Cotton Mill Blues -- Wilmer Watts and the Lonely Eagles
    Faded Coat of Blue, The -- Owen Mills
    Jesus Is Precious to Me -- Vaughan Quartet
    Little Old Sod Shanty -- Whitey Johns (John White)
    Reuben, Oh Rueben -- Emry Arthur
    S. O. S. Vestris -- Welling and Schannen
    Shady Grove -- Kentucky Thorobreds
    Stack-O-Lee [I 15] -- Fruit Jar Guzzlers
    Strawberry Roan, The [B 18] -- Rex Kelly

    JEMF 103: This was the first LP reissue not issued by a major label to explore the repertory of a particular record company: the Paramount label. Though this was one of the preeminent media for blues and gospel recordings in the '20s and '30s (Paramount 14000s are collectors' gold for blues fans), the label also featured a less-successful hillbilly 3000 series. This anthology was programmed to demonstrate the range of that material; consequently its historical value probably overshadows its aesthetic appeal. Nevertheless there are some gems: the beautiful Civil War song, "Faded Coat of Blue" perhaps the most memorable, but the selections by Emry Arthur and Wilmer Watts also fine pieces. "Cabin Home" represents the ragtimey approach to early hillbilly music at its charming best, while "Alabama Square Dance" is an instrumental piece embedded in a bit of a humorous sketch--a device frequently explored in the late 1920s and not always without embarrassing results. (The LP was, in fact, criticized for including a piece that seemed to demean Southern mountain culture by its stereotyped portrayals.) The lengthy brochure includes a Paramount 3000 numerical listing and a history of the company as well as detailed notes on the performers and the selections and text/tune transcriptions.

474a   Label Name/Number: Marimac [cass] 9100
Title: *A Joyful Noise, Vol. 1*
Editor: [Larry MacBride]
Source and Date of Recordings: From commercial 78s, 1920s-'30s
Date of Publication: 1984
Selections:

    Banks of the River -- Flat Creek Sacred Singers
    Beautiful -- Garland Bros. & Grinstead
    Bringing in the Sheaves -- Eva Quartet
    Coronation -- Daniels-Deason Sacred Harp
    Gabriel's Trumpet -- Morris Bros. with Eunice
    God Leads His Dear Children -- Joseph Callender
    Home of the Soul -- Cliff and Tommy Carlisle
    I Want To Go There Don't You? -- Blue Ridge Singers
    I'll Lead a Christian Life -- Elder G(olden) P. Harris
    Jacob's Ladder -- Chumbler Family
    Little Black Train Is Coming, The -- Emry Arthur

Music in My Soul -- Bush Brothers
My Prayer -- Carolina Gospel Singers
Old Ship of Zion, The -- Allison's Sacred Harp
Outshine the Sun -- (Roy) Harvey, (Bob) Hoke, and (Posey) Rorer
Rejoicing All the Way -- Avondale Mills Quartet
Religion Is a Fortune -- Alabama Sacred Harp
That Lonesome Valley -- Carolina Ramblers
We'll Be at Home Again -- Mr. & Mrs. R. N. Grisham
Will There Be Any Stars in My Crown -- Harkreader & Moore

474b   Label Name/Number: Marimac 9101 [cass]
Title: *A Joyful Noise, Vol. 2*
Editor: [Larry MacBride]
Source and Date of Recordings: From commercial 78s, 1920s-'30s
Date of Publication: 1984
Selections:

Beyond the Clouds -- Gordon County Quartet
Down to Jordan -- Dixie Mountaineers
Dunlap [My God, the Springs of All My Joys] -- Elder G(olden) P. Harris
Everybody Will Be Happy over There -- Deal Family
Glory Is Rising in My Soul -- Blue Ridge Singers
I Belong to This Band -- Allison's Sacred Harp
I'm Going Home To Die No More -- Giddens Sisters
Jesus Leads I'll Follow On -- Buffalo Ragged Five
Joy Among the Angels -- Deal Family
Just over the River -- Garland Bros. & Grinstead
Little Black Train, The -- Harmon E. Helmick
Lonesome Valley, Pt. 2 -- Dixie Reelers
Odem -- Roswell Sacred Harp Singers
On the Glory Road -- Bush Brothers
On the Streets of Glory -- (Roy) Harvey, (Bob) Hoke, and (Posey) Rorer
Present Joys -- Alabama Sacred Harp Singers
Sailing Ship, The -- Crowder Brothers
Shining City over the Water -- Dorsey & Beatrice Dixon
To the Lamb -- Ridgel's Fountain Citians
When the Gates of Glory Open -- Bush Brothers

Mar [cass] 9100: / [cass] 9101: These two collections represent the first publications in nearly two decades to tap the treasures of sacred song recorded along with other types of hillbilly music in the 1920s and '30s. The range of styles is remarkably broad and prompts some speculations about the modus operandi of the commercial record companies of the period that allowed such diverse material to be issued. The selections, recorded between about 1927 and 1940, range from the distinctive fa-sol-la style of the Alabama Sacred Harp Singers and the rather stiff and ponderous sound of the Bush Brothers or Deal Family to the more fluid stringband approach of Roy Harvey's group, the solo fiddle/vocal of G. P. Harris, and the comfortable gospel sound of the Carlisles. More notable than the stylistic range is the lack of professional polish of many of the groups--their simple homeyness denotes performers who were used to singing only in their own homes and churches and not in any commercial context. It is amazing that so many of them were interested in appearing before the microphones of the roving field crews of OKeh, Columbia, Brunswick, and others--or, more remarkable still--traveled to more remote cities for studio engagements. Several artists were relatively popular, judging by the number of their recordings: for example, there were 10 singles issued by both the Bush Brothers and the Deal Family. Others, like the Daniels-Deason, Gordon County, and Garland Brothers groups, had no more than a couple sides apiece. Among the loveliest selections are those featuring Cliff Carlisle and his very young son, Tommy; and the Morris Brothers with their friend, Eunice Ayers--two of the youngest singers on early hillbilly recordings. Also quite striking are the two fiddle/vocal pieces by G. P. Harris. A few groups (Crowder Brothers, Carlisles, Harvey, Harkreader) are better known for their secular recordings, but most of these artists recorded religious material almost exclusively. The lack of any notes is a disappointment.

475a   Label Name/Number: Marimac 9104 [cass]
Title: *The Cold-Water Pledge, Vol. 1: Songs of Moonshine and Temperance Recorded in the Golden Age*
Editor: Pat Conte
Source and Date of Recordings: From commercial 78s, 1925-37
Date of Publication: 1984
Annotations: Brief insert leaflet; separately sold booklet
Selections:
   Bootlegger's Story -- Rambling Duet (Howard Dixon and Frank Gerald)
   Carolina Moonshiner -- Al Hopkins & his Buckle Busters
   Drunkard's Doom, The -- Ted Chestnut
   Enforcement Blues, The -- Allen Brothers
   Father's a Drunkard -- Walter Coon
   Goodbye Booze -- Gid Tanner & Fate Norris
   Got the Drunken Blues -- Bill Cox
   Got the Jake Leg Too -- Ray Brothers
   Home Brew Rag -- Lowe Stokes and his North Georgians
   I Ain't a Bit Drunk -- George Roark
   I Want Some Home Brew -- Orla Clark
   I'll Never Get Drunk Anymore -- Piedmont Log Rollers
   Jim and Me -- A. P. Cranford and Bob Thompson
   Kentucky Bootlegger -- Fruit Jar Guzzlers
   Likes Likker Better Than Me -- Woodie Brothers
   Mountain Dew -- Bascom Lamar Lunsford
   Prohibition, Yes or No (Pts 1/2) -- Gid Tanner and his Skillet Lickers
   We Have Moonshine -- Earl Shirkey and Roy Harvey
   Wrong Road, The -- Hall Brothers

475b   Label Name/Number: Marimac 9105 [cass]
Title: *The Cold-Water Pledge, Vol. 2: Songs of Moonshine and Temperance Recorded in the Golden Age*
Editor: Pat Conte
Source and Date of Recordings: From commercial 78s, 1925-37
Date of Publication: 1984
Annotations: Brief insert leaflet; separately sold booklet
Selections:
   Al Smith for President -- Carolina Night Hawks
   Bay Rum Blues -- Ashley & Foster
   Bootlegger's Dream of Home -- Earl Shirkey & Roy Harvey
   Drunkard's Child, The -- J. Frank Smith
   Drunkard's Dream -- Morgan Denmon
   Drunken Hiccoughs [= I've Only Been Down to the Club] -- Holland Puckett

Drunken Hiccoughs -- Fiddlin' John Carson
Jake Leg Blues -- Mississippi Sheiks
Moonshine Blues -- Jimmie Tarlton
No Business of Mine -- Smoky Mountain Ramblers
"Nol Pros" Nellie -- Bascom Lamar Lunsford
Old Home Brew, The -- Dixon Brothers
Old Whisker Bill, the Moonshiner -- Buell Kazee
Poor Fish -- Charlie Craver
Poor Little Bennie -- Bel Lam and his Green County Singers
Prohibition Is a Failure -- Lowe Stokes and his Pot Lickers
She Took My Licker from Me -- Fiddlin' John Carson
Stop Drinkin' Shine -- Gid Tanner
Virginia Bootlegger -- Red Fox Chasers

Mar 9104 / 9105:   Although the period during which the 18th Amendment prohibited alcoholic beverages in the United States lasted only from 1920 to 1933, the controversy surrounding the morality or lack thereof of liquor began much earlier, in the mid-19th century; in fact, by 1917, 27 states had their own "dry" laws. Thus, temperance and tippling were a common subject in song (popular as well as folk) from the 1870s on, though given greater relevance during the '20s. In the southern mountains, fiercely independent fundamentalist Scots-Irish descendents were torn between favoring bans on the evil drink and resenting governmental interference in their pursuit of their own private vices. These two cassettes offer an enjoyable sampling of musical commentary on the subject, about evenly divided, pro and con. 9105 includes a cut by the Mississippi Sheiks, one of the few black stringbands to record during the 1920s. In their day they entertained both black and white audiences with a musical repertoire that could fit either crowd. Most of the other artists are represented on other albums in this discography. 9104 includes Bascom Lunsford's original composition, "[Good Old] Mountain Dew," a piece that has since entered oral tradition. In Lunsford's original version--as well as in his other offering on 9105--his lawyer's background is readily apparent. Also on 9104 is a two-part skit by the Skillet Lickers, in which Clayton McMichen takes the part of the moonshine-advocating mountaineer who bests the temperance lecturer played by Columbia A&R man Dan Hornsby. Many such skits were recorded during the 20s, but this one is unusual for the high ratio of talk to music--and to the fervor of the arguments presented. A separately sold 16-page booklet by W. K. McNeil provides biographical background on the artists and brief notes on the sources of the songs.

476   Label Name/Number: Marimac 9106 [cass]
Title: *Make Me a Cowboy Again for a Day*
Editor: Frank Mare
Source and Date of Recordings: From commercial 78s, 1920s and '30s
Date of Publication: [1984]
Annotations: 1 p. insert by Bob Bovee
Selections:
Arizona Girl I Left Behind, The [P 1a] -- Billie Maxwell
Bury Me Out on the Prairie [B 2] -- Edward L. Crain
Falling Leaf -- L. K. Reeder
Great Grand Dad -- John White
Home on the Range -- Ken Maynard
Last Longhorn, The -- Carl T. Sprague
Little Joe, the Wrangler [B 5] -- Goebel Reeves
Little Old Sod Shanty -- Jules Allen
Lonely Cowboy Pts 1/2, The -- Arthur Miles

Make Me a Cowboy Again -- Peg Moreland
Night Guard, The -- Jack Webb
Night Herding Song -- Marc Williams
O Bury Me Not on the Lone Prairie [B 2] -- Carl T. Sprague
Old Black Steer, The -- "Powder River" Jack Lee
On the Red River Shore [M 26] -- Patt Patterson and Lois Dexter
Out on the Lone Star Cow Trail -- Dick Devall
Texas Trail, The -- Jack Weston
Trail to Mexico, The [B 13] -- Harry McClintock
Wandering Cowboy, The -- Cartwright Brothers

Mar [cass] 9106: Most of the well-known cowboy songs and ballads originated during the decades of the long cattle drives--primarily the last three decades of the 19th century. The proliferation of the railroads and mechanization in the next century radically changed the cowboy's life. Many of the songs on this collection date from that era. An exception is "Great Grand Dad," written in 1925; and though Bovee in his notes asserts "Make Me a Cowboy Again" is also from the '20s, it was probably composed in the 1890s. The performers were, for the most part, experienced cowpunchers--or at least grew up in the southwest and had first-hand experience of what they sang about. A few (e. g., Moreland) were strictly studio performers. Some (Maynard, McClintock, Reeves, Patterson and Dexter) had some range experience but were better known for their later professional entertainment careers. Of some (Miles, Weston, Reeder), biographical information has yet to emerge. Cowboying being a profession that attracted out west a great many well-educated young men seeking their fortunes or a dash of excitement, many of the songs were written by poets of some literary skills and subsequently set to music (generally older, traditional tunes) by singers of modest musical abilities. This is not to deny that those poets did not subscribe wholly to the standards of the day, which set high store on sentiment and even bathos. A number of cowboy ballads were recompositions of older stories--such as "On the Red River Shore," about a murderous father's objections to his daughter marrying a cowboy, and the ever-popular "Bury Me Not on the Lone Prairie," an 1870s rewrite of an earlier "The Ocean Burial."

477   Label Name/Number: Marimac 9109 [cass]
Title: *Johnny's Gone to War: Old-Time War Songs Recorded in the Golden Age*
Editor: Pat Conte
Source and Date of Recordings: From commercial 78s, 1920s-'30s
Date of Publication: [1984]
Selections:
Annie Dear I'm Called Away -- Blind Jack Mathis
Battleship Maine, The -- Richard Harold
Battleship of Maine -- Piedmont Log Rollers
Bloody War -- Jimmy Yates' Boll Weevils
Boy in Blue, The -- Stuart Hamblen
By a Cottage in the Twilight -- Harvey & Johnston
Captain Won't You Let Me Go Home -- Darby & Tarlton
Cuban Soldier, The -- Carter Family
Dixie Division -- Fiddlin' John Carson
Dying Soldier, The -- Buell Kazee
He Is Coming to Us Dead -- Grayson & Whitter
I Once Had a Sweetheart -- Reed Children
Johnson Boy -- Grant Brothers and Their Music
Kaiser and Uncle Sam, The -- Charlie Oaks
Maple in the Lane -- "Peg" Moreland

Marching Through Flanders -- Charlie Oaks
Off to the War I'm Going -- Carolina Twins
Sailor Man Blues -- Norwood Tew
When the Roses Bloom Again -- Watts and Wilson
Write a Letter to My Mother -- North Carolina Ramblers

Mar [cass] 9109: It is surprising that before this cassette no one had tried to program a collection of ballads and songs on the theme of war, drawn from hillbilly 78s. This set includes pieces from the three wars commented upon in hillbilly music--Civil, Spanish-American, and First World Wars--as well as some that are not easily tied to a particular historic period and are only loosely classified as war songs. The collection includes some of the very few reissues by Charlie Oaks, an early hillbilly recording artist important for his repertoire; nothing has been learned about his identity.

478a   Label Name/Number: Marimac 9110 [cass]
Title: *It'll Never Happen Again (Old Time String Bands, Vol. 1)*
Editor: Bill Dillof
Source and Date of Recordings: From commercial 78s, 1927-37
Date of Publication: [ca. 1985]
Annotations: Discographic data only
Selections:

Because He Loved Her So -- Cofer Brothers
Billy in the Lowground -- Dr. Humphrey Bate and his Possum Hunters
Duck Shoes Rag -- Grinnell Giggers
Franklin County Blues -- Dixie Ramblers
Give Me a Chaw Tobacco -- Carter Brothers and Son
Hell Amongst the Yearlings -- Dilly and His Dill Pickles
How Long? -- Cofer Brothers
I Want My Black Baby Back -- Walter Couch and Wilkes Ramblers
I've Got No Honey Babe Now -- Frank Blevins and his Tarheel Rattlers
It'll Never Happen Again -- Binkley Brothers Dixie Clodhoppers
Magnolia Waltz -- Cherokee Ramblers
McDonald's Farm -- Caplinger's Cumberland Mountain Entertainers
Ragtime Annie -- Floyd County Ramblers
Ridin' in an Old Model "T" -- Dixie Ramblers
Rose with a Broken Stem, The -- Clay Everhart and the North Carolina Cooper Boys
Sally Aim [= Sally Ann] -- Frank Blevins and his Tarheel Rattlers
Second Class Hotel -- Ozarkers
Step Stone -- Floyd County Ramblers
Suzanna Gal -- Dad Blackard's Moonshiners
Tail of Halley's Comet -- Happy Hayseeds

478b   Label Name/Number: Marimac 9111 [cass]
Title: *Goin' Up Town (Old Time String Bands, Vol. 2)*
Editor: Bill Dillof
Source and Date of Recordings: From commercial 78s, 1924-37
Date of Publication: [ca. 1985]
Annotations: Discographic information only
Selections:

Aunt Dinah's Quilting Party -- Floyd County Ramblers
Bill Morgan and His Gal -- Buster Carter and Preston Young

Chesapeake Bay -- Walter Couch and the Wilkes Ramblers
Dawn Waltz, The -- Jack Cawley's Oklahoma Ridge Runners
Don't Get Trouble in Your Mind -- Frank Blevins and His Tarheel Rattlers
Goin' Down the Road Feelin' Bad -- Cherokee Ramblers
Goin' Up Town -- Dr. Humphrey Bate and His Possum Hunters
I've Got a Gal in Baltimore -- Georgia Crackers
Johnny Goodwin -- Bull Mountain Moonshiners
Keno, the Rent Man -- Cofer Brothers
Last Shot Got Him, The -- Chenoweth's Cornfield Symphony Orchestra
Leather Breeches -- Carter Brothers and Son
Old Aunt Betsey -- Frank Blevins and His Tarheel Rattlers
Plow Boy Hop -- Grinnell Giggers
She's a Flower from the Fields of Alabama -- Emry & Henry Arthur
Take Your Foot Out of the Mud and Put It in the Sand -- Dr. Humphrey Bate and His Possum Hunters
When I Had But Fifty Cents -- Binkley Brothers' Dixie Clodhoppers
White River Stomp -- Jack Cawley's Oklahoma Ridge Runners
Whoa Back Buck -- Annie, Judy, and Zeke Canova
Working on the Railroad -- Blankenship Family

Mar [cass] 9110 / 9111: These two cassettes offer a wide variety of styles that were to be heard on 78s during the late 1920s and early '30s. As the Depression decade wore on, these highly distinctive regional bands tended to disappear and be replaced by a fewer number of more homogeneous sounds, until on eve of World War II one could speak of an emerging country/western musical style that was certainly southeastern but could not be further pinpointed. The bands are from Georgia, the Carolinas, Kentucky, Tennessee, Oklahoma, and the Ozarks. Judy Canova, better known for her work as a comedienne on radio and in movies, is shown here in her earlier career as part of a family of musical entertainers. A handful of the songs are older fiddle tunes, but music of the early 20th century predominates.

479a   Label Name/Number: Morning Star 45003
Title: *Wink the Other Eye: Kentucky Fiddle Band Music, Vol. 1*
Editors: Gus Meade and Richard Nevins
Source and Date of Recordings: From commercial 78s, 1927-33
Date of Publication: 1980
Annotations: Same 12 p. brochure by Meade and Nevins in all three volumes
Selections:
B Flat Rag -- Madisonville String Band
Cumberland Gap -- Rutherford, Burnett and Moore
Forked Deer -- Taylor's Kentucky Boys
Gate To Go Through -- Jimmie Johnson's String Band
Gray Eagle -- Taylor's Kentucky Boys
Let Her Go, I'll Meet Her -- Rutherford and Foster
Monroe County Quickstep -- Rutherford and Foster
Old Blind Dog -- Jimmie Johnson's String Band
Pretty Little Girl -- Hack's String Band
Richmond Blues -- Rutherford and Foster
Soap in the Washpan -- Jimmie Johnson's String Band
Soldier's Joy -- Taylor's Kentucky Boys
Washington's Quadrille -- Jimmie Johnson's String Band
Wink the Other Eye -- Hack's String Band

479b   Label Name/Number: Morning Star 45004
Title: *Wish I Had My Time Again: Kentucky Fiddle Band Music, Vol. 2*
Editors: Gus Meade and Richard Nevins
Source and Date of Recordings: From commercial 78s and test pressings, 1927-33
Date of Publication: 1980
Annotations: Same 12 p. brochure by Meade and Nevins in all three volumes
Selections:

Black Snake Moan -- Cobb and Underwood
Bow Legged Irishman -- Ted Gossett's String Band
Brick Yard Joe -- Doc Roberts
Eighth of January -- Ted Gossett's String Band
Fate of Ellen Smith, The [F 11] -- Green Bailey
Fire in the Mountain -- Ted Gossett's String Band
Fox Chase -- Ted Gossett's String Band
Going Across the Sea -- Henry L. Bandy
If I Die a Railroad Man -- Green Bailey
Knoxville Rag -- Taylor, Burnette and Moore
Old Buzzard -- Doc Roberts
Sail Away Ladies -- Henry L. Bandy
Wild Hog in the Woods -- Lonesome Luke and Farmhands
Wish I Had My Time Again -- Hatton Brothers

479c   Label Name/Number: Morning Star 45005
Title: *Way Down South in Dixie: Kentucky Fiddle Band Music, Vol. 3*
Editors: Gus Meade and Richard Nevins
Source and Date of Recordings: From commercial 78s and test pressings, 1927-33
Date of Publication: 1980
Annotations: Same 12 p. brochure by Meade and Nevins in all three volumes
Selections:

And the Cat Came Back -- Doc Roberts
Cuttin' at the Point -- Charlie Wilson and Hayloft Boys
Five Up -- Henry L. Brandy
Glide Waltz -- Green's String Band
Lost Love -- Asa Martin
Monkey Show -- Henry L. Brandy
New Money -- Doc Roberts
Old Flannagan -- Blue Ridge Mountaineers
Old Voile -- Blue Ridge Mountaineers
Shaker Ben -- Walter Family
Stove Pipe Blues -- Kentucky String Ticklers
That's My Rabbit, My Dog Caught It -- Walter Family
Way Down South in Dixie -- Doc Roberts
We'll Understand It Better Bye and Bye -- Kentucky String Choristers

MS 45003/4/5: This wonderful set is mostly the result of Gus Meade's passionate interest in fiddle music of Kentucky and his indefatigable field and library work tracking down the musicians who made these rare recordings. All the selections on these discs, featuring 24 different groups of musicians, were made for the Richmond, Indiana-based Gennett label and its subsidiaries. Meade notes that Kentucky contributed the largest number of artists to the Gennett stable, and, correspondingly, the majority of Kentucky artists who made recordings were associated with Gennett.

Many of the artists made only a few recordings, and some are exceedingly rare--more than half the 78s used in preparing these three LPs are the only known existing copies. Henry Bandy (1876-1943) was an early performer on WLS's Grand Ole Opry; he made four recordings in 1928 that were never issued. His family kept test pressings of those recordings, and they are issued here for the first time. Other tracks are all dubbed from rare 78s. Some of the groups (e. g., the Blue Ridge Mountaineers) made no other recordings than those reissued here. The Draper Walter family recorded eight sides, but only two have been recovered. A few of the bands--Martin and Roberts and their associates, and Rutherford and Burnett, for example--were widely popular and well represented on discs. Taylor's Kentucky Boys (the trio's eponymous manager was not one of the musicians) is of particular interest for being one of the very few old-time stringbands to record with a black breakdown fiddler, Jim Booker. The Booker family was one of several black groups of central Kentucky that were apparently very influential in the (largely Anglo-American) stringband musical style of the region. The 12" x 12" brochure that accompanies all three albums includes Meade's biographical and stylistic discussions of the musicians; several photos; a map of Kentucky showing the residences of the various musical groups; and some general comments on Gennett, the music, the project, and the fieldwork involved by Nevins. This is an outstanding regional survey; the scratchy nature of several of the tracks is regrettable but unavoidable, since alternate sources of the recordings are non-existent. [JEMFQ 64-WS]

480   **Label Name/Number:** Morning Star 45008
Title: *When I Was a Cowboy: Songs of Cowboy Life*
Editor: Richard Nevins
Source and Date of Recordings: From commercial 78s, 1920s-'30s
Date of Publication: 1984
Annotations: Liner notes by Richard Nevins
Selections:
    'Long Side the Santa Fe Trail -- Jules Allen
    Bandit Cole Younger [E 3] -- Edward L. Crain
    Bury Me out on the Prairie -- Delmore Brothers
    Cowboy, The -- Carl T. Sprague
    Dixie Cowboy [B 3] -- Aulton Ray
    Dying Ranger [A 14] -- Cartwright Brothers
    Get Along Little Dogies -- Cartwright Brothers
    Goodbye Old Paint -- Harry McClintock
    Lone Star Trail, The -- Ken Maynard
    Out on a Western Range -- Uncle Pete and Louise
    Sporting Cowboy, The [E 17] -- Watts and Wilson
    Tom Sherman's Barroom [B 1] -- Dick Devall
    Tying a Knot in the Devil's Tail [B 17] -- Powder River Jack and Kitty Lee
    Utah Carroll [B 4] -- Cartwright Brothers

M S 45008: Morning Star's anthology of cowboy ballads and songs offers compositions from the late 19th century--the cowboy's heyday, eschewing any later songs from the hillbilly era or the sagebrush screen. Except for southeasterners Watts and Wilson, the Delmores, and Aulton Ray (and probably Uncle Pete and Louise), the artists are from the southwest and mostly traditional. Maynard, in spite of his movie career, probably learned his songs from traditional sources. Nevins' very general comments on cowboy music and life provide no information about the performers or the specific songs included.

481   **Label Name/Number:** New World Records NW 236
Title: *Going Down the Valley: Vocal and Instrumental Styles in Folk Music from the South*

Editor: Norm Cohen
Source and Date of Recordings: From studio recordings, 1926-38
Date of Publication: 1977
Annotations: 6 p. sewn-in notes by Norm Cohen
Selections:

Banjo Pickin' Girl -- Coon Creek Girls
Billy Grimes, the Rover -- Shelor Family
By the Cottage Door -- Perry County Music Makers
Carve That Possum -- Uncle Dave Macon and His Fruit Jar Drinkers
Corrina, Corrina -- Ashley and Abernathy
Cotton-Eyed Joe -- Carter Brothers and Son
George Washington -- Pope's Arkansas Mountaineers
Going Down the Valley -- Ernest V. Stoneman and His Dixie Mountaineers
I Truly Understand, You Love Another Man -- Shortbuckle Roark and Family
Katie Dear (Silver Dagger) [M 4 / G 21] -- Callahan Brothers
Little Maggie -- Wade Mainer, Zeke Morris, and Steve Ledford
Little Maud -- Bela Lam and His Greene County Singers
Milwaukee Blues -- Charlie Poole and the North Carolina Ramblers
Molly Put the Kettle On -- Gid Tanner and his Skillet Lickers
Nancy Jane -- Fort Worth Doughboys
New Salty Dog, A -- Allen Brothers
Old Joe Clark -- Ben Jarrell and DaCosta Woltz's Southern Broadcasters
Sweet Rose of Heaven -- Taylor-Griggs Louisiana Melody Makers

NW 236: Like RCA Victor LPV 552, after which it was patterned, this album aimed to present a variety of old-time stringband styles in a program illustrating to some extent chronological development and regional characteristics--except that the editor could draw upon most of the labels of the period, not just Victor. Thus, the older Anglo-American styles of the Shelors, Stonemans, Southern Broadcasters, and Carters, give way to minstrel (Macon), blues (Ashley and Abernathy, Poole, the Allens), and jazz (Doughboys) influences. [JEMFQ 51]

482 Label Name/Number: Old Homestead OHCS 141
Title: *West Virginia Hills -- Early Recordings from West Virginia*
Source and Date of Recordings: From commercial 78s, ca. 1927-32
Date of Publication: 1982
Annotations: Liner notes by Ivan M. Tribe
Selections:

Chicken -- McClung Brothers
Footprints in the Snow -- Bernice Coleman and West Virginia Ramblers
Give My Love to Nell -- David Miller
Ida Red -- Three Tweedy Brothers
Jackson County -- Billy Cox
Kanawha March -- Kessinger Brothers
Little Indian Napanee -- David Miller
Logan County Blues -- Frank Hutchison
Mary Dear -- Richard Harold
May I Sleep in Your Barn Tonight Mister? -- Miller Wikel
Moatsville Blues -- Moatsville String Ticklers
Old Account Was Settled, The -- Welling and McGhee
Preacher and the Bear -- John McGhee
Sweet Bird -- West Virginia Night Owls

We Have Moonshine -- Roy Harvey and Earl Shirkey
We'll Meet on the Beautiful Shore -- Billy Cox
West Virginia Hills -- Moatsville String Ticklers
Wreck of the Old 97, The -- Frank Hutchison

483   Label Name/Number: Old Homestead OHCS-177
Title: *Home in West Virginia: West Virginia Project, Vol. 2*
Artist(s): Various
Source and Date of Recordings: From commercial 78s, 1928-52
Date of Publication: 1987
Annotations: Jacket notes by Ivan M. Tribe
Selections:
　　Atlanta Bound -- Frank Dudgeon
　　Bake That Chicken Pie -- Jackson County Barn Owls
　　Come Take a Trip in My Airship -- Fred Pendleton & the West Virginia Melody Boys
　　Frail Wildwood Flower -- Miller Wikel with John JcGhee
　　High Silk Hat and a Gold Walking Cane -- Billy Cox
　　I Hate To Be Called a Hobo -- Frank Dudgeon
　　Kentucky Boot Leggers -- Fruit Jar Guzzlers
　　Little Lulie -- Dick Justice
　　My Little Home in West Virginia -- Ellis Hall and Bill Addis
　　Nobody's Business -- Warren Caplinger's Cumberland Mountain Entertainers
　　Old Fashioned Cottage -- Blind Alfred & Arville Reed
　　Prison Sorrows -- Weaver Brothers
　　Three Nights Experience [C. 274] -- John B. Evans
　　When a Boy from the Mountains -- Blaine & Cal Smith
　　Wreck of the C. & O. *Sportsman* -- Roy Harvey with Branch & Coleman
　　Wreck of the West Bound Airliner -- Fred Pendleton & West Virginia Melody Boys
　　You Came Back to Me -- Weaver Brothers
　　You'll Miss Me -- Blind Alfred Reed & Arville Reed

OHCS 141 / 177: These two albums were collaborations between John Morris's Old Homestead label and country music historian Ivan Tribe, whose book, *Mountaineer Jamboree* (1984), did much to document the history of country music in West Virginia. The two albums's selections were recorded between 1928 and 1936 (except for one selection on 177 recorded in 1952). Of these, the Night Owls, Tweedys, McClungs, Harold, Weavers, Evans, the Barn Owls, Hall and Ellis, Wikel, and Dudgeon had never appeared on LP previously. The oldest songs on Vol. 1 are from the 1880s, and include Coleman's "Footprints in the Snow" (credited on the original 78 rpm issue to Roy Harvey and the West Virginia Ramblers, and there titled "Little Footprints")--which became a bluegrass warhorse in the 1950s and later. The older selections on Vol. 2 include Justice's "Little Lulie," a demodalized version of "Darling Corey"/"Little Maggie;" Evans's "Three Nights Experience" [Child 274]; and the Weaver Brothers' "Prison Sorrows," a variant of the "Seven Long Years in Prison"/"Prisoner's Song" complex. Hutchison's "Old 97" is a previously unissued harmonica instrumental. Tribe's liner notes give brief biographical information on the musicians, many of whom have not been discussed in print before and comments on the songs themselves.

484   Label Name/Number: Old Timey 100
Title: *The String Bands, Vol. 1*
Editor: [Chris Strachwitz]
Source and Date of Recordings: From commercial 78s, 1920s-'30s
Date of Publication: 1962

Annotations: 1 p. insert by Chris Strachwitz
Selections:
   Allen Brothers Rag -- Allen Brothers
   Chinese Rag -- Spooney Five
   Crowley Waltz -- Hackberry Ramblers
   Dickson County Blues -- Arthur Smith Trio
   Down Yonder -- Hershel Brown and His Washboard Band
   Hawkins Rag -- Gid Tanner and His Skillet Lickers
   Home Town Blues -- Roane County Ramblers
   Hungry Hash House -- Charlie Poole and the North Carolina Ramblers
   If the River Was Whiskey -- Charlie Poole and the North Carolina Ramblers
   Japanese Breakdown -- Scottdale String Band
   Moatsville Blues -- Moatsville String Ticklers
   Nobody Loves Me -- Hershel Brown and His Washboard Band
   Tickle Her -- Hackberry Ramblers
   Train 45 -- Grayson and Whitter
[Also one other Cajun number]

485   Label Name/Number: Old Timey 101
Title: *The String Bands, Vol. 2*
Editor: Chris Strachwitz
Source and Date of Recordings: From commercial 78s, 1922-50s
Date of Publication: 1965
Annotations: Liner notes by Chris Strachwitz
Selections:
   All Night Long -- Earl Johnson's Clodhoppers
   Alto Waltz -- Darby and Tarlton
   Bath House Blues -- Ashley's Melody Men
   Black Bottom Strut -- Three Stripped Gears
   Carbolic Rag -- Scottdale String Band
   Cue Ball Blues--Little Joe Arwood
   Darkie's Wail -- Riley Pucket
   Hackberry Trot -- Hackberry Ramblers
   I'll Roll in My Sweet Baby's Arms -- Buster Carter and Preston Young
   Jamestown Exhibition -- Bayless Rose
   Lay Down Baby, Take Your Rest -- Carolina Tar Heels
   My Little Girl -- Spooney Five
   Rubber Dolly Rag -- Uncle Bud Landress
   Sally Gooden -- Eck Robertson
   Three Men Went a-Huntin' -- Byrd Moore and His Hot Shots
[Also one other Cajun stringband]

   OT 100 / 101: OT 100 was one of the first bootleg hillbilly anthologies to appear after the Folkways "Anthology." Both 100 and 101 reflect strongly the aesthetic tastes of Old Timey's proprietor, Chris Strachwitz, who had been a stout admirer of Cajun and blues music as well as old-timey. I have omitted from each LP listing one selection that is entirely in the Cajun idiom, but have included the selections by the Hackberry Ramblers, who straddled the dividing line between country and Cajun music throughout their long career. I've also included the tune by the Missis-sippi Mud Steppers: although they were an African-American band, their stringband music could have fitted into a contemporary program of hillbilly music. In general, both albums include a large proportion of tunes and styles strongly reflecting blues, ragtime, and jazz influences. OT 101 includes Eck Robertson's "Sally Gooden," his first recording and to the best of our knowledge the first commercial recording by a traditional rural artist.

486   Label Name/Number: Old Timey 102
Title: *Ballads and Songs*
Editor: Chris Strachwitz
Source and Date of Recordings: From commercial 78s, 1925-39
Date of Publication: 1965
Annotations: Liner notes by Toni Brown
Selections:
   Black Jack David [C. 200] -- Cliff Carlisle
   Deep Elm -- Lone Star Cowboys
   Frankie Dean [I 3] -- Tom Darby and Jimmie Tarlton
   Frankie Silvers [E 13] -- Byrd Moore and His Hot Shots
   Franklin Roosevelt's Back Again -- Bill Cox and Cliff Hobbs
   Handsome Molly -- Grayson and Whitter
   It's Hard To Leave You Sweet Love -- Lewis McDaniel and Gid Smith
   Little Love, A -- Wade Mainer
   Little Maggie -- Grayson and Whitter
   Old Reuben -- Wade Mainer
   On the Old Plantation [= Lorena] -- Blue Sky Boys
   Pretty Polly [P 36b] -- Lily Mae Ledford and the Coon Creek Girls
   Rose Conley [F 6] -- Grayson and Whitter
   Roy Dixon -- Jimmie Tarlton
   School House Fire -- Dixon Brothers
   That Fatal Courtship [P 24] -- Ephraim Woodie and the Hen-pecked Husbands

      OT 102:   OT 102 includes a number of fine old ballads and songs, including a rousing performance of "Pretty Polly" and Cliff Carlisle's steel-guitar-accompanied "Black Jack David," and three incomparable renditions by G. B. Grayson, since more fully represented on other albums. One of the most interesting items is the 1936 paean to Franklin D. Roosevelt, whose election promised an end to Prohibition, thereby earning him many a mountaineers' undying gratitude. [JAF 314--DKW]

487   Label Name/Number: RCA 2100-2-R [CD]
Title: *Something Got a Hold of Me: A Treasury of Sacred Music*
Editor: Billy Altman
Source and Date of Recordings: Studio recordings, 1927-41
Date of Publication: 1990
Annotations: 10 p. enclosed booklet by Altman
Selections:
   Always Lift Him Up and Never Knock Him Down -- Blind Alfred Reed
   Cryin' Holy unto My Lord -- Bill Monroe and His Blue Grass Boys
   Farther Along -- Wade Mainer and the Sons of the Mountaineers
   Heavenly Train, The -- Bill Carlisle
   I Didn't Hear Nobody Pray -- Dixon Brothers
   I'm Working on a Building -- Carter Family
   Just One Way to the Pearly Gates -- Uncle Dave Macon
   Just Over in the Glory Land -- J. E. Mainer's Mountaineers
   Mansions in the Sky -- Wade Mainer and the Sons of the Mountaineers
   On That Old Gospel Ship -- Monroe Brothers

Only One Step More -- Blue Sky Boys
Something Got a Hold of Me -- Carter Family
There'll Be No Distinction There -- Blind Alfred Reed
Tramp on the Street -- Grady and Hazel Cole
What Would You Give in Exchange? -- Monroe Brothers
Where the Soul of Man Never Dies -- Blue Sky Boys

RCA 2100-2-R [CD]: Following the warm reception given RCA/BMG's new reissue series (see following two items), editor Billy Altman produced two companion albums designated "sacred" and "gospel" music, by which he meant to distinguish between Anglo-American and African-American performers and traditions, respectively, in programs of religious music. This, the former disc, includes some of the most popular hillbilly artists in the 1930s on RCA's budget-priced Bluebird label--the Mainers, Monroes, Carter Family, Uncle Dave, and Blue Sky Boys. More significant is Hazel and Grady Cole's 1939 composition, "Tramp on the Street," an outstanding example of country music social theology that has since become a country standard and also entered oral tradition. A decade or more earlier are two titles by one of the less successful recording artists, Alfred Reed, a musically endowed Methodist minister from West Virginia, some of whose songs achieved wide popularity for a while. "There'll Be No Distinction There" promises social equality in the hereafter for those who have suffered poverty, discrimination and other hardships in the present world.

488   Label Name/Number: RCA 8416-2-R [CD]
Title: *Ragged But Right: Great Country String Bands of the 1930's*
Editor: Billy Altman
Source and Date of Recordings: Studio recordings, 1933-38
Date of Publication: 1988
Annotations: 14-p. enclosed brochure by Altman
Selections:

Blue River -- Prairie Ramblers
Go Easy Blues -- Prairie Ramblers
Hawkins' Rag -- Ted Hawkins and Riley Puckett
Ida Red -- Gid Tanner and His Skillet Lickers
Johnson's Old Grey Mule -- J. E. Mainer's Mountaineers
Kentucky Blues -- Prairie Ramblers
Maple on the Hill -- J. E. Mainer's Mountaineers
Mitchell Blues -- Wade Mainer and the Sons of the Mountaineers
Montana Plains -- Patsy Montana
On Tanner's Farm -- Gid Tanner and His Skillet Lickers
Ragged But Right -- Riley Puckett and Ted Hawkins
Riding on That Train 45 -- Wade Mainer, Zeke Morris, and Steve Ledford
Seven and a Half -- J. E. Mainer's Mountaineers
Shady Grove My Darling -- Prairie Ramblers
Short Life and It's Trouble -- Wade Mainer and Zeke Morris
Soldier's Joy -- Gid Tanner and His Skillet Lickers
Tex's Dance -- Prairie Ramblers
Tokio Rag -- Ted Hawkins and Riley Puckett

489   Label Name/Number: RCA 8417-2-R [CD]
Title: *Are You from Dixie? Great Country Brother Teams of the 1930's*
Editor: Billy Altman
Source and Date of Recordings: Studio recordings, 1930-39

Date of Publication: 1988
Annotations: 18-p. enclosed booklet by Altman
Selections:
 Are You from Dixie? -- Blue Sky Boys
 Blow Yo' Whistle, Freight Train -- Delmore Brothers
 Crawdad Song -- Lone Star Cowboys
 Deep Elm Blues -- Lone Star Cowboys
 Down with the Old Canoe [D 24?] -- Dixon Brothers
 Have a Feast Here Tonight -- Monroe Brothers
 I'm Just Here To Get My Baby out of Jail -- Blue Sky Boys
 I've Got the Big River Blues -- Delmore Brothers
 Intoxicated Rat, The -- Dixon Brothers
 Jake Walk Blues -- Allen Brothers
 Just Because -- Lone Star Cowboys
 Katie Dear [M 4] -- Blue Sky Boys
 New Salty Dog, A -- Allen Brothers
 Nine Pound Hammer Is Too Heavy -- Monroe Brothers
 Roll Down the Line -- Allen Brothers
 Roll in My Sweet Baby's Arms -- Monroe Brothers
 The Nashville Blues -- Delmore Brothers
 Weave Room Blues -- Dixon Brothers

   RCA 8417-2-R [CD] / RCA 8416-2-R [CD]:   Following the discontinuance of its Vintage Series in the early 1970s, RCA embarked on another, shorter-lived reissue program resurrecting the old Bluebird label and logo of the 1930s. A few 1930s country and western swing albums enjoyed a brief existence before that series, too, was discontinued. No further systematic reissue programs were undertaken until after RCA was purchased by the German BMG corporation. In the late 1980s, Billy Altman, a young journalist who specialized in writing about music, persuaded BMG to hire him on contract to reissue some of RCA's archival hillbilly and blues material. These two CDs were the first in the new series. The stringband set is divided among the Skillet Lickers, the Prairie Ramblers and Patsy Montana, J. E. Mainer's Mountaineers, and Wade Mainer groups. The Skillet Lickers exemplified the wild stringband style that thrived in North Georgia at the hands of such celebrated entertainers as Tanner and Puckett themselves, Fiddlin' John Carson, Earl Johnson, Clayton McMichen, Lowe Stokes, and others. They are represented here by six of their most successful numbers, all recorded in 1934: Puckett's rendition of the title song; the group's rendition of "On Tanner's Farm," a variant of the traditional "Down on Penny's Farm"; Ted Hawkins' mandolin compositions, "Hawkins' Rag" and "Tokio Rag"; and the dance tunes "Soldier's Joy" (with Tanner on banjo) and "Ida Red." North Carolina also had a thriving stringband tradition, generally (but not always) represented by a smoother singing style and fiddle and a picked rather than a frailed banjo. Brothers J. E. Mainer (fiddle) and Wade Mainer (banjo) were among the most popular among old-time tarheel recording artists--first together, as J. E. Mainer's Mountaineers (1935-6), and then, after they parted, heading separate ensembles. The earlier group is represented by one of their best sellers, the 19th-century sentimental favorite, "Maple on the Hill," J. E.'s "Seven and a Half" (better known as "Hook and Line," or "Shout Lulu") and an exuberant "Johnson's Old Grey Mule." The Mainers were among the earliest groups to learn from recordings of other hillbilly artists, and Wade Mainer's "Riding on That Train Forty Five," and "Mitchell Blues" were probably taken from the versions by Grayson and Whitter and by Narmour and Smith (originally titled "Carroll County Blues"), respectively. A wildly different approach to stringband music was pursued by the Kentucky group, the Prairie Ramblers, whose country jazz had more in common with the western swing bands of Milton Brown and Bob Wills than with any well-known Kentucky bands of the period. Though all such groups are best-known for their treatment of 30s pop and jazz material, the Ramblers' roots lay in the same stratum of traditional Anglo-American instrumental dance music that underlay the music of the Skillet Lickers and Mainer bands. Their rousing "Shady Grove My Darling" comes from this wellspring. Featuring the flashy fiddling of Tex Atchison, plectrum banjo or mandolin by Chick Hurt, guitar or harmonica by Salty Holmes, and vocals by Patsy Montana, they were one of the most successful country acts of the mid-'30s.

The companion CD features a half dozen of the best known exponents of one of the most widespread formats during the '30s, brother duets: the Allens (from Tennessee), Attleseys (Texas; here as the Lone Star Cowboys, later known as the Shelton Brothers), the Delmores (Alabama), Dixons (South Carolina), Monroes (Kentucky), and Bolicks (Blue Sky Boys, from North Carolina). Each but one featured a different instrumental combination: Allens, guitar and banjo; Attleseys, mandolin and jug or uke, with guitar backup; Delmores, guitar and tenor guitar; Dixons, guitar and steel guitar; Monroes and Bolicks, both mandolin and guitar -- but with vastly different styles. Each team is represented by some of their best-known material. Although we think of these artists and their repertoires as being largely traditional, it is worth remembering that most of them composed or reworked much of their own material: more than half the selections in this sampler were new to the 1930s. Both CDs include a brochure by Altman with discographic data, photos, and good background notes. [JAF 409]

490 Label Name/Number: RCA Victor LPV 507
Title: *Smoky Mountain Ballads*
Editor: John A. Lomax
Source and Date of Recordings: Studio recordings, 1930-38
Date of Publication: 1964 (originally issued as 78 rpm set P-79 in 1941)
Annotations: Liner notes by Ed Kahn
Selections: (All but asterisked titles appeared in the 1941 album)
    Chittlin' Cookin' Time in Cheatham County -- Arthur Smith Trio
    Cumberland Mountain Deer Race -- Uncle Dave Macon
    Darling Corey -- Monroe Brothers
    Down in the Willow [F 6] -- Wade Mainer and Zeke Morris
    Down with the Old Canoe [D 24?] -- Dixon Brothers *
    East Virginia Blues, The -- Carter Family
    I'm Bound to Ride -- Arthur Smith Trio *
    Ida Red -- Gid Tanner and His Skillet Lickers
    Intoxicated Rat -- Dixon Brothers
    On a Cold Winter's Night [G 26] -- J. E. Mainer's Mountaineers
    On Tanner's Farm -- Gid Tanner and Riley Puckett *
    Railroadin' and Gamblin' -- Uncle Dave Macon *
    Riding on That Train Forty-Five -- Wade Mainer, Zeke Morris, and Steve Ledford
    There's More Pretty Girls Than One -- Arthur Smith Trio *
    Where Is My Sailor Boy? -- Monroe Brothers *
    Worried Man Blues -- Carter Family

RCA LPV 507: John Lomax's carefully edited album, *Smoky Mountain Ballads*, was one of the first repackagings of traditional southeastern rural music for a sophisticated urban northern audience. The album went out of print a few years after its issue and was not available again until 1964, when the Vintage Series album was issued, with six more titles added to the eight Lomax had originally chosen. Mercifully, Lomax's notes were not reprinted; his overly romanticized prose offered little substantive information about the songs themselves and nothing at all about the performers or the details of the original recordings. Readers were told nothing about commercial vs. field recordings in general or about the sources of these selections in particular. Probably it was an unimportant question to Lomax, who must have had some information from Victor's files at his disposal yet evidently chose to ignore it. Comparison of Ed Kahn's 1964 notes shows how much more we had learned about hillbilly music in the intervening years; we have learned that much more again since 1964.

491   Label Name/Number: RCA Victor LPV 522
Title: *Authentic Cowboys and Their Western Folksongs*
Editor: Fred Hoeptner
Source and Date of Recordings: Studio recordings, 1925-34
Date of Publication: 1965
Annotations: Liner notes by Fred G. Hoeptner
Selections:
> Bill Was a Texas Lad [dB 41] -- J. D. Farley
> Bucking Broncho (My Love Is a Rider) -- Mildred and Dorothy Good (The Girls of the Golden West)
> Cowboys's Dream, The -- Jules Allen
> Following the Cow Trail -- Carl T. Sprague
> Haunted Hunter -- Billie Maxwell
> Mormon Cowboy, The -- Carl T. Sprague
> Night Guard, The -- Jack Webb
> Old Chisholm Trail, The -- 'Mac' McClintock
> Powder River, Let 'Er Buck -- Powder River Jack and Kitty Lee
> Sam Bass [E 4] -- 'Mac' McClintock
> Texas Ranger [A 8] -- Cartwright Brothers
> There's a Brown Skin Girl down the Road Somewhere -- A. C. (Eck) Robertson
> Tying a Knot in the Devil's Tail [B 17] -- Powder River Jack and Kitty Lee
> Utah Carroll [B 4] -- Carl T. Sprague
> When the Work's All Done This Fall [B 3] -- Carl T. Sprague
> Zebra Dun [B 16] -- Jules Allen

RCA LPV 522:   In 1964, RCA Victor inaugurated its Vintage Series, a high-price line directed toward the specialist record collector. The series was the brainchild of producer and long-time jazz enthusiast Brad McCuen. There were 84 carefully programmed albums planned in the next eight years, though the last few were never issued. Among these LPs were a comparatively few devoted to folk-derived music. LPV 502 reissued some vintage recordings of Woody Guthrie from 1940-41, and LVP 507 (see above) reissued a classic album programmed by John A. Lomax. Another five were devoted to archival material from RCA's extensive hillbilly/country/bluegrass catalog, four of which are discussed here. For each one, RCA selected a recognized folk music authority and gave him free rein over choice of material and liner notes. Here, Fred Hoeptner programmed an album heavy in cowboy balladry from the last half of the 19th century--the era during which this kind of music flourished. Texas cowboy fiddler Eck Robertson's contribution is the one instrumental selection on the album. Musically the most striking piece is the Cartwrights' fiddle/vocal duet on "Texas Ranger." Recorded in the hauntingly echoic space of Camden, New Jersey, Trinity Church, the piece is one of the gems from the "golden age" of hillbilly music. In terms of popularity, the award must go to Sprague's "When the Work's All Done This Fall," one of the first cowboy ballads recorded by a traditional performer and a near-million seller at a time when such sales figures were rare indeed. [JAF 283--DKW]

492   Label Name/Number: RCA Victor LPV 532
Title: *The Railroad in Folksong*
Editor: Archie Green
Source and Date of Recordings: Studio recordings, 1926-40

Date of Publication: 1966
Annotations: Liner notes by Archie Green
Selections:

Cannon Ball, The -- Delmore Brothers
Crime of the D'Autremont Brothers -- Johnson Brothers
Davis Limited, The -- Jimmie Davis
Engine One-Forty-Three [G 3] -- Carter Family
If I Die a Railroad Man -- Tenneva Ramblers
Jerry, Go Ile That Car -- Harry 'Mac' McClintock
Little Red Caboose Behind the Train, The -- Paul Warmack and His Gully Jumpers
Longest Train, The -- J. E. Mainer's Mountaineers
McAbee's Railroad Piece -- Palmer McAbee
Nine Pound Hammer Is Too Heavy -- Monroe Brothers
Orange Blossom Special -- Rouse Brothers
Peanut Special -- Byron Parker and His Mountaineers
Red and Green Signal Lights, The -- G. B. Grayson and Henry Whitter
Train's Done Left Me, The -- Carolina Tar Heels
Wreck of the Old 97 [G 2] -- Vernon Dalhart
Wreck of the Virginian, The -- Blind Alfred Reed

RCA LPV 532: Archie Green, authority on labor lore and occupational folksong, programmed two albums on railroad songs at about the same time: this one, drawn from commercial recordings, and one for the Library of Congress (L61; see Section II) utilizing entirely noncommercial field recordings. Some of country music's best-loved train songs are here, including the two trainwreck ballads by Dalhart and the Carter Family, the original recording of the Rouse Brothers' own composition, "Orange Blossom Special," now a fiddler's showpiece, the Monroe Brothers' lively rendition of a song tied closely to the John Henry legend. Reed's trainwreck composition describes a local West Virginia tragedy that never achieved wide popularity despite its haunting melody; "McAbee's Railroad Piece" is a harmonica instrumental by a performer whose ethnicity is still uncertain. [JAF 317--DKW]

493 Label Name/Number: RCA Victor LPV 548
Title: *Native American Ballads*
Editor: D. K. Wilgus
Source and Date of Recordings: Studio recordings, 1925-39
Date of Publication: 1967
Annotations: Liner notes by D. K. Wilgus
Selections:

Cold Penitentiary Blues [I 4] -- B. F. Shelton
Death of Floyd Collins [G 22] -- Vernon Dalhart
Down on the Banks of the Ohio [F 5] -- Red Patterson's Piedmont Log Rollers
Dying Hobo, The [H 3] -- Travis B. Hale and E. J. Derry, Jr.
Jesse James [E 1] -- Harry 'Mac' McClintock
Leavin' Home [I 3] -- Swingbillies
Little Mo-Hee [H 8] -- Hall Brothers
My Name Is John Johanna [H 1] -- Kelly Harrell
Seven Long Years in Prison -- Tenneva Ramblers
Sweet Betsy from Pike [B 9] -- Bradley Kincaid
They Say It Is Sinful To Flirt [G 19] -- Delmore Brothers
Tom Sherman's Barroom [B 1] -- Dick Devall
Two Soldiers, The [A 17] -- Carl T. Sprague

Wild and Reckless Hobo [H 2] -- Jimmie Davis
Wreck of the Six Wheeler -- Newton Gaines
[Also 1 African-American performance]

RCA LPV 548: On this album, Wilgus strove to present a well-balanced sampling of the native American balladry genre as preserved in RCA's vaults from the period of 1925 to 1939. Compared with lyric song and instrumental music, the LP demonstrates that balladry was not Victor's forte. Most of the ballads are fairly well-known in Anglo-American tradition. Several ballads presumably of African-American origin are also included (I 3, I 4, I 16/dI 25), but only one selection on the LP features black performers (Jazz Gillum's "Big Katy Adams"). The musical highlight of the album is Dick Devall's "Tom Sherman's Barroom," one of the few unaccompanied ballads commercially recorded by a white singer. Devall recorded a shorter version of the same ballad for John A. Lomax in 1946. The liner notes are what we have come to expect from Wilgus, who was, at the time, one of the few album editors who treated the back of a record jacket as the appropriate place for scholarship. [JAF 323]

494   Label Name/Number: RCA Victor LPV 552
Title: *Early Rural String Bands*
Editor: Norm Cohen
Source and Date of Recordings: Studio recordings, 1922-49
Date of Publication: 1968
Annotations: Liner notes by Norm Cohen
Selections:
    Alabama Jubilee -- Bill Helms and His Upson County Band
    Big Bend Gal -- Shelor Family
    Black-Eyed Susie -- J. P. Nester and Norman Edmonds
    Bring Me a Leaf from the Sea -- Carolina Tar Heels
    Charlie, He's a Good Old Man -- Kelly Harrell and the Virginia String Band
    How Many Biscuits Can I Eat? -- Gwen Foster
    Jaw Bone -- Pope's Arkansas Mountaineers
    Leather Breeches -- W. A. Hinton
    Medley of Reels -- Henry Ford's Old Time Dance Orchestra
    Mitchell Blues -- Wade Mainer and Sons of the Mountaineers
    New Salty Dog, A -- Allen Brothers
    Ragtime Annie -- A. C. (Eck) Robertson
    Tanner's Hornpipe -- Gid Tanner and His Skillet Lickers
    Up Jumped the Devil -- Byron Parker and His Mountaineers

RCA LPV 552: This survey of hillbilly instrumental music was programmed to open with an unaccompanied fiddle solo ("Ragtime Annie") and unaccompanied banjo solo ("Leather Breeches,") followed by a fiddle/banjo duet ("Black-Eyed Susie"), then selections including, successively, guitar, mandolin, and other instruments in approximate order of their historical introduction to southeastern instrumental music. Stylistic developments were also recapitulated in movement from older, clearly Anglo-American styles to later ones that showed African-American influence from minstrel stage ("Jaw Bone") to blues, jazz, ragtime, and swing. [JAF 325--AJ]

495   Label Name/Number: Rounder 1026
Title: *Rich Man, Poor Man: American Country Songs of Protest*
Source and Date of Recordings: From commercial 78s, 1920s and '30s
Date of Publication: 1981
Annotations: Liner notes by Mark Wilson

Selections:

All I've Got Is Gone -- Ernest V. Stoneman
Breadline Blues -- Slim Smith
Cotton Mill Blues -- Wilmer Watts and the Lonely Eagles
Death of Mother Jones, The -- Gene Autry
Farmer Is the Man That Feeds Them All, The -- Fiddlin' John Carson
Farmer Is the Man, The -- Wheeler and Lamb
Fifty Years from Now -- Harry McClintock
Forgotten Soldier Boy, The -- Monroe Brothers
Marion Massacre, The -- Welling and McGhee
Miner's Prayer, A -- Hart Brothers
Money Cravin' Folks -- Blind Alfred Reed
Poor Man, Rich Man -- Dave McCarn
Riley the Furniture Man -- Georgia Crackers
Shut Up in Coal Creek Mine -- Green Bailey
Spinning Room Blues -- Dixon Brothers
We're up against It Now -- Uncle Dave Macon

Rndr 1026: To the social historian, hillbilly recordings are a potential treasure trove of musical commentary on contemporary events and movements of the period from 1925 to World War II. Most reissue anthologies are organized on principles of region of performers' origins or musical styles. There is a great deal of material still awaiting examination in an historical context. These 16 songs are all the creations of local poets--generally the musicians who recorded them--dramatizing the plight of the poor working classes at about the time of the Great Depression. They are protest songs, surely, in their artful though not covert complaints of the inequities in the social system or in the temporary economic setbacks that befall their narrators. But they are neither propagandistic nor militant. Protest is not part of a program of social reform; there is no "larger issue" to be addressed. There is simply protest--sometimes, as in McCarn's several compositions growing out of his years' experience in the cotton mills, with more than a touch of humor and irony. A few of the pieces--for example "Shut Up in Coal Creek Mine"--are especially moving, particularly when the textual understatement is supplemented by some historical facts that were probably well known to the recording's original audience. Today, we are not certain which of the several underground explosions at Fraterville/Cross Mountain in the period of 1902-1911 the song memorializes, but its text was ostensibly based on the last messages scribbled by the miners and later found when their bodies were recovered. Autry's paeon of tribute to Mother Jones (1830-1930), the one-time beacon of strength of the unionization movement seems grossly incongruous in view of his later commercial and financial successes; at the time, he was just a struggling performer singing someone else's composition about a popular figure. [JEMFQ #61--DN]

496 Label Name/Number: Rounder 1029
Title: *Banjo Pickin' Girl, Vol. 1*
Source and Date of Recordings: From commercial 78s, 1924-38
Date of Publication: 1978
Annotations: Liner notes by Patricia A. Hall and Charles Wolfe
Selections:

All Night Long -- Roba Stanley
Banjo on My Knee Blues -- Louisiana Lou
Banjo Pickin' Girl -- Coon Creek Girls
Bucking Broncho -- Girls of the Golden West
Christine LeRoy [H 31] -- Blue Ridge Mountain Singers
Cowboy's Wife -- Billie Maxwell

Export Gal [P 35] -- Louisiana Lou
I Wish I Had Never Met You -- Blue Ridge Mountain Singers
Last Gold Dollar -- Moonshine Kate
Montana Plains -- Rubye Blevins (Patsy Montana)
Old Lonesome Blues -- Bowman Sisters
Poor Girl's Story, The -- Moonshine Kate
Single Life -- Roba Stanley
Sowing on the Mountain -- Coon Creek Girls
Waltz of the Hills -- Rubye Blevins (Patsy Montana)
Big Eyed Rabbit -- Eva David and Samantha Bumgarner

Rndr 1029: The compilers of this album tried to satisfy two aims simultaneously: to survey the role of female performers in early country music and to offer examples of song lyrics that reflect the role of women in society. The 16 selections reissued feature 10 performers or groups who recorded between 1924 and 1938. The artists range from the historically important but musically rather stiff Eva Davis and Samantha Bumgarner, and Roba Stanley--among the earliest female country recording artists--to the thoroughly professional and highly popular Coon Creek Girls and Girls of the Golden West. Uneven as the performers are in their artistry, so are they in their importance, historically speaking: Bumgarner and Stanley were significant only for their chronological priority; Patsy Montana, for her great popularity through the '30s; others, like Louisiana Lou and Billie Maxwell, were unquestionably minor figures. Thematically, the songs touch on some important issues concerning the social role of women. Roba Stanley's "Single Life" is the familiar statement of a young unmarried who states proudly, "I am single and no man's wife, and no man shall control me." By contrast, "Cowboy's Wife" is the sad recital of a hard-working housewife who vainly hopes that her cowboy husband will notice her new dress as he comes home but resigns herself to providing him his supper uncomplainingly because she knows that's the way to his heart. The two previously unissued titles by the Blue Ridge Mountain Singers are charmingly done and interesting as well, However, I would strongly question the speculation in the brochure notes that they were not originally issued because they both deal "indirectly, with adultery." Adultery is, I think, a far too specific label to attach to either story; infidelity, of course, but nothing more specific that the oft-recorded "There'll Come a Time," or "Rock All Our Babies to Sleep," or "May I Sleep in Your Barn Tonight Mister." Moonshine Kate's "Poor Girl's Story" is basically Carson Robison's "Railroad Boomer," slightly altered to present the image of a female, rather than a male, wanderer. And the Coon Creek Girls' song that gives the album its title "conjures up the image of another fun-loving, wander-lusting mountain girl--the Appalachian equivalent of the jazz age's flapper." Millie and Dolly Good's "Bucking Broncho," about a young cowboy and his sweetheart, has often been described as a double entendre piece, but I find the suggestion of a second, sexual, meaning unconvincing. The all-too familiar subject of murdered sweethearts is represented by "Export Gal," a variant of "Knoxville Girl." As of this writing (1993), Vol. 2 has yet to be issued. [JEMFQ 55]

497   Label Name/Number: Rounder 1033
Title: *Tennessee Strings*
Editor: [Charles Wolfe]
Source and Date of Recordings: From commercial 78s, 1920s-'30s
Date of Publication: 1979
Annotations: Liner notes by Charles Wolfe
Selections:
Alecazander -- Johnson Brothers
Bum on the Bum -- Ramblin' Red Lowery
Chattanooga Blues -- Allen Brothers

Death of William Jennings Bryan, The -- Charlie Oaks
Free a Little Bird -- Ridgel's Fountain Citians
Goin' To Stop Drinkin' When I Die -- Fleming and Townsend
Hickman Rag, The -- Charlie Bowman with the Hill Billies
In the Steps of Light -- Vaughan Quartet
Little Willie Green (from New Orleans) -- Swift Jewel Cowboys
Maybelle Rag -- Young Brothers and Homer Davenport
Old Joe -- Dr. Humphrey Bate and His Possum Hunters
Tell Her To Come Back Home -- Uncle Dave Macon and His Fruit Jar Drinkers
Tell It to Me Boys -- Grant Brothers
Tennessee Jubilee -- Uncle Dave Macon and Sid Harkreader
Tribulation -- Southern Melody Boys
Times Ain't What They Used To Be -- Tom Ashley and Gwen Foster

Rndr 1033: This album, intended as a companion to Charles Wolfe's *Tennessee Strings* (University of Tennessee Press, 1977), a history of country music in Tennessee, is a "sampler of the diverse forms of old-time music in Tennessee during the 1920s and 1930s." In its preparation, Wolfe tried to avoid duplication of titles already reissued and to "produce a collection that will appeal both to the serious student and collector of old-time music as well as to the general listener." In both respects he succeeded admirably. Although several of the artists had never appeared on previous reissue albums, the musical strengths of the sampling are remarkable. The two 1925 recordings of "Hickman Rag," with Charlie Bowman's hard-driving fiddling, and"Maybelle Rag," with Jess Young's fiddling and Homer Young's astonishing 3-finger banjo-picking, are both particularly noteworthy. Both, incidentally, are circle-of-fifths-based tunes, a form which is the most common justification in country music for the appellation of "rag." Tom Ashley was from Tennessee, though he is generally associated with the group of western North Carolina musicians that went by the name of the Carolina Tar Heels. Charlie Oaks's piece may not set the feet of many listeners tapping but it is an important piece historically, dealing with the Scopes trial. Oaks himself was an important early artist about whom far too little is known. In his notes, Wolfe tries to make a case for five distinct musical regions in Tennessee by the end of the 1920s: (1) the area in eastern Tennessee around Bristol, Kingsport,and Johnson City (Ashley, Bowman, Johnson Brothers, Grant Brothers); (2) the area around Knoxville (Oaks, Ridgel); (3) the Chattanooga area, near the Alabama and Georgia borders (Young, Allen Brothers); (4) the Nashville area (Macon, Bate); and (5) the Memphis region in the southwest (Fleming and Townsend, Lowery, Swift Jewel Cowboys). The two religious recordings by the Vaughan Quartet and the Southern Melody Boys seem to fall through the cracks of this division. There is something to be said for this categorization (although one needs more examples than the handful on this disc to gain any confidence in the divisions); however, by the early 1930s chronological distinctions seem to have become as important as regional ones.   [JEMFQ 62]

498   Label Name/Number: Rounder 1035
Title: *Work Don't Bother Me: Old Time Comic Songs from North Georgia*
Editor: Charles Wolfe
Source and Date of Recordings: From commercial 78s and test pressings, 1926-31
Date of Publication: 1986
Annotations: Liner notes by Charles Wolfe
Selections:
   All Gone Now -- Clyde Evans
   Charming Betsy -- Georgia Organ Grinders
   Cotton Mill Blues -- Lee Brothers Trio
   Georgia Hobo, The [H 2] -- Cofer Brothers

How I Got My Gal -- Clyde Evans
I Lost My Girl (New Cut Road) -- Earl Johnson's Dixie Entertainers
I Shall Not Be Moved -- Gid Tanner Band (*)
It Just Suits Me -- Lowe Stokes and his North Georgians
Just Married -- Riverside String Band (*)
Long Way to Tipperary -- Fiddlin' John Carson
Prohibition Blues -- Clayton McMichen (*)
She's a Beaut -- Earl Johnson's Dixie Entertainers
She's Killing Me -- Nichols Brothers
Soldier Will You Marry Me -- Skillet Lickers
Way Down in Georgia -- Earl Johnson's Dixie Entertainers
Work Don't Bother Me -- Gid Tanner Band (*)

Rndr 1035:   The title of this album suggests a much more specific subject than its contents justify. In fact, this is simply a selection of light-hearted songs and ballads on a variety of subjects, of which courtship and marriage is most prominent--all by musicians associated with one of the most prolific centers of early hillbilly recorded music. Four of the recordings (marked by asterisks) were never issued prior to this collection--including McMichen's "Prohibition Blues," which can be considered "comic" only by considerable stretching of the definition.

499   Label Name/Number: Rounder 1037
Title: *Kentucky Country: Old Time Music from Kentucky, Original 1927-1937 Recordings*
Editor/Producer: Charles Wolfe
Source and Date of Recordings: From commercial 78s and test pressings, 1927-37
Date of Publication: 1983
Annotations: Liner notes by Charles Wolfe
Selections:

Beaver Valley Breakdown -- Lonesome Luke and his Farm Boys
Cold Penitentiary Blues [I 4] -- B. F. Shelton
Crossed Old Jordan's Stream -- Bird's Kentucky Corn Crackers
Going Home This Evening -- Karl and Harty
Hard for To Love -- Appalachia Vagabond
I Truly Understand -- Shortbuckle Roark and Family
I Want To Go Where Jesus Is -- Ernest Phipps and his Holiness Quartet
Lady Gay [C. 79] -- Buell Kazee
Nobody's Business -- Walker's Corbin Ramblers
Peddlar and His Wife [F 24] -- Appalachia Vagabond
Roundin' Up the Yearlings -- Slim Miller with the Cumberland Ridge Runners
Run Them Coons into the Ground -- Cliff Gross and Muryel Campbell
Shady Grove -- Prairie Ramblers
Shortinin' Bread -- Fiddlin' Doc Roberts
Western Kentucky Limited -- Hack String Band
Wild Horse or Stoney Point -- Jilson Setters

Rndr 1037:   This cross section of old-time music (16 commercial records, one previously unissued) includes some of the most popular recording hillbilly artists of the day as well as some almost unknown ones. Styles range from banjo/vocals by Buell Kazee (whose rendition of "Lady Gay" I have already praised as one of the finest on record), Hayes Shepard, George Roark, and B. F. Shelton; and a fiddle tune by Jilson Setters (J. W. Day), to fiddle/guitar instumentals by Doc Roberts and Cliff Gross, a smooth vocal duet by Karl and Harty, and stringband music by Walker's Corbin Ramblers and the Prairie Ramblers. This is an excellent anthology that deserves booklet-length annotation, but much more information can be found in Wolfe's *Kentucky Country: Folk and Country Music of Kentucky* (University Press of Kentucky, 1982). [JAF 391]

500   Label Name/Number: Vetco 103
Title: *Songs of the Railroad Recorded 1924-1934*
Source and Date of Recordings: From commercial 78s, 1924-34
Date of Publication: [ca. 1971]
Annotations: Liner notes by Bob Hyland
Selections:

    C. and O. Excursion -- Frank Hutchison
    C. C. and O. Number 558 -- Al Hopkins and His Buckle Busters
    Casey Jones [G 1] -- Gid Tanner and His Skillet Lickers
    Double Headed Train -- Henry Whitter
    Engineer Frank Hawk -- Rainey Old Time Band
    Engineer's Dream, The -- Vernon Dalhart
    Engineer's Last Run, The -- Blue Ridge Mountain Singers
    Home Again Medley -- Red Mountain Trio
    I'm Nine Hundred Miles from Home -- Fiddlin' John Carson
    Little Red Caboose Behind the Train, The -- Pickard Family
    Nine Pound Hammer, The -- Al Hopkins and His Buckle Busters
    Railroad Blues -- Roy Harvey and Earl Shirkey
    Southern Number 111 -- Roane County Ramblers
    When the Train Comes Along -- Uncle Dave Macon and Sam and Kirk McGee
    Wreck of the 1256 -- Vernon Dalhart
    Wreck of the Royal Palm Express, The [dG 51] -- Vernon Dalhart

Vetco 103:   On commercial hillbilly recordings of the late '20s and 1930s railroads were a favorite topic, subjects ranging from the heroic figures like Casey Jones, to tragic trainwrecks, pathetic stories of unfortunate travelers, programmatic imitations, and religious imagery.   This album includes a smattering of all, and more.   It is particularly rich in music imitating railroad sounds ("Engineer Frank Hawk," "C. C. and O. No. 558," "Southern Number 111," "C. and O. Excursion," "Double Headed Train").   Record collector Hyland provides brief notes on the performers and the context of the songs, but there is clearly room for more extensive commentary.

ARTIST INDEX

[Underlined names/numbers designate albums devoted entirely (or primarily) to the indicated artists.]

Abbot, Francis H.: LC AFS L68

Abernathy, Will: NWR NW 236

Adams Family Quartet: TFS-108

Adams, Finley: BRI 004

Adams, Howard, and Thornton Regular Baptist Church Congregation: NWR NW 294

Adams, James Taylor: BRI 004

Adams, Kenneth "Bill": N&T 1001

Agins, Sam: NWR NW 314/315

Aiken County String Band: Cty 531

Aitken, Lea: Ok OK 76004

Akers, Rev. Robert: LC AFC L69-L70

Alabama Sacred Harp Singers: Atl SD-1346, Atl SD-1347, Atl SD-1349, Mar 9100, Mar 9101, Prst INT 25007

Alden, Ray: Her XXXIII

Allen Brothers: BF 15501, Mar 9105, NWR NW 236, OT 100, RCA 8417-2-R [CD], RCA LPV 552, Rndr 1033

Allen, Alice: MFP 002

Allen, Jules Verne: BF 15502, Mar 9106, MS 45008, NWR NW 314/315, RCA LPV 522

Allen, Pug: HMM LP001, HMM LP002

Allen, Rex: NWR NW 314/315

Allery, Alec: MFP 002

Allison's (J. T.) Sacred Harp Singers: Mar 9100, Mar 9101, NWR NW 245

Alston, Israel: Rndr 0237

Altizer, Maude: FPrm 41942

Ambassadors: OFA TALP-001

Anderson, Arthur: TFS-106

Anderson, Long Pete: Ok OK 75003

Anderson, Virgil: Cty 777, Cty 787

Anderson, Willard: Cty 787

Anthony, "Chubby": SmFwys CD SF 40038

Appalachia Vagabond: Rndr 1037

Arizona Wranglers: NWR NW 314/315

Arkansas Barefoot Boys: Cty 518

Arm and Hammer String Band: Her XXXIII

Armstrong, Lena: FLeg FSA-22, FLeg FSA-23

Arthur, Emry: Cty 522, JEMF 103, Mar 9100, Mar 9111, OH OHCS 190.

Arthur, Henry: Mar 9111

Arthur, Tanner, and His Blue Ridge Cornshuckers: NWR NW 245

Arwood, Garrett and Noah: HMM LP002

Asher, McKinley: Rndr 0237

Ashlaw, Ted: Philo 1022

Ashley, Clarence ("Tom"): Cty 502, Cty 525, Fwys FA 2951, Fwys FA 2953, Fwys FA 2350, Fwys FA 2355, Fwys FA 2359, Fwys FA 2390, Fwys FA 2435, Mar 9104, NWR NW 236, NWR NW 245, Rndr 1033, Van VRS-9147

Ashley's Melody Men: Cty 503, Cty 518, OT 101

Atcher, Bob: TFS-105

Atwood, Kenneth Ward: NWR NW 291, Ok OK 76004

Austin, Lonnie: Ldr LEE 4045

Austin, Mrs. Morris: NWR NW 239

Autry, Gene: CMH 106, NWR NW 314/315, Rndr 1026

Avery, Sam: TFS-108

Avondale Mills Quartet: Mar 9100

Ayers, Cap: Rndr 0057

Bachor, Paul: Ok OK 76004

Back, Rev. I. D., and the Mount Olive Regular Baptist Church Congregation: Atl SD-1349, Prst INT 25011

Backwoods Band: Her XXXIII

Bailey, Franklin, and Tennessee Pals: Prst FL 14030

Bailey, Green: CT 6001, Cty 502, MS 45004, Rndr 1026

Bailey, Wheeler: TFS-106

Baird, Bertha: TFS cass

Baker, Bob, and Pike Cty Boys: SmFwys CD SF 40038

Baker, Etta: Trad 1007

Baker, Lawrence: MFFA 1001

Baker, Mr. and Mrs. J. W.: Cty 522, CMF 011-L, TFS-105

Baldwin, Jones: Rndr 0058

Ballance, Maurice: Fwys FS 3848

Ball, Estil C.: Atl SD-1346, Atl SD-1347, Atl SD-1349, Atl SD-1350, LC AFS L1, LC AFS L2, LC AAFS L9, NWR NW 291, Prst INT 25003, Prst INT 25009, Rndr 0026, Rndr

0028, Rndr 0072, Rndr SS-0145

Ball, Orna: Atl SD-1349, Atl SD-1350, LC AFS L2, Rndr SS-0145, Rndr 0072

Bandy, H. L.: MS 45004, MS 45005

Barbee, Eldia: PB 003, PB 004, PB 006, TFS-103

Barbee, Oscar: PB 005, PB 006, TFS-103

Barker, Horton: BRI 002, Fwys FA 2362, LC AFS L1, LC AFS L7, LC AAFS L54

Barnes' (H. M.) Blue Ridge Ramblers: BRI 005

Barry, Michael F.: LC AFS L60

Barton, Elmer: JEMF 105, LC AFS L62, MC #1

Basil, Troy: Mer 1001-2

Basnight, Mary: Fwys FS 3848

Bate, Dr. Humphrey, and His Possum Hunters: Cty 531, Cty 541, Mar 9110, Mar 9111, Rndr 1033

Batts, Floyd: Prst INT 25009

Beaudoin, Lois and Wilfred: JEMF 105

Bebee, Jim: MFP 002

Beck, Rev. I. D.: NWR NW 294

Beeker, H. J.: LC AAFS L54

Begley, Justus: LC AAFS L9, LC AFS L7, NWR NW 226

Bellbrook String Band: OHS (No #)

Bell, William: UIP cass

Benfield, Neriah and Kenneth: Fwys FA 2365, NWR NW 226, Van VRS-9182

Benford, Mac: Ldr LEA 4012

Bentley Boys: Fwys FA 2951

Bice Family: PB 006

Billings, William: NWR NW 205

Binkley Brothers' Dixie Clodhoppers: Cty 504, Cty 541, Mar 9110, Mar 9111

Bird, W. E.: LC AFS L68

Bird's Kentucky Corn Crackers: Rndr 1037

Birkhead and Lane: Cty 520

Birns, Roy Everett: Prst INT 25004, Prst INT 25009

Bivens, John A.: Fwys FES 34151

Blackard's (Dad) Moonshiners: Cty 504, CMF 011-L, Mar 9110

Blackburn, "Uncle" Rufus: Fwys FA 2435

Blair, Bob: ArkTrad [No #]

Blankenship Family: Mar 9111

Blankenship, Rance: ArkTrad [No #]

Bledsoe, Tommy R.: JnAp JA 049

Bledsoe, W. A.: Miss AH-002

Blevins, Frank and his Tarheel Rattlers: Col CS 9660, Mar 9110, Mar 9111

Blevins, Haywood: BRI 005, Rndr 0058

Blevins, Jont: Rndr 0058

Blevins, Rubye (Patsy Montana): NWR NW 314/315, Rndr 1029, RCA 8416-2-R [CD]

Blind Andy: *see* Jenkins, Andy

Bloxham, Earsel: MFP 001

Bluegrass Buddies: Fwys FS 3832

Blue Grass Mountain Boys: Fwys FA 2434

Blue Ridge Corn Shuckers: CMF 011-L

Blue Ridge Highballers: Col CS 9660, Cty 407, Cty 501, FC-014, MS 45005

Blue Ridge Mountain Singers: Rndr 1029, Vet 103

Blue Ridge Singers: Mar 9100, Mar 9101

Blue Sky Boys (Bill and Earl Bolick): BB AXM2-5525, Cam CAL 797, JEMF 104, Rndr CD 11536, Rndr 1006, OT 102, RCA 2100-2-R [CD], RCA 8417-2-R [CD]

Blum, Sid: Rndr 0064

Boarman, Andrew F: Jn Ap JA 025

Boggs, Dock: Asch AH 3903, Brun 59001, BRI 002, Cty 511, Fwys FA 2392, Fwys FA 2953, Fwys RBF 654, Van VRS-9147

Bogtrotters (Crockett Ward, Fields Ward, Eck Dunford, Dr. W. P. Davis, Walter Alderman, Marvin Evans, Dr. W. E. Dalton): Bio RC-6003

Bolick, Bill and Earl: *see* Blue Sky Boys

Bonner, Patrick: LC AFS L62

Booker Orchestra: Cty 531

Borusky, Pearl Jacobs: LC AFS L1, LC AAFS L55, LC AAFS L58

Bossie, Bob: Rndr 0237

Bowlen, Charles: LC AAFS L55

Bowlen, Granville: Fwys FA 2317

Bowles, Jim: Mer 1001-2

Bowman, Charlie: Col CS 9660, Cty 507, Cty 525, Cty 527, Rndr 1033

Bowman, Vergil and Geneva: OHS (No #)

Bowman Sisters: Rndr 1029

Box, T. J. "Uncle Jake": TFS-103

Boyd, Bill, and His Cowboy Ramblers: NWR NW 226

Boyd, Ted: HMM LP001, Rndr 0057

Boyle, Margaret Y.: Ok OK 75003

Branch, Dave: AFF AFF 33-1

Branch, Ernest: OH OHCS-177

Brandon, Willie: PB 003, PB 004

Breeding, Dennis: JnAp JA 030

Brewer, Kahle, with Stoneman's Dixie Mountaineers: CMF 011-L, Cty 507

Bright Light Quartet: Prst INT 25009

Brown, James: NWR NW 239, UIP cass

Brown, John: Miss AH-002:

Brown, Linda: Fwys FA 2358

Brown, Noble B.: LC AAFC L26/27, LC AFS L61

Brown, Ross: Fly LP 546, Fwys FE 34161

Brown's (Hershal) Washboard Band: Cty 544, OT 100

Broyles, Gilbert (Gib): N&T 1001

Broyles, Jerome: N&T 1001

Bruce, W. Guy: Fwys FE 34161

Bruesoe, Leizime: LC AFS L62

Brushy Mtn. Boys: Fwys FA 2434

Brushy River Boys: Fwys FA 2435

Bryan, Art: Bio RC 6004

Bryant, Don: SmFwys CD SF 40037

Bryant, Jack: Rndr 0001

Bryant, Mrs. T. M.: LC AAFS L54

Buck Mountain Band (Wade Ward, Charlie Higgins, and Dale Poe): Fwys FA 2435

Buckner, Elic: LC AAFS L9

Buffalo Ragged Five: Mar 9101

Bull Mountain Moonshiners: CMF 011-L, Mar 9111

Bumgarner, "Aunt" Samantha: Riv RLP 12-610, Rndr 1029

Bundy, Winifred: LC AAFS L55

Burckhart, Jacob: NWR NW 226

Burditt, Phyllis: MC #1

Burke, John: Kicking Mule KM 204

Burke, S. C. H.: UTP [cass, no #]

Burnett, Richard D.: Col CS 9660, Cty 501, Cty 504, Cty 511, Cty 522, Cty 527, Fwys FA 2951, Hist HLP 8003, MS 45003, Rndr 1004

Busby, Abraham John: Ok OK 75003, LC AAFS L30

Bush Brothers: Mar 9100, Mar 9101

Butler, Street: Mer 1001-2

Byrne, Jerry: LC AAFS L16

Cadle, Tillman: TFS-108

Cagle, A. Marcus: LC AAFS L11, NWR NW 205

Cahan, Andy: Cty 791, Her 070, Her XXXIII

Caldwell, Hubert: Ldr LEA 4012

Caldwell, Walter and Lola: NWR NW 223

Callahan Brothers: OH OHS 90031, NWR NW 236

Callender, Joseph: Mar 9100

Campbell, Booth: LC AAFS L20

Campbell, Fred A.: UIP cass

Campbell, Larry, and Country Playboys: Prst FL 14030

Camp Creek Boys: Cty 709

Canova, Annie, Judy, and Zeke: Mar 9111

Canoy, Enos, Lola, and Tim: LC AAFS L9, Miss AH-002

Cantrell, J. B.: TFS-106

Cantrell, Peanut: PB 003

Caplinger's (Warren) Cumberland Mountain Entertainers: Cty 531, Mar 9110, OH OHCS-177

Caraco, Cliff: Fwys FS 3832

Carawan, Guy: Rndr 0064

Carl, Leon "Fritz": JEMF 105

Carlisle, Bill: RCA 2100-2-R [CD]

Carlisle, Cliff: Mar 9100, OT 102

Carlisle, Mrs. Irene: LC AAFS L30

Carlisle, Tommy: Mar 9100

Carlton, Gaither: Cty 717, Fwys FA 2390, Rndr 0028, Van VRS-9182

Carmack, Effie M.: Ok OK 75003

Carolina Buddies: BF 15521, Cty 522, Col CS 9660, FC-014

Carolina Gospel Singers: Mar 9100

Carolina Night Hawks: Mar 9105

Carolina Ramblers: JEMF 103, Mar 9100

Carolina Springs Primitive Baptist Church: UNC 0-8078-4083-1

Carolina Tar Heels: BF 15507, Cty 504, Cty 511, FLeg FSA-24, Fwys FA 2951, GHP LP 1001, OT 101, RCA LPV 532, RCA LPV 552

Carolina Twins: Mar 9109

Carpenter, Bob: Atl SD-1346, Atl SD-1347, Prst INT 25004

Carpenter, Ernie: AH AHR 003

Carpenter, French: FProm [no #]

Carper, Janie: BRI 005

Carrico, Stuart: Rndr 0058

Carr, Bill: LC AAFS L54

Carroll County Ramblers: Hist HLP 8003

Carson Creek, Alleghany Cty, NC Congregation: LC AFC L69-L70

Carson, Fiddlin' John: Cty 514, Cty 525, Cty 544, Mar 9104, Mar 9109, NWR NW 245, Rndr 1026, Rndr 1035, Rndr 1003, UIP [no #] [cass], Vet 103

Carter Brothers and Son: Cty 518, Cty 528, Mar 9110, Mar 9111, NWR NW 236

Carter Family: BRI 004, Cam ACLI-0047(e), Cam ACLI-0501, Cam CAL 586, Cam CAL

2473, Cam CAL 2554(e), CMF 011-L, CMH 107, CMH 112, CMH 116, CMH 118, De DL 4404, De DL 4557, Fwys FA 2951/51/53, Har HL 7280/HS 11332, Har HL 7300, Har HL 7344, Har HL 7396, Har HL 7422, JEMF 101, Mar 9109, MCA [Japan] VIM-4012, OH OHCS 111, OH OHCS 112, OH OHCS 116, OH OHCS 117, OH OHS 90045, OTC 6001, RCA LPM 2772, RCA 2100-2-R, RCA LPV 507, RCA LPV 532, TL TLCW-06

Carter, Buster, and Preston Young: FC-014, Fwys FA 2951, Mar 9111, OT 101

Carter, Janette and Joe: JnAp JA0059C

Carter, Maybelle: Van VRS-9147

Carter, Will: NWR NW 314/315

Cartwright Brothers: Mar 9106, MS 45008, RCA LPV 522

Carver Boys: CT 6001, JEMF 103

Case, Clyde: AH AHR 010

Caudell, Ike, and Congregation of Mount Olivet Regular Baptist Church: NWR NW 294

Caudill, Clell: Rndr 0058

Caudill, Hus: Rndr 0058

Cave, Arthur: UNC 0-8078-4084-X

Cave, Betty: UNC 0-8078-4084-X

Cave, Rosalee: UNC 0-8078-4084-X

Cave, Welford: UNC 0-8078-4084-X

Cawley's Jack Oklahoma Ridge Runners: Mar 9111

Cawthorn, Mabel: Fwys FE 34162

Chancey/Chancy, Chesley: Fwys FE 34162, GV SC 03

Chancey, Don: Fwys FE 34162

Chancey, Joe: Fwys FE 34162

Chancey, Ralph: Fwys FE 34162

Chandler, Dillard: Fwys FA 2309, Fwys FA 2418

Chandler, Lloyd: Rndr 0028

Chapman, Willie: Fwys FA 2317

Chappell, Wavie: AH AHR 009

Chase, Richard: Trad 1007

Chastain, Homer and Calvin, and band: PB 005

Chelf, J. E.: Mer 1001-2

Chenoweth's Cornfield Symphony Orchestra: Mar 9111

Cherokee Ramblers: Mar 9110, Mar 9111

Chestnut, Ted: Mar 9105

Childers, Bobby: Fwys FE 34162

Childers, George: Fwys FE 34162

Childress, Ray, and Carolina Foothill Ramblers: Prst FL 14030

Christeson, R. P.: GyEg 101

Christianson, Ernest: MFP 002

Chumber, Coker, and Rice: JEMF 103

Chumbler Family: Mar 9100

Cickram, Grover and Marvin: Rndr 0057

Clark Family Orchestra: Ok OK 76004

Clark, Angie: NWR NW 291

Clark, Orla: Mar 9105

Clarks Creek Progressive Primitive Baptist Church, Ararat, VA Congregation: LC AFC L69-L70

Claunch, W. E.: LC AFS L2, Miss AH-002

Claus, Jeff: Her XXXIII

Clem, Harman: LC AAFS L9

Cleveland, Sara: FLeg FSA-33, Philo 1020, NWR NW 239

Clifton, Elder Bennie and Edrie: UNC 0-8078-4083-1

Clifton, Fred: Rndr 0057

Clifton, Verlen: Cty 791

Cobb and Underwood: MS 45004

Cockerham, Fred: Cty 717, Cty 713, Cty 723, Cty 741, Her XXXIII, Rndr 0001, Rndr 0028

Cockram, Darrell: Rndr 0057

Cockram, Helen: BRI 004

Cofer Brothers: Cty 544, Mar 9110, Mar 9111, Rndr 1035

Coffee, Lester A.: LC AAFS L55, LC AFS L61

Coffey, John: Bio RC 6004

Coffey, O. L.: LC AAFS L9

Coffman, Mose: Her XXXIII, Rndr 0018

Cohen, John: Van VRS-9147

Colburn, Howard: AlaTrad 103

Colby, Pete: Bio RC 6004

Cole, Calvin: LC AAFS L9, Rndr 0058

Cole, Dutch: Cty 518

Cole, Grady and Hazel: RCA 2100-2-R [CD]

Coleman and Harper [Joe Evans and Arthur McLain]: Hist HLP 8002

Coleman, Bernice: Hist HLP 8002, OH OHCS-177

Coleman, Bernice, and West Virginia Ramblers: OH OHCS-141

Colvin, Hiter: Cty 503, Cty 520

Comber, Chris: CMH 106

Combs, Alfred "Badeye": JnAp JA 030

Community Baptist Church, Alleghany Cty, NC Congregation: LC AFC L69-L70

Condie, Vernon: Ok OK 76004

Connor, Sam: HMM LP001, HMM LP002, Rndr 0057

Conroy, Tari: MFP 002

Converse, Neal: JEMF 105

Conway, Rev. Archie: LC AFS L60

Coon Creek Girls: NWR NW 236, OT 102, Rndr 1029

Coon, Walter: Mar 9104

Cooper, Wilma Lee: Rndr 0143

Cope Brothers: TFS-105

Copeland, Leonard: Cty 523

Cormier, Joseph: JEMF 105

Cornett, "Banjo" Bill: Fwys FA 2317

Correct Tone String Band: Her XXXIII

Cottrell, Jenes: FProm [no #], Her 12, Van VRS-9147

Cottrell, Noah: FProm 41942

Couch, Walter, and Wilkes Ramblers: Mar 9110, Mar 9111

Cowden, Noble: Ark Trad 002, ArkTrad [No #]

Cox, Bill: Kan 305, Mar 9105, OH OHCS-141, OH OHCS-177, OT 102,

Cox, Eugene: SmFwys CD SF 40037

Cox, Veronica Stoneman: SmFwys CD SF 40037

Craig, Gray: Ldr LEA 4012, Ldr LEA 4040

Crain, Edward L.: Fwys FA 2951, Mar 9106, MS 45008

Cramp, Bill: NWR NW 223

Crandall, Horace: AFF AFF 33-2

Crandall, Myron: Ok OK 75003, Ok OK 76004

Cranfill, J. B.: Cty 517

Cranford, A. P.: Mar 9105 *see also* Red Fox Chasers

Cranford, Miles and Thompson: *see* Red Fox Chasers

Crase, James: Fwys FA 2317

Craver, Charlie: Mar 9104

Crawford, Bob: N&T 1001

Crawford, Jennifer: BRI 005

Creed, Kyle: Mtn 302, Mtn 304, Mtn 303

Crisp, Palmer: LC AAFS L20

Crisp, Rufus: Fwys FA 2342, LC AAFS L20, LC AAFS L21

Critchlow, Slim: NWR NW 314/315

Crockett Family: *see* Crockett's Kentucky Mountaineers

Crockett, Dad: Brun 59009, Hist HLP 8003

Crockett, George: Hist HLP 8003

Crockett, Johnny and Albert: Cty 523

Crockett's Kentucky Mountaineers: Brun 59009, Cty 501, Cty 503

Cronin, Paddy: JEMF 105

Crook Brothers String Band: Cty 542

Cross Roads Primitive Baptist Church, Baywood, VA Congregation: LC AFC L69-L70

Crowder Brothers: Mar 9101

Crowder, Monte: Ala Trad 103

Cruise, Michael: LC AFS L62

Culis, Ed ("Doc"): PB 004

Cunningham, Howard: Fwys FE 34161

Curry, Lula M.: Fwys FA 2358

Da Costa Woltz's Southern Broadcasters: Cty 508, Cty 524, Hist HLP 8003, NW NWR 236

Dalhart, Vernon: BRI 004, RCA LPV 532, RCA LPV 548, Vet 103

Dalton, Frank: Rndr 0057

Daniels-Deason Sacred Harp: Mar 9100

Danville Primitive Baptist Church: UNC 0-8078-4083-1

Darby, Tom: Col CS 9660, BF 15504, Mar 9109, NWR NW 223, OT 101, OT 102, OT 112

Davenport, Clyde: Cty 786, Cty 788, DU 33014

Davenport, Homer: *see* Young Brothers

Davidson, George: Fwys FA 2358

Davis, Asa: MC #1

Davis, Eva: Rndr 1029

Davis, George: Fwys FA 2317, Fwys FTS 31016, LC AFS L60

Davis, Grandma Pearlie: Fwys FA 2434, Prst FL 14030

Davis, Henry: OHS (No #)

Davis, Jimmie: RCA LPV 532, RCA LPV 548

Davis, Luther: Her 070, Rndr 0058

Davis, Mary and Cora: LC AAFS L54

Davis, Walt: HMM LP001

Day, J. W.: *see* Setters, Jilson

Day, Newell: Ok OK 76004

Day, Rose: Fwys FA 2358

Day, Stella: Ok OK 76004

Deal Family: Mar 9101

Dean, Ruby, and Journeymen's Quartet: Fwys FA 2358

Delmore Brothers (Alton and Rabon): Cty 508, MS 45008, NWR NW 223, OTC 6002, RCA 8417-2-R [CD], RCA LPV 532, RCA LPV 548

Delp, Hobart, and Band: Asch AH 3831

Denmon, Morgan: Mar 9104

Denny, Clyde: JnAp JA 030

Denny, Mary: JnAp JA 030

Denoon, Jimmy: LC AAFS L20, LC AAFS L30

Denoon, Ray R.:   NWR NW 223

De Noyer, Emery: LC AFS L1, LC AAFS L55

Denson, Howard: NWR NW 205

Denson, Paine: LC AAFS L11

Denson, S. M.:   NWR NW 205

Denson Quartet: NWR NW 223

Devall, Dick: LC AAFS L20, Mar 9106, MS 45008, RCA LPV 548

Dickens, H. N.:   Fwys FA 2315

Dickinson, Wes: JEMF 105

Dilleshaw, John: Cty 523, Hist HLP 8002

Dillingham, J. D.:   NWR NW 291

Dillon, John W.:   LC AFS L68

Dilly, Seven Foot and His Dill Pickles (probably A. A. Gray, John Dilleshaw):   Hist HLP 8003, Mar 9110, NWR NW 226

Dimmery, Ira: Arh 5011

Dinwiddie, Wayne: LC AAFS L21

Dixie Mountaineers: *see* Stoneman's Dixie Mountaineers

Dixie Ramblers: Fwys FA 2434, FC-014, Mar 9110

Dixie Reelers: Mar 9101

Dixon Brothers (Dorsey and Howard):   CT 6000, CT 6002, Cty 508, Mar 9104, OT 102, RCA 2100-2-R [CD], RCA 8417-2-R [CD], RCA LPV 507, Rndr 1026

Dixon, Dorsey and Beatrice: Mar 9101

Dixon, Dorsey: Tst T-3301, Van VRS-9147

Dixon, Howard: Tst T-3301 *see also* Rambling Duet

Dixon, Nancy: Tst T-3301

Dixon, Samuel Clay: NWR NW 291

Donaldson, Findlay: TFS-108

Doss, Willy: Van VRS-9182

Douglas, Wilson: Her 12, Rndr 0047, Rndr SS-0145

Downer, James T.:   LC AFS L60

Draheim, Sue: Ldr LEA 4012

Draughn, Ella: LC AFC L69-L70

Driver, Bill: UMP

Drye, Joe: Cty 720

Drysen, Jesse, leading the Alabama Sacred Harp Singers: Prst INT 25011

Dubois, Camile: JEMF 105

Dudgeon, Frank: OH OHCS-177

Dunford, Pat: KM 204

Dunford, "Uncle" Eck: CMF 011-L, Fwys FA 2951, NWR NW 291

Dunham's (Mellie) Orchestra: JEMF 105

Dupree's Rome Boys: Cty 514

Dusenbury, Emma: LC AAFS L54, LC AAFS L58

Dwyer, Everett: JEMF 105

Dye, John M.:   LC AAFS L11

Dykes, Clyde: N&T 1001

Dykes Magic City Trio: Cty 503, OH OHCS 191

East, Ernest, and Pine Ridge Boys: Cty 718, Her XXXIII

East Texas Serenaders: Cty 410, Cty 517, Cty 527

Easter, J. B.:   TFS-106

Ebenezer Baptist Church Mass Choir: OFA TALP-001

Eddy, Bill: GyEg 101

Edgin's (George) Corn Dodgers: Cty 520

Edmonds, Jimmy: Bio RC-6002

Edmonds, Norman: Cty 535, DU DU-33002, Fwys FA 2434, Fwys FA 2435, Prst FL 14030, Prst INT 25003, RCA LPV 552

Edmonds, Paul: Prst INT 25003

Edwards, Bert, and Randolph Music Club Band: Prst FL 14030

Edwards, Billy: Fwys FA 2435

Edwards, Dot: Fwys FA 2435

Edwards, George: Asch AA 3/4

Edwards, Kenneth, and Sunny Mountain Boys: Fwys FA 2434, Prst FL 14030

Elam, Stelle: UICFC CFC 301

Elk Horn Four: LC AFC L69-L70

Eller, Lawrence: Fly LP 546, Fwys FE 34161

Eller, Leatha: Fwys FE 34161

Eller, Vaughn: Fly LP 546, Fwys FE 34161

Elridge, Charlie: Prst INT 25006

Emerson, Bill: Prst INT 13038, Prst INT 13049

Enloe, Lyman: GyEg 101

Entrekin, Ben: GV SC 03

Ephesus Primitive Baptist Church: UNC 0-8078-4083-1

Etheridge, Isabel: Fwys FS 3848

Eva Quartet: Mar 9100

Evans, Cliff: Asch AH 3831

Evans, Clyde: Rndr 1035

Evans, Joe: Hist HLP 8002

Evans, John B.:   OH OHCS-177

Evans, Mutt: Cty 508
Evening Breezes Sextet: LC AFS L60
Everhart, Clay, and the North Carolina Cooper Boys: Col CS 9660, Mar 9110
Everidge, Charles: Atl SD-1346, Prst INT 25003, NWR NW 223

Fahey, John: Rndr 0032
Falcon, Joseph, with Clemo and Ophy Breaux: OT 100
Farley, J. D.: RCA LPV 522
Farmer, Mary Franklin: LC AAFS L54
Farnes, Ralph: MFP 002
Ferguson, Hank: FLeg FSA-13
Ferrill, Clarence: Cty 787, TFS-103
Fincham, Delores Hurt: UNC 0-8078-4084-X
Finnemore, Charles: MC #1
Finster, Rev. Howard: Fwys FE 34162
Flat Creek Sacred Singers: Mar 9100
Fleming and Townsend: Rndr 1033
Flesher, Bob: Mtn 303
Fletcher, David: BF 15505, Cty 523
Flippen, Benton, and the Smoky Mountain Boys: HMM LP002
Floyd County Ramblers: BRI 004, Cty 502, Cty 531, Mar 9110, Mar 9111
Ford, Elizabeth Walker: Fwys FE 4001
Ford, Fred: TFS-105
Ford, Warde H.: Fwys FE 4001, LC AAFS L30, LC AAFS L57, LC AAFS L58, LC AFS L29, LC AAFS L54, LC AFS L61
Ford's (Henry) Old Time Dance Orchestra: RCA LPV 552
Foreacre, Louise: Fwys FA 2315
Forster, Omer: TFS-103
Fort Worth Doughboys: NWR NW 236
Foster, Gwen: BF 15505, Cty 523, Mar 9104, NWR NW 245, RCA LPV 552, Rndr 1033
Foster, John: Cty 502
Fountain, Buzz: KM 204
Four Pickled Peppers: FC-014
Four Virginians: FC-014
Fowler, J. C.: LC AAFS L9
Fox Chasers: Cty 531
Fraley, Annadeene: Her XXXIII, Rndr 0037, Rndr SS-0145
Fraley, J. P.: Her XXXIII, Rndr 0037
Franklin, Lewis: Cty 707
Franklin, Major: Cty 707
Freeman, "Fiddling" Tom: AlaTrad 103
Freeny's Barn Dance Band: Cty 529

Friendly City Playboys: Fwys FA 2434
Frost, Irma: CMF 011-L
Fruit Jar Guzzlers: JEMF 103, Mar 9105, OH OHCS-177
Fulp, Preston: TFS-106
Fulton, Buck: TFS-106

Gabisch, Muriel: MFP 002
Gage, Jim: JnAp JA 037
Gaines, Newton: RCA LPV 548
Galbraith, Art: Hoop 101, Rndr 0133, Rndr 0157, Rndr 0158
Gallop, Dile: Fwys FS 3848
Galt, Nellie: LC AFS L68
Gant Family: LC AAFS L54
Gardner, Gail: AFF AFF 33-1
Gardner, James: Rndr 0008
Gardner, Mary: Atl SD-1350
Gardner, Mattie: Atl SD-1350
Gardner, Robert: Brch 1944
Garland Brothers and Grinstead: Mar 9100, Mar 9101
Garrett, Bud: Mer 1001-2
Garrish, Jule: Fwys FS 3848
Gartin, G. C.: LC AFS L60
Gaultney, Munsey: Rndr 0058
Gellert, Dan: KM 204
Gentry, Henry: Riv RLP 12-610
George, Elmer: MC #1
George, Franklin: Kan 307
George, Robert: GV SC 03
Georgia Crackers: Cty 514, Mar 9111, Rndr 1026
Georgia Organ Grinders: Cty 544, Rndr 1035
Georgia Yellow Hammers: Cty 504, Cty 514, Cty 544, Rndr 1032
Gerald, Frank: *see* Rambling Duet
Gerrard, Alice: Cty 791, Her 070
Gevedan, Monroe: LC AAFS L54
Gibson, Lifus: Rndr 0237
Giddens Sisters: Mar 9101
Giessler, Val: MFP 001
Gifford, Larkin: Ok OK 76004
Gilbert, Kay: NWR NW 239
Gilbert, Ollie: NWR NW 294, Prst INT 25003, Prst INT 25004, Prst INT 25006, Prst INT 25011, Rim Rlp-495
Gilliland, Henry: Cty 517
Gillum, Frances: NWR NW 226, Rndr SS-0145
Gilmore, Tony: UMP

Girls of the Golden West (Millie and Dolly Good): NWR NW 314/315, RCA LPV 522, Rndr 1029, <u>Sytn</u> STR <u>202</u>
Givens, W. M. (Billy): LC AFS L68
Gladden, Mrs. Texas: Asch AA 3/4, BRI 002, LC AFS L1, LC AFS L7, LC AAFS L68, NWR NW 294, Prst INT 25004, Prst INT 25011
Glancy, Joe: LC AFS L60
Goforth, Gene: GyEg 101
Golden, Katie: Fwys FA 2435
Golden Melody Boys (Demps and Phil): Hist HLP 8002, JEMF 103
Golding, Katie: Mtn 303
Good, Mildred and Dorothy: *see* Girls of the Golden West
Goodman, Don: AFF 33-3
Goodson, Thaddeus: Rndr 0237
Goodwin, Cecil: UICFC CFC 301
Goodwin, Doug: JEMF 105
Goodwin, Jim: UICFC CFC 301
Gordon County Quartet: Mar 9101
Gossett's Ted Band: Cty 527, Cty 531, MS 45004
Gott, Peter: Rndr 0064
Graham, Addie: <u>JnAp JA</u> 020
Graham, George Vinton: LC AAFS L54
Grant Brothers: Mar 9109, Rndr 1033
Gravely, Spud: Asch AH 3831, Fwys FS 3832
Graves, John: Mer 1001-2
Graves, Josh: JnAp JA 030
Grayson, G. B.: Fwys FA 2951
Grayson, G. B., and Henry Whitter: Cty 502, Cty 503, <u>Cty 513</u>, Cty 522, Cty 525, <u>DU 33033</u>, Hist HLP 8003, <u>OH OHCS 157</u>, OT 100, OT 102, Mar 9109, RCA LPV 532
Green, Bud: TFS-108
Green, Sam and Charley: TFS-108
Green's String Band: MS 45005
Greene, Alva: NWR NW 226, Rndr SS-0145
Greene, Clarence: Cty 511
Greene, Ottie "Coot": FLeg FSA-23
Greer, Prof. I. G.: LC AAFS L12, LC AAFS L14, LC AFS L7
Greer, Prof. and Mrs. I. G.: CT 6001
Gregory, W. L.: <u>DU 33014</u>
Grenfell, Ray: MFP 001
Grey, Larsen: Her XXXIII
Griffin, Henry: Fwys FES 34151
Griffin, John R., and Arthur Griffin: GV SC 03

Griffin, Mrs. G. A.: LC AAFS L54, LC AAFS L58
Grimm, Flarrie: Fwys FES 34151
Grinnell Giggers: Mar 9110, Mar 9111
Grisby, Corbett: Fwys FA 2317
Grisham, Mr. and Mrs. R. N.: Mar 9100
Gross, Cliff, and Muryel Campbell: Rndr 1037
Gross, Levi: JnAp JA0059C
Grover, Carrie: LC AAFS L21, LC AAFS L58, NWR NW 291
Guillemette, Ben: JEMF 105
Guillette, Wilfred, and Maurice Campbell: NWR NW 239
Gunning Sara Ogan: <u>FLeg FSA-26</u>, Rndr <u>0051</u>, Rndr SS-0145, Van VRS-9182, TFS-108
Guthrie, Woody: LC AFS L1

Hackberry Ramblers: OT 100, OT 101
Hack's String Band: Rndr 1037, MS 45003
Hagie, Mrs. Lloyd Bare: NWR NW 245
Hale, Theron, and Daughters: Cty 542
Hale, Travis B., and E. J. Derry, Jr.: RCA LPV 548
Haley, James Edward: <u>Rndr 1010</u>
Hall Brothers: Mar 9104, RCA LPV 548
Hall, A. L., Band: Fwys FA 2434
Hall, Ellis, and Bill Addis: OH OHCS-177
Hall, Howard: HMM LP001, Rndr 0058
Hall, Martha: Fwys FA 2317
Hall, Roy: Her XXXIII
Hall, Wendell: CMH 106
Hamblen, Stuart: Mar 9109
Hamil, Howard: AlaTrad 103
Hamilton, Diane: Grnhys GR714
Hamilton, Mrs. Goldie: NWR NW 223
Hamilton, Y. Z.: AlaTrad 103
Hammond, John: Cty 522
Hammons, Burl: Her XXXIII, <u>LC AFS L65-L66</u>, Rndr <u>0018</u>
Hammons, Edden: <u>WVUP 001</u>
Hammons, Sherman: <u>LC AFS L65-L66</u>, Rndr <u>0018</u>
Hammontree, Doney: LC AAFS L12
Hampton, Nell: NWR NW 291, NWR NW 294
Hanby, Ray: LC AAFS L9
Hand, Judge Learned W.: LC AFS L29
Hannah, John: GFS 901
Hanson, Delbert: MFP 002
Happy Hayseeds: Mar 9110
Hardesty, Cliff and Telford: GFS 901
Hargis, Wesley: NWR NW 245

Harkreader, Sid, and Grady Moore: Cty 541, JEMF 103, Mar 9100, Rndr 1033

Harmon, "Aunt" Dora: Fwys FA 2358

Harmon, Austin: LC AFS L61, Rndr 0237

Harmon, Buddy: Rndr 0005

Harmon, Dick: Rndr 0005

Harper, Doc: Cty 517

Harmon, Lena: TFS cass

Harmon, Margie: FLeg FSA-23

Harmon, R. L.: FLeg FSA-23

Harmon, Samuel: LC AAFS L54, LC AAFS L57

Harmon, Walter: N&T 1001

Harold, Richard: Mar 9109, OH OHCS-141

Harper, Oscar: Cty 517, LC AAFS L9

Harper, Roy: TFS-105

Harrell, Kelly: BF 15508/9/10, BRI 002, BRI 004, CMH 106, Cty 408, Cty 502, Cty 504, Cty 508, Cty 522, FC-014, Fwys FA 2951, RCA LPV 548, RCA LPV 552

Harris, Elder G. P.: Mar 9100, Mar 9101

Hart Brothers: Rndr 1026

Harvey, Roy: Cty 508, Cty 523, Hist HLP 8002, JEMF 103, Mar 9100, Mar 9101, Mar 9104, Mar 9105, Mar 9109, OH OHCS-141, OH OHCS-177, Vet 103

Harwood, Tom: MFP 002

Hascall, Carol: GyEg 101

Hash, Albert: Rndr 0058

Hash, Worley: Rndr 0058

Hatcher, John: LC AFS L62, Miss AH-002

Hatcher, Sam: TFS-106

Hatton Brothers: MS 45004

Hauser, Wayne: Cty 733

Hawkes, Sarah: Asch AH 3831

Hawkins, Ezra "Ted": NWR NW 226, RCA 8416-2-R [CD]

Hawkins, F. LeRoy: OFA TALP-001

Hawks, Carlton: Fwys FE 4001

Hawks, Charles, and Brushy River Boys: Prst FL 14030

Hawks, Ray: LC AAFS L54

Hayes, Nap, and Matthew Prater: Hist HLP 8002

Helmick, Harmon E.: Mar 9101

Helms, Bill, and His Upson County Band: RCA LPV 552, Cty 514

Helms, Horace: Fwys FES 34151

Helms, Karen: Fwys FES 34151

Helms, *see*: Fwys FES 34151

Helton, Ernest: LC AFS L68, JnAp JA 030, Rndr 0237

Helton, George: UMP

Helton, Osey: Rndr 0237

Henderson, Jerry: TFS-105

Henderson, Louis: Fwys FS 3809

Hendley, Fisher: Cty 515

Hendren, Alva Lee: MFFA 1001

Hendricks, Maidy Kelly: UTP [cass, no #]

Henthorne, Harold: OFA TALP-001

Herald, John: Fwys FA 2434, Van VRS-9152

Herbert, Didier: Fwys FA 2953

Herbert, Morris, and the Twin County Boys: Prst FL 14030

Herdman, Curley: Kan 310

Hickok, Elgia: Van VRS-9182

Hickory Nuts: Cty 522

Hicks, Besford/Bessford: Cty 786, TFS-104

Hicks, Buna: FLeg FSA-22, FLeg FSA-23, TFS cass

Hicks, Captain: FLeg FSA-23

Hicks, Dee: Cty 787, Cty 789, TFS-104, TFS-103, TFS-105

Hicks, Delsie: TFS-103

Hicks, Delta: Cty 789, TFS-104

Hicks, Joe: TFS-104

Hicks, Lily Mae: TFS-104

Hicks, Stanley: HMM LP002

Hicks, Viola: FLeg FSA-23

Higgins, Branch W.: BRI 004

Higgins, Elder and Mrs. Jess B.: LC AFC L69-L70

Higgins, "Uncle" Charlie: Atl SD-1346, Atl SD-1347, Fwys FA 2434, Fwys FS 3832, Prst INT 25003, Prst INT 25004

High, Otis: Fwys FES 34151

Highnight, Luke, and His Ozark Strutters: Cty 531, Cty 519

Highwoods String Band: Her 12

Hiles, Ruth: OFA TALP-001

Hillbillies: BRI 005, Cty 405, Cty 501, Cty 525, Rndr 1033

Hill Brothers and Willie Simmons: Cty 508

Hill, Matt: AlaTrad 103

Hilt, John: Ldr LEA 4012

Hilton, L. M.: Fwys FA 2036, LC AAFS L30

Hinton, Sam D.: LC AAFS L21

Hinton, W. A.: Cty 515, RCA LPV 552

Hobbs, Cliff: OT 102

Hobbs, Smiley: SmFwys CD SF 40037, SmFwys CD SF 40038

Hobson, John, and the Glen Ayre Ramblers: HMM LP002

Hockmeyer, Jake and Russ Orchard: MFFA 1001

Hodges Brothers (Felix, Ralph, and James Hodges and John White): Arh F5001

Hoffmann, John: Her XXXIII

Hoke, Bob: Mar 9100, Mar 9101

Holbert, Jim: LC AFS L61

Holcomb, Odabe: Fwys FA 2317

Holcomb, Roscoe: Fwys FA 2317, Fwys FA 2390, Fwys FA 2363, Fwys FA 2368, Fwys FA 2374

Holland, Floyd: Shoe SGB 1

Holland, Jerry: Rndr SS-0145

Holland, Thomas, and The Crossroad Boys: Prst FL 14030

Hollis, D. Dix: AlaTrad 103

Holly, Rev. A. B.: LC AFS L68

Holyoak, Van: AFF AFF 33-2, AFF 33-3, NWR NW 314/315, Rndr SS-0145

Hometown Boys: Cty 544

Hommon, Rollie: GFS 901, OFA TALP-001

Honeycutt, James E.: TFS-108

Honeycutt, Lonzo: TFS-108

Hood, Alex, and His Railroad Boys: Cty 531

Hooven, Herb: Prst FL 14010

Hopkins, Al and His Buckle Busters: Brun 59009, Mar 9105, Vet 103

Hopkins, Doc: Brch 1945

Hopson, Mitchel: HMM LP002

Hornsby, R. M.: LC AAFS L11

Horton, Green Berry: MFFA 1001

Hoskins, Theophilus G.: Rndr 0237

House, Bob: TFS-106

Houston, Sonny: JnAp JA 030

Howard, Clarence: Rndr 0009

Howard, Clint: Fwys FA 2390, Fwys FA 2435, Rndr 0009, Van VSD-107/108, Van VRS-9147

Howard, Dave: Her XXXIII

Howard, Edgar: Fwys FS 3848

Howard, Elizabeth: Fwys FS 3848

Howard, Lake: Cty 409

Howard, Lawton: Fwys FS 3848

Hubbard, Joe: BRI 002

Hudelston, Jesse: TFS-103

Hughes, Delbert: Her XXXIII

Hughes, Ella: PB 004

Hughes, Joe: Cty 517

Hughes, Lena: NWR NW 226

Hundley, Holley: AH AHR 009

Hunter, Ed: TFS-108

Hunter, Max: FLeg FSA-11

Hunter, Tommy: Prst INT 13020, Prst INT 13030,

Hunt, J. M. (Sailor Dad): LC AFS L2, LC AAFC L26/27

Huntington, Gale: NWR NW 239

Hunt's (Prince Albert) Ramblers: Fwys FA 2952

Hurst, Margaret Caudil, and daughter: Fwys FA 2358

Hurt, Belvin: UNC 0-8078-4084-X

Hurt, Zack: CT 6001

Hutchins, Esker, and Surrey County Ramblers: Cty 757, Fwys FA 2434, Prst FL 14030

Hutchison, Frank: Cty 511, Cty 523, Fwys FA 2951, OH OHCS-141, Rndr 1007, Vet 103

Hylton Thessalonia Primitive Baptist Church: UNC 0-8078-4083-1

Hyman, Judy: Her XXXIII

Inboden, Woody: OFA TALP-001

Ingalls, Jeremiah: NWR NW 205

Ingenthron, Charles: LC AAFS L12, LC AAFS L14, LC AAFS L20, LC AAFS L30

Isaacs, Clyde: Rndr 0001

Isley, Tex: Fwys FA 2350, Ldr LEA 4012, Ldr LEA 4040

Jackson County Barn Owls: OH OHCS-177

Jackson, "Aunt" Molly: LC AFS L2, LC AFS L61, LC AAFS L54, LC AAFS L57, Rndr 1002

Jackson, Gene: GV SC 03

Jackson, Harry: Fwys FH 5723, NWR NW 314/315

Jackson, Johnny: Fwys FA 2435

Jackson, Vestal: N&T 1001

Jacobs, Ollie: LC AAFS L58

Jagoe, Sam: UIP cass

James, J. S.: NWR NW 205

Jarrell, Ben: see DaCosta Woltz's Southern Broadcasters

Jarrell, Benny, and Flint Hill Playboys: Her XXXIII

Jarrell, Tommy: Cty 717, Cty 757, Cty 713, Cty 723, Cty 741, Cty 748, Cty 756, Cty 778, Cty 791, Mtn 302, Her XXXIII, HMM LP002

Jarvis, Ward: Her XXXIII, TALP TALP-001

Jeffus, Daniel: UTP [cass, no #]

Jenkins' (Frank) Pilot Mountaineers: Cty 522

Jenkins, Blind Andy: CT 6001

Jenkins, Frank: Cty 507, Cty 515 *see also* DaCosta Woltz's Southern Broadcasters

Jenkins, Oren: SmFwys CD SF 40037

Jenkins, Oscar: Cty 507, Cty 713, Cty 723, Cty 741

Jenkins, Snuffy: <u>Arh 5011</u>, <u>Rndr 0005</u>, Rndr SS-0145, SmFwys CD SF 40037

Jenks, Orville J.: LC AFS L60

Jepson, James: Ok OK 75003

Johnson Brothers: CMF 011-L, RCA LPV 532, Rndr 1033

Johnson Family: AlaTrad 103

Johnson, Earl: Cty 503, Cty 507, <u>Cty 543</u>

Johnson, Earl, and His Clodhoppers: Cty 531, Cty 544, Hist HLP 8003, OT 101

Johnson, Earl, and His Dixie Entertainers: Cty 514, Rndr 1035

Johnson, Jack: TFS-108

Johnson, Jess: Cty 508, Cty 523, Mar 9109

Johnson, John: <u>AH AHR 001</u>

Johnson, Linnie: TFS-105

Johnson, Polly: BRI 002

Johnson, Sam: LC AFS L60

Johnson, Vesta: GyEg 101, MFFA 1001

Johnson's (Jimmie) String Band: MS 45003

Johnston, Dean: GyEg 101

Joines, "Aunt" Polly: Asch AH 3831

Joines, Paul: Asch AH 3831

Jones, Etta: FLeg FSA-22, FLeg FSA-23

Jones, Lewis W.: Ok OK 75003

Jones, Louie: Cty 786

Jones, Morgan: LC AAFS L16

Jones, "Uncle" George: LC AFS L60

Jones, Vester: Fwys FS 3811

Jordan, Lon: LC AFS L62

Josey, Albert: Rndr 0237

Judd, Mr. and Mrs. Vernon: NWR NW 226, Rndr SS-0145

Justice, Dick: Cty 511, Fwys FA 2951, OH OHCS-177

Karl and Harty: Rndr 1037

Karnes, Alfred G.: CMF 011-L, Cty 508

Kartchner, K. C.: Ok OK 75003

Kartchner Sisters: Ok OK 76004

Kazee, Buell: Brun 59001, Cty 515, Fwys FA 2951, Fwys FA 2953, <u>Fwys FS 3810</u>, <u>JnAp JA 009</u>, KM 204, Mar 9104, Mar 9109, Rndr 1037

Keating, William E.: LC AAFS L16

Keith, Leonard: AlaTrad 103

Kelly, Rex: JEMF 103

Kemp, Cordell: TFS-103

Kentucky String Choristers: MS 45005

Kentucky String Ticklers: MS 45005

Kentucky Thorobreds: JEMF 103

Kerr, Janet: Ldr LEA 4012, Ldr LEA 4040

Kessinger Brothers (Clark and Luches): Cty 503, Cty 504, Cty 527, <u>Cty 536</u>, <u>Kan 600</u>, OH OHCS-141

Kessinger, Clark: <u>Cty 733</u>, <u>Kan 306</u>

Keys, Will: N&T 1001

Kilgore, Mrs. Esco: LC AFS L61

Kimble Family (Taylor, Stella, Ivery, Doris, Pearl Wagoner Richardson): Her XXII, Her XXXIII, Rndr 0057

Kincaid, Bradley: Brun 59009, <u>OH OHCS 107</u>, <u>OH OHCS-314</u>, <u>OH OHCS-315</u>, <u>OH OHCS-316</u>, <u>OH OHCS-317</u>, RCA LPV 548

Kingery, Pat: Mer 1001-2

King, Henry, and family: LC AFS L2, LC AAFS L20

Kirbo, Larry: Hoop 101

Kirby, Edward: NWR NW 239

Kirkpatrick, Jim: LC AAFS L56

Kittrell, Frank (with Mollie Kittrell): Miss AH-002

Kizzar, Tim AFF 33-3

Kline, Michael: JnAp JA0059C

Knicely, Jim: AH AHR 010

Knight, Charlie, and His Country Music Boys: Fwys FA 2434

Knight, Ray: Fwys FE 34162

Lacy, Noah: AlaTrad 103

Lambert, L. W. J., and Bluegrass Partners: Prst FL 14030

Lamb, Frosty: KM 204

Lamb, Monroe: CT 6001, Rndr 1026

Lam, Bela, and His Green County Singers: Mar 9104, NWR NW 236

Lancaster, M. L. A.: NWR NW 205

Lancaster, Sarah: NWR NW 205

Landers, George: Rndr 0028

Landress, "Uncle" Bud: OT 101

Largen, Marshall Family: LC AFC L69-L70

Larkan, Fiddlin' Bob, and Family: Cty 519

Larsen, Grey: JnAp JA 018

Larson, A. Karl: Ok OK 76004

Lathrop, Carl: LC AAFS L56

Laurel Glenn Regular Baptist Church, Alleghany Cty, NC Congregation: LC AFC L69-L70

Lawson, Clorine: Mer 1001-2

Lawson, Richard: LC AFS L60

Lay, George: LC AFS L61

Leake County Revelers: Col CS 9660, Cty 501, Cty 511, Cty 529, Cty 532

Ledford, Lilly May: Cty 712, Grnhys GR712 *see also* Coon Creek Girls

Ledford, Rosie: Cty 712

Ledford, Steve: NWR NW 236, RCA LPV 507, RCA 8416-2-R [CD], Rndr 0008

Ledford, Susie: Cty 712

Ledford, Wayne: Rndr 0008

Le Doux, Chris: NWR NW 314/315

Lee Brothers Trio: Rndr 1035

Lee, Buck: Ok OK 75003

Lee, Joe: AlaTrad 103

Lee, "Powder River" Jack and Kitty: Mar 9106, MS 45008, NWR NW 314/315, RCA LPV 522

Lee, Troy P., (with Rex and Ray Offutt): Hoop 101, MFFA 1001

Lehman, Pickles: MFP 002

Leming, Carl: Ldr LEA 4012

Lemon, Charlie Bill: Kan 306

Leslie, Sam: LC AAFS L20

Lewey, Fred: LC AFS L68

Lewis Brothers (Dempson and Denmon): Cty 503, Cty 517

Lewis Brothers: TFS-103

Lewis, John: TFS-106

Liberty Church Sacred Harp Singing: GV SC 03

Lifus Gibson: Rndr 0237

Lilly Brothers: Cty 729, Fwys FA 2433, Prst FL 14010, Prst FL 14035

Lilly, Bea: SmFwys CD SF 40038

Lilly, Everett Allan: Prst FL 14010

Lindsey, James: Mtn 303, Prst FL 14030

Lineberry, Audine: Mtn 302

Lissman, Pete: Mtn 303

Lobdell, Hamilton: LC AAFS L55

Logan, Tex: SmFwys CD SF 40038

Logue, Seamus: NWR NW 239

Lomax, John A.: LC AAFS L28

Lone Star Cowboys: OT 102, RCA 8417-2-R [CD]

Lonesome Luke and his Farm Boys: MS 45004, Rndr 1037

Long, Charles (and Sam Neal): Miss AH-002

Long, Howard: BF 15505

Long, Fiddlin' Sam: Cty 520

Long, Lola: TFS-106

Long, Mrs. Maud: LC AAFS L14, LC AAFS L21

Loomis, Dan: Her XXXIII

Louise, Edmonds: Fwys FA 2434

Louisiana Honeydrippers (Jim Smoak, Bucky Wood, Dewey Edwards, Lum York, V. J. Myers, J. C. Myers): Arh 5010, Prst INT 13035

Louisiana Lou: Rndr 1029

Love, Daddy John: NWR NW 245

Lovell, Merle: LC AFS L61

Lowe, Charlie: Cty 757

Lowe, Lawrence: Her XXXIII

Lowery, Ramblin' Red: Rndr 1033

Luebke, Adele: TFS-108

Lund, Kelly: Fwys FS 3832

Lund, Lewis: NWR NW 239

Lundy, Emmett W.: Cty 535, Str STR 802

Lundy, Geedy: Cty 535

Lundy, Jerry: Rndr 0036

Lundy, Kelly: Cty 535

Lundy, Ted: Rndr 0020

Lunsford, Bascom Lamar, and the Laurel River Band Boys: Fwys FA 2434

Lunsford, Bascom Lamar: Asch AA 3/4, Brun 59001, CT 6001, Cty 515, Fwys FA 2952, Fwys FA 2953, Fwys FP 40 (FA 2040), LC AAFS L20, LC AAFS L21, LC AFS L29, LC AAFS L54, LC AFS L68, Mar 9104, Mar 9105, Riv RLP 12-645, Rndr 0065

MacDonald, Wilmot: UIP cass

Macedonia Union Baptist Church, Alleghany Cty, NC Congregation: LC AFC L69-L70

Macon, "Uncle" Dave: BF 15503, BF 15518, BF 15519, BF BFX 15214, Brun 59001, Brun 59009, Cty 515, Cty 502, Cty 541, Cty 542, Cty 521, Cty 545, De DL 4760, Fwys RBF 51, Fwys FA 2953, Hist HLP 8006, NWR NW 236, RCA 2100-2-R [CD], RCA LPV 507, Rndr 1026, Rndr 1028, Rndr 1033, TFS-105, Vet 101, Vet 103, Vet 105

Madisonville String Band: MS 45003

Mainer, J. E., and his Mountaineers: Alp ALP 201, Alp ALP 202, Arh F5002, Atl SD-1350, Fwys FA 2435, OT 106/07, Prst INT 25003, Prst INT 25009, Prst FL 14030, RCA 2100-2-R [CD], RCA 8416-2-R [CD], RCA LPV 507, RCA LPV 532

Mainer, Wade: Cty 404, OH OHS 90001, NWR NW 236, OT 102, RCA LPV 507

Mainer, Wade and Julia: JnAp JA0059C

Mainer, Wade and Sons of the Mountaineers: NWR NW 245, RCA LPV 552, RCA 2100-2-R [CD], RCA 8416-2-R [CD]

Maitland, Richard: LC AAFC L26/27

Mandel, Ben: NWR NW 239

Mangrum, Blind Joe: Cty 542

Mann, Mary C.: LC AFS L68

Mann, Mrs. M. L.: LC AAFS L11

Mann, Thomas: LC AAFS L9

Manning, Leola: TFS-105

March, William: LC AFS L60

Marks, Phyllis: AH AHR 008

Marlor, I. N. (Nick): LC AAFS L54, NWR NW 223

Marshall, Jim and Artie: BRI 004, LC AFC L69-L70

Marshall, William: Fwys FS 3832, HMM LP001, HMM LP002, Rndr 0058

Martin, Asa: MS 45005, NWR NW 245

Martin, Asa and Cumberland Rangers (Buz Brazeale, Jim Gaskin, Earl Barnes): Rndr 0034, Rndr SS-0145

Martin, Marcus: LC AAFS L21, LC AFS L62

Martin, Mrs. W. L.: LC AAFS L54

Martin, Reed: KM 204

Marvin, Frankie: CMH 106

Massengale, John: NWR NW 205

Mastin, Bruce, and Band: Fwys FS 3832

Mathis, Blind Jack: Mar 9109

Matrin, Doug: GV SC 03

Matthews, Sloan: LC AAFS L28

Maxwell, Billie: Mar 9106, RCA LPV 522, Rndr 1029

Mayfield, Doris and Lyle: CFC UI 301

May, Basil: LC AFS L1

May, William: AH AHR 010

Maynard, Ken: Fwys FA 2953, Mar 9106, MS 45008, NWR NW 314/315

McAbee, Palmer: NWR NW 226, RCA LPV 532

McAlexander, Eunice Yeatts: BRI 002, HMM LP001

McArthur, Rudger: LC AAFS L30

McBee, Hamper: TFS-103

McBride, Bill: LC AAFS L56

McCann, Gordon: Hoop 101, Rndr 0158

McCarn, Dave: BF 15505, Rndr 1026

McCarroll, "Uncle" Jimmy: TFS-103

McCartt Brothers and Patterson: Cty 503

McCauley, Clara J.: TFS-106

McClintock, Harry 'Mac': CMH 106, Fwys FD 5272, LC AFS L61, Mar 9106, MS 45008, NWR NW 314/315, RCA LPV 522, RCA LPV 532, RCA LPV 548, Rndr 1009, Rndr 1026

McCloud, Paralee: Fwys FE 34161

McClung Brothers: OH OHCS-141

McCool, Jay C: HMM LP001

McCord, May Kennedy: LC AAFS L54, LC AFS L61, LC AAFS L12, UTP [cass, no #]

McCutcheon, John: JnAp JA 010, JnAp JA 018, JnAp JA 037, Grnhys GR714

McDaniel, Lewis: OT 102

McDowell, Mrs. L. L.: LC AAFS L54

McFarland, Lester: Brch 1944

McGee, Clifton: Arh 5012

McGee, Kirk: BF 15517, Cty 541, Cty 541, Fwys FA 2379, Fwys FTS 31007, Vet 103

McGee, Sam: Arh 5012, BF 15517, Cty 502, Cty 511, Cty 523, Cty 541, Cty 542, Fwys FA 2379, Fwys FTS 31007, Vet 103

McGhee, John: OH OHCS-177, OH OHCS-141, Rndr 1026

McGuire, Audrey: TFS-103

McKinney, Bonnie: AH AHR 010

McKinney, Lee Finis Cameron "Tip": MFFA 1001

McLain, Arthur: Hist HLP 8002

McMahan, Pete: GyEg 101

McMichen, Clayton: Col CS 9660, Cty 501, Cty 507, Cty 527, Cty 544, Rndr 1035, Van VRS-9183

McMinnville Garment Factory Workers' Band: LC AAFS L20

McNally, Elsie Sherfey: UNC 0-8078-4084-X

McNeil, Sam: Rndr 0057

McPeak, Udel: Fwys FA 2435

McVay and Johnson: Cty 508

Meade, Gene: Cty 733

Medlin, Julian "Greasy": Arh 5011, Rndr 0005

Melton, Ivor: Asch AH 3831, Fwys FA 2435

Miles, Arthur: Mar 9106

Miller, Dave: Cty 729

Miller, David: Cty 523, JEMF 103, OH OHCS-141

Miller, John: Rndr 0021

Miller, Kenny: SmFwys CD SF 40037

Miller, Slim, with the Cumberland Ridge Runners: Rndr 1037

Miller, Smokey Joe: Fwys FES 31089, Fwys FE 34162

Miller, Sonny: Fwys FA 2435
Miller, Susie: NWR NW 291
Miller, Wikel: OH OHCS-141, OH OHCS-177
Mills, Owen: *see* Miller, David
Ming, Floyd, and His Pep-Steppers: Cty 528, Fwys FA 2952
Mississippi Possum Hunters: Cty 528
Mississippi Sheiks (African-American group): Mar 9104
Moatsville String Ticklers: OH OHCS-141, OT 100
Mobley, Olive: Fwys FA 2358
Mobley, Pleaz: Fwys FA 2358, LC AAFS L12, LC AAFS L14
Molsky, Bruce: Her XXXIII
Moncrief, Maude: LC AAFS L11
Monday, Isham: Mer 1001-2
Monroe Brothers (Bill and Charlie): <u>BB AMX2-5510</u>, RCA 2100-2-R [CD], RCA 8417-2-R [CD], RCA LPV 507, RCA LPV 532, Rndr 1026
Monroe, Bill, and his Blue Grass Boys: <u>Cam CAL 719</u>, RCA 2100-2-R [CD]
Montana, Patsy: *see* Blevins, Rubye
Montgomery, Will: GV SC 03
Moody, Mack: NWR NW 239
Mooney, M.: CMF 011-L
Moonshine Kate (Carson): Rndr 1029
Moore, Alex: LC AFS L1
Moore, Ashley: TFS-106
Moore, Byrd: Cty 504, Cty 527, MS 45003, OT 101, OT 102, Cty 503
Moore, Grady: Cty 541, JEMF 103, Mar 9100
Moore, Jack: TFS-106
Moore, Jess: AlaTrad 103
Moore, Spence/Spencer: BRI 002, BRI 004, Prst INT 25004, Prst INT 25009
Moreland, "Peg": Mar 9106, Mar 9109
Morgan, Albert: LC AAFS L16
Morgan, David: NWR NW 205
Morgan, Mrs. Minta: LC AFS L29, LC AFS L61
Morgan, Tom: Prst INT 13038, Prst INT 13049
Morgan, Tom, Scott, and Mary: PB 004
Morgan, William J.: LC AAFS L55
Morris Brothers: Her 12
Morris Brothers and Eunice [Ayer]: Mar 9100
Morris, Dave: Her 12
Morris, Jess: LC AAFS L28
Morris, Jimmy: LC AAFS L58
Morris, John: Her 12

Morris, Neil: Atl SD-1346, Atl SD-1347, Atl SD-1349, NWR NW 223, Prst INT 25003, Prst INT 25006, Prst INT 25009
Morris, William T.: LC AAFS L30
Morris, Zeke: NWR NW 236, RCA LPV 507, RCA 8416-2-R [CD]
Morrison, Absy: Prst INT 25003, Prst INT 25006
Morrison, David: LC AFS L60
Morrison Twin Brothers String Band: Cty 518
Morton, Coy: Her XXXIII
Moseley, Arthur: LC AAFS L55
Moser, Artus: <u>RRT LP-8073</u>, Riv RLP 12-617
Mountain Ramblers (Joe Drye, Carson Cooper, James Lindsey, Jim McKinnon, Thurman Pugh): Atl SD-1346, Atl SD-1347, Atl SD-1349, Atl SD-1350, <u>Cty 720</u>, Fwys FA 2434, Fwys FA 2435, NWR NW 294, Prst INT 25011
Mountain View Baptist Church, Lowgap, NC Congregation: LC AFC L69-L70
Moving Star Hall Singers: Van VRS-9182
Moyer, Phyllis: JnAp JA 030
"Mrs. B.D.": TFS-103
Muldowney, James: LC AAFS L16
Mullins, Ira: Her 12
Mulvihill, Brendan: NWR NW 239
Murphy, Otho: Ok OK 75003
Myers, Fulton: Cty 717, Rndr 0058
Myers, Jim F.: LC AAFS L9, Miss AH-002
Myers, Sidny/Sidna: Cty 717, Rndr 0028

Nail, Euna Vee Denson: LC AAFS L11
Napier, Ray: Fwys FA 2358
Nares, James: NWR NW 205
Narmour and Smith: Cty 503, Cty 511, Cty 528, Cty 529
Nashville Washboard Band: LC AAFS L9
Nations Brothers: Cty 529
Neaves, Glen: Asch AH 3831, Fwys FS 3811, Fwys FS 3832
Neaves, Mrs. Glen: Fwys FS 3832
Neely, Bill: Hoop 101
Neese, J. J.: Fwys FA 2315
Nelstone's Hawaiians (Herbert Nelson and James Touchstone): Fwys FA 2951, NWR NW 245
Nestor, J. P.: CMF 011-L, Cty 535, Fwys FA 2953, RCA LPV 552
New Ballard Fife and Drum Band: Rndr 0057
New Rubatonic Entertainers: Her XXXIII

Nicholas, Arthur: FProm 41942

Nicholas, General Custer: FProm 41942

Nichols Brothers: Rndr 1035

Nicholson, Bill: LC AAFS L14

Norman, John: LC AAFS L56

Norman, Thomas: Mtn 303

Norris, Fate: Mar 9105

Norris, Land: Cty 515

North Carolina Boys (Gray Craig, Kinney Rorrer, Doug Rorrer): Ldr LEA 4040

North Carolina Ramblers: *see* Poole, Charlie

Norton, Dellie: HMM LP001, HMM LP002, Rndr 0028

Norton, Henry: Cty 508

Norton, Morris: HMM LP001

Nye, Captain Pearl R.: NWR NW 291, OHS (No #), LC AFS L29

Oaks, Charlie: Mar 9109, Rndr 1033

O'Connor, John: UIP cass

Odem, L. P.: LC AAFS L11

Offutt, Ray: MFFA 1001

Offutt, Rex: MFFA 1001

Ogan, Sara(h): NWR NW 245 [*see also* Gunning, Sara Ogan]

Ohl, Lew: MFP 001

Ohrlin, Glenn: Hoop 101, CFCUI CFC 301, Philo 1017, Rndr 0158, NWR NW 314/315, Shoe SGB 1, Van VRS-9183

Ohrlin, Kay: Philo 1017

Older, Lawrence: FLeg FSA-15, NWR NW 239

Old Harp Singers of Eastern Tennessee: Fwys FA 2356

Old Regular Baptist Church Congregation: Fwys FA 2317

Old Republican Primitive Baptist Church: UNC 0-8078-4083-1

Ollie, Bunn: Cty 507

Ornstein, Lisa: Her XXXIII

Osborne, Johnny C.: JnAp JA 049

Osborne, R.: NWR NW 205

Osborne, "Uncle" Charlie: JnAp JA 049

Owen, Dock: LC AAFS L11

Owens, Missy: UNC 0-8078-4084-X

Owens, Tex: NWR NW 314/315

Ozarkers: Mar 9110

Pace, Gladys: Mcr 1001-2

Palmer, Estella: Shoe SGB 1

Parham, "Chub": LC AFS L2 [*see also* Parham, Walter]

Parham, Red, and the Haywood Cty Ramblers: Fwys FA 2434

Parham, Walter "Red": Riv RLP 12-610, Riv RLP 12-617, Riv RLP 12-650, Rndr 0065

Parish, Leone: Her 070

Parish, Roscoe: Her 070

Parker, Byron, and His Mountaineers: Cty 503, RCA LPV 532

Parker, Chet: Van VRS-9182

Parker, "Chubby": Fwys FA 2951

Parker, Maggie Hammons: LC AFS L65-L66, Rndr 0018

Parker, Mrs. Ella: Fwys FS 3809

Parks, Oscar: Fwys FS 3809, LC AAFS L54

Parsons, Phoeba: FProm 41942, Her 12, Van VRS-9183

Parsons, Roscoe: FProm 41942, Van VRS-9183

Pate, Fiddlin' Jim: Cty 517

Patterson, Bobby: Mtn 302, Mtn 303

Patterson, James: GV SC 03

Patterson, Joe: Van VRS-9182

Patterson, Pat, and Lois Dexter: Mar 9106

Patterson, "Uncle" John: Arh 5018, Fwys FE 34162, Fwys FES 31089, GV SC 03, Rndr 0058, Rndr SS-0145

Patterson's (Red) Piedmont Log Rollers: Cty 502, Mar 9105, Mar 9109, FC-014, RCA LPV 548

Patton, Gary: BRI 005

Payne Brothers and Blaustein: TFS-103

Peaceful Valley Quartet: LC AFC L69-L70

Pegram, George: Fwys FA 2435, Riv RLP 12-610, Riv RLP 12-617, Riv RLP 12-650, Rndr 0001, Rndr 0065

Pendleton, Buddy: Ldr LEA 4012

Pendleton, Calvin: Her XXXIII, Rndr 0057

Pendleton, Delmar: Her XXXIII, Rndr 0057

Pendleton, Fred, and West Virginia Melody Boys: OH OHCS-177

Pendleton, Harry: Cty 201

Perkins, Lucinda: Fwys FA 2358

Perkins, Marieda: Fwys FA 2358

Perkins, Terry: Fwys FA 2358: Fwys FA 2358

Perry County Music Makers (Nonnie Presson, Bulow Smith, Virginia Clayborne): Cty 520, DU 33009, NWR NW 236,

Perry, Duane: JEMF 105

Perry, Frances: LC AAFS L55

Perry, Wayne: LC AFS L62

Peters, Homer: LC AAFS L9

Peters, J. L.: LC AAFS L55
Peterson Brothers Stringband: Ok OK 76004
Peterson, Emery: Ok OK 76004
Peterson, Pete: Her XXXIII
Pettyjohn, Betty: AFF 33-4
Pettyjohn, Bunk: AFF 33-3, AFF 33-4
Phelps, Harvey: OFA TALP-001
Phillips, Lacey: Trad 1007
Phipps' (Ernest) Sacred Singers: Fwys FA 2952
Phipps Family (A. L., Kathleen, Helen, Leemon): Fwys FA 2375, Van VRS-9183
Phipps, Ernest, and his Holiness Quartet: CMF 011-L, Cty 508, NWR NW 245, Rndr 1037
Pickard Family: Vet 103
Pickard, Obed: NWR NW 226
Pick, Forest: Her XXXIII
Pickow, Jon: Grnhys GR714
Pickow, Peter: Grnhys GR714
Piedmont Log Rollers: *see* Patterson's Piedmont Log Rollers
Pierce, J. C.: BRI 004
Pike, Russ: LC AAFS L20, LC AFS L2
Pilla, John: Van VRS-9213
Pine River Boys (Foy James Lewis, Maybelle Harris, Abe Horton, Walter Morris, Howard Hall): Mtn 305
Pipers Gap Ramblers: Cty 535
Pitt, Everett: Mar [cass] 9200
Platt, Moses (Clear Rock): LC AAFS L54
Plemmons, Ruby Bowman: BRI 002
Plum, Cecil: GFS 901
Plymouth Vermont Old Time Barn Dance Orchestra: JEMF 105
Poe, Charley: Atl SD-1346, Atl SD-1347
Poe, Dale: Prst INT 25003
Politte, Joe: MFFA 1001
Poole, Charlie, and the North Carolina Ramblers: Col CS 9660, Bio BLP 6005, Cty 501, Cty 502, Cty 504, Cty 505, Cty 509, Cty 516, Cty 540, FC-014, Fwys FA 2951, Hist HLP 8003, Hist HLP 8005, Mar 9109, NWR NW 236, OT 100
Popejoy, Columbus: TFS-106
Pope's Arkansas Mountaineers: Cty 518, NWR NW 236, RCA LPV 552
Poplin Family (China Poplin, Edna Poplin Elmore, Bill Poplin, David Jackson): Fwys FA 2306
Porter, "Granny": Asch AH 3831

Posey, Delilah Denson: LC AAFS L11
Powell, Lester: NWR NW 291
Powers, Ada: JnAp JA0059C
Powers, Fiddlin,' and Family: Cty 525
Powers, Turner: OHS (No #)
Prairie Ramblers: RCA 8416-2-R [CD], Rndr 1037
Presnell, Edd: Trad 1007
Presnell, Hattie: FLeg FSA-22, TFS cass
Presnell, Lee Monroe: FLeg FSA-22, FLeg FSA-23
Presnell, Rosa: FLeg FSA-22, FLeg FSA-23
Presson, Nonnie: TFS-103
Price, Chester: UIP cass
Price, Edith B.: MC #1
Price, Fred: Fwys FA 2390, Rndr 0009, Van VSD-107/108, Van VRS-9147
Price, Kenneth: Rndr 0009
Prillaman, Ted: BRI 004
Proffitt, Frank: FLeg FSA-1, FLeg FSA-36, Fwys FA 2360, Rndr 0028, Van Vrs 9183
Propps, Louis H.: NWR NW 226
Prude, Johnny G.: NWR NW 314/315, LC AAFS L28
Puckett, Holland: Mar 9104
Puckett, Riley: Col CS 9660, Cty 411, Cty 501, Cty 507, Cty 515, Cty 527, Cty 544, NWR NW 226, OT 101, OH OHCS 114, RCA LPV 507, RCA 8416-2-R [CD], Rndr 1035
Purdy, J. D.: LC AFS L68
Puryear Brothers Band: Her XXXIII

Quesinbery, Rufus: Prst INT 25003
Quinn, John L.: LC AAFS L16

Rada, Andrew: LC AAFS L16
Rainey Old Time Band: Vet 103
Rambling Duet (Howard Dixon and Frank Gerald): Mar 9105
Ramey, Bob: Fwys FA 2358
Ramsey, Evelyn: HMM LP001
Ramsey, Obray: Prst INT 13020, Prst INT 13030, Riv RLP 12-649, Riv RLP 12-610, Riv RLP 12-617
Randolph, Vance: LC AAFS L30
Rasmusson, Bernie: MFP 002
Ratliff, Shorty, and the Bluegrass Mountain Boys: OFA TALP-001
Ray Brothers: Cty 528, Mar 9105
Ray, Aulton: MS 45008
Ray, "Lost John": Fwys FA 2435

Raymond, Little "Doc", and the Coleman Pardners: BRI 004

Read, Daniel: NWR NW 205

Rea, Bill: Arh 5011

Reaves White County Ramblers: Cty 519

Rector, John: LC AFS L62,

Rector, John: Bio RC-6002, Cty 535, Rndr 0058

Red Fox Chasers (Cranford, Miles, and Thompson): Cty 502, Cty 510, Hist HLP 8003, Mar 9104

Red Headed Fiddlers: Cty 515, Cty 517, Cty 527

Red Mountain Trio: Vet 103

Redman, Wash, Lawrence, and James: TFS-108

Reeder, L. K.: Mar 9106

Reed Children: Mar 9109

Reed, Alan: Rndr 0021

Reed, Arville: Cty 522, OH OHCS-177

Reed, Bill and Belle: Fwys FA 2951

Reed, Blind Alfred: CMF 011-L, Cty 502, Cty 522, OH OHCS-177, RCA 2100-2-R [CD], RCA LPV 532, Rndr 1001, Rndr 1026

Reed, Bud: Fwys FA 2493, Rndr 0021, Rndr 0077

Reed, David: Fwys FA 2493, Rndr 0021, Rndr 0077

Reed, Frank: MFFA 1001

Reed, Ola Belle: Fwys FA 2493, Her 12, Rndr 0077, Rndr 0021, KM 204, Rndr SS-0145

Reedy, Blair C.: LC AAFS L9, Atl SD-1349

Reedy, Jack, and His Walker Mountain String Band: Cty 504

Reedy, Wade: Rndr 0028

Reese, Belton: Rndr 0237, Rndr 0237

Reese, Marion: NWR NW 226

Rees, H. S.: NWR NW 205

Reeves, Goebel: CMH 106, Mar 9106

Reeves, Kilby: Asch AH 3831

Reid, Boone: Trad 1007

Reid, Gordon: JnAp JA 030

Reinhart, Dick: Brun 59001

Reynolds, Cathy and Lloyd: CFCUI 301

Reynolds, Shorty Ralph: KM 204

Rhythm Wranglers: Ok OK 76004, Ok OK 76004

Rice, Glen, and his Beverly Hill Billies: NWR NW 314/315

Rice, Orrin: LC AAFS L12

Richards, Dora: LC AAFS L55

Richardson, Lacey: Atl SD-1349

Richardson, Larry: Fwys FA 2435, SmFwys CD SF 40037

Richmond, Fritz: Prst FL 14010

Riddle, Almeda: Atl SD-1350, ArkTrad 003, Fwys FA 2390, Min JD-203, Rndr 0017, Rndr 0083, Van VRS-9158, NWR NW 245, NWR NW 291, NWR NW 294, Prst INT 25003, Prst INT 25004, Prst INT 25006, Prst INT 25009, Prst INT 25011, Rndr SS-0145, Van VRS-9183

Riders in the Sky: NWR NW 314/315

Ridge Rangers: LC AFS L61, OHS (No #)

Ridgel's Fountain Citians: Mar 9101, Rndr 1033

Riggs, Clyde C.: TALP TALP-001

Riley, Bartow: Cty 703

Rindlisbacher, Mr. and Mrs. Otto: LC AAFS L55

Ritchie, Edna: FLeg FSA-3, Van VRS-9183

Ritchie, Jean: Elek EKLP-2, Fwys FA 2301, Fwys FA 2301, Fwys FA 2426, Fwys FA 2427, Grnhys GR714, Jn Ap JA 037, JnAp JA0059C, LC AAFS L14, LC AAFS L57, Riv RLP 12-620,, Van VRS-9183 Westm SWN 18021

Ritchie's (Grandpa Isom) Church Congregation: NWR NW 223

Ritter, Tex: NWR NW 314/315

Rittler, Dick: SmFwys CD SF 40037

Riverside String Band: Rndr 1035

Roane County Ramblers: Col CS 9660, Cty 403, Cty 501, Cty 507, OT 100, Vet 103

Roanoke Jug Band: Cty 531

Roark, George "Shortbuckle", and His Family: CT 6001, Mar 9105, NWR NW 236, Rndr 1037

Roberts, Fiddlin' Doc: Cty 511, Cty 527, DU 33015, Her XXXIII, MS 45004, MS 45005, Rndr 1037

Roberts, Frances: AFF 33-1, AFF 33-2

Roberts, James: Her XXXIII, NWR NW 245

Roberts, Pete: SmFwys CD SF 40037, SmFwys CD SF 40038

Robertson, A. C. ("Eck"): Cty 202, Cty 507, Cty 517, Cty 527, Fwys FA 2952, OT 101, RCA LPV 522, Sytn STR 201

Robinette, Melvin: Cty 527

Robinson, Captain Leighton and group (Alex Barr, Arthur Brodeur, Leighton McKenzie): NWR NW 223

Robinson, Capt. Leighton: LC AAFC L26/27

Robinson, Sunshine: LC AAFS L54

Rodgers, Jimmie: CMF 011-L, CMH 106, NWR NW 314/315

Rodriguez, Joe and Bennie: AFF 33-1

Rogers, Berthie: Fwys FE 34161

Rogers, Grant: FLeg FSA-27, Kan 308, Kan 313, NWR NW 239

Rogers, Paul: LC AAFS L14

Rogers, Ralph AFF 33-3

Roheim, Anund: MFP 002

Rorer, Posey: CT 6001, Cty 508, FC-014, Mar 9100, Mar 9101 *see* also Charlie Poole and North Carolina Ramblers

Rorick, Dorothy: BRI 002, Rndr 0058

Rorie, Kenneth: ArkTrad [No #]

Rorrer, Doug: Ldr LEA 4012, Ldr LEA 4040

Rorrer, Kinney: Ldr LEA 4040

Rose, Artie: Prst INT 13038, Prst INT 13049

Rose, Bayless: OT 101

Rosenbaum, Art: Fwys FE 34162

Ross Cty Farmers (Lonnie Seymour, Tony Ellis, Jeff Goehring): Mar [cass] 9013

Rossi, Neil: Her XXXIII, Bio RC 6004

Roswell Sacred Harp Singers: Mar 9101

Rouse Brothers: RCA LPV 532

Royce, Luther: LC AAFS L55

Roy Pope and the Carolina Homeboys: Fwys FES 34151

Ruby, Texas: NWR NW 314/315

Ruffner, Alva: LC AAFS L9

Russell, Burt: Rndr 0036

Russell, Robert: BRI 002

Russell, S. F.: BRI 002

Rutherford, Betsy: Bio RC 6004

Rutherford, Leonard: Col CS 9660, Cty 501, Cty 504, Cty 511, Cty 522, Cty 527, Fwys FA 2951, Hist HLP 8003, MS 45003, Rndr 1004

Rutherford, Leonard, and John Foster: MS 45003

Sacred Harp Singers: Fwys FA 2953, Van VRS-9182

Sampson, Homer: AH AHR 009

Sandage, Virgil: Fwys FS 3809

Savakus, Russ: Van VRS-9213, Van VRS-9239

Schaffer, Gus: LC AAFS L56

Schartiger, Holly: FProm 41942

Schlautman, Lou: MFP 001

Schoolcraft, Sara: FProm 41942

Schreiber, Fred: Cty 542

Schuyler, Calswell Family: LC AFC L69-L70

Schwarz, Tracy: Her 12, Van VRS-9147

Scottdale String Band: OT 100, OT 101

Scott, Bill: LC AFC L69-L70

Scott, Mrs. Ben: LC AFS L62

Scruggs, Junie: SmFwys CD SF 40037

Scruggs, Thelma, Beatrice, and Irene: NWR NW 291

Seeger, Mike: Grnhys GR712, Grnhys GR714, SmFwys CD SF 40037, Her 12, SmFwys CD SF 40038

Seegmiller, Ella J.: Ok OK 75003

Setran, Ben: MFP 002

Setters, Jilson [J. W. Day]: Fwys FA 2952, Rndr 1037

Seven Foot Dilly and His Dill Pickles: *see* Dilly

Sexton, Lee: Fwys FA 2317, JnAp JA0059C

Sexton, Morgan: JnAp JA0055, JnAp JA0059C

Seymour, Lonnie: GFS 901

Shady Grove Primitive Baptist Church: UNC 0-8078-4083-1

Shakers (Sister R. Mildred Barker and others): Rndr 0078

Shannon, Carlos: Prst INT 25006

Sharp, Arnold: GFS 901

Sharp, Hardy (with Horace Kinard or Douglas Williams): Miss AH-002

Sharp, Hinman and Sharp: Cty 527, Cty 531

Sharp, John, and Band: Cty 787

Shaw, Bessie: LC AFS L68

Shaw, Rosalie: NWR NW 239

Sheehan, Shorty and Juanita: Fwys FS 3809

Shelor Family (Clarice, Jesse, Bill, Jimmy, Paul, Joe, Susan): Her XXII, Her XXXIII

Shelor Family: BRI 005, CMF 011-L, NWR NW 236, RCA LPV 552

Shelor, Bill: Rndr 0057

Shelor, Claris and Joe: Rndr 0057

Shelton, B. F.: Cty 502, Cty 522, CMF 011-L, Hist HLP 8003, RCA LPV 548, Rndr 1037

Shelton, Elisha: Fwys FA 2309

Sherfey, Denise: UNC 0-8078-4084-X

Sherfey, Don: UNC 0-8078-4084-X

Sherfey, John: UNC 0-8078-4084-X

Sherfey, Pauline: UNC 0-8078-4084-X

Sherfey, Tammy: UNC 0-8078-4084-X

Sherrill, Homer: Arh 5011, Rndr 0005, Rndr SS-0145

Shippee, "Uncle" Joe: JEMF 105

Shirkey, Earl Mar 9105, Mar 9104, OH OHCS-141, Vet 103

Shores Southern Trio: Cty 514

Short, Mrs. Lillian: LC AAFS L12

Shuffler, George: Cty 739

Shupe, James, Family: Ok OK 76004

Sidle, Kenny: GFS 901

Simmons, Matt: TFS-106

Simon, Billy: AFF 33-2

Sims, Aaron: TFS-105

Singleton, Kitty Ritchie: LC AAFS L54

Sisson, Allen: NWR NW 226

Sizemore, George "Curly": LC AFS L60

Sizemore, Whit, and the Shady Mountain Ramblers: JnAp JA0059C

Skeens, Mrs. Lee: LC AAFS L57

Skillet Lickers: *see* Tanner, Gid

Slagle, Tom: N&T 1001

Slaughter, Matokie: Cty 717, Cty 757

Small, Dol: LC AAFS L58

Small, J.: Cty 515

Smathers, Luke String Band (Smathers, Harold Smathers, J. T. Smathers, Charles Gidney, Bea Smathers, David Holt): JnAp JA 032

Smeck, Roy: NWR NW 245

Smelser, Vern: Fwys FS 3809

Smith, Arthur: Cty 546/7, Fwys FA 2379, Fwys FTS 31007

Smith, Arthur, and His Dixieliners (Alton and Rabon Delmore): Cty 507, NWR NW 226

Smith (Arthur) Trio: OT 100, RCA LPV 507

Smith, Betty: GV SC 03, JnAp JA 018

Smith, Blaine and Cal: OH OHCS-177

Smith, Blaine: PB 003, PB 004, PB 005

Smith, Bulow: TFS-103

Smith, Curley: Fwys FA 2358

Smith, Edgar S.: OHS (No #)

Smith, J. Frank: Mar 9104

Smith, Gid: Rndr 1026

Smith, Glen: Asch AH 3831, Cty 757, Fwys FS 3811, Fwys FS 3832

Smith, Hobart: Asch AA 3/4, Atl SD-1350, BRI 004, BRI 005, FLeg FSA-17, Fwys FA 2390, LC AFS L7, NWR NW 226, NWR NW 294, Prst INT 25003, Prst INT 25004, Prst INT 25009, Prst INT 25011, Trad 1007, Van VRS-9182

Smith, Joyce: NWR NW 205

Smith, L. D.: LC AAFS L14

Smith, Oliver: Elek EKL-316

Smith, Ollan, and Dennis Brewer: TFS-105

Smith, Preston: NWR NW 294, Prst INT 25011

Smith, R. B. and S. J. Allgood: Cty 515

Smith, Smith: OT 102

Smith, Walter (Kid): Cty 508, Cty 522, BF 15521, FC-014

Smith, Wesley: UIP cass

Smith's (Dr.) Hoss Hair Pullers: Cty 519

Smith's Garage Fiddle Band: Cty 517

Smoke, Herbert: LC AFS L2

Smokey Valley Boys: Her XXXIII

Smoky Mountain Ramblers: Mar 9104

Snow, Kilby: Fwys FA 2365, Asch AH 3902

Snow, Mac: Cty 723, Her XXXIII

Solomon and Hughes: Cty 501

Solomon, Ervin: Cty 517

Solomon, Jim: Cty 517

Solomon, Norman: Cty 707

Solomon, Vernon: Cty 703

Somerville, Andrew: Ok OK 75003

Sons of the Pioneers: NWR NW 314/315

Southern Melody Boys: Rndr 1033

Southern Mountain Boys (Ted Lundy, Bob Paisley, Jerry Lundy, Wes Rineer, John Haftl): Fwys FA 2435, Rndr 0020

Southland Ladies Quartette: NWR NW 223

Spangler, Dudley "Babe": Cty 201

Spangler, George, and the Thornton Regular Baptist Church Congregation: Prst INT 25011

Spangler, J. W. "Babe": Cty 201

Spencer, Ed: Fwys FS 3811

Spencer, Emily P.: JnAp JA0059C, Mtn 304

Spencer, J. A. S.: LC AFS L68

Spencer, Paul: Rndr 0058

Spencer, Thornton: JnAp JA0059C, Rndr 0058

Spencer, Tom: TFS-105

Spilkia, Dave: Her XXXIII

Spooney Five: OT 100, OT 101

Spradlin, Retta: Cty 786

Sprague, Carl T.: BF BCD 15456, Mar 9106, MS 45008, NWR NW 314/315, RCA LPV 522, RCA LPV 548

Sprague, Harold: MFP 002

Sprung, Joan: Ldr LEA 4012

Sprung, Roger: Ldr LEA 4012, Riv RLP 12-620, Fwys FA 2426

Stamm, Leona: Rndr 0032

Stamper, Corbit: Rndr 0058

Stamper, I. D.: JnAp JA 010, NWR NW 226

Stamps-Baxter School of Music, Members of: NWR NW 223

Stanley Brothers (Carter and Ralph): BRI 002, BRI 004, Cty 739, Fwys FA 2390

Stanley, Jerrel: LC AFS L60

Stanley, Raymond: TFS-106

Stanley, Roba: Rndr 1029

Stanley, Shag: Cty 723, Cty 741

Starling, Delmer: Fwys FA 2434

Steele, Pete: Fwys FS 3828, LC AAFS L21, LC AFS L1, LC AFS L2, NWR NW 226, OHS (No #)

Steele, Mrs. Pete: OHS (No #)

Steel, Ben, and His Bare Hands: Her XXXIII

Stephens, Harry: LC AAFS L28

Stephens, "Uncle" Bunt: Cty 541, Fwys FA 2952

Stephenson, John: NWR NW 205

Stepp, W. M.: LC AFS L62, Rndr 0237

Stewart, Donnie: Fwys FA 2358

Stewart, Florrie: PB 003, PB 004

Stewart, Goldie: Arh 5012

Stewart, Joe: SmFwys CD SF 40037

Stikeleather, James G.: LC AFS L68

Stikeleather, Nancy Weaver: LC AFS L68

Stinnett, Cyril: GyEg 101, UMP

Stokes, Lowe: Col CS 9660, Cty 501, Cty 507, Cty 514, Cty 544

Stokes, Lowe, and his (Georgia) Potlickers: Cty 514, GV SC 03, Mar 9105

Stokes, Lowe, and His North Georgians: Cty 504, Cty 511, Cty 523, Mar 9104, Rndr 1035

Stoneman Family: Fwys FA 2315, Fwys FA 2953

Stoneman, Ernest V.: CMF 011-L, Cty 535, Cty 507, Fwys FA 2365, Hst HLP 8004, Hist HLP 8003, OH OHCS 172/73, Rndr 1008, Rndr 1026

Stoneman, Ernest V. and His Dixie Mountaineers: BRI 004, CMF 011-L, Cty 508, Mar 9101, NWR NW 236

Stoneman, Ernest V. and the Blue Ridge Corn Shuckers: BRI 002

Stoneman, George: Cty 757, Fwys FA 2435, Prst INT 25003

Stoneman, Mr. and Mrs. Ernest: Fwys FA 2953

Stoney Mountain Boys: Fwys FA 2435

Storm, Arnold Kieth: FLeg FSA-18

Storm, Gail Stoddard: NWR NW 239

Stover, Don: Cty 729, Fwys FA 2433, Prst FL 14010, SmFwys CD SF 40038

Stover, Hazel: AH AHR 009

Stowe, Charles: Fwys FS 3848

Strange, Rusty: Bio RC 6004

String Band from Ft. Thomas, KY: OHS (No #)

Stripling Brothers (Charles and Ira): Cty 503, Cty 507, Cty 401

Stripling, Charlie: AlaTrad 103

Strong, Luther: LC AFS L2, LC AFS L62, NWR NW 226: NWR NW 226

Stuart, Jerry: SmFwys CD SF 40038

Stuart, Joe: JnAp JA 030

Stubblefield, Blaine: LC AFS L61

Sturgill, Kate Peters: BRI 002

Sturgill, Virgil: Riv RLP 12-617

Styes, Archie: LC AAFS L54

Sullivan, Mary: LC AAFS L57, LC AAFS L54, LC AFS L61

Summers, John W.: Fwys FS 3809, Kan 307, Rndr 0194

Sumner, Marion: Fwys FA 2317, JnAp JA 030, JnAp JA 037, JnAp JA0059C

Sunny Mountain Boys: Fwys FA 2435

Sutphin, J. C.: Fwys FA 2315, SmFwys CD SF 40037

Sutphin, Vernon:

Sutterfield, Barry: NWR NW 223

Sutton, Julius: LC AFS L68

Sutton, Lannis F.: LC AAFS L30

Swafford, Johnson: PB 004

Swamp Rooters: Cty 514, Cty 527

Swann, Wallace, and his Cherokee String Band: LC AFS L2

Sweet Brothers: Cty 535

Swift Jewel Cowboys: Rndr 1033

Swingbillies, with Charlie Poole, Jr.: RCA LPV 548

Swinney, Raymond: Rndr 0237

Sykes, Robert, and the Surry Cty Boys: HMM LP002

Taggart, George S.: Ok OK 75003

Tanner, Gid: Cty 515, Mar 9104, Mar 9105

Tanner, Gid and His Skillet Lickers: Col CS 9660, Cty 506, Cty 514, Cty 526, Cty 544, FSSM FSSMLP 15001-D, Mar 9105, NWR NW 236, OH OHCS 192, OH OHCS 193, OT 100, RCA 8416-2-R [CD], RCA LPV 507, RCA LPV 552, Rndr 1005, Rndr 1023, Rndr 1035, Vet 103, Vet 107

Tanner, Gordon: Fwys FE 34162, Fwys FES 31089

Tanner, Phil and the Jr. Skillet Lickers: Fwys FES 31089

Tarlton, Jimmie: <u>BF</u> 15504, Col CS 9660, Cty 511, GV SC 03, Mar 9104, Mar 9109, NWR NW 223, OT 102, OT 101, <u>OT</u> 112, <u>Tst</u> <u>T-3302</u>

Tarwater, Rebecca: LC AFS L1, LC AAFS L54

Tate, Dan: BRI 002, Cty 757, Her XXXIII, HMM LP001, HMM LP002, LC AAFS L9

Tate, Rob: HMM LP001

Tatum Macedonia Primitive Baptist Church: UNC 0-8078-4083-1

Taylor-Griggs Louisiana Melody Makers: NWR NW 236

Taylor Chapel A. M. E. Church: Mer 1001-2

Taylor, Burnette and Moore: MS 45004

Taylor, Earl, and Stony Mountain Boys: SmFwys CD SF 40038

Taylor, Kevin: NWR NW 239

Taylor's Kentucky Boys: Cty 501, Hist HLP 8003, MS 45003

Teague, Ed: Fwys FE 34162

Teague, Howe: GyEg 101

Temple, L. Parker ("Pick"): LC AAFS L28

Tennessee Mountaineers: CMF 011-L

Tennessee Ramblers: Brun 59009, Cty 504

Tenneva Ramblers: CMF 011-L, <u>Pu PU</u> <u>3001</u>, RCA LPV 532, RCA LPV 548

Tesinsky, Andy: MFP 002

Tew, Norwood: Mar 9109

Thacker, Maude: Fwys FE 34161

Thatcher, Bill: Van VRS-9182

Thomas, Buddy: Her XXXIII, <u>Rndr</u> <u>0032</u>, Rndr SS-0145

Thomas, Gilbert: Rndr 0034

Thomas, Lois "Granny": AFF 33-3

Thomas, Rod: Rndr 0032

Thomas, Tony: <u>Tak</u> <u>A</u> <u>1013</u>

Thomas, W. H., and group: TFS-106

Thomasson, Benny: Cty 703, Cty 724

Thompson, Bob: Mar 9105 *see also* Red Fox Chasers

Thompson, George T.: Ok OK 75003

Thompson, Mildred and Beverly: Cty 757

Thompson, Thelma: BRI 005

Thompson, Tommy: KM 204

Thompson, "Uncle" Jimmy: Cty 542

Three Stripped Gears: OT 101

Thrower, John "Doodle", and the Golden River Grass (James Watson, Bill Kee, Lyn Elliott): GV SC 03

Tillett, Dick: Fwys FS 3848

Tincher, Diane: Fwys FA 2358

Tipton, Ernestine: LC AAFS L11

Tobacco Workers: TFS-106

Todd, Clarence: Cty 507

Tolman, Harvey and Rose Tolman: NWR NW 239

Tolman, Newton F.: NWR NW 239

Toppers, Rocky: Cty 786

Tracy, Clara Hawks: Fwys FE 4001

Traywick, Bascom: Fwys FES 34151

Trentham, Lee, and band: PB 005

Trivett, Joseph Able: <u>FLeg FSA-2</u>

Trotchie, Mary: MFP 002

Trowbridge, Ken: MFP 001

Troxell Brothers (Ralph and Clyde): <u>Mar</u> <u>[cass]</u> <u>9025</u>

Troxell, Clyde: Cty 786

Tucker, George: <u>Rndr</u> <u>0064</u>

Tucker, Stephen B.: LC AFS L62, Miss AH-002

Turbyfill, Lena Bare: LC AFS L7, NWR NW 245

Turner, Clay: PB 003

Turner, Della: Ok OK 76004, Ok OK 76004

Turner, Wesley J.: LC AFS L60

Tuttle, Mrs. Mildred: LC AAFS L12

Tweedy Brothers, Three: OH OHCS-141

"Uncle" Pete and Louise: MS 45008

Underhill, Mrs. Anna: Fwys FS 3809

Underwood, Charles: LC AFS L60

Underwood, Marion: Cty 515

Ungar, Jay: Her XXXIII

Union Primitive Baptist Church: UNC 0-8078-4083-1

Vance's Tennessee Breakdowners: Cty 525

Vandergriff, Russ: TFS-105

Van Arsdale, Phil, Paul, and Sterle: NWR NW 239

Varney, Dave: Fwys FA 2358

Vass, Ruby: Asch AH 3831, NWR NW 294, Prst INT 25003, Prst INT 25011

Vaughan Quartet: JEMF 103, Rndr 1033

Virginia Dandies: CT 6001

Virginia Mountain Boys (Glen Neaves, Cullean Galyean, Bobby Harrison, Ivor Melton, David Lambeth, John Jackson, Jerry Steinberg, Herman Dalton, Marvin Cockram): <u>Fwys FA 3830</u>, <u>Fwys FA 3833</u>, <u>Fwys FS 3839</u>, <u>Fwys FS 3829</u>

Virginia Playboys: Fwys FA 2435
Vowell, G. D.: LC AAFS L57

Waddell, J. M.: LC AAFS L28
Walburn and Hethcox: Cty 544
Walden, Charlie: GyEg 101
Walker Family (Sammie, Bernice, Ivan, and
     Rickie Walker, Nell Walker Fernandez):
     Mer 1001-2
Walker, Marie: TFS-106
Walker, Robert: Fwys FE 4001, LC AAFS L55
Walker, William: NWR NW 205
Walker's Corbin Ramblers: Rndr 1037
Wallace, Eugene: TFS-106
Wallace, Gusty: Mer 1001-2
Wallin, Berzilla: Fwys FA 2309
Wallin, Cas: Fwys FA 2309, HMM LP001,
     HMM LP002
Wallin, Doug: HMM LP002
Wallin, Lee: Fwys FA 2309
Wallin, Virgie: HMM LP002
Walsh, Bob: GyEg 101
Walsh, Daniel: LC AAFS L16
Walsh, Dock: Col CS 9660, Cty 508, Cty 515
Walsh, Philip: UIP cass
Walter Family: MS 45005, NWR NW 226
Walters, Bob: UMP
Walters, Clay: LC AAFS L58
Ward Family: Cty 534
Ward, A. E. and His Plowboys: Cty 519
Ward, Fields: Bio RC-6002, Bio RC-6003,
     Fwys FS 3832, Hst HLP 8001, Rndr 0036,
     NWR NW 245, Rndr SS-0145
Ward, Mr. and Mrs. Crockett: NWR NW 245
Ward, Mrs. Crockett: LC AAFS L57
Ward, Nancy: Rndr 0036
Ward, Tab: FLeg FSA-23
Ward, Wade: Asch AH 3831, Atl SD-1346, Atl
     SD-1347, Bio RC-6002, Bio RC-6003, Cty
     534, Cty 535, Cty 757, Fwys FA 2363, Fwys
     FA 2380, Fwys FS 3811, Fwys FS 3832, LC
     AFS L2, Prst INT 25003, Prst INT 25004,
     Rndr 0028
Warmack, Paul, and His Gully Jumpers: Cty
     541, RCA LPV 532
Watkins, Dr. C. L.: LC AAFS L54
Watkins, Joseph H.: LC AAFS L30, Ok OK
     75003
Watson Family (Doc Watson, Rose Lee Wat-
     son, Arnold Watson, Mrs. Annie Watson,
     Gaither Carlton, Sophronie Miller Greer,

Dolly Greer, Merle Watson, Tina Greer):
     Sm/Fwys SF 40012 [CD], Tpc 12TS336
Watson, Arnold: Van VRS-9182
Watson, Doc: Fwys FA 2426, Fwys FA 2390,
     SmFwys SF 40012 [CD], Topic 12TS336,
     Van VCD-45/46, Van VRS-9147, Van VRS-
     9152, Van VRS-9170, Van VRS-9182, Van
     VRS-9213, Van VRS-9239, Van VSD-9/10,
     Van VSD-107/108, Van VSD-6576
Watson, El: CMF 011-L
Watson, Merle: SmFwys SF 40012 [CD], Topic
     12TS336, Van VCD-45/46, Van VRS-9152,
     Van VRS-9170, Van VRS-9213, Van
     VRS-9239, Van VSD-9/10, Van VSD-6576
Watson, Willard: Cty 717
Watts, Wilmer and the Lonely Eagles: JEMF
     103, NWR NW 245, Rndr 1026
Watts (Wilmer) and Wilson: Cty 522, Mar
     9109, MS 45008
Weaver Brothers: OH OHCS-177
Weaver, Ed: HMM LP001, HMM LP002
Webb, Jack: Mar 9106, RCA LPV 522
Weeks, L. O.: JEMF 105, LC AFS L62
Weems, Ace, and his Fat Meat Boys: Her
     XXXIII
Weems String Band: Cty 501, Cty 520
Weissberg, Eric: SmFwys CD SF 40037,
     SmFwys CD SF 40038, Van VSD-6576
Welling and Schannen: JEMF 103
Welling, Frank: OH OHCS-141, Rndr 1026
Wells, Lee: LC AAFS L11
Wells, Lester: LC AAFS L56
West, Harry and Jeanie: Fwys FA 2352, Fwys
     FA 2357, Prst INT 13038, Prst INT 13049,
     Riv RLP 12-617, Riv RLP 12-610,
West, Hedy: BF 15003, FLeg FSA-3, Tpc
     12T146, Van VRS 9124, Van VRS 9162
West, Ron: JEMF 105
West Virginia Coon Hunters: CMF 011-L
West Virginia Night Owls: OH OHCS-141
Weston, Jack: Mar 9106
Wheeler, Frank: CT 6001, Rndr 1026
Wheeler, Jimmy: GFS 901
Whitaker, Orland: N&T 1001
Whited, Ralph: AlaTrad 103
Whitehead, Red: Cty 518
White and Searcy: NWR NW 205
White, B. F.: NWR NW 205
White, Dan: Fwys FS 3809
White, Everett: AH AHR 007
White, John: JEMF 103, Mar 9106, NWR NW
     245, NWR NW 314/315

White, Mr.: LC AFS L61

Whitten, Mike Cty 514

Whitter, Henry: BRI 004, CMF 011-L, Cty 502, Cty 503, Cty 522, Cty 525, Cty 513, Cty 522, Cty 525, DU 33033, OH OHCS 157, Hist HLP 8003, Mar 9109, OT 100, OT 102, RCA LPV 532, Vet 103

Widner, Jimmy: MFP 002

Wiggins, Gene: Fwys FE 34162

Wilkins, A.: LC AFS L68

Williams Family: ArkTrad 004

Williams, "Aunt" Alice: Fwys FA 2358

Williams, B. G.: N&T 1001

Williams, Doc: Rndr 0057

Williams, Marc: Mar 9106, NWR NW 314/315

Williams, Phil: Grnhys GR712

Williams, Vivian: Grnhys GR712

Williams, Walter: Rndr 0237

Williamson and Curry: Fwys FA 2951

Willingham, Thaddeus C.: LC AFS L2, NWR NW 245, Rndr 0237

Wills, Bob, and the Texas Playboys: NWR NW 314/315

Wilson, "Aunt" Jenny: Her XXXIII

Wilson, Charlie, and Hayloft Boys: MS 45005

Wilson, Clyde (Slim): LC AAFS L54

Wilson, Mrs. A. P.: NWR NW 291

Wilson, Nile: GyEg 101

Wimmer, Dent: HMM LP001, HMM LP002, Rndr 0057

Wimmer, Sherman: HMM LP001, Rndr 0057

Winans, Bob: KM 204

Wine, Melvine: Her XXXIII

Winger, Betty Bush: LC AFS L68

Winningham, Nancy Hicks: TFS-104

Winston, Dave: Her XXXIII

Winters, Margaret: Fwys FA 2358

Wise, Russell: LC AFS L61

Womack, Don: MFFA 1001

Wombell, Mrs. Ollie: LC AAFS L54

Wood, Emmanuel, and Family: MFFA 1001

Wood, George: Rndr 0057

Wood, Maggie: Cty 201

Woodbridge, Tim: Bio RC 6004

Woodie, Ephraim, and the Hen-pecked Husbands: OT 102

Woodie Brothers: Mar 9105

Woodlieff, Norman: Cty 508, Ldr LEE 4045

Woods, Charlie: HMM LP001, Rndr 0057

Workman, Molly: JnAp JA0059C

Workman, Nimrod: JnAp JA 001, JnAp JA0059C, Rndr 0076, Rndr SS-0145

Wright, Jack: JnAp JA 018, JnAp JA 037

Wright, Eugene: Rndr 0089

Wright, Oscar: Cty 717, Cty 757, Rndr 0089

Wyatt, Clarence H.: LC AFS L61

Yadkin Cty Ramblers: Fwys FA 2434

Yates' (Jimmy) Boll Weevils: Mar 9109

Yellin, Bob: SmFwys CD SF 40038

Yerman, Brian: Mtn 304

Young Brothers and Homer Davenport: Rndr 1033

Young, Martin: Fwys FA 2317

Zeh, Dorothy: BRI 005

TITLE INDEX

In this alphabetical index, most spellings have been normalized to facilitate finding. E.g., "git" to "get," "dem" to "them," "goin'" to "going." Other elided gerunds, "...in'" have been changed to "...ing." Such common usages as "gonna", "holler," "ain't" or "bile" are retained where standardization would produce overly awkward results. Initial "A," "An," or "The" have been omitted--except in a few cases where the resulting abridged reading would look ambiguous or too strange (e.g., "The Walls," or "The Lord Will Provide"). In all cases, the article has been moved to the end of the title so alphabetization commences on the noun rather than the article. Alphabetization follows the "dictionary" rather than the "telephone book" principle--i.e., spaces are ignored, so that "New York" follows, rather than precedes, "Newton." Numerals in titles have been spelled out--except occasionally for dates, which are placed where they would fall had they been spelled out. Spellings have been made uniform regardless of what was given in the sources. Thus, both "travelling" and "traveling" are rendered as "traveling"; "cuckoo" and "coo-coo" are both given as "cuckoo." "Black Eyed Susie," "Blackeyed Susie," and "Black-Eyed Susie" are combined.

In the main listings the titles as given on the albums are generally retained. It should be noted, however, that the titles given on the albums are often not reliable: collectors may misunderstand the names the informants give them, or may choose to give "standard" titles. Album compilers, particular of reissues of commercial 78 rpm recordings, may change titles--generally because of a conviction that there is another proper title (e.g., "Always Marry Your Lover" to "Girl I Left Behind"), but also out of carelessness (one finds, for example, different titles on the record label and the jacket listing) or, occasionally for fear of offending readers (e.g., "Nigger in the Woodpile" to "In the Woodpile.") When an informant has not renamed a song but simply garbled its title, one is tempted to ask what, indeed, is the title of the song? On commercial 78s, often standard titles were altered for business reasons or simply for novelty: a nonce title would make a standard tune copyrightable--e.g., "Tanner's Hornpipe" and "On Tanner's Farm" are, respectively, versions of "Rickett's Hornpipe" and "On Penny's Farm." Some record label renderings suggest scribal errors, as in "Sally Aim" for "Sally Ann."

Different, but closely related, titles of the same song are grouped together for convenience. E.g., the square brackets in "Big Ball In Boston [Memphis] [Town] [Uptown]" indicate four variant titles. Parentheses indicate optional wordings: "Bring Back My (Blue Eyed) Boy (to Me)" indicates that variant titles may include "Bring Back My Boy," "Bring Back My Blue Eyed Boy," "Bring Back My Boy to Me," or "Bring Back My Blue Eyed Boy to Me." Common alternate titles are often referred to by "see also" following the album listings. These are not exhaustive; nor can the reader be certain that all listings for a single title (particularly in the case of instrumental tunes) are indeed closely related. An exhaustively cross-referenced index is virtually impossible, because tunes and lyric songs can vary gradually from one distinct entity to another. In the case of ballads indexed by Child or Laws, the bracketed reference number following the title obviates the need for "see also" citations.

In the case of labels that use prefixes identical with their abbreviations (BF, BRI, CMH, TFS), the duplication has been eliminated. Thus, Bear Family BF 15001 appears in the Index as BF 15001 rather than BF BF 15001.

Ace of Spades: Cty 703
Acorn Stomp: Cty 410
Across the Rocky Mountain: Fwys FA 2317
Across the Shining River: Tst T-3301
Adeline Waltz: Cty 410
Adieu False Heart: Cty 546
Administration Blues: Tst T-3302

Adrain's Hornpipe: UMP No #
After My Laughter Came Tears: OFA TALP-001
After the Ball: BF 15504, OH OHCS 107, Rndr CD 11536
After the Sinking of the Titanic [D 24]: BF 15504

Aggravating Papa: Rndr 0089

Ain't Going To Lay My Armor Down: Cty 508

Ain't Going To Work Tomorrow: Fwys FA 2365, Rndr 0058

Ain't Gonna Be Treated This-a-Way: FLeg FSA-24

Ain't Gonna Rain No More: Rndr 0009

Ain't It a Shame To Gamble on a Sunday: Tst T-3302

Ain't It a Shame To Keep Your Honey out in the Rain: BF 15518

Ain't It Awful: Cty 787

Ain't Nobody Gonna Miss Me: SmFwys SF 40038

Ain't Nobody's Business: Cty 543

Ain't No Grave Can Hold My Body Down: Rndr 0026

Ain't No Sense You High Hatting Me: Rndr 0009

Ain't That Skipping and Flying: BF 15501

Ain't That Trouble in Mind: Bio RC-6003, Cty 534, Hist BC 2433-1

Ain't We Crazy: OH OHCS 107, Rndr 1009

Airplane Ride: NW 294

Alabama Bound: Van VSD-6576

Alabama Gal (Won't You Come out Tonight): UIP [cass, no #], JEMF 101, Rndr 0028

Alabama Jubilee: JnAp 032, RCA LPV 552, Rndr 0005

Alabama Square Dance, Pt. l: JEMF 103

Alabama Trot: Cty 403

Alabama Waltz: Miss AH-002

Alan (Allen) Bain: Ph 1022, Prst INT 25006, Rndr 0083

Alberta: Van VRS-9213, Van VCD-45/46 *see also* Tempie

Al Bowen: Rndr SS-0145

Al Smith for President: Mar 9105

Alecazander: Rndr 1033

Alex and Maureen: MFP MFP 002

Alexandria: Ok OK 76004

Alice Brown: JnAp JA 049

Alimony Woman: Kan 305

All Aboard: Alp ALP 201

All Are Talking of Utah: Ok OK 75003

All Around the Cedar: PB 004

All Around the World and Back to Citico: Ala Trad 103

All at One Shot: JnAp JA 049

All Bound down in Birmingham Jail: Tst T-3302

Allen Brothers Rag: OT 100

Allen Clan, The [E 5]: Bio RC-6002

All God's Children Got To Humble Down: LC AFS L68

All Go Hungry Hash House: BF 15519, Cty 516, OT 100, Rndr 1008

All Gone Now: Rndr 1035

All Hid: NW 291

All I (I've) Got's Gone: Fwys FA 2365, OH OHCS-172, Rndr 1026

All in down and out Blues: Fwys RBF RF 51

All My Sins Are Taken Away: BF 15510

All Night Long (Blues),: Cty 504, OT 101, Rndr 1007, Rndr 1029 *see also* Richmond Blues

All the Good Times Are Passed and Gone: BB AXM2-5510, SmFwys SF 40038

All the Way to Galway: Kan 307

Alto Waltz: OT 101

Always Be Waiting for You: CT 6000

Always Lift Him Up and Never Knock Him Down: RCA 2100-2-R, Rndr 1001

Amarillo Waltz: Sytn STR 201

Amazing Grace: Ark Trad 003, Bio RC 6004, FLeg FSA-23, Fwys FA 2317, Fwys FA 2356, Fwys FA 2357, Fwys FA 2358, Fwys FA 2359, Fwys FA 2362, Fwys FA 2426, Fwys FS 3810, GV SC 03, JnAp JA 009, NW 294, Rndr 0064, Shoe SGB 1, Trad TLP 1007, UNC 0-8078-4083-1, Van VRS-9147

Amber Tresses: Fwys FS 3848, OTC 6001

American and Spanish Fandango: Cty 515

American Frigate [A 4]: Mar 9200

Amos Johnson Rag: Fwys FTS 31007

Amsterdam: NW 205, Prst INT 25007

Anchored His Love: Van VRS-9183

Anchored in Love: Cam CAL 2554(e), CMH 107, OH OHCS 116

And Am I Born To Die: Tpc 12TS336

And Now, Old Serpent, How Do You Feel?: NW 239

Andrew Batan [C. 250]: Fwys FE 4001, LC AAFS L58

And the Cat Came Back: MS 45005

Angel Band: FLeg FSA-23

Angeline (the Baker): DU 33002, Kan 307

Anger in the Land: Van VRS 9162

Annie Dear I'm Called Away: Mar 9109

Annie Laurie: Rndr 0089

An Old Man Came Courting Me: FLeg FSA-3

Answer to Greenback Dollar: OT 106

Answer to Weeping Willow: CMH 116, MCA VIM-4012, MCA MCAD-10088 [CD]

Antioch: Atl SD-1349

Apple Blossom: Cty 707, Rndr 0028

Apple Brandy: TFS 104

Apples in the Summertime: UICFC CFC 201

Apple Tree Song: NW 291

Apron String Blues: BF 15507

Arcade Blues: Hist HLP 8006

Arcade Building Moan: TFS 105

Are You from Dixie?: Cam CAL 797, RCA 8417-2-R, Rndr 1006, Rndr CD 11536

Are You Happy or Lonesome?: DU 33014

Are You Lonesome Tonight?: CMH 112, OH OHS 90045

Are You Sure?: Cty 508

Are You Tired of Me (My) Darling?: Brch 1944, CMH 118, Cty 729

Are You Washed in the Blood of the Lamb?: BF 15518, CMF 011-L, Cty 508, Rndr 0001, Rndr 1008

A-Riding Old Paint: NW 314/315

Arizona Girl I Left Behind [P 1a]: Mar 9106

Arizona Stomp: Cty 410

Arkansas Sheik: Rndr 1023

Arkansas Traveler: Atl SD-1350, Brun 59000, Cty 514, Cty 517, Cty 723, Fwys FA 2315, Fwys 2363, Fwys FA 2380, Her 12, Kan 307, Mtn 305, OFA TALP-001, Riv RLP 12-610, Sytn STR 201, Tak A 1013, WVUP 001

Arkansas Turnback: Rndr 0133

Arnold's Tune: Tpc 12TS336

A-Roving on a Winter's Night: Tpc 12TS336

A-Roving, or The Amsterdam Maid: LC AAFC L26/27

Art Wooten's Quadrille: UMP No #

Arthur Berry: Rndr 0194

As I Walked out into Her Hall: TFS 104

As I Walked out One Morning in Spring: Fwys FE 34161

As I Walked over London's Bridge [C. 209]: BRI 002

As I Went Walking One Morning for Pleasure: Fwys FH 5723

As Joseph Was A'Walking [C. 54]: FLeg FSA-3

Asleep in the Briny Deep: Cam CAL 797, Rndr 1006

As Time Draws Near: Cty 757

As We Sat Beneath the Maple on the Hill: CT 6001, FC FC-014

As Willie and Mary Strolled by the Seashore: BF 15517

At the End of Jimmy's Bar: FLeg FSA-27

At the End of the Hobo's Trail: CMH 106

At the Foot of Yonders Mountain: Fwys FA 2362

At Twilight Old Pal of Yesterday: ACM ACM-1

Atlanta Bound: OH OHCS-177

Audition, The: Arb 201

Aunt Dinah's Quilting Party: Mar 9111, Rndr 0026

Aunt Emmy's Tea Party: Kan 313

Aunt Liza's Favorite: Rndr 0005

Aunt Rhodie R.I.P.: GnHys GR714 *see also* Go Tell Aunt Rhody

Aunt Sal's Song: FLeg FSA-3

Autoharp Special: Asch AH 3902

Avalon Quick Step: Cty 528

Avondale Mine Disaster, The [G 6]: LC AAFS L16

Awake, Arise You Drowsy Sleeper (My Old True Lover) [M 4]: LC AAFS L55, Fwys FA 2309, FLeg FSA-22, Riv RLP 12-610

Away out on the Mountain: OH OHCS 114

Away out on the Old Saint Sabbath: Cam ACL1-0501

Away out West in Kansas: Fwys FS 3809

Away over in the Promised Land: Fwys FA 2375

Baa Baa Black Sheep: LC AAFS L20

Baa Nanny Black Sheep: Tpc 12TS336

B-A-Bay: NW 291

Babe: Cty 410, Cty 517

Babes in the Woods: GnHys GR712, Van VRS-9158

Babies in the Mill: BF 15003, Tst T-3301

Baby Girl: OTC 6002

Baby Let Your Hair Roll Down: Fwys FA 2368

Baby-O: Fwys FA 2360, HMM LP002, Riv RLP 12-620

Baby Rose (Just Keep Waiting till the Good Time Comes): Cty 540

Bachelor's Hall: Rndr 1003, Wstm SWN 18021

Bachelor's Reply: FLeg FSA-27

Back in the Saddle Again: NW 314/315

Back Step Cindy: Cty 748, HMM LP002

Back to Johnson City: OT 107

Back to the Blue Ridge: Cty 523

Back Up and Push: Cam CAL 719, OH OHCS 192, Tak A 1013

Backwater Blues: KM 204

Backwoodsman [C 19]: Mar 9200

Bacon Rind: Tak A 1013

Bad Companions [E 15]: BF BCD 15456

Bad Girl's Lament [Q 26]: BRI 002, Ph 1022

Bailiff's Daughter of Islington, The [C. 105]:
    MC 1

Bake That Chicken Pie: BF 15503, Cty 542, OH
    OHCS-177

Baldheaded End of the Broom: FLeg FSA-23

Ballad of Bascom Lunsford: JnAp 018

Ballad of Braswell Boys: TFS 103

Ballad of Fancy Gap: BRI 004

Ballad of Jay Legg: FPrm 41942

Ballad of Jesse James [E 1]: UTP [cass, no #]

Ballad of Peace: Fwys FA 2358

Ball and Chain: Fwys FA 2342

Ballstown: LC AAFS L11

Baltimore Fire: Cty 509

Baltzell's Tune: GFS GFS 901

Bandit Cole Younger [E 3]: MS 45008

Banging Breakdown: Atl SD-1350

Bangum and the Wild Boar [C. 18]: LC AAFS
    L57, JnAp JA0059C

Banjo Clog: Fwys FA 2392, HMM LP001

Banjo on My Knee Blues: Rndr 1029

Banjo Picking Girl: Cty 712, GnHys GR712,
    Mtn 305, NW 236, Rndr 1029 *see also*
    Going Round the World; Sugar Babe

Banjo Solo: Rndr 0237

Banjo Tramp: Her 33

Bankhead Blues: Cty 529

Banks of Old Tennessee: Rndr 0009

Banks of the Arkansas -- Atl SD-1346

Banks of the Ohio [F 5]: Cty 522, Fwys FS
    3832, OHCS-172, Riv RLP 12-617, Tst
    T-3302, Van VSD-9/10, Prst INT 25003,
    Prst INT 13049 *see also* Down on the ...

Banks of the River: Mar 9100

Banks of the Wabash: Rndr 0089

Baptismal Anthem: NW 205

Baptizing at Carson Creek: LC AFC L69-L70

Baptizing down by the River: Atl SD-1349

Barbara Allen [C. 84]: Asch AH 3831, BRI 002,
    FLeg FSA-32, Fly LP 546, Fwys FA 2317,
    Fwys FA 2358, Fwys FA 2368, Fwys FA
    3830, JnAp JA 010, KM 204, LC AAFS L14,
    LC AFS L1, LC AAFS L54, Min JD-203,
    NW 223, OH OHCS 107, OH OHCS 314,
    Ph 1022, Rim Rlp-495, Rndr 0064, RRT
    LP-8073, Tak A 1013, TFS cass [no #]
    Wstm SWN 18021

Barber's Blues: CMH 106

Barefoot Boy: AFF 33-3

Barker's Creek [B 10]: Rndr 0028

Barlow Knife, Mar 9025

Barney McCoy: Cty 533

Barnyard, The: LC AAFS L21

Barnyard Serenade: AH AHS 001, OHCS-157

Bashful Bachelor: BF 15505

Bathe in That Beautiful Pool: Cty 508

Bath House Blues: Cty 518, OT 101

Battle Axe and the Devil [C. 278]: Kan 305

Battle of Antietam Creek: LC AFS L29

Battle of King's Mountain, The [L 4]: Prst INT
    13020

Battle of Mill Springs [A 13]: AH AHR 009,
    FLeg FSA-26

Battle of New Orleans [A 7]: AFF 33-4

Battle of Pea Ridge [A 12b]: FLeg FSA-11

Battle of Shiloh: Her 12

Battle of Stone River: Fwys FS 3809

Battleship Maine: Mar 9109

Battleship of Maine: Mar 9109, FC FC-014

Bay Rum Blues: BF 15505, Mar 9105

Bear Creek Blues: Har HL 7300, TL TLCW-06

Bear Creek Sally Goodin: MFFA 1001

Bear Creek's Up: Miss AH-002

Bear Me Away on Your Snowy Wings: BF
    15518 *see also* Life's Evening Sun

Be at Home Soon Tonight: BF 15508, Tst
    T-3301

Beaumont Rag: Cty 202, Cty 410, Cty 517, Cty
    703, Hoop 101, JnAp 030, Rndr 0005, Van
    VRS-9170, Van VCD-45/46

Beautiful: Mar 9100, Rndr CD 11536

Beautiful Beautiful Brown Eyes: BB
    AXM2-5525, OH OHCS 112

Beautiful Damsel: AH AHR 009

Beautiful Golden Somewhere: SH
    SH-CD-3779

Beautiful Home: Har HL 7396

Beautiful Isle o'er the Sea: Har HL 7396, TL
    TLCW-02

Beautiful Life, A: BB AXM2-5510, Mar 9013,
    Prst INT 13035

Beautiful Stars: CT 6000

Beautiful Utah: Ok OK 76004

Beaver Cap: Ark Trad 002, Roots 701

Beaver Dam Road: Fwys FA 2360

Beaver Valley Breakdown: Rndr 1037

Because He Loved Her So: Mar 9110

Bed Bug Blues: Cty 777, DU 33014

Beefsteaks: Rndr 0009

Bee Hunt on Hell-for-Sartin Creek, A: FSSM
FSSMLP 150001-D
Been a Long Time a-Traveling (Here Below):
Riv RLP 12-620, NW 223, JnAp JA 020
Been on the Job Too Long: NW 245
Been to the East, Been to the West: Cty 529
Before the Daylight in the Morning: FLeg
FSA-33
Behind the Eight Ball: Cty 720
Behind These Prison Walls of Love: Rndr CD
11536
Behind Those Stone Walls: Har HL 7422
Belled Buzzard: Tak A 1013
Belle Election: Rndr 0058
Belle Gunness: Rndr 0158
Belle of Lexington: Str STR 802
Beneath the Old Southern Sky: Prst FL 14010
Beneath the Weeping Willow Tree: BF 15509
see also Bury Me Beneath
Benfield Hoedown: Fwys FA 2365
Benjamin Deane [F 32]: UIP cass
Bessie the Heifer: FLeg FSA-27
Betsy Brown: Rndr 0064
Better Farther On: OH OHCS 116
Betty Baker: AH AHS 003
Betty Larkin: Riv RLP 12-620
Beware: Rndr 1001
Beyond Black Smoke: CT 6000
Beyond the Clouds: Mar 9101
B Flat Rag: MS 45003
Bibb County Hoedown: NW 226
Bible's True, The: TFS 105, Vet 101
Big Ball in Boston [Memphis] [Town]
[Uptown]: Atl 1347, Cty 504, Cty 506, PB
005
Big Bend Gal: BRI 005, RCA LPV 552
Big Bend Tragedy: TFS 105
Big Combine: UICFC CFC 301
Big Crap Game: Ark Trad [No #]
Big-Eared Mule: Arh 5011, SmFwys SF 40037
Big Eyed Rabbit: Cty 401, Cty 717, Mar 9025,
Rndr 0008, Rndr 1029
Big Fancy: WVUP 001
Big Footed Nigger (Man) (In a Sandy Lot): Cty
401, Miss AH-002, NW 226
Big Indian Hornpipe: Rndr 0032
Big John McNeil: GyEg 101
Big Liza: Mtn 304
Big Rock Candy Mountain: CMH 106, LC AFS
L61, Rndr 1009
Big Scioty: Rndr 0018

Big Tilda: Atl 1347
Big Tracy: Kan 310
Biler and the Boar [C. 18]: Rndr 0076
Bile Them Cabbage Down: AFF 33-3, Ala
Trad 103, Arh 5001, Cty 723, Fwys FA 2315,
Fwys FA 2365, Fwys FA 2379, LC AAFS L9,
Rndr 0237, SmFwys SF 40038, Van VRS-
9183, Vet 107
Bill Banks: Tpc 12TS336
Bill Cheatham: Arh 5010, BF 15501, Cty 507,
Cty 515, Cty 542, Fwys FA 2435, Fwys FS
3839, Van VSD-9/10, JnAp 030
Bill Driver Tune: GyEg 101
Bill in the Lowground: JnAp 032 *see also* Billy
in ...
Bill Katon's Reel: GyEg 101
Bill Mason: Col CS 9660, Cty 509
Bill Morgan and His Gal: FC FC-014, Mar
9111
Bill Staples [H 1]: TFS 104
Bill Was a Texas Lad: RCA LPV 522
Billy Boy: Fwys FA 2358, OH OHCS 314
Billy Grimes (the Rover): CMF 011-L, LC
AAFS L14, NW 236
Billy in the Low Ground [Lowland]: AH AHS
001, Cty 202, Cty 501, Cty 507, Cty 703, Cty
733, DU 33014, DU 33015, Mar 9110, Fwys
FA 2380, GyEg 101, Kan 310, Prst FL 14010,
Rndr 0021, Rndr 0133, Rndr 1004, Sytn STR
201, UICFC CFC 201, Van VSD-9/10 *see
also* Bill ...
Billy Richardson's Last Ride: AH AHR 009,
UICFC CFC 201
Billy the Kid: AFF 33-2
Billy Venero [B 6]: AFF 33-1, AFF 33-3, CMH
106, LC AAFS L55, Ph 1017, Rndr 1009,
Shoe SGB 1
Billy Wilson: Cty 542
Birdie: Cty 741, Rndr 0037
Birds Are Returning: Hist BC 2433-1 *see also*
Sweet Bird, Sweet Fern
Birds' Song, The: Fwys FS 3809
Birmingham: Cty 518 *see also* Sugar Babe
Birmingham Jail, No. 2: OT 112
Birmingham Rag: OT 112
Birmingham Town: OT 112
Biscuits: Tpc 12TS336
Bishop of Canterbury [C. 45]: LC AAFS L57
Bitter Creek: Cty 724
Black and Blue Blues: Rndr 1001
Black and White Rag: Cty 724

Black Annie: FLeg FSA-17, Rndr 1032

Blackberry Blossom: Arh 5012, Fwys FA 2435, Her 33, Mtn 303, NW 225, Cty 547, Rndr 1004, Van VCD-45/46

Blackberry Rag: Fwys FA 2366

Blackberry Wine: FLeg FSA-36

Black Bottom Strut: OT 101

Black Dog Blues: Fwys FA 2315

Blackest Crow: FLeg FSA-3

Blackeyed Peas and Cornbread: GyEg 101 *see also* Peas and Cornbread

Black Eyed Susie (Susan): AH AHR 010, Brun 59000, Cty 405, Cty 535, Cty 713, CMF 011-L, DU 33015, DU 33002, Fwys FA 2317, HMM LP002, JnAp JA0059C, Mtn 305, RCA LPV 552, Rndr 0194, Vet 107

Blackey Rag: JnAp 030

Black Hawk Waltz: Kan 306

Black Hills Waltz: Ok OK 75003

Blackie's Gunman: TL TLCW-06

Black Is the Color: Elek EKLP-2, HMM LP001

Black Jack Davey (David) [C. 200]: FLeg FSA-2, Fwys FA 2418, Har HL 7422, JnAp JA 009, OT 102, Prst INT 13020, Riv RLP 12-645, RRT LP-8073, TFS cass, TL TLCW-02, Van VRS-9158

Black Lung Song: Rndr 0076

Black Market Reel: Kan 313

Black Mountain Blues: LC AAFS L20

Black Mountain Rag: Cty 703, Fwys FA 2380, Van VRS-9152, Van VCD-45/46

Black Oak Ridge: PB 003

Black Pine Waltz: BF 15505

Black Satin: DU 33009

Black Sheep: BF 15504, NW 223, UICFC CFC 201

Black Snake Moan: MS 45004

Black Waters: JnAp 018

Blessed, Thrice Blessed: Rndr 0078

Blind Baggage Blues: Kan 305

Blind Child: FLeg FSA-18, FPrm 41942, OH OHCS 107

Blind Girl: AFF 33-4

Blind Man: JnAp JA 009

Blind Man and His Child: Cty 510

Blood of Old Red Rooster, The [C. 13]: Rndr 0083

Blood on the Saddle: Fwys FH 5723

Bloody War: Mar 9109

Blow Boys Blow: LC AAFC L26/27, LC AFS L68

Blow the Man Down: LC AAFC L26/27

Blow Ye Gentle Winds: Tpc 12T146

Blow Yo' Whistle, Freight Train: RCA 8417-2-R

Blue: Bio RC 6004

Blue and Low: Kan 305

Bluebell: AH AHR 008

Blue Eagle: Cty 707

Blue Eyed Boy: GnHys GR712

Blue Eyed Ella: BF 15508 *see also* Fair Eyed Ellen

Blue-Eyed Gal (Girl): Cty 525, Fwys FA 2342, LC AAFS L20, JnAp JA 009 *see also* Fly Around My Pretty Little Miss

Blue Eyes: JEMF 103

Bluefield Murder: Bio BLP 6005

Blue Goose: Fwys FA 2342, Rndr 0032

Bluegrass Breakdown: Prst FL 14010

Blue-Haired Jimmy: Fwys FA 2362

Blue Monday: LC AFS L60

Blue Moon of Kentucky: Prst INT 13049

Blue Mule: Rndr 0133

Blue Railroad Train: Van VCD-45/46, Van VRS-9213

Blue Ridge Cabin Home: NW 225

Blue Ridge Mountain Blues: Elek EKL-316, FLeg FSA-11, OT 107, Van VCD-45/46

Blue Ridge Rambler's Rag: BRI 005

Blue River: RCA 8416-2-R

Blues: NW 226

Blues Don't Mean a Thing: Fwys FA 2306

Blues in My Mind: Rndr 0021

Blues in the Morning: Rndr 0072

Blues Take Off Your Shoes: Rndr 0008

Blue Tail Fly, The: OH OHCS 316

Blue Yodel No. 7: Cam CAL 719

Boarding House Bells Are Ringing Waltz: Kan 600

Boating up Sandy: Cty 525, Cty 788, Fwys FA 2358, Her 12

Boatsman: Kan 307

Boat's up the River: Fwys FA 2368, KM 204, Rndr 0077

Bobby Halsey: NW 291

Bob Murphy: Arh 5018

Body and Soul: NW 225

Boggy Road to Texas: Arh 5011

Bogue Chitto Fling Ding: Arh 5001

Boil Them Cabbage Down: *see* Bile ...

Bolakins (Lamkin) [C. 93]: LC AFS L7, TFS cass, Fwys FA 2360

Bold McCarthy, *or* The City of Baltimore [K 26]: NW 223

Bold McIntyres: LC AAFS L55

Bold Sea Captain [O 25]: JnAp JA 001

Bold Soldier [M 27]: Mar 9200, FLeg FSA-27

Boll Weevil [I 17]: Cty 741

Boll Weevil: Mar 9025

Bonaparte's March: FLeg FSA-15, JEMF-105

Bonaparte's March into Russia: Rndr 0057

Bonaparte's Retreat: AFF 33-3, AH AHS 001, Cty 202, Cty 546, Cty 703, Cty 756, FLeg FSA-17, Fwys FA 2366, Her 33, LC AAFS L21, LC AFS L62, PB 005, Sm/Fwys SF 40012, Str STR 802, Tak A 1013

Bonnet Trimmed in Blue: FLeg FSA-15

Bonnie Black Bess [L 9]: FLeg FSA-15

Bonnie Blue Eyes: CMH 112, JEMF 101, MCA MCAD-10088 [CD], Rndr 0237, Riv RLP 12-617

Bonnie George (James) Campbell [C. 210]: Fwys FA 2358, FLeg FSA-1

Bonny Labouring Boy [M 14]: Asch AA 3/4

Boogie: Fwys FTS 31007

Booneville Stomp: Cty 518

Booth Killed Lincoln: LC AFS L29

Booth Killed Lincoln (*fiddle tune*): LC AFS L29

Bootlegger's Dream of Home: Mar 9105

Bootlegger's Story: CT 6000, Mar 9104

Boots and Saddle: Cty 411

Booze Yacht: Fwys FS 3848

Border Affair: AFF 33-2

Born in Hard Luck: Arh 5011

Born To Serve the Lord: Rndr 0026

Bosky Steer: AFF 33-1

Boss of the Section Gang: LC AFS L61

Boston Burglar [L 16b]: Ark Trad [No #], BF BCD 15456, Mar 9200, Riv RLP 12-610, Riv RLP 12-617, UTP [cass, no #], Van VRS 9162

Bow and Balance [C. 10]: Fwys FA 2362

Bow and Balance to Me [C. 10]: AH AHR 008

Bow Down, O Zion: Rndr 0078

Bow Legged Irishman: MS 45004

Boy in Blue: Mar 9109

Boys, Be Good to Dear Old Dad: Bio RC 6004

Boys on the Hill: LC AAFS L16

Boy That Lives Here, The: Ph 1020

Boy Who Could Never Come Home, The: FLeg FSA-18

Brady Why Didn't You Run?: Her 22

Bragg's Retreat: Miss AH-002

Brave Boys [K 21]: NW 239

Brave Engineer: JEMF 103

Bravest Cowboy: Cty 741

Brazos River: LC AAFS L30

Breadline Blues: Rndr 1026

Bread of Heaven: Fwys FS 3810

Breakdown: Prst FL 14030

Breaking Up Christmas: Cty 723, DU 33002, Mtn 302, Prst INT 25003, Rndr 0057

Break Melody: Hist HLP 8002

Breeze: Elek EKL-316

Brennan on the Moor [L 7]: Fwys FE 4001, LC AAFS L55

Bretheren, We Meet Again: Prst INT 25011

Briarpicker Brown: Rndr 0032

Brickyard Joe: DU 33015, MS 45004, UMP No #

Brigham, Brigham Young: Ok OK 75003

Bright and Morning Star: NW 223

Brighter Days: Fwys FA 2342

Brightest and Best: JnAp 037

Bright Morning Stars Are Rising: Rndr 0064

Bright Sherman Valley: BF 15509 *see also* Red River Valley

Brilliancy Medley (*includes* Billy Wilson, Bill Cheatham): Cty 507, Fwys FA 2952, Sytn STR 201

Bring Back My (Blue Eyed) Boy (To Me): Ark Trad [No #], Cty 729, CMH 107, De DL 4557 *see also* Wandering Boy

Bringing Back the Sheep: LC AFS L65-L66

Bringing in the Sheaves: Mar 9100

Bring Me a Leaf from the Sea: BF 15507, RCA LPV 552

Brisk Young Farmer, The [N 30]: Rndr 0083

Brisk Young Soldier, The [M 27]: AH AHR 007

Bristol Tennessee Blues: Cty 405

British American Fight [H 20]: AH AHR 010

Broken Down (Brokedown) Brakeman: Rndr 0083

Broken Down Gambler: Cty 526

Broken Down Tramp: CMH 112, JEMF 101 *see also* The Tramp

Broken Engagement: BF 15509, JEMF 101, OH OHCS 111 *see also* Standing by a Window

Broken Hearted Blues: OT 107

Broken Hearted Lover: BF 15521, Cty 402, Har HL 7344, OHCS-172, OTC 6001 (*n.b.*: 4 different songs)

Broken Token, The [N 42]: LC AAFS L21

Broken Wedding: Cty 522

Brother Ephus: FLeg FSA-32

Brother Green: AH AHR 009

Brother Jim Got Shot: Fwys FA 2392

Brother Jonah: LC AFS L68

Brown Button Shoes: Rndr 0032

Brown Eyes: Cam ADL 2-0726(e)

Brown Girl, The [C. 73]: AH AHR 007, TFS cass, Van VRS 9124

Brown Kelley Waltz, Parts 1 and 2: Sytn STR 201

Brown's Dream: HMM LP002, JnAp JA 049, Rndr 0008

Brown's Ferry Blues: AFF 33-3, Cty 542, Fwys FA 2306, Kan 305, Van VSD-9/10 *see also* Dog House Blues

Brown Skin Blues: Cty 511

Brown Waltz: AFF 33-1

Brush the Dust from that Old Bible: OH OHCS 316

Brushy Fork: GFS GFS 901

Brushy Run: Rndr 0047

Buck: Ldr LEA 4012

Buck Creek Girls: Fwys FA 2317

Buck Dancer's Choice: Arh 5012, Fwys FA 2379

Buck Dancing Charlie: Miss AH-002

Buck Eyed Rabbits: Cty 525 *see also* Prettiest Girl in the County

Bucking Broncho (My Love Is a Rider): RCA LPV 522, Rndr 1029, Sytn STR 202

Bucking Mule: Arh 5018, PB 005, PB 006, SmFwys SF 40037, Vet 107 *see also* McCarroll's Breakdown, Whoa Mule

Budded Roses: Asch AH 3831, Asch AH 3902, Cty 516

Buddies in the Saddle: Har HL 7300

(Buddy Won't You) Roll down the Line: BF 15501, Cty 545, Fwys FA 2953, Hist HLP 8006, RCA 8417-2-R

Buffalo Boy: LC AAFS L21

Buffalo Gals: Cty 533, JnAp JA 025, MFP MFP 002, Prst INT 25006, LC AFS L62 *see also* Alabama Gals, Round Town Gals

Buffalo Nickel: UICFC CFC 201

Buffalo Skinners [B 10]: LC AAFS L28, UICFC CFC 301

Bugerboo [O 3]: HMM LP001

Buggerman in the Bushes: Fwys FTS 31016

Bugle Call Rag: Prst INT 13035, SmFwys SF 40037

Building on the Sand: Fwys FA 2352

Bull at the Wagon: Cty 503, Cty 517

Bulldog (Down) in Sunny Tennessee: FLeg FSA-24, GHP LP 1001 *see also* Girl I Left in Sunny Tennessee

Bull Riders in the Sky: UICFC CFC 301

Bullseye Bill: FLeg FSA-27

Bull Whackers: Ok OK 75003

Bully of the Town [I 14]: BF BFX 15215, Cty 526, Cty 543, JEMF 103, JnAp 032, Trad 1007

Bumblebee in the Gourdvine: Cty 724

Bum Hotel: Vet 105

Bummer's Reel: LC AFS L62

Bum on the Bum: Rndr 1033

Bum Song: CMH 106, Rndr 1009

Bum Song, No. 2: CMH 106, Rndr 1009

Bunch of Chickens: Rndr 0194

Bunker Hill: MFFA 1001

Burglar Bold: Arh 5012

Burglar Man [H 23]: JnAp JA 001, Tst T-3301, Prst INT 25004

Burial of Wild Bill: Cty 522, Ph 1017

Burly Banks of Barbry-O, The [C. 14]: MC 1

Bury Me Beneath [Under] the (Weeping) Willow: CMF 011-L, Fwys FA 2427, N&T 1001, OH OHCS 111, Prst INT 13049, Riv RLP 12-617, Rndr 0143, RCA LPM 2772

Bury Me Not (out) on the Lone Prairie [B 2]: AFF 33-1, JnAp 018, Mar 9106, Rndr 0036, Van VRS 9124

Bury Me out on the Prairie: MS 45008, OH OHCS 316

Busted: FLeg FSA-13

Butcher Boy [P 24]: BF 15508, BB AXM2-5525, BRI 002, Cam CAL 797, FLeg FSA-27, Fwys FA 2951, Fwys FS 3810, Mar 9200, Prst FL 14035, Rndr 0077, Rndr 0017, Rndr CD 11536

By a Cottage in the Twilight: Mar 9109

Bye and Bye You Will Soon Forget Me: BF 15509 *see also* Fond Affection

Bye Bye Blues: Cty 787

By the Cottage Door: DU 33009, NW 236

By the Old Oaken Bucket, Louise: BF 15504

By the Touch of Her Hand: Har HL 7422

C. & N. W. Railroad Blues: Rndr 0005

Cabin Home: JEMF 103

Cabin in Gloryland: JnAp JA 001

Cabin in the Valley: Rndr 0026

Cabin on Hill: Atl SD-1349

Cabin with the Roses at the Door: CT 6001, Rndr 1004

Cackling Hen (and Rooster Too): Cty 506, Fwys FA 2435, Fwys FES 34151, GnHys GR712, JnAp JA0059C, KM 204, Mar 9025, Mtn 303, Riv RLP 12-650, Rndr 0009, SmFwys SF 40037, Van VSD-107/108

Calinda: Arh 5010

Callahan: Cty 788, Fwys FTS 31016, GnHys GR712, Her 22, Rndr 0237

Callahan Rag: Cty 403

Callahan's Reel: JnAp JA 049, OH OHCS 191

Called to the Foreign Field: Cty 508

Call Me Back Pal of Mine: ACM ACM-1, OH OHCS 114

Call of the Road: Van VRS-9213

Call Your Dogs and Let's Go Hunting: GyEg 101

Calvary: Asch AH 3903, Atl SD-1349, Van VRS-9182

Cambric Shirt [C. 2]: Fwys FA 2358, RRT LP-8073

Camp Chase: AH AHS 001, AH AHR 007, FPrm (No #), LC AFS L65-L66, Rndr 0047

Camping in Canaan's Land: Fwys FA 2357

Camp Nelson Blues: Cty 531

Camp Run: AH AHS 003

Canadian Rose: FLeg FSA-27

C. and N. W. Railroad Blues: Cty 503

C. and O. Excursion (Train): Rndr 1007, Vet 103

Candy Girl (Gal): Cty 541, Cty 786

Can I Sleep in Your Barn: Cty 509 *see also* May I Sleep in Your Barn Tonight Mister

Cannonball: Asch AH 3902, OTC 6001, Har HL 7422, OH OHS 90045, RCA LPV 532

Cannon Ball Blues: Cty 511, TL TLCW-06 *see also* Whitehouse Blues

Cannonsville Dam: FLeg FSA-27

Can the Circle Be Unbroken: Har HL 7280, TL TLCW-06

Can't Hit Lucky: Fwys FES 34151

Can't You Remember When Your Heart Was Mine [C. 243]: BF 15507

Captain Devin [L 13a]: FLeg FSA-26, Rndr SS-0145

Captain George Has Your Money Come: Cty 529

Captain Karo: Fwys FES 34151

Captain Webster: FLeg FSA-33

Captain Won't You Let Me Go Home: Mar 9109

Caravan: BRI 005

Carbolic Rag: OT 101

Careless [Loveless] Love: Asch AH 3903, Cty 504, Cty 511, Hist HLP 8004, Fwys FA 3830, Riv RLP 12-610, SmFwys SF 40037 *see also* I Have No Loving Mother Now, Lonesome Day Today

Carolina Cannonball: Fwys FS 3848

Carolina Lady, The [O 25]: Fwys FA 2418

Carolina Moonshiner: Mar 9104

Carolina Rag: Cty 720

Carolina Stompdown: Cty 531 *see also* Soldier's Joy

Caroline of Edinboro' Town [P 27]: LC AAFS L14

Carroll County Blues: Arh 5001, Cty 511, Cty 528, GyEg 101, Rndr 0009, Tak A 1013

Carter's Blues: CMH 118

Carve That Possum: Cty 545, De DL 4760, NW 236

Casey Jones [G 1]: AFF 33-2, Fwys FS 3848, LC AFS L68, Mar 9013, Van VRS-9182, Vet 103

Casey's Hornpipe: UMP No #

Cat Came Back, And the: see And the Cat Came Back

Catfish: Fwys FA 2306, NW 291 *see also* Banjo Sam

Catfish Blues: Van VRS-9182

Cat's Meow: Rndr 0034

Cattle Call: NW 314/315

Cave Love Has Gained the Day: BF 15510, Cty 408

C. C. and O. Number 558: Cty 405, Vet 103

Celebrated Workingman, A: LC AAFS L16

Change All Around, A: OT 106

Changing Business: AFF 33-3

Chapel Hill March: Str STR 802

Chapel Hill Serenade: Cty 791, Her 070

Chariot: NW 291

Charles Guiteau [E 11]: BF 15510, Cty 408, Cty 522, Fwys FA 2951, Fwys FA 2368, Fwys FA 2375, LC AFS L29, Mer 1001-2, Riv RLP 12-617

Charleston No. 1: Cty 503, Cty 529

Charley, He's a Good Old Man: BF 15510, Cty 408

Charlie: Riv RLP 12-620 *see also* Charlie, Charlie's Neat

Charlie and Nellie: CMH 116, MCA MCAD-10088 [CD], OH OHCS 117 see also Charlie Brooks

Charlie (Charley) Brooks: Kan 308, OH OHCS 111 see also Charlie and Nellie

Charlie, He's a Good Old Man: RCA LPV 552 see also Charlie's Neat, Charlie

Charlie Lawson [F 35]: Rndr 0065

Charlie Mason Pogie Boat: Fwys FS 3848

Charlie's Neat: Fwys FA 2317 see also Charlie, Charlie He's a Good Old Man

Charlotte Hot-Step: Cty 523

Charmaine: MFP MFP 002

Charming Betsy: Arh 5001, Arh 5011, Fwys FS 3839, GnHys GR712, Cty 515, Rndr 1035

Charming Bill: BF 15517, Fwys FTS 31007

Charming Little Girl [M 3]: FPrm 41942

Chase the Squirrel: PB 004

Chattanooga: PB 003

Chattanooga Blues: Rndr 0089, Rndr 1033

Cheat 'Em: see Bill Cheathem

Cheatham County Breakdown: Cty 546

Cherish the Ladies: NW 239

Cherokee: OFA TALP-001

Cherokee Polka: Rndr 1010

Cherry Blossom Waltz: Rndr 0005

Cherry Mountain Hoedown: Tak A 1013

Cherry River Line: FPrm 41942, FPrm (No #) (related to Little Maggie)

Cherry River Rag: Rndr 1010

Cherry Tree Carol [C. 54]: AH AHR 008, Fwys FA 2302, LC AAFS L14, LC AAFS L57, Riv RLP 12-617

Chesapeake Bay: Mar 9111

Chevrolet Car: BF 15517, Cty 541

Chevrolet Six: Rndr 1007

Chewing Gum: Cty 409, OTC 6001, Rndr 1028

Chick-a-la-le-o: Atl SD-1350, NW 245, Van VRS-9158

Chicken: BF BCD 15456, OH OHCS 141

Chicken: Tak A 1013

Chicken in the Barnyard (Bread Tray): Ala Trad 103, Cty 733, Rndr 0058

Chicken Pie: Arh 5010

Chicken Reel: Fwys FA 2380, Mer 1001-2, N&T 1001, Riv RLP 12-650, Rndr 0047, Rndr 0194, SmFwys SF 40037

Chickens Don't Roost Too High: Ala Trad 103

C-H-I-C-K-E-N Spells Chicken: BF 15517

Chickens (They) Grow Tall: UICFC CFC 301, Van VRS-9183

Childhood Play: Van VRS-9239

Child of Desertion, A: Fwys FTS 31016

Children of the Heav'nly King: LC AFC L69-L70, Min JD-203

Chillicothe Two-Step: GFS GFS 901, Mar 9013

Chilly Winds: Atl 1347, Cty 535, Cty 778, Fwys FA 2380, LC AFS L2

Chinese Breakdown: Fwys FTS 31007, JEMF 101, OH OHCS 117 see also Chinese Rag

Chinese Rag: OT 100 see also Chinese Breakdown

Ching Chong: Arh 5012

Chinky Pin: Cty 733

Chinquapin Hunting: DU 33002

Chinquapin Pie: FLeg FSA-17

Chisholm Trail: BF 15502

Chittlin' Cooking Time in Cheatham County: Cty 547, RCA LPV 507

Choctaw Bill: PB 003

Chow Time: The, Rndr 0026

Christian Pilgrim: Fwys FES 34151

Christine LeRoy: Rndr 1029

Christmas Cake: Tst T-3301

Christmas Eve: GnHys GR712, Mer 1001-2

Christmas Eve in the East Side: Rndr 1002

Christmas Holiday: HMM LP001

Christmas Lullaby: SH SH-CD-3779

Christmas Time in the Morning: Miss AH-002

Christmas Time Will Soon Be Over: Cty 514

Christ Was a Wayworn Traveler: FLeg FSA-26

Christ Was Born in Bethlehem: Wstm SWN 18021

Chum's Hornpipe: Mar 9013

Church in the Wildwood: CMH 118

Cider Mill: Cty 709, Cty 713

Cimarron: JnAp 032

Cincinnati: PB 003

Cincinnati Blues: Cty 777

Cindy: Brun 59000, Cty 405, Cty 544, FLeg FSA-17, Fwys FA 2314, Fwys FA 2360, Fwys FS 3811, Fwys FS 3832, HMM LP001, LC AFS L2, OH OHCS 317, PB 005, Prst FL 14030, Rndr 0065 see also Get Along Home Cindy, I Get My Whiskey from Rockingham, Tell Her To Come Back Home

Cindy Gal: Fwys FA 2306

Cindy in the Summertime: Fly LP 546, Fwys FE 34161, GV SC 03

Circus Days: Rndr 1009

Circus Piece: Miss AH-002

Citaco: Cty 527, TFS 103, PB 006 see also Swamp Cat Rag

City Boarders: NW 314/315

City Four Square: Fwys FA 2362, Rndr 0076

City of Sighs and Tears: Shoe SGB 1

City on the Hill: Alp ALP 201, Cty 787

Civil War March: Fwys FA 2358

Claude Allen [E 6]: Prst INT 25009, BRI 004, LC AFS L7, Fwys FA 2355

Claudie Banks [N 40]: AH AHR 007

Clayhole Waltz: Ok OK 76004

Clayton Boone [C. 200]: Fwys FH 5723

Clay Town Farm: AFF 33-3

Cleveland's March: Her 070, Str STR 802

Clinch Mountain: Fwys FA 3833

Clinch Mountain Backstep: JnAp JA 025

Clouds Are Gwine To Roll Away: Van VSD-9/10

Clover Blossoms: OH OHCS 114

Club Meeting: BF BCD 15456

Cluck Old Hen: Brun 59000, Cty 405, Cty 501, DU 33033, Cty 739, Cty 756, FLeg FSA-1, Fwys FA 2317, Fwys FA 2350, Fwys 2363, Fwys FA 2380, Fwys FS 3811, Her 12, HMM LP001, Prst INT 25004, Rndr 0237, Rndr 0037

Coal Black Mining Blues: Rndr 0076

Coal Creek March: Cty 515, Cty 788, Fwys FS 3828, LC AFS L2, N&T 1001, OHS OF-1001

Coal Loading Blues: LC AFS L60

Coal Loading Machine: LC AFS L60

Coal Mine Blues: Cty 401

Coal Miner's Blues: De DL 4404, Fwys FA 2352, MCA MCAD-10088 [CD], OH OHCS 117, TL TLCW-02

Coal Miner's Boogie: Fwys FTS 31016

Coal Miner's Child: FLeg FSA-32

Coal Miner's Goodbye: LC AFS L60

Cock Robin: Fwys FS 3810

Code of the Mountains: AH AHR 010

Coffee Blues: Van VRS-9183

Coke Oven March: Asch AH 3903

Cold Frosty Morning: Miss AH-002

Cold Icy Floor: Bio RC-6002, Bio RC-6003

Cold Penitentiary Blues [I 4]: RCA LPV 548, Rndr 0064, Rndr 1037

Cole Younger [E 3]: Fwys FA 2392, Fwys FA 2951, Ph 1017

Colley's Run-I-O [C 17c]: LC AAFS L28

Columbus Stockade Blues: Fwys FA 2435, FLeg FSA-17, Prst INT 25009, GV SC 03, *see also* Go and Leave Me If You Wish To

Combination Rag: Cty 410

Combs Hotel Burned Down: Fwys FA 2368

Come All Ye Lewiston Factory Girls: BF 15003

Come All Ye Texas Rangers [A 8]: Min JD-203

Come All You Coal Miners: NW 245

Come All You Maidens: FLeg FSA-33

Come Be My Rainbow: Roots 701

Come, Come Ye Saints: Fwys FA 2036

Come Dearest the Daylight Is Dawning/Nobody's Darling: Rndr 1028

Come Home: Rndr 0020

Come Life, Shaker Life: Rndr 0078

Come on Buddie, Don't You Want To Go: Rndr 1028

Come Take a Trip in My Airship: Ark Trad 002, OHCS-177

Come, Thou Fount of Every Blessing: Ark Trad 003, Mar 9013

Come Thou Long-expected Jesus: UNC 0-8078-4083-1

Come Up Horsey: NW 291

Comical Ditty, A: Rndr 0083

Coming down from Denver: MFFA 1001

Coming from the Ball: Fwys FA 2379

Coming Round the Mountain: Vet 105 *see also* She'll Be ...

Coming Up the Pike: Rndr 0133

Commentary: NW 205 ??

Common Bill: LC AAFS L14

Concord Rag: Fwys FA 2435, OT 107

Condescension: Firmly I Stand on Zion's Hill: UNC 0-8078-4083-1

Coney Island (Isle): Fwys FA 2368, Rndr 0005, Rndr 1007

Conservation Hornpipe: Kan 313, Ldr LEA 4012

Contented Bachelor: Ok OK 76004

Conversation with Death: Fwys FA 2309, Rndr 0028

Convict and the Rose: Cam ADL 2-0726(e)

Coo-Coo: see Cuckoo

Coon Dog: Cty 201

Coon from Tennessee: Cty 540 *see also* Tennessee Coon

Coon in a Treetop: GFS GFS 901

Coon on a Rail: Ala Trad 103

Cora Ellen: Mar 9025

Cora Is Gone: Prst INT 13035

Corina, Corina: JEMF 104, Fwys FA 2359, NW 236, Van VSD-107/108

Corn Dodger Special No. 1: Cty 520

Corn Licker and Barbecue, Part 2: Rndr 1003

Corn Licker Rag: OH OHS 90031

Corn Licker Still in Georgia, A: Cty 506

Corn Song: Cty 786

Coronation: Mar 9100

Cottage Hill: GFS GFS 901

Cotton Blossom: Rndr 0036

Cotton Eye(d) Joe: Atl 1347, Cty 506, Cty 518, Cty 520, Cty 528, Cty 544, Cty 709, Cty 756, Fwys FA 2317, Fwys FS 3832, HMM LP002, LC AFS L62, NW 236, OH OHCS 191, PB 005, Prst INT 25006, Prst FL 14030, Prst INT 13035, Rndr 0047, SmFwys SF 40037

Cotton in the Crib: PB 003

Cotton Mill Blues [Colic]: BF 15505, JEMF 103, JEMF 104, NW 245, Rndr 1026, Rndr 1035 *see also* Poor Man, Rich Man

Cottom Mill Girls: Van VRS 9124

Cotton Patch: Cty 544, OH OHCS 192

Cotton Patch Rag: Cty 707, Hist HLP 8002

Couderay Jig: LC AAFS L55

Country Blues: Fwys FA 2953, Fwys RBF 654, OT 107, Van VCD-45/46, Van VRS-9152 *see also* Darling Cora

Country Girl Valley: BF 15504

Country Ham and Red Gravy: Vet 101

Count the Days I'm Gone: Fly LP 546

County Jail: Asch AH 3831

County Road Gang: Rndr 0036

Courting Case: FLeg FSA-23, FLeg FSA-2, Fwys FA 2358

Courting in the Rain: JnAp JA0059C, FLeg FSA-24

Courting Song: Mer 1001-2

Cousin Sally Brown: Cty 717, Her 070, Sm/Fwys SF 40012

Covered Wagon Rolled Right Along: Arh 5011

Cowards over Pearl Harbor: Rndr 0143

Cowboy in Church: Ph 1017

Cowboy Jack [B 24]: Fwys FH 5723, OH OHCS 111, RCA LPM 2772, Sytn STR 202, UTP [cass, no #]

Cowboys' Christmas Ball: Rndr 0158

Cowboy's Dream: MFP 0001, RCA LPV 522

Cowboy's Lament: BF 15502

Cowboy's Life Is a Very Dreary Life: LC AAFS L28

Cowboy's Meditation: Mtn 304

Cowboy Song: NW 314/315

Cowboy's Shirttail: AFF 33-3

Cowboy Stomp: NW 314/315

Cowboy's Wife: Rndr 1029

Cowboy's Wild Song to His Herd: Cam ACL1-0501, CMH 118

Cowboy, The: MS 45008, NW 314/315, Ph 1017, UICFC CFC 301

Cowgirl's Dream: Sytn STR 202

Cowhand's Last Ride: NW 314/315

Cowman's Prayer: BF BCD 15456, Ph 1017

Cowman's Troubles: AFF 33-1

Cowtrail to Mexico: BF 15502

Coyote, The: Ok OK 76004

Cranberry Rock: Rndr 0018

Cranberry Song: LC AAFS L55

Crawdad (Song) (Hole): Fwys FA 2306, Fwys FA 2359, SH SH-CD-3786, TFS 106, Van VSD-107/108, RCA 8417-2-R

Crawling and Creeping: NW 245

Crazy Creek: Her 33

Crazy Fingers: Rndr 0072

Crazy Jim: Rndr 0194

Creole Girl, The [H 9]: Ark Trad [No #]

Crescent Limited: FLeg FSA-24

Cricket on the Hearth: DU 33002, SmFwys SF 40038, Fwys FA 2435

Crime of the D'Autremont Brothers: RCA LPV 532

Cripple Creek: AH AHS 003, Cty 703, Cty 717, Cty 720, DU 33015, FLeg FSA-23, Fly LP 546, Fwys FA 2426, Fwys FA 3830, Fwys FS 3811, LC AAFS L20, LC AFS L2, Prst INT 13030, Riv RLP 12-610, Riv RLP 12-649, Rndr 0058, SmFwys SF 40037, Trad TLP 1007, Van VRS-9182, Vet 107 *see also* Going Up Cripple Creek, Going Up Brushy Fork

Cripple Creek & Shooting Creek: HMM LP 001

Crocodile's Mouth: TFS 104

Croquet Habit: Cty 529 *see also* Take a Drink on Me, Tell It to Me

Crossbones Skully: Rndr 1002

Crossed Old Jordan's Stream: Rndr 1037

Cross-Eyed Butcher and Cackling Hen: De DL 4760, Hist HLP 8002 *see also* Cackling Hen

Cross Mountain Mines Explosion [G 9]: TFS 106

Crow Creek: UICFC CFC 201

Crowley Waltz: OT 100

Cruel Slavery Days: Bio RC-6002

Cruel War Is Raging, The [O 33]: LC AAFS L20

Cruel Willie: Ark Trad 004, Rndr SS-0145

Crying Holy unto My Lord: Alp ALP 202, RCA 2100-2-R

Cuba: Asch AH 3903

Cuban Soldier: De DL 4557, Mar 9109

Cuckoo [Coo-Coo] (She's a Fine Bird): BF 15509, Elek EKLP-2, FLeg FSA-17, FLeg FSA-3, Fwys FS 3828, Fwys FA 2953, Fwys FA 2359, Sm/Fwys SF 40012, Van VSD-6576, Van VRS-9182, Van VRS-9147

Cuckoo's [Coo-Coo's] Nest: Fwys FS 3809, KM 204, Rndr 1010

Cumberland [A 26]: Mar 9200

Cumberland Blues: Cty 511, DU 33015, GFS GFS 901

Cumberland Gap: BRI 005, Cty 527, Cty 723, DU 33014, Fwys FA 2315, Fwys FA 2342, Fwys FA 2363, Fwys FA 2379, Fwys FA 2435, Fwys FS 3810, Fwys FTS 31089, Kan 307, LC AFS L62, MS 45003, Mtn 304, OH OHCS 111, OH OHCS 192, PB 005, PB 006, Riv RLP 12-610, Rndr 0028, Rndr 0058, Rndr 0089, Rndr 1005 *see also* Cumberland Gap on a Bucking Mule

Cumberland Gap on a Bucking Mule: Rndr 1023 *see also* Cumberland Gap

Cumberland Land: Cty 786

Cumberland Mountain Deer Race: Fwys RBF RF 51, RCA LPV 507

Cumberland's Crew, The [A 18]: LC AFS L29

Curb Stone: FPrm 41942

Curley Headed Baby: Cty 411, OH OHCS 114, Rndr 0052, Fwys FA 2352, Rndr 0143

Curley Headed Woman (Hesitation Blues): Cty 511

Curtains of Night: Pu PU 3001

Cusseta: NW 205, Prst INT 25007

Custer's Last Charge: LC AAFS L30

Cutting at the Point: MS 45005

Cyclone of Rye Cove: BRI 004, CMH 107, JEMF 101, OH OHCS 111

Dabbling in the Dew: GnHys GR714

Daddy Blues: Rndr 0157

Dakota Land: UICFC CFC 301

Dallas Bound: Cty 517

Dallas Stamper: GyEg 101

Dally Roper's Song: Fwys FH 5723

Dan Carter Waltz: Cty 723, Ldr LEE 4045

Dance All Night (with a Bottle in Your Hand): Cty 401, Cty 733, Cty 778, Fwys FTS 31007, Fly LP 546, Vet 107 *see also* Give the Fiddler a Dram

Dance All Night with the Fiddler's Gal: HMM LP002

Dance Around Molly: Cty 720, MFFA 1001

Dance Boatman Dance: Her 070

Dancing Waves Schottische: JnAp JA 025

Dan Doo [C. 279]: AH AHR 008, Fwys FA 2360, TFS 108

Dandy Jim: Mar 9025

Dangerous Blues: Prst INT 25009

Dang My Pop-Eyed Soul: Kan 305

Dango: FLeg FSA-24

Daniel O'Connell's Welcome to Parliament: JEMF-105

Daniel Prayed: Fwys FA 2359, NW 225

Danny Boy: Rndr 0089

Dan Tucker: JnAp JA 049

Danville Girl [H 2]: Fwys FA 2392, Fwys RBF 654

Darby's Ram: Ark Trad 004, JnAp 018

Dark and Stormy Weather: CMH 118, OH OHCS 117

Dark Eyes: CT 6000

Dark Haired True Lover: MCA MCAD-10088 [CD], MCA VIM-4012, OH OHCS 111

Dark Holler Blues: Cty 502, Cty 525

Darkie's Wail: OT 101, OH OHCS 114

Dark Road Is a Hard Road To Travel: Cty 513

Dark Scenes of Winter: Asch AA 3/4

Darktown Dandies: JnAp JA 025

Dark Town Strutters' Ball: Ldr LE 4040

Dark Was the Night and Cold the Ground: UNC 0-8078-4083-1

Darling: Mer 1001-2

Darling Child: Col CS 9660, Cty 407 *see also* Love Somebody, Too Young To Marry

Darling Cora (Corey): AH AHR 010, BB AXM2-5510, Cty 502, Fwys FA 2374, Fwys FS 3810, Fwys FA 2366, JnAp JA 010, LC AAFS L14, RCA LPV 507, Rndr 0076, Sm/Fwys SF 40012 *see also* Country Blues

Darling Don't You Know That's Wrong: JnAp JA 020

Darling Honey: Mar 9013

Darling Little Joe: Cam CAL 2473 *see also* Little Joe

Darling Nellie, Across the Sea: Rndr 0020

Darling Nellie Gray: JnAp JA 025, JnAp JA 030

Darling Six Months Ain't Long: Cty 712

Darling Where You Been So Long: Pu PU 3001 *see also* I Wish I Was a Mole in the Ground

Darneo: Cty 407, Cty 501 *see also* Sail Away
    Ladies, Sally Ann
Davenport: Asch AH 3903
David's Lamentation: LC AAFS L11, NW 205,
    Prst INT 25007
Davis Limited: RCA LPV 532
Davison-Wilder Blues: FLeg FSA-32
Davy Crockett: AH AHR 010, FLeg FSA-26,
    Rndr 0051, TFS 103
Davy, Davy: Cty 520 *see also* Going down the
    River
Davy Dugger: Rndr 0089
Dawn Waltz: Mar 9111
Dawsonville Jail: Fwys FE 34162
Day I Fought Dwyer: Mar 9200
Day Is Past and Gone: FLeg FSA-22, Riv RLP
    12-620
Days of '49: BF 15502, Ok OK 75003, Rndr
    0158, UICFC CFC 301
D-Bar-2 Horse Wrangler: NW 314/315
Deacon Jones: Cty 410
Deadheads and Suckers: Bio RC-6003
Dead Horse, The, or Poor Old Man: LC
    AAFC L26/27, N&T 1001
Deaf Woman's Courtship: Str STR 802
Dear Companion: FLeg FSA-3, Riv RLP
    12-620
Dear Daddy You're Gone: OH OHS 90001
Dear Friends Farewell: JnAp JA 020
Dear Heart: Ok OK 76004
Dear Old Dixie: SmFwys SF 40037
Death Is Only a Dream: OH OHCS 116
Death of Edward Hawkins: Rndr 0034
Death of Floyd Collins [G 22]: RCA LPV 548,
    TFS 105, Rndr 0064
Death of Jerry Damron: Fwys FA 2392
Death of John Henry [I 1]: Brun 59001, Cty
    545, Hist HLP 8006, Rndr 1028
Death of Mother Jones: Rndr 1026
Death of Queen Jane [C. 170]: LC AAFS L21,
    Fwys FP 40
Death of the Blue Eagle: Fwys FA 2317, Fwys
    FTS 31016
Death of the Lawson Family [F 35]: Asch AH
    3831
Death of the Old Sow: MFFA 1001
Death of William Jennings Bryan: Rndr 1033
Deceiver/Box the Fox: Her 12 ??
Deep down in My Heart: LC AFS L68
Deep Elem (Elm) Blues: Arh 5018, Mar 9025,
    OT 102, RCA 8417-2-R

Deep River Blues: Van VRS-9152, Van
    VSD-9/10
Deer Song: RRT LP-8073
Defellum Blues: see Deep Elem Blues
Deliverance Will Come: BF 15518
Del Rio: JEMF 101
Democratic Donkey: Kan 305
Denver Belle: Her 33
Derby Polka: JnAp JA 025
Derby Ram: Brun 59001, HMM LP001, LC
    AAFS L12, Riv RLP 12-645
Devil and Farmer's Wife, The [C. 278]: Rndr
    0076, FLeg FSA-17, LC AAFS L58, Her 12,
    Van VRS-9147
Devil and the Old Woman [C. 278]: AH AHR
    008
Devil Chased Me Around the Stump: PB 003
Devil in Georgia: Her 12
Devil in the Strawstack: Cty 756
Devilish Mary [Q 4]: LC AAFS L14, Cty 506,
    Cty 510, Fwys FS 3811, Riv RLP 12-617,
    Fwys FA 2362
Devil Perceived: BF 15003
Devil's Dream: LC AAFS L9, FLeg FSA-15,
    Kan 306, Kan 307, Ldr LEA 4012
Devil's Nine Questions [C. 1]: BRI 002, LC
    AFS L1
Devotion: Poor and Afflicted, Lord Are Thine:
    UNC 0-8078-4083-1
Devotion: 'Twas on That Dark, That Doleful
    Night: UNC 0-8078-4083-1
Dew Drop: Ala Trad 103, Arh 5012
Dewy Dens of Yarrow, The [C. 214]: FLeg
    FSA-11
Diamond Joe: Cty 514
Diamond(s) in the Rough: BF 15518, Cam
    CAL 586, JEMF 101
Dickson County Blues: OT 100
Dickson County Blues, #2: Cty 546 *see also*
    Sleeping Lulu, etc.
Did Christ o'er Sinners Weep: SH
    SH-CD-3779
Did He Ever Return: UIP [cass, no #]
Did the Rum-Do-Daddy: Van VRS-9183
Did You Ever See the Devil, Uncle Joe: Cty
    510, DU 33015, Rndr 0058 *see also* Hop
    Light Ladies, Miss McLeod's Reel
Die in the Field of Battle: Cty 534
Diesel Train: NW 225
Dig a Hole in the Meadow: Prst FL 14035
Digging Potatoes: WVUP 001

Dill Pickles Rag: BRI 005, Cty 707, NW 225, Van VRS-9239

Dim Narrow Trail: NW 314/315

Dinah: JnAp 032

Dineo: Ark Trad 004, Rndr 0057

Dissatisfied: OH OHCS 114

Distant Land To Roam, A: Cam CAL 2473, OH OHS 90045

Dixie: Cty 526

Dixie Blossom: MFFA 1001, Rndr 0133

Dixie Blues: Mar 9013

Dixie Boll Weevil: UIP [cass, no #]

Dixie Cowboy [B 3]: MS 45008

Dixie Darling: OH OHCS 117

Dixie Division: Mar 9109

Dixie Hoedown: Kan 310, MFP MFP 002

Dixie Mail: OT 112

Dixie, There's No Place Like Home: Arh 5011

Dixon Said to Jackson [L 4]: JnAp JA 001

Dixon County Blues: AH AHS 001

Doc Jessup's Schottische: Rndr 0157

Doc's Guitar: Van VRS-9152, Van VSD-9/10

Dog and Cat Rag: TFS 103

Dog and Gun (*or* The Jolly Farmer) [N 20]: OH OHCS 316, TFS 104

Doggett's Gap: RRT LP-8073

Dog House Blues: Cam CAL 719

Do, Little Bobby: Fwys FA 2342

Do Little Bobby, Do: LC AAFS L21

Do Lord Remember Me: Mer 1001-2

Done Gone: Cty 202, Cty 507, Kan 306, Rndr 1010, Sytn STR 201, UMP No #

Don't Cause Mother's Hair to Turn Gray: Rndr 0008

Don't Forget Me (Little Darling): Har HL 7422

Don't Forget This Song [E 15]: CMH 107, OH OHCS 117, TL TLCW-06

Don't Get Trouble in (Your) Mind: HMM LP001, Mar 9111, OT 106

Don't Get Weary Children: Cty 515

Don't Go down That Lonesome Road: Van VRS 9162

Don't Go Out: OT 107

Don't Go Out Tonight My Darling: Fwys FA 3830, Cty 513

Don't Go Riding down that Old Texas Trail: Fwys FE 34161, Fly LP 546

Don't Grieve After Me: Cty 508

Don't Leave Me Alone: Cty 404

Don't Leave Me This Way: Alp ALP 201

Don't Let the (Your) Deal Go Down: Bio RC-6002, Cty 505, Cty 525, Cty 724, Fwys FS 3832, Fwys FTS 31007, Her 22, JnAp JA 025, Kan 600, SmFwys SF 40037, Van VSD-9/10

Don't Let Your Deal Go down Medley: Arb 201

Don't Love Nobody: SmFwys SF 40037

Don't Make Me Go to Bed and I'll Be Good: OH OHCS 315

Don't Mind the Weather: Fwys FA 2426

Don't Put Off Salvation Too Long: NW 223

Don't Say Goodbye If You Love Me: Rndr 1006, SH SH-CD-3795

Don't This Road Look Rough and Rocky: Rndr 0052

Don't Trade: Rndr CD 11536

Don't Try It for It Can't Be Done: OH OHCS 114

Don't You Cry My Honey: Cty 514

Don't You Hear Jerusalem Moan?: FSSM FSSMLP 150001-D, Rndr 1023

Don't You Look for Trouble: Rndr 1028

Don't You Remember?: Fwys FA 2309

Don't You Remember the Time?: Cty 529

Doodle Bug: Sm/Fwys SF 40012

Doon Reel: JEMF-105

Do Remember Me Baby: Mer 1001-2

Do Round My Lindy: Rndr 1003

Double Headed Train: Vet 103

Double Quick March: BRI 005

Double Tragedy: Ok OK 75003

Down beside the Ohio [F 5]: Prst INT 13030

Down by the Greenwood Side [C. 20]: FLeg FSA-11

Down by the Railroad Track: FLeg FSA-27, OH OHCS 107

Down by the Riverside [P 18]: AH AHR 010

Down by the Sea Shore [K 17]: FLeg FSA-11, Riv RLP 12-649 *see also* I Never Will Marry

Down Came an Angel: FLeg FSA-3

Down, Down, Down: LC AAFS L16

Downfall of Paris: DU 33009, Riv RLP 12-650

Down Home Waltz: Rndr 0133

Down in a Coal Mine: LC AAFS L16

Down in Arkansas: Prst INT 25004

Down in Florida on a Hog: OT 112 *see also* Lonesome Road Blues

Down in the Lowly Vale: Rndr 0078

Down in the Mire: Van VRS-9183

Down in the Tennessee Valley: OH OHCS 190

Down in the Valley: Fwys FA 2358, Fwys FA 2360, OH OHCS 192, OH OHCS 314, Riv RLP 12-650

Down in the Valley To Pray: Rndr 0051, Van VRS-9239, Van VCD-45/46

Down in the Willow (Garden) [F 6]: Asch AA 3/4, Fleg FSA 23, RCA LPV 507

Down on Penny's Farm: Fwys FA 2951 see also On Tanner's Farm

Down on the Banks of the Ohio [F 5]: Cam CAL 797, RCA LPV 548, Rndr 1006 see also Banks of the Ohio

Down on the Picket Line: FLeg FSA-26

Down South Blues: Cty 511, Fwys RBF 654, JnAp JA 010

Down the Old Plank Road: Fwys FA 2953

Down the Road: SmFwys SF 40037, Fwys FA 2366, HMM LP002, Sm/Fwys SF 40012

Down to Jordan: Mar 9101

Down to the Deep and Rolling River: Rndr 0078

Downward Road [H 6]: Rndr 0051

Down with the Old Canoe [D 24?]: Ark Trad 004, RCA LPV 507, RCA 8417-2-R

Down Yonder: OH OHCS 192, OT 100 see also Georgia Blues

Doxology: LC AFC L69-L70

Do You Call That Religion: Rndr 0026

Dragging the Bow: Arh 5018, JnAp 030

Drake's Reel: FLeg FSA-24

Dreadful Memories: FLeg FSA-26

Dreadnaught, The [D 13]: NW 239

Dreaming of the Georgiana Moon: JnAp 030

Dream of the Miner's Child: Fwys FS 3829, FLeg FSA-18, SH SH-CD-3795, Van VRS-9170

Dreamy Georgiana Moon: Rndr 0005, Rndr 0034

Dreary Black Hills: LC AAFS L28

Dr. Ginger Blue [Ginger Blues]: NW 245, Rndr 0034

Drifting Too Far from the Shore: BB AXM2-5510, SmFwys SF 40038

Drill Man Blues: LC AFS L60

Drink 'Er Down: UICFC CFC 201

Drinking from the Fountain: Fwys FA 3830

Drinking of the Wine: Rndr 0065

Driving Saw-Logs on the Plover [dC 29]: Ph 1022

Drowsy Sleeper [M 4]: Van VRS 9124

Drummer Boy: Fwys FTS 31007

Drunkard's Child, The: Mar 9105

Drunkard's Courtship: Fwys FA 2362

Drunkard's Doom: Bio RC 6004, Mar 9104

Drunkard's Dream: Ark Trad 002, Fwys FA 3830, Mar 9105, Rndr 0051

Drunkard's (Drunken) Hiccoughs: Alp ALP 202, Cty 519, Cty 724, Cty 756, LC AFS L62, OT 107, Prst INT 25004, Trad TLP 1007 see also Rye Whiskey, etc.

Drunkard's Hell: Ark Trad [No #]

Drunkard's Lone Child: Mer 1001-2 , Van VRS-9147, Rndr 0076

Drunkard's Wife: FLeg FSA-11

Drunken Driver: Fwys FA 2418, Rndr 0008

Drunken Hiccoughs [= Down to the Club]: Mar 9105

Drunken Hiccoughs: Mar 9105

Drunken Sailor: LC AAFC L26/27

Dry and Dusty: Cty 518, Cty 724

Dry Bones: Fwys FA 2952

Dryland Farmers: Ok OK 76004

Dry Town Blues: Cty 532

Duck Shoes Rag: Mar 9110

Ducks on (In) the (Mill) Pond: Cty 748, Mtn 302, Rndr 0089, Str STR 802

Dummy, The: JnAp JA 020

Dunbar: Rndr 1010

Dunlap: Mar 9101, UNC 0-8078-4083-1

Duplin County Blues: Cty 409 see also I Don't Love Nobody

Durang's Hornpipe #2: Rndr 0157

Durang's Hornpipe: Cty 707, GFS GFS 901, JEMF-105, Kan 306, MFFA 1001, Rndr 0237, Rndr 0194

Dusty Miller: Cty 202, Cty 724, Fwys FA 2379, GyEg 101, Her 12, Miss AH-002, Rndr 0037

Dying Boy's Prayer: OH OHS 90001

Dying Cowboy, The [B 1]: LC AAFS L20, NW 314/315, MFP MFP 002, BF 15502

Dying Girl: Fwys FE 34162

Dying Girl's Farewell: OH OHS 90031, Rndr 1008

Dying Hobo [H 3]: BF 15509, RCA LPV 548, LC AFS L61

Dying Mine Brakeman: LC AFS L60

Dying Mother: Har HL 7300

Dying Ranger, The [A 14]: Asch AH 3903, LC AAFS L28, MS 45008, Ph 1017

Dying Soldier: Mar 9109

Earl Johnson's Arkansaw Traveler: Cty 543 *see also* Arkansas Traveler

Early Bird Always Gets Worm: Rndr 0026

Early, Early in the Spring [M 1]: Rndr 0028, Tpc 12TS336

Early in the Morning: Prst INT 25009

East Bound Train: Hist HLP 8004, Rndr 0009, Van VSD-107/108

Easter Day: CT 6000

East Tennessee Blues: Fwys FA 2355, GyEg 101

East Texas Drag: Cty 410

East Virginia (Blues): Cty 712, Cty 739, Fwys FA 2317, Fwys FA 2953, Fwys FS 3810, Fwys FS 3828, Fwys FS 3829, GnHys GR712, Rndr 0237, OH OHS 90045, RCA LPV 507

East Virginia Blues No. 2: Har HL 7422, TL TLCW-02

Easy Rider: BF 15517, Fwys FTS 31007

Ebenezer: JnAp JA0059C

Echo Canyon *or* Hooray Hoorah the Railroad Is Begun: Fwys FA 2036, LC AAFS L30

Echoes of the Ozarks: Cty 520

Edom: LC AAFS L11

Edward [C. 13]: Fwys FA 2302, MC 1, GnHys GR714, LC AAFS L12, LC AAFS L57

Eighteen-O-Nine (1809): Asch AH 3831

Eighth Day of January: Fwys FS 3832

Eighth of January: Cty 518, Cty 527, Cty 531, Cty 541, GyEg 101, MS 45004, Miss AH-002, Prst INT 25006, LC AFS L2

Elder Bordee [C. 167]: FLeg FSA-15

Elephant March: BF BFX 15214

Eleven Cent Cotton: Rndr 1028

Elfin Knight, The [C. 2]: Fwys FS 3809

Elkhorn Ridge: Cty 717

Elk River Blues: AH AHS 003

Ella's Grave: Fwys FA 2365, Van VRS-9182

Ellen Smith [F 11]: Fly LP 546, Fwys FS 3828

Elzic's Farewell: Rndr 0047, KM 204, FPrm (No #)

Empty Cot in the Bunkhouse: Sytn STR 202

End of My Journey: Fwys FA 2352

Enforcement Blues, The: Mar 9104

Engineer Frank Hawk: Vet 103

Engineer on the Mogull: Rndr 1003

Engineer's Dream: Vet 103

Engineer's Last Run: Vet 103

Engineer, The: LC AFS L61

Engine One-Forty-Three [G 3]: Cam CAL 2473, Fwys FA 2951, RCA LPV 532

Erin-Go-Bragh [Q 20]: NW 239

Erin's Green Shore [Q 27]: BF 15003, Van VRS 9124

Essie Dear: Rndr 0065

Eternity (from the White Pilgrim): Fwys FS 3810

Eugene Butcher: AH AHR 007

Evalina Waltz: DU 33009

Evening Bells Are Ringing: RCA LPM 2772

Evening Rainbow Waltz: Rndr 0058

Evening Shade: Fwys FTS 31007, LC AAFS L11, Mar 9013

Evening Star Waltz: Cty 524, Her 22, Str STR 802

Evergreen Shore: JnAp 037

Everybody's Got To Be Tried: FLeg FSA-36

Everybody to the Puncheon: Cty 536

Everybody Two-Step: Cty 403

Everybody Will Be Happy over There: Mar 9101

Everybody Works but Father: Elek EKL-316, Roots 701

Every Day Dirt [Q 9]: BF 15505, Fwys FA 2366, Sm/Fwys SF 40012

Every Rose Grows Merry in Time [C. 2]: FLeg FSA-33

Every Time I Kneel and Pray: Rndr 0072

Exile of Arion: TFS 104

Expert Town (*or* The Oxford Girl) [P 35]: LC AAFS L12

Explosion in the Fairmount Mines: Rndr 1001

Export Gal [P 35]: Rndr 1029

Eyes Like Cherries: Fwys FA 2306

Factory Girl: Tst T-3301

Faded Coat of Blue: Bio RC 6004, CMH 107, JEMF 103

Faded Flowers: Cam ACL1-0501

Faded Picture on the Wall: Rndr 0008

Faded Roses: Fwys FA 2350

Fair and Tender Ladies: FLeg FSA-2, FLeg FSA-3, Fwys FS 3829, TL TLCW-06, Van VRS 9162

Fair Annie of Lochroyan [C. 76]: Fwys FA 2301

Fair at Batesland: Rndr 0158

Fair Ellender [C. 73]: UTP [cass, no #]

Fair Eyed Ellen [F 1a]: Cam CAL 797, Rndr 1006

Fair Fannie Moore [O 38]: NW 239, UICFC CFC 201

Fair Miss in the Gardens [N 42]: Fwys FA 2368

Fair Rosamund: FLeg FSA-32

Faithful Soldier: Tpc 12TS336, Van VRS-9170

Fall, Fall, Build Me a Boat [K 12]: Fwys FA 2342

Falling by the Wayside: Cty 540

Falling Leaf: Mar 9106

Falling of the Pine: LC AAFS L56

Fall on My Knees: Cty 709, Cty 741, Her 33

Falls of Richmond: WVUP 001

False Hearted Lover [F 1]: Ark Trad 002

False Hearted Lover's Blues: Fwys RBF 654

False Knight Upon Road [C. 3]: LC AAFS L21

False Sir John [C. 4]: Fwys FA 2301

Fame Apart from God's Approval: Hist HLP 8006

Famous Wedding: Fwys FE 34161

Fancy Nancy: BF 15505

Fanny Hill: Rndr 0058

Far Beyond the Blue Skies: OH OHCS 191

Far Beyond the Starry Sky: Fwys FA 2352, Rndr 0143

Fare Thee Well: Van VRS 9124

Fare Thee Well Old Ely Branch: Rndr 1002

Farewell, Earthly Joy: Rndr 0078

Farewell Mary Ann: Miss AH-002

Farewell Nellie: MCA VIM-4012

Farewell to Old Beaver: Fwys FA 2342

Farewell Waltz: DU 33015

Farewell Whiskey: Miss AH-002

Farmer Is the Man: Rndr 1026

Farmer Is the Man That Feeds Them All: Rndr 1026, NW 245

Farmer's Curst Wife [C. 278]: Atl SD-1346, BRI 002, FLeg FSA-22, Fwys FA 2362, LC AFS L1, Mar 9200 [cass], MC 1, NW 239, Ok OK 76004, Ph 1022

Farmer's Daughter: Rndr 1023

Farm Girl Blues: Cty 511, GHP LP 1001

Farm Land Blues: Fwys FA 2951

Farm Relief: De DL 4760

Farther Along: RCA 2100-2-R, SH SH-CD-3779, UICFC CFC 201, Van VRS 9162

Fatal Courtship [P 24]: OT 102

Fatal Derby Day, The: OH OHCS 314

Fatal Flower Garden [C. 155]: Fwys FA 2951

Fatal Wedding: Ark Trad [No #], Cty 517, OH OHCS 107

Fatal Wreck of the Bus: OT 107

Fat Back Meat and Dumplings: Rndr 0157

Fate of Chris Lively and Wife: Cty 522

Fate of Dewey Lee: BRI 004, CMH 116

Fate of Ellen Smith [F 11]: Cty 502, MS 45004

Fate of Talmadge Osborne: BRI 004, OHCS-173

Fate of the Battleship Maine: Brch 1945

Father Adieu: Atl SD-1349

Father Get Ready: Riv RLP 12-620

Father Grumble [Q 1]: LC AAFS L14

Father, Jesus Loves You: Atl SD-1349

Father's a Drunkard: Mar 9104

Fathers Have a Home Sweet Home: Rndr 0072

Father's Maid: Van VRS-9183

Fathers, Now Our Meeting Is Over: FLeg FSA-22

Fat Meat and Dumplings: MFFA 1001

Feast Here Tonight: SmFwys SF 40038, Mar 9013

Felipe: AFF 33-1

Few More Years Shall Roll, A: JnAp 037

F. F. V. [G 3]: AH AHR 009, Van VRS-9239

Fiddle-I-Fee: LC AAFS L14

Fiddler a Dram: TFS 103, Van VRS-9170

Fiddler's Blues: Cty 546

Fiddler's Convention in Georgia, A: Vet 107

Fiddler's Dream: Cty 547, Rndr 0020

Fiddling Soldier, The [P 14]: Kan 305

Fifty Miles of Elbow Room: Cam ACL1-0501, CMH 118

Fifty Year Ago Waltz: Rndr 0005

Fifty Years Ago: Ala Trad 103

Fifty Years from Now: Rndr 1026

Fifty Year Waltz: Arh 5001

Filipino Baby: Kan 305

Fillmore: LC AAFS L11

Fine Sally [P 9]: Fwys FA 2309

Fine Times at Our House: Fwys FS 3809, LC AFS L65-L66, WVUP 001, GFS GFS 901

Fingerprints Upon the Window Pane: OH OHCS 315

Finger Ring: LC AFS L68, Riv RLP 12-610

Fingers on Fire: Fwys FA 2306

Finley Preston: Rndr 0009

Fireman Save My Child: Rndr 1009

Fire on the Hillside: Fwys FES 34151

Fire on [In] the Mountain: Cty 709, Cty 791, Fwys FS 3811, Fwys FS 3839, Her 22, MS 45004, Prst FL 14030, Van VRD-107/108 *see also* Hog Eye, Sal Let Me Chaw Your Rosin

Firmly I Stand on Zion's Hill: UNC 0-8078-4083-1

First Lady Waltz: Arh 5018

First Whippoorwill Song: Kan 308, OH OHCS 314

Fisherman's Luck: CT 6002

Fisher's Hornpipe: Arh 5010, BRI 005, Cty 405, Cty 707, Cty 756, Kan 307, LC AFS L62, Str STR 802

Fish in the Mill-pond: Tpc 12TS336

Five Hundred Miles: Fwys FE 34162, Van VRS 9124

Five Leaf Clover: Rndr 0194

Five Miles: Cty 788

Five Miles out of Town: Cty 787

Five Nights Drunk [C. 274]: FLeg FSA-22

Five to My Five: Fwys FE 34162

Five Up: MS 45005

Flat Footed Charlie: Arh 5018

Flatwoods: Cty 756, Cty 788, Her 070, PB 005, Rndr 0020, Rndr 1005, Str STR 802

Flim-a-Lim-a-Lee [C. 2]: FLeg FSA-15

Flippin' Jenny: AH AHS 003

Floating down the Streams of Time: Alp ALP 202

Flock of Birds: Rndr 0157

Flop-Eared Mule: Ala Trad 103, Arb 201, Asch AH 3902, Bio BLP 6005, Cty 407, Cty 533, Cty 733, Fwys FA 2365, Ldr LE 4040, Ldr LEE 4045, OH OHCS 193, Rndr 0021 *see also* Karo, Ranger's Hornpipe, Roscoe Trillion

Flop House Blues: Rndr 0158

Florella [F 1]: TFS 106

Florida Blues: Cty 546, Her 22

Flower from My Angel Mother's Grave, A: BF 15517

Flower of the Morning: Rndr 1010

Flowers from Heaven: Rndr 0157

Flower from the Fields of Alabama: Cty 788

Flowers of Edinburgh: Rndr 0133, NW 239

Fly Around My Pretty Little Miss [Blue Eyed Girl]: BRI 005, Col CS 9660, Fly LP 546, FLeg FSA-23, Ldr LE 4040, Prst INT 25004, Riv RLP 12-650, Rndr 0021, Riv RLP 12-645, Riv RLP 12-610, Vet 107 *see also* Blue-Eyed Girl, Washing Mama's Dishes, Your Blue Eyes Run Me Crazy

Flying Clouds: Cty 540, Ldr LEE 4045

Flying Cloud, The [K 28]: Fwys FE 4001

Flying Engine: Cty 519

Flying Indian: Rndr 0057, Her 22

Flying U Bull: AFF 33-1

Fod: LC AFS L2

Foggy Mountain Breakdown: Prst FL 14010

Foggy Mountain Top: RCA LPM 2772, Riv RLP 12-650, SmFwys SF 40038, TL TLCW-02 *see also* On Some Foggy Mountain Top

Foggy Valley: MFP MFP 002

Following the Cowtrail [B 13]: BF BCD 15456, RCA LPV 522

Fond Affection: OTC 6001

Footprints in the Snow: Fwys FA 2355, Van VSD-107/108, OH OHCS 141, OH OHCS 314

Ford One Step: GyEg 101

Foreign Lander: FLeg FSA-3, Fwys FA 2317

Foreman Monroe [C 1]: Fwys FE 4001

For Goodness Sakes Don't Say I Told You: BF 15518

Forgotten Soldier Boy: Rndr 1026

Forgotten Waltz: GyEg 101

Forked Buck: FPrm (No #), Rndr 0047

Forked [Forky] Deer: AH AHS 001, AH AHS 003, Cty 202, Cty 501, Cty 527, Cty 707, Cty 756, GyEg 101, Kan 600, MS 45003, Ldr LEE 4045, Rndr 0028, Rndr 0037, Rndr 0058, Rndr 0194, Rndr 1010, Str STR 802, WVUP 001

Forked Horn Deer: Kan 307

Forks of Sandy: Hist HLP 8005, Rndr 0089

Forsaken Love: Cam CAL 586, Cty 409, Rndr 0143

Forsaken Lover: Fwys FA 2375

For Seven Long Years I've Been Married: BF 15510, Cty 408

Fort Benning Blues: Tst T-3302

Fort Smith: MFFA 1001

Fort Smith Breakdown: Cty 519

Fortune: Bio RC-6003, Cty 709, Cty 718, Cty 778, Fwys FA 3830, Fwys FS 3811, Prst FL 14030, Rndr 0028 *see also* Once I Had a Fortune

Fortunes: Fwys FA 2493

Forty: JnAp JA 001

Four Cent Cotton: Cty 506, Cty 514

Four Marys [C. 173]: GnHys GR714, LC AFS L7, Rndr 0017

Fourteen Days in Georgia: Cty 407, Ldr LE 4040, GyEg 101 *see also* Sixteen Days in Georgia

Fourth of July at a Country Fair: Rndr 1032

Fourth of July Waltz: Rndr 0133

Four Thousand Years Ago: OH OHCS 107, OH OHCS 314 *see also* I Was Born ...

Fox, The: PB 004, Rndr CD 11536

Fox Chase: Cty 789, FPrm 41942, Fwys FA 2317, Fwys FA 2368, Fwys FA 2380, Her 33, MS 45004, MFFA 1001, Prst INT 25004, SmFwys SF 40038, Van VRS-9182

Fox Horn / Cherokee Song of Welcome: Fwys FA 2358

Fox on the Run: NW 225

Fragments: Van VRS 9124

Frank Barbee Hornpipe: PB 006

Frank Bole: AFF 33-3

Frank DuPree: CT 6001

Frankie: Rndr 0032, Rndr SS-0145

Frankie [I 3]: OH OHCS 191

Frankie and Johnnie [I 3]: OH OHCS 112, OH OHCS 114, Fwys FA 2374

Frankie Baker [I 3]: Cty 741

Frankie Dean: Col CS 9660, OT 102

Frankie Silvers [E 13]: Fwys FA 2350, OT 102, Tpc 12T146

Frankie Was a Good Girl [I 3]: Fwys FA 2315

Frank James: FLeg FSA-2

Frank James, the Roving Gambler [L 16b]: LC AAFS L14

Franklin Blues: Arh 5012

Franklin County Blues: Mar 9110

Franklin D. Roosevelt's Back Again: Kan 305, OT 102

Frail Wildwood Flower: see Wildwood Flower

Freckles: AFF 33-3

Fred's Rambling Blues: Van VRS-9182

Free Again: Alp ALP 201

Free (a) Little Bird: BF 15501, Brch 1945, Col CS 9660, Cty 403, Cty 503, Fwys FA 2352, Fwys FA 2359, Fwys FA 2368, OH OHCS 191, Rndr 0065, Rndr 1033 *see also* I'm As Free ...

Freight #1262: FLeg FSA-27 *see also* Wreck of the 1262

Freighting from Wilcox to Globe: LC AAFS L30

Freight Train Moan: Cty 547

French Four: LC AFS L62

French Waltz: Cty 786, Mar 9025

Fresno Blues: Cty 523

Friendly Beasts, The: AH AHR 008

Frisco Blues: BF 15501

Frisky Jim: UMP No #

Frog and the Mouse: Mar 9200 [cass]

Froggie Went A-Courting: AH AHR 008, Atl SD-1350, BRI 002, Fwys FES 34151, JnAp JA 055, LC AAFS L12, Min JD-203, NW 239, NW 291, TFS 104, SH SH-CD-3786, Van VRS-9158, Van VRS-9239, Van VCD-45/46, Wstm SWN 18021

Frog in the Spring: FLeg FSA-15

Frolic: JnAp JA 049

From Earth to Heaven: Fwys RBF RF 51

From Jerusalem to Jericho: Rndr 1028, Vet 101

From Texas to Alaska: Kan 308

Frosty Morn: Sm/Fwys SF 40012 [CD]

Fruit Jar Drinkers: Brun 59001

Fuller Blues: Arh 5012

Funny When You Feel That Way: De DL 4404, OH OHCS 117

Fun's All Over: Rndr 0037

Fuzzy Rag: OH OHCS 114

Gabriel's Trumpet: Mar 9100

Galilee: Fwys FS 3828, OHS OF-1001

Gal I Left Behind [P 1b]: BF 15502, Fwys FH 5723

Gal That Got Stuck on Everything She Said: Fwys RBF RF 51

Gambler, The [E 14]: BF BCD 15456

Gambler's Lament: CT 6001

Gambler's Yodel: Van VSD-6576

Gambling Jim: OT 112

Gambling Man [H 4]: FLeg FSA-32

Gambling on the Sabbath Day [E 14]: Elek EKL-316

Garfield March: Cty 536, Kan 600

Garley's Fox Chase: FLeg FSA-24

Gary Dawson's Tune: HMM LP002

Gastonia Gallop: BF 15505

Gastony Song: Fwys FA 2418

Gate To Go Through: MS 45003

Gathering Buds: SH SH-CD-3779

Gathering Flowers (from the Hillside): Fwys FA 2418, Har HL 7280, OTC 6002

Gather Round the Camp Fire, Brethren: Fwys FA 2036

Gayest Old Dude in Town: BF 15503

Gay Paree: Ok OK 75003

Gee Whiz What They Done to Me: FLeg FSA-26

General Grant's Grand March: BRI 005

Gentle Annie: Rndr 0089

Gentle Boy, The: Ph 1022

Gentle Fair Jenny [C. 277]: Fwys FA 2302, Wstm SWN 18021, FLeg FSA-3

Gentle Maiden: JnAp 018

George Allen [C. 85]: Asch AH 3831

George Allen [G 3]: LC AFS L61

George Booker: Her 12

George Collins [C. 85]: Bio BLP 6005, Cty 502, FLeg FSA-22, Fwys FA 2360, Prst INT 13020, TFS cass

George Gann: PB 005

George Washington: Ark Trad 004, Cty 504, NW 236

Georgia Blues: Cty 514 *see also* Down Yonder

Georgia Buck: Her 22, Riv RLP 12-650, Rndr 0065, Van VRS-9152

Georgia Camp Meeting: Cty 201, Cty 532 *see also* Peaches down in Georgia

Georgia Hobo [H 2]: Rndr 1035

Georgia Man: Cty 544

Georgia Railroad: FSSM FSSMLP 150001-D, Rndr 0008

Georgia Row: Rndr 0032

Georgia's Three-Dollar Tag: Rndr 1003 *see also* Hesitation Blues

Georgia Volunteer, A: Ph 1020

Georgia Wagoner: Ala Trad 103, OH OHCS 192, Vet 107 *see also* Tennessee Wagoner, Texas Wagoner, Wagoner

Georgia Wobble Blues: Hist HLP 8003

Georgie: Cty 757, Tpc 12TS336

Georgie [C. 209]: LC AFS L68, Van VRS-9239

Get a Little Dirt on Your Hands: FLeg FSA-13

Get Along: OH OHCS 192

Get Along down to Town: LC AAFS L20

Get Along Home (Miss) Cindy: ACM ACM-1, Cty 518 *see also* Cindy

Get Along Little Doggies: MS 45008, MFP 0001, Rndr 1009

Get Away, Old Man, Get Away: OH OHCS 316, Rndr 0064

Get off Your Money: Ala Trad 103

Getting on the Train: Mer 1001-2

Getting up the Stairs: Cty 786

Get Up and Bar the Door [C. 275]: AH AHR 008, RRT LP-8073

Get Up in the Cool: Cty 202

Gid Tanner's Bucking Mule: Fwys FTS 31089 *see also* Bucking Mule

Ginseng: JnAp JA 001

Gippy Get Your Hair Cut: Cty 536

Gipson Davy [C. 200]: MFFA 1001

Girl I Left Behind (Me): LC AAFS L9, PB 004, Trad TLP 1007, FLeg FSA-17, Mar 9025, PB 005

Girl I Left Behind Me [*Original title*: Always Marry Your Lover] [P 1b]: Brun 59001

Girl I Left Behind [P 1b]: Prst INT 25004

Girl I Left in Danville [H 2]: CT 6000, Tst T-3301

Girl I Left (Loved) in Sunny Tennessee: BF BCD 15456, Cty 540, OHCS-173, Prst INT 13038

Girl I Love Don't Pay Me No Mind: Cty 547

Girl in Blue Velvet Band, The: Prst INT 13035, Prst INT 13038

Girl in the Hillbilly Band: Kan 305

Girl of Constant Sorrow: Van VRS-9182

Girl on the Greenbriar Shore: CMH 118

Girl That Wore the Waterfall, The [H 26]: AH AHR 007

Git Along Little Dogies: *see* Get Along ...

Give an Honest Irish Lad a Chance: Mar 9200 [cass], NW 239

Give Him One More As He Goes: Har HL 7300

Give Me a Chaw Tobacco: Mar 9110

Give Me Back My Fifteen Cents: Cty 541

Give Me Back My Five Dollars: BF 15519

Give Me Just a Little More Time: Rndr 0026

Give Me One More Chance: Fwys FA 2358

Give Me the Roses Now: Prst INT 13049

Give Me Your Love and I'll Give You Mine: CMH 112, OH OHCS 112 *see also* You Give Me ...

Give My Love to Nell: OH OHCS 107, OH OHCS 141, OH OHCS 317

Give the Fiddler a Dram: Cty 518, Fwys FA 2317, LC AAFS L20, Mer 1001-2, Tpc 12TS336 *see also* Dance All Night ...

Glen's Chimes: Atl SD-1350

Glide Waltz: MS 45005

Glory in the Meeting House: Fwys FTS 31016, LC AFS L2

Glory Is Rising in My Soul: Mar 9101

Glory Land: Fwys FA 2392

Glory Land Road: PB 006

Glory to God, My Son's Come Home: LC AFS L68

Glory to the Lamb: Har HL 7396

Go Away from Me, Young Man: FLeg FSA-2

God Be with You till We Meet Again: AFF 33-4

God Bless Them Moonshiners: Riv RLP 12-620

God Gave Noah the Rainbow Sign: Cam CAL 586, Cty 791, Har HL 7396, OH OHCS 117,

Riv RLP 12-649, TL TLCW-06, Van VRS-9183

God Holds the Future in His Hands: BB AXM2-5510

Go Dig My Grave: Fwys FA 2427

God Leads His Dear Children: Mar 9100

God Moves in a Windstorm: Rndr 0051, TFS 108

Go Down Moses: Rndr 0072

Go Down to Old Ireland: AH AHR 008

God Put a Rainbow in the Clouds: Rndr 0021

God's Gonna Ease My Troubling Mind: Fwys FA 2355

God's Gonna Trouble the Waters: OH OHCS 111

Go Easy Blues: RCA 8416-2-R [CD]

Go Home Little Girl: Rndr 0021

Go in and out the Window: PB 004

Going Across the Mountain: FLeg FSA-1

Going Across the Sea: Cty 521, Cty 542, MS 45004, Rndr 1004, Cty 787, Mer 1001-2

Going Around the (This) World (Baby Mine): Cty 787, Fwys FS 3828, OH OHCS 190, Rndr 1004 *see also* Banjo Picking Girl, Sugar Babe

Going Away Tomorrow [N 8]: FLeg FSA-23

Going Back to Alabama: Rndr 0034

Going Back to Jericho: Cty 515

Going Back to Kentucky: Rndr 0037

Going Back to Mississippi: Sytn STR 202

Going Back to My Texas Home: OH OHCS 111

Going Back to Sumter: Fwys FA 2306

Going Back to Texas: JEMF 101

Going Back West in the Fall: OT 107

Going Crazy: Cty 514 *see also* I Don't Love Nobody, Henpecked Man

Going down That Lonesome Frisco Line: BF 15504

Going down the Lee Highway: Cty 503, DU 33033

Going down the River: Cty 519, Rndr 0037 *see also* Davy Davy

Going down the (This) Road (Feeling Bad): Fwys FA 2418, Fwys FE 34162, Mar 9111, Trad 1007, Van VCD-45/46

Going down the Valley (One by One): ACM ACM-1, Cty 508, Cty 712, NW 236

Going down to Lynchburg Town: Cty 407

Going (Gwine) Back to Dixie: Cty 521

Going Home: Rndr 0058

Going Home This Evening: Rndr 1037

Going (on) down (in) Town: JnAp JA0055, Vet 107

Going Round This World: JnAp JA 010

Going to Boston: Van VRS-9183

Going to Chattanoogie: PB 006

Going to Georgia: FLeg FSA-24, Fly LP 546

Going to Jail: Cty 531

Going to See Friel Lowe: Her 070

Going to Stop Drinkin' When I Die: Rndr 1033

Going to Town: Cty 546

Going to Write Me a Letter: Rndr 0077

Going up Brushy Fork: Cty 536, Kan 600 *see also* Cripple Creek

Going up (down to) Cripple Creek: Rndr 1008 *see also* Cripple Creek

Going up to Hamburg: Miss AH-002

Going up Town: Mar 9111

Gol Darn Wheel [dB 38]: AFF 33-2, NW 314/315, Ok OK 75003, Ph 1017

Golden Bells: AH AHS 001

Golden Pen: Fwys FA 2315

Golden Slippers: BRI 005, KM 204, Ldr LEE 4045, OH OHCS 191, Van VRS-9182

Golden Willow Tree [C. 286]: FLeg FSA-2, LC AFS L7, LC AAFS L58, TFS cass

Gold Rush: Hoop 101, JnAp 030

Gold Watch and Chain: GV SC 03, OH OHCS 117

Go Long Mule: Cty 545

Gone to Kansas: Mar 9200 [cass]

Gone to View That Land: MFFA 1001

Gonna Catch That Train an' Ride: Arh 5011

Gonna Lay Down My Old Guitar: Van VRS-9170

Gonna Quit My Rowdy Ways: OH OHS 90031

Gonna Row My Boat: Fwys FA 2375

Gonna See My Mama: Mar 9013

Gonna Swing on the Golden Gate: Rndr 1003

Goodbye Booze: Cty 516, FSSM FSSMLP 150001-D, Mar 9104

Goodbye Dear Old Stepstone: Rndr 0065

Goodbye Little Bonnie: Cty 510, Hist BC 2433-1 *see also* Goodbye My Bonnie Goodbye

Goodbye Liza Jane: Cty 516, Rndr 0020

Goodbye Maggie: BB AXM2-5510, Prst FL 14035

Goodbye Mary Dear: Cty 516 *see also* Mary Dear

Goodbye My Bonnie [Lover] Goodbye: BF 15507, OH OHCS 190 *see also* Goodbye

Little Bonnie, There's More Pretty Girls Than One

Goodbye My Honey I'm Gone: Pu PU 3001

Goodbye Old Paint: LC AAFS L28, MS 45008, Rndr 0158, Rndr 1009

Goodbye Old Stepstone: OHCS-172

Goodbye to the Plains: CMH 112

Good Fellow: Cty 532

Good Morning and Old Owl: JnAp JA 001

Goodnight Waltz: Kan 600, Tak A 1013

Good Old Days of Adam and Eve: NW 239

Good Old Limburger Cheese: Kan 308

Good Old Man: TFS 104

Good Old Mountain Dew: Riv RLP 12-610

Good Old Rebel: LC AAFS L20

Good Old State of Maine: NW 239

Go On, Nora Lee: Rndr 1028

Gooseberry Pie: OH OHCS 107

Gospel Cannonball: OTC 6002

Gospel Is Advancing: Rndr 0078

Gospel Kindred, How I Love You: Rndr 0078

Gospel Plow: FPrm (No #)

Gospel Ship: Har HL 7280, TL TLCW-06

Go Tell Aunt Nancy: Atl SD-1350

Got No Honey (Sugar) Baby Now: Fwys FA 2374, FLeg FSA-36

Got the Drunken Blues: Mar 9104

Got the Jake Leg Too: Mar 9104

Go to Italy: Riv RLP 12-645

Go to Sleep Little Baby: Atl SD-1350, NW 291

Got the Farmland Blues: BF 15507

Got the Money, Too: Cty 545

Governor Al Smith: Cty 521

Go Wash in That Beautiful Pool: FLeg FSA-24, Rim Rlp-495

G Rag: Rndr 1032

Grandfather's Clock: SH SH-CD-3795

Grand Hornpipe: Rndr 0194

Grandma's Advice: Fwys FES 34151

Grandma's Chickens: MFP MFP 002

Grandpa's Quadrille: Ok OK 76004

Grandpa's Waltz: JEMF-105

Grand Picnic: MFFA 1001

Granny, Take a Look at Uncle Sam: Rndr 0037

Granny Went to Meeting with Her Old Shoes On: NW 226, Rndr SS-0145

Granny Will Your Dog Bite?: Cty 531, Cty 791, UMP No # *see also* Old Jake Gillie

Grapevine Twist: KM 204

Grasshopper Sitting on a Sweet Potato Vine: Her 070

Grave on the Green Hillside: Cam CAL 586

Graveyard Blues: HMM LP001, Prst INT 25004

Gravy and Bread: FLeg FSA-27

Gray Eagle: Hist HLP 8003, MS 45003, Mar 9013

Gray Goose: NW 291

Greasy Coat: Rndr 0018

Greasy String: CMF 011-L, Cty 756

Greasy Wagon: Cty 523

Great Big Billy Goat: Arh 5010

Great Big Taters (in Sandyland): Miss AH-002, Sytn STR 201 *see also* Sally Ann, etc.

Great Big Yam Potatoes: Miss AH-002

Great Explosion: FLeg FSA-18

Great Grand Dad: Mar 9106

Great Milwaukee Fire, The [G 15]: Ph 1020

Great Reaping Day: Cty 508, Fwys FA 2365

Great Speckle(d) Bird: Fwys FA 2427

Great Titanic, The [D 24?]: Brch 1945, Fwys FA 2375, FLeg FSA-17

Greenback Dollar: Arh F5002, Asch AH 3902, Cty 501, Cty 520, Cty 718, PB 005, Prst INT 13038, Prst INT 13020

Green Backed Dollar Bill: Cty 541

Green Bed, The [K 36]: TFS 106

Green Coffee: PB 004

Green Corn: AFF 33-4, Rim Rlp-495, UICFC CFC 201

Green Fields (of America): Fwys FA 2356, Ldr LE 4040, UICFC CFC 201

Green Ford Blues: Cty 777

Green Grass Grew All Around, And The: SH SH-CD-3786

Green Gravel: PB 004

Green Grows the Violets: Prst INT 13038

Green Grows the Willow Tree: Riv RLP 12-620

Green Grow the Lilacs: Rndr 0052

Green Mountain: Mer 1001-2

Green Mountain Polka: Cty 407

Green River March: Cty 403

Green Rolling Hills of West Virginia: BF 15003

Green Sally: Up: Atl SD-1350

Green Valley Waltz: Cty 503, Fwys FA 2379 *see also* Little Red Shoes

Greenwich: NW 205, Prst INT 25007

Green Willow Tree [C. 286]: Asch AH 3831

Grey Cat on the Tennessee Farm: Cty 521

Grey Eagle: Cty 202, Cty 409, Cty 703, Her 33, Kan 307, LC AAFS L21, OFA TALP-001, Rndr 0009, Rndr 0194, TFS 103

Grey Eagle Jig: Rndr 1010

Griffin's Fiddle Medley: GV SC 03
Grigsby's Hornpipe: Cty 202
Groundhog: Cty 504, Cty 713, Fwys FA 2366,
    Fwys FA 2314, Fwys FA 2360, Fwys FS 3811,
    JnAp JA 010, NW 226, Sm/Fwys SF 40012,
    Van VRS-9147, Van VCD-45/46
Grub Springs: LC AFS L2, LC AFS L62, Miss
    AH-002
Guide Me O Thou Great Jehovah: AH AHR
    009, JnAp JA 020, NW 294, Prst INT 25011,
    Riv RLP 12-620
Guitar Instrumental: UICFC CFC 301
Guitar Picking Sam: Elek EKL-316
Guitar Rag: Cty 523, Hist HLP 8002 see also
    Steel Guitar Rag
Guitar Waltz: Fwys FA 2379
Gunboat: AH AHS 003
Guy Reed [C 9]: UIP cass
Gyps of David [C. 200]: FLeg FSA-1
Gypsy (Gypsum) Davy [C. 200]: Elek EKLP-2,
    FLeg FSA-15, LC AFS L1
Gypsy Laddie [C. 200]: Fwys FA 2301
Gypsy Rag: DU 33009
Gypsy's Warning: Fwys FA 2427, OH OHCS
    315, Prst INT 13038
Gypsy's Wedding Day, The [O 4]: Fwys FA
    2362

Hackberry Trot: OT 101
Had the Key to the Kingdom: Alp ALP 202
Hairy Buck: Cty 789
Hale's Rag: Cty 542
Half Shaved: KM 204, KM 204, Fwys FA 2380,
    Rndr 0028
Half Shaved Nigger: HMM LP001
Hallelujah: NW 205
Hallelujah I'm a Bum: CMH 106, Rndr 1009
Hallelujah Side: Fwys FA 2315, Rndr 1008
Ham Beats All Meat: Cty 531
Hambone: Atl SD-1350
Hamilton's Special Breakdown: Ala Trad 103
Hammer Ring: Fwys FA 2306
Hand Cart Song: Fwys FA 2036, LC AAFS
    L30, Ok OK 75003
Hand in Hand We Have Walked Along
    Together: GHP LP 1001
Hand Me Down My Old White Hat: Rndr 0237
Hand Me Down My Walking Cane: BF 15509,
    CMH 106, Cty 718, FSSM FSSMLP
    150001-D, OHCS-172

Handsome Molly: Cty 513, DU 33033, FLeg
    FSA-1, Fwys FA 2355, Fwys FS 3811, OT
    102, Van VCS-45
Hanging Around the Kitchen 'Til the Cook
    Comes Home: GyEg 101
Hanging Johnny: NW 223
Hanging of Georgie [C. 209]: Asch AH 3831
Hang John Brown: Fwys FA 2315
Hangman Ballad [C. 95]: Fwys FA 3830, Fwys
    FA 2301, Fwys FH 5723, Mer 1001-2, Prst
    INT 25009, Van VRS-9183
Hannamariah: Fwys FA 2306
Happiest Days of All: Cam ACL1-0501, CMH
    107, OH OHCS 112, TL TLCW-06
Happy in Prison: CMH 112, OH OHCS 116
Happy or Lonesome: CMH 118, OH OHS
    90045
Hard, Ain't It Hard: SmFwys SF 40037
Hard for To Love: Rndr 1037
Hard Luck Blues: Fwys FA 2350, Fwys RBF
    654
Hard Road to Texas: Miss AH-002
Hard Times: Fwys FS 3828, TFS 108
Hard Times Blues: Hoop 101
Hard Times Come Again No More: Fwys FA
    2036
Hard Times in Coleman's Mines: Rndr 1002
Hard Times in Here: Tst T-3301
Hard Times in the Charleston Jail: Rndr 0018
Hard Working Miner: LC AFS L60
Harlan County Blues: Fwys FTS 31016, LC
    AFS L60
Hassett's Retreat: AH AHS 001
Haste to the Wedding: LC AAFS L9, LC AFS
    L62, UICFC CFC 201
Haul Away: LC AFS L68
Haul Away My Rosy: LC AFS L2
Haul the Bowline: LC AAFC L26/27
Haul the Wood Pile Down: LC AFS L68
Haunted Hunter: RCA LPV 522
Haunted Road Blues: NW 245
Haunted Wagon: Rndr 0018
Haunted Woods: AH AHR 007, Fwys FA 2355
Have a Feast Here Tonight: BB AXM2-5510,
    Prst FL 14010, Prst INT 13038, RCA
    8417-2-R
Have Courage To Only Say (My Boy To Say)
    No: CT 6002, Fwys FA 2036
Have No Desire to Roam: BB AXM2-5525
Haven of Rest: GnHys GR714
Hawaiian March: Tst T-3302

Hawaiian Nights: DU 33009

Hawk Caught (Got) the Chicken [and Gone]: Cty 202, Cty 712

Hawkins County Jail: Prst INT 25009

Hawkins' Rag: OH OHCS 193, OT 100, RCA 8416-2-R [CD]

Hawks and Eagles: DU 33002

Hearing Aid: Ok OK 76004

Heart of City That Has No Heart: OH OHCS 190

Heart That Was Broken: CMH 116

Heave Away: LC AAFC L26/27

Heave-Ho the Anchor: OH OHCS 190

Heaven Bells Are Ringing: MFFA 1001, OH OHS 90001

Heavenly Train: RCA 2100-2-R [CD]

Heavenly Vision: LC AAFS L11

Heaven's Radio: Har HL 7300

Heavy Hearted Blues: OT 112

Heavy-Loaded Freight Train: LC AAFS L21

Heel and Toe Polka: GFS GFS 901, GyEg 101

Heffinger's Fox Chase: Ldr LEE 4045

He Is Coming to Us Dead: Cty 513, Mar 9109

Hell Among the Round Peakers: Cty 718

Hell Among the Yearlings: Cty 202, Cty 733, Fwys FA 2379, Fwys FS 3811, Mar 9110

Hell Bound for Alabama: Cty 525 *see also* Rattler Treed a Possum, Shoot That Turkey Buzzard

Hell Bound Train: Rndr 1007, UICFC CFC 301

Hell Broke Loose in Georgia: Cty 526, Mar 9025

He'll Hold to My Hand: PB 006

Hell in Texas: UMP No #

Hello Central (Give My Heaven): Cam CAL 2554(e)

Hello Stranger: De DL 4404, OH OHCS 112, MCA MCAD-10088 [CD], TL TLCW-06

He'll Set Your Fields on Fire: Fwys FA 2357

Hell up Hickory Holler: Rndr 0089

Hen and the Rooster: Ok OK 76004

Hen Cackle: Arh 5018, Fwys FTS 31089, Cty 503, Cty 543 *see also* Cackling Hen, etc.

He Never Came Back: MCA VIM-4012, TL TLCW-06

Henpecked Man: BF 15510, Cty 408 *see also* Going Crazy, I Don't Love Nobody

Henry Clay Beattie: BF 15509, Cty 408, Cty 502

Henry Lee [C. 68]: Fwys FA 2951

Henry Whitter's Fox Chase: CMF 011-L

He Rambled: Cty 505

Herding Sheep for Granville Pace: Ok OK 76004

Here and There: Rndr 0072

Here Goes a Bluebird: HMM LP002

Her Name Was Hula Lou: BF 15507

He's Coming After Me: OHCS-172

He's Coming from Vietnam: Rndr 0008

Hesitation Blues: FPrm (No #), LC AFS L68 *see also* Georgia's Three Dollar Tag, Curley Headed Woman

He's up with the Angels Now: BF 15503

He Took a White Rose from Her Hair: Har HL 7344

He Went in Like a Lion: BF 15521, Ldr LEE 4045

He Who Died on Calvary's Mountain: Cty 789

He Will Set Your Fields on Fire: BB AXM2-5510

He Won the Heart of My Sarah Jane: BF 15519, Vet 105

Hey, Hey, I'm Memphis Bound: NW 223

Hey, Mr. Banjo: SmFwys SF 40037

Hicarmichael: Fwys FA 2418

Hiccup Oh Lordy: GnHys GR712

Hickman Rag: Rndr 1033

Hickman's Boys: TFS 105

Hickory Bow Story: GyEg 101

Hicks Carmichael: TFS 106

Hicks' Farewell: Fwys FA 2309, NW 294, Prst INT 25011

Hide-a-Me: FLeg FSA-24

Higgins' Farewell: Mer 1001-2

High Atmosphere: Rndr 0028

High Chin Bob: Ph 1017

High Grass Town: OH OHCS 315

Highlander's Farewell: Str STR 802

Highland Fling: LC AFS L62

High on a Mountain: Fwys FA 2493, Rndr 0021

High Silk Hat and a Gold Walking Cane: OH OHCS-177

High-Toned Dance: Hoop 101, AFF 33-2, Rndr 0158

Hightower: Fwys FA 2356

Highway 52: BRI 004

Highwayman, The [I 4]: Cty 516

Hignite Blues: LC AFS L60

Hill Lone and Gray, A: Cam ACL1-0047

Hills and Home: NW 225

Hills of Mexico: Fwys 2363

Hills of Old New Hampshire, The: OH OHCS 317

Hills of Roane County: Fwys FA 2352, TFS 103

Hink Cogar's Deer Ride: Rndr 0018

Hinkey Dinkee Dee: OH OHCS 193

Hiram Hubbard: Fwys FA 2426, Riv RLP 12-620

Hi Said the Blackbird: Fwys FA 2358

Hi Yo, Hi Yo: Sytn STR 202

Hobo Jack the Rambler: CT 6002

Hobo John: Bio RC-6002

Hobo Life: BF 15505

Hobo's Life, A: Ph 1022

Hobo Tramp: BF 15504

Hoedown: OHS OF-1001, Prst INT 13035

Hog Drivers: UICFC CFC 301

Hog Eye: Cty 518 *see also* Fire on the Mountain, Sal Let Me Chaw Your Rosin

Hog-Eyed Man: LC AFS L62, JnAp JA0059C

Hogs in a Corn Field: OHS OF-1001

Hold Fast to the Right: Brch 1944, CMH 116, MCA MCAD-10088 [CD], N&T 1001, Prst INT 13030

Holding to His Hand of Love: LC AFC L69-L70

Hold My Dying Head: TFS 108

Hold on to the Sleigh: Vet 101

Hold That (the) Wood Pile Down: Cty 545, Fwys RBF RF 51, Vet 101, Van VSD-9/10

Hold to God's Unchanging Hand: Rndr 0072

Hold Watcha Got: NW 225

Ho Lilly Ho [N 7]: Asch AH 3831

Holler Jimmy Riley Ho: Fwys FES 34151

Holliding (Hollyding) [Cindy]: Cty 757, Her 33, Rndr 0058 *see also* Back Step Cindy

Hollow Poplar: Fwys FA 2379, JnAp 030

Home Again Blues: Ala Trad 103

Home Again Medley: Vet 103

Home Brew Rag: Mar 9104

Home by the Sea: Cam CAL 2473

Home in Heaven, A: LC AFC L69-L70

Home in Louisiana: Arh F5002

Home in Tennessee: Cam CAL 2473

Home in the Sky: ACM ACM-1

Home of the Soul: Mar 9100

Home on the Range: BF 15502, BF BCD 15456, Mar 9106, MFP 0001

Homesick for Heaven: Rndr 0009

Homestead on the Farm: CMH 116, OH OHCS 112, RCA LPM 2772, Prst INT 13049

Home Sweet Home: Cty 515, Cty 524, Fwys FS 3848, JnAp JA 025, Rndr 0028, SmFwys SF 40037

Hometown Blues: Cty 403, OT 100

Hometown Rag: Cty 544

Home Valley Home: Rim Rlp-495

Homeward Bound: LC AAFC L26/27, NW 205

Honest Confession Is Good for the Soul: Vet 105

Honest Farmer: Rndr 1003

Honey Babe: JEMF 101

Honey Babe Blues: Fwys FA 2355

Honey in the Rock: CMH 112

Honeysuckle: Cty 540, Cty 709, Cty 741

Honeysuckle Rag: Fwys FA 2435

Honeysuckle Time: Cty 510, Hist HLP 8003

Honky Tonk Swing: Cam CAL 719

Hoof It: Tak A 1013

Hook and Line: Fwys FA 2368, Fwys FES 34151, JnAp JA0055, OH OHCS 191

Hooker's Hornpipe: UMP No #

Hooknose in Town [= Big Balls in Town]: Arh 5001

Hop High (Light) Ladies, the Cake's All Dough: BF 15503, Bio RC-6003, Cty 201, Hist HLP 8006, Hist HLP 8004, OH OHCS 193, Rndr 0057, Riv RLP 12-620, UIP [cass, no #] *see also* Miss McLeod's Reel, Did You Ever See the Devil, Mountain Reel

Hop, Old Rabbit, Hop: Fwys FA 2362

Horney Ewe, The: AH AHS 003

Horrid Boy, The: Ark Trad 002

Horse Shoe Bend: Cty 401

Hot Corn: Cold Corn: OHS OF-1001

Hot Times: Mer 1001-2

Hound Chase: GFS GFS 901

Hounds in the Horn: HMM LP001

House Carpenter [C. 243]: Ark Trad [No #], AH AHR 009, BRI 002, FLeg FSA-22, Fwys FA 2301, Fwys FA 2350, Fwys FA 2366, Fwys FA 2426, Fwys FA 2951, Fwys FS 3828, LC AFS L1, LC AFS L1, OH OHCS 316, OHS OF-1001, Prst INT 25003, Rndr 0051, Rndr 0058, Sm/Fwys SF 40012, TFS 103, TFS cass, Tpc 12T146, Van VRS-9147, Van VRS-9158

Housekeeper's Tragedy, The: OH OHCS 317

House of David Blues: Cty 547, Fwys FA 2379

House of Gold: PB 006, Rndr 0026

Howard Carey [E 23]: UIP cass

How Beautiful Heaven Must Be: Her 070, OH OHCS 317, Rndr 1028

How Came That Blood on Your Shirt Sleeve? [C. 13]: Rim Rlp-495, FS cass, FLeg FSA-11

How Can a Broke Man Be Happy?: CT 6000

How Can a Poor Man Stand Such Times and Live?: BF 15003, Rndr 1001

How Come You Do Me Like You Do?: Cty 411

How Firm a Foundation: Ark Trad 003, Van VRS-9158

How Great Thou Art: Arh 5012

How Happy Are They: LC AFC L69-L70

How Happy Is the Sportsman: LC AAFS L55

How I Got My Gal: Rndr 1035

How Long: Mar 9110

How Lovely Are the Faithful Souls: Rndr 0078

How Many Biscuits Can You [I] Eat?: Cty 712, RCA LPV 552

How Tedious and Tasteless the Hours: Rndr 0017

Hubbard: Van VRS 9162

Huckleberry Blues: OH OHCS 191

Hull's Victory: JEMF-105, LC AFS L62

Humansville: GyEg 101

Humpbacked Mule: Fwys FA 2359

Humphrey's Jig: Rndr 1010

Hungry and Faint and Poor: JnAp JA 020

Hungry Disgusted Blues: Rndr 1002

Hungry Hash House: see All Go Hungry Hash House

Hunky Dory: NW 226, Rndr SS-0145

Hunters of Kentucky, The [A 25]: OH OHCS 315, TFS 105

Hunting the Buck: Riv RLP 12-620

Husband and Wife Were Angry One Night: Hist HLP 8005

Hushabye: Mar 9200 [cass], Tpc 12TS336

Hush Little Baby (Don't You Cry): BF 15518, Elek EKLP-2, Wstm SWN 18021

Hutchison's Rag: Rndr 1007

Hymn My Mother Sang: ACM ACM-1

Hymns My Mother Sang: BB AXM2-5525

I Ain't a Bit Drunk: Mar 9104

I Ain't Going To [Gonna] Work Tomorrow: CMH 118

I Ain't Got Long To Stay: BF 15518

I Ain't Got No Use for the Women: Fwys FH 5723

I Ain't No Better Now: OH OHCS 193, Rndr 1023

I Ain't Nobody's Darling: Cty 535

I Am a Girl of Constant Sorrow:

I Am a Little Scholar: JnAp JA 020

I Am a Man (Girl) of Constant Sorrow: FLeg FSA-26, OH OHCS 190

I Am an Old Time Trapper: Ok OK 76004

I Am a Pilgrim: Riv RLP 12-617, Riv RLP 12-649, Van VSD-9/10

I Am a Poor Wayfaring Stranger: NW 294, Prst INT 25011

I Am a Traveling Creature: JnAp JA 001, Rndr 0051

I Am Bound for the Promised Land: CMF 011-L

I Am Gonna Marry That Pretty Little Girl: Hist BC 2433-1

I Am O'ershadowed by Love: NW 223

I Am on My Way to Heaven: Cty 508

I Am Ready To Go: ACM ACM-1

I Am Resolved: Cty 533

I Believe: Rndr 0021

I Believe It: ACM ACM-1

I Belong to This Band: Mar 9101

Iberia Breakdown: UMP No #

I Bless the Day: Rndr 0078

I Cannot Be Your Sweetheart: Cam CAL 2473, JEMF 101, OH OHCS 112 *see also* Pale Moonlight

I Can't Change It: JnAp JA 010

I Can't Stay Here by Myself: Ark Trad [No #]

I Can't Tell Why I Love Her: BF 15504,

I Can't Tell Why I Love You: CT 6000

Icy Mountain: OFA TALP-001

Ida Red: Arh 5001, Cty 791, Fwys FA 2380, Fwys FS 3811, Fwys FS 3828, JnAp JA 020, JnAp JA 049, Mer 1001-2, OH OHCS 141, OH OHCS 191, OH OHCS 192, RCA 8416-2-R, RCA LPV 507, Rndr 1008, PB 006

I Didn't Hear Anybody (Nobody) Pray: CT 6000, RCA 2100-2-R [CD]

I'd Like To Be in Texas: OH OHCS 316

I'd Like To Be Your Shadow in the Moonlight: Prst INT 13049

I Done Quit Drinking: Mer 1001-2

I Don't Drink-a Your Whiskey: Fwys FA 2306

I Don't Let the Girls Worry My Mind: ACM ACM-1

I Don't Like the Blues No How: GHP LP 1001

I Don't Love Nobody: DU 33015, Rndr 0133, Rndr SS-0145 *see also* Going Crazy, Henpecked Man

I Don't Want To Get Married: Fwys FA 2306

I Don't Want Your Greenback Dollar: JEMF 104

I Feel the Need of a Deeper Baptism: Rndr 0078

If He's Gone Let Him Go God Bless Him: Rim Rlp-495

If I Could Hear My Mother Pray Again: OH OHS 90001, Rndr 0052, Rndr CD 11536

If I Could Only Blot Out the Past: BF 15517

If I Die a Railroad Man: MS 45004, Pu PU 3001, RCA LPV 532

If I Lose Let Me Lose: Arh F5002, Cty 509

If I Was a Mining Man: FLeg FSA-24

I Found You Among the Roses: Har HL 7300

If the Light Has Gone Out in Your Soul: NW 245

If There Wasn't Any Women in the World: Rndr 0008

If the River Was Whiskey: Cty 509, OT 100

If the Wind Had Only Blown the Other Way: AH AHR 010

If You Believe: Rndr 0072

If You Want To Go A-Courting: FSSM FSSMLP 15001-D, Cty 405

If You Want To Make a Preacher Cuss: TFS 106

I Gave My Love a Cherry: OH OHCS 314

I Get My Whiskey from Rockingham: Cty 507, Cty 543 *see also* Cindy

I Got a Bulldog: Hist BC 2433-1

I Got Her Boozy: OH OHS 90031

I Hate the Capitalist System: Rndr 0051 *see also* I Hate the Company Bosses

I Hate the Company Bosses: FLeg FSA-26 *see also* I Hate the Capitalist System

I Hate To Be Called a Hobo: OH OHCS-177

I Have An Aged Mother: CMH 107, OH OHCS 117

I Have Letters from My Father: FLeg FSA-26

I Have Lost You Darling, True Love: DU 33033, OHCS-157

I Have No Loving Mother Now: BF 15510, Cty 408, OH OHCS 116 *see also* Careless Love

I Have No Mother Now: Cty 712, GnHys GR712

I Have No One To Love Me (but the Sailor on the Deep Blue Sea): Cam CAL 2554(e), CMH 107

I Heard My Mother Weeping: Tpc 12TS336

I Heard Somebody Call My Name: BF 15510

I Heard the Voice of Jesus Say: UNC 0-8078-4083-1

I Hear the Low Winds Sweeping: Rndr 0051

I Hope I Live a Few More Days: Asch AH 3903

I Hunger and Thirst: Rndr 0078

Ike Ward: PB 003

I Know My Name Is There: Rndr 1008

I Left Her at the River: BF 15504

I'll Be All Smiles Tonight: Ark Trad 004, BF 15501, CMH 107

I'll Be Glad When You're Dead You Rascal You: N&T 1001

I'll Be Home Some Day: Cam CAL 2554(e)

I'll Be Satisfied: OHCS-173

I'll Be There: AH AHS 001

I'll Be True to the One That I Love: Cty 739

I'll Be Washed: BF 15507

I'll Hit the Road Again, Boys: NW 239

I'll Keep Loving You: JnAp 032

I'll Keep My Skillet Good and Greasy: see Keep My ...

I'll Lead a Christian Life: Mar 9100

I'll Live On: SH SH-CD-3779

I'll Meet My Mother After All: Bio BLP 6005

I'll Never Be Lonesome in Heaven: Fwys FA 2358

I'll Never Forsake You: Har HL 7344

I'll Never Get Drunk No More: FLeg FSA-1, Mar 9104

I'll Not Marry at All: Prst INT 13020

I'll Remember You, Love, in My Prayers: OH OHCS 314

I'll Rise When the Rooster Crows: Cty 504

I'll Roll in My Sweet Baby's Arms: OT 101

I'll Sell My Hat, I'll Sell My Coat: LC AAFS L55

I'll Spend and Be Spent: Rndr 0078

I'll Tickle Nancy: BF 15519

I Looked and Lo a Lamb: Rndr 0078

I Lost My Girl (New Cut Road): Rndr 1035

I Love Coal Miners, I Do: Rndr 1002

I Loved You Better Than You Knew: OH OHCS 317

I Loved You So True: BF 15521 *see also* I'll Remember You Love, in My Prayers

I Love Little Willie: Rndr 0051

I Love Mother: I Love Her Way: Rndr 0078

I Love My Mountain Home: GHP LP 1001

I Love My Rooster: Fwys FA 2358, OH OHCS 314

I Love My Sweetheart the Best: BF 15509

I Love To Talk to Jesus: OHCS-173

I'm A-Going Away in the Morn: De DL 4760

I'm Alone, All Alone: Fwys FA 2365

I'm Alone in This World: JnAp 037

I'm a Long Time Traveling Away from Home: NW 245

I'm a Long Time Traveling Here Below: Rndr 0083, FLeg FSA-36

I'm Always Whistling the Blues: BF 15501

I'm an Old Bachelor: Tpc 12T146

I Married Me a Wife: TFS 106

I'm As Free a Little Bird As I Can Be: N&T 1001 *see also* Free Little Bird

I'm a Swede from North Dakota: UICFC CFC 301

I'm Bound To Ride: Cty 546, RCA LPV 507

I'm Coming Back, but I Don't Know When: Prst INT 13049

I'm Drifting Farther from You: Rndr 1028

I Mean To Live for Jesus: Rndr 1001

I Met a Handsome Lady: Fwys FA 2315

I'm Free, I've Broken the Chains: Rndr 1028

I'm Getting Ready To Go: Cty 411, OH OHCS 114

I'm Glad My Wife's in Europe: Fwys FA 3833, Rndr 1003

I'm Glory Bound: Rndr 0026

I'm Going Away in the Morn: Cty 541

I'm Going Back to Jericho: Fwys FA 2355

I'm Going Back to North Carolina: BF 15508, FLeg FSA-1 *see also* My Home's Across the Blue Ridge Mountains

I'm Going down by the River of Jordan: LC AFC L69-L70

I'm Going Home To Die No More: Mar 9101

I'm Going That Way: FLeg FSA-23

I'm Going to Georgia: BF 15507, Fwys FE 34161, OH OHCS 114, Pu 3001 *see also* Fly Around My Pretty Little Miss, The Girl I Left Behind Me

I'm Going To Leave Old Arkansas: Cty 519

I'm Going To Organize: FLeg FSA-26

I'm Going To Take the Train to Charlotte: UIP [cass, no #]

I'm Goin' To Walk with My Lord: Fwys FS 3839

I'm Gonna Leave Old Texas Now: Fwys FH 5723

I'm Gonna Lay My Burdens Down: SH SH-CD-3779

I'm Gonna Let It Shine: Fwys FA 2357

I'm Gonna Ride on that Cloud: Prst INT 13020

I'm Gwine Back to Dixie: Cty 532

I'm Just Here To Get My Baby out of Jail: Arh F5002, OHS OF-1001, BB AXM2-5525, RCA 8417-2-R, Rndr CD 11536

I'm Leaving You, Sweet Florine: Rndr 0034

I'm Leaving You Woman: Cty 777

I'm Living on Higher Ground: PB 006

I'm Nine Hundred Miles from Home: Rndr 1003, Vet 103

I'm Nobody's Darling on Earth: Cty 408

I'm Not Ashamed To Own My Lord: UNC 0-8078-4083-1

I'm Not Living: FLeg FSA-13

I'm Not Turning Backward: OH OHS 90001

I'm Old but I'm Awfully Tough: MFFA 1001

I'm Only on a Journey Here: Fwys FA 2357

I'm on My Journey Home: NW 223, Prst INT 25011

I'm Ragged but I'm Right: Cty 411

I'm Redeemed-Alcoa Quartet: CMF 011-L

I'm Running on the River: NW 291

I'm Sad and Blue: Cty 520, DU 33009

I'm Satisfied: OH OHCS 192, Rndr 1005

I'm S-A-V-E-D: Rndr 1032, Rndr CD 11536

I'm Sitting on Top of the World: JEMF 101, Prst INT 13049

I'm So Glad He Found Me: PB 006, UNC 0-8078-4084-X

I'm Standing on the Solid Rock: OFA TALP-001

I'm the Child To Fight: De DL 4760, Hist HLP 8006

I'm the Man That Rode the Mule Around the World: Cty 540, Fwys FA 2350 *see also* I Was Born About Ten Thousand Years Ago, Four Thousand Years Ago

I'm Thinking Tonight of My Blue Eyes: Cam CAL 586, Har HL 7422, OH OHCS 111

I'm Troubled: Fwys FA 2366, Sm/Fwys SF 40012 [CD]

I'm Tying the Leaves So They Won't Come Down: Brch 1944

I'm Working on a Building: OH OHS 90045, RCA 2100-2-R, OTC 6001

In a Cottage by the Sea: BF 15521

In a Little Village Church Yard: CMH 112, OT 107, Prst INT 13049

In a Lonely Graveyard: Rndr 0008

In a Village by the Sea: OH OHCS 315

In Bonny Scotland [N 2]: FLeg FSA-33

In Came the Owl: TFS 104

Indiana Hero, The [F 16]: Fwys FS 3809

Indian Creek: Cty 547

Indian Eat the Woodpecker: Miss AH-002

Indian Love Call: JnAp 032

"Indian" Songs: Rndr 0051

Indian Tribes of Tennessee: JnAp JA 020

Indian War Whoop: Cty 520, Cty 528, Fwys FA 2952, Miss AH-002

In Dublin City [L 12]: FLeg FSA-23

I Need the Prayers: BB AXM2-5525

I Never Did Believe: Rndr 0078

I Never Go There Anymore [The Bowery]: Cty 545

I Never Will Marry [K 17]: Cam CAL 2554(e), OH OHCS 117, Fwys FA 2375

In London City [P 24]: Fwys FA 2374

In My Dear Old Southern Home: BB AXM2-5510

In My Old Cabin Home: UIP [cass, no #]

In New York: Arb 201

In Scotland Town [C. 17]: LC AFS L65-L66

Interstate 40: FLeg FSA-13

In the Blue Hills of Virginia (on the Trail of the Lonesome Pines): OTC 6002

In the Concert Garden: Rndr 0036

In the Golden Bye and Bye: OHCS-173

In the Hills of Roane County: Cam CAL 797, Rndr 1006, Rndr CD 11536

In the Last Chance Saloon: Kan 308

In the Pines: Cam CAL 719, Col CS 9660, Cty 547, Cty 789, Fwys FA 2368, Fwys FA 3833 *see also* The Longest Train

In the Resurrection Morning: Fwys FES 34151

In the Shadow of Clinch Mountain: MCA VIM-4012, MCA MCAD-10088 [CD]

In the Shadow of the Pine: BF 15510, Cty 408, Cty 504, CMH 112, MCA VIM-4012

In the Steps of Light: Rndr 1033

In the Studio: Arb 201

In the Sweet Bye and Bye: Rndr 0001

In the Woodpile: Cty 506

Intoxicated Rat: RCA LPV 507, RCA 8417-2-R, Van VRS-9147, Van VRS-9152

In Zepo Town [M 32]: Fwys FA 2309

I Once Had a Sweetheart: Mar 9109

I Once Loved a Sailor: Hist HLP 8005

I Once Loved a Young Man: OT 107

I Only Want a Buddy (Not a Sweetheart): Elek EKL-316, OH OHCS 112

Iowna: Her 22

Ireland's Green Shore [Q 27]: Rndr 0018

I Remember Calvary: OHCS-172

I Ride an Old Paint: Fwys FH 5723

Irish Police: BF 15504

Irish Washerwoman: AFF 33-2, LC AAFS L9, PB 005, SmFwys SF 40037

I Rode Southern, I Rode L. & N.: LC AFS L61

Iron Merrimac: LC AFS L29

Isaac Medler: LC AFS L68

I Saw a Man at the Close of Day: Rndr 0009, Van VSD-107/108, Cty 513

I Saw the Face of Jesus: UNC 0-8078-4084-X

I Saw the Light: GV SC 03

I Saw the Wood: Tst T-3301

I See God in Everything: Rndr 0026

I Shall Know by the Prints of the Nails in His Hand: OH OHCS 190

I Shall Not Be Moved: Riv RLP 12-645, Rndr 1035, UNC 0-8078-4084-X

Island Unknown, Parts 1 and 2: Sytn STR 201

It Ain't Gonna Rain No Mo': Vet 107

Italy: CT 6001

I Tickled Her Under the Chin: Rndr 0034

It Is Better Farther On: CMH 116

It Is No Secret: BF BCD 15456

It Just Suits Me: Rndr 1035

It'll Aggravate Your Soul: CMH 107, TL TLCW-06

It'll Never Happen Again: Mar 9110

It Might Have Been Worse: DU 33009

It Rained a Mist [C. 155]: Prst INT 25003, Rim Rlp-495, Rndr 0020

It Rained Five Days: Fwys FES 34151

I Truly Understand You Love Another Man: CT 6001, Rndr 1037, NW 236

It's a Beautiful Doll: JnAp JA 055

It's a Long, Long Road To Travel Alone: Har HL 7300

It's a Long Way to Tipperary: Vet 107

It's a Shame To Whip Your Wife on Sunday: Rndr 1003

It's a Wonder: FLeg FSA-27

It's Hard To Leave You Sweet Love: BF 15521, OT 102

It's Just the Same Today: TFS 108

It's Moving Day: Cty 509

It's Nobody's Business: Rndr 0237

It's None of Your Business: Cty 409

It's Sinful To Flirt: Hist HLP 8004

It Was Midnight on the Stormy Deep [M 1]: Rndr CD 11536

It Won't Be Long: Arh 5001

It Won't Be Long till My Grave Is Made: Cty 508

I've Always Been a Rambler [P 1b]: Cty 502, Cty 513, Rndr 0021

I've Been a Hard-Working Pilgrim: Rndr 0072

I've Endured: Fwys FA 2493, Rndr 0077, Her 12

I've Got a Gal in Baltimore: Mar 9111

I've Got a Gal on Sourwood Mountain: Cty 544

I've Got a Mother: Riv RLP 12-620

I've Got No Honey Babe Now: Mar 9110

I've Got the Big River Blues: RCA 8417-2-R [CD]

I've Got the Mourning Blues: Fwys RBF RF 51

I've Had a Big Time Today: Cty 546

I've Had a Big Time Tonight: Fwys FTS 31007

I've Lost My Love: Cty 409 *see also* Careless Love

I Want a Nice Little Fellow: BF 15509, FC FC-014

I Want My Black Baby Back: Mar 9110

I Want My Rib: Rndr 0005

I Want Some Home Brew: Mar 9104

I Want To Be a Cowboy's Sweetheart: NW 314/315

I Want To Be a Real Cowboy Girl: NW 314/315, Sytn STR 202

I Want To Be Loved: OH OHCS 112

I Want To Be Where You Are: OH OHS 90031

I Want To Go Home: Prst INT 13030

I Want To Go There Don't You: Mar 9100

I Want To Go Where Jesus Is: CMF 011-L, Rndr 1037

I Want To Go Where Things Are Beautiful: Rndr 0076

I Want To Know More About My Lord: Rndr 0072

I Want To Love Him More: Van VCD-45

I Was a Stranger: Van VCD-45

I Was Born Four (Ten) Thousand Years Ago: BF 15508, FLeg FSA-24 *see also* I'm the Man That Rode the Mule Around the World, Four Thousand Years Ago

I Was Born in Pennsylvania [E 15]: BF 15508

I Went Out a'Hunting: AFF 33-4

I Went To See My Suzie: FLeg FSA-23

I Went To See My Sweetheart: BF 15521 [= If One Won't Another One Will]

I Went up on the Mountain: Riv RLP 12-617

I Will Arise: Ark Trad 004, Asch AH 3902

I Will Meet You in the Morning: OHCS-173

I Will Walk with My Children: Rndr 0078

I Wish I Had Never Met You: Rndr 1029

I Wish I Was a Mole (In the Ground): Fwys FA 2953, Fwys FE 34162, LC AAFS L21 *see also* Darling Where You Been So Long

I Wish I Was a Single Girl Again: BF 15508, UTP [cass, no #]

I Wish I Was in Heaven Sitting Down: Van VRS-9183

I Wish I Was Single Again: Cty 411, N&T 1001

I Wish I Were a Single Girl: Prst INT 13030

I Wish I Were a Single Girl Again: Fwys FA 2317

I Wish My Baby Was Born: Rndr 0028

I Wonder How the Old Folks Are at Home: Prst FL 14010

I Wonder If You Feel the Way I Do: Cam CAL 719

I Wonder When I Shall Be Married: FLeg FSA-3, OH OHCS 316

I Wonder Where My Darling Is Tonight: OTC 6002

I Won't Be Worried: Cty 404

I Wouldn't Mind Dying: JEMF 101

Jack and Joe: Fwys FES 34151, JnAp JA 010, Rndr 0020

Jack and Mae: Prst FL 14035

Jackaro [N 7]: FLeg FSA-3, Wstm SWN 18021

Jack Danielson's Reel: GyEg 101, UMP No #

Jack Haggerty [C 25]: LC AAFS L56

Jackie's Gone A-Sailing [N 7]: LC AAFS L21

Jack (Jackie) Monroe [N 7]: Cty 534, Rndr 0064

Jack of Diamonds: AH AHS 003, BF 15502, Cty 723, Cty 724, Fwys FH 5723, JEMF 104, LC AAFS L14, Tak A 1013, Van VRS-9182 *see also* Rye Whiskey, etc.

Jackson County: OH OHCS 141 *see also* Uncle Dave's Travels, Pt. 2

Jacob's Ladder: Fwys FA 2365, Mar 9100

Jailer's Daughter: Kan 305

Jailhouse Blues: CMH 106

Jailhouse Rag: Cty 523

Jake and Roanie: Hoop 101

Jake and Rooney and the Bald-Faced Steer: Shoe SGB 1

Jake Gillie: Cty 717, Rndr 0057 *see also* Old Jake Gillie, Granny Will Your Dog Bite

Jake Leg Blues: Mar 9105

Jake Leg Wobble: Cty 528

Jake Walk Blues: BF 15501, RCA 8417-2-R [CD]

James Bird [A 5]: Ph 1020
James MacDonald: Ph 1020
Jamestown Exhibition: OT 101
Jam on Gerry's Rock [C 1]: AH AHR 007, LC
    AAFS L56, NW 239
Japanese Breakdown: OT 100
(Old) Jaw Bone: Cty 518, Fwys FA 2317, RCA
    LPV 552
Jay Gould's Daughter: JnAp JA 009
Jay Legg: LC AFS L65-L66
J. B. Marcum [E 19]: Brch 1945
Jealous Brothers [M 32]: FLeg FSA-22
Jealous Hearted Me: De DL 4404, OH OHS
    90045, TL TLCW-06
Jealous Lover [F 1]: BRI 002
Jealous Mary: Cty 540
Jealous Sweetheart: CMF 011-L
Jed Hobson: FLeg FSA-15
Jeff Davis: PB 003
Jefferson St. Rag: Cty 523
Jennie Jenkins: Atl 1347, Fwys FP 40, LC AFS
    L2, Fwys FA 2352, Mer 1001-2
Jenny Get Around: JnAp JA0055
Jenny Johnson: Her 33
Jenny Lind Polka: Cty 201
Jenny Lynn: SmFwys SF 40037
Jenny in the Cotton Patch: Cty 788, DU 33014
Jenny on the Railroad: Cty 528
Jenny Put the Kettle On: Fwys FS 3832, Mer
    1001-2, MFFA 1001
Jerry, Go (Will You) Ile That Car: LC AFS
    L61, RCA LPV 532, Rndr 1009
Jerusalem Mourn: HMM LP001
Jesse James [E 1]: Arh 5012, Bio RC-6003,
    Brch 1945, Fwys FS 3832, LC AAFS L20,
    SmFwys SF 40037, RCA LPV 548
Jesus Appeared in a Barroom: Fwys FTS 31016
Jesus, Grant Us All a Blessing: JnAp 037
Jesus Is a Rock: UNC 0-8078-4083-1
Jesus Is Coming Soon: LC AFC L69-L70
Jesus Is My Only Friend: LC AFS L68
Jesus Is Precious to Me: JEMF 103
Jesus Is Real: OFA TALP-001
Jesus Leads I'll Follow On: Mar 9101
Jesus Reigns: JnAp JA 020
Jesus Says Go: Fwys FA 2418
Jig: NW 226, Rndr 0194
Jigs in E Minor: JEMF-105
Jim Along Josie: FLeg FSA-15, GnHys GR712
Jim and Me: Mar 9104, NW 294, Prst INT
    25011

Jim Blake's Message: De DL 4557 see also Jim
    Blake the Engineer; Jim Blake
Jim Blake the Engineer: CT 6001 see also Jim
    Blake's Message; Jim Blake
Jim Blake (Your Wife Is Dying): FLeg FSA-18,
    Fwys FA 2427 see also Jim Blake's Mes-
    sage; Jim Blake the Engineer
Jim Chapman Schottische: Rndr 0034
Jim Crack Corn: NW 291
Jim Gunther and the Steer: Prst INT 13020,
    Riv RLP 12-617
Jimmie and Sallie: CT 6000
Jimmie Brown the Newsboy: OTC 6001
Jimmie's Blue Heaven: Tst T-3302
Jimmie Settleton: FLeg FSA-24
Jimmy Clark: Mtn 303
Jimmy in the Swamp: UMP No #
Jimmy Johnson: AH AHS 001, AH AHS 003,
    LC AFS L65-L66
Jimmy Randal (Randolph) [C. 12]: Mar 9200,
    Rim Rlp-495
Jimmy Rogers Mixture: AH AHS 001
Jimmy's Texas Blues: Van VSD-9/10
Jimmy Sutton: Atl 1347, Cty 534, Cty 757, Cty
    534, Tpc 12TS336 see also Old Jimmy Sut-
    ton
Jim Sapp Rag: Fwys FA 2379
Jinny Nettles: UMP No #
Jobal Hunter [C. 18]: TFS cass
Jobbin' Getting There: Cty 542
Job I Left Behind: Van VRS-9182
Joe Bowers [B 14]: FLeg FSA-2, JnAp JA 049,
    LC AAFS L30, Ph 1022, Tst T-3302, Tpc
    12T146
John Brown: Atl 1347
John Brown's Dream: Cty 524, Cty 713, Cty
    717, Mtn 302, Trad TLP 1007
John Greer's Tune: FLeg FSA-17
John Hardy (Was a Desperate Little Man) [I 2]:
    Asch AH 3903, Bio RC-6002, Bio RC 6004,
    Cty 741, Cty 748, Cty 757, FLeg FSA-17,
    FPrm 41942, Fwys FA 2360, Fwys FA 2433,
    Fwys FA 2951, Fwys FA 3833, Fwys FS 3810,
    Fwys FS 3832, GnHys GR712, Hist BC
    2433-1 Rndr 0021, Rndr 0237
John Henry (Hardy) [I 2]: FLeg FSA-11
John Henry [I 1]: Alp APL 202, Atl 1347, Bio
    RC-6003, Brch 1945, Cty 502, Cty 543, Cty
    729, Cty 748, Cty 757, Fly LP 546, Fwys FA
    2315, Fwys FA 2317, Fwys FA 2365, Fwys
    FA 2392, Fwys FA 2435, Fwys FA 2951,

Fwys FES 34151, Fwys FS 3810, Fwys FS 3839, GnHys GR712, JnAp JA0055, JnAp JA 010, LC AFS L2, Mtn 305, OH OHS 90031, OHS OF-1001, Riv RLP 12-610, Riv RLP 12-645, Rndr 0001, Rndr 1005, SH SH-CD-3786, SmFwys SF 40037 (2 versions), Trad 1007, Tst T-3302, Rndr 0237

John J. Curtis [G 29]: LC AAFS L16

John Lover Is Gone: Fwys FA 2380, Fwys FS 3832

Johnnie Get Your Gun: Cty 544

Johnny and Jane, Parts 1 and 2: Rndr 1007

Johnny Boker (Booger): Cty 786, LC AAFC L26/2, Rndr 0018

Johnny Carroll's Camp: LC AAFS L56

Johnny Cuckoo: Atl SD-1350

Johnny Don't Come Home Drunk: GyEg 101

Johnny Doyle [M 2]: FLeg FSA-22, Fwys FA 2309

Johnny Goodwin: CMF 011-L, Mar 9111

Johnny Gray: Cty 545, Fwys RBF RF 51

Johnny Lover: Cty 531

Johnny, Oh, Johnny: FLeg FSA-22

Johnny O'Lou: Fwys FS 3848

Johnny Randall [C. 12]: FLeg FSA-15

Johnny Sands [Q 2]: Tpc 12T146

Johnny's Gone to War: Cty 717, Mtn 305

Johnny Troy [L 21]: TFS-106

Johnny Was a Miller Boy: PB 004

Johnny Wilson: Rndr 0064

John Rawl Jamieson: Rndr 0032

Johnson Boys: Cty 405, Cty 757, Mar 9109, FLeg FSA-23, Fwys FA 2360, Fwys FS 3811, Pu 3001, Trad TLP 1007

Johnson City Blues: Cty 511

Johnson City Rag: Cty 403, Cty 501, Cty 507

Johnson Gal: Col CS 9660, Cty 529

Johnson's Old Gray Mule: Atl SD-1350, Cty 543, Prst INT 13035, Prst FL 14030, Riv RLP 12-650, Rndr 0001, Rndr 1032, RCA 8416-2-R

Johnson's Road: FLeg FSA-15

Johnstown Flood [G 14]: NW 239

John's Trip to Boston: UIP [cass, no #]

John the Baptist: Rndr 0026

Join the C. I. O.: Rndr 1002

Joke on the Puppy: Miss AH-002, Cty 756 *see also* Rye Straw

Joking Henry: Cty 513

Jolly Blacksmith: Cty 542

Jolly Old Dutchman, The: AH AHR 010

Jolly Old Time Farmer: FLeg FSA-13

Jones County: Miss AH-002

Jordan Is a Hard Road to Travel: Fwys RBF RF 51, Vet 105 *see also* Other Side of Jordan

Josh and I: Cty 536

Joy Among the Angels: Mar 9101

Juba: Fwys FA 2309

Jubilee: Elek EKLP-2, GnHys GR714, Rndr 0072, Wstm SWN 18021

Juice of the Forbidden Fruit: Prst INT 25006

Julie Ann Johnson: Str STR 802

Julie Girl: FC FC-014

Julie Jenkins: Fwys FA 2360, Tpc 12TS336

Jump Fingers: UMP No #

Jump Jim Crow: Her 33

June Apple: Cty 709, Cty 713, Cty 718, Fwys FA 2380, Prst INT 25004, Mtn 302

June Rose Waltz: Cty 401

Just a Closer Walk with Thee: Elek EKL-316

Just a Few More Days: JEMF 101, MCA VIM-4012, OH OHCS 116

Just a Little Talk with Jesus: Rndr 1002

Just Another Broken Heart: De DL 4557, Fwys FA 2375, OH OHCS 112, OH OHS 90045

Just as the Sun Went Down: OHCS 315

Just a Strand from a Yellow Curl: Rndr 0052

Just Because: Fwys FA 2306, Rndr 0001, RCA 8417-2-R [CD]

Just Break the News to Mother: BF BCD 15456

Just from the Fountain: Rndr 0157

Just Keep Waiting 'Til the Good Time Comes: Hist HLP 8003

Just Married: Rndr 1035

Just One Way to the Pearly Gates: Cty 521, RCA 2100-2-R [CD]

Just over in the Gloryland: OT 106, RCA 2100-2-R [CD]

Just over the River: Mar 9101

Just Plain Folks: OHCS 315

Just the Same Today: FLeg FSA-26, Rndr 0064

Kaiser and Uncle Sam: Mar 9109

Kanawha County Rag: Cty 536

Kanawha March: Kan 306, OH OHCS 141

Kansas City Blow: Elek EKL-316

Kansas City Blues: Rndr 1007

Kansas City Kitty: MFP MFP 002, Rndr 0005, SmFwys SF 40037

Kansas City Railroad: Cty 411

Kansas City Reel: Cty 519

Kansas City Stomp: Cty 546

Karo: Cty 542 *see also* Flop Eared Mule, *etc.*

Kate and the Cowhide [N 22]: TFS 104

Katie Dear (Silver Dagger) [M 4/G 21]: Ark Trad 004, Cam ADL 2-0726(e), Cam CAL 797, NW 236, RCA 8417-2-R, Rndr 1006

Katie Morey [C. 112 / N 24]: Ph 1022, Van VRS-9239

Katy Bar the Door: Her 070

Katy Cline (Kline): BB AXM2-5510, Cty 510, Fwys FS 3811, Fwys FES 34151, Mtn 304, SmFwys SF 40038, Van VRS-9182

Katy Did: Cty 514

Katy Hill: Ala Trad 103, Cam CAL 719, Her 33, PB 006, Prst FL 14010, Rndr 0089, SmFwys SF 40038 *see also* Sally Johnson

Kaw River: Cty 707

K. C.: see Kansas City

Keep a Light in Your Window Tonight: Fwys FTS 31007

Keep in the Middle of the Road: Sm/Fwys SF 40012 [CD]

Keep My Skillet Good and Greasy: BF 15503, BF 15519, Prst INT 13035, Riv RLP 12-610, Rndr 0065

Keep on the Firing Line: Cam ACL1-0047, LC AFC L69-70

Keep on the Sunny Side: Har HL 7280, JEMF 101, OH OHCS 111, OH OHCS 112, OH OHCS 116, OH OHS 90045, RCA LPM 2772, Riv RLP 12-649, TL TLCW-06

Keep Your Gal at Home: OH OHCS 193, Rndr 1005

Keep Your Garden Clean: Elek EKLP-2, UTP [cass, no #]

Keith and Hiles Line: Fwys FE 4001

Kelly Schottische: UMP No #

Kennedy Rag: Cty 401

Kenny Wagner Surrender [E 8]: Hist HLP 8003, OHCS-173

Keno, the Rent Man: Mar 9111

Kentucky: Rndr CD 11536

Kentucky Blues: RCA 8416-2-R [CD]

Kentucky Bootlegger(s): Mar 9104, OH OHCS-177

Kentucky Boys: TFS 104

Kentucky Moonshiner: Rndr 0064

Kentucky Waltz: MFFA 1001

Ketter Gun: Cty 789

Keys of Canterbury: Fwys FA 2358

Kickapoo Medicine Show, Pts. 1/2: Rndr 1023

Kicking Mule: AFF 33-3, BF 15517, Mtn 304, LC AAFS L20

Kilby Jail: Fwys FA 2379

Killiekrankie: GnHys GR714

Kimball House: NW 226, OH OHCS 193

Kingdom's Come: Fwys FA 2435

King in North America: UTP [cass, no #]

King John and the Bishop [C. 45]: MC 1

King Kong Kitchie: Fwys FA 2951

Kings Highway: OH OHCS 116

King's Love-Letter [C. 208]: LC AAFS L58

King William Was King George's Son: NW 245

Kirby Cole: TFS-105

Kissing: BF BCD 15456

Kissing Cousins: Arh 5010

Kissing Is a Crime: Har HL 7300, OH OHCS 111, OH OHS 90045, TL TLCW-06

Kissing on the Sly: De DL 4760

Kiss Me Cindy: OT 106 *see also* Cindy

Kiss Me Goodbye If You Love Me: Alp ALP 201

Kiss Me Quick: Cty 514

Kiss Waltz: Hist HLP 8005, Cty 540

Kitchen Girl: Rndr 0089

Kittie Clyde: Mtn 302

Kitty Alone: Fwys FA 2317

Kitty and the Baby: GV SC 03

Kitty Blye: Bio BLP 6005

Kitty Puss: Cty 788, Rndr 0032

Kitty Sharp: FLeg FSA-27

Kitty Waltz: Cam CAL 586

Kitty Waltz Yodel: Arb 201

Kitty Wells: Fwys FS 3848, Hist HLP 8004

Kneel at the Cross: BB AXM2-5525

Knit Stockings: NW 239

Knocking on the Henhouse Door: FLeg FSA-24

Knoxville Blues: Cty 523, Fwys FA 2379

Knoxville Girl [P 35]: Cty 718, Fwys FA 3833, JnAp 018, Prst FL 14035, Prst INT 13035, Riv RLP 12-617, TFS-103

Knoxville Rag: Mar 9025, MS 45004, Rndr 1004

Ladies' Fancy: Rndr 0133

Ladies on the Steamboat: Col CS 9660, Cty 788, DU 33014, Rndr 1004

Ladies' Walpole Reel: NW 239

Lady Beauty Bride [M 3]: Rim Rlp-495

Lady Beauty Bright [M 3]: Van VRS 9162

Lady Be Good: JnAp 030

Lady Bride and Three Babes [C. 79]: Fwys FES 34151

Lady Gay [C. 79]: Brun 59001, Rndr 1037, JnAp JA 001, Van VRS-9158, JnAp JA 009

Lady Isabel and the Elfin Knight [C. 4]: JnAp 018

Lady Margaret [C. 74]: FLeg FSA-11, Riv RLP 12-620, Rndr 0017, TFS 104

Lady of Carlisle [O 25]: LC AFS L1

Lady's Fancy: Cty 703

Lafayette: Fwys FTS 31007

Lakes of Ponchartrain [H 9]: Arh 5010

Lament for Barney Graham: FLeg FSA-32

Lamplighting Time in the Valley: Rndr 0077

L. and N. Rag: Cty 531

Land of Pleasure: Fwys FE 4001

Lantern in the Ditch: UMP No #

Larry O'Gaff: FLeg FSA-27

Lass of Loch Royale [C. 76]: Prst INT 25003

Lass of Mohea [H 8]: Mer 1001-2

Last Chance: FLeg FSA-17

Last Days in Georgia: Cty 527

Last Fierce Charge [A 17]: BF BCD 15456, Rndr 0083

Last Gold Dollar: Rndr 1029

Last Great Roundup: BF BCD 15456

Last Letter: JEMF 101, Rndr CD 11536

Last Longhorn: Mar 9106

Last Mile of Way: Cam ADL 2-0726(e)

Last Night I Was Your Only Darling: OTC 6002

Last of Callahan: JnAp JA0055, LC AFS L2 *see also* Callahan

Last of Sizemore: NW 226

Last Old Dollar: Brch 1945

Last Old Shovel: Rndr 0020

Last Pay Day at Coal Creek: Fwys FS 3828

Last Scene of the Titanic: Rndr 1007

Last Shot Got Him: Cty 528, Mar 9111

Last Words of Copernicus: Prst INT 25007, NW 205

Late Last Night When (My) Willie Came Home: Cty 545, De DL 4760, Fwys FA 2315, Fwys FTS 31007

Late One Evening [M 32]: NW 223

Lather and Shave [Q 15]: Cty 789

Laughing Boy: Cty 703

Laugh Your Blues Away: Rndr 1028

Laurel Mountain Breakdown: GFS GFS 901

Lawson Family Murder [F 35]: Prst INT 25009, Van VSD-6576, Rndr 0052

Lay Around the Kitchen 'Til the Cook Comes In: Rndr 0034

Lay Down Baby, Take Your Rest: OT 101

Lay My Head Beneath the Rose: CMH 112

Lay Your Good Money Down: Rndr 0157

Lazarus [C. 56]: LC AAFS L57

Lazy Farmer Boy: Fwys FA 2951

Lazy Kate: UMP No #

Lazy Mary: PB 004

Leaf from the Sea: Rndr 0065

Leake County Blues: Cty 511

Leather Breeches [Britches]: Cty 201, Cty 506, Cty 515, Cty 532, Cty 543, Cty 707, Cty 733, Fwys FA 2435, Fwys FES 34151, GyEg 101, Hist HLP 8003, Mar 9111, Miss AH-002 RCA LPV 552, SmFwys SF 40038, TFS-108

Leave It There: Asch AH 3903

Leaves Is Falling on the Ground, The: Arh 5001

Leaving Dear Old Ireland: Cty 516, Rndr 0036

Leaving Home [I 3]: Cty 505, RCA LPV 548

Lee Highway Blues: Fwys FA 2359, OHCS-157

Lee's Ferry: Rndr 0158, Rndr 0237

Lee Tharin's Bar Room [B 1]: Tpc 12T146

Left All Alone Again Blues: Cty 511

Legend of Slide Mountain: FLeg FSA-27

Legend of the Robin's Red Breast, The: OHCS 314, OHCS 316

Let Her Go, God Bless Her: OT 106 *see also* Let Her Go, I'll Meet Her

Let Her Go, I'll Meet Her: MS 45003 *see also* Let Her Go, God Bless Her

Let Me Be Your Salty Dog: Rndr 0052 *see also* Salty Dog

Let Me Fall: Cty 709, Cty 723, Mtn 304

Let Me Have Mother's Gospel: Rndr 0078

Let Old Drunkards Be: Cty 757

Let's Be Friends Again: BF 15504

Let Me Be Your Teddy: Rndr 1002

Let's Go Hunting: PB 004

Let's Go To Bury: LC AFS L68

Let's Keep the Holler Alive: Fwys FS 3848

Letter Edged in Black: Ldr LE 4040, UICFC CFC 201

Letter from down the Road: Van VRS 9124

Letter That Never Came: Cty 505

Let That Circle Be Unbroken: Fwys FS 3839 *see also* Will the ....

Let the Church Roll On: OH OHCS 111

Let the Spirit Descend: PB 006

Let Us Be Lovers Again: Prst Int 13049

Lewiston Factory Mill Girls: Van VRS 9162
Lexington: DU-33009
Lexington Murder [P 35]: NW 245
Liberty: Cty 526, Cty 544, FSSM FSSMLP
    150001-D, Fwys FA 2356, Ldr LEA 4012,
    Mtn 304, Prst INT 13035
Liberty Hornpipe: Tak A 1013
Life and Death of Charlie Poole: BRI 004
Life and Death of Jesse James: BF 15503
Life Gits Teejus Don't It: Van VSD-9/10
Life Is Like a River: SH SH-CD-3795
Life of Jimmy [sic] Rodgers, The: OHCS 317
Life's Evening Sun: ACM ACM-1
Life's Railway to Heaven: OHCS 315, UICFC
    CFC 201
Lighthouse: MFFA 1001
Lightning Express: AFF 33-4, LC AFS L61,
    Cam CAL 797, Rndr 1006, UIP [cass, no #]
Lights in the Valley: Alp ALP 201, NW 226
Likes Likker Better Than Me: Mar 9104
Lily of the West [P 29]: Cty 789, Fwys FE
    34161, HMM LP001, Rndr 0065
Lily Shaw: Fwys FS 3839 see also Ballad of
    Finley Preston
Lily Schull: NW 245 see also Ballad of Finley
    Preston
Lime Street Blues: DU 33014
Lincoln Was a Union Man: Cty 787
Linda Sue: Cty 720
Link of Chain: Her 33
Liquor Seller: Her 070
Listen to the Mockingbird: Fwys FTS 31089,
    Kan 306, Riv RLP 12-650
Little Annie: Cty 409, Cty 729, Fwys FA 2433
Little Bessie: AH AHR 010, Ark Trad 002, BB
    AXM2-5525, BF 15504, Cam ADL 2-
    0726(e), FC FC-014, Fwys 2368, JnAp JA
    055, OFA TALP-001
Little Betty Brown: Cty 536
Little Birdie: Bio RC-6002, Cty 712, Cty 717,
    Cty 757, FLeg FSA-36, Fwys FA 2317, Fwys
    FA 2363, Fwys FA 2390, Fwys FA 3833,
    Fwys FS 3828, JnAp JA 055, OHS OF-1001
Little Black Train (Is Coming): Fwys FA 2392,
    Har HL 7396, Mar 9100, Mar 9101
Little Bonnie: Rndr 0020
Little Book: Alp ALP 202
Little Box of Pine on the 7:29: Elek EKL-316,
    Kan 308
Little Brown Bulls [C 16]: Fwys FE 4001, LC
    AFS L1, LC AAFS L56, LC AAFS L55

Little Brown Jug: Cty 757, Cty 778, JnAp JA
    049, Ldr LEE 4045
Little Carpenter, The: Van VRS 9162
Little Children: Rndr 0078
Little Church Aisle: UNC 0-8078-4084-X
Little Church House on the Hill: Arh 5001
Little Cory: Elek EKLP-2
Little Dappled Cow: Atl SD-1350
Little Darling Pal of Mine: Cam CAL 2554(e),
    Cty 510, Har HL 7280, OH OHS 90045, Van
    VRS-9213
Little Devils [C. 278]: Elek EKLP-2, Fwys FA
    2302, Wstm SWN 18021
Little Dogies: LC AAFS L20
Little Dove: LC AFS L2
Little Family: NW 294, Prst INT 25011
Little Farmer Boy: Fwys FA 2418
Little Fisherman: HMM LP001
Little Frankie Baker [I 3]: Fwys FA 3833
Little Frankie [I 3]: JnAp JA 055
Little Girl That Played on My Knee: MCA
    VIM-4012 [Japan]
Little Grave in Georgia: Cty 543
Little Grey Mule: Fwys FA 2363
Little Guinea Gay Haw [C. 13]: TFS cass
Little Hillside: Fwys FA 2350
Little Honey: HMM LP002
Little Indian Napanee: OH OHCS 141
Little Iron Monitor: Mar 9200
Little Joe: BB AXM2-5510, De DL 4404, Fwys
    FA 2352, TL TLCW-06 see also Darling
    Little Joe
Little Joe the Wrangler [B 5]: AFF 33-4, BF
    15502, FLeg FSA-18, Fwys FH 5723, Mar
    9106, MFP 0001
Little Joe the Wrangler's Sister Nell [dB 36]:
    Fwys FH 5723
Little Johnny [K 36]: AH AHR 007
Little Liza Jane: JnAp 018, Rndr 0037, Mtn 304
Little Log Cabin by the Sea: Cam CAL
    2554(e), CMF 011-L
Little Log Cabin in the Lane: Fwys FA 2350
Little Lonie [F 4]: AH AHR 009
Little Log Hut in the Lane: CMH 107
Little Love, A: OT 102
Little Love: Fwys FS 3811
Little Lulie: OH OHCS-177 see also Darling
    Cora
Little Lump of Coal: BF 15003, Fwys FTS
    31016
Little Maggie: Fly LP 546, Her 33, Mtn 303,
    NW 236, OHCS-157, OT 102, Prst INT

13035, Riv RLP 12-610, Rndr 0008 SmFwys SF 40037, Tpc 12TS336

Little Margaret [C. 74]: Fwys FP 40, JnAp 018, Prst INT 13030, Prst INT 13038, Riv RLP 12-649, Van VRS 9162

Little Massie Grove [C. 81]: BRI 002

Little Matty Groves [C. 81]: Tpc 12T146

Little Maud: NW 236

Little Mohea [H 8]: AFF 33-3, Fwys FS 3810, FLeg FSA-2, RCA LPV 548

Little More Sugar in the Coffee: UIP [cass, no #]

Little Moses: Atl SD-1349, Cam CAL 586, Fwys FA 2952

Little Musgrave [C. 81]: Fwys FA 2302

Little Old Log Cabin in the Lane: OHCS-173, Rndr 0001, Rndr 1008, Rndr 1003, Sytn STR 202

Little Old Log Shack I Always Call My Home: NW 314/315

Little Old Man Lived out West [C. 277]: Van VRS 9162

Little Old Sod Shanty: BF 15502, JEMF 103, Mar 9106, LC AAFS L20

Little Omie (Wise) [F 4]: Ark Trad 002, Asch AH 3903, LC AFS L65-L66, Van VCD-45 *see also* Omie Wise

Little Orphan Girl: Van VCD-45, Van VRS-9147, Van VSD-107/108

Little Pal: Rndr 0009

Little Pink: AH AHR 010

Little Poplar Log House on the Hill: Har HL 7344, OH OHS 90031

Little Rabbit: Cty 501

Little Red Barn: FLeg FSA-27, Kan 313

Little Red Caboose Behind Train: RCA LPV 532, Vet 103

Little Red Shoes: BB AXM2-5510, Fly LP 546

Little River Stomp: Tak A 1013 *see also* Green Valley Waltz

Little Rock Getaway: JnAp 030

Little Rooster: NW 291

Little Rosa Lee: LC AAFS L9

Little Rose: Rndr 0047

Little Rosebuds: OH OHS 90001

Little Rosewood (Rosebud) Casket: FLeg FSA-18, Fwys FA 2427

Little Sadie [I 8]: Cty 791, Fwys FA 2315, Fwys FA 2359, Fwys FA 2363, Van VRS-9147, Van VRS-9170, Van VSD-9/10

Little Sally Walker: LC AAFS L9

Little Sally Water: NW 291

Little Satchel Suzanna Gal: Cty 713

Little Scholar: JnAp JA 001

Little Schoolboy [C. 49]: Prst INT 25003

Little Ship [C. 286]: Fwys FE 34161

Little Shirt (That) My Mother Made for Me: AH AHR 007, OH OHCS 107, OHCS 314

Little Sod Shanty: AFF 33-4

Little Soldier [M 27]: HMM LP001

Little Sparrow: Asch AH 3831, HMM LP002, JnAp JA 055, Prst INT 13030

Little Stream of Whiskey [H 3]: Van VRS-9170, Rndr 0036, Rndr 1004

Little Sunshine: Fwys FA 2317

Little Sydney (Cindy): Fwys FS 3848

Little Things: Her 070

Little Turtle Dove: Cty 515

Little Waltz in A: AFF 33-4

Little Whiskey: GyEg 101

Little White Robe: FLeg FSA-36

Little Willie: Fwys FS 3829, SmFwys SF 40038, Van VRS 9124

Little Willie Green (from New Orleans): Rndr 1033

Little Willow Green: Rim Rlp-495

Live and Let Live: Ldr LEA 4012

Liza Jane: Arh 5010, Atl 1347, Cty 757, KM KM 204, OHS OF-1001, PB 005, Cty 520, SmFwys SF 40037, SH SH-CD-3786 *see also* Goodbye Liza Jane, etc.

Liza up a Simmon Tree: OH OHCS 107, OHCS 314

Lloyd Bateman [C. 53]: LC AAFS L57

Locks and Bolts [M 13]: GnHys GR714, Rndr 0083, Van VRS-9158

Logan County Blues: Cty 523, OH OHCS 141 *see also* Spanish Fandango

Logan County Jail [E 17]: AH AHR 007

Log Chain: Mar 9013

London City Where I Did Dwell [P 24]: JnAp JA 055

Londonderry Hornpipe: Kan 307

Lone Cow Trail: Cty 789

Lonely Cowboy Pts 1/2: Mar 9106

Lonely Grave: Pu PU 3001

Lonely Tombs: Asch AH 3902, Cty 404, Prst INT 25011

Lone Pilgrim: Fwys FA 2366, Rndr 1002, Sm/Fwys SF 40012 [CD]

Lone Prairie: Fwys FA 2363, Fwys FA 2380

Lonesome Blues: Cty 532, SmFwys SF 40037

Lonesome Day: Asch AH 3831

Lonesome Day Today: Cty 546

Lonesome Dove: Prst INT 25006, Rndr 0051, Rndr 0083

Lonesome for You Darling: Har HL 7422

Lonesome Homesick Blues: CMH 118

Lonesome Hungry Hash House: Fwys FTS 31089

Lonesome in the Pines: OT 112

Lonesome Jailhouse Blues: Rndr 1002

Lonesome Moonlight Waltz: MFP MFP 002

Lonesome Pines: Rndr 0018

Lonesome Pine Special: Cam CAL 2473

Lonesome Railroad: OT 112

Lonesome Road Blues: Cty 524, Cty 709, Cty 778, SmFwys SF 40037, Fwys FA 2315, Fwys FA 3833, Riv RLP 12-649, Rndr 0005, SmFwys SF 40037

Lonesome Scenes of Winter [H 12]: JnAp JA 020, JnAp JA 055

Lonesome Valley: Atl SD-1349, Fly LP 546, Har HL 7280, OH OHS 90045, TL TLCW-02 *see also* You've Got To Walk That ...

Lonesome Valley, Pt. 2: Mar 9101

Lonesome Weary Blues: Cty 523

Lone Star Trail: Fwys FA 2953, MS 45008, NW 314/315

Long and a Country Jake: JnAp JA 020

Long Black Veil: FLeg FSA-13, Prst FL 14035

Long Eared Mule: FC FC-014

Longest Train (I Ever Saw): CMF 011-L, Pu 3001, Alp ALP 201, RCA LPV 532 *see also* in the Pines

Longing for Old Virginia: RCA LPM 2772

Long Journey Home: Arh 5011, Cty 729, Cty 739, Van VSD-107/108

Long Lonesome Way: JnAp 037

Long, Long Ago: TFS-108

Long Side the Santa Fe Trail: BF 15502, MS 45008

Long Sought Home: UNC 0-8078-4083-1

Long Time Ago: LC AAFC L26/27

Long Time Gone: Arh 5011

Long Way to Tipperary: Rndr 1035

Look Away from the Ocean: Har HL 7396

Look Before You Leap: Cty 516

Look down That Lonesome Road: Sm/Fwys SF 40012 [CD]

Look for Me: Rndr 0008

Look How This World Made a Change: MCA VIM-4012 [Japan]

Look on and Cry: Cty 404

Look up, Look down That Lonesome Road: JnAp JA 009

Look up, Look down That Old Railroad: FLeg FSA-23

Lord Barnett [C. 68]: Fwys FS 3809

Lord Bateman [C. 53]: Fwys FA 2301, Rndr 0076, LC AAFS L12, LC AAFS L57, MC 1, Rim Rlp-495, Mar 9200

Lord, Build Me a Cabin in Glory Land: UICFC CFC 201

Lord Daniel [C. 81]: JnAp JA 001, Rndr 0076

Lord, I'm in Your Care: CMH 112, OH OHCS 116

Lord Joshuay [C. 95]: Rndr 0065

Lord Level [C. 75]: AH AHR 009

Lord Lovel [C. 75]: AH AHR 008, Fwys FA 2301, FLeg FSA-36, Fwys FA 2358, LC AAFS L55, Mar 9200

Lord Promised Me a Place in the Sky, The: Alp ALP 201

Lord Randall [C. 12]: FLeg FSA-1, Fwys FA 2302

Lord Thomas and Fair Ellender [C. 73]: FLeg FSA-2, Fwys FA 2301, Fwys FA 2362, LC AFS L7, RRT LP-8073, TFS cass

Lord Will Make a Way Somehow, The: LC AFC L69-L70

Lord Will Provide, The: JnAp JA 020

Lord, You've Been So Good to Me: Fwys FA 2358

Loss of the "New Columbia": LC AAFS L21

Lost Boy Blues: NW 226

Lost Child: Cty 401, Cty 507

Lost Gander: Cty 789

Lost Girl, The: Str STR 802

Lost Goose: Cty 202

Lost Indian: Cty 202, Cty 534, Cty 724, Fwys FA 2317, Her 33, Mtn 304, NW 226, Rndr 0018, Rndr 0157, Rndr 1010

Lost Jimmie Whalen [C 8]: Fwys FE 4001

Lost John: Ala Trad 103, DU 33014, Fwys FA 2315, Fwys FA 2434, JnAp JA 010, Mar 9025, Miss AH-002, Riv RLP 12-610, Riv RLP 12-650, Rndr 0034, Rndr 0065, Rndr 1004, Van VSD-9/10

Lost Love: MS 45005

Lost Love Blues: Fwys RBF 654

Lost Soul, The: Fwys FA 2366, Sm/Fwys SF 40012 [CD]

Lost Train Blues: Cty 524, Cty 546, Fwys FA 3833 *see also* New Lost Train Blues

Louisiana Earthquake: Fwys FA 2355
Louisville Burglar [L 16b]: Cty 522
Love Has Brought Me to Despair [P 25]: Fwys FA 2309
Love Henry [C. 68]: AH AHR 009
Love Is Little: Rndr 0078
Love Lifted Me: OH OHCS 190
Lovely Jimmy: Mar 9200
Lovely Mansion: Hoop 101
Love Me Darling (Love Me): Cty 409, Fwys FA 3833
Love, More Love: Rndr 0078
Love Nancy: WVUP 001
Love of Polly and Jack Monroe [N 7]: Fwys FTS 31016
Love of Rosanna McCoy: Fwys FA 2358
Love Please Come Home: NW 225
Lover of the Lord: LC AAFS L11
Lover's Farewell: Cty 409
Lover's Lane: MCA VIM-4012 [Japan]
Lover's Return: OTC 6001
Love Somebody: Mtn 303
Loving Hannah: JnAp JA0059C
Loving Henry [C. 68]: Rndr 0076
Loving Jesus: NW 205, Prst INT 25007
Loving Nancy: Asch AH 3903
Loving Nancy [K 14/P 5]: FLeg FSA-26
Low down in the Valley: Rndr 0078
Lowe Bonnie [C. 68]: OT 112, Tst T-3302
Lowlands Low, The, *or* The Golden Willow Tree [C. 286]: Fwys FE 4001
Lowlands of Holland [C. 92]: LC AAFS L21
Low Low in This Pretty Path: Rndr 0078
Lucky Tiger Ointment: TFS-103
Lucy Neil: DU-33002
Lula Walls: Cam CAL 586, Har HL 7280
Lullaby Medley: Riv RLP 12-620
Lumberjack Dance Tune: LC AAFS L55
Lumberjack's Alphabet: LC AAFS L56
Lunatic Asylum: TFS-103
Lye Soap Breakdown: Hist HLP 8003
Lynchburg Town: Arb 201, Bio BLP 6005, OHS OF-1001 *see also* Going down to ..., Monkey Show

Maggie Walker Blues [P 1b]: Fwys FA 2355
Magnolia One-Step: Cty 529
Magnolia Waltz: Mar 9110
Maiden's Lament: FLeg FSA-33
Maid of Kildare: LC AFS L62
Make Me a Cowboy Again: Mar 9106

Make Me a Pallet on the Floor: Bio RC-6003
Make Room in the Lifeboat for Me: OTC 6002
Makin' Hay: Rndr 0008
Mama Blues: Prst INT 13035, Rndr 0065, SH SH-CD-3786, Van VRS-9170
Mama Buy Me a Chiney Doll: Atl SD-1350
Mama Scolds Me for Flirting: FLeg FSA-24
Mama Won't [Don't] Allow No Low Down Hanging Around: Arh F5002 *see also* No Low Down Hanging Around
Mandola Polka: Ok OK 76004
Mangrum and Mynatt [E 17]: TFS-106
Manhattan Blues: Elek EKL-316
Man of Constant Sorrow: Cty 786, Cty 789, FLeg FSA-36, Fwys FA 2363, Fwys FA 3830, Prst INT 13030, Rndr 0017, Rndr 1010
Man of Galilee, The: Fwys FA 2357
Mansions in the Sky: Cty 404, RCA 2100-2-R [CD]
Man That (Who) Rode the Mule 'Round the World: BF 15503, Mtn 305
Mantle So Green [N 38]: Ph 1022
Maple in the Lane: Mar 9109
Maple on Hill: Arh F5002, Alp ALP 201, BF 15518, Fleg FSA 23, Fwys FA 2427, Fwys FS 3829, OH OHCS 111, OH OHS 90031, RCA 8416-2-R
Maple on the Hill, No. 2: OT 106
Maple Sugar: JEMF-105
March Around the Throne: PB 006
Marching Jaybird: Trad TLP 1007
Marching through Flanders: Mar 9109
Marching through Georgia: JnAp JA 010, Mar 9025
Margie: Rndr 0020
Marion Massacre: Rndr 1026
Marmaduke's Hornpipe: MFFA 1001, GyEg 101, UMP No #
Married Life Blues: Fwys 2368, JnAp JA 010
Married Man's Blues: Cty 534
Martha Campbell: Her 33, Rndr 0032
Marthy Won't You Have Some Good Old Cider: Tpc 12TS336
Mary Dear: OH OHCS 141 *see also* Goodbye Mary Dear
Mary Dowell: AH AHR 009
Mary Mack: Atl SD-1350
Mary of the Wild Moor [P 21]: AH AHR 008, Cam ADL 2-0726(e), Cam CAL 797, Mar 9200
Massa Bill: MFFA 1001

Massa Run Away: HMM LP001
Matilda Jane Lee: Fwys FS 3848
Matthew Twenty-Four: Fwys FA 2357
Matty Groves [C. 81]: Fwys FA 2309, FLeg
    FSA-2, TFS cass, Van VRS-9239
Maudaline: DU-33009
Maybelle Rag: Rndr 1033
May Day Carol: FLeg FSA-3
May I Go with You, Johnny? [O 33]: FLeg
    FSA-26
May I Sleep in Your Barn Tonight Mister?:
    Arb 201, Bio BLP 6005, OH OHCS 141,
    OHCS-173, Ark Trad 002, Fwys FA 2350,
    Fwys FA 2365, Fwys FA 2434, Kan 313 *see
    also* Can I Sleep ...
McAbee's Railroad Piece: RCA LPV 532
McCarroll's Breakdown: Cty 403 *see also*
    Bucking Mule, Whoa Mule
McCraw's Ford: Rndr 0133
McDonald's Farm: Mar 9110
McKenzie Case: Rndr 0237
McKinley: HMM LP001
McKinley March: Rndr 0036
McMichen's Reel: Her 33
Me and My Old Wife Had a Little Falling Out:
    Cty 786
Mean Women: Asch AH 3902
Mear: LC AAFS L11
Medley: Fwys FTS 31089, JnAp JA 025, Ldr
    LEA 4012
Medley of Reels: RCA LPV 552
Meet Her When the Sun Goes Down: UIP
    [cass, no #]
Meeting in the Air: Har HL 7300
Meeting Is Over: Fwys FA 2418, JnAp 037
Meet Me by the Ice House Lizzie: JnAp 032
Meet Me by the Moonlight Alone: CMH 116
Meet Me in Rose Time Rosie: FLeg FSA-17
Meet Me There: UNC 0-8078-4084-X
Meet Me Tonight: JnAp JA 010
Meigs County Reel: Kan 310
Me Johnny Mitchell Man: LC AAFS L16
Melancholy Day: NW 205, Prst INT 25007
Memorial Service: NW 205
Memory Lane: Cty 404
Memphis Blues: Fwys FTS 31007, JnAp 032,
    Van VRS-9170
Mercian Tittery-Ary-A: LC AFS L65-L66
Meriweather: Cty 788
Mermaid, The [C. 289]: LC AAFS L58, TFS
    cass

Merrimac at Sea [C. 289]: Rndr 0017
Merry Brown Field [C. 43]: Mar 9200
Merry Girl: Cty 524, Cty 778
Merry Golden Tree [C. 286]: Fwys FA 2301,
    Prst INT 25006, Riv RLP 12-645, RRT
    LP-8073
Methodist Pie: OHCS 314
Mexicali Rose: Tak A 1013
Mexican Rag: OT 112
Mexican Tune: Ph 1017
Mexican Waltz: Kan 600
Mexico: JnAp JA 055
Michigan I-O [C 17b]: LC AAFS L56
Mickey Brannigan's Pup: Ph 1022
Middlegrove: MFFA 1001
Midnight on the Stormy Deep (Sea): CMF
    011-L, Mar 9013, BB AXM2-5525, Fwys FA
    2433
Midnight on the Water: Cty 724
Midnight Serenade: Cty 201
Midnight Shuffle: MFFA 1001
Midnight Special: JEMF 104
Midnight Waltz: Kan 600
'Mid the Green Fields of Virginia: RCA LPM
    2772
Milford: LC AAFS L11, NW 205, Prst INT
    25007
Milk Cow Blues: Arh 5018, Fwys FA 2374,
    Fwys FTS 31007, Rndr 0005
Milk 'em in the Evening Blues: Fwys FTS
    31007
Milk White Steed [C. 75]: LC AFS L68
Miller's Cave: Prst FL 14010
Miller's Reel: Arh 5011, Cty 707, Rndr 0037
Miller's Will [Q 21]: Fwys FA 2362, Riv RLP
    12-645, Rndr 0051
Milwaukee Blues: Cty 504, Cty 516, NW 236
Milwaukee Fire: LC AAFS L55
Mind Your Own Business: AFF 33-3
Mineola Rag: Cty 410, Cty 527
Miner Hill: Ph 1022
Miner's Blues: Rndr 1007
Miner's Doom: LC AAFS L16
Miner's Dream: Cty 777
Miner's Dream Come True: Fwys FTS 31016
Miner's Farewell (Poor Hardworking Miners):
    Van VRS 9124
Miner's Prayer: Rndr 1026
Mines of Irvingdale [G 6]: Ph 1020
Minnow on the Hook: FPrm (No #)
Minstrel Boy: Kan 307

Miss Brown: Cty 528

Miss Dare: Mer 1001-2 *see also* Charlie Brooks, Send Back My Wedding Ring

Mission: LC AAFS L11

Mississippi Baby: Arh 5001

Mississippi Breakdown: Cty 528, Cty 532

Mississippi Echoes: Cty 528

Mississippi Flood: UICFC CFC 201

Mississippi Heavy Water Blues: Fwys FA 2374

Mississippi Jubilee: Cty 531 *see also* Mississippi Sawyer

Mississippi Sawyer: Arh F5002, Asch AH 3831, Cty 201, Cty 510, Cty 535, Cty 718, Cty 748, Cty 791, FLeg FSA-23, Fwys FA 2363, Fwys FA 2380, Fwys FS 3811, Her 22, Kan 307, Kan 600, LC AAFS L9, LC AFS L68, Ldr LEE 4045, Miss AH-002, Mtn 303, Mtn 305, OH OHCS 192, PB 005, Rndr 0001, Rndr 1023, UICFC CFC 201, WVUP 001 *see also* Mississippi Jubilee

Mississippi Square Dance (Sally Ann): Cty 529

Mississippi Valley Waltz: Rndr 0237

Miss Lisa Poor Gal: Pu PU 3001 *see also* Liza Jane, Goodbye Miss Liza

Miss McCloud's Reel: JEMF-105, JnAp JA0059C, FSSM FSSMLP 150001-D *see also* Hop Light Ladies, Did You Ever See the Devil Uncle Joe?

Missouri Mud: UMP No #

Miss Sally at the Party: Miss AH-002

Mister Bartender: Rndr 0051

Mister Rabbit: NW 291

Mistreated Blues: BF 15521

Mistreated Mama Blues: Fwys FA 2390

Mitchell Blues: RCA 8416-2-R, RCA LPV 552, Rndr 0008

Mixed Blues: Fwys FA 2392

Moatsville Blues: OH OHCS 141, OT 100

Model T Blues: Rndr 0005

Mole in the Ground: Fwys FP 40, Riv RLP 12-617, SH SH-CD-3786

Molly Bawn [O 36]: BF 15003, FLeg FSA-33

Molly Bender [O 36]: AH AHR 008, AH AHR 009

Molly Brooks: Trad TLP 1007

Molly Darling: Brch 1944

Molly Hare: Asch AH 3902

Molly Married a Traveling Man: BF 15503

Molly Musk: MFFA 1001

Molly [Polly] Put the Kettle On: Cty 506, Cty 529, FSSM FSSMLP 150001-D, Her 070, NW 236, Rndr 0058, Str STR 802

Molly Van [O 36]: HMM LP002

Mona Lisa: JnAp 032

Money Craving Folks: Rndr 1026

Money Musk: JEMF-105, LC AFS L62

Monkey in the Dog Cart: Cty 532

Monkey on a String: Cty 509

Monkey Show: MS 45005 *see also* Lynchburg Town

Monroe County Quickstep: MS 45003 *see also* Taylor's Quickstep

Montana Is My Home: Van VRS-9183

Montana Plains: RCA 8416-2-R, Rndr 1029

Montgomery: LC AAFS L11, NW 205, Prst INT 25007

Monticello: DU 33014

Moonlight on the River Colorado: MFP MFP 002

Moonlight Waltz: Kan 310

Moonshine: FLeg FSA-1

Moonshine Blues: Mar 9105

Moonshiner: Fwys FA 2363

Moonshiner and His Money: Col CS 9660, Cty 507

Moonshiner's Dream: OH OHCS 114

Moonshiner's Lament: Van VRS 9162

Moonshiner Song: Fwys FS 3810

Moonshine Steer: AFF 33-1

More Pretty Girls Than One: FLeg FSA-23, Fwys FS 3829, N&T 1001, Prst INT 13035

More Pretty Girls Than One, Part 3: CT 6000

Mormon Cowboy: Mtn 304, RCA LPV 522

Morning Blues: Rndr 0064

Morning Fair: FLeg FSA-1

Morning of 1845 [C 19]: Fwys FS 3809

Morning Trumpet: Fwys FA 2356, NW 205, Prst INT 25007

Most Fair Beauty Bright [M 3]: Fwys FA 2427

Mother Came To Get Her Boy from Jail: OH OHS 90001

Mother in Bright Glory: JnAp 037

Mother-In-Law: FLeg FSA-2

Mother Is Gone: Van VRS-9182

Mother Jones' Will: Rndr 0076

Mother Knows Best: Rndr 0020

Motherless Children: Fwys FA 2374, RCA LPM 2772

Mother's Going To Leave You Bye and Bye: OH OHCS 190

Mother's Grave: Rndr SS-0145

Mother's (Last) Farewell Kiss: Cty 540, Hist HLP 8005

Mother's Love: TFS-108
Mother's Plea for Her Son: FC FC-014
Mother the Queen of My Heart: Kan 313
Mountain Clog: Her 22
Mountain Dew: Mar 9104, Van VSD-107/108
Mountaineer's Courtship: Fwys FA 2953,
    OHCS-173, CMF 011-L *see also* Old Grey
    Beard
Mountain Fox Chase: Riv RLP 12-617
Mountain Picking: Cty 739
Mountain Reel: Cty 505 *see also* Hop Light
    Ladies, *etc.*
Mountains of Tennessee: Cam ACL1-0501,
    CMH 118
Mountain Top: Rndr 0005
Mount Zion: LC AAFS L11
Mourning Tears: GnHys GR714
Moving On: Van VSD-9/10
Moving on down the River: GnHys GR714
Mr. Garfield: Fwys FP 40, LC AFS L29
Mt. Zion: Prst INT 25007, Rndr 0009
Muck on My Heel: HMM LP002
Muddy Roads: Fwys FA 2366, LC AFS L65-
    L66, Sm/Fwys SF 40012 [CD]
Mud Fence: Rndr 0037
Mulberry Gap: Fwys FE 34162, TFS-108, GV
    SC 03
Mulberry Hill: LC AFS L68
Mule Skinner Blues: Cam CAL 719, Fwys FA
    2365,
Mule Skinning Blues: LC AFS L60
Murder of the Lawson Family [F 35]: BF
    15521, Col CS 9660, FC FC-014
Music in My Soul: Mar 9100
Muskrat: Cty 777, Van VCD-45, Van
    VRS-9170, Van VRS-9182
Must Jesus Bear the Cross Alone: LC AFC
    L69-L70
My Bearded Lover: Kan 313
My Bones Gonna Rise Again: BF 15505
My Bonny Bon Boy [C. 12]: FLeg FSA-33
My Boy Willie: Elek EKLP-2
My Brushy Mountain Home: FLeg FSA-24
My Buddy: Rndr SS-0145
My Carrie Lee: Mtn 304
My Christian Friends: Fwys FS 3810
My Clinch Mountain Home: Har HL 7280,
    RCA LPM 2772
My Cross-Eyed Beau: Sytn STR 202
My Daughter Wished To Marry: Fwys RBF RF
    51

My Dear Old Arizona Home: NW 314/315,
    Sytn STR 202
My Dear Old Southern Home: SH
    SH-CD-3795
My Dixie Darling: De DL 4404, OH OHS
    90045, TL TLCW-06
My Doney Where Have You Been So Long:
    Rndr 0077, KM KM 204
My Epitaph: Fwys FA 2493, Rndr 0021
My Evolution Girl: BF 15521
My Family Has Been a Crooked Set: BF 15517
My Father Doesn't Love Me Anymore: BF
    15521
My First Bicycle Ride: OHCS-172
My Ford Sedan: UIP [cass, no #]
My Friend Jim: SH SH-CD-3795
My God the Spring of All My Joys: UNC
    0-8078-4083-1
My Good Old Man [Q 2]: Tpc 12T146
My Grandfather's Clock: OHCS 315
My Grandmother Green: LC AAFS L21
My Gypsy Girl [O 4]: Cty 509
My Harding County Home: Rndr 0158, Rndr
    0237
My Head and Stay (Is Called Away): JnAp JA
    020, JnAp 037
My Heart's Tonight in Texas: CMH 118
My Home Among the Hills: Fwys FA 2375,
    Har HL 7344, TL TLCW-06
My Home in Montana: UICFC CFC 301
My Home Is Not in South Carolina: Fwys FA
    2306
My Home, My Sweet Home in Zion: Rndr
    0078
My Home's Across the Blue Ridge Mountains:
    De DL 4557, GHP LP 1001, Fwys FA 2359,
    Van VSD-107/108, Van VRS-9183 *see also*
    I'm Going Back to North Carolina
My Home's in Charlotte, North Carolina: Fly
    LP 546
My Honey Lou: CMH 112
My Horse Ain't Hungry: BF 15509 *see also*
    Wagoner's Lad, Pretty Polly
My Last Dollar: Rndr 1009
My Last Dollar Is Gone: Arh 5010
My Last Letter: BB AXM2-5525 *see also* The
    Last Letter
My Little Dony: Miss AH-002
My Little Girl: OT 101, UICFC CFC 201
My Little Home in Tennessee: Cam CAL 2473,
    Kan 308

My Little Home in West Virginia: OH OHCS-177

My Little Rooster: Atl SD-1350

My Long Journey Home: BB AXM2-5510

My Lord Keeps a Record: NW 294, Prst INT 25011

My Lord What a Morning: Prst INT 13020, Riv RLP 12-649

My Main Trial: Rndr 0052

My Mama Always Talked to Me: Cty 522

My Mama Scolds Me for Flirting: BF 15507

My Mama's Gone (Gambler's Yodel): Van VSD-107/108

My Man John: NW 239

My Man Will Be Home Some Old Day: HMM LP002

My Mind Is To Marry: DU 33033, OHCS-157

My Mother and My Sweetheart: Bio BLP 6005

My Mother Is Waiting: OH OHS 90001

My Mother's Beautiful Hands: OH OHCS 107

My Mother Was a Lady: Ark Trad 002

My Name Is John Johanna [H 1]: BF 15510, Cty 408, Fwys FA 2951, RCA LPV 548

My Native Home: De DL 4557, OH OHS 90045

My Old Brown Coat and Me: FLeg FSA-15

My Old Cottage Home: Ark Trad 003, Rndr 0017, Cam ACL1-0047

My Old Dog's Trailing up a Squirrel: Miss AH-002

My Old Kentucky Home: AFF 33-4

My Old Stetson Hat: Rndr 0158, Rndr 0237

My Old Virginia Home: Har HL 7344

My Only Sweetheart: Cty 534, Hist BC 2433-1, OHCS-172

My Ozark Mountain Home: Ark Trad 004, Cty 520

My Parents Raised Me Tenderly [P 1a]: LC AAFS L12, TFS-103

My Prayer: Mar 9100

My Pretty Little Gal Is Gone: Prst INT 25006

My Pretty Little Pink: NW 226, Rndr 0076

My Rough and Rowdy Ways: Van VCD-45, Van VSD-6576

My Soul's Full of Glory: Tpc 12T146

Mysteries of the World: Rndr 1028

My Sweetheart in Tennessee: Rndr 1004

My Sweetheart Is a Shy Little Miss: BF 15521

My Sweetheart's a Cowboy: LC AAFS L20

My Sweet Iola: OHCS 315

My Texas Girl: Har HL 7344, TL TLCW-06

My Virginia Rose Is Blooming: CMH 116, OH OHCS 111

My Wife Died Saturday Night: Cty 541 *see also* Way down on the Old Plank Road

My Wife Has Gone [Went Away] and Left Me: BF 15510, Cty 408, Cty 516

Nancy Ann: JnAp JA 049, Kan 307

Nancy Blevins: Fwys FA 2380, Rndr 0058

Nancy Dalton: Mer 1001-2

Nancy Jane: NW 236

Nancy Rollin [Rowland]: Cty 520, Cty 528, FSSM FSSMLP 150001-D, Rndr 1023, Rndr 0005

Nancy's Fancy: LC AAFS L9

Nancy's Got a Party Dress On: Prst INT 25006

Naomi Wise [F 4]: Cty 510, LC AAFS L12

Nashville Blues: TFS-103, Van VRS-9152, RCA 8417-2-R [CD]

Nashville Picking: Van VRS-9213

Natchez Under the Hill: SmFwys SF 40038, LC AFS L62

Nathan Killed the Bell Cow: AH AHR 008

Natural Bridge Blues: Her 33

N-Bar-N, The: MFP MFP 002

Needlecase: Fwys FA 2379

Neighbor Girl: Fwys FA 2309

Nellie Cropsey [F 1c]: Fwys FS 3848

Nellie Grey: Mtn 304

Never Alone Waltz: Arh 5001

Never Be As Fast As I Have Been: Cty 525, OHCS-157

Never Grow Old: Rndr 0001

Never Let the Deal Go Down: TFS-106

Never Let the Devil Get the Upper Hand of You [P 35]: De DL 4557

Never Make Love No More: Hist HLP 8006

Never Miss Your Mother: JnAp JA 049

Never No More Blues: Van VRS-9213

Never Seen the Like Since Getting Upstairs: Rndr 1023

New Birmingham Jail: BF 15504

New Chattanooga Mama: Cty 409

New Coon in Town: FC FC-014

New Dixie: Rndr 1023 *see also* Dixie

New Five Cents: Cty 787

New Ford Car: Vet 105

New Harmony: NW 205

New Huntsville Jail: Hist HLP 8002

New Lost Train Blues: Cty 507, OT 107 *see also* Lost Train Blues

Newlywed Reel: JEMF-105

New Market Reel: Rndr SS-0145
Newmarket Wreck: CMF 011-L, Cty 522,
    TFS-105
New Money: DU 33015, MS 45005
New Prisoner's Song: Fwys RBF 654
New River Song: BRI 004
New River Train: BB AXM2-5510, BF 15508,
    CMH 106, Cty 533, Cty 778, Hist BC 2433-1,
    Fwys FA 2315, LC AFS L61, Fwys FA 2363,
    Fwys FS 3829, OHS OF-1001, SmFwys SF
    40038, Van VSD-107/108
New Salty Dog: NW 236, RCA 8417-2-R, RCA
    LPV 552
News Boy: OFA TALP-001
New Spanish Twostep: Ok OK 76004
New Talking Blues: Rndr 0064
New Titanic: FPrm (No #)
New York Hobo: BF 15504
Nickety, Nackety: AH AHR 010
Nigger in the Woodpile: Cty 724, Tak A 1013,
    TFS-108
Nigger Trader: Fwys FA 3830
Nigger Trader Boatman: HMM LP001
Night Guard: Mar 9106, RCA LPV 522
Night Herding Song: Mar 9106, LC AAFS L28
Night in a Blind Tiger: Cty 526
Nightingales of Spring [N 29]: Fwys FE 4001
Nightingale Song [P 14]: Rndr 0017
Nine Hundred Miles: JnAp JA 010
Nine Miles out of Louisville: Rndr 0032
Nine-Pound Hammer (Is Too Heavy): BB
    AXM2-5510, Cty 513, Cty 739, FLeg
    FSA-13, SmFwys SF 40038, Fwys FA 2352,
    Riv RLP 12-617, RCA 8417-2-R, RCA LPV
    532, Vet 103
Nineteen Years Old [cf. H 24]: TFS 104
Ninety and Nine: FLeg FSA-18, Fwys FA 2360,
    Rndr 0077, SH SH-CD-3779
Nobody: AH AHR 008
Nobody Loves Me: OT 100
Nobody's Business: Ldr LEA 4012, OH
    OHCS-177, OH OHCS 190, Rndr 1037
Nobody's Darling: DU 33033, OH OHCS 112,
    Rndr 1028, Fwys FA 3833
Nobody's Darling but Mine: Rndr 0143
Nobody's Darling on Earth: Ark Trad 002
Nobody's Darling on Earth: BF 15510
No Business of Mine: Mar 9105
No Depression (In Heaven): De DL 4557, OH
    OHS 90045
No Disappointment in Heaven: Brch 1944,
    Fwys FA 2392

No Drunkard Can Enter There: Cty 508
No Home Cried the Little Girl: Rndr 0089
Nola Shannon: Ark Trad [No #]
No Letter in the Mail (Today): Cam CAL 719,
    Cty 739, Fwys FA 2317
No Low Down Hanging Around: BF 15501,
    Rndr 0036 *see also* Mama Don't Allow ...
"Nol Pros" Nellie: Mar 9105
No More Goodbyes: TL TLCW-06
No More the Moon Shines on Lorena: Cam
    ACL1-0501
None Can Preach the Gospel Like the
    Mormons Do!: Ok OK 75003
No One Loves You As I Do: Hist BC 2433-1
No One To Love Me [K 12]: Mtn 303
No One To Welcome Me Home: OH OHCS
    116
No Other's Bride I'll Be: Har HL 7344
North Carolina Boys: Ldr LE 4040
Northfield: Fwys FA 2356, LC AAFS L11, NW
    205, GV SC 03
North Port: NW 205
Norway Bum: UIP cass
No Sir: Fwys FA 2427
Not A-Gonna Lay My Religion Down: LC AFS
    L68
No Tears in Heaven: Asch AH 3902, Rndr
    SS-0145
No Telephone in Heaven: OH OHCS 112, SH
    SH-CD-3795
Not Far from Ballston: FLeg FSA-15
Nothing but the Blood: UNC 0-8078-4084-X
Nothing Doing: Hist HLP 8002
Nothing to It: Van VRS-9213
Nottingham Fair: LC AAFS L20
Nowhere Road: FLeg FSA-2
No Work for a Tramp: OHS OF-1001

O. and K. Train Song: JnAp JA 020
O Brighter Than the Morning Star: Rndr 0078
O Bury Me Not on the Lone Prairie [B 2]: Mar
    9106
Ocean: Fwys FA 2356
Odem: Mar 9101
O'Donnell Abu: Kan 307
Off She Goes: JEMF-105, LC AAFS L9
Off to (the) War I'm Going: BF 15505, Mar
    9109
O'Gaff's Jig: JEMF-105
O Give Me a Little Love: Rndr 0078
Oh Babylon Oh Babylon!: Fwys FA 2036

Oh Baby You Done Me Wrong: Cty 545

Oh Blue: NW 291

Oh Come See Me When You Can: HMM LP001

Oh Death: BRI 002, FLeg FSA-26, JnAp JA 001, OH OHCS 117, Van VRS-9147

Oh Fly Around My Pretty Little Miss: LC AAFS L9 *see also* Fly Around ... etc.

Oh for the Wild and Woolly West: CMH 106

Oh Hide You in the Blood: Fwys FA 2357, Fwys FA 2433

Oh How I Hate It: GHP LP 1001

Oh I'm a Jolly Irishman Winding on the Train: LC AFS L61

Oh John the Spirit of the Lord: TFS-108

Oh Lord Ellie: HMM LP001

Oh Lord What a Morning: FLeg FSA-36

Oh Loving Babe: Rndr 1028

Oh Marry in Time [C. 2]: JEMF 104

Oh Miss I Have a Very Fine Farm: FLeg FSA-11

Oh Molly Dear (Go Ask Your Mother) [M 4]: BF 15509, CMF 011-L, Hist HLP 8003

Oh My Little Darling: NW 245

O Holy Father: Rndr 0078

Oh Pray Doctor: Fwys FS 3848

Oh Pretty Monkey: BF 15509

Oh Soldier, Soldier: Wstm SWN 18021

Oh Take Me Back: De DL 4404

Oh Those Tombs: JEMF 104

Oklahoma Kid: CMH 106

Old Abe: Fwys FA 2360

Old Account Was Settled (Long Ago): Van VRS-9147, OH OHCS 141, PB 003

Old Age: NW 225

Old Age Pension: UICFC CFC 201

Old Age Pension Blues: Fwys FA 2317

Old and Faded Picture: OH OHS 90001

Old and Only in the Way: Cty 516

Old Arm Chair, The: AH AHR 007

Old Aunt Betsey: Mar 9111

Old Aunt Jenny: JnAp JA 055

Old Aunt Katy: JnAp JA 049

Old Bangum [C. 18]: Cty 787, Fwys FA 2301

Old Bill Moser's Ford: Rndr 0064

Old Black Crow in the Hickory Nut Tree: BF 15501

Old Black Steer: Mar 9106

Old Blind Dog: MS 45003 *see also* Old Grey Mare ...

Old Blue: Prst INT 13035

Old Blue Sow: LC AAFS L9, Miss AH-002

Old Blue Was Gray Horse: Fwys FH 5723

Old Brady [I 9]: TFS 104

Old Buck: Cty 778

Old Bunch of Keys: Cty 713

Old Buzzard: DU 33015, MS 45004

Old Chain Gang: ACM ACM-1

Old Chimney Sweeper: FLeg FSA-3

Old Chisholm Trail: MFP 0001, NW 314/315, RCA LPV 522, Rndr 1009, Sytn STR 202

Old Christmas Morning: FPrm (No #), Rndr 0047

Old Churchyard: Rndr 0017

Old Clay Pipe: Bio BLP 6005

Old Coon Dog: Mar 9013, UICFC CFC 201

Old Corn Liquor: HMM LP001

Old Cotton Eyed Joe: DU-33002

Old Country Church: Atl SD-1349

Old Cow Died in the Forks of the Branch, The: Cty 788

Old Crossroads: Asch AH 3902

Old Crumley [Q 1]: FLeg FSA-3

Old Cumberland Land: TFS-105

Old Dad: Cty 535, LC AFS L62

Old Dan Tucker: Arh 5010, BF 15519, Mer 1001-2, Rndr 0064, Rndr 0194, Rndr 0237

Old Devil, The [C. 278]: TFS cass

Old Dubuque: Rndr 0157

Old East Virginia: JnAp JA 055

Old Elm Tree: Shoe SGB 1

Old Eve She Did the Apple Pull: TFS-108

Old Faithful: OH OHCS 111

Old Fashioned Cottage: OH OHCS-177

Old Fashioned Locket: Brch 1944

Old Fashioned Meeting: ACM ACM-1

Old Field Rabbit: Miss AH-002

Old Flannagan: MS 45005

Old Gospel Ship: NW 294, Prst INT 25011

Old Grandpaw Yet: NW 291

Old Granny Hare: LC AFS L68

Old Gray Horse: NW 226

Old Greasy Coat: WVUP 001

Old Grey Beard: JnAp JA 055

Old Grey Goose: GHP LP 1001

Old Grey Mare (Kicking out of the Wilderness): Cty 543, Fwys FS 3810, LC AFS L68 *see also* Old Blind Dog

Old Grumble [Q 1]: TFS-106

Old Hat, The: Cty 532

Old Hen Cackled and Rooster's Going To Crow: Hist HLP 8002, Rndr 1003

Old Hickory Cane: Atl 1347

Old Home Brew: CT 6002, Mar 9105

Old Home down on the Farm: Brch 1944

Old Homeplace: Rndr 0020

Old House, The: FPrm 41942

Old Ireland [N 30]: BRI 002

Old Iron Pants Pete: Fwys FH 5723

Old Jack Frost: FLeg FSA-26

Old Jake Gillie: Cty 536, Kan 306 *see also*; Granny Will Your Dog Bite

Old Jaw Bone: Cty 520 *see also* Jawbone

Old Jimmy Johnson: FPrm 41942

Old Jimmy Sutton: Bio RC-6003, DU 33033, Fwys FA 2363, Fwys FA 2380, Fwys FS 3811, Rndr 0028 *see also* Jimmy Sutton

Old Joe: Cty 541, Rndr 1033, UMP No #

Old Joe Clark: AFF 33-4, Atl SD-1350, Brun 59000, Cty 524, Cty 709, Cty 723, FLeg FSA-32, Fwys FA 2317, SmFwys SF 40038, Fwys FA 2342, Fwys FA 2365, Fwys FA 2380, Fwys FA 2433, Fwys FS 3811, Fwys FS 3832, Her 070, Kan 310, LC AFS L2, LC AFS L62, Ldr LE 4040, Mtn 305, NW 236, PB 005, Prst INT 25004, Riv RLP 12-650, Rndr 0065, Rndr 1008, Tak A 1013, Van VRS-9183, Wstm SWN 18021

Old Joe's Barroom [B 1]: Fwys FA 2392

Old John Hardy [I 2]: Cty 525 *see also* John Hardy

Old John the Rabbit: NW 291

Old Kimball [Q 22]: LC AFS L1

Old King Cole: AH AHR 008, FLeg FSA-3

Old Ladies' Home: JEMF 101, OH OHCS 111

Old Lady and Devil [C. 278]: Fwys FA 2951

Old Lady Sitting in the Dining Room: LC AAFS L9

Old Liberty: Mer 1001-2

Old Lonesome Blues: Rndr 1029

Old Maid and the Burglar: Hist HLP 8004

Old Man at the Mill: Fwys FA 2435, Fwys FA 2355

Old Man Below: Sm/Fwys SF 40012, Van VRS-9239

Old Man, Can I Have Your Daughter?: Rndr 0018

Old Man from the North Country [C. 10]: Riv RLP 12-645

Old Man Old Woman: GyEg 101

Old Man Portell's Tune: MFFA 1001

Old Man Satan/Drive Old Satan Away: LC AFS L68

Old Man's Drunk Again: Fwys RBF RF 51

Old Man Who Lived in West [C. 277]: MFFA 1001

Old Master's Runaway [Year of Jubilo]: BF 15517, Cty 542

Old Melinda: UMP No #

Old Miner's Refrain: LC AAFS L16

Old Miss Sally: Miss AH-002

Old Mister Rabbit: Cty 788

Old Molly Hare: Cty 501, Cty 527, Cty 791, Kan 307, Rndr 0058

Old Mother Flanagan: Rndr 0047

Old Mother Hippletoe: NW 291

Old Mother Rhyme: Rndr 0064

Old Mountain Dew: OTC 6002, Rndr 0065

Old Ninety-Seven [G 2]: LC AFS L68, Cty 741

Old Number Nine [G 26]: Alp ALP 201

Old Oly Mathieus: MFP MFP 002

Old One-Step: MFP MFP 002

Old Pine Tree: Fwys FA 2375

Old Pinto and Me: Kan 305

Old Rachel: Rndr 1007

Old Rattler: Riv RLP 12-650, Rndr 0065

Old Reuben [Ruby]: Cty 404, Cty 748, Fwys FA 2306, Fwys FA 2355, Fwys FA 2363, Fwys FA 2380, Fwys FS 3811, OT 102, Riv RLP 12-610

Old Richmond: Fwys FA 2434, Her 22

Old Rock Jail Behind Old Iron Gate: Rndr 1032

Old Rock Road: MFFA 1001

Old Rooney's Calf's a Bawling: AFF 33-2

Old Rub Alcohol Blues: Fwys RBF 654

Old Rugged Cross: GyEg 101

Old Sally Brown: LC AAFS L9

Old Shep: Brch 1944

Old Ship of Zion: Mar 9100

Old Shoes and Leggings: FLeg FSA-15

Old Shop: Fwys FA 2418

Old Sledge: AH AHS 003, LC AFS L65-L66

Old Smokey: Fwys FA 2363, LC AAFS L14, Tpc 12T146

Old Southern Town: FLeg FSA-26

Old Sow: AH AHR 010

Old Sow (Jumped over Fence, the Little Ones Crawled Under): Fwys FS 3848

Old Spinning Wheel: Cty 411

Old Susannah: GV SC 03

Old Swinging Bridge: Rndr 0020

Old Ties: Hist HLP 8006

Old Time Backstep Cindy: Cty 791

Old Time Corn Shucking, Pts. 1 & 2: CMF 011-L

Old Time Fire on the Mountain: Rndr 0057

Old Time Medley: Cty 503

Old Time Reel: Prst FL 14030

Old Time Religion: Rndr 0072

Old Time Sally Ann: Cty 791

Old Time Schottische: UMP No #

Old True Love: Cty 757

Old Tucky Buzzard: Fwys FS 3848

Old Tyler: FLeg FSA-3

Old Virginia March: Rndr 0057

Old Virginia Waltz: Ldr LEA 4012

Old Virginny: Elek EKLP-2, FLeg FSA-23

Old Voile: MS 45005

Old Whisker Bill: Mar 9105

Old Zeke Perkin: Rndr 0036

O Lord Don't 'Low Me To Beat 'Em: LC AFS L1

O Love Is Teasing: Elek EKLP-2

Omie Let Your Bangs Hang Down: Cty 717

Omie Wise [F 4]: Cty 513, Fwys 2368, Fwys FA 2951, JnAp JA 020, JnAp JA 049, JnAp JA 055, Prst INT 13020, Tpc 12TS336, Van VRS-9152

On a Bright and Summer's Morning: LC AAFS L21, Rndr 0065

On a Cold Winter's Night [G 26]: RCA LPV 507

On a Hill Lone and Gray: OH OHCS 116, OTC 6001

Once I Courted a Charming Beauty Bright [M 3]: LC AAFS L55

Once I Had a Fortune: Hist HLP 8004

Once I Had and Old Grey Mare: Fwys FE 34161

Once I Lived in Cottonwood: Ok OK 75003

Once I Lived in Old Virginia: HMM LP001

Once in the Saddle [B 1]: TFS 104

Once More A-Lumbering Go: FLeg FSA-15, LC AAFS L56

One and a Few: Ph 1020

One Dark Stormy Night: BF 15505

One Day I Will: Rndr 0072

One Dime Blues: Trad TLP 1007

One Eyed Rosie: Cty 788

One Eyed Sam: Bio RC-6002

One John Riley: FPrm 41942

One Life's As Long As Any Man Can Live: FLeg FSA-13

One Little Word: JEMF 101, OH OHCS 117

One Moonlight Night: Cty 509

One More Kiss Before You Go: BF 15521

One More Ride: NW 314/315

One More River To Cross: Hist HLP 8006, Rndr SS-0145

One Morning in May [or The Nightingale] [P 14]: AH AHR 008, Elek EKLP-2, Fwys FA 2953, LC AFS L1, Tpc 12TS336, Wstm SWN 18021

One Night in Cleveland: OHS OF-1001

On Johnny Mitchell's Train: LC AAFS L16

On Jordan's Stormy Banks: UNC 0-8078-4083-1

On Learning Songs: Rndr 0078

Only As Far As the Gate (Dear Ma): BF 15519, OHCS 317

Only a Step to the Grave: BF 15517

Only Girl I Ever Cared About: CMH 112

Only Girl I Ever Loved: Hist HLP 8005

Only One Step More: BB AXM2-5525, Fwys FA 2357, RCA 2100-2-R [CD], Rndr CD 11536

Only the Leading Role Will Do: Rndr 0077

On My Way To See Nancy: WVUP 001

On Praying Ground: SH SH-CD-3779

On Sister Paulina Springer: Rndr 0078

On Some Foggy Mountain Top: BB AXM2-5510

On Tanner's Farm: RCA 8416-2-R, RCA LPV 507 *see also* Down on Penny's Farm

On That Old Gospel Ship: BB AXM2-5510, RCA 2100-2-R

On the Banks of the Ohio [F 5]: Arh 5001, BB AXM2-5510, OH OHS 90031, Fwys FP 40

On the Banks of (the) Old Tennessee: CT 6001, DU 33033, Fwys FA 3830, OHCS-157, UIP [cass, no #], Van VSD-107/108

On the Beach: DU-33009

On the Dixie Bee Line: Rndr 0064, Vet 101

On the Glory Road: Mar 9101

On the Lake of Pontchartrain [H 9]: LC AAFS L55

On the Old Plantation: OT 102

On the Other Side of Jordan: see Other Side of Jordan

On the Red River Shore: Mar 9106

On the Road to California or The Buffalo Bull Fight: LC AAFS L30

On the Rock Where Moses Stood: Cam CAL 586, Har HL 7396, TL TLCW-06

On the Sea of Galilee: Cam ACL1-0047, OH OHCS 116

On the Streets of Glory: Mar 9101

On the Train: Arb 201

On Top of Old Smoky: Fwys FS 3810, Riv RLP 12-617

On Zion's Holy Ground: Rndr 0078

Ooze up to Me: OT 112

Open the Door: FLeg FSA-11

Open up Them Pearly Gates (for Me): Van VSD-9/10, Prst FL 14035

Opera Reel: Kan 313, Rndr 0194

Opossum ... *see* Possum ...

Orange Blossom Special: Cam CAL 719, Prst FL 14030, RCA LPV 532

Orphan Child: OH OHCS 117

Orphan Girl: AH AHR 008, BF BCD 15456, Cty 515, JnAp JA 009, Min JD-203, Van VRS-9158

Orvetta Waltz: GyEg 101

O the Gospel of Mother: Rndr 0078

Other Side of Jordan: Cty 411, LC AFC L69-L70, OH OHCS 114 *see also* Jordan Is a Hard Road To Travel

O, Thou in Whose Presence: JnAp JA 009

Otto Wood the Bandit: BF 15521, Cty 522, Van VRS-9170

Our Goodman [C. 274]: LC AAFS L12

Our Johnny: Tst T-3301

Out of My Bondage: Fwys FTS 31089

Out on a Western Range: MS 45008

Out on Old Saint Sabbath: OH OHCS 111

Out on the Lone Star Cow Trail: Mar 9106

Outshine the Sun: Mar 9100

Over the Garden Wall: RCA LPM 2772

Over the Mountain: BF 15518, Rndr 1028, Vet 101

Over There: Tpc 12T146

Over the River to Charley's: Rndr 0157 *see also* ...To Charley's

Over the River To Feed My Sheep: GnHys GR714

Over the Road I'm Bound To Go: Cty 542, Fwys RBF RF 51

Over the Sea Waltz: Tak A 1013

Over the Waves: Cty 733, DU 33014, Rndr 0001

Over the Woods and through the Snow: MFFA 1001

Over Yonder in the Graveyard: Rndr 0077

Oxbow Quadrille: Ldr LEA 4012

Oxford Girl [P 35]: Min JD-203

Oxford Merchant [C. 283]: LC AAFS L58

Oxford Minuet: UMP No #

Oyster River Quadrille: UMP No #

Ozark Mountain Waltz: GyEg 101

Ozark Rag: Cty 410

Ozark Waltz: Cty 518

Pacific Slope: UMP No #

Paddy Doyle: Fwys FA 2362, LC AAFC L26/27

Paddy Get Back: LC AAFC L26/27

Paddy on the Handcar: Cty 527

Paddy on the Turnpike: Fwys FA 2435, Fwys FS 3832, HMM LP002, Kan 306, Rndr 0047

Paddy's Hollow: Fwys FS 3848

Paddy, Won't You Drink Some Cider?: Col CS 9660, Rndr 1023

Pale Moonlight: Cty 404

Pallet on the Floor: Cty 401

Palms of Victory: LC AFC L69-L70

Pa, Ma, and Me: Rndr 1032

Panhandle Country: OFA TALP-001

Panhandle Rag: Fwys FA 2306

Pans of Biscuits: BF 15003, Van VRS 9162

Panther in the Rock: Rndr 0018

Papa, Papa Build Me a Boat [K 12]: Fwys FA 2392

Papa's Billy Goat: Rndr 0051, UIP [cass, no #]

Paper of Pins: AH AHR 008, Atl SD-1350, Fwys FA 2358

Parkersburg Landing: Rndr 1010

Parson Burrs: Prst INT 25004

Parson's Farewell: GnHys GR714

Parson's Rock: LC AFS L65-L66

Parting Hand: Rndr 0026

Pass Around the Bottle and We'll All Take a Drink: Rndr 1005

Passing Policeman, A: CMF 011-L

Passing thru the Garden: JnAp JA 001

Patched Up Old Devil: FLeg FSA-18

Pateroller Song: Trad TLP 1007

Pathway of Teardrops, A: NW 225

Pat Malone [Q 18]: FLeg FSA-15, Kan 308

Pat McBraid: FLeg FSA-27

Patrick County Blues: Cty 201

Patsy Beasley: Fwys FES 34151

Patty on the Turnpike: Cty 525

Paul Bachor's Serenade: Ok OK 76004

Paving the Highway with Tears: Kan 308

Paw Paw Patch: Fwys FA 2358

Pay Day at Coal Creek: LC AFS L2

Payday at the Mine: LC AFS L60

Peachbottom Creek: Fwys FA 2363

Peach Bottom Creek: Fwys FA 2380

Peaches down in Georgia: Rndr 1032

Peacock Rag: Cty 547, Fwys FTS 31007, NW 226

Pea Fowl: Cty 786

Peanut Special: RCA LPV 532

Pearl Bryan [F 1a]: Mer 1001-2

Pearl Bryan [F 2]: Brch 1945

Pearl Bryan [F 2?]: Fwys FA 2375

Pearl Bryan(t) [F 1b]: Cty 522, OHCS 317, Prst INT 13030

Pearly Blue: Rndr 0058

Pearly Dew: NW 226

Pearly Gates: BB AXM2-5510

Pedlar and His Wife [F 24]: Rndr 1037

Peek-a-Boo (Waltz): AFF 33-2, BF 15503, OHCS-172, Vet 105, Rndr 0036, Rndr 0133

Peeler Creek Waltz: Ldr LEA 4012

Peel Her Jacket: JEMF-105

Peg and Awl: BF 15507, BF 15508, Fwys FA 2951, FLeg FSA-15, FLeg FSA-17, Prst INT 25004, Rndr 0009

Peggy Gordon: Ph 1022

Peggy of Glasgow [C. 228]: Rndr 0017

Paggy Walker [P 1b]: Asch AH 3903

Penitentiary Blues [I 8]: Arh 5012

Perry's Victory: LC AFS L62

Philadelphia Lawyer: SmFwys SF 40038, Fwys FS 3839

Phil Sheridan: LC AFS L29

Phyllis Gayle Breakdown: GyEg 101

Pick and a Shovel down in the Mines: PB 003

Picking and Blowing: Riv RLP 12-617

Picking My Way to Georgia: Ldr LEE 4045

Picking the Guitar: Elek EKL-316

Picture on the Wall: RCA LPM 2772, Rndr 1032

Pictures from Life's Other Side: OH OHCS 107, Rndr 1006

Piedmont: Rndr 0157

Pig Ankle Rag: Arh 5012

Pig (at Home) in the Pen: Asch AH 3831, Cty 547, Cty 718, Cty 739, DU 33014, Fwys FTS 31007, Fwys FA 2314, Fwys FS 3839, Rndr 0065

Pig Schottische: LC AAFS L55

Pigtown Fling: JEMF-105, LC AAFS L9 *see also* Wild Horse, Stoney Point

Pike's Peak: Cty 527 *see also* Rat Cheese Under the Hill

Pilgrim: UNC 0-8078-4083-1

Pin Ball Machine: Tst T-3301

Pine Ridge Breakdown: PB 005

Pinery Boy: LC AAFS L55

Piney Woods Gal [Girl] (of North Carolina): Bio RC-6003, Prst INT 25004, Rndr 0036, Rndr 0058, Str STR 802

Pinnacle Mountain Silver Mine: BRI 004

Pioneer Courtship: Fwys FES 34151

Piper on the Hearth: Van VRS-9183

Pisgah: Amazing grace! How Sweet the Sound: UNC 0-8078-4083-1

Pisgah: I'm Not Ashamed To Own My Lord: UNC 0-8078-4083-1

Place Called Hell: FLeg FSA-27

Plain Golden Band [H 17]: UIP cass

Plain Old Country Lad: Rndr 0072

Plains, Georgia Rock: Arh 5018

Plains of Waterloo : AH AHR 009

Plant Some Flowers by My Graveside: N&T 1001

Play Parties: Fwys FS 3809

Pleasant Hill: Fwys FA 2356

Please Come Back, Little Pal: Mar 9013, SmFwys SF 40037

Please Let Me Stay a Little Longer: Atl SD-1349

Please Mama Please: N&T 1001

Please Meet Me Tonight: Shoe SGB 1

Please Papa Come Home: Bio BLP 6005

Please, Papa, Don't Whip Little Benny: GnHys GR712

Ploughboy down at the Farm: TFS-108

Plow Boy Hop: Mar 9111

Poca River Blues: Cty 733

Poison in a Glass of Wine [P 30]: HMM LP002

Poison Serpent [Pizen Sarpent] (Springfield Mountain) [G 16]: TFS 104

Polecat Blues: Her 33, Ldr LE 4040, TFS-103

Polecat's Den: Cty 788

Policeman: Cty 713, KM KM 204, Mtn 302

Polk County Breakdown: Cty 720

Polly Ann: Fwys FA 2379

Polly [O 14]: FLeg FSA-32

Polly Put the Kettle On: Cty 741, Fwys FA 2380, Fwys FS 3811, Riv RLP 12-649

Pompey Is Dead: LC AAFS L55

Poor and Afflicted, Lord Are Thine: UNC 0-8078-4083-1

Poor and Rambling Boy [L 12]: Fwys FA 2427

Poor Boy [I 4]: Cty 411, JEMF 104

Poor Boy in Jail: Fwys FA 2392

Poor Drunkard's Dream: Cty 404, NW 245

Poor Ellen Smith [F 11]: Atl 1347, Brch 1945, Cty 748, Cty 791, Fleg FSA 23, Fwys FA 2360, Fwys FA 3830, Fwys FS 3811, Prst INT 13038, Prst INT 25003, Rndr 0065

Poor Ellen Smith [F 11]: OH OHCS 191

Poor Fish: Mar 9105

Poor Girl's Story: Rndr 1029

Poor Goins: BRI 004

Poor Jesse James [E 1]: Riv RLP 12-645

Poor Little Bennie: Mar 9105

Poor Little Ellen [F 11]: Riv RLP 12-610

Poor Little Joe: FLeg FSA-18

Poor Little Johnny's Gone to the War: Her 070

Poor Little Lost Baby: Van VRS 9162

Poor [Pore] Little Mary Setting in the Corner: LC AAFS L9

Poor Little Orphaned Boy: Cam ACL1-0047

Poor Little Turtle Dove: Rndr 0064

Poor [Pore] Man: Arh 5010, FLeg FSA-36, Van VRS-9183

Poor Man, Rich Man: BF 15505, Rndr 1026 *see also* Cotton Mill Colic

Poor Man's Song: Cty 789

Poor Old Dad: BF 15503

Poor Omie [F 4]: Fwys FA 2359

Poor Orphan Child: CMF 011-L, RCA LPM 2772

Poor Pilgrim of Sorrow: JnAp 037

Poor [Po'] Lazarus: Prst INT 25009

Poor [Po'] Mourner: BF 15502 *see also* Shout Monah ..., When the Good Lord Sets You Free, You Shall Be Free

Poor Rambler: Fwys FA 3833

Poor Scotchee [C. 68]: PB 004

Poor Sinners, Fare You Well: Vet 101

Poor Soldier: FLeg FSA-36

Poor Tramp: Rndr 1008

Poor Tuckahoe, The: AH AHR 007

Poor Wayfaring Stranger: Atl SD-1349, Min JD-203

Pop Goes the Weasel: PB 004

Pork Chops: BF 15504

Portland Fancy: JEMF-105

Portsmouth Hornpipe: JEMF-105

Possum on the Rail: Cty 528 *see also* Racoon on a Rail

Possum Trot: Rndr 0057, Rndr 0157

Possum up a Gum Stump: Ala Trad 103, Arh 5011 *see also* Rabbit up a Gum Stump

Possum up a 'Simmon Tree: Rndr 0032

Pot Licker Blues: CMF 011-L

Pot Wrassler: Fwys FH 5723, NW 314/315

Powder River Let 'Er Buck: RCA LPV 522, Rndr 0158, Rndr 0237

Powers' Waltz: JnAp JA0059C

Prayer of a Miner's Child: Asch AH 3903

Prayer of Drunkard's Little Girl: Rndr 1001

Preacher and the Bear: Fwys FA 2306, OH OHCS 141

Preacher Blues: BF 15501

Preacher Got Drunk and Laid His Bible Down: Cty 504

Preaching by the Road Side: Alp ALP 202, UNC 0-8078-4084-X

Preach the Gospel: Fwys FA 2357

Precious Jewel: Cty 404, Fwys FA 2365, OTC 6002

Precious Lord: SH SH-CD-3779

Precious Memories: FLeg FSA-23, Fwys FA 2427, Ldr LE 4040, OH OHS 90001, UNC 0-8078-4084-X

Present Joys: Fwys FA 2952, Mar 9101

Prettiest Little Girl in the County-O [Country]: Fwys FE 34162, Rndr 1023 *see also* Buck Eyed Rabbits

Pretty Aggie [C. 4]: AH AHR 007

Pretty Betty Martin: Fwys FA 2427

Pretty Crowing Chicken [C. 248]: FLeg FSA-22, Rndr 0028, TFS cass

Pretty Fair Miss [N 42]: Prst INT 13030

Pretty Green Island: Rndr 0064

Pretty Little Girl: DU-33002, HMM LP001, MS 45003, Tst T-3302

Pretty Little Girl I Left Behind Me: AH AHS 003

Pretty Little Girl with the Blue Dress On: Rndr 0194

Pretty Little Indian: OFA TALP-001

Pretty Little Miss: Ark Trad 002

Pretty Little Pink: Fwys FA 2355, Van VSD-107/108

Pretty Little Widow: Cty 526, Cty 720, Rndr 0009

Pretty Little Willow: Fwys FS 3811

Pretty Pink: Mar 9025

Pretty Polly: Cty 510 *see also* Wagoner's Lad, My Horses Ain't Hungry

Pretty Polly [N 14]: Prst INT 25004

Pretty Polly or the False-Hearted Knight [C. 4]: Fwys FE 4001, TFS 104

Pretty Polly [P 36b]: Asch AH 3831, Brun 59001, Cty 522, Cty 522, Cty 712, Cty 739, FPrm 41942, Fwys FA 2314, Fwys FA 2358, Fwys FS 3811, Fwys FS 3828, Fwys RBF 654, GyEg 101, JnAp JA 010, JnAp JA 020, LC AFS L1, Mtn 303, OT 102, Prst INT 13035, Prst INT 25009, Riv RLP 12-610, Rndr 0072, TFS-106, Trad TLP 1007, Wstm SWN 18021

Pretty Saro: Fwys FA 2309, GnHys GR714, Prst INT 13030, Sm/Fwys SF 40012, Tpc 12T146, Tpc 12TS336, Van VRS-9239

Pretty Suzie: FLeg FSA-11

Price of Cotton (Blues): BF 15501, OT 115

Printer's Bride: Fwys FA 2427

Prisoner at the Bar: ACM ACM-1, Ark Trad 002

Prisoner for Life, A: BF 15502

Prisoner's Call: Rndr 1002

Prisoner's Dream: OT 115, BB AXM2-5525, BF 15501, OH OHCS 111

Prisoner's Plea: CT 6002

Prisoner's Song: Fwys FA 2350, Fwys FS 3839, LC AFS L68

Prison Sorrows: OH OHCS-177

Prison Warden's Secret: FLeg FSA-18

Prodigal's Career: Rndr 0083

Prodigal Son: Fwys FA 2358

Prohibition Blues: Rndr 1035

Prohibition Is a Failure: Mar 9105

Prohibition, Yes or No (Sketch; Pts 1/2): Mar 9104

Promised Land: Tpc 12T146

Property Auction: Her 070

Protecting the Innocent: Rndr 0089

Pumpkin Vine: GFS GFS 901

Puncheon Floor: Miss AH-002

Punching the Dough: BF 15502, Rndr 0158, Rndr 0237

Put Me in My Little Bed: BF 15518

Put My Little Shoes Away: AFF 33-4, Ark Trad 002, Roots 701, UICFC CFC 201

Puttin' on the Style: Kan 313

Put-Together Blues: Tst T-3302

Put Your Little Foot: UICFC CFC 301

Quadrille: LC AFS L62

Quadrille in C & F: UMP No #

Quadrille Melody: UMP No #

Quaker's Cow: Van VSD-9/10

Queen Jane [C. 52]: FLeg FSA-33

Queen of the Earth and Child of the Stars: WVUP 001

Queen Sally [C. 295 / P 9]: BRI 002

Queenstown Warning [H 14]: Ph 1020

Quil O'Quay [C. 18]: JnAp JA 001

Quinn's Reel: JEMF-105

Quit That Tickling Me: Rndr 0058, Rndr CD 11536

Rabbit: NW 291

Rabbit in a Log: Cty 739, Fwys FA 2390, Prst INT 13035

Rabbit in the Pea Patch: Cty 521, NW 291

Rabbit up a Gum Stump: Cty 503, Cty 520 *see also* Possum up a Gum Stump

Rabbit, Where's Your Mammy?: Arh 5010 *see also* Little Rabbit Where's Your Mammy?, There's No Hell in Georgia

Raccoon on a Rail: Cty 544 *see also* Possum on a Rail

Rachel: Her 22, Kan 310

Radio Theme Song: Sytn STR 201

Raftman's Song: TFS 105

Ragged but Right: OH OHCS 114, RCA 8416-2-R

Ragged [Raggedy] Ann: Mtn 303 *see also* Ragtime Annie

Ragging the Wires: Rndr 0026

Raging Sea, How It Roars [C. 289]: BRI 002, Cty 534, Rndr 1008

Ragtime Annie: Cty 501, Cty 507, Cty 509, Cty 733, Fwys FA 2380, Fwys FS 3832, MFP MFP 002, Mar 9110, RCA LPV 552, Sytn STR 201, Van VRS-9170 *see also* Ragged Ann

Railroad Bill [I 13]: Asch AA 3/4, Cty 515, Rndr 1007, Prst INT 25009, Trad TLP 1007, Van VRS-9182

Railroad Blues: Alp ALP 201, Arb 201, Arh 5012, Cty 511, Fwys FA 2379, Vet 103

Railroad Boomer: Roots 701

Railroader (for Me): LC AAFS L20, LC AFS L61

Railroading and Gambling: BF 15519, Cty 541, RCA LPV 507

Railroading on the Great Divide: TL TLCW-06

Railroad through the Rocky Mountains: Mer 1001-2

Railroad Tramp: Fwys FA 2392

Rain and Snow: Bio RC 6004, Fwys FA 2418, Prst INT 13020

Rainbow Division: OT 112 *see also* Birmingham Jail

Rainbow mid the Willows [M 13]: Prst INT 25003

Rainbow Schottische: Cty 777

Rainbow Sign: Cty 791

Rainbow Waltz: OH OHCS 192

Rain Crow Bill: Van VRS-9239

Raindrop Waltz: OH OHCS 193

Raise a Ruckus [Rough House] Tonight: Arh 5010, NW 225, Rndr 1032

Rake and Rambling Boy [L 12]: Rndr 1023, Tpc 12T146

Raker's Hornpipe: Miss AH-002

Raleigh and Spencer: Cty 756 *see also* Riley...

Rambling Blues: Cty 505 *see also* Beale Street Blues, Tennessee Blues

Rambling Boy: Cty 404, Cty 411

Rambling Boy [L 12]: LC AFS L7, Riv RLP 12-649

Rambling Gambler: CT 6002

Rambling Hobo: Rndr 0028, Rndr 0058, Sm/Fwys SF 40012, Tpc 12TS336, Van VRS-9147, Van VCD-45

Rambling Reckless Hobo [H 2]: Rndr 1004

Ramshackle Shack (on the Hill): Alp ALP 202, Arh F5002, Cty 404, Cty 739 *see also* Sparkling Blue Eyes

Randy Riley [C. 278]: FLeg FSA-15

Ranger's Command: Rndr 0077

Ranger's Hornpipe: Cty 401 *see also* Flop Eared Mule

Rank Stranger: Van VSD-107/108

Rare Willie Drowned in the Yarrow [C. 215]: GV SC 03, Rndr 0017

Rat Cheese Under the Hill: Cty 503, Cty 536 *see also* Pike's Peak

Rats in the Meal Barrel: Miss AH-002

Rattle Down the Acorns: Her 33 *see also* Rattling ..., Shaking ...

Rattler Treed a Possum: Ark Trad 004, Cty 519 *see also* Hell Bound for Alabama, Shoot That Turkey Buzzard

Rattlesnake: Ok OK 75003

Rattlesnake and the Texas Pony: MFFA 1001

Rattlesnake Bill: Ark Trad 004, JnAp JA 010

Rattlesnake Song [G 16]: Ark Trad [No #]

Rattling Down the Acorns: Cty 786 *see also* Rattle ..., Shaking ...

Rawhide: Prst FL 14030

Reckless Motorman: De DL 4557

Reckless Night Blues: BF 15501

Red and George Breakdown: Rndr 0065

Red and Green Signal Lights: Fwys FA 3833, DU 33033, OHCS-157, RCA LPV 532 *see also* Engineer's Child

Red Apple Rag: Cty 547

Red Bird: Cty 733

Red Hawk Waltz: Rndr 0157

Red Headed Irishman: Rndr 0037

Red Hill Special: OHS OF-1001

Red Hot Breakdown: Cty 543, Hist HLP 8003

Red Jacket Mine Explosion: Fwys FA 2375

Red Mountain Wine: Her 22

Red River Valley: BF BCD 15456, AFF 33-3, Fwys FA 2365 *see also* Bright Sherman Valley

Red River Valley/Rio Jarmana: BF 15003

Red River Waltz: Cty 401

Red Rocking Chair: Cty 712, Fwys FA 3833

Red Rose Rag: BF 15505, Cty 523

Red Steer: OH OHCS 191

Red Whiskey: LC AAFS L20

Redwing: Fwys FTS 31007, JnAp JA 010, Ldr LE 4040

Red Wing: Roots 701

Reidsville Blues: Ldr LEA 4012

Rejoicing All the Way: Mar 9100

Religion Is a Fortune: Mar 9100

Religious Song: Fwys FS 3810

Remember and Do Pray for Me: Rndr 0028

Remember What You Told Me, Love: Rndr 0076

Resignation: JnAp 037

Resurrection, The: CMF 011-L, OHCS-172

Returning Sweetheart [N 42]: Asch AH 3831

Reuben Ranzo: LC AAFC L26/27

Reuben's Train or Reuben: AH AHR 010, Cty 713, FLeg FSA-1, SmFwys SF 40037, Fwys FA 2434, JEMF 103, Mtn 302, Rndr 0001, Rndr 0237, Tpc 12TS336, Van VSD-107/108

Reuben Wright and Phoebe Brown: LC AAFS L55

Rich and Rambling Boy [L 12]: Prst INT 13020

Rich Girl, Poor Girl: FLeg FSA-13

Rich Irish Lady [P 9]: FLeg FSA-32

Richmond: Cty 718, Ldr LEA 4012, Ldr LEE 4045

Richmond Blues: Fwys FA 2355, MS 45003

Richmond Cotillion: Cty 524 *see also* Richmond Square, Green Mountain Polka

Richmond Square: Alp ALP 202, Bio BLP 6005 *see also* Richmond Cotillion, Green Mountain Polka

Rich Mountain: Her 22, Rndr 0057

Rich Old Farmer [P 1a]: LC AFS L1

Rich Old Lady [Q 2]: Ark Trad [No #]

Rickett's Hornpipe: Kan 307, LC AFS L62, Ldr LEE 4045 *see also* Tanner's Hornpipe

Riddle Song: SH SH-CD-3786, Van VRS-9213, FLeg FSA-3

Riddles & Where's the Ox At?: HMM LP002

Ride Old Buck to Water: Cty 526

Ridge Running Roan: NW 314/315, Fwys FH 5723

Riding in an Old Model "T": Mar 9110

Riding on a Humpback Mule: Ok OK 76004

Riding on My Saviour's Train: Cty 729

Riding on That Train 45: RCA 8416-2-R, RCA LPV 507 *see also* Train Forty-Five

Riley and Spencer: Bio RC-6002, Rndr SS-0145

Riley's Hen House Door: Cty 411

Riley the Furniture Man: Rndr 1026

Ring Dang Rantigan: Rndr 0051

Ring the Bells: Her 070

Rio Grande: LC AAFC L26/27

Rise When the Rooster Crows: Fwys RBF RF 51, Vet 101

Rising Sun (Blues): Fwys FA 2359, Fwys 2363, Van VRS-9170, Van VCD-45 [= House of the Rising Sun]

Risselty Rosselty: NW 223

River Driver's Song: Fwys FE 4001

River of Jordan: CMH 107, Har HL 7396, OH OHCS 116, OH OHCS 117, Fwys FA 2306

River Stay Away from My Door: Fwys FA 2434

Road That's Walked by Fools: Asch AH 3902

Road to Washington: *see* Unlucky Road ...

Roaming Boy [P 1b]: Prst INT 13030

Roane County Prisoner: AH AHS 001

Roane County Rag: Cty 403

Roan Mountain Breakdown: Rndr 0008

Robertson County: Cty 541

Robin Hood and the Peddler [C. 132]: NW 291

Robin Hood Rescuing the Three Squires [C. 140]: MC 1

Robinson County: Cty 520, Cty 531

Rochester Schottische: Cty 756

Rock About, My Sarah [Saro] Jane: Brun 59001, Cty 521 *see also* Sara Jane

Rock All the Babies To Sleep: Prst INT 25006

Rock Creek Girl: Mer 1001-2

Rockhouse Gambler: Rndr 0036

Rock House Joe: Fwys FA 2379

Rocking Chair Money: Fwys FTS 31016

Rockingham Cindy: Cty 713, Cty 748, Mtn 302

Rocking in a Weary Land: Her 070

Rockin' the Boat: DU 33014

Rock Little Julie: JnAp JA 009

Rock That Cradle Lucy: Cty 506, Cty 544

Rock the Cradle and Cry: Rndr 0076

Rock the Cradle Joe: Cty 201

Rockville Waltz: Ok OK 76004

Rocky Island: Fwys FA 2317

Rocky Mountain: Her 070

Rocky Mountain Goat: Rndr 0018

Rocky Mountain Hornpipe: Rndr 0133

Rocky Pallet [Possum and Taters]: Cty 526

Rocky Road: Fwys FA 2952, Van VRS-9182

Rocky Road through Georgia: Mer 1001-2

Rocky Road to Denver: GyEg 101

Rocky Road to Dublin: DU 33014, Her 12, Rndr 0047

Rocky Run: SmFwys SF 40038

Rocus's Reel: Kan 310

Rogers' Gray Mare [P 8]: FLeg FSA-23

Rogers' Hornpipe: FLeg FSA-27

Roll Along Prairie Moon: Sytn STR 202

Roll down the Line: *see* Buddy Won't You ...

Roll 'Em on the Ground: Rndr 1005

Rolling Deep: Rndr 0078

Rolling Hills of Border: JnAp 018

Rolling Home: LC AAFC L26/27

Rolling Mills Are Burning Down: Rndr 0028

Rolling On: BB AXM2-5510, Prst FL 14010

Rolling on the Rye Grass: LC AAFS L16

Rolling Pin Woman: Kan 305

Rolling Store: FLeg FSA-2

Roll in My Sweet Baby's Arms: BB AXM2-5510, RCA 8417-2-R, Prst FL 14035, Van VSD-6576 *see also* I'll Roll..

Roll on Boys: GHP LP 1001

Roll on Buddy: BB AXM2-5510, Cty 525, Cty 718, Fwys FA 2374, Fwys FA 2379, LC AFS L61, Riv RLP 12-650, Rndr 0065, Van VSD-9/10

Roll on Daddy, Roll On: BF 15507

Roll on John: Fwys FA 2342, JnAp JA 009

Roll on Little Dogies: BF BCD 15456, Fwys FH 5723

Roll on the Ground: LC AFS L2

Roll on Weary River, Roll On: BF 15003

Roll the Cotton Down: LC AAFC L26/27

Roll the Old Chariot Along: LC AFS L68

Rolly Trudum: Fwys FA 2362, LC AAFS L12

Rome County: Rndr 0017

Room in Heaven for Me: CMH 107
Roosian Rabbit: Rndr 0037
Root Hog or Die [B 21]: LC AAFS L30
Rosa Lee McFall: Fwys FA 2352
Roscoe Trillion: *see* Flop Eared Mule, etc.
Rose Conley [F 6]: OT 102, OHCS-157
Rose in Grandma's Garden: Fwys FA 2315
Roses in the Morning: Cty 788
Roses While I'm Living: Asch AH 3903
Rose Waltz: UMP No #
Rose with a Broken Stem: Mar 9110
Rosewood Casket: Atl 1347, SmFwys SF 40037, Prst FL 14035, Rndr 0021
Rough Neck Blues: OT 115
Rough Scotsman: GyEg 101
Rounded Up in Glory: BF BCD 15456
Rounders Luck: OH OHS 90031 *see also* Rising Sun Blues, House of the Rising Sun
Rounding Up the Yearlings: Rndr 1037
Round the Mountain: Fwys FS 3848
Round to Maryanne's: NW 291
Round Town Girls [Gals]: Asch AH 3902, Bio RC-6002, Cty 405, Cty 407, HMM LP002, Kan 307, Prst FL 14030 *see also* Alabama Gals, Buffalo Gals
Round-Up Cook: Fwys FH 5723
Roustabout: Cty 717, Rndr 0057, Her 33, Mtn 304
Route, The: LC AFS L65-L66
Rove Riley Rove: Rndr 0237
Roving Boy [P 1b]: TFS 106
Roving Cowboy [P 1a]: JnAp JA 009
Roving Cunningham: Ph 1022
Roving Gambler [H 4]: Asch AH 3831, BF 15508, TFS 106
Roving Piper: AH AHS 001
Roving Ranger [A 8]: Asch AH 3831
Rowan County Crew [E 20]: Rndr 0034
Row Us over the Tide: BF 15510, Cty 408, Cty 508, Mer 1001-2
Roxie Anne: NW 291
Roy Dixon: OT 102
Rubber Dolly: AFF 33-3
Rubber Dolly Rag: OT 101
Rubber-Tired Buggy: PB 003
Ruben's Train: see Reuben's Train
Rude and Rambling Man [L 12]: Fwys FA 2350, GHP LP 1001
Rufus: OH OHCS 192
Rufus Blossom: BF 15517 *see also* Whistling Rufus

Rufus Rastus: Cty 528
Run Banjo: NW 226
Run Boy [Smoke] Run: see Run Nigger Run
Run Mountain: Arh F5002
Run Nigger [Boy] [Johnnie] [Smoke] Run: Arh 5010, Cty 526, DU 33015, Fwys FS 3839, Ldr LE 4040, LC AFS L62, PB 003, Rndr 0005, Rndr 0037, Rndr 1005, Sytn STR 201, Vet 105 *see also* Run Boy Run, Run Slave Run
Running Bear: Kan 310
Run Rabbit Run: Kan 310
Run Sinner and Hide Your Face: TFS 106
Run, Slave, Run: Van VRS 9162
Run Them Coons into the Ground: Rndr 1037
Russian Rabbit: see Roosian Rabbit
Russian Roulette: HMM LP001
Rustic Dance: Cty 723, Ldr LEE 4045, UMP No #
Rusty Spurs: NW 314/315
Rutherford's Reel: Rndr 0034
Rutherford's Waltz: DU 33014
Rutland's Reel: Ldr LEA 4012
Rye Straw: AH AHS 003, Cty 527, Cty 788, Fwys FS 3809, Miss AH-002, Rndr 1005, Tak A 1013
Rye Whiskey: AFF 33-4, Cty 202, FLeg FSA-1, Tak A 1013 *see also* Jack O'Diamonds, Drunkard's Hiccoughs, My Horses Ain't Hungry
Rymer's Favorite: NW 226

Sabula Blues: Hist HLP 8002
Sad and Lonesome Day: Har HL 7344
Saddle Old Paint: Her 33
Sadie Goodwin: Mtn 303
Sago Lily: Fwys FA 2036
Sail Away Ladies: Brun 59000, Cty 521, Cty 756, Fwys FA 2952, FPrm (No #), GyEg 101, Her 070, MS 45004, Mtn 304, PB 003, Rndr 0037
Sailing on the Ocean: Cty 531 *see also* Sugar Hill
Sailor Boy [K 13]: CMH 118, Fwys FS 3848
Sailor Man Blues: Mar 9109
Sailor on the Deep Blue Sea [K 12]: JnAp JA0059C, Prst INT 13020, Riv RLP 12-617, Riv RLP 12-645
Sailor's Alphabet: LC AAFC L26/27
Saint Anne's Reel / Growling Old Man, Growling Old Woman: Her 33
Saint James Hospital [B 1]: Van VCD-45/46, Van VRS-9152

Saint Joe Hornpipe: UMP No #

Saint Louis Blues: BRI 005, Fwys FA 2317, OH OHS 90031

Saint Patrick's Day in the Morning: JEMF 105

Saint Regious Girl: De DL 4557

Saints Go Marching In: Fwys FA 2433 *see also* When the Saints ...

Salem's Bright King: AH AHR 009

Sales Tax Toddle: Cty 529

Sal Let Me Chaw Your Rosin Some: FSSM FSSMLP 150001-D, Vet 107

Sally [P 9]: FLeg FSA-26

Sally Ann: Cty 405, Cty 717, Cty 718, Cty 720, Cty 723, Cty 748, DU 33015, FLeg FSA-3, FLeg FSA-17, Fwys FA 2355, Fwys FA 2363, Fwys FA 2380, Fwys FA 2434, Fwys FA 2435, Fwys FS 3832, JnAp 032, KM 204, Mar 9110, Mtn 302, Mtn 305, Prst FL 14030, Prst INT 25003, Rndr 0058, SmFwys SF 40037, SmFwys SF 40037, SmFwys SF 40038 *see also* Sail Away Ladies, Great Big Taters, Big Footed Man in the Sandy Lot

Sally Ann Johnson: AH AHS 001, Cty 733

Sally Brown: LC AFS L2

Sally [Sallie] Gooden [Goodin] [Goodwin]: Arh F5002, Brun 59000, Cty 703, Cty 733, DU 33033, Fwys FA 2358, Fwys FA 2380, Fwys FE 34162, Fwys FS 3811, Fwys FS 3832, GyEg 101, Hist HLP 8004, HMM LP001, JnAp 030, LC AAFS L9, LC AFS L68, Ldr LEE 4045, OT 101, Prst FL 14030, Prst INT 25003, SH SH-CD-3786, SmFwys SF 40037, SmFwys SF 40037, Sytn STR 201, Tak A 1013 Trad TLP 1007, UICFC CFC 201 *see also* Tennessee Breakdown

Sally in the Garden: Brun 59000

Sally in the Green Corn: Mar 9100

Sally Johnson: Col CS 9660, Cty 202, Cty 501, Cty 517, Cty 544, Cty 703, DU 33014, Fwys FTS 31007, Rndr 0005 *see also* Katy Hill

Sally Long: Fwys FA 2379

Sal's Gone to the Cider Mill: Cty 506

Salt Lake City Blues: Cty 541

Salt River: Cty 527, Cty 707, Cty 733, Kan 307, Rndr 0057, Van VSD-9/10

Salty Dog Blues: BF 15517

Sal, Won't You Marry Me?: Her 33

Sam Bass [E 4]: LC AAFS L30, RCA LPV 522

Same Time Today As It Was Yesterday: Fwys FS 3809

Sam McGee Stomp: Arh 5012

Sammie, Where Have You Been So Long: Fwys RBF 654

Sam's Rag: Rndr SS-0145

Sam's "Waiting for a Train" [H 2]: UICFC CFC 301

San Antonio Rose: JnAp JA 025

Sand Mountain Blues: Fwys FS 3829

Sandy Boys: WVUP 001, LC AFS L65-L66

Sandy River: Cty 717, Cty 733, LC AAFS L21

Sandy River Belle(s): CMF 011-L, Cty 407, Cty 504, Her 22, Rndr 0057

Sanford Barney [H 1]: LC AFS L7

Santa Fe Trail: Ph 1017

Sardinia: Prst INT 25011

Sardis: LC AAFS L11

Saro: Cty 201

Saro [Sarah] (Jane): Cty 531, Mtn 304, Rndr 1004, Rndr 0057, Rndr 0058

Sassy Sam: BF 15518

Satan, Your Kingdom Must Come Down: FLeg FSA-36, LC AFC L69-L70, Rndr 0028

Satisfied: Elek EKL-316, LC AAFS L9

Satisfied at Last: CT 6002

Saturday Night Breakdown: Cty 532

Saturday Night Waltz: Cty 519

S-A-V-E-D: FSSM FSSMLP 150001-D *see also* I'm   S-A-V-E-D

Save My Mother's Picture from the Sale: BF 15519

Say Darling Say: Cty 535, Cty 791, Fwys FA 2315, Hist BC 2433-1

Say Old Man, Can You Play a Fiddle?: Cty 202

Scab's Toast, A: Rndr 0064

School House Fire: OT 102

Schoolhouse Song: TFS 103

Schottische: Cty 201, OFA TALP-001

Schottische Time: Fwys FA 2392

Scolding Wife, [C. 278]: Fwys FS 3828

Scotch Musick: Prst INT 25003

Scotland: Prst FL 14030

Scott Number One: UMP No #

Scott Number Two: UMP No #

Sea Fowl: Cty 789

Sea Gulls and Crickets: Fwys FA 2036

Sea of Galilee: Har HL 7300

Sea of Life: Fwys FA 2357

Searching for a Pair of Blue Eyes: OT 106

Searching for a Soldier's Grave: Rndr 0052

Searcy County Rag: Cty 503, Cty 518

Seashell Song: Rndr 0083

Second Class Hotel: Mar 9110

See God's Ark: Van VRS-9182

Seeing Nellie Home: Brch 1944, Fwys FA 2435 *see also* Aunt Dinah's Quilting Party

See That My Grave Is Kept Clean: NW 294, Prst INT 25011

Send Back My Wedding Ring: OH OHCS 114 [= Nellie Dare and Charlie Brooks] *see also* Charlie Brooks, Miss Dare

Seneca Square Dance: Ark Trad 004, Cty 520

Serenaders Waltz: Cty 410

Serves 'Em Fine: BF 15505

Seth Thomas Clock: Rndr 0157

Set Me Free: JnAp JA0059C

Setting in the Chimney Jamb: Rndr 1005

Seven and a Half: Arh F5002, OT 106, RCA 8416-2-R

Seven Long Years in Prison [E 17]: Pu 3001, RCA LPV 548

Seventy-Two: Fwys FS 3848

Shackles and Chains: FLeg FSA-13, Fwys FS 3829

Shady Grove (My Darling): Asch AH 3902, Atl 1347, BF 15003, Cty 717, Fwys FA 2342, Fwys FA 2359, Fwys FS 3828, Her 070, HMM LP002, JEMF 103, JnAp JA0059C, Mtn 304, Prst INT 13020, RCA 8416-2-R, Riv RLP 12-620, Rndr 0028, Rndr 0089, Rndr 1037, SH SH-CD-3786, Sm/Fwys SF 40012, Trad TLP 1007, Van VCD-45, Van VRS 9124

Shake 'em Down: Van VRS-9182

Shake Hands with Mother (Again): FLeg FSA-36, Mtn 305, OH OHS 90001

Shake My Mother's Hand for Me: Arh F5002

Shaker Ben: MS 45005

Shaking down (off) the Acorns: Rndr 0018, WVUP 001 *see also* Rattle ..., Rattling ...

Shall We Gather at the River: De DL 4760, Tak A 1013

Shamus O'Brien: Rndr 0133

Shanghai in China: BF 15507

Shanghai Rooster: Alp ALP 201, Rndr 0008

Shannon Waltz: Cty 410

Shantyman's Life: LC AAFS L55

Shanty Town: Ldr LE 4040

Sharp's Hornpipe: Cty 787

Shaving a Dead Man: Cty 757

Shear Them Sheep Even: Van VRS-9182

She Came Rolling down the Mountain: OH OHS 90031

Sheeps and Hogs Walking through the Pasture: Rndr 0032

Sheep Shell Corn (by the Rattlin' of His Horn): Her 070, Str STR 802

Sheepy and the Goat: Tpc 12TS336

Sheffield Apprentice [O 39]: Mar 9200

She Is Gone: JnAp 037

She Just Kept Kissing On: BF 15510

Shelburne Reel: JEMF 105

She'll Be Coming 'Round the Mountain: Fwys FA 2365

Shelving Rock: AH AHS 003, FPrm (No #), Rndr 0047, Rndr 0089

She Ought To Been a Lady: MFFA 1001

Sherburne: LC AAFS L11, NW 205, Prst INT 25007

Sherman's Retreat: Fwys FS 3809

She's a Beaut: Rndr 1035

She's a Flower from the Fields of Alabama: Hist HLP 8003, Mar 9111

She's Got the Money Too: Vet 101

She's Killing Me: OH OHS 90031, Rndr 1035

She Sleeps Beneath the Norris Dam: TFS 105

She's Mean I Mean: TFS 108

She's My Curly Headed Baby: Alp ALP 202

She's My Curly Headed Baby, No. 3: OH OHS 90031

She Tickled Me: CT 6002

She Took My Licker from Me: Mar 9105

She Wouldn't Be Still: BF 15507

She Wouldn't Give Me Sugar in My Coffee: Hist HLP 8006

Shine on Me: ACM ACM-1, Fwys FA 2952

Shining City over the River: CT 6002, Mar 9101

Shining for the Master: OH OHCS 190

Ship Carpenter [C. 243]: LC AAFS L58

Ship in the Clouds: DU-33002, Her 22

Ship Sailing Now: OH OHS 90001

Ship Set Sail for North America: [C. 286]: LC AAFS L58

Ship That Never Returned, The [D 27]: SH SH-CD-3795

Shirley's Tune: Ok OK 76004

Shoes and Leggins: Fwys FA 2951

Shoo Fly Don't (You) Bother Me: BF 15519, Cty 536, Bio RC-6003, LC AAFS L21, Her 070, Fwys FA 2342, LC AAFS L16

Shooting Creek: Cty 501, Cty 505, Rndr 0057 *see also* Cripple Creek

(Shoot That) Turkey Buzzard: Cty 405, Fwys FE 34162, JnAp JA 049

Shoot the Buffalo: PB 004

Short Creek: Ph 1017

Shortening: Her 12

Shortening Bread: Cty 519, Cty 526, Cty 543, Her 22, Mar 9013, OH OHCS 111, OH OHCS 191, Rndr 1037, Fwys FA 2365, OHS OF-1001, Riv RLP 12-649, Rndr 0057, TFS 103, FPrm 41942, Prst INT 13030, Rndr 0089, Van VRS-9183, Rndr 0005, Rndr 0237, SmFwys SF 40037, Mer 1001-2

Short Life of (and It's) Trouble: RCA 8416-2-R, Rndr 1004, Cam CAL 797, Cty 513, FLeg FSA-17, Arh F5002, Fly LP 546, SmFwys SF 40038, Elek EKLP-2

Short Time Here: Fwys FA 2418

Shout (Little) Lulie (Lula): Cty 789, DU 33033, Fly LP 546, Fwys FA 2342, Fwys FA 2350, Fwys FE 34161, LC AAFS L21, Mer 1001-2, Rndr 0005 *see also* Hook and Line

Shout Monah, You Shall Be Free: Vet 101 *see also* You Shall Be Free, Poor Mourner, *etc.*

Shucking Up the Corn: Mer 1001-2

Shuffle Feet Shuffle: Cty 515

Shull's Mills: FLeg FSA-36

Shut Up in (the Mines at) Coal Creek Mine [G 9]: CT 6001, Rndr 1026, FLeg FSA-32, TFS 105

Sidney Allen [E 5]: BRI 004

Signal Light: SH SH-CD-3795

Silk and Satin: TFS 108

Silk Merchant's Daughter [N 10]: AH AHR 007, HMM LP001

Silly Bill: Atl 1347, Cty 405, Ldr LEE 4045

Silver Bell(s): DU-33009, Ldr LE 4040

Silver Dagger [G 21]: AH AHR 009, Rndr 0051

Silver Dollar: OTC 6002

Silver Threads Among the Gold: Ldr LEA 4012

Since Baby's Learned To Talk: BF 15503

Since the Angels Took My Mother Far Away: BB AXM2-5525

Sinful To Flirt [G 19]: Mtn 304, Mer 1001-2, Rndr 0143 *see also* It's ...

Singing Alphabet: LC AAFS L12

Singing Birds: Her 33, Rndr 0018

Single-Footing Horse: Fwys FTS 31007

Single Girl, Married Girl: BF 15003, CMF 011-L, FLeg FSA-36, Fwys FA 2953, LC AFS L68, OH OHS 90045, OTC 6001, Prst Int 13038, Van VRS 9124, Wstm SWN 18021

Single Life: Rndr 1029

Sing Me a Song: Fwys FA 2493, Rndr 0077

Sing Song Kitty: SH SH-CD-3786, Van VRS-9239

Sing to Me of Heaven: Riv RLP 12-620

Sinking in the Lonesome Sea [C. 286]: Har HL 7422, OH OHCS 112, TL TLCW-06

Sinking of the Cumberland [A 26]: Fwys FE 4001

Sinking of the Merry Golden Tree [C. 286]: Fwys FA 2375

Sinner's Friend: Prst INT 25007

Sinner You Better Get Ready: BB AXM2-5510, Fwys FA 2433

Sioux Indians [B 11]: NW 314/315, LC AFS L1

Sir Lionel [C. 18]: FLeg FSA-22

Sir Patrick Spens [C. 58]: TFS 106

Sissy in the Barn: LC AAFS L9

Sisters Thou Art Mild and Lovely: JnAp JA 020

Sit at Home: Fwys FA 2306

Sitting on Top of the World: Hist HLP 8002, OH OHCS 117, FLeg FSA-17, Tak A 1013, Van VRS-9152, Van VSD-107/108

Six Feet of Earth: Elek EKL-316

Six Month Ain't Long: Cty 502

Six More Miles: Prst Int 13038

Six Nights Drunk [C. 274]: TFS cass

Sixteen Days in Georgia: Cty 536, Kan 600

Sixteen on Sunday: Fwys FA 2379

Sixteen Tons: Fwys FTS 31016

Six Thousand Years Ago: Van VRS-9152 *see also* I Was Born About 4000 Years Ago

Six White Horses: Arh 5001, Cam CAL 719

Skidd More: Cty 407

Skillet Good and Greasy: Fwys FA 2355

Skillet Licker Breakdown: OH OHCS 192

Skipping and Flying: see Ain't That Skipping and Flying; *see also* Ain't That Trouble in Mind

Skipping through the Frost and the Snow: Cty 786

Skip to Ma (My) Lou, (My Darling): CMF 011-L, Cty 534, Cty 534, Fwys FS 3832, Mtn 305, OHCS-172, PB 004, Trad TLP 1007

Sleep, Baby, Sleep: CMF 011-L, SH SH-CD-3795

Sleeping Lulu: Cty 786, DU 33014, Rndr 1005

Sleepy Joe: UMP No #

Sleepy Lou: De DL 4760, Hist HLP 8006 *see also* Dickson County Blues, L. and N. Rag

Slewfoot: Van VSD-107/108

Slim Gal: Cty 544

Slow Buck: Rndr 1005 *see also* Chicken Reel

Smile a While: JnAp JA 025

Smith's Rag: Cty 547

Smith's Reel: Cty 707

Smoke Above the Clouds: Ala Trad 103

Smoke Among the Clouds: Rndr 0009

Smoke Behind the Clouds: PB 006

Snapping Bug: OHS OF-1001

Snowbird: Fwys FE 34161

Snowbird on (in) the Ashbank: Arh 5018, Rndr 0089, HMM LP002

Snow Dove: SmFwys SF 40038

Snowdrop: Fwys FA 2379, KM 204

Snowshoes: GFS GFS 901

Snuffy's Talking Blues: Arh 5011

Soap in the Washpan: MS 45003

Soapsuds over the Fence: Her 33

Soar Away: NW 205

Sockeye: PB 005

Softly Come the Gypsy: JnAp 018

So Handy, Me Boys, So Handy: LC AAFC L26/27

Soldier and Lady [P 14]: Fwys FS 3809, TFS 108, FLeg FSA-23, Prst INT 25006, Rndr 0021

Soldier John: FLeg FSA-23

Soldier of the Legion: Min JD-203, Van VRS-9158

Soldier's Joy: AFF 33-2, AFF 33-4, Col CS 9660, Cty 405, Cty 405, Cty 407, Cty 506, Cty 514, Cty 709, Cty 756, FLeg FSA-17, FPrm (No #), Fwys FA 2317, Fwys FA 2390, Fwys FA 2426, Fwys FES 34151, Fwys FS 3811, Fwys FS 3832, GFS GFS 901, GV SC 03, GyEg 101, JnAp JA 025, LC AAFS L9, LC AAFS L20, Ldr LEA 4012, Miss AH-002, MS 45003, Mtn 305, Prst INT 13035, RCA 8416-2-R, Trad 1007 Trad TLP 1007 *see also* Carolina Stompdown

Soldier (Soldier) (Will [Won't] You Marry Me): Atl SD-1350, LC AFS L2, Rndr 1035

Soldier's Sweetheart: JEMF 101, OH OHCS 117

Soldier's Sweetheart [N 42]: TFS 106

Soldier Traveling from the North [C. 299]: Fwys FA 2309

Somebody, but You Don't Mean Me: BF 15502

Somebody's Been Beating My Time: Fwys FA 2306

Somebody's Tall and Handsome: FLeg FSA-3, GHP LP 1001

Somebody's Waiting for You: OH OHCS 107

Somebody Touched Me: Tst T-3301

Someday We'll Meet Again Sweetheart: Fwys FA 3830

Some Glad Day: BB AXM2-5510

Some Have Fathers over Yonder: Fwys FE 34162

Some Little Bug Is Going To Get You Some Day: OH OHCS 107

Someone Else May Be there While I'm Gone: BF 15517

Something Doing: Hist HLP 8002

Something Got a Hold of Me: OH OHCS 112, RCA 2100-2-R

Sometimes: Atl SD-1350

Somewheres in West Virginia: JnAp JA 025

Somewhere Somebody's Waiting: Fwys FA 2352

Song of a Lost Hunter [C. 68]: FLeg FSA-1

Song of the Cove Creek Dam: TFS 106

Song of the Doodle Bug: Rndr 1032

Song of the French Broad River: Riv RLP 12-649

Sons of Sorrow: Ark Trad 003

Sopping the Gravy: Cty 703, Kan 600

S. O. S. Vestris: JEMF 103

Sourwood Mountain: Asch AH 3902, Brun 59000, Cty 778, FLeg FSA-1, Fwys FA 2342, Fwys FA 2363, Fwys FA 2380, Fwys FS 3811, Hist HLP 8002, JnAp JA 010, LC AAFS L12, LC AAFS L21, Riv RLP 12-650, Rndr 1008, Trad TLP 1007, Van VRS-9183, Wstm SWN 18021

Sourwood Mountain Medley--Part 1: De DL 4760

South: Mtn 303

Southbound: Sm/Fwys SF 40012, Van VRS-9213, Van VSD-9/10

Southern Medley: Cty 540, Hist HLP 8005

Southern Moon: ACM ACM-1

Southern No. 111: Cty 403, Vet 103

Southern Rose Waltz: KM 204

Southern Skies: Cty 729

Southern Soldier: LC AFS L29

Sow 'Em [Sowing] on the Mountain: CMH 118, Rndr 1029

Sow Took the Measles: TFS 104

Spanish Fandango: Arh 5011, NW 226, OHS OF-1001, Cty 523, Hist HLP 8002, SmFwys SF 40037 *see also* American and Spanish Fandango, Logan County Blues

Spanish Merchant's Daughter: Fwys FA 2953

Sparkling Blue Eyes: OH OHCS 117, OT 106

Sparkling Blue Eyes, No. 2: OT 106
Sparrow's Question: FLeg FSA-18
Spikedriver Blues: Fwys FA 2426, Van VSD-9/10
Spinning Room Blues: Rndr 1026
Spirit of Love: OH OHCS 116
Spokane Waltz: MFFA 1001
Sporting Bachelors: JnAp JA 009
Sporting Cowboy [E 17]: Ph 1017, Shoe SGB 1
Sporting Molly: FLeg FSA-11
Sport in New Orleans: Fwys FA 2418
Spotted Pony: GyEg 101
Springfield Mountain [G 16]: Asch AA 3/4, Fwys FP 40, Mar 9200
Springhill Disaster: NW 225
Spring of '65: Fwys FA 2317
Springtime of (My) Life: Fwys FA 2493, Rndr 0021
Sprinkle Coal Dust on My Grave: LC AFS L60
Squire's Daughter [C. 10]: Fwys FA 2358
Stack O'Lee [Stackalee] (Was a Bully) [I 15]: Fwys FA 2951, Fwys FE 34162, JEMF 103, Rndr 1010, Van VSD-6576
Stand Boys Stand: Mar 9013
Standing by a Window: Col CS 9660 *see also* Broken Engagement
Standing on the Promises: CMF 011-L
Star of Bethlehem: Ark Trad 003
Starry Night for Ramble, A: JnAp 018
Starving to Death on a Government Claim: LC AAFS L30
Staten Island Hornpipe: Ldr LEA 4012
State of Arkansas [H 1]: Rndr 0064
Station House Blues: Cty 777
Station Will Be Changed after a While: Vet 105
Stay All Night: Cty 741
Steam Arm: TFS 105
Steel A-Going Down: JnAp JA 009
Steel Guitar Rag: Fwys FA 2306, JnAp 030, Tst T-3302 *see also* Guitar Rag
Step Back Cindy: Cty 756
Step High Waltz: Cty 403
Step It Up and Go: Arh 5011
Step Stone: Mar 9110
Stern Old Bachelor: De DL 4404, Mer 1001-2
Steven's Waltz Number Two: UMP No #
St. George: LC AAFS L30
Stillhouse: Cty 717, Rndr 0057, Her 33
Stillhouse Brown: Rndr 0032
Still There's a Spark of Love: Rndr 0143
Stingy Woman Blues: Fwys FA 2317

Stolen Love: Cty 510
Stone [Stone's] Rag: Cty 541, GyEg 101, Tak A 1013, TFS 103
Stoney Creek: Fwys FA 2435
Stoney Point: MFFA 1001, Rndr 0089, UICFC CFC 201, UMP No # *see also* Wild Horse
Stoney Ridge Stomp: Rndr 0089
Stoney's Waltz: Fwys FA 2315
Stoney's Wife: Fwys FA 2365
Stop Drinkin' Shine: Mar 9105
Stop That Knocking at My Door: BF 15518
Storms Are on [Stormy Rose] the Ocean: FLeg FSA-17, Prst Int 13038, Prst FL 14010, TL TLCW-06, Van VRS-9147 *see also* It's Hard To Leave You Sweet Love
Story of Freeda Bolt: BRI 004
Story of the Flood: BRI 004
Story of the Knoxville [P 35]: Cam CAL 797
Story of the Mississippi: OHCS-173
Stove Pipe Blues: MS 45005
Stratfield: LC AAFS L11
Strawberry Roan [B 18]: AFF 33-3, NW 314/315, MFP 0001, OK 75003, Fwys FH 5723
Straw Breakdown: Cty 546 *see also* Turkey in the Straw
Streamline Mama: Cty 409
Stream of Time: JnAp 037
Streets of Glory: Rndr 0009, Ldr LEE 4045
Streets of Laredo [B 1]: NW 314/315, LC AAFS L28, Fwys FH 5723
Stumptown Stomp: Cty 202
St. ... see Saint ...
Sugar Babe [Baby]: Fwys FA 2953, Fwys RBF 654, Fwys FA 2392, LC AFS L65-L66, Rndr 0018, Van VRS-9147 *see also* Banjo Picking Girl, Birmingham
Sugar Barrel: GFS GFS 901, Mar 9013
Sugar Blues: Asch AH 3903
Sugar Cane Mama: Fwys FA 2352
Sugarfoot Rag: Cty 791, Rndr 0072
Sugar Gal: PB 003
Sugar Grove Blues: LC AFS L65-L66
Sugar Hill: Bio RC-6003, Brun 59000, Cty 534, Cty 741, Cty 757, Fwys FS 3811, Hist HLP 8003, Mtn 302, Rim Rlp-495, Str STR 802 *see also* Sailing on the Ocean
Sugar in the Gourd: Cty 507, Cty 720, Her 070, JnAp JA 049, LC AFS L62, Ldr LEA 4012, Rndr 1003
Sugar on the Floor: Fwys FA 2426

Sugar Tree Stomp: Cty 547

Sullivan's Hollow: Cty 529

Summer Evening in Aalhus, A: MFP MFP 002

Summerland: Arh 5018

Summertime on the Beeno Line: BF 15503

Sumter Rag: Fwys FA 2306

Sunday Night Reel: Rndr 0133

Sundown: Mer 1001-2, Riv RLP 12-645

Sunny Home in Dixie: Cty 507

Sunnyside: Cty 703

Sunny Side of Life: Cam CAL 797, Rndr 1006

Sunny Side of the Mountain: Fwys FA 3833

Sunny South: SmFwys SF 40037 *see also* Sweet
    Sunny South

Sunny Tennessee : Cty 502, Rndr 0009, Van
    VSD-107/108 *see also* Girl I Loved in ...

Sun of the Soul: OTC 6001

Sun's a Gonna Shine: AFF 33-3

Sunset March: Arb 201

Sunset Memories: DU-33009

Sun's Gonna Shine in My Back Door: TL
    TLCW-06

Sunshine in the Shadows: Cam CAL 2554(e),
    CMH 107

Surely I Will: Rndr 0009

Susan Loller on Judio: Mer 1001-2

Susanna Gal: Cty 201, Her 22, Mtn 302, Str
    STR 802

Susan (Susie) Girl: Cty 789, Riv RLP 12-620

Susie Lee: Cty 545

Susie Licked the Ladle Clean: Shoe SGB 1

Suwanee River: Rndr 0089

Suzanna Gal: Cty 718, Mar 9110

Swamp Cat Rag: Cty 514 *see also* Citaco

Swamper's Revenge on the Windfall: LC AAFS
    L55

Swannanoa Tunnel (Swanno Mountain): Fwys
    FP 40, Fwys 2368

Swap a Little Sugar: Rndr 0008

Sweeping through the Gates: Rndr 1008

Sweet Allalee: Rndr 1006

Sweet As the Flowers in May Time: Cam
    ACL1-0047, CMH 107

Sweet Betsy from Pike [B 7]: RCA LPV 548

Sweet Bird [Fern]: Cam CAL 586, Cty 510, OH
    OHCS 141, Rndr 0036 *see also* Birds Are
    Returning

Sweet Bunch of Daisies: Kan 306, Rndr 0034

Sweet Bunch of Violets: Cty 533

Sweet Bye and Bye: Fwys FA 2357

Sweet Eloise: Kan 305

Sweetest Flower Waltz: Cty 410

Sweetest Gift (a Mother's Smile): Arh 5011,
    Fwys FA 2435, Rndr CD 11536

Sweet Fern: see Sweet Bird

Sweet Georgia Brown: JnAp 030, Van
    VRS-9213

Sweetheart Mountain Rose: Rndr CD 11536

Sweet Heaven in My View: De DL 4404

Sweet Heaven When I Die: Pu 3001

Sweet Jane: Van VRS 9124

Sweet Kiss Waltz: Fwys FA 2306

Sweet Kitty Wells: OHCS 317 *see also* Kitty
    Wells

Sweet Lovely Jane: FLeg FSA-11

Sweet Marie: Fwys FA 2365

Sweet Mary: Fwys FA 2362

Sweet Milk and Peaches: Cty 529

Sweet Rivers: Ark Trad 003

Sweet Rivers of Redeeming Love: JnAp 037

Sweet Rose of Heaven: Cty 532, NW 236

Sweet Rosie: Rndr 0076

Sweet Rosie O'Grady: DU 33033

Sweet Sadie [I 8]: AH AHR 010 (*see also*
    Little Sadie)

Sweet Sixteen: Cty 505

Sweet Soldier Boy [K 12]: FLeg FSA-22

Sweet Summer's Gone Away: OHCS-173

Sweet Sunny South: Cty 502, Cty 505, Cty 748,
    Ldr LEA 4012, Her 22, Mer 1001-2, Mtn
    303, Rndr 0032 *see also* Sunny South, Take
    Me Home to the Sweet Sunny South

Sweet William (and Fair Ellen) [C. 7]: Bio
    RC-6002, CT 6001, Cty 534, LC AAFS L12,
    NW 245

Sweet William and Lady Margaret [C. 74]:
    Fwys FA 2302

Sweet William [N 8]: LC AAFS L21

Sweet Willie: Fwys FA 2317, Fwys FA 2427

Sweet Wine: NW 223

Swing and Turn Jubilee: Ark Trad [No #]

Swing Low, Chariot: Riv RLP 12-645

Swing Nine Yards of Calico: Rndr 0037

Sycamore Shoals: N&T 1001

Tail of Halley's Comet: Mar 9110

Take a Drink on Me: Cty 505 *see also* Tell It
    to Me

Take a Look at That Baby: Hist HLP 8002

Take Me Back to My (Old) Carolina Home:
    Rndr 1028

Take Me Back to Renfro Valley: ACM ACM-1

Take Me Back to Tennessee: Cty 546

Take Me Back to Tulsa: AFF 33-3

Take Me [Home] Back to the Sweet Sunny South: Hist HLP 8003, OH OHS 90001

Take Me Home Poor Julia: Cty 521

Take Me in the Life Boat: Alp ALP 201

Take Me to Lincoln: DU-33009

Take Me to the Land of Jazz: Cty 523

Take Them for a Ride: BF 15505

Take the News to Mother: FLeg FSA-18, OH OHS 90031

Take This Hammer: Prst Int 13049

Take Up Thy Cross: BB AXM2-5525

Take Your Foot out of the Mud and Put It in the Sand: Mar 9111

Take Your Time and Think It Over: Kan 308

Take Your Time Miss Lucy: Cty 712

Tales of My Grandad: FLeg FSA-27

Talk About Suffering: Van VRS-9152

Talkin' Guitar: SH SH-CD-3786

Talking Memphis: UICFC CFC 301

Tall Timber: Her 33

T. and P. Line: LC AFS L61

Tanner's Boarding House: OH OHCS 193, Rndr 1005

Tanner's Hornpipe: RCA LPV 552 *see also* Rickett's Hornpipe

Tanner's Rag: OH OHCS 193

Tater Patch: Cty 757, Cty 778

Taxes on the Farmer Feeds Them All: UIP [cass, no #]

Taylor's Quickstep: DU 33014, Mar 9025, Rndr 1004

Teardrops in My Eyes: Fwys FA 2434

Teasdale Quadrille: Ok OK 76004

Teetotaller: Kan 307

Television: Arh 5011

Tell Her To Come Back Home: De DL 4760, Rndr 1033 *see also* Cindy

Tell It to Me (Boys): Rndr 1033, Pu 3001 *see also* Take a Drink on Me

Tell Mother I Will Meet Her: CMF 011-L, Cty 533

Temperence Reel: Van VRS-9182

Tempie (Roll Down Your Bangs): Cty 748, Cty 791 *see also* Alberta

Ten Cent Piece: Cty 519

Tenderfoot: Ph 1017, AFF 33-2

Tennessee Blues: Arb 201, Bio BLP 6005, Cam CAL 719 *see also* Rambling Blues

Tennessee Breakdown: Cty 525 *see also* Sally Gooden

Tennessee Coon: Rndr 1032 *see also* Coon from Tennessee

Tennessee Gambler: Fwys FA 2352

Tennessee Girl: OH OHCS 191

Tennessee Jubilee: De DL 4760, Rndr 1033 *see also* Ain't Nobody's Business, Turkey in the Straw, Straw Breakdown

Tennessee (Mountain) (Red) Fox Chase: Cty 525, Vet 101 *see also* Fox Chase

Tennessee Stud: SH SH-CD-3786, Van VRS-9213

Tennessee Wagoner (Wagner): GyEg 101, Cty 720, Rndr 0157

Tennessee Waltz: Cty 403

Ten Thousand Cattle: UICFC CFC 301

Ten Thousand Miles: Asch AH 3831, LC AFS L2, Rndr 0083

Terry Sloan: AFF 33-2

Testimony: LC AFC L69-L70

Texahoma Boogie: JnAp 030

Texas Belle(s): AFF 33-3, AFF 33-4, LC AFS L2

Texas Bound: GnHys GR712

Texas Farewell: Cty 517

Texas Gales/Blackberry Rag: Sm/Fwys SF 40012

Texas Gales [Gals]: Cty 405, Cty 741, Fwys FA 2366, Her 12, Van VSD-6576

Texas Hop: OH OHCS 192

Texas Quick-Step: Cty 517, Rndr 0005

Texas Ranger(s) [A 8]: LC AAFS L28, RCA LPV 522

Texas Wagoner: Cty 202, Cty 527, Sytn STR 201 *see also* Tennessee Wagoner, Georgia Wagoner

Tex's Dance: RCA 8416-2-R

T for Texas: BRI 005

Thank You Jesus: Van VRS-9183

That Bloody War: FLeg FSA-2

That Fatal Courtship: see Fatal Courtship

That French-Canadian Tune: MFP MFP 002

That Last Move for Me: CMH 112

That Little Lump of Coal: LC AFS L60

That Lonesome Valley: Mar 9100

That Silver Haired Daddy of Mine: Sytn STR 202, SH SH-CD-3795

That's My Rabbit, My Dog Caught It: MS 45005, NW 226

That Star Belongs to Me: Prst FL 14010

That's What It's Like To Be Lonesome: TL TLCW-06

That Thirty Inch Coal: Rndr 0064

That Was the Last Thing on My Mind: Van VRS-9213

Them Two Gals of Mine: BF 15518

There Ain't No Use Working So Hard: BF 15507

There Is a Happy Land: Ark Trad 003

There Lived an Old Lord [C. 10]: Fwys FA 2302

There'll Be Joy, Joy, Joy: Cam ACL1-0047, JEMF 101 *see also* Within My Father's House

There'll Be No Distinction There: Har HL 7396, RCA 2100-2-R, Rndr 1001

There'll Be Some Changes Made: JnAp 030

There'll Come a Time: Cty 509, Hist HLP 8004, Prst FL 14035

There Once Was an Owl: JnAp 018

There's a Big Wheel: TL TLCW-06

There's a Brown Skin Girl down the Road Somewhere: Sytn STR 201, RCA LPV 522

There's a Hard Time Coming: Rndr 1003

There's a Lock on the Chicken Coop Door: Her 22

There's a Man Going Round Taking Names: GHP LP 1001

There's a Mother Always Waiting You at Home: FLeg FSA-18

There's a Place in My Home for Mother: CT 6002

There's a Red Light Ahead: OHCS 316

There's More in Heaven for Me: OH OHCS 116

There's More Pretty Girls Than One: Cty 547, RCA LPV 507, LC AAFS L21, Rndr 0034, Van VSD-107/108

There's No Hell in Georgia: Cty 519

There's No Hiding Place down Here: Cam CAL 2554(e)

There's No One Like Mother to Me: MCA VIM-4012

There's No One Like the Old Folks: Rndr 1004

There's No Place Like Home: OHCS 315

There's No Place Like Home for the Married Man: Rndr 0034

There's Someone A-waiting: OTC 6001

There's Trouble on My Mind Today: OTC 6002

There Was An Old and Wealthy Man [C. 272]: LC AAFS L58

There Was an Old Lady [Q 2]: Fwys FA 2362

There Was an Old Man Lived in the West [C. 277]: TFS 104

There Was an Old Woman: Wstm SWN 18021

They Call Her Mother: MCA VIM-4012

They're After Me: BF 15519

They're All Going Home but One: ACM ACM-1

They're at Rest Together: Prst Int 13049, SmFwys SF 40038

They Sang That Old Time Religion: Ark Trad 003

They Say It Is Sinful To Flirt [G 19]: Ark Trad 002, RCA LPV 548

They Sent Her Gun to War: Kan 305

Things I Don't Like To See: BF 15519

Thirty Pieces of Silver: Fwys FA 2357

This Gospel How Precious: Rndr 0078

This Is Like Heaven to Me: OH OHCS 116, RCA LPM 2772

This Is the Place: Ok OK 75003

This Little Light of Mine: Mer 1001-2, UNC 0-8078-4084-X

This Morning, This Evening, Right Now: FLeg FSA-24 *see also* How Many Biscuits Can I Eat?

This What the Union Done: LC AFS L60

Thompson's Mule: AH AHR 008

Those Blue Eyes I Love So Well: Alp ALP 202

Those Cruel Slavery Days: Hist BC 2433-1

Those Dark Eyes: Prst Int 13038

Three Babes [C. 79]: BRI 002, LC AAFS L58, LC AFS L7

Three Babes [C. 79]: HMM LP001, JnAp JA 020, Prst INT 25004, Rim Rlp-495, RRT LP-8073

Three-Day Blues: Fwys FTS 31016

Three Dulcimer Numbers (Poor Ellen Smith, Down in the Willow Garden, Maple on the Hill): FLeg FSA-23

Three Forks of Cheat: LC AFS L65-L66

Three Forks of Reedy: AH AHS 001

Three Forks of Sandy: Kan 306

Three-In-One Two-Step: Cty 410, Cty 517

Three Maids [C. 11]: BRI 002

Three Men (They) Went A-Hunting: AH AHR 008, NW 239, OT 101

Three Nights Drunk [C. 274]: FLeg FSA-27, Prst INT 25003, OH OHCS 192

Three Nights Experience [C. 274]: OH OHCS-177

Three Way Hornpipe: Cty 787

Three Wishes, The (or Better Than Gold): OHCS 316

Throw the Old Cow over the Fence: Cty 541 *see also* Robertson County

Throw the Soapsuds in the Corner of the Fence: Miss AH-002

Thunderbolt Hornpipe: UMP No #

Thunder Road: FLeg FSA-13

Tickle Her: OT 100

Tiehacker Rag: GyEg 101

Tiehacker's Tune No. 2: GyEg 101

Tie Up Those Broken Chords: Hist BC 2433-1

Tiger Rag: JnAp 032

Tillies and Turnies [E 18]: Ark Trad 004

Till the Snowflakes Fall: OHCS-172

Tim Brooks [H 27]: CT 6001

Time Draws Near: HMM LP002

Time Has Made a Change in Me: Ark Trad 003

Times Ain't What They Used To Be: Rndr 1033

Tinker's Story [Q 2]: Mar 9200

Tipperary: Rndr 0158

Tipple Blues: BF 15501, *see also* Deep Elem Blues

Tishomingo County Blues: Miss AH-002

'Tis Sweet To Be Remembered: Brch 1944

'Tis the Gift To Be Simple: Rndr 0078, Van VRS-9183

Titanic, The: TL TLCW-06

Tittery-Irie-Aye: LC AAFS L30, Ok OK 75003

T Model Ford and Train: Rndr 0065

Tobacco Union: FLeg FSA-23

To Be a Farmer's Boy [Q 30]: TFS 104

Today Is Monday: NW 291

Tokio Rag: OH OHCS 193, RCA 8416-2-R

Tomahawk: Mar 9013

Tom and Jerry: Cty 545, Cty 707, Cty 724, De DL 4760, Fwys RBF RF 51

Tom Daniels: Fwys FS 3848

Tom Dooley [F 36]: DU 33033, OHCS-157, Van VCD-45/46, FLeg FSA-1, Fwys FS 3811, Van VRS-9152

Tommy Love: Cty 201, Her 22, Rndr 0057

Tommy's Waltz: Cty 720

Tom Plum's Run: AFF 33-3

Tom Plum's Song: AFF 33-3

Tom Sherman's Barroom [B 1]: Min JD-203, MS 45008, RCA LPV 548

Tom Watson Special: UIP [cass, no #]

Took My Gal A-Walking: Cty 505

Too Late: Cty 533

Too Young To Marry: Cty 713, FC FC-014

Too Young To Understand the Sorrow: Kan 308

Top Hand: Ph 1017

Top of Cork Road: Kan 307

Tossing the Baby So High: Vet 105

To the Lamb: Mar 9101

To the Work: CMF 011-L

Tough Luck: Fwys FA 2359, Rndr 0009

To Wear a Green Willow [P 31]: FLeg FSA-33

Tragedy of Spring City: TFS 105

Tragic Romance: Cty 729, Fwys FA 2365, Fwys FS 3839, Van VSD-6576

Trail of the Lonesome Pine: DU-33009

Trail to Mexico [B 13]: Shoe SGB 1, UICFC CFC 301

Train 45: Alp ALP 201, OHCS-157, OT 100, DU 33033, SmFwys SF 40037, Fwys FA 3833, Mar 9025, N&T 1001, Prst FL 14030

Train A-Pulling Crooked Hill: Fwys FS 3828

Train Blues: LC AFS L61

Train Is off the Track: LC AFS L61

Train (No.) 111: Alp ALP 202, Atl SD-1350, OT 107, TFS 103

Train on the Island: Cty 778, DU-33002, Fwys FA 2953, Fwys FS 3832, Her 070, HMM LP002, Rndr 0057

Train That Carried My Girl from Town: Fwys FA 2366, Fwys FA 2374, Rndr 0036, Rndr SS-0145, Sm/Fwys SF 40012, Van VRS-9147

Train, The: LC AFS L2

Tra-La-La-La: OH OHCS 193

Tramp on the Street: Bio RC 6004, Prst Int 13038, UICFC CFC 201, RCA 2100-2-R, Rndr 0052

Trap Hill Tune: Rndr 0058

Traveling Creature: JnAp JA0059C

Traveling down the Road: BF 15503, Vet 105

Traveling Man: Van VSD-6576

Traveling On: NW 205, Prst INT 25007

Traveling on My Mind: Rndr 1028

Traveling to the Grave: Her 070

Tree in Wood: LC AAFS L12

Tribulation(s): Rndr 1033, Atl SD-1349

Trifling Woman: FLeg FSA-1

Triple Blues: BF 15501

Triplett Tragedy: Fwys FA 2366, Sm/Fwys SF 40012

Trip to New York, A: Arb 201

Trouble(s): Cty 777, Her 22

Trouble at the Coal Creek Mines: Brch 1945

Trouble in Mind: Fwys 2363

Trouble Just Got in My Way: FLeg FSA-13

Trouble on My Mind: Fwys FA 2342

Troubles, Trials, Tribulations: Rndr 0026

Trouble Trouble: Prst FL 14035

Truckdriver's Song: DU-33009

True and Trembling Brakeman, The: OHCS 317

True Blue Bill: TFS 104

True Born Irishman: FPrm 41942

True Love: Fwys 2363

True Lover's Farewell: JnAp 018

True Lovers [G 21]: Fwys FA 2355

Trumpey's Hoedown: GFS GFS 901

Tucker's (Old) Barn: Rndr 0008, Tpc 12TS336

Tug Boat: Cty 724

Tunes from Home Schottische: UMP No #

Tupelo Blues: Cty 528

Turkey Foot: Ala Trad 103

Turkey in a Peapatch: Rndr 0032

Turkey in the Straw: AFF 33-2, AFF 33-3, Asch AH 3903, Fwys FA 2358, Fwys FA 2435, Fwys FS 3809, GFS GFS 901, JnAp JA 025, Kan 307, Kan 310, Kan 600, LC AFS L65-L66, NW 223, Prst INT 25006, Riv RLP 12-650, Rndr 0057, SmFwys SF 40037, Sytn STR 201 *see also* Straw Breakdown, Tennessee Jubilee

Turkey Knob: Cty 733

Turkish Lady [C. 53]: Wstm SWN 18021

Turkish Rebelee [C. 286]: BRI 002, Fwys FA 2362

Turner's Camp on the Chippewa [C 23]: LC AAFS L56

Turnip Greens: Prst INT 25006

Turn Your Radio On: BRI 005, Rndr 1006

TVA Song: TFS 105

'Twas on That Dark, That Doleful Night: UNC 0-8078-4083-1

Twelfth [12th] Street Blues: Cty 514

Twenty-One Years [E 16]: Brch 1944, Elek EKL-316, NW 225

Twenty Years Behind Time: Kan 308

Twilight Is Falling: LC AFC L69-L70

Twilight Is Stealing: Ark Trad 003, OH OHCS 191

Twinkle (Twinkle) Little Star: Arh 5011, Fwys FA 2434, GyEg 101, MFFA 1001, SmFwys SF 40037

Twin Sisters: AH AHS 003, Cty 717, Rndr 0028, Rndr 0057, Rndr 0058

Two Brothers [C. 49]: LC AFS L7, NW 239

Two-Cent Coal: LC AFS L60

Two Dollar Bill: Fwys FA 3830

Two Drummers: FLeg FSA-18, Kan 313

Two Dukes A-Roving: Riv RLP 12-620

Two Faithful Lovers: Rndr 1004

Two-In-One Chewing Gum: Fwys RBF RF 51

Two Little Angels: JnAp JA 001

Two Little Boys: CT 6002, PB 004

Two Little Children: Fwys FA 2427, OHCS-173

Two Little Girls in Blue: OH OHCS 107

Two Little Lads: Ark Trad [No #]

Two Little Orphans: OHCS 315

Two Little Rosebuds: CT 6002

Two Lovers [N 28]: Van VRS-9158

Two More Years and I'll Be Free: Cty 739

Two Old Freight Trains Side by Side: Rndr 0034

Two Old Soldiers: Rndr 0064

Two Sisters [C. 10]: FLeg FSA-22, LC AAFS L57, LC AFS L7, TFS cass

Two Sons of North Britain [J 12]: Ph 1022

Two-Step Schottische: LC AFS L62

Two Sweethearts: OH OHCS 117, OTC 6001

Two-Timing Blues: Asch AH 3902

Two White Nickels / Three Thin Dimes: Her 33

Tying a Knot in the Devil's Tail [B 17]: AFF 33-1, Fwys FH 5723, MS 45008, MFP 0001, NW 314/315, RCA LPV 522

Uncle Bud: Rndr 1005

Uncle Buddy: Fwys FTS 31007

Uncle Charlie's Breakdown: Prst INT 25003

Uncle Dave's Beloved Banjo: BF 15518

Uncle Dave's Travels, Parts 1/2/3/4: BF 15503

Uncle Dave's Travels, Pt 1: De DL 4760

Uncle Eef's Got a Coon: Fwys 2363, Rndr 0064

Uncle Joe: Mar 9013

Uncle Joe and His Hounds: Tst T-3302

Uncle John's Rock: Arh 5018

Uncle John's Waltz: Arh 5018

Uncle Mitt: Mar 9013

Uncle Ned: Cty 748, JnAp JA0055

Unclouded [Uncloudy] Day: AFF 33-4, FLeg FSA-17, Fwys FA 2375, Fwys FS 3828, Prst Int 13049, SH SH-CD-3779

Underneath the Weeping Willow: Arh 5010

Under the Double Eagle: Arb 201, Bio BLP 6005, Cty 407, Fwys FTS 31007, Kan 306, Kan 310, Ldr LEA 4012, Ldr LEE 4045, SmFwys SF 40037

Union Man: LC AAFS L16

Unloved and Unclaimed: Rndr 0052

(Unlucky) Road to Washington: Hist HLP 8004, OHCS-173 *see also* Whitehouse Blues, McKinley

Unnamed Breakdown: UMP No #

Unnamed D Tune: Cty 202

Unnamed Schottische: MFFA 1001

Unnamed Tune: Fwys FS 3809

Unnamed Tune in D, A, & G: UMP No #

Unnamed tune (similar to Devil in the Straw-stack): Her 070

Unnamed tune (version of Bonaparte Crossing the Rhine): Her 070

Unnamed tune (version of Cuckoo's Nest): Her 070

Unquiet Grave [C. 79]: JEMF 104

Unruly Wife [?]: PB 004

Up Jumped the Devil: HMM LP002, RCA LPV 552

Up the Lazy River: JnAp 030, JnAp 032

Utah Carl [Carol] [B 4]: AFF 33-2, BF BCD 15456, FLeg FSA-18, Fwys FH 5723, MS 45008, Ph 1020, Rim Rlp-495, RCA LPV 522

Utah Iron Horse: LC AAFS L30

Vain World Adieu: Ark Trad 003, LC AAFS L11

Vance Song [F 17]: BRI 004

Varsouviana: Ph 1017

Ven'mous Viper [G 16]: AH AHR 008

Victoria: Prst INT 25007

Victory Rag: Van VRS-9239

Village Churchyard: Fwys FA 2374

Village School: NW 245

Virgin Ditch: Ok OK 76004

Virginia Bootlegger: Mar 9105

Visits: Her 33

Vulture, The: Cty 789

Wabash Cannon Ball: Cam CAL 586, FLeg FSA-13, Fwys FA 2426, Van VSD-9/10

Wade's Fox Chase: Bio RC-6002

Wagoner: Cty 707, Rndr 0005 *see also* Georgia Wagoner, Tennessee Wagoner, Texas Wagoner

Wagoner's Lad: Fwys FS 3810, Prst INT 13020 *see also* My Horses Ain't Hungry

Waiting for a Train [H 2]: FLeg FSA-13

Waiting for the Evening Mail: Cty 411

Waiting for the Lord To Come: Fwys FS 3809

Wait 'Til the Clouds Roll By: Hist HLP 8006

Wait 'Til the Sun Shines Nellie: OH OHCS 114

Wait 'Til You Hear This One, Boy: UMP No #

Wake Up Jacob: Fwys FA 2952 *see also* Wild Horse, Stoney Point, etc.

Wake (Up) Susan: Cty 720, GnHys GR712, Kan 307, LC AFS L62, GyEg 101, Her 12, Rndr 1010

Walburn Stomp: Cty 544

Waldo: GyEg 101

Walk Along John: MFFA 1001, Rndr 0157, Tak A 1013

Walk and Talk Together: Mer 1001-2

Walk Around My Bedside: Fwys FA 2374

Walking Boss: Fwys FA 2359

Walking in Jerusalem: Van VSD-107/108

Walking in My Sleep: Cty 201, Cty 778, Fwys FA 2435, Fwys FS 3832, GyEg 101, JnAp 032, Ldr LE 4040

Walking in Sunlight: Cty 521

Walking in the King's Highway: De DL 4557

Walking in the Light: Cty 409

Walking in the Parlor: Asch AH 3831, Ala Trad 103, Cty 756, DU-33002, Fwys FA 2435, Fwys FS 3832, Her 070, Rndr 0018, Rndr 0047, Rndr 0089

Walking in the Way with Jesus: CMF 011-L, Rndr 1001

Walking John: AFF 33-3, Rndr 0158, UICFC CFC 301

Walking My Lord up Calvary's Hill: Fwys FA 2357

Walk in the Park, A: Prst FL 14030

Walk Light Ladies: Fwys FA 2342

Walk on Boy: Van VRS-9213

Walk Tom Wilson Walk: BF 15519

Walk up Georgia Row: JnAp JA 049

Walls of Jericho: Rndr 0057, Rndr 0058

Walls, The: FLeg FSA-13

Waltz: Fwys FA 2365

Waltz of Shannon: Ok OK 76004

Waltz of the Hills: Rndr 1029

Waltz of the Wildflowers: MFP MFP 002

Waltz You Saved for Me: GyEg 101, JnAp 030

Wandering Boy: Cty 524, Fwys FA 2368, Fwys FA 2435, MFFA 1001, OH OHCS 190 *see also* Bring Back to Me My Blue Eyed Boy

Wandering Gypsy Girl [O 4]: OH OHCS 190

Wanted Man: Van VSD-107/108

Want To Go to Cuba but I Can't Go Now: KM 204

Want To Go to Memphis So Bad: Rndr 0157

Warfare: Rndr 0028

Warfield: Her 33

Warhorse Game: Rndr 1032 *see also* Old Hen Cackled

War Is A-Raging [O 33]: Asch AH 3831, Fwys FA 2315, Fwys FS 3828, Prst INT 13030

Warning Song: Fwys FA 2358

Wars by the Numbers: Kan 308

Washing Mama's Dishes: GHP LP 1001 *see also* Fly Around My Pretty Little Miss, *etc.*

Washington's March: WVUP 001

Washington's Quadrille: MS 45003

Washington the Great: LC AFS L29

Watcha Gonna Do When Your Licker Gives Out?: Rndr 1003

Watch and Pray: Cty 534, Hist BC 2433-1

Waterbound: Fwys 2363 *see also* Way down in North Carolina

Watergate Boogie: Rndr SS-0145

Water Is Wide, The: Min JD-203

Watermelon (Hanging) (Smiling) on the Vine: Alp ALP 202, Arh 5001, Arh 5011, BF 15519, BB AXM2-5510, Cty 526, Ok OK 75003, Prst FL 14030, Rndr 1005

Waverley: Rndr 0133

Waves on Sea [C. 289]: Fwys FA 2433

Waves on the Ocean: Cty 535, Rndr 0058, Str STR 802

Way back in the Hills: AFF 33-3

Way down in Arkansas: Hist HLP 8002

Way down in Georgia: Rndr 1035

Way down in North Carolina: Cty 534, Hist BC 2433-1 *see also* Waterbound

Way down in the Country: Fwys FA 2365

Way down on the Island: Riv RLP 12-610

Way down on the Mango Farm: Rndr SS-0145

Way down South in Dixie: MS 45005

Way down the Old Plank Road: Cty 521 *see also* My Wife Died Saturday Night

Way Downtown: Fwys FA 2359, Van VSD-107/108, Van VCD-45/46

Wayfaring Pilgrim: Rndr 0021

Wayfaring Stranger: Fwys FA 2317, Fwys FA 2362, Fwys FS 3829, UNC 0-8078-4083-1

Waynesboro [Waynesburgh] (Reel): Cty 703, DU 33015, WVUP 001, Her 33

Way out in Free Hill: Mer 1001-2

Way out in Idaho: LC AFS L61

Way out There: OH OHS 90031

Ways of the World: LC AFS L62, LC AFS L2

Wayward Boy: FC FC-014

Wealthy Squire [N 20]: FPrm 41942

We Are Anchored by the Roadside (Jim): Fwys FE 4001, Fwys FE 4001

We Are Up Against It Now: see We're Up Against It Now

Wearing of the Green: Kan 307

Weary Angel of Death: Rndr 0020

Weary Blues: Van VRS-9170

Weary Lonesome Blues: ACM ACM-1

Weave Room Blues: CT 6000, RCA 8417-2-R, Tst T-3301, Van VRS-9147

Weaver's Life: Tst T-3301

Webb's Tune: Mar 9013

We Can't Be Darlings Anymore: Alp ALP 202

Wednesday Night Waltz: Cty 501, Cty 532, Cty 733, DU 33015, Fwys FS 3839, Tak A 1013

We Done Quit: LC AFS L60

Weeping Lady: Kan 313

Weeping Willow (Tree): BB AXM2-5510, Cty 729, DU 33014, Fly LP 546, Fwys FA 2365, Prst FL 14035, Riv RLP 12-645, Riv RLP 12-649 *see also* Bury Me Beneath the ...

Weevily Wheat: PB 004, Rndr 0089

We Have Moonshine: Mar 9104, OH OHCS 141

We Left Our Homes in Utah: Ok OK 76004

Welcome: AH AHR 010

We'll All Sing Hallelujah: Prst INT 25007

We'll Be at Home Again: Mar 9100

We'll Camp a Little While in the Wilderness: HMM LP002

We'll Meet at the End of the Trail: Sytn STR 202

We'll Meet on the Beautiful Shore: OH OHCS 141

Well Met, My Old True Love [C. 243]: LC AAFS L58

We'll Talk About One Another: BF 15521

We'll Understand It Better Bye and Bye: MS 45005

We'll Work 'Til Jesus Comes: SH SH-CD-3779

We Must Be Meek: Rndr 0078

Went To Go to Meeting: Miss AH-002

Went up on the Old Hillside: JnAp JA 020

We Parted by the Riverside: OH OHCS-172

We're Going To Pump Out Lake Erie: OHS OF-1001

We're Marching Around the Levees

We're Stole and Sold from Africa: JnAp JA 020

We're Up Against It Now: BF 15518, Rndr 1026

We Shall All Be Reunited: Van VRS-9170

We Shall Meet Some Day: Prst FL 14010

We Shall Rise: Har HL 7344

Wes Muir's Tune: GyEg 101

Western Country: Bio RC-6003, Fwys FA 2380, Fwys FS 3832

Western Kentucky Limited: Rndr 1037

Western Mount Pleasant: Fwys FA 2356

West Fork Girls: FPrm 41942, Rndr 0047

Westphalia Waltz: JEMF 105

West Virginia Highway: Rndr 1008

West Virginia Hills: OH OHCS 141

West Virginia Hornpipe: Kan 306

West Virginia Mine Disaster: Bio RC 6004

West Virginia Special: Cty 536

We've Just Got To Have 'em, That's All: Rndr 1001

We Will All Go Home with You: Rndr 0078

We Will March through the Streets of the City: CMH 107

We Will Miss Him: OT 106

What a Friend We Have in Jesus: Rndr 0001

What a Friend We Have in Mother: Fwys FA 3830

What Are They Doing in Heaven Today?: Fwys FA 2357

What a Time We're Living In: LC AFC L69-L70

What Does the Deep Sea Say?: Rndr 0052, Van VSD-107/108

What Is a Home Without Love?: BB AXM2-5510

What Is Home Without Babies?: Hist HLP 8005

What Is That Blood on Your Shirt Sleeve? [C. 13]: Rndr 0076

What'll I [You] Do with the Baby-O?: Cty 778, JnAp JA 009, Rndr 0143, Fwys FA 2426 *see also* What You Gonna Do ...

What'll Ye Do: Van VRS-9183

What's the Use of Repining?: Fwys FA 2036

What Would You Give in Exchange?: BB AXM2-5510, JEMF 101, OH OHS 90001, RCA 2100-2-R, Fwys FA 2433, Fwys FS 3829

What You Gonna Do with the Baby?: Cty 513, Hist HLP 8003 *see also* What'll I Do ...

What You Gonna Name That Pretty Baby?: Fwys FE 34161

Wheel Hoss: Cty 729

Wheels: Arh 5012

When a Boy from the Mountains: OH OHCS-177

When a Fellow Is out of a Job: FLeg FSA-27

When a Man Is Married: Pu 3001

When I Can Read My Titles Clear: Rndr 0026, Rndr 0077

When I Die: Fwys FA 2366, Sm/Fwys SF 40012

When I Get Home: Atl SD-1349

When I Had but Fifty Cents: Mar 9111

When I Lay My Burdens Down: BF 15003

When I'm Gone You'll Soon Forget Me: Cty 411

When I Reach My Home Eternal: OT 107

When I Take My Vacation in Heaven: Rndr 0052

When I Was a Baby: FC FC-014

When Jesus Christ Was Here on Earth: NW 294, Prst INT 25011

When Jones's Ale Was New: LC AAFC L26/27

When Kentucky Had No Union Men: Fwys FTS 31016

When Moses and the Israelites: Fwys FS 3810, JnAp JA 020

When Our Lord Shall Come Again: BB AXM2-5510, Fwys FA 2357, JEMF 101

When Reubin Come to Town: Cty 545

When Silver Threads Are Gold Again: CMH 112

When Sorrows Encompass Me 'Round: Cty 723

When the Bees Are in the Hive: ACM ACM-1, Ark Trad 004, Bio BLP 6005

When the Birds Begin Their Singing in the Trees: Rndr 1032

When the Breaker Starts Up Full Time: LC AAFS L16

When the Bumblebee Backed Up to Me and Pushed: Rndr 0005

When the Gates of Glory Open: Mar 9101

When the Good Lord Sets Me Free: BF 15507

When the Harvest Days Are Over: BF 15519

When the Palefaces Came: AH AHR 008

When the Redeemed Are Gathering In: LC AFC L69-L70, OHCS-172

When the Roll Is Called up Yonder: OH OHCS 116, AFF 33-4

When the Roses Are Blooming: OH OHCS 112

When the Roses Bloom Again: Brch 1944, Fwys FA 3830, Mar 9109, OHCS-173

When the Roses Bloom in Dixieland: BB AXM2-5525, Cam ACL1-0501

When the Roses Come Again: Cam CAL 2473

When the Saints Go Marching In: Cty 729

When the Snowflakes Fall Again: Kan 313

When the Springtime Comes: Fwys FA 2315

When the Stars Begin To Fall: NW 294, Prst INT 25011

When the Train Comes Alone: Cty 545, Fwys RBF RF 51, Vet 103

When the Wagon Was New: Arh 5012

When the Whippoorwill Was Whispering Good Night: Bio BLP 6005

When the Work's All Done This Fall [B 3]: AFF 33-1, BF BCD 15456, Fwys FH 5723, MFP 0001, NW 314/315, Ph 1022, RCA LPV 522, Van VSD-9/10

When the World's on Fire: CMH 118

When They Ring the (Those) Golden Bells: CMF 011-L, JnAp 018, JnAp JA 025

When This Evening Sun Goes Down: MCA VIM-4012

When This World Comes to an End: LC AFS L65-L66

When You and I Were Young, Maggie: MFP MFP 002, UIP [cass, no #]

When You Ask a Girl To Leave Her Happy Home: Cty 524

When You Leave, You'll Leave Me Sad: BF 15501

Where Are You Going Alice? [cf. N 40]: Cty 513, Fwys FS 3839

Where Could I Go but to the Lord?: Rndr 0001

Where'd You Get Your Whisky?: LC AAFS L9

Where I Shall Be?: CT 6002

Where Is My Sailor Boy?: BB AXM2-5510, RCA LPV 507, Fwys FA 2433

Where Is the Gem?: Rndr 0078

Where No One Stands Alone: OFA TALP-001

Where Shall I Be?: OTC 6001

Where the Catskills Reach Their Summits: Kan 308

Where the Gates Swing Outward Never: OH OHCS 190

Where the Irish Potatoes Grow: Cty 519

Where the Old Red River Flows: Prst Int 13049

Where the Silvery Colorado Winds Its Way: CMH 112, OH OHCS 190

Where the Soul of Man Never Dies: FLeg FSA-23, RCA 2100-2-R

Where the Sun Will Never Go Down: FLeg FSA-22

Where the Whip-poor-will Is Whispering Goodnight: Hist HLP 8005

Where the Wild, Wild Flowers Grow: Rndr 0077

Whip-Poor-Will Song: OHCS-173

Whiskers: Rndr 0157

Whiskey Before Breakfast: MFFA 1001, GyEg 101

Whiskey Joe: N&T 1001

Whiskey Took My Daddy Away: Fwys FA 2434

Whisky Johnny: LC AAFC L26/27

Whispering: JnAp 030

Whispering Hope: BB AXM2-5525, Rndr CD 11536

Whistle, Daughter, Whistle: Tpc 12T146

Whistling Rufus: Fwys FTS 31007, N&T 1001, Van VRS-9170

Whistling Songbird: BF 15504

White Cafe: UIP cass

Whitehouse Blues: Col CS 9660, Cty 505, Fwys FA 2951, Fwys FA 3833, SmFwys SF 40038, Van VCD-45/46 *see also* Cannonball Blues, Unlucky Road to Washington

White Kitty: Rim Rlp-495

White Lightning: Cty 544

White Oak Mountain: Cty 712

White Oak Stomp: HMM LP001

White Pilgrim: JnAp 037

White River: GyEg 101

White River Stomp: GV SC 03, Mar 9111

White Rose Waltz: Rndr 0037

White Shotgun: Fwys FTS 31016

White Water: GyEg 101

Whoa Back Buck: Mar 9111

Whoa! Ha! Buck & Jerry Boy: Fwys FA 2036

Whoa Larry Whoa: TFS 108

Whoa, Mule (Whoa): Arh 5010, Atl SD-1350, Fwys FA 2350, Fwys FA 2434, Fwys FA 2435, GyEg 101, JnAp JA 025, OH OHCS 193, Rndr 0009, Rndr 1032, *see also* Bucking Mule

Who Broke the Lock (on the Henhouse Door)?: Bio RC-6003

Whoopee-Ti-Yi-Yo: NW 245, NW 314/315

Whoop 'Em Up Cindy: Fwys FA 2379, Vet 105 *see also* Cindy

Whoopie Ti Yi Yo: Sytn STR 202 *see also* Get Along Little Dogie

Whore's Lament [Q 26]: BF 15003

Who Said I Was a Bum: CMH 106

Who's Been Here Since I've Been Gone?: Rndr 0018

Who's Going down to Wilmingtown?: Prst INT 13035

Who's Gonna Kiss Your Lips Dear Darling?: GHP LP 1001

Who's Gonna Shoe Your Pretty Little Feet (Foot)?: Rndr 0143, JEMF 104, ArFF AFF 33-4

Who's Sorry Now?: JnAp 030

Who's That Knocking on My Window? [M 4]: JEMF 101, MCA VIM-4012

Who Will Bow and Bend Like the Willow?: NW 239, Rndr 0078

Why Are You Leaving?: Fwys FTS 31016

Why Did You Wander?: NW 225, Prst FL 14010

Why Don't You Bob Your Hair, Girls?, No. 2: Rndr 1001

Why Do You Bob Your Hair, Girls?: OT 106, Rndr 1001

Why Do You Cry Little Darling?: CMH 118

Why Do You Stand There in the Rain?: FLeg FSA-26

Why Must I Wear This Shroud?: NW 294

Why Not Confess?: BB AXM2-5525

Why There's a Tear in My Eye: JEMF 101

Wideman's Quickstep: Rndr 0157

Widow Haley: Fwys FTS 31007

Widow's Old Broom: LC AAFS L12

Wife of Usher's Well [C. 79]: MC 1, FLeg FSA-32

Wife Wrapped in a Wether's Skin [C. 277]: RRT LP-8073, FLeg FSA-32

Wild and Reckless Hobo [H 2]: Cty 739, JEMF 104, RCA LPV 548

Wild Barbaree [K 33] LC AAFS L21

Wild Bill Jones [E 10]: Arh F5002, BF 15508, Brch 1945, Cty 404, Cty 712, Cty 777, Cty 786, FLeg FSA-1, Fwys FA 2350, Fwys FS 3829, GnHys GR712, Mar 9025, Prst INT 13020, Riv RLP 12-617, TFS 106

Wild Boar's Den [C. 18]: LC AAFS L57, TFS cass

Wild Buckaroo: Rndr 0158

Wild Cat Mama: CMH 106

Wild Colonial Boy [L 20]: Fwys FE 4001

Wildflower of the Mountain: JnAp JA 025

Wild Goose Chase: Cty 786, Cty 777, Str STR 802

Wild Hog in the Woods: Her 33, MS 45004

Wild Hog in the Woods [C. 18]: BRI 002,

Wild Hogs in the Red Brush: Rndr 1007

Wild Horse: AH AHS 003, Cty 509, Rndr 1037, FPrm (No #), Rndr 0237 *see also* Stoney Point, Nigger in the Woodpile, *etc.*

Wild Horse in the Red Brush: AH AHS 001

Wild Mustard River [C 5]: LC AAFS L56

Wild Rose of the Mountain: Rndr 0037

Wild Rose Waltz: Rndr 0157

(Frail) Wildwood Flower: ArFF AFF 33-4, Cam CAL 586, Cty 739, Fwys FA 2365, Har HL 7280, OH OHCS-177, Prst FL 14010, Riv RLP 12-649, Riv RLP 12-650, Rndr 0001, RRT LP-8073, SmFwys SF 40037, TL TLCW-06

Wilkes County Blues: BF 15505

William Hall [N 30]: FLeg FSA-22, Van VRS 9162

Willie Brennan [L 7]: Prst INT 25009

Willie down by the Pond [G 19]: FLeg FSA-27

Willie Moore: Ark Trad [No #], Col CS 9660, Fwys FA 2426, Fwys FA 2951, TFS 104, Van VSD-6576

Willie My Son [C. 12]: AH AHR 008

Willie Was As Fine a Sailor: Ph 1022

Will My Mother Know Me There?: OH OHCS 116

Willow Garden [F 6]: Prst INT 25003, Shoe SGB 1 *see also* Down in the ...

Willow Green: Prst INT 25006

Willow Tree: Fwys 2368

Will Sweethearts Know Each Other There: Fwys RBF 654

Will the Circle Be Unbroken?: BB AXM2-5510, OH OHCS 111, Bio RC 6004, FLeg FSA-36, JEMF 104, PB 003, Riv RLP 12-650, Tst T-3301, Van VSD-107/108

Will There Be Any Stars?: N&T 1001

Will There Be Any Stars in My Crown?: Mar 9100

Will There Be Any Yodelers in Heaven?: Sytn STR 202

Will the Roses Bloom in Heaven?: Cam CAL 2554(e)

Will the Weaver [Q 9]: Kan 308, Van VRS-9158

Willy Brook: AH AHR 009

Will You Always Love Me, Darling?: Fwys FA 2352

Will You Be Lonesome Too: OTC 6002

Will You Be True?: Ldr LE 4040

Will You Miss Me (When I'm Gone?): Cty 739, OFA TALP-001, OH OHCS 111, Har HL 7422, RCA LPM 2772, TL TLCW-06

Wilson's Clog: LC AFS L65-L66

Wilson's Hornpipe: Kan 306

Wind and Rain [C. 10]: Ark Trad 004, Asch AH 3902, BRI 002

Windham: LC AAFS L11, Prst INT 25007

Wind That Shook the Barley: LC AFS L62

Windy and Warm: Van VRS-9213, Van VSD-9/10

Windy Bill [dB 41]: Rndr 0158, UICFC CFC 301, Fwys FH 5723

Winking Eye: Bio RC-6002

Wink the Other Eye: MS 45003

Wino's Last Prayer: Kan 305

Wintergrace: GnHys GR714

Winter's Night: Van VRS-9239

Wise County Jail: Fwys FA 2392

Wish I Had My Time Again: MS 45004

Wish I Had Stayed in the Wagon Yard: Cty 504

Wish to the Lord I Had Never Been Born: Cty 407

With a New Tongue: Rndr 0078

Within My Father's House: Cty 409 *see also* There'll Be Joy, Joy, Joy

Wolves (A-)Howling: Cty 401, Cty 503, Miss AH-002

Woman from Yorkshire [Q 2]: FLeg FSA-15

Woman's Been After Man Ever Since: Rndr 1001

Wonderful Day, A: CT 6000

Wonderful Love: Her 33

Wonder Who's Kissing Her Now, Pt. 2: CT 6002

Wondrous Love: Fwys FA 2356, Fwys FA 2362, LC AAFS L11, NW 205, Prst INT 25007

Won't You Come over to My House?: Hoop 101

Woodchuck in the Deadning: Arh 5010

Wooden Shoe Story: GyEg 101

Woodrow for President: Asch AH 3902

Woodsman's Alphabet: Ph 1020

Work Don't Bother Me: BF 15521, Rndr 1035

Working for My Lord: BF 15519

Working on a Building: Alp ALP 202, Rndr 0001

Working on the Railroad: Mar 9111

Working on This Old Railroad: Rndr 0076

Worldwide Peace: Ark Trad 003

Worried Blues: Rndr 1007

Worried Man: Prst INT 13030

Worried Man Blues: Cam ACL1-0047, Har HL 7280, OH OHCS 111, RCA LPV 507, Rndr CD 11536, TL TLCW-06

Worrysome Woman [C. 248]: HMM LP002

Worthy of Estimation: Cty 521

Wouldn't Mind Working from Sun to Sun: JnAp JA 020

Wreck of Lady Sherbrooke: Fwys FE 4001

Wreck of Main Line Number 4: Fwys FTS 31016

Wreck of Number Nine [G 26]: AFF 33-4, FLeg FSA-13, Fwys FA 2365, Van VSD-6576

Wreck of Old 97 [G 2]: Riv RLP 12-650, BRI 004, FLeg FSA-13, JnAp JA 025, Tst T-3301, Fwys FA 2315, RCA LPV 532

Wreck of the C & O Sportsman: OH OHCS-177

Wreck of the Number Nine [G 26]: SH SH-CD-3795

Wreck of the Royal Palm [dG 51]: LC AFS L61

Wreck of the Shenandoah [dG 52]: FPrm 41942

Wreck of the Six Wheeler: RCA LPV 548

Wreck of the Tennessee Gravy Train: Fwys RBF RF 51

Wreck of the Titanic: Brch 1945

Wreck of the 1256: BRI 004, Vet 103

Wreck of the 1262: Van VSD-9/10

Wreck of the Virginian: Cty 502

Wreck of the West Bound Airliner: OH OHCS-177

Wreck on the C. & O. [G 3]: Brch 1945, OHCS 317

Wreck on the Highway: Fwys FA 2427, Tst T-3301, Van VRS-9147

Wreck on the Mountain Road: Cty 502

Write a Letter to My Mother: Cty 516, Mar 9109, OT 106

Wrong Road, The: Mar 9104

Yellow Barber: GFS GFS 901, Rndr 0032

Yellow Cat: Her 22

Yellow Pups (Fox Chase): Fwys FS 3810

Yellow Rose of Texas: Cty 524, Hist HLP 8003, Mer 1001-2

Yes Ma'am [Bed Time Quiz]: LC AFS L68

Yes Sir, She's My Baby: JnAp JA 025

Yew Piney Mountain: AH AHS 001, AH AHS 003, FPrm (No #), Rndr 0047, Her 12

Yielding and Simple: Rndr 0078
Yodeling Ranger: CMH 106
Yonder He Goes: GV SC 03
You Ain't Heard Nothing Yet: FLeg FSA-13
You Ain't Talking to Me: Cty 540, Hist HLP 8005
You Are My Flower: De DL 4404, OH OHCS 112
You Been Gone So Long: Cty 777
You Better Let That Liar Alone: De DL 4557
You Came Back to Me: OH OHCS-177
You Could Be a Millionaire: Rndr 0052
You'd Better Wake Up: NW 225
You Denied Your Love: CMH 116, OH OHCS 112
You Don't Tell Me That You Love Me Anymore: Rndr 0021
You Give Me Your Love: BB AXM2-5525 *see also* Give Me Your Love
You Gotta Quit Kicking My Dawg Around: Rndr 1023
You Gotta See Your Momma Every Night: Fwys FA 2306
You Got To Stop Drinking Shine: FSSM FSSMLP 15001-D, Rndr 1023
You Led Me to the Wrong: Rndr 0077
You'll Miss Me: OH OHCS-177
You May Forsake Me: Cty 404
You Must Be a Lover of the Lord: Hist BC 2433-1
You Must Come in at the Door: SH SH-CD-3779
You Must Unload: Rndr 1001
You Never Miss Your Mamma [Mother] ('Till She's Gone): OHCS-157, Rndr 0057
Young and Tender Ladies: Fwys FA 2317
Young Beham [C. 53]: FLeg FSA-22, TFS cass
Young Boy Left His Home One Day, A: Hist HLP 8005
Young Charlotte (Carlotta) [G 17]: Fwys FS 3809, LC AAFS L14, Van VRS-9158
Young Edmund: Mar 9200
Young Emily [M 34]: Fwys FA 2418, Rndr 0028
Young Freda Bolt: CMH 116

Young Henerly [C. 68]: LC AFS L65-L66
Young Johnny [G 16]: LC AAFS L55
Young Johnny [K 38]: Fwys FE 4001
Young Johnny Sailed from London [K 36]: Cty 789
Young John Riley [N 37]: Mer 1001-2
Young Ladies Take Warning: Fwys FES 34151
Young Lady Who Married a Mule Driver: LC AFS L60
Young Man Who Wouldn't Hoe Corn [H 13]: Ark Trad 004, Fwys FS 3809
Young Men and Maids [G 21]: Asch AH 3831
Young Timmy the Miller [P 8]: AH AHR 007
Young Repoleon [J 5]: Cty 787
You're a Flower Blooming in the Wildwood: Prst Int 13038
You're a Little Too Small: BF 15507
You're Gonna Be Sorry You Let Me Down: Cam CAL 2473
You're Nothing More to Me: CMH 116
Your Long Journey: Fwys FA 2366, Sm/Fwys SF 40012, SH SH-CD-3795
Your Low Down Dirty Ways: Cty 504
Your Mother Still Prays for You Jack: CMH 116
Your Old Standby: NW 225
Your Saddle Is Empty Old Pal: Cty 739
You Tied a Love Knot in My Heart: Cam CAL 2473
You Tried To Ruin My Name: Rndr 0143
You've Been a Friend to Me: De DL 4404, TL TLCW-06
You've Got To Righten That Wrong: CMH 116, TL TLCW-06
You've Got To Walk That Lonesome Valley: ACM ACM-1

Zack, the Mormon Engineer: Fwys FA 2036
Zebra Dun [B 16]: AFF 33-1, Fwys FH 5723, LC AAFS L28, Mtn 304, MFP 0001, Ph 1017, RCA LPV 522
Zelma Waltz: OH OHCS 192
Zolgotz: LC AFS L29
Zollie's Retreat: Cty 786

INDEX OF CHILD BALLADS

[Records listed together following one title are the same recording. Recordings are not indexed here if only the tune, without words, is rendered.]

1	Devil's Nine Questions, BRI 002, LC AFS L1	12	My Bonny Bon Boy: FLeg FSA-33
2	Cambric Shirt: Fwys FA 2358	12	Willie My Son: AH AHR 008
2	Every Rose Grows Merry in Time: FLeg FSA-33	13	Edward: Fwys FA 2302
2	Flim-a-Lim-a-Lee: FLeg FSA-15	13	Edward: GnHys GR714
2	Oh Marry in Time: JEMF 104	13	Edward: LC AAFS L12
2	Cambric Shirt: RRT LP-8073	13	Edward: LC AAFS L57
2	Elfin Knight: Fwys FS 3809	13	Edward: MC 1
3	False Knight upon the Road: LC AAFS L21	13	How Come That Blood?: FLeg FSA-11
4	False Sir John: Fwys FA 2301	13	How Came That Blood on Your Shirt Sleeve: Rim Rlp-495
4	Lady Isabel and the Elfin Knight: JnAp 018		
4	Pretty Aggie: AH AHR 007	13	How Came That Blood on Your Shirt Sleeve?: TFS cass [no #]
4	Pretty Polly: Fwys FE 4001		
4	Pretty Polly (Six Kings' Daughters): TFS 104	13	Little Guinea Gay Haw: TFS cass [no #]
7	Sweet William: Bio RC-6002	13	Blood of the Old Red Rooster: Rndr 0083
7	Sweet William: Cty 534		
7	Sweet William (Earl Brand): LC AAFS L12	13	What Is That Blood on Your Shirt Sleeve?: Rndr 0076
7	Sweet William: NW NWR 245	14	Burly Banks of Barbry-O: MC 1
7	Sweet William and Fair Ellen, Pts 1/2: CT 6001	17	In Scotland Town: LC AFS L65-L66
		18	Bangum and the Boar: LC AAFS L57
10	Bow and Balance: Fwys FA 2362	18	Biler and the Boar: Rndr 0076
10	Bow and Balance to Me: AH AHR 008	18	Jobal Hunter: TFS cass [no #]
10	Old Man from the North Country: Riv RLP 12-645	18	Old Bangum: Cty 787
		18	Old Bangum: Fwys FA 2301
10	Squire's Daughter: Fwys FA 2358	18	Quil O'Quay: JnAp JA 001
10	There Lived an Old Lord: FA 2302	18	Sir Lionel: FLeg FSA-22
10	Two Sisters: FLeg FSA-22	18	Wild Boar: LC AAFS L57
10	Two Sisters: LC AFS L7	18	Wild Boar's Den: TFS cass [no #]
10	Two Sisters: LC AAFS L57	18	Wild Hog in the Woods: BRI 002
10	Two Sisters: TFS cass [no #]	20	Down By the Greenwood Side: FLeg FSA-11
10	Wind and Rain: Ark Trad 004		
10	Wind and Rain: Asch AH 3902	43	Merry Brown Field: Mar 9200 [cass]
10	Wind and Rain: BRI 002	45	King John and the Bishop: MC 1
11	Three Maids: BRI 002	45	Bishop of Canterbury: LC AAFS L57
12	Jimmy Randal: Mar 9200 [cass]	49	Little Schoolboy: Prst INT 25003
12	Jimmy Randolph: Rim Rlp-495	49	Two Brothers: LC AFS L7
12	Johnny Randall: FLeg FSA-15	49	Two Brothers: NW NWR 239
12	Lord Randall: FLeg FSA-1	52	Queen Jane: FLeg FSA-33
12	Lord Randall: Fwys 2302	53	Lloyd Bateman: LC AAFS L57
		53	Lord Baseman: Rndr 0076
		53	Lord Bateman: Fwys FA 2301
		53	Lord Bateman: LC AAFS L12

53   Lord Bateman: LC AAFS L57
53   Lord Bateman: MC 1
53   Lord Bateman: Rim Rlp-495
53   Lord Beekman: Mar 9200 [cass]
53   Turkish Lady: Wstm SWN 18021
53   Young Beham: FLeg FSA-22
53   Young Beham: TFS cass [no #]
54   As Joseph Was A-Walking: FLeg
         FSA-3
54   Cherry Tree Carol: AH AHR 008
54   Cherry Tree Carol: Fwys FA 2302
54   Cherry Tree Carol: LC AAFS L14
54   Cherry Tree Carol: LC AAFS L57
54   Cherry Tree Carol: Riv RLP 12-617
56   Lazarus: LC AAFS L57
58   Sir Patrick Spens: TFS-106
68   Henry Lee: Fwys FA 2951
68   Lord Barnett: Fwys FS 3809
68   Love Henry: AH AHR 009
68   Loving Henry: Rndr 0076
68   Lowe Bonnie: OT 112
68   Lowe Bonnie: Test T-3302
68   Song of a Lost Hunter: FLeg FSA-1
68   Poor Scotchee: PB 004
68   Young Henerly: LC AFS L65-L66
73   Brown Girl: AH AHR 007
73   Brown Girl: TFS cass [no #]
73   Brown Girl: Van VRS 9124
73   Fair Ellender: UTP cass no #
73   Lord Thomas and Fair Ellender:
         FLeg FSA-2
73   Lord Thomas and Fair Ellender: Fwys
         FA 2301
73   Lord Thomas and Fair Ellender: Fwys
         FA 2362
73   Lord Thomas and Fair Ellender: LC
         AFS L7
73   Lord Thomas and Fair Ellender:
         RRT LP-8073
73   Lord Thomas: TFS cass [no #]
74   Lady Margaret: FLeg FSA-11
74   Lady Margaret: Riv RLP 12-620
74   Lady Margaret: Rndr 0017
74   Lady Margaret: TFS 104
74   Little Margaret: Fwys FP 40
74   Little Margaret: JnAp 018
74   Little Margaret: Prst INT 13030
74   Little Margaret: Prst INT 13038
74   Little Margaret: Riv RLP 12-649
74   Little Margaret: Van VRS 9162
74   Sweet William and Lady Margaret:
         Fwys FA 2302

75   Lord Level: AH AHR 008
75   Lord Lovel: AH AHR 009
75   Lord Lovel: FLeg FSA-36
75   Lord Lovel: Fwys FA 2301
75   Lord Lovel: LC AAFS L55
75   Lord Lovell: Fwys FA 2358
75   Lord Lover: Mar 9200 [cass]
75   Milk White Steed: LC AFS L68
76   Fair Annie of Lochroyan: Fwys FA
         2301
76   Lass of Loch Royale: Prst INT 25003
78   Unquiet Grave: Fwys FA 2302
79   Lady Bride and Three Babes: Fwys
         FES 34151
79   Lady Gay: Brun 59001, Rndr 1037
79   Lady Gay: JnAp JA 001
79   Lady Gay: JnAp JA 009
79   Lady Gay: Van VRS-9158
79   Three Babes: BRI 002
79   Three Babes: LC AAFS L58
79   Three Babes: LC AFS L7
79   Three Little Babes: HMM LP001
79   Three Little Babes: JnAp JA 020
79   Three Little Babes: Prst INT 25004
79   Three Little Babes: Rim Rlp-495
79   Three Little Babes: RRT LP-8073
79   Unquiet Grave: JEMF 104
79   Wife of Usher's Well: FLeg FSA-32
79   Wife of Usher's Well: MC 1
79   Wife of Usher's Wells: Fwys FA 2302
81   Little Massie Grove: BRI 002
81   Little Matty Groves: Tpc 12T146
81   Little Musgrave: Fwys FA 2302
81   Lord Daniel: JnAp JA 001
81   Lord Daniel: Rndr 0076
81   Massey Grove: TFS cass [no #]
81   Mathie Grove: Fwys FA 2309
81   Mathy Grove: FLeg FSA-2
81   Matty Groves: Van VRS-9239
84   Barbara Allen: BRI 002
84   Barbara Allen: FLeg FSA-32
84   Barbara Allen: Fly LP 546
84   Barbara Allen: Fwys FA 2317
84   Barbara Allen: Fwys FA 2433
84   Barbara Allen: Fwys FA 3830
84   Barbara Allen: KM KM 204
84   Barbara Allen: LC AAFS L14
84   Barbara Allen: LC AFS L1
84   Barbara Allen: LC AAFS L54 (30 ver-
         sions)
84   Barbara Allen: Min JD-203

84	Barbara Allen:	NW NWR 223
84	Barbara Allen:	OH OHCS 107
84	Barbara Allen:	OHCS 314
84	Barbara Allen:	Ph 1022
84	Barbara Allen:	Rndr 0064
84	Barbara Allen:	RRT LP-8073
84	Barbara Ellen:	Fwys FA 2358
84	Barbrie Allen:	Rim Rlp-495
84	Barbry Allen:	Asch AH 3831
84	Barbry Allen:	TFS cass [no #]
84	Barbry Allen:	Wstm SWN 18021
84	Barbry Ellen:	Fwys FA 2301
84	Barbry Ellen:	TFS cass [no #]
84	Barbry Ellen:	TFS cass [no #]
85	George Allen:	Asch AH 3831
85	George Collins:	Cty 502
85	George Collins:	TFS cass [no #]
	(2 versions)	
85	George Collins:	FLeg FSA-22
85	George Collins:	Fwys FA 2360
85	George Collins:	Prst INT 13020
85	Story of George Collins:	Bio BLP-6005
92A	Lowlands of Holland:	LC AAFS L21
93	Bolakins (Lamkin):	LC AFS L7
93	Bo Lamkin:	Fwys FA 2360
93	Bolamkin:	TFS cass [no #]
95	Hangman:	Fwys FA 2301
95	Hangman:	Mer 1001-2
95	Hangman:	Van VRS-9183
95	Hangman Ballad:	Fwys FA 3830
95	Hangman Tree:	Prst INT 25009
95	Hangman's Song:	Fwys FH 5723
95	Lord Joshuay, Rndr 0065	
105	Bailiff's Daughter of Islington MC 1	
112/N24	Katie Morey: Ph 1022	
132	Robin Hood and the Peddler:	NW NWR 291
140	Robin Hood Rescuing the Three Squires: MC 1	
155	Fatal Flower Garden:	Fwys FA 2951
155	It Rained a Mist:	Prst INT 25003
155	It Rained a Mist:	Rim Rlp-495
155	It Rained a Mist:	Rndr 0020
167/250	Andrew Bataan: LC AAFS L58	
167	Elder Bordee:	FLeg FSA-15
170	Death of Queen Jane:	Fwys FP 40
170	Death of Queen Jane:	LC AAFS L21
173	Four Marys:	GnHys GR714
173	Four Marys:	LC AFS L7
173	Four Marys:	Rndr 0017
200	Blackjack Daisey:	TFS cass [no #]
200	Black Jack Daisy:	Fwys FA 2418
200	Black Jack Davey:	Van VRS-9158
200	Black Jack David:	FLeg FSA-2
200	Black Jack David:	Har HL-7422
200	Black Jack David:	OT 102
200	Black Jack Davy:	JnAp JA 009
200	Black Jack Davy:	Prst INT 13020
200	Black Jack Davy:	Riv RLP 12-645
200	Black Jack Davy:	RRT LP-8073
200	Clayton Boone:	Fwys FH 5723
200	Gipson Davy:	MFFA 1001
200	Gyps of David:	FLeg FSA-1
200	Gypsy Laddie:	Fwys FA 2301
200	Gypsum Davy:	Elek EKLP-2
200	Gypsy Davy:	FLeg FSA-15
200	Gypsy Davy:	LC AFS L1
208	King's Love-Letter: LC AAFS L58	
209	As I Walked over London's Bridge: BRI 002	
209	Georgie: LC AFS L68	
209	Georgie: Van VRS-9239	
209	Hanging of Georgie: Asch AH 3831	
210	Bonnie George Campbell: Fwys FA 2358	
210	Bonnie James Campbell: FLeg FSA-1	
214	Dewy Dens of Yarrow: FLeg FSA-11	
215	Rare Willie Drowned in the Yarrow: GV [cass] SC 03	
215	Rare Willie Drowned in Yarrow: Rndr 0017	
228	Peggy of Glasgow: Rndr 0017	
243	Can't You Remember When Your Heart Was Mine?: BF 15507	
243	House Carpenter:	AH AHR 009
243	House Carpenter:	BRI 002
243	House Carpenter:	FLeg FSA-22
243	House Carpenter:	Fwys FA 2301
243	House Carpenter:	Fwys FA 2350
243	House Carpenter:	Fwys FA 2366
243	House Carpenter:	Fwys FA 2426
243	House Carpenter:	Fwys FA 2951
243	House Carpenter:	Fwys FS 3828
243	House Carpenter:	LC AFS L1
243	House Carpenter:	OHCS 316
243	House Carpenter:	OHS OF-1001
243	House Carpenter:	Prst INT 25003
243	House Carpenter:	Rndr 0051
243	House Carpenter:	Rndr 0058
243	House Carpenter:	Sm/Fwys CD SF 40012

243   House Carpenter: TFS-103
243   House Carpenter: TFS cass [no #]
           (2 versions)
243   House Carpenter: Tpc 12T146
243   House Carpenter: Van VRS-9147
243   House Carpenter: Van VRS-9158
243   House Carpenter's Wife: Ark Trad
           [no #]
243   Little Farmer Boy: Fwys FA 2319
243   Ship Carpenter: LC AAFS L58
243   Well Met, My Old True Love: LC
           AAFS L58
248   Pretty Crowin' Chicken: TFS cass
           [no #]
248   Pretty Crowing Chicken: FLeg
           FSA-22
248   Pretty Crowing Chicken: Rndr 0028
248   Worrysome Woman: HMM LP002
250   Andrew Batan: Fwys FE 4001
272   There Was an Old and Wealthy Man:
           LC AAFS L58
274   Five Nights Drunk: FLeg FSA-22
274   Four Nights' Experience: Fwys FTS
           31089
274   Our Goodman: LC AAFS L12
274   Six Nights Drunk: TFS cass [no #]
274   Three Nights Drunk: FLeg FSA-27
274   Three Nights Drunk: OH OHCS 192
274   Three Nights Drunk: Prst INT 25003
274   Three Nights Experience: OHCS-177
274   Get Up and Bar the Door: AH AHR
           008
275   Get Up and Bar the Door: RRT
           LP-8073
277   Dandoo: AH AHR 008
277   Dan Do: Fwys FA 2360
277   Dan Doo: TFS-108
277   Gentle Fair Jenny: FLeg FSA-3
277   Gentle Fair Jenny: Fwys FA 2302
277   Gentle Fair Jenny: Wstm SWN 18021
277   Little Old Man Lived Out West: Van
           VRS 9162
277   Old Man Who Lived in the West:
           MFFA 1001
277   There Was an Old Man Lived in the
           West: TFS 104
277   Wife Wrapped in a Wether's Skin:
           RRT LP-8073
277   Wife Wrapt in Wether's Skin: FLeg
           FSA-32
278   Devil and the Farmer's Wife: Her 12

278   Devil and the Old Woman: AH AHR
           008
278   Farmer's Curst Wife: Atl SD 1346
278   Farmer's Curst Wife: Mar 9200 [cass]
278   Little Devils: Fwys FA 2302
278   Little Devils: Wstm SWN 18021
278   Randy Riley: FLeg FSA-15
278   Devil and the Farmer: Rndr 0076
278   Devil and the Farmer's Wife: FLeg
           FSA-17
278   Devil and the Farmer's Wife: Van
           VRS-9147
278   Devil and the Farmer's Wife: LC
           AAFS L58
278   Farmer's Curst Wife: Atl SD-1346
278   Farmer's Curst Wife: BRI 002
278   Farmer's Curst Wife: FLeg FSA-22
278   Farmer's Curst Wife: Fwys FA 2362
278   Farmer's Curst Wife: LC AFS L1
278   Farmer's Curst Wife: MC 1
278   Farmer's Curst Wife: NW NWR 239
278   Farmer's Curst Wife: Ok OK76004
278   Farmer's Curst Wife: Ph 1022
278   Little Devils: Elek EKLP-2
278   Old Devil: TFS cass [no #]
278   Old Lady and the Devil: Fwys FA
           2951
278   Scoldin' Wife: Fwys FS 3828
283   The Oxford Merchant: LC AAFS L58
286   Ship Set Sail for North America, A:
           LC AAFS L58
286   Golden Willow Tree: TFS cass [no #]
286   Green Willow Tree: Asch AH 3831
286   Merry Golden Tree: Fwys FA 2301
286   Merry Golden Tree: Prst INT 25006
286   Sinking in the Lonesome Sea: Har
           HL-7422, OH OHCS 112
286   Sinking of the Merry Golden Tree:
           Fwys FA 2375
286   Golden Willow Tree: FLeg FSA-2
286   Golden Willow Tree: LC AAFS L58
286   Golden Willow Tree: LC AFS L7
286   Little Ship: Fwys FE 34161
286   Lowlands Low: Fwys FE 4001
286   Merry Golden Tree: Riv RLP 12-645
286   Merry Golden Tree: RRT LP-8073
286   Turkish Rebelee: BRI 002
286   Turkish Rebilee: Fwys FA 2362
289   Mermaid: TFS cass [no #]
289   Mermaid: LC AAFS L58
289   Merrimac at Sea: Rndr 0017

289   Raging Sea, How It Roars: BRI 002,
      Cty 534, Rndr 1008
289   Waves on the Sea: Fwys FA 2433

295/P9   Queen Sally: BRI 002
299   Soldier Travelling from the North:
      Fwys FA 2309

INDEX OF LAWS BALLADS

[Record label/numbers together following one title indicate the same recording. Recordings are not indexed here if only the tune, without words, is rendered.]

A 4 American Frigate: Mar 9200 [cass]

A 5 James Bird: Ph 1020

A 7 Battle of New Orleans: AFF AFF 33-4

A 8 Come All Ye Texas Rangers: Min JD-203

A 8 Roving Ranger: Asch AH 3831

A 8 Texas Ranger: RCA LPV-522

A 8 Texas Rangers: CMH 106, Rou 1009

A 8 Texas Rangers: LC AAFS L28

A 12b Battle of Pea Ridge: FLeg FSA-11

A 13 Battle of Mill Spring: FLeg FSA-26

A 14 Dying Ranger: Asch AH 3903

A 14 Dying Ranger: LC AAFS L28

A 14 Dying Ranger: MS 45008

A 14 Dying Ranger: Ph 1017

A 17 Last Fierce Charge: Rndr 0083

A 17 Last Fierce Charge: BF BCD 15456

A 17 Two Soldiers, The: RCA LPV-548

A 18 Cumberland's Crew: LC AFS L29

A 25 Hunters of Kentucky: TFS 105

A 26 Cumberland: Mar 9200 [cass]

A 26 Sinking of the Cumberland: Fwys FE 4001

B 1 Cowboy's Lament: FV 12502

B 1 Lee Tharin's Barroom: Tpc 12T146

B 1 Old Joe's Barroom: Fwys FA 2392

B 1 Once in the Saddle: TFS 104

B 1 Saint James' Hospital: Van VRS-9152, Van VCD 45/46

B 1 Streets of Laredo: NW NWR 314/315

B 1 Dying Cowboy: LC AAFS L20

B 1 Lee Tharin's Bar Room: Tpc 12T146

B 1 Streets of Laredo: LC AAFS L28

B 1 Streets of Loredo: Fwys FH 5723

B 1 Tom Sherman's Barroom: Min JD-203

B 1 Tom Sherman's Barroom: MS 45008, RCA LPV-548

B 2 Bury Me Not on the Lone Prairie: AFF AFF 33-1

B 2 Bury Me Not on the Lone Prairie: JnAp 018

B 2 Bury Me Not on the Lone Prairie: Rndr 0036

B 2 Bury Me Out on the Prairie: Mar 9106 [cass]

B 2 Bury Me Not on the Lone Prairie: Van VRS 9124

B 2 Dying Cowboy: LC AAFS L28

B 2 Dying Cowboy: BF 15502, FV 12502

B 2 Dying Cowboy: NW NWR 314/315

B 2 O Bury Me Not on the Lone Prairie: Mar 9106 [cass]

B 3 Dixie Cowboy: MS 45008

B 3 When the Work's All Done This Fall: Ph 1022

B 3 When the Work's All Done This Fall: MFP 0001

B 3 When the Work's All Done This Fall: AFF AFF 33-1

B 3 When the Work's All Done This Fall: Fwys FH 5723

B 3 When the Work's All Done This Fall: RCA LPV-522

B 3 When the Work's All Done This Fall: NW NWR 314/315

B 3 When the Work's All Done This Fall: BF BCD 15456

B 4 Utah Carl: AFF AFF 33-2

B 4 Utah Carl: FLeg FSA-18

B 4 Utah Carl: Fwys FD 5272

B 4 Utah Carl: Ph 1020

B 4 Utah Carl: Rim Rlp-495

B 4 Utah Carol: BF BCD 15456

B 4 Utah Carrol: RCA LPV-522

B 4 Utah Carroll: Fwys FH 5723

B 4 Utah Carroll: MS 45008

B 5 Little Joe, the Wrangler: AFF AFF 33-4

B 5 Little Joe, the Wrangler: FLeg FSA-18

B 5 Little Joe, the Wrangler: Fwys FH 5723

B 5 Little Joe, the Wrangler: BF 15502, FV 12502

B 5 Little Joe, the Wrangler: MFP 0001

B 5 Little Joe, the Wrangler: Mar 9106 [cass]

B 6   Billie Venero: Shoe SGB 1
B 6   Billy Vanero: LC AAFS L55
B 6   Billy Venero: CMH 106
B 6   Billy Venero: AFF AFF 33-1
B 6   Billy Venero: AFF AFF 33-3
B 6   Billy Venero: Ph 1017
B 6   Billy Venero: CMH 106, Rou 1009
B 7   Lonely Cowboy, The, Pts 1/2: Mar 9106 [cass]
B 7   Wandering Cowboy, The: Mar 9106 [cass]
B 8   Ranger's Command, The: Rou 0077
B 9   Sweet Betsy from Pike: RCA LPV-548
B 10   Barker's Creek: Rndr 0028
B 10   Buffalo Skinners: UICFC CFC 301
B 10   Buffalo Skinners: LC AAFS L28
B 11   Sioux Indians: NW NWR 314/315
B 11   Sioux Indians: LC AFS L1
B 13   Cow Trail to Mexico, BF 15202, FV 12202
B 13   Trail to Mexico: Mar 9106, Rou 1009
B 13   Trail to Mexico: Shoe SGB 1
B 13   Trail to Mexico: UICFC CFC 301
B 13   Following the Cow Trail: BF BCD 15456
B 13   Following the Cow Trail: RCA LPV-522
B 14   Joe Bowers: FLeg FSA-2
B 14   Joe Bowers: JnAp JA 049
B 14   Joe Bowers: LC AAFS L30
B 14   Joe Bowers: Ph 1022
B 14   Joe Bowers: Test T-3302
B 14   Joe Bowers: Tpc 12T146
B 15   Bucking Bronco: RCA LPV 522, Rndr 1029, Sytn STR 202
B 16   Zebra Dun: Fwys FH 5723
B 16   Zebra Dun: LC AAFS L28
B 16   Zebra Dun: AFF AFF 33-1
B 16   Zebra Dun: Ph 1017
B 16   Zebra Dun: RCA LPV-522
B 16   Zebra Dunn: MFP 0001
B 17   Tying a Knot in the Devil's Tail: Fwys FH 5723
B 17   Tying a Knot in the Devil's Tail: MFP 0001
B 17   Tying a Knot in the Devil's Tail: NW NWR 314/315
B 17   Tying a Knot in the Devil's Tail: MS 45008, RCA LPV-522
B 17   Tying Knots in the Devil's Tail: AFF AFF 33-1

B 18   Strawberry Roan: AFF AFF 33-3
B 18   Strawberry Roan: Fwys FH 5723
B 18   Strawberry Roan: JEMF 103
B 18   Strawberry Roan: NW NWR 314/315
B 18   Strawberry Roan: MFP 0001
B 18   Strawberry Roan: Ok OK 75003
B 21   Root Hog Or Die: LC AAFS L30
B 23   My Heart's Tonight in Texas: Cam CDN-5111
B 24   Cowboy Jack: Fwys FH 5723
B 24   Cowboy Jack: OH OHCS 111
B 24   Cowboy Jack: RCA LPM-2772
B 24   Cowboy Jack: Sytn STR-202
B 24   Cowboy Jack: UTP [cass no #]
dB 36   Little Joe the Wrangler's Sister Nell: Fwys FH 5723
dB 38   Gol Darn Wheel: Ok OK 75003
dB 38   Gol Darn Wheel: Ph 1017
dB 38   Gol-Durned Wheel: AFF AFF 33-2, NW NWR 317/318
dB 41   Bill Was a Texas Lad: RCA LPV-522
dB 41   Windy Bill: Rndr 0158
dB 41   Windy Bill: Rndr 0237

C 1   Foreman Monroe: Fwys FE 4001
C 1   Jam on Gerry's Rock: AH AHR 007
C 1   Jam on Gerry's Rock: NW NWR 239
C 1   Jam on Gerry's Rocks (2 versions): LC AAFS L56
C 5   Wild Mustard River: LC AAFS L56
C 8   Lost Jimmie Whalen: Fwys FE 4001
C 9   Guy Reed: UIP cass [no #]
C 16   Little Brown Bulls: Fwys FE 4001
C 16   Little Brown Bulls: LC AAFS L55
C 16   Little Brown Bulls: LC AFS L1
C 16   Little Brown Bulls: LC AAFS L56
C 17b   Michigan I-O: LC AAFS L56
C 17c   Colley's Run-I-O: LC AAFS L28
C 19   Backwoodsman: Mar 9200 [cass]
C 19   Morning of 1845: Fwys FS 3809
C 19   Spring of '65: Fwys FA 2317
C 23   Turner's Camp on the Chippewa: LC AAFS L56
C 25   Jack Haggerty: LC AAFS L56
dC 29   Driving Saw-Logs on the Plover: Ph 1022

D 13   Dreadnaught: NW NWR 239
D 24   Great Titanic: Fwys FA 2375
cf. D 24 After the Sinking of the Titanic: BF 15504, FV 12504

cf. D 24 Down with the Old Canoe: RCA LPV-507, RCA 8417-2-R
cf. D 24 Last Scene of the Titanic: Rou 1007
D 27 Ship That Never Returned, The: SH SH-CD-3795

E 1 Ballad of Jesse James: UTP [cass no #]
E 1 Jesse James: Atl SD-1346
E 1 Jesse James: Arh 5012
E 1 Jesse James: Brch 1945
E 1 Jesse James: Fwys FS 3832
E 1 Jesse James: LC AAFS L20
E 1 Jesse James: RCA LPV-548
E 1 Jessie James: Bio RC-6003
E 1 Life and Death of Jesse James: BF 15503, FV 12503
E 1 Poor Jesse James: Riv RLP 12-645
E 3 Bandit Cole Younger: Fwys FA 2951
E 3 Bandit Cole Younger: MS 45008
E 3 Cole Younger: Fwys FA 2392
E 3 Cole Younger: Ph 1017
E 4 Sam Bass: LC AAFS L30
E 4 Sam Bass: RCA LPV-522
E 5 Sidney Allen: BRI 004
E 5 Allen Clan: Bio RC-6002
E 6 Claude Allen: BRI 004
E 6 Claude Allen: Fwys FA 2355
E 6 Claude Allen: Fwys FA 2390
E 6 Claude Allen: LC AFS L7
E 6 Claude Allen: Prst INT 25009
E 7 Kenny Wagner: Atl SD-1346
E 8 Kenny Wagner Surrender: Hist HLP 8003
E 10 Wild Bill Jones: Arh F5002
E 10 Wild Bill Jones: BF 15508
E 10 Wild Bill Jones: Brch 1945
E 10 Wild Bill Jones: Cty 410
E 10 Wild Bill Jones: Cty 712
E 10 Wild Bill Jones: Cty 777
E 10 Wild Bill Jones: Cty 786
E 10 Wild Bill Jones: FLeg FSA-1
E 10 Wild Bill Jones: Fwys FA 2350
E 10 Wild Bill Jones: Fwys FS 3829
E 10 Wild Bill Jones: GnHys GR712
E 10 Wild Bill Jones: Mar 9025 [cass]
E 10 Wild Bill Jones: Prst INT 13020
E 10 Wild Bill Jones: Riv RLP 12-617
E 10 Wild Bill Jones: TFS 106
E 11 Charles Guiteau: BF 15510, Cty 408, Cty 522, Fwys FA 2951

E 11 Charles Guiteau: Fwys FA 2368
E 11 Charles Guiteau: Fwys FA 2375
E 11 Charles Guiteau: LC AFS L29
E 11 Charles Guiteau: Mer 1001-2
E 11 Charles Guiteau: Riv RLP 12-617
E 13 Frankie Silvers: Fwys FA 2350
E 13 Frankie Silvers: OT 102
E 13 Frankie Silvers: Tpc 12T146
E 14 Gambling on the Sabbath Day: Elek EKL-316
E 14 Gambler, The: BF BCD 15456
E 15 Bad Companions: BF BCD 15456
E 15 Don't Forget This Song: CMH 107, OH 117
E 15 I Was Born in Pennsylvania: BF 15508
E 16 Twenty-One Years: Elek EKL-316
E 16 Twenty-One Years: NW NWR 225
E 17 Logan County Jail: AH AHR 007
E 17 Mangrum and Mynatt: TFS 106
E 17 Prisoner's Dream: BF 15501, FV 12501
E 17 Prisoner's Dream: OT 115
E 17 Seven Long Years in Prison: OT 115
E 17 Sporting Cowboy: Cty 522, MS 45008
E 17 Sporting Cowboy: Ph 1017
E 18 Tillies and Turnies: Ark Trad 004
E 19 J. B. Marcum: Brch 1945
E 20 Rowan County Crew: Rndr 0034
E 23 Howard Carey : UIP cass [no #] (2 versions)

F 1a Blue Eyed Ella, BF 15508
F 1a Fair Eyed Ellen: Cam CAL-797, Rou 1006
F 1a False Hearted Lover: Ark Trad 002
F 1a Florella: TFS 106
F 1a Pearl Bryan: Mer 1001-2
F 1a Jealous Lover: BRI 002
F 1b Pearl Bryan: Cty 522
F 1b Pearl Bryan: OHCS 317
F 1b Pearl Bryant: Prst INT 13030
F 1c Nellie Cropsey: Fwys FS 3848
F 2 Pearl Bryant: Brch 1945
F 2 + Pearl Bryan: Fwys FA 2375
F 4 Naomi Wise: Fwys FA 2951
F 4 Naomi Wise: LC AAFS L12
F 4 Ommie Wise: Cty 513, Fwys FA 2951
F 4 'Omie Wise: JnAp JA 049
F 4 Little Lonie: AH AHR 009
F 4 Little Oma: Ark Trad 002
F 4 Little Omie: LC AFS L65-L66

F 4   Little Ommie Wise: Asch AH 3903
F 4   Omie Wise: Fwys 2368
F 4   Omie Wise: JnAp JA0055
F 4   Omie Wise: JnAp JA 020
F 4   Omie Wise: Prst INT 13020
F 4   Omie Wise: Tpc 12TS336
F 4   Omie Wise: Van VRS-9152, Van
          VCD 45/46
F 4   Poor Omie: Fwys FA 2359
F 5   Banks of the Ohio [I'll Never Be
          Yours]: Cty 522
F 5   Banks of the Ohio: Fwys FS 3832
F 5   Banks of the Ohio: OHCS-172
F 5   Banks of the Ohio: Prst INT 13049
F 5   Banks of the Ohio: Prst INT 25003
F 5   Banks of the Ohio: Riv RLP 12-617
F 5   Banks of the Ohio: Test T-3302
F 5   Banks of the Ohio: Van VSD-9/10
F 5   Down Beside the Ohio: Prst INT
          13030
F 5   Down on the Banks of the Ohio: Cam
          CAL 797, Cam ADL2-0726(e),
          Rou 1006
F 5   Down on the Banks of the Ohio: RCA
          LPV-548
F 5   On the Banks of the Ohio: Arh 5001
F 5   On the Banks of the Ohio: Cam
          CAL-774, BB AMX2-5510
F 5   On the Banks of the Ohio: Fwys FP
          40
F 5   On the Banks of the Ohio: OH OHS
          90031
F 6   Down in the Willow Garden: Asch
          AA 3/4
F 6   Down in the Willow: RCA LPV-507
F 6   Rose Conley: OT 102, OHCS-157
F 6   Willow Garden: Shoe SGB 1
F 11   Ellen Smith: Fly 546
F 11   Ellen Smith: Fwys FS 3828
F 11   Poor Ellen Smith: Atl 1347
F 11   Poor Ellen Smith: Brch 1945
F 11   Poor Ellen Smith: Cty 748
F 11   Poor Ellen Smith: Cty 791
F 11   Poor Ellen Smith: Fwys FA 2360
F 11   Poor Ellen Smith: Fwys FA 3830
F 11   Poor Ellen Smith: Fwys FS 3811
F 11   Poor Ellen Smith: OH OHCS 191
F 11   Poor Ellen Smith: Prst INT 13038
F 11   Poor Ellen Smith: Prst INT 25003
F 11   Poor Ellen Smith: Rndr 0065
F 11   Poor Little Ellen: Riv RLP 12-610

F 11   Fate of Ellen Smith: Cty 502, MS
          45004
F 16   Indiana Hero: Fwys FS 3809
F 17   Vance Song: BRI 004
F 24   Peddler and His Wife: Rndr 1037
F 31   [Murder of] Naomi Wise: Cty 510
F 32   Benjamin Dean (3 versions): UIP cass
          [no #]
F 35   Charlie Lawson: Rndr 0065
F 35   Death of the Lawson Family: Asch
          AH 3831
F 35   Lawson Family Murder: Van
          VSD-6576
F 35   Lawson Family Tragedy: Rou 0052
F 35   Lawson Murder: Prst INT 25009
F 35   Murder of the Lawson Family: FC
          FC-014
F 35   Murder of the Lawson Family: BF
          15521, Co CS 9660
F 36   Tom Dooley: DU 33033, OH
          OHCS-157
F 36   Tom Dooley: FLeg FSA-1
F 36   Tom Dooley: Fwys FS 3811
F 36   Tom Dooley: Van VRS-9152, Van
          VCD 45/46

G 1   Casey Jones: AFF AFF 33-2
G 1   Casey Jones: Asch AH 3903
G 1   Casey Jones: Fwys FD 5752
G 1   Casey Jones: LC AFS L68
G 1   Casey Jones: Vet 103
G 2   Old Ninety Seven: LC AFS L68
G 2   Wreck of the Old 97: BRI 004
G 2   Wreck of the Old 97: FLeg FSA-13
G 2   Wreck of the Old Ninety-Seven: Fwys
          FA 2315
G 2   Wreck of the Old 97: OH OHCS 141
G 2   Wreck of the Old 97: Riv RLP 12-650
G 2   Wreck of the Old 97: Test T-3301
G 2   Wreck of the Old 97: RCA LPV-532
G 3   Brave Engineer: JEMF 103
G 3   George Allen: LC AFS L61
G 3   Engine One-Forty-Three: Fwys FA
          2951, Cam CAL 2473, RCA
          LPV-532, RCA CPM1-2763
G 3   F. F. V.: Van VRS-9239
G 3   FFV, The: AH AHR 009
G 3   Wreck on the C. & O.: Brch 1945
G 3   Wreck on the C & O Road: OHCS
          317
G 6   Mines of Irvingdale: Ph 1020

G 6   Avondale Mine Disaster: LC AAFS
       L16

G 9   Shut Up in Coal Creek Mine: CT
       6001, Rou 1026

G 9   Cross Mountain Mines Explosion:
       TFS 106

G 11b Reckless Motorman: De DL-4557

G 14   Johnstown Flood: NW NWR 239

G 15   Great Milwaukee Fire: Ph 1020

G 15   Milwaukee Fire: LC AAFS L55

G 16   Springfield Mountain: Asch AA 3/4,
       Fwys FA 2040 (FP 40)

G 16   Springfield Mountain: Mar 9200 [cass]

G 16   Pizen Sarpent (Springfield Mountain):
       TFS 104

G 16   Rattlesnake Song: Ark Trad [no #]

G 16   Ven'mous Viper: AH AHR 008

G 16   Young Johnny: LC AAFS L55

G 17   Young Carlotta: Van VRS-9158

G 17   Young Charlotte: Fwys FS 3809

G 17   Young Charlotte: LC AAFS L14

G 19   He Took a White Rose from Her Hair:
       Ha HL 7344

G 19   It's Sinful To Flirt: Hist 8004

G 19   Sinful Flirt: Mtn 304

G 19   Sinful To Flirt: Mer 1001-2

G 19   Sinful To Flirt: Rndr 0143

G 19   They Say It Is Sinful To Flirt: Ark
       Trad 002

G 19   They Say It Is Sinful To Flirt: RCA
       LPV-548

G 19   Willie down by the Pond: FLeg
       FSA-27

G 21   Silver Dagger: AH AHR 009

G 21   Silver Dagger: Rndr 0051

G 21   True Lovers: Fwys FA 2355

G 21   Young Men and Maids: Asch AH
       3831

G 21   Printer's Bride: Fwys FA 2427

G 22   Death of Floyd Collins: RCA
       LPV-548

G 22   Death of Floyd Collins: Rndr 0064

G 22   Death of Floyd Collins: TFS 105

G 22   Death of Floyd Collins: UIP cass

G 26   Old Number Nine: Alp ALP-201

G 26   On a Cold Winter's Night: RCA
       LPV-507

G 26   Brave Engineer: JEMF 103

G 26   Wreck of Old #9: FLeg FSA-13

G 26   Wreck of Old Number 9: Van
       VSD-6576

G 26   Wreck of Number Nine: Fwys FA
       2365

G 26   Wreck of the Number 9: AFF AFF
       33-4

G 26   Wreck of the Number Nine: SH
       CD-3795

G 29   John J. Curtis: LC AAFS L16

dG 51 Wreck of the Royal Palm: LC AFS
       L61

dG 51 Wreck of the Royal Palm: Vet 103

dG 52 Wreck of the Shenandoah: FPrm
       41942

H 1   My Name Is John Johanna: BF 15510,
       Cty 408, Fwys FA 2951, RCA
       LPV-548

H 1   Sanford Barney: LC AFS L7

H 1   State of Arkansas: Rndr 0064

H 1   Uncle Dave's Travels, Pt. 1 (Misery in
       Arkansas): De DL-4760

H 1   Way down in Arkansas: Hist BC-2433

H 2   Danville Girl: Fwys FA 2392

H 2   Danville Girl: Fwys RBF 654

H 2   Georgia Hobo: Rou 1035

H 2   Girl I Left in Danville: CT 6000, Test
       T-3301

H 2   New York Hobo: BF 15504, FV 12504

H 2   Rambling Reckless Hobo: Rndr 1004

H 2   Sam's "Waiting for a Train": UICFC
       CFC 301

H 2   Waiting for a Train: FLeg FSA-13

H 2   Wild and Reckless Hobo: Cty 739

H 2   Wild and Reckless Hobo: JEMF 104

H 2   Wild and Reckless Hobo: RCA
       LPV-548

H 3   Little Stream of Whiskey: Van
       VRS-9170

H 3   Dying Hobo: BF 15509, RCA
       LPV-548

H 3   Dying Hobo: LC AFS L61

H 3   Little Stream of Whiskey: Rndr 0036

H 3   Little Stream of Whiskey: Rndr 1004

H 4   Gambling Man: FLeg FSA-32

H 4   Roving Gambler: Asch AH 3831

H 4   Roving Gambler: TFS 106

H 4   Rovin' Gambler [2 versions]: BF
       15508

H 4   Roving Cunningham: Ph 1022

H 6   Downward Road: Rndr 0051

H 8   Lass of Mohea: Mer 1001-2

H 8   Little Mohea: AFF AFF 33-3

H 8	Little Mohee: Fwys FS 3810		I 1	John Henry Was a Little Boy: Alp ALP 202
H 8	Little Mo-hee: RCA LPV-548			
H 8	Little Mohee: FLeg FSA-2		I 2	John Hardy: Asch AH 3903
H 9	Lakes of Ponchartrain: Arh 5010		I 2	John Hardy: Bio RC 6004
H 9	On the Lake of Pontchartrain: LC AAFS L55		I 2	John Hardy: Cty 533, Hist 8001
			I 2	John Hardy: Cty 741
H 9	Creole Girl: Ark Trad [no #]		I 2	John Hardy: Cty 748
H 12	Lonesome Scenes of Winter: JnAp JA 020		I 2	John Hardy: FPrm 41942
			I 2	John Hardy: Fwys FA 2360
H 13	Young Man Who Wouldn't Hoe Corn: Fwys FS 3809		I 2	John Hardy: Fwys FA 2433
			I 2	John Hardy: Fwys FA 2951
H 13	Young Man Who Wouldn't Hoe Corn: Ark Trad 004		I 2	John Hardy: Fwys FA 3810
			I 2	John Hardy: Fwys FS 3832
H 14	Queenstown Warning: Ph 1020		I 2	John Hardy: Fwys FS 3833
H 17	Plain Golden Band: UIP cass [no #]		I 2	John Hardy: GnHys GR712
H 20	British American Fight: AH AHR 010		I 2	John Hardy: Hist BC 2433-1
H 23	Burglar Man: JnAp JA 001		I 2	John Hardy: OH OHCS 112
H 23	Burglar Man: Prst INT 25004		I 2	John Hardy Was a Desperate Little Man: RCA CPM-2763
H 23	Burglar Man: Test T-3301			
H 23	Old Maid and the Burglar: Hist 8004		I 2	John Henry (Hardy): FLeg FSA-11
cf. H 24	Nineteen Years Old: TFS 104		I 2	Old John Hardy: Cty 525
H 26	Girl That Wore the Waterfall, The: AH AHR 007		I 3	Frankie: OH OHCS 191
			I 3	Frankie Baker: Cty 741
H 27	Tim Brooks: CT 6001		I 3	Frankie and Johnny: Fwys FA 2374
H 30	Jerry Go Ile That Car: RCA LPV-532		I 3	Frankie and Johnny: OH OHCS 114
H 31	Christine Le Roy: Rou 1029		I 3	Frankie Dean: OT 102
			I 3	Frankie Was a Good Girl: Fwys FA 2315
I 1	Death of John Henry: Brun 59001, Cty 502, Cty 545, Hist HLP 8006			
			I 3	Leaving Home: Cty 505
I 1	Death of John Henry: BFX 15214		I 3	Leaving Home: RCA LPV-548
I 1	Death of John Henry: Rou 1028		I 3	Little Frankie Baker: Fwys FA 3833
I 1	Gonna Die with My Hammer in My Hand: Fwys FA 2951		I 3	Little Frankie: JnAp JA 055
			I 4	Cold Penitentiary Blues: RCA LPV-548, Rndr 1037
I 1	John Henry: Atl 1347			
I 1	John Henry: Bio RC-6003		I 4	Cold Penitentiary Blues: Rndr 0064
I 1	John Henry: Brch 1945		I 4	Gambler's Lament: CT 6001
I 1	John Henry: Cty 543		I 4	Gamblin' Jim: OT 112
I 1	John Henry: Cty 729		I 4	Highwayman: Cty 516
I 1	John Henry: Fly 546		I 4	Poor Boy, Cty 411
I 1	John Henry: Fwys FA 2317		I 4	Poor Boy: JEMF 104
I 1	John Henry: Fwys FA 2392		I 4	Poor Boy: Fwys FD 5272
I 1	John Henry: Fwys FS 3810		I 4	Poor Boy in Jail: Fwys FA 2392
I 1	John Henry: Fwys FS 3839		I 8	Little Sadie: Cty 791
I 1	John Henry: GnHys GR712		I 8	Little Sadie: Fwys FA 2315
I 1	John Henry: JnAp JA 010		I 8	Little Sadie: Fwys FA 2359
I 1	John Henry: OH OHS 90031		I 8	Little Sadie: Fwys FA 2363
I 1	John Henry: Riv RLP 12-610		I 8	Little Sadie: Van VRS-9147
I 1	John Henry: Riv RLP 12-645		I 8	Little Sadie: Van VRS-9170
I 1	John Henry: Rndr 0001		I 8	Little Sadie: Van VSD-9/10
I 1	John Henry: Rndr 1005		I 8	Penitentiary Blues: Arh 5012
I 1	John Henry: Test T-3302		I 8	Sweet Sadie: AH AHR 010

I 9   Been on the Job Too Long: NW
       NWR 245
I 9   Old Brady: TFS 104
I 13   Railroad Bill: Asch AA 3/4
I 13   Railroad Bill: Prst INT 25009
I 13   Railroad Bill: Rndr 1007
I 13   Railroad Bill: Van VRS-9182
I 14   Bully of the Town: Cty 526
I 14   Bully of the Town: Cty 543
I 14   Bully of the Town: JEMF 103
I 15   Stackalee: Fwys FA 2951
I 15   Stack O'Lee: Van VSD-6576
I 15   Stackolee: Rndr 1010
I 15   Stagolee Was a Bully: Fwys FE 34162
I 16   Wreck of the Six Wheel Driver: RCA
       LPV-548
I 17   Boll Weevil: Cty 741
I 17   Dixie Boll Weevil: UIP [cass no #]

J 5   Young Repoleon: Cty 787
J 12   Two Sons of North Britain: Ph 1022

K 12   Fall, Fall, Build Me a Boat: Fwys FA
       2342
K 12   I Have No One To Love Me (But the
       Sailor in the Deep Blue Sea):
       Cam CAS(e) 2554, CMH 107
K 12   No One To Love Me: Mtn 303
K 12   Papa, Papa Build Me a Boat: Fwys
       FA 2392
K 12   Sailor on the Deep Blue Sea: Prst
       INT 13020
K 12   Sweet Soldier Boy: FLeg FSA-22
K 12   Sailor on the Deep Blue Sea: Riv
       RLP 12-645
K 12   Sailor on the Deep Blue Sea: Riv
       RLP 12-617
K 13   Sailor Boy: CMH 118
K 13   Sailor Boy: Fwys FS 3848
K 14/P 5 Loving Nancy: FLeg FSA-26
K 17   Down by the Sea Shore: Riv RLP 12-
       649
K 17   I Never Will Marry: Cam CAS(e)
       2554, OH OHCS 117
K 17   I Never Will Marry: Fwys FA 2375
K 17   Down by the Sea Shore: FLeg FSA-11
K 21   Brave Boys: NW NWR 239
K 26   Bold McCarthy, *or* City of Baltimore:
       NW NWR 223
K 28   Flying Cloud: Fwys FE 4001
K 33   Wild Barbaree: LC AAFS L21

K 36   Green Bed: TFS 106
K 36   Little Johnny: AH AHR 007
K 36   Young Johnny Sailed from London:
       Cty 789
K 38   Young Johnny: Fwys FE 4001
K 43   Sailor Being Tired: Fwys FA 2309

L 4   Dixon Said to Jackson: JnAp JA 001
L 4   Battle of King's Mountain: Prst INT
       13020
L 7   Brennan on the Moor: Fwys FE 4001
L 7   Brennan on the Moor: LC AAFS L55
L 7   Willie Brennan: Prst INT 25009
L 9   Bonnie Black Bess: FLeg FSA-15
L 12   In Dublin City: FLeg FSA-23
L 12   Poor and Ramblin' Boy: Fwys FA
       2427
L 12   Rake and Rambling Boy: Rou 1023
L 12   Rake and Rambling Boy: Tpc 12T146
L 12   Rambling Boy: LC AFS L7
L 12   Rambling Boy: Riv RLP 12-649
L 12   Ramblin' Boy: Cty 404
L 12   Rich and Rambling Boy: Prst INT
       13020
L 12   Rude and Rambling Man: Fwys FA
       2350
L 12   Rude and Rambling Man: GHP LP-
       1001
L 13a Captain Devin: FLeg FSA-26
L 13a Captain Devin: Rndr SS-0145
L 16b Boston Burglar: Ark Trad [no #]
L 16b Boston Burglar: BF BCD 15456
L 16b Boston Burglar: Mar 9200 [cass]
L 16b Boston Burglar: Riv RLP 12-617
L 16b Boston Burglar: Riv RLP 12-610
L 16b Boston Burglar: UIP [cass no #]
L 16b Boston Burglar: UTP [cass no #]
L 16b Boston Burglar: Van VRS 9162
L 16b Frank James: FLeg FSA-2
L 16b Frank James, the Roving Gambler
       (Boston Burglar): LC AAFS L14
L 16b Louisville Burglar: Cty 522
L 20   Wild Colonial Boy: Fwys FE 4001
L 21   Johnny Troy: TFS 106

M 1   Early, Early in the Spring: Rndr 0028
M 1   Early, Early in the Spring: Tpc
       12TS336
M 1   It Was Midnight on the Stormy Deep:
       Rndr CD 11536
M 1   Midnight on the Stormy Sea: BB
       AXM2-5525

M 2   Johnny Doyle: FLeg FSA-22
M 2   Johnny Doyle: Fwys FA 2309
M 3   Charming Little Girl: FPrm 41942
M 3   Don't You Remember?: Fwys FA
              2309
M 3   Once I Courted a Charming Beauty
              Bright: LC AAFS L55
M 3   Most Fair Beauty Bright: Fwys FA
              2427
M 3   Lady Beauty Bride: Rim Rlp-495
M 3   Lady Beauty Bright: Van VRS 9162
M 4   Awake, Arise You Drowsy Sleeper:
              LC AAFS L55
M 4   Awake, Awake: Fwys FA 2309
M 4   Awake, Awake, My Old True Lover:
              FLeg FSA-22
M 4   Drowsy Sleeper: Van VRS 9124
M 4/G 21 Katie Dear (Silver Dagger): NW
              NWR 236
M 4   Katie Dear: Ark Trad 004
M 4   Katie Dear: Cam CAL-797, Cam
              ADL2-0726(e), RCA 8417-2-R
M 4   O Molly Dear: CMF-011-L, Hist HLP
              8003
M 4   Oh Molly Dear, Go Ask Your Mother:
              BF 15509
M 4   Who's That Knocking?: JEMF 101
M 4   Who's That Knocking on My Window?:
              MCA VIM-4012
M 13   Locks and Bolts: GnHys GR714
M 13   Locks and Bolts: Rndr 0083
M 13   Locks and Bolts: Van VRS-9158
M 13   Rainbow 'mid the Willows: Prst INT
              25003
M 14   Bonny Labouring Boy: Asch AA 3/4
M 26   On the Red River Shore: Mar 9106
              [cass]
M 27   Bold Soldier: Mar 9200 [cass]
M 27   Little Soldier: HMM LP001
M 27   Bold Soldier: FLeg FSA-27
M 27   Brisk Young Soldier, The: AH AHR
              007
M 32   In Zepo Town: Fwys FA 2309
M 32   Late One Evening: NW NWR 223
M 32   Jealous Brothers: FLeg FSA-22
M 34   Young Emily: Fwys FA 2418
M 34   Young Emily: Rndr 0028

N 2   In Bonny Scotland: FLeg FSA-33
N 7   Ho Lilly Ho: Asch AH 3831
N 7   Jack Monroe: Rndr 0064

N 7   Jackaro: FLeg FSA-3
N 7   Jackie Munroe: Cty 534
N 7   Jackie's Gone A-Sailing: LC AAFS
              L21
N 7   Love of Polly and Jack Monroe: Fwys
              FTS 31016
N 7   Jackero: Wstm SWN 18021
N 8   Going Away Tomorrow: FLeg
              FSA-23
N 8   Sweet William: LC AAFS L21
N 10   Silk Merchant's Daughter: AH AHR
              007
N 10   Silk Merchant's Daughter: HMM
              LP001
N 14   Pretty Polly: Prst INT 25004
N 20   Dog and Gun (Jolly Farmer): TFS
              104
N 20   Dog and Gun: OHCS 316
N 20   Wealthy Squire: FPrm 41942
N 22   Kate and the Cowhide: TFS 104
N 24   Katie Morey: Van VRS-9239
N 28   As Willie and Mary Strolled by the
              Seashore: BF 15517
N 28   Two Lovers: Van VRS-9158
N 29   Nightingales of Spring: Fwys FE 4001
N 30   Old Ireland: BRI 002
N 30   Brisk Young Farmer: Rndr 0083
N 30   William Hall: FLeg FSA-22
N 30   William Hall: Van VRS 9162
N 37   Young John Riley: Mer 1001-2
N 38   Mantle So Green: Ph 1022
N 40   Claudie Banks: AH AHR 007
cf. N 40 Where Are You Going, Alice?: Cty
              513
cf. N 40 Where Are You Going, Alice?: Fwys
              FS 3839
N 42   Fair Miss in the Gardens: Fwys 2368
N 42   Pretty Fair Miss All in a Garden:
              Fwys FA 2390
N 42   Pretty Fair Miss: Prst INT 13030
N 42   Returning Sweetheart: Asch AH 3831
N 42   Broken Token: LC AAFS L21
N 42   Soldier's Sweetheart: TFS 106

O 3   Bugerboo: HMM LP001
O 4   My Gypsy Girl: Cty 509
O 4   Gypsy's Wedding Day: Fwys FA 2362
O 4   Wandering Gypsy Girl: OH
              OHCS-190
O 14   Polly: FLeg FSA-32
O 25   Bold Sea Captain: JnAp JA 001

O 25 Carolina Lady: Fwys FA 2418
O 25 Lady of Carlisle: LC AFS L1
O 33 May I Go with You, Johnny: FLeg FSA-26
O 33 Cruel War Is Raging: LC AAFS L20
O 33 War Is a-Ragin' for Johnny: Fwys FS 3828
O 33 War Is a-Raging: Asch AH 3831
O 33 War Is a-Raging: Fwys FA 2315
O 33 War Is a-Raging: Prst INT 13030
O 36 Molly Bawn: FLeg FSA-33
O 36 Molly Bawn: BF 15003
O 36 Molly Bender: AH AHR 008
O 36 Molly Bender: AH AHR 009
O 36 Molly Van: HMM LP002
O 38 Fair Fannie Moore: NW NWR 239
O 38 Fair Fanny Moore: UICFC CFC 201
O 39 Sheffield Apprentice: Mar 9200 [cass]

P 1a Arizona Girl I Left Behind Me: Mar 9106 [cass]
P 1a My Parents Raised Me Tenderly: LC AAFS L12
P 1a My Parents Raised Me Tenderly: TFS 103
P 1a Rich Old Farmer: LC AFS L1
P 1a Roving Cowboy: JnAp JA 009
P 1b Gal I Left Behind, The: Fwys FH 5723
P 1b Girl I Left Behind [or Always Marry Your Lover]: Brun 59001
P 1b Girl I Left Behind: Prst INT 25004
P 1b I've Always Been a Rambler: Cty 502, Cty 513
P 1b I've Always Been a Rambler: Rndr 0021
P 1b Maggie Walker Blues, Fwys FA 2355
P 1b Peggy Walker: Asch AH 3903
P 1b Roving Boy: TFS 106
P 1b Roaming Boy: Prst INT 13030
P 8 Rogers' Gray Mare: FLeg FSA-23
P 8 Young Timmy the Miller: AH AHR 007
P 9 Fine Sally: Fwys FA 2309
P 9 Queen Sally: BRI 002 [v. also C. 295]
P 9 Sally: FLeg FSA-26
P 9 Rich Irish Lady: FLeg FSA-32
P 14 One Morning in May (or Nightingale): Elek EKLP-2 (2 versions)
P 14 One Morning in May: Tpc 12TS336
P 14 Soldier and the Lady: TFS 108

P 14 Nightingale Song: Rndr 0017
P 14 One Morning in May: AH AHR 008
P 14 One Morning in May: Wstm SWN 18021
P 14 Soldier and the Lady: FLeg FSA-23
P 14 Soldier and the Lady: Fwys FS 3809
P 14 Soldier and the Lady: Prst INT 25006
P 14 Soldier and the Lady: Rndr 0021
P 18 Down by the Riverside: AH AHR 010
P 21 Mary of the Wild Moor: AH AHR 008
P 21 Mary of the Wild Moor: Cam CAL-797, Cam ADL2-0726(e)
P 21 Mary of the Wild Moor: Mar 9200 [cass]
P 24 Butcher Boy: Fwys FS 3810
P 24 Butcher Boy: Mar 9200 [cass]
P 24 Butcher Boy: Prst FL 14035
P 24 Butcher's Boy: BF 15508
P 24 Butcher's Boy: BRI 002
P 24 Butcher's Boy: BB AXM2-5525, Cam CAL-797, Cam ADL2-0726(e)
P 24 Butcher's Boy: FLeg FSA-27
P 24 Butcher's Boy: Fwys FA 2951
P 24 Butcher's Boy: Rndr 0017
P 24 Butcher's Boy: Rndr 0077
P 24 Fatal Courtship: OT 102
P 24 In London City: Fwys FA 2374
P 24 London City Where I Did Dwell: JnAp JA 055
P 25 Love Has Brought Me to Despair: Fwys FA 2309
P 27 Caroline of Edinboro' Town: LC AAFS L14
P 29 Lily of the West: Cty 789
P 29 Lily of the West: Fwys FE 34161
P 29 Lily of the West: HMM LP001
P 29 Lily of the West: Rndr 0065
P 30 Poison in a Glass of Wine: HMM LP002
P 31 To Wear a Green Willow: FLeg FSA-33
P 35 Expert Town (Oxford Girl): LC AAFS L12
P 35 Export Gal: Rndr 1029
P 35 Knoxville Girl: Cty 718
P 35 Knoxville Girl: Fwys FA 3833
P 35 Knoxville Girl: JnAp 018
P 35 Knoxville Girl: Prst INT 13035
P 35 Knoxville Girl: Riv RLP 12-617
P 35 Knoxville Girl: TFS 103

P 35   Never Let the Devil Get the Upper
         Hand of You: De DL-4557
P 35   Lexington Murder: NW NWR 245
P 35   Oxford Girl: Min JD-203
P 35   Story of the Knoxville Girl: Cam
         CAL-797, Cam ADL2-0726(e),
         Rou 1006
P 36b Pretty Polly: Asch AH 3831
P 36b Pretty Polly: Brun 59001, Fwys RBF
         654
P 36b Pretty Polly: Cty 522
P 36b Pretty Polly: Cty 712
P 36b Pretty Polly: Cty 739
P 36b Pretty Polly: FPrm 41942
P 36b Pretty Polly: Fwys FA 2314
P 36b Pretty Polly: Fwys FA 2358
P 36b Pretty Polly: Fwys FS 3811
P 36b Pretty Polly: Fwys FS 3828
P 36b Pretty Polly: JnAp JA 010
P 36b Pretty Polly: JnAp JA 020
P 36b Pretty Polly: LC AFS L1
P 36b Pretty Polly: Mtn 303
P 36b Pretty Polly: OT 102
P 36b Pretty Polly: Prst INT 13035
P 36b Pretty Polly: Prst INT 25009
P 36b Pretty Polly: Riv RLP 12-610
P 36b Pretty Polly: Rndr 0072
P 36b Pretty Polly: TFS 106
P 36b Pretty Polly: Wstm SWN 18021
P 38   James MacDonald: Ph 1020

Q 1   Father Grumble: LC AAFS L14
Q 1   Old Crumley: FLeg FSA-3
Q 1   Old Grumble: TFS 106

Q 2   My Good Old Man: Tpc 12T146
Q 2   Rich Old Lady: Ark Trad [no #]
Q 2   There Was an Old Lady: Fwys FA
         2362
Q 2   Tinker's Story: Mar 9200
Q 2   Woman from Yorkshire: FLeg
         FSA-15
Q 3   Johnny Sands: Tpc 12T146
Q 4   Devilish Mary: Cty 506
Q 4   Devilish Mary: Cty 510
Q 4   Devilish Mary: Fwys FA 2362
Q 4   Devilish Mary: LC AAFS L14
Q 4   Devilish Mary: Riv RLP 12-617
Q 4   Dev'lish Mary: Fwys FS 3811
Q 9   Every Day Dirt: Sm/Fwys SF 40012
Q 9   Everyday Dirt: BF 15505, FV 12505
Q 9   Everyday Dirt: Fwys FA 2366
Q 9   Will the Weaver: Van VRS-9158
Q 15   Lather and Shave: Cty 789
Q 18   Pat Malone: FLeg FSA-15
Q 18   Pat Malone: Kan 308
Q 20   Erin-Go-Bragh: NW NWR 239
Q 21   Miller's Will: Fwys FA 2362
Q 21   Miller's Will: Riv RLP 12-645
Q 21   Miller's Will: Rndr 0051
Q 22   Old Kimball: LC AFS L1
Q 26   One Morning in May: LC AFS L1
Q 26   Bad Girl's Lament: Ph 1022
Q 26   Bad Girl: BRI 002
Q 26   Whore's Lament: BF 15003
Q 27   Erin's Green Shore: BF 15003
Q 27   Erin's Green Shore: Van VRS 9124
Q 27   Ireland's Green Shore: Rndr 0018
Q 30   To Be a Farmer's Boy: TFS 104

ALBUMS INDEXED BY LABEL/NUMBER

Label/Number	Sequence	Artists
Alabama Traditions 103	207	Various
Alpine ALP 201	403a	J. E. Mainer
Alpine ALP 202	403b	J. E. Mainer
Arhoolie 5001	53	Hodges Bros
Arhoolie 5010 [< Folklyric LP 122]	84	Louisiana Honeydrippers
Arhoolie 5011 [< Folklyric LP 123]	69	Jenkins/Sherrill
Arhoolie 5012	96	Sam McGee
Arhoolie 5018	109	Uncle John Patterson
Arhoolie F5002	92	J. E. Mainer
Arizona Friends of Folklore AFF 33-1	208	Various
Arizona Friends of Folklore AFF 33-2	209	Various
Arizona Friends of Folklore AFF 33-3	210	Various
Arizona Friends of Folklore AFF 33-4	113	Bunk and Becky Pettyjohn
Arkansas Traditions 003	131	Almeda Riddle
Arkansas Traditions 004	203	Williams Family
Arkansas Traditions [No #]	211	Various
Arkansas Traditions 002	23	Noble Cowden
Asch AA 3/4	212	Various
Asch AH 3831	213	Various
Asch AH 3902	155	Kilby Snow
Asch AH 3903	13	Dock Boggs
Atlantic SD-1346	214	Various
Atlantic SD-1347	215	Various
Atlantic SD-1349	216	Various
Atlantic SD-1350	217	Various
Aug. Her. AHR 003	18	Ernie Carpenter
Augusta Heritage AHR 001	71	John Johnson
Augusta Heritage AHR 007	202	Everett White
Augusta Heritage AHR 008	93	Phyllis Marks
Augusta Heritage AHR 009	218a	Various
Augusta Heritage AHR 010	218b	Various
Bear Family BCD 15456	157	Carl T. Sprague
Bear Family BF 15003	196	Hedy West
Bear Family BF 15503	392	Uncle Dave Macon
Bear Family BF 15504	439	Darby and Tarlton
Bear Family BF 15505	407	Dave McCarn and Gwen Foster
Bear Family BF 15507	343	Carolina Tar Heels
Bear Family BF 15508	382a	Kelly Harrell
Bear Family BF 15509	382b	Kelly Harrell
Bear Family BF 15510	382c	Kelly Harrell
Bear Family BF 15517	409	Sam and Kirk McGee
Bear Family BF 15518	393	Uncle Dave Macon
Bear Family BF 15519	394	Uncle Dave Macon
Bear Family BF 15521	434	Carolina Buddies
Bear Family BFX 15214	91	Uncle Dave Macon
Bear Family BF 15501	332	Allen Brothers
Bear Family BF 15502	333	Jules Allen

Biograph BLP 6005	412	North Carolina Ramblers
Biograph RC-6002	176	Fields and Wade Ward
Biograph RC-6003	177	Original Bogtrotters
Biograph RC 6004	146	Betsy Rutherford
Birch 1944	90	McFarland and Gardner
Birch 1945	56	Doc Hopkins
Blue Ridge Institute BRI 002	219	Various
Blue Ridge Institute BRI 004	220	Various
Blue Ridge Institute BRI 005	221	Various
Brunswick 59000	443	Various
Brunswick 59001	444	Various
CMH CMH 106	445	Various
CMH CMH 107	351	Carter Family
CMH CMH 112	352	Carter Family
CMH CMH 116	353a	Carter Family
CMH CMH 118	353b	Carter Family
Columbia CS 9660	446	Various
Country Music Foundation CMF 011-L	447	Various
Country Turtle 6000	373	Dixon Brothers
Country Turtle 6001	448	Various
Country Turtle 6002	374	Dixon Brothers
County 201	156	J. W. Spangler
County 202	141	Eck Robertson
County 401	438	Stripling Brothers
County 403	422	Roane County Ramblers
County 404	405	Wade Mainer
County 405	384	Hillbillies
County 407	335	Blue Ridge Highballers
County 408	383	Kelly Harrell
County 409	385	Lake Howard
County 410	376	Various
County 411	418	Riley Puckett
County 501	449	Various
County 502	450	Various
County 503	451	Various
County 504	452	Various
County 505	413	Charlie Poole
County 506	425	Skillet Lickers
County 507	453	Various
County 508	454	Various
County 509	414	Charlie Poole
County 510	420	Red Fox Chasers
County 511	455	Various
County 513	379	Grayson and Whitter
County 514	456	Various
County 515	457	Various
County 516	415	Charlie Poole
County 517	458	Various
County 518	459a	Various
County 519	459b	Various
County 520	459c	Various

County 521	395	Uncle Dave Macon
County 522	460	Various
County 523	461	Various
County 524	371	D. C. Woltz's So. Broadcasters
County 525	462	Various
County 526	426	Skillet Lickers
County 527	463	Various
County 528	464a	Various
County 529	464b	Various
County 531	465	Various
County 532	391	Leake County Revelers
County 533	466a	Ernest V. Stoneman & others
County 534	466b	Ward Family & others
County 535	466c	Various
County 536	388	Kessinger Brothers
County 540	416	Charlie Poole
County 541	467a	Various
County 542	467b	Various
County 543	387	Earl Johnson
County 544	468	Various
County 545	396	Uncle Dave Macon
County 546	433a	Fiddlin' Arthur Smith, Vol. 1
County 547	433b	Fiddlin' Arthur Smith, Vol. 2
County 703	223	Riley / Solomon / Thomasson
County 707	224	Franklin / Franklin / Solomon
County 709	16	Camp Creek Boys
County 712	77	Coon Creek Girls
County 713	61	Cockerham, Jarrell, and Jenkins
County 717	225	Various
County 718	32	Ernest East
County 720	100	Mountain Ramblers
County 723	62	Cockerham, Jarrell, and Jenkins
County 724	168	Benny Thomasson
County 729	80	Lilly Brothers
County 733 [< Folk Prom. FP 828]	74	Clark Kessinger
County 739	159	Stanley Brothers
County 741	63	Cockerham, Jarrell, and Jenkins
County 748	64	Tommy Jarrell
County 756	65	Tommy Jarrell
County 757	226	Various
County 777	1	Virgil Anderson
County 778	66	Tommy Jarrell
County 786	227a	Various
County 787	227b	Various
County 788	28	Clyde Davenport
County 789	50	Dee and Delta Hicks
County 791	67	Tommy Jarrell
Davis Unlimited DU-33002	33	Norman Edmonds
Davis Unlimited DU-33009	112	Perry County Music Makers
Davis Unlimited DU 33014	42	Gregory and Davenport
Davis Unlimited DU 33015	423	Fiddling Doc Roberts

Davis Unlimited DU 33033	380	Grayson And Whitter
Decca DL 4404	354	Carter Family
Decca DL 4557	355	Carter Family
Decca DL 4760	397	Uncle Dave Macon
Elektra EKL-316	154	Oliver Smith
Elektra EKLP-2 (10")	132	Jean Ritchie
Flyin' Cloud FC-014	369	Various
Flyright LP 546	34	Eller Bros. & Ross Brown
Folk Legacy FSA-1	118	Frank Proffitt
Folk Legacy FSA-2	169	Joseph Able Trivett
Folk Legacy FSA-3	140	Edna Ritchie
Folk Legacy FSA-11	58	Max Hunter
Folk Legacy FSA-13	35	Hank Ferguson
Folk Legacy FSA-15	106	Lawrence Older
Folk Legacy FSA-17	153	Hobart Smith
Folk Legacy FSA-18	161	Arnold Kieth Storm
Folk Legacy FSA-22	228a	Various
Folk Legacy FSA-23	228b	Various
Folk Legacy FSA-24	17	Carolina Tar Heels
Folk Legacy FSA-26	43	Sara Ogan Gunning
Folk Legacy FSA-27	142	Grant Rogers
Folk Legacy FSA-32	195	Hedy West
Folk Legacy FSA-33	20	Sara Cleveland
Folk Legacy FSA-36	119	Frank Proffitt
Folk Promotions 41942	229	Various
Folk Promotions [no #]	230	Various
Folksong Society of Minn. MFSSLP 15001-D	427	Gid Tanner & Skillet Lickers
Folkways FA 2036 (FP 36)	52	L. M. Hilton
Folkways FA 2040 (FP 40)	88	Bascom Lamar Lunsford
Folkways FA 2301	135a	Jean Ritchie
Folkways FA 2302	135b	Jean Ritchie
Folkways FA 2306	117	Poplin Family
Folkways FA 2309	231	Various
Folkways FA 2315	233	Various
Folkways FA 2317	234	Various
Folkways FA 2342	27	Rufus Crisp
Folkways FA 2350	5	Ashley and Isley
Folkways FA 2352	198	Harry and Jeannie West
Folkways FA 2355	3	Clarence Ashley
Folkways FA 2356	105	Old Harp Singers
Folkways FA 2357	199	Harry and Jeanie West
Folkways FA 2358	236	Various
Folkways FA 2359	4	Clarence Ashley
Folkways FA 2360	120	Frank Proffitt
Folkways FA 2362	10	Horton Barker
Folkways FA 2363	237	Various
Folkways FA 2365	238	Various
Folkways FA 2368	54	Roscoe Holcomb
Folkways FA 2374	55	Roscoe Holcomb
Folkways FA 2375	114	Phipps Family
Folkways FA 2379	97	McGee Brothers and Arthur Smith

Folkways FA 2380	178	Wade Ward
Folkways FA 2390	239	Various
Folkways FA 2392	12	Dock Boggs
Folkways FA 2418	19	Dillard Chandler
Folkways FA 2426	137	Jean Ritchie
Folkways FA 2427	136	Jean Ritchie
Folkways FA 2433	81	Lilly Brothers
Folkways FA 2434	240	Various
Folkways FA 2435	241	Various
Folkways FA 2493	124	Ola Belle Reed
Folkways FA 2951 (FP 251)	470a	Various
Folkways FA 2952 (FP 252)	470b	Various
Folkways FA 2953 (FP 253)	470c	Various
Folkways FA 3830	172	Virginia Mountain Boys
Folkways FA 3833	173	Virginia Mountain Boys
Folkways FD 5272	95	Harry McClintock
Folkways FE 4001	246	Various
Folkways FE 34161	248a	Various
Folkways FE 34162	248b	Various
Folkways FES 31089	164	Gordon Tanner et al.
Folkways FES 34151	247	Various
Folkways FH 5723	60	Harry Jackson
Folkways FS 3809	242	Various
Folkways FS 3810	72	Buell Kazee
Folkways FS 3811	243	Various
Folkways FS 3828	160	Pete Steele
Folkways FS 3829	175	Virginia Mountain Boys
Folkways FS 3832	244	Various
Folkways FS 3839	174	Virginia Mountain Boys
Folkways FS 3848	245	Various
Folkways FT 1007	98	McGee Brothers and Arthur Smith
Folkways FTS 31016 (FA 2343)	29	George Davis
Folkways RBF 51	398	Uncle Dave Macon
Folkways RBF 654	336	Dock Boggs
Gambier Folklore Society GFS 901	249	Various
GHP LP 1001	342	Carolina Tar Heels
Global Village SC 03	250	Various
Greenhays GR712	78	Lily May Ledford
Greenhays GR714	138	Jean Ritchie
Grey Eagle (U. of Missouri) 101	251	Various
Harmony HL 7280/HS 11332	356	Carter Family
Harmony HL 7300	357	Carter Family
Harmony HL 7344	358	Carter Family
Harmony HL 7396	359	Carter Family
Harmony HL 7422	360	Carter Family
Heritage 12	252	Shelor / Kimble
Heritage 070	108	Davis, Parish, and Parish
Heritage XXII	253	Various
Heritage XXXIII	254	Various
Historical HLP 8001 (BC 2433-1)	442	Fields Ward
Historical HLP 8002 (BC 2433-2)	471	Various

Historical HLP 8003	472	Various
Historical HLP 8004	435	Ernest V. Stoneman
Historical HLP 8005	417	Charlie Poole
Historical HLP 8006	399	Uncle Dave Macon
Home-Made Music LP001	255a	Various
Home-Made Music LP002	255b	Various
Hoopsnake 101	256	Various
JEMF 103	473	Various
JEMF 104 (< Cap. T 2483)	14	Blue Sky Boy
JEMF 105	257	Various
JEMF 101	361	Carter Family
June Appal JA0055	149	Morgan Sexton
June Appal JA0059C	258	Various
June Appal JA 001	204	Nimrod Workman
June Appal JA 009	73	Buell Kazee
June Appal JA 010	158	I. D. Stamper
June Appal JA 018	152	Betty Smith
June Appal JA 020	41	Addie Graham
June Appal JA 025	11	Andrew F. Boarman
June Appal JA 030	163	Marion Sumner
June Appal JA 032	151	Luke Smathers String Band
June Appal JA 037	139	Jean Ritchie
June Appal JA 049	107	Uncle Charlie Osborne
June Appal JAA001 [3 LP box]	257x	Various
June Appal JAA002 [3 LP box]	257x	Various
June Appal JAA003 [3 LP box]	257x	Various
Kanawha 305	24	Billy Cox
Kanawha 306	75	Clark Kessinger
Kanawha 307	39	Franklin George & John Summers
Kanawha 308	143	Grant Rogers
Kanawha 310	49	Curley Herdman
Kanawha 313	144	Grant Rogers
Kanawha 600	389	Kessinger Brothers
Kicking Mule KM 204	259	Various
Leader LEA 4012	260	Various
Leader LEA 4040	101	North Carolina Boys
Leader LEE 4045	6	Austin & Woodlieff
Library of Congress AFS L1	261	Various
Library of Congress AFS L2	262	Various
Library of Congress AFS L7	263	Various
Library of Congress AAFS L9	264	Various
Library of Congress AAFS L11	265	Various
Library of Congress AAFS L12	266	Various
Library of Congress AAFS L14	267	Various
Library of Congress AAFS L16	268	Various
Library of Congress AAFS L20	269	Various
Library of Congress AAFS L21	270	Various
Library of Congress AAFC L26/27	271	Various
Library of Congress AAFS L28	272	Various
Library of Congress AFS L29	273	Various
Library of Congress AAFS L30	274	Various

Library of Congress AAFS L54	275	Various
Library of Congress AAFS L55	276	Various
Library of Congress AAFS L56	277	Various
Library of Congress AAFS L57	278a	Various
Library of Congress AAFS L58	278b	Various
Library of Congress AFS L60	279	Various
Library of Congress AFS L61	280	Various
Library of Congress AFS L62	281	Various
Library of Congress AFS L65-L66	46	Hammons Family
Library of Congress AFS L68	282	Various
Library of Congress AFC L69-L70	283	Various
Marimac 9013	145	Ross County Farmers
Marimac 9025	170	Troxell Brothers
Marimac 9100	474a	Various
Marimac 9101	475b	Various
Marimac 9104	475a	Various
Marimac 9105	475b	Various
Marimac 9106	476	Various
Marimac 9109	477	Various
Marimac 9110	478a	Various
Marimac 9111	478b	Various
Marimac 9200	116	Everett Pitt
MCA MCAD-10088	363	Carter Family
MCA VIM-4012	362	Carter Family
Meriweather 1001-2	284	Various
Middlebury Collge #1	285	Various
Minstrel JD-203	129	Granny Riddle
Mississippi Dept. of Arch. & Hist. AH-002	286	Various
Missouri Friends of Folk Arts 1001	287	Various
Montana Folklife Project MFP 001	288	Various
Montana Folklife Project MFP 002	289	Various
Morning Star 45003	479a	Various
Morning Star 45004	479b	Various
Morning Star 45005	479c	Various
Morning Star 45008	480	Various
Mountain 302	68	Tommy Jarrell et al.
Mountain 303	25	Kyle Creed et al.
Mountain 304	26	Kyle Creed et al.
Mountain 305	115	Pine River Boys
New World NW 205	148	Sacred Harp
New World NW 223	290	Various
New World NW 226	291	Various
New World NW 236	481	Various
New World NW 239	292	Various
New World NW 245	293	Various
New World NW 291	294	Various
New World NW 294	295	Various
New World NW 314/315	296	Various
Now and Then 1001	297	Various
Ohio Historical Society OF 1001	299	Various
Ohio Traditional Arts TALP-001	298	Various

Okehdokee OK 75003	300	Various
Okehdokee OK 76004	301	Various
Old Homestead OHCS-314	76a	Bradley Kincaid
Old Homestead OHCS-315	76b	Bradley Kincaid
Old Homestead OHCS-316	76c	Bradley Kincaid
Old Homestead OHCS-317	76d	Bradley Kincaid
Old Homestead OHCS 107	390	Bradley Kincaid
Old Homestead OHCS 111	364a	Carter Family
Old Homestead OHCS 112	364b	Carter Family
Old Homestead OHCS 114	419	Riley Puckett
Old Homestead OHCS 116	365	Carter Family
Old Homestead OHCS 117	366	Carter Family
Old Homestead OHCS 141	482	Various
Old Homestead OHCS 157	381	G. B. Grayson & Henry Whitter
Old Homestead OHCS 172	436a	Ernest V. Stoneman
Old Homestead OHCS 173	436b	Ernest V. Stoneman
Old Homestead OHCS 177	483	Various
Old Homestead OHCS 190	334	Emry Arthur
Old Homestead OHCS 191	375	Dykes "Magic City" Trio
Old Homestead OHCS 192	428	Gid Tanner & Skilet Lickers
Old Homestead OHCS 193	429	Gid Tanner & Skilet Lickers
Old Homestead OHS 90001	406	Wade Mainer
Old Homestead OHS 90031	341	Various
Old Homestead OHS 90045	367	Carter Family
Old Time Classics OTC 6001	368	Carter Family
Old Time Classics OTC 6002	372	Delmore Brothers
Old Timey 100	484	Various
Old Timey 101	485	Various
Old Timey 102	486	Various
Old Timey 106	404a	Mainer's Mountaineers
Old Timey 107	404b	Mainer's Mountaineers
Old Timey 112	440	Tom Darby And Jimmie Tarlton
Philo 1017	103	Glen Ohrlin
Philo 1020	21	Sara Cleveland
Philo 1022	2	Ted Ashlaw
Pine Breeze 003	302	Various
Pine Breeze 004	303	Various
Pine Breeze 005	304	Various
Pine Breeze 006	9	Barbee/Bice Family
Prestige Folklore 14010	82	Lilly Brothers
Prestige Folklore 14030	305	Various
Prestige Folklore 14035	83	Lilly Brothers
Prestige INT 13020	122	Obray Ramsey
Prestige INT 13030	123	Obray Ramsey
Prestige INT 13035	85	Louisiana Honeydrippers
Prestige INT 13038	200	Jeanie West
Prestige INT 13049	201	Harry and Jeanie West
Prestige INT 25003	306	Various
Prestige INT 25004	307	Various
Prestige INT 25006	308	Various
Prestige INT 25007	147	Alabama Sacred Harp Singers

Prestige INT 25009	309	Various
Prestige INT 25011	310	Various
Puritan PU 3001	441	Tenneva Ramblers
RCA 2100-2-R	487	Various
RCA 8416-2-R	488	Various
RCA 8417-2-R	489	Various
RCA Bluebird AMX2-5510	410	Monroe Brothers
RCA Bluebird AXM2-5525	337	Blue Sky Boys
RCA Camden ACL1-0047(e)	349	Carter Family
RCA Camden ACL1-0501	350	Carter Family
RCA Camden CAL 586	346	Carter Family
RCA Camden CAL 719	411	Bill Monroe
RCA Camden CAL 797	338	Blue Sky Boys
RCA Camden CAL 2473	347	Carter Family
RCA Camden CAL 2554(e)	348	Carter Family
RCA Victor LPM 2772	369	Carter Family
RCA Victor LPV 507	490	Various
RCA Victor LPV 522	491	Various
RCA Victor LPV 532	492	Various
RCA Victor LPV 548	493	Various
RCA Victor LPV 552	494	Various
Rich-R-Tone LP-8073	99	Artus Moser
Rimrock Rlp-495	40	Aunt Ollie Gilbert
Riverside RLP 12-610	311	Various
Riverside RLP 12-617	312	Various
Riverside RLP 12-620	133	Jean Ritchie
Riverside RLP 12-645	89	Bascom Lamar Lunsford
Riverside RLP 12-649	121	Obray Ramsey
Riverside RLP 12-650	110	Pegram & Parham:
Rounder 0001	111	George Pegram
Rounder 0005	70	Jenkins and Sherrill
Rounder 0008	79	Steve Ledford
Rounder 0009	57	Clint Howard & Fred Price
Rounder 0017	128	Almeda Riddle
Rounder 0018	47	Hammons Family
Rounder 0020	87	Ted Lundy
Rounder 0021	125	Ola Belle Reed
Rounder 0026	7	E. C. Ball
Rounder 0028	313	Various
Rounder 0032	166	Buddy Thomas
Rounder 0034	94	Asa Martin & Cumberland Rangers
Rounder 0036	179	Fields Ward
Rounder 0037	36	J. P. and Annadeene Fraley
Rounder 0047	31	Wilson Douglas
Rounder 0051	44	Sara Ogan Gunning
Rounder 0057	314a	Various
Rounder 0058	314b	Various
Rounder 0064	171	George Tucker
Rounder 0065	315	Lunsford / Pegram & Parham
Rounder 0072	8	E. C. and Orna Ball
Rounder 0076	205	Nimrod Workman

Rounder 0077	126	Ola Belle Reed
Rounder 0078	150	Early Shaker Spirituals
Rounder 0083	130	Almeda Riddle
Rounder 0089	206	Oscar and Eugene Wright
Rounder 0133	37	Art Galbraith
Rounder 0143	22	Wilma Lee Cooper
Rounder 0157	38	Art Galbraith
Rounder 0158	104	Glen Ohrlin
Rounder 0194	162	John W. Summers
Rounder 0237	316	Various
Rounder 1001	421	Blind Alfred Reed
Rounder 1002	59	Aunt Molly Jackson
Rounder 1003	344	Fiddlin' John Carson
Rounder 1004	340	Burnett and Rutherford
Rounder 1005	430	Gid Tanner and Skillet Lickers
Rounder 1006	339	Blue Sky Boys
Rounder 1007	386	Frank Hutchison
Rounder 1008	437	Ernest V. Stoneman
Rounder 1009	408	Harry K. McClintock
Rounder 1010	45	Ed Haley
Rounder 1023	431	Gid Tanner and Skillet Lickers
Rounder 1026	495	Various
Rounder 1028	400	Uncle Dave Macon
Rounder 1029	496	Various
Rounder 1032	377	Georgia Yellow Hammers
Rounder 1033	497	Various
Rounder 1035	498	Various
Rounder 1037	499	Various
Rounder CD 11536	15	Blue Sky Boys
Rounder SS-0145	317	Various
Shoestring Tape SGB 1	318	Various
Smiths/Fwys CD SF 40037 (FA 2314)	232	Various
Smiths/Fwys CD SF 40038 (FA 2318)	235	Various
Smiths/Fwys SF CD 40012	180	Watson Family
Sonyatone STR 201	424	Eck Robertson
Sonyatone STR 202	378	Girls of the Golden West
String STR 802	86	Emmett Lundy
Sugar Hill SH-CD-3779	190	Doc Watson
Sugar Hill SH-CD-3786	191	Doc Watson
Sugar Hill SH-CD-3795	192	Doc Watson
Takoma A 1013	167	Tony Thomas
Tenn. Folklore Society TFS 104	51	Hicks Family
Tenn. Folklore Society [cass, no #]	319	Various
Tenn. Folklore Society TFS-103	320	Various
Tenn. Folklore Society TFS-105	321	Various
Tenn. Folklore Society TFS-106	322	Various
Tenn. Folklore Society TFS-108	323	Various
Testament T-3301	30	Dorsey Dixon
Testament T-3302	165	Jimmie Tarlton
Time-Life TL CW-06	370	Carter Family
Topic 12T146	197	Hedy West

Topic 12TS336	181	Watson Family
Tradition TLP 1007	324	Various
U. of Ill. Campus Folksong Club CFC 201	222	Various
U. of Ill. Campus Folksong Club CFC 301	102	Glen Ohrlin
U. of Illinois Press [cass, no #]	325	Various
U. of Illinois Press [no #]	345	Fiddlin' John Carson
U. of Missouri Press	326	Various
U. of No. Carolina Press 0-8078-4083-1	327	Various
U. of No. Carolina Press 0-8078-4084-X	328	Various
U. of Texas Press [cass, no #]	329	Various
Vanguard VCD-45/46	187	Doc Watson
Vanguard VRS-9147	330	Various
Vanguard VRS-9152	182	Doc Watson
Vanguard VRS-9158	127	Almeda Riddle
Vanguard VRS-9170	183	Doc Watson
Vanguard VRS-9182	331a	Various
Vanguard VRS-9183	331b	Various
Vanguard VRS-9213	184	Doc Watson
Vanguard VRS-9239	185	Doc Watson
Vanguard VRS 9124	193	Hedy West
Vanguard VRS 9162	194	Hedy West
Vanguard VSD-9/10	186	Doc Watson
Vanguard VSD-107/108	188	Watson, Howard, and Price
Vanguard VSD-6576	189	Doc Watson
Vetco 101	401	Uncle Dave Macon
Vetco 103	500	Various
Vetco 105	402	Uncle Dave Macon
Vetco 107	432	Gid Tanner and Skillet Lickers
Westminister SWN 18021	134	Jean Ritchie
West Virginia Univ. Press Sound Arch. 001	48	Edden Hammons